Richard Sennett, Henry J. Oram

The Marine Steam Engine

Richard Sennett, Henry J. Oram

The Marine Steam Engine

ISBN/EAN: 9783954272167
Erscheinungsjahr: 2012
Erscheinungsort: Bremen, Deutschland

THE

MARINE STEAM ENGINE

A TREATISE FOR ENGINEERING STUDENTS
YOUNG ENGINEERS, AND OFFICERS OF THE ROYAL NAVY
AND MERCANTILE MARINE

BY THE LATE

RICHARD SENNETT

ENGINEER-IN-CHIEF OF THE NAVY; FELLOW OF THE ROYAL SCHOOL OF NAVAL
ARCHITECTURE AND MARINE ENGINEERING; MEMBER OF THE INSTITUTIONS OF CIVIL AND
MECHANICAL ENGINEERS; VICE-PRESIDENT OF THE INSTITUTION OF NAVAL
ARCHITECTS; LATE INSTRUCTOR AND LECTURER IN MARINE
ENGINEERING AT THE ROYAL NAVAL COLLEGE

AND

HENRY J. ORAM

SENIOR ENGINEER INSPECTOR AT THE ADMIRALTY; INSPECTOR OF MACHINERY IN H.M. FLEET
MEMBER OF THE INSTITUTION OF CIVIL ENGINEERS
MEMBER OF THE INSTITUTION OF NAVAL ARCHITECTS; LECTURER ON MARINE
ENGINEERING AND LATE INSTRUCTOR IN MARINE ENGINE DESIGN
AT THE ROYAL NAVAL COLLEGE; ETC.

WITH NUMEROUS DIAGRAMS

1899

Bibliographical Note.

First Edition, March 1882.

Second Edition, with Additions and Corrections, October 1885.

*Third Edition, Revised and largely Rewritten by H. J. Oram,
January* 1898.

Fourth Edition, with Additions and Modifications, June 1899.

INTRODUCTORY NOTE

To THE many who knew the late Richard Sennett, my old friend and pre-decessor in office, and appreciated his work and worth, and regretted the all too early closing of his brilliant career, it will be a source of gratification that the revision of this book has been undertaken by so capable a marine engineer as Inspector of Machinery H. J. Oram, R.N.

Mr. Oram has acquired a vast amount of special knowledge and experience of marine machinery of the latest types, and it is believed this has been incorporated in the present edition in a manner that will make it of great value to students, young engineers, and officers of the Royal and Mercantile Navies in carrying on their studies and duties.

A. J. DURSTON,
Engineer-in-Chief of H.M. Navy.

ADMIRALTY, LONDON.

NOTE TO NEW EDITION.

THE demand for a new edition of this work coming so soon
indicates a measure of appreciation of its contents which is highly
valued by the writer. In revising for the present edition, the
suggestions of reviewers who kindly expressed them have been
kept in view as far as possible, and it is hoped in the future to
do this more fully. Some modifications have been made, and
such additions as the progress of engineering appeared to warrant,
such, for example, as the Marine Steam Turbine, the development of which will be watched with interest. As a figure was
given in the preface for the I.H.P. of water-tube boilers constructed or ordered for the Royal Navy, it may be mentioned
that this figure is now practically 1,500,000, I.H.P.

H. J. ORAM.

LONDON: *April* 1899.

PREFACE

This work, originally written by the late Mr. Richard Sennett, was never revised, owing at first to the pressure of his official duties, and subsequently by reason of his death, so that it had become obsolete, on account of the very great changes which have taken place in marine engineering, more especially in the naval machinery with which it originally dealt.

When considering the preparation either of an independent new work or the thorough revision and modernisation of the old one, the latter course was chosen, as there appeared to be features in the work and its arrangement which offered advantages over others of its kind, although this course has involved practically rewriting it.

The style and arrangement have, however, been preserved, and the result appears in the present volume as a practically new book, which it is hoped will be of service to students of engineering, and enjoy a measure of popularity equal to that received and so well deserved by the original work.

The amount of printed matter and also the number of illustrations have been considerably increased, as in the writer's opinion ample illustration is essential to the proper understanding of written descriptions of engineering details. The illustrations have generally been specially prepared for the work, and alteration of type and size of page have been made to keep the book within convenient size, owing to the increased contents.

These illustrations and the subject matter have also been made more general in character, and been drawn from the practice of the most successful makers of mercantile marine, as well as naval, machinery. The fact may be noted that during recent years there has been, as regards the engines of large vessels, a much nearer approximation to identity in mercantile and naval practice than was usual previously, showing that valuable features have been mutually borrowed.

The growing importance of water-tube boilers has caused this subject to be dealt with at considerable length, and this part of the book exemplifies the great changes that have taken place since the work was first published. It may be observed in passing, as indicating the national importance of this section, that in the Royal Navy there are now about 1,000,000 I.H.P. of water-tube boilers, either built, building, or about to be commenced.

A new feature is the detailed description of the care and management of, and the treatment of defects in, marine engines and boilers, which it is expected will be found of value to students of engineering and young engineers. It is not pretended, however, that this part of the duties of engineers can be adequately learnt from books, for actual experience in the engine rooms will alone completely supply the requisite instruction. What is given will, however, prepare young engineers for such experience, and give information on points which they are at first more or less unacquainted with.

In the preparation of a work of this kind, one becomes indebted to many friends for assistance of various kinds, and to these I tender my best thanks, especially to Mr. P. Marrack, R.N., Engineer Inspector, Admiralty, who has kindly read over most of the proof sheets.

H. J. ORAM.

London, 1898.

CONTENTS.

THE MECHANISM.

THE PROPELLER.

GENERAL.

APPENDIX.

THE

MARINE STEAM-ENGINE.

CHAPTER I.

HISTORY AND PROGRESS.

THE earliest steam-engines were simply reciprocating engines, and for many purposes such engines are still used even at the present day. Until, however, a suitable method of turning reciprocating into rotative motion had been discovered and utilised not any progress was made in adapting the steam-engine to the propulsion of vessels. The adoption of the crank effected this desirable object, enabled the power of the engine to be transmitted to the propeller smoothly and without shock, and was an indispensable step in the progress of steam navigation.

The *marine* steam-engine may justly be considered as a production of the present century. In the latter part of the eighteenth century several attempts were made to adapt the steam-engine for the propulsion of boats, but none of them were quite successful. The first practical steamboat was built on the Clyde, in 1801, by William Symington, for Lord Dundas. She was called the 'Charlotte Dundas,' and was worked for some time with success as a tug on the Forth and Clyde Canal, but was withdrawn from this service in consequence of an apprehension that the banks of the canal would suffer from the wash of the propeller. This boat was fitted with a single paddle-wheel placed near the stern, driven by a horizontal direct-acting engine, with connecting-rod and crank, and the general arrangement of her machinery would be considered creditable even at the present day.

The first recorded instance of steam navigation proving commercially successful was in America, where, in 1807, Robert Fulton built a steam vessel called the 'Clermont,' propelled by paddles driven by a Boulton & Watt engine. In 1812 Henry Bell built a vessel called the 'Comet,' which was successfully worked on the Clyde as a passenger steamer between Glasgow and Greenock. The 'Comet' was propelled by two pairs of paddles, each paddle having four floats or blades, somewhat resembling a pair of canoe paddles, crossed at right angles. The paddles were driven by an engine of somewhat peculiar design, which, however, approximated to the side-lever engine of a later day. This small boat was the first passenger steamer in Europe.

B

From this date the success of steam navigation may be said to have been secured, and the advancement that has been made since has not consisted so much in the discovery of new principles as in the extension of old ones, and the introduction and development of improved mechanism and workmanship, with consequent economy of fuel. The result has been a progressive increase in the size, power, and speed of steamships and in the extent of their voyages; so that at the present day we have ships displacing 19,500 tons, and capable of being driven at a speed of 22 knots by engines developing more than 30,000 indicated horse-power, while even larger vessels are under construction.

Side-lever engine.—The propeller used in the earlier steamships was invariably the paddle-wheel, and the type of engine existing and giving satisfaction on land was naturally adapted at first to rotate

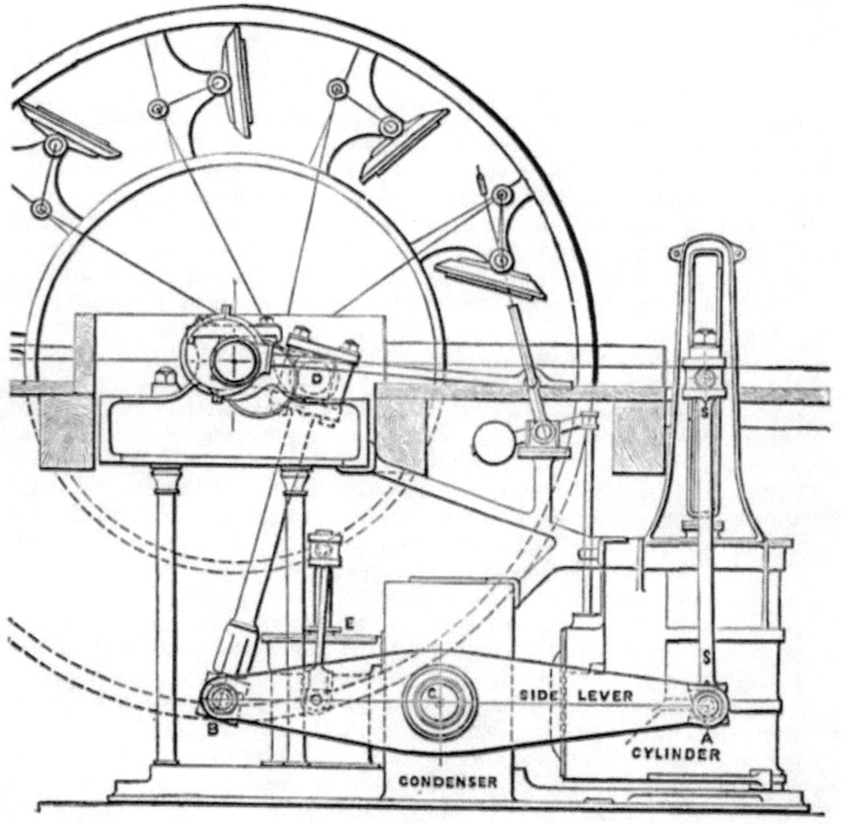

Fig. 1.

these paddle-wheels. Almost all these early engines were, therefore, of the *beam* type. In America the beam was generally placed over the crank, while in this country it was placed below the crank. The latter type of engine was known as the *side-lever engine*. The general arrangement of the side-lever engine is shown in outline in Fig. 1, and it represents the type usually fitted not only in the first steam vessels, but also for some years after.

On the top of the piston-rod is fixed a crosshead with side-rods, s, attached at each end, which, passing down on either side of the cylinder, are connected to the ends, A, of a beam or side-lever, A B, oscillating on a fulcrum or gudgeon at its centre, C. The opposite ends, B, of these side-levers are fitted with journals carrying the crosstail, to the centre of which, one end of the connecting-rod B D is attached, the other end working on the crankpin D. The air-pump E is worked by side-rods from intermediate points in the side-levers, the upper ends of the air-pump side-rods being jointed to the opposite ends of the air-pump crosshead, to the centre of which the air-pump rod is secured. The piston-rod crosshead works in vertical guides to insure parallelism, and the parallel-motion rods used in land beam engines are dispensed with.

Grasshopper engines.—The arrangement of the side-levers was sometimes varied by making them levers of the third order, the gudgeon or fulcrum being at one end and the steam cylinder placed between the gudgeon and connecting-rod. These engines were commonly known as *grasshopper engines.*

The side-lever type of engine, though very heavy and occupying a large space for the power developed, was safe and reliable, securing a sufficient length of connecting-rod, and having its moving parts practically in equilibrium. It consequently continued in general use for a great number of years, but was at length superseded by the direct-acting type, which was lighter and more compact.

Introduction of steam war vessels.—Steam vessels were introduced into the Royal Navy in the year 1820, when the 'Monkey,' a vessel of 210 tons, was built at Rotherhithe and fitted by Messrs. Boulton & Watt with engines of 80 nominal horse-power. There were two cylinders, about $35\frac{1}{2}$ in. diameter and 3 ft. 6 in. stroke, working at $26\frac{1}{2}$ revolutions per minute, giving a mean piston speed of 185 ft. per minute. She was followed in 1822 by the 'Active,' of 80 nominal horse-power, by the same firm, and in 1823 by the 'Lightning,' of 100 horse-power, by Messrs. Maudslay, and some others whose names appeared for the first time in the Official Navy List for March 1828. These early steam vessels were mainly used for towing and general purposes, and could scarcely be classed as war vessels. Between this date and 1840 seventy other steam vessels were added to the Navy, the majority being fitted with flue boilers and slow-moving side-lever engines worked with steam at a pressure of 4 lbs. per square inch above the atmosphere.

The 'Rhadamanthus,' one of these ships, was fitted with side-lever engines and flue boilers by Messrs. Maudslay, Sons, & Field in 1832. The nominal horse-power was 220, but the engines were capable of being worked up to 400 I.H.P., or 1·8 times the nominal power. The load on the safety valves was 4 lbs. per square inch, and the number of revolutions per minute when working at full power $17\frac{1}{2}$, giving a mean piston speed of 175 ft. per minute. The total weight of the machinery was 275 tons, or 13·75 cwts. per I.H.P. developed.

Between 1840 and 1850 tubular boilers were introduced. In these boilers a group of small tubes was substituted for the long winding flue, to convey the heated gases from the furnaces to the chimney. The boilers were thus made lighter and more compact, and the working pressures of steam generally were increased to from 10 to 15 lbs. per square inch above the atmosphere.

Abandonment of side-lever engines.—Attempts were soon made to reduce the space required by the machinery, and the side-levers were abandoned and *direct-acting engines* fitted for rotating the paddle-wheels. Several arrangements of this kind were fitted, the two best known being the double-cylinder engine by Messrs. Maudslay and the oscillating engine adopted by Messrs. Penn. Fig. 2 shows the *double-cylinder engine*, which consisted of two equal cylinders side by side, the piston-rods from the two cylinders being connected to a single cross-head. In order to get sufficient length of connecting-rod, the cross-head was of peculiar form and passed down between the cylinders, having a journal at its lower end, on which one end of the connecting-rod worked, the other end being attached to the crankpin.

Fig. 3 shows the general arrangement of the *oscillating engine*, which is the simplest and most compact type for driving paddle-wheels. This type of engine, although first fitted for marine purposes by Messrs. Maudslay, Sons, & Field, who in 1828 fitted a pair of oscillating engines into the steamship 'Endeavour,' and subsequently in several other ships, was adopted and perfected by the late eminent engineer, Mr. John Penn, with whose name it is now generally associated. In these engines the connecting-rod is altogether dispensed with, the upper end of the piston-rod being fitted with brasses to work directly on the crankpin, and the cylinder itself is carried on trunnion bearings, to allow the necessary oscillation to suit the motion of the crank. The trunnions are hollow, and the steam is admitted to and exhausted from the cylinders through them. In this type of engine space and weight have been economised as far as is possible for paddle-wheel engines, and the majority of engines now made for paddle-wheel vessels are on this plan.

The 'Magicienne' was one of the best specimens of the steam war-vessels of that period. She was fitted with oscillating engines by Messrs. Penn in 1850. The pressure of steam in the boilers was 14 lbs. per square inch, number of revolutions per minute at full power $20\frac{1}{2}$, giving a mean piston speed of 287 ft. per minute, with a maximum I.H.P. of 1,300. The total weight of the machinery was 275 tons, or 4·23 cwts. per I.H.P.

Defects of paddle-wheels —The paddle-wheel possessed many practical disadvantages which interfered with progress beyond a certain point. Its performance was much affected by the variation of draught of the ship during a voyage, as the coal and stores were consumed, and the paddle-boxes offered resistance to the progress of the vessel. For fighting ships paddle-wheels were particularly unsuitable. The wheels themselves were exposed to danger from shot and shell, and the paddle-boxes interfered seriously with the training and working of the guns, while the shafting and many parts of the engines had to be considerably above the water-line, much of it above the upper deck. The paddle-wheel also is not a form of propeller well adapted for the application of high powers.

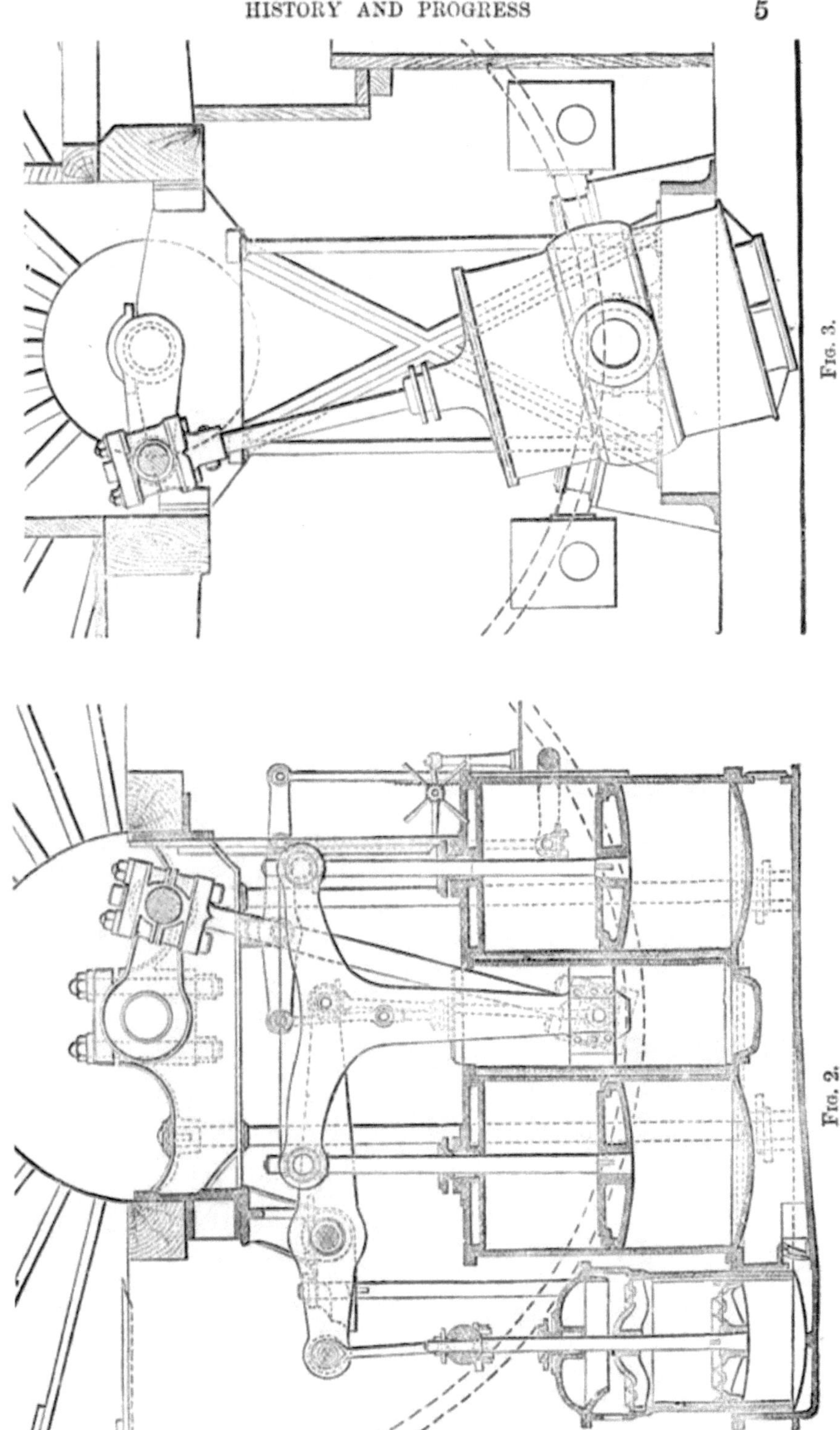

Fig. 3.
Fig. 2.

Adoption of the screw propeller.—The adoption of the screw propeller in lieu of the paddle-wheel was the most important step taken in the progress of marine engineering, for this rendered many subsequent advances possible. Its principal advantages, as compared with the paddle-wheel, are, that it is comparatively little affected by the rolling, or by the variation of the draught of the ship during a voyage, and it is equally capable of application to either great or small powers. It is not exposed to damage by projectiles, and also permits of the engines being kept below the water-line, which is very important in unarmoured warships. Screw engines, whether horizontal or vertical, can be further protected, if necessary, by being kept below the steel armour deck, with armour gratings in the necessary engine-room hatchways and other openings, while in the larger class of war vessels, such as the battleships and large cruisers, their height is so moderate that efficient protection can be given them by armour, even when the engines are vertical and the cylinders above the water-line. With screw engines the decks are also kept clear for the guns.

The substitution of the screw propeller for the paddle-wheel began to grow general about the period 1845–50. The screw propeller had been invented long before, but its practical utility had not been generally recognised, and it was still regarded as being in the experimental stage. The first notable experiments as to the comparative efficiencies of paddle-wheels and screw propellers were made in 1840, when the 'Archimedes,' with a screw propeller, beat the paddle-wheel boat 'Ariel' between Dover and Calais by five to six minutes under steam and sail. The 'Archimedes' afterwards beat the paddle-wheel steamers 'Beaver' and 'Swallow,' but was beaten slightly by the 'Widgeon.' The Admiralty, in 1843, caused some important experiments to be carried out with the screw ship 'Rattler' and the paddle-wheel ship 'Alecto,' and, in 1849, with the screw ship 'Niger' and paddle-wheel vessel 'Basilisk.' The results in each case were in favour of the screw propeller, and many valuable conclusions were deduced from the trials.

From that time the use of the screw propeller gradually became more general, till at the present day it is almost solely employed for marine propulsion, the paddle-wheel only being applied in special cases. It is not too much to say that ships of the class now traversing the ocean in all directions, both in the royal and mercantile navies, would not have been possible had not the screw superseded the paddle.

Gearing for screw engines and its abandonment.—In order to attain the same speed of ship the screw propeller had to be driven at a much greater speed than the paddle-wheel, and as it was not possible in the then condition of mechanical engineering to drive the pistons at a sufficiently high speed to enable the engine shaft to be connected directly to the propeller shafting, the earlier engines used for working screw propellers were *geared*, so that the screw shaft was caused to revolve at a much higher rate of speed than the engine shaft. A large spur wheel, keyed on the crank-shaft of the engine, worked into a pinion on the screw propeller shafting, so that the speed of the engine shaft could be multiplied on the screw shaft as might be necessary.

Before long, however, such improvements in workmanship and mechanical details were effected, that the speeds both of piston and of revolution could be sufficiently increased to allow *direct engines* to be fitted. In these the gearing is left out, and the crank-shaft connected direct to the screw shafting. In many marine engines at the present day, even of the largest size, the mean piston speeds are as high as from 800 to 950 ft. per minute at the maximum power, while in the fast-running engines supplied for torpedo boats and destroyers it rises as high as 1,200 ft. per minute, and in extreme cases to 1,400 ft. It is probable that in the future of marine engineering the speeds may be increased even beyond this, in order to attain increased economy.

Horizontal engines.—The paddle-wheel engines were either vertical or inclined ; but when the screw propeller was introduced, and it became possible to place the whole of the propelling apparatus below the water-line, the engine was placed horizontally, and from that time, for about thirty years, the engines of warships were almost always of the horizontal type. One of the great obstacles that had then to be overcome in connecting the crank-shaft of the horizontal engine direct to the screw shafting was the close proximity in which the cylinder was necessarily placed to the centre-line of the ship, owing to the limitation of the beam of the ship, which made it difficult to get a connecting-rod of suitable length to work between the cylinder and the crank.

Trunk engines.—Mr. John Penn solved this difficulty by his invention of the trunk engine. In this engine a large hollow trunk, cast on or bolted to the piston, and working through a steam-tight stuffing-box on the end of the cylinder, was substituted for the piston-rod, and the connecting-rod was attached directly to a journal or gudgeon in the centre of the piston itself, as shown in Fig. 4. Though the use of a large trunk of this description does not at first sight appear desirable, yet the engines of this type have generally worked in a satisfactory manner, and they were amongst the most smooth-working and efficient marine engines employed. With the introduction of high-pressure steam, however, they became obsolete, owing to the difficulty of keeping the trunks in a steam-tight condition.

Return connecting-rod engines.—This kind of engine was adopted by the majority of marine engineering firms to enable the horizontal cylinders to be brought close to the crank-shaft, and, as usually fitted, is shown in Fig. 5. There were two rods to each piston, one passing above, the other below the crank-shaft, to the opposite side of the ship, while the further ends of the piston-rods were fixed to a cross-head, having a journal at its centre, from which the connecting-rod worked back to the crank.

In some later examples, in order to obviate the disadvantage of having more than one stuffing-box for each cylinder, and simplify the design of the piston, a single piston-rod was fitted, attached to a cross-head between the cylinder and the crank-shaft, from which two rods were carried, one above, the other below, the shaft, to a similar cross-head on the opposite side, as in the ordinary return connecting-rod arrangement.

Direct-acting engines.—The *direct-acting engine* shown in Fig. 6, having the connecting-rod between the cylinder and the crank, was often employed, especially by Messrs. Humphrys, in the later horizontal examples, the parts being stowed as compactly as possible in the limited

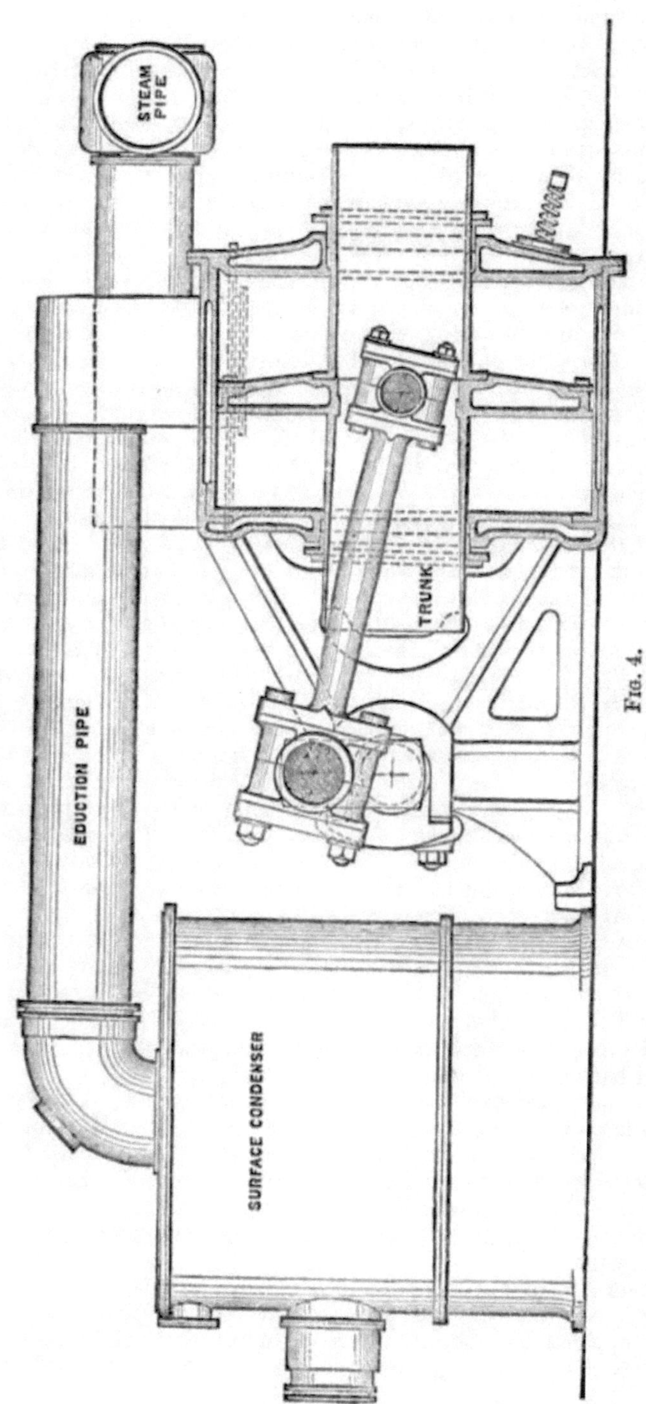

Fig. 4.

DISCHARGE PIPE
SURFACE CONDENSER
EDUCTION PIPE
INLET FOR CIRCULATING WATER
PISTON ROD
CYLINDER

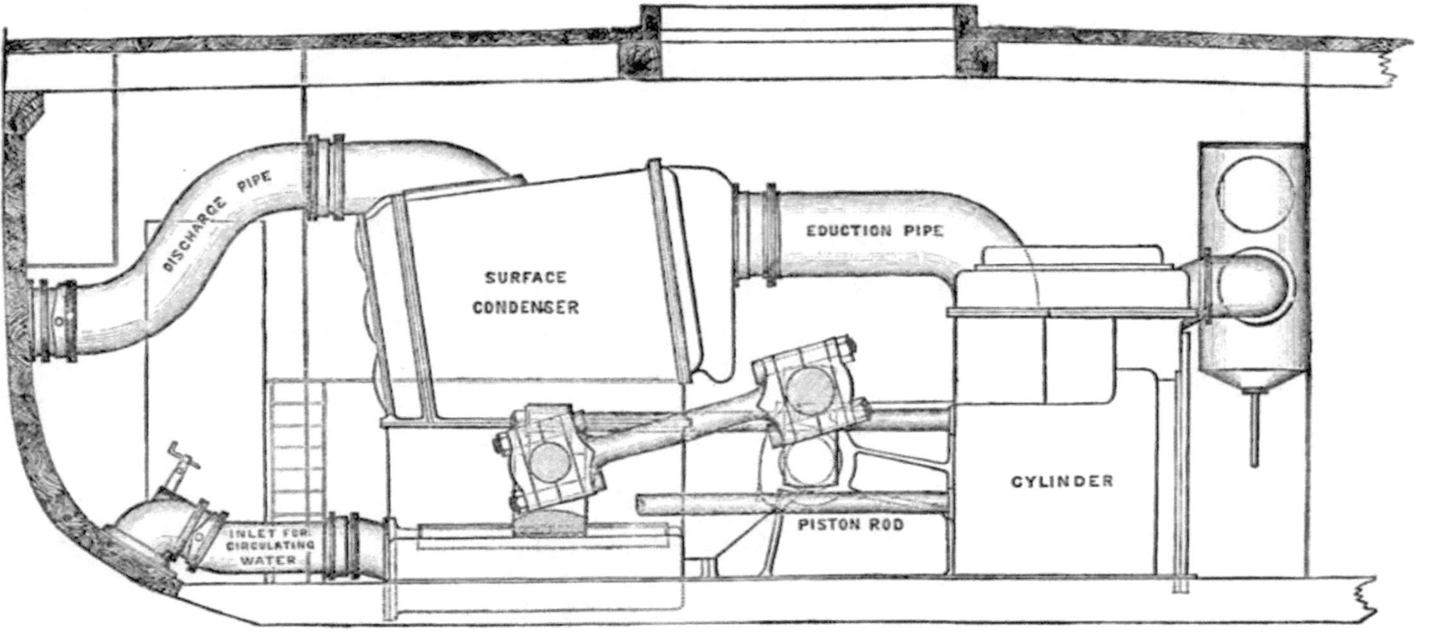

Fig. 5.

space available, and a short connecting-rod fitted. It is the simplest type, and the most suitable for general work, and, whenever sufficient room can be obtained, it is usually adopted. For vertical engines, with the cylinders at the top working down to the crank-shaft, which are now generally fitted for marine purposes, this type is universally adopted.

Early screw engines.—The majority of steamers, both war and mercantile, built during the years 1850–60, were fitted with horizontal screw propeller engines worked with steam of from 20 to 25 lbs. pressure per square inch. The engines had jet injection condensers, and were not remarkable for economy of fuel, but they were much lighter, and occupied considerably less space, than the paddle-wheel engines that preceded them. The mean piston speed in this type of engine was generally about 400 ft. per minute, and the weight of machinery about $3\frac{3}{4}$ cwts. per I.H.P.

Surface condensation.—The adoption of surface condensation, which became general about 1860, formed a most important step in marine engineering. Its value consisted not so much in the economy effected by the avoidance of loss from the brining of boilers, as in the fact that by its eliminating the element of danger resulting from deposit of solid non-conducting matter on the heating surfaces, it rendered possible the use of higher steam pressures in marine boilers, and led eventually to the introduction of cylindrical boilers and compound engines. When surface condensation was first introduced, the old flat-sided boilers, made to fit the section of the ship, were still retained, but were strengthened by fitting additional stays to enable them to carry steam pressures of 30 to 35 lbs. per square inch, and the majority of warships built during the years 1860–70 were fitted with surface-condensing engines worked with steam of this pressure. The piston speeds were also considerably increased, especially in the larger ships in which a long stroke could be obtained. With this type of engine the mean piston speeds varied from 500 to 665 ft. per minute. To promote economy of fuel the cylinders were usually steam-jacketed, and made large enough to allow for considerable expansion at full power, and the boilers were fitted with superheaters. The average weight of the machinery of this type, including the water in boilers and condensers, was about 3 cwts. per I.H.P.

Compound or double expansion engines.—After the introduction of the surface condenser, attention was directed to the use of higher steam pressures and greater expansion of steam, as theoretical considerations showed that considerable gain could thus be effected. The result was that the steam pressure was increased from 30 or 35 lbs. to 60 lbs., while cylindrical boilers were fitted to safely carry the increased pressure, and the engine was changed to the compound type. Compound engines were fitted to nearly all warships from 1870 to 1885.

In this type of engine the expansion is conducted in stages ; the steam, after being admitted to a small cylinder and expanding therein, is led to a larger cylinder, where it expands still further prior to exhaust, so that the stresses on the framing and journals are decreased and the loss from liquefaction of steam in the cylinders reduced

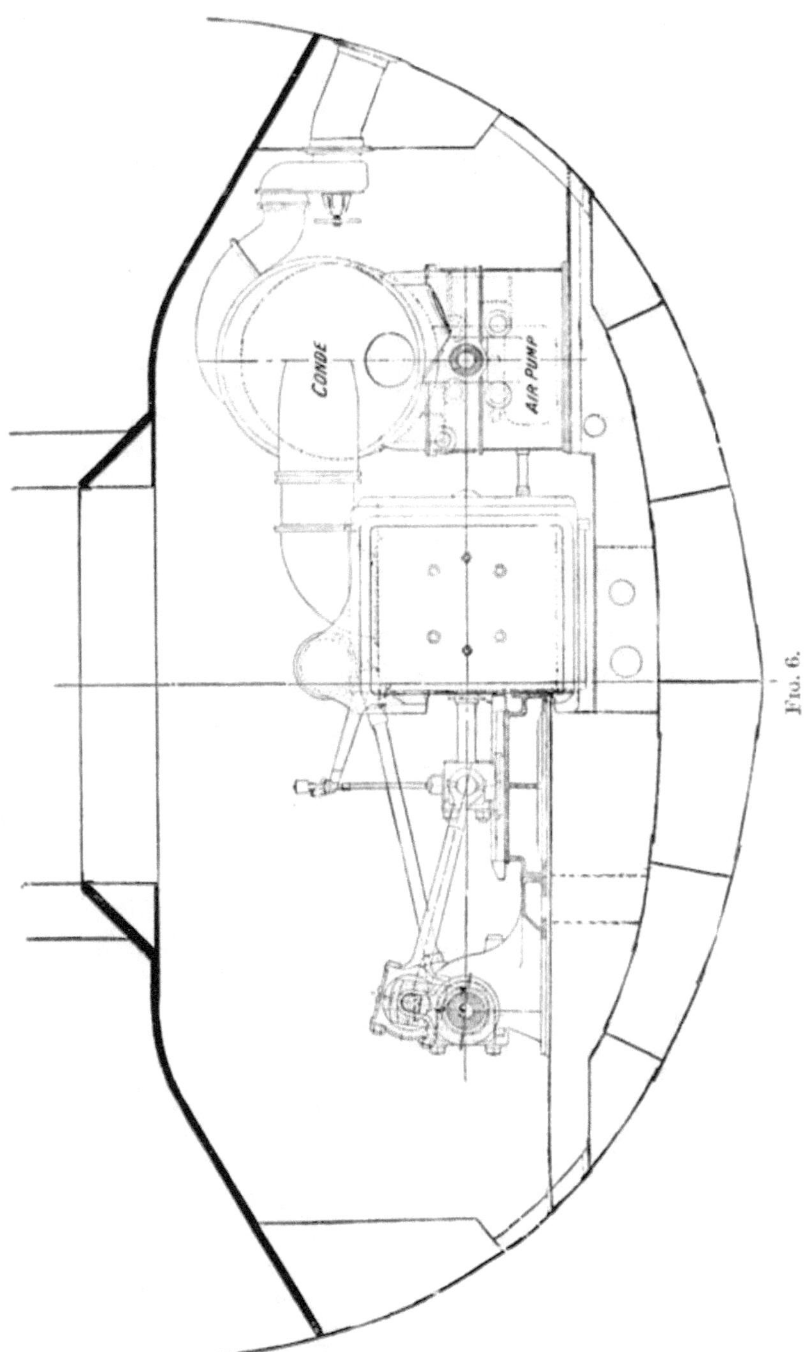

Fig. 6.

to a minimum. The following summary of its advantages is confirmed by experience :—

1. Reduction of the maximum stresses on the framing, shafting, and bearings, and consequent reduction of weight and cost.

2. Increased regularity of turning moment, and consequent increased efficiency of the propeller in the water.

3. More economical use of the steam in the cylinders and consequent increase of power from a given expenditure of heat.

The working steam pressure in the Royal Navy with this type of engine was originally 60 lbs. per square inch. This has been gradually increased from time to time, till in about the year 1880 it was 90 lbs., while in the last of this type fitted the pressure was increased to 120 lbs.

From the adoption of compound engines and higher steam pressures a considerable economy of fuel at once resulted. The gain in economy by the use even of the 60-lb. compound engines over the ordinary surface-condensing engines worked with steam of 30 lbs. pressure may be taken to be at least 30 per cent.

This gain was well authenticated, and the average amounts claimed by the principal Engineers and Steamship Companies, in reply to questions by an Admiralty Committee in 1872, was 30 to 35 per cent.

Vertical engines.—The vertical type of engine, with cylinders at the top and crank-shaft below, was adopted for merchant ships long before it was introduced into the Royal Navy, because it was a necessity in most warships that all the machinery should be kept below the water-line, and horizontal engines alone satisfied this condition. Figs. 7 and 8 show a vertical engine of the type fitted in the mercantile marine. Vertical engines possess many practical advantages over horizontal engines, especially in connection with the working of the cylinders and pistons, and general accessibility of the engine. When, therefore, the twin-screw system was adopted for armour-clad ships, vertical compound engines were fitted, with a middle line water-tight bulkhead separating the two sets. By dividing the power into two parts, each set of engines, even in a ship of great power, would be of moderate dimensions, and although the whole of the machinery might not in all cases be entirely below the water-line, the parts above would be protected, not only by armour plating, but by a body of coal in addition, the coal-bunkers being continued on each side of the engine room. This extension of the use of vertical engines has continued and been applied to all classes of vessel, and special means for protecting the cylinders have often been fitted. At the present time new engines for the Navy are being made vertical for all classes of vessel.

Three-cylinder compound engines.—As the power of compound engines increased the dimensions of the low-pressure cylinders became so great that it was found desirable to fit two low-pressure cylinders instead of one, in consequence of the difficulties experienced in obtaining sound castings of large size, and to keep the size of the reciprocating parts as small as possible. This led to what is known as the *three-cylinder compound engine*, which is simply a modification of the ordinary two-cylinder compound engine. Figs. 9 and 10 show a vertical compound engine of the three-cylinder type.

Triple expansion engines.—With initial steam pressures above

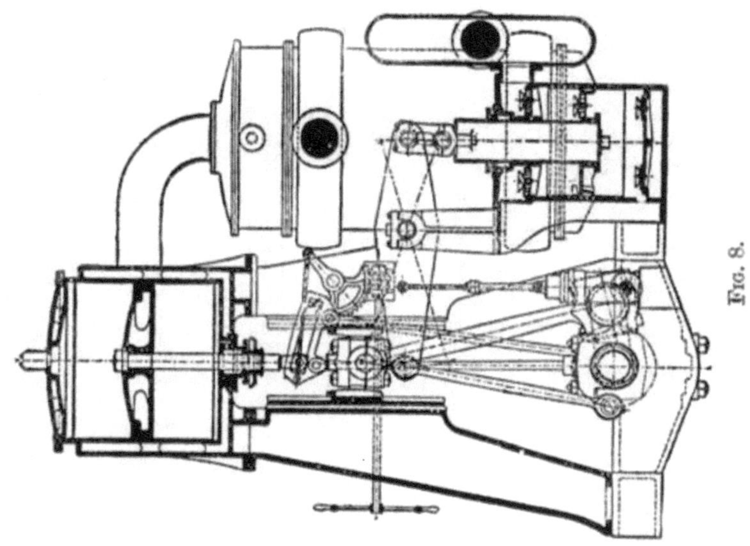

Fig. 8.

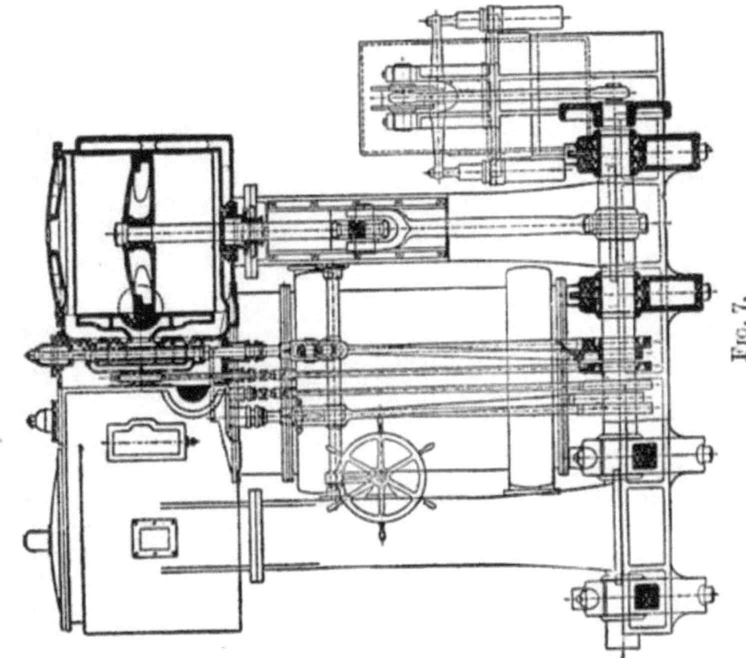

Fig. 7.

100 lbs. per square inch, the variation of temperature in each cylinder of an ordinary compound engine again becomes great, so that the full economy due to the high pressure cannot be attained in consequence of the loss from liquefaction. It was therefore soon found desirable to extend the compound system, and divide the expansion into three stages, carried out in separate cylinders, so as to reduce the range of temperature in each.

Engines on this system are usually known as *triple expansion* or *triple compound engines*. They were first introduced by the late Dr., then Mr., A. C. Kirk, of Messrs. R. Napier & Sons, Glasgow, who, in 1874, fitted them on board the s.s. 'Propontis,' to utilise steam of 150 lbs. pressure, supplied by Rowan & Horton's water-tube boilers. These engines gave good economical results, but the boilers unfortunately gave trouble, and were ultimately taken out. Very little further was done in this direction, until, in 1881, Mr. Kirk fitted a set of triple expansion engines on board the s.s. 'Aberdeen,' for the trade to Australia and China. The results in this instance were so satisfactory that other engines of the same type followed, and the system was soon largely adopted in the mercantile marine. Since 1885 the new ships for the Royal Navy have been fitted with triple expansion engines, which type is now the most general for marine purposes. The steam pressure first used with them in the Navy was 130 lbs., which was gradually increased to 155 lbs. in the year 1887. From this date to 1895 large numbers of triple expansion engines were added to the Navy, all with 155 lbs steam pressure. In the mercantile marine, however, 180 lbs. steam pressure is now largely used, and in many cases 200 lbs.

In the two large cruisers 'Powerful' and 'Terrible,' commenced in 1893, and tried in 1896–97, a boiler pressure of 260 lbs. is adopted, reduced to 210 lbs. at the engines, while in cruisers of 1895, and subsequently, these pressures have been increased to 300 and 250 lbs. respectively. Triple expansion engines are fitted, the low-pressure cylinders being divided into two parts.

The gain in economy effected by the triple expansion engine, worked with steam of 130 lbs. to 150 lbs. pressure, over the ordinary compound engine worked at 90 to 100 lbs. pressure, may be taken at from 15 to 20 per cent., while with the higher pressures it will be still greater. Figs. 11 and 12 show the general arrangement of a triple expansion engine.

Quadruple expansion engines.—In many cases in the mercantile marine the stage expansion principle is carried still further, and quadruple expansion engines fitted, dividing the expansion into four stages, the boiler pressures being generally 200 lbs. per square inch, and in some cases 250 lbs. per square inch.

These engines are more suitable for the mercantile marine, where the range of powers required from the engines is limited, than for the Navy, where this range is large ; also as regards the Navy generally, evidence does not show that the additional complication thus introduced, and the extra length of engine room required, together with the additional engine friction, is compensated for by a sufficient gain in economy. They are gradually being introduced into the mercantile marine, but in the Navy only one torpedo boat and some smaller craft have been so fitted.

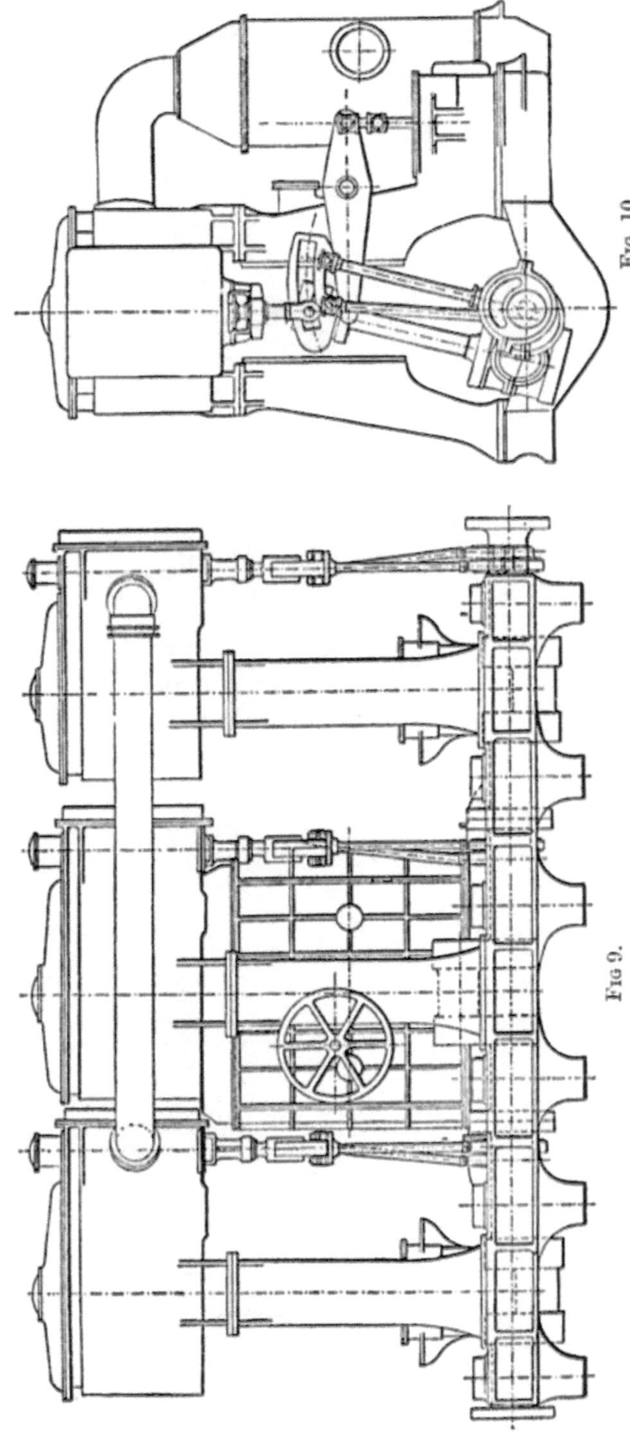

Fig. 10.

Fig 9.

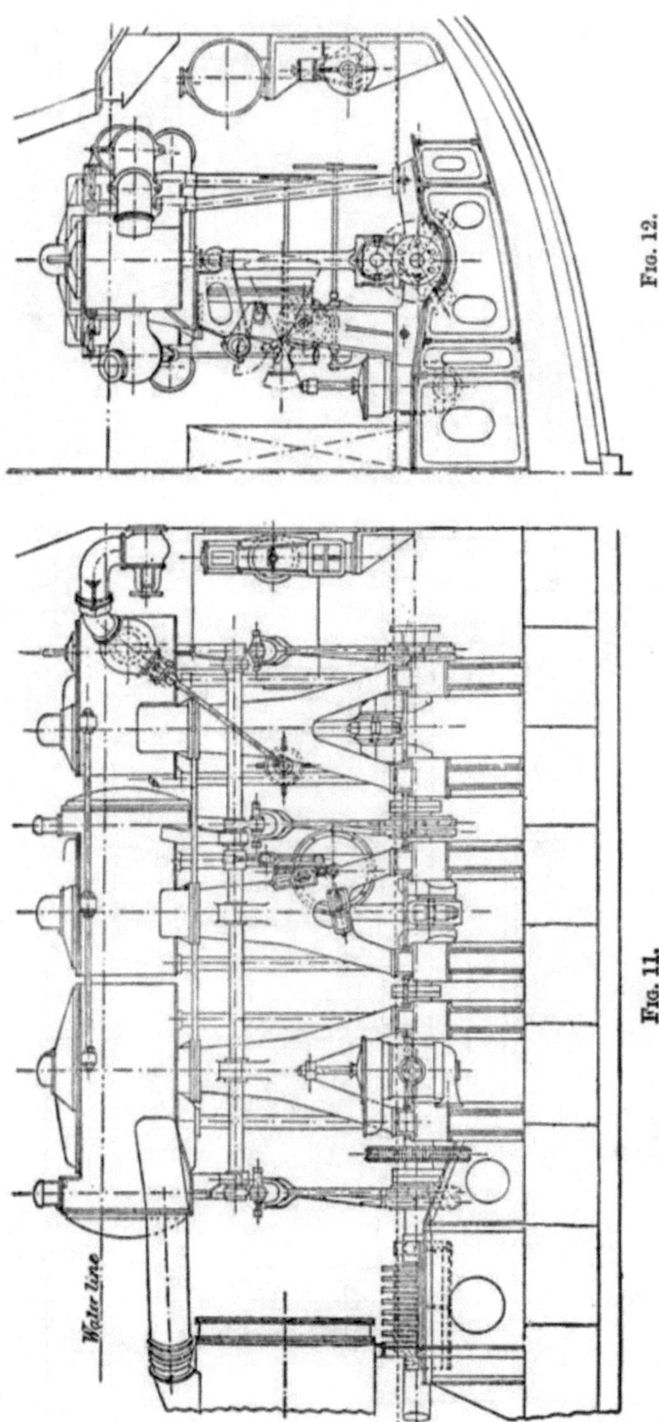

Fig. 12.

Fig. 11.

Improvements in economy.—In consequence of the improvements effected, the consumption of coal with the most recent engines is less than one-third that required for the engines generally used before 1860, and the effect on warships of this great reduction of coal expenditure has been twofold :—

a. The increased distance ships are able to steam without exhausting their coal supply has rendered seagoing mastless armour-clad ships possible.

b. The reduced quantity of coal necessary to be carried for the same radius of action has enabled space and weight which would formerly have been required for coals to be devoted to other objects in order to increase their offensive or defensive powers.

Corresponding benefits have also been derived by the mercantile marine.

Forced draught.—The conditions of service of ships in the Royal Navy render it necessary to provide for the development of high power and speed on special occasions, such as the events of action, chasing, &c., although the greater portion of the work of the ship has to be performed at comparatively low powers. It is therefore desirable in warships to provide special means of forcing the boilers when the full speed is required. Formerly a steam jet in the chimney was used for this purpose, but this wastes a lot of fresh water. In 1882 the system of forming the stokeholds into closed compartments, and keeping them under air-pressure by means of blowing fans was adopted and continued to the present day, with results that are satisfactory, provided only a moderate pressure of air be used, and by this means the steam generating powers of the boilers have been largely increased. Details of the fittings required for this purpose are given in Chapter V. The introduction of *forced draught* has enabled the weight of machinery to be considerably reduced, and the average weight of machinery for the latest modern warships fitted with circular boilers is about $1\frac{3}{4}$ cwt. per I.H.P. developed with moderate forced draught. A lesser weight than this, viz., $1\frac{1}{2}$ cwt., was at one period allowed, but this is not now recommended.

From this brief sketch a general idea may be formed of the progress that has been made in marine engineering. The machinery of the 'Salamander,' built in 1832, weighed 275 tons, developed 400 I.H.P., and consumed 7 to 8 lbs. of coal per horse-power. In modern warships, machinery of the same weight would, under moderate forced draught, be capable of developing satisfactorily at least 3,000 I.H.P., with about one-fourth the consumption of coal per horse-power, and the space occupied would be considerably less. Another important feature is the great increase in the total power now available for the propulsion of vessels at high speeds. For example, in H.M.S. 'Terrible,' which in 1845 represented the finest type of steam warship of the day, the I.H.P. was less than 2,000, and her speed about 10 knots, while in the present H.M.S. 'Terrible,' a first-class cruiser, the horse-power is 25,600, and the speed 22·8 knots. In a later series of cruisers, the 'Drake' class, the power is still greater, viz. 30,000 I.H.P.

Future progress.—Quite recently water-tube boilers, of various types, have been adopted in the Navy with steam pressure in boilers of 300 lbs. and engines working at 250 lbs. per square inch. A great impetus will probably be given to the use of higher steam pressures by the more extended use of this type of boiler, since there is then, within moderate limits, but little increase of boiler weights involved by higher pressures, the only increase of importance being in the engine. Probably the near future will see a general advance of steam pressure coupled with the use of the water-tube boiler, and, especially in the mercantile marine, the development of quadruple expansion engines.

Considerable progress is still possible as regards the boiler in the reduction of the great waste of heat which now takes place, due either to incomplete combustion, or the inability of the heat-absorbing surfaces, as now arranged, to prevent a serious loss of heat in the escaping gases. Further reductions in coal expenditure may be expected in the future under each of these heads.

More attention seems necessary also as regards the mechanical efficiency of the engines used in large vessels. Careful tests in this direction would probably point out many ways in which improvement would result.

CHAPTER II.

WORK AND EFFICIENCY.

Force, work, and energy.—Force is that which acts in producing or resisting motion in a body, and may be represented by a pressure or a pull. The British unit of force is the weight of one pound avoirdupois, and forces are therefore expressed generally as being equal to so many pounds weight.

A force is said to perform work when by its action resistance is overcome and motion produced. This union of force and motion is essential to the conception of *work.* However great the pressure applied, unless the body acted on be moved, no work is done. *Energy* is the term used to signify the capacity of a body for doing work. For example, if a force acts through a certain distance it is said to *exert energy,* while the resistance overcome through a certain distance by means of this exertion is the *work done.*

Measurement of work and energy.—The amount of work done is measured by multiplying the magnitude of the resistance—or, in other words, the force opposing the motion—by the distance through which the resistance is overcome, estimated in the direction of the resistance. Energy is measured in a similar manner.

The British unit of work is the foot-pound, which is a very convenient term, implying the combination of force and motion, which is the essential condition for the performance of work. One foot-pound represents the amount of work done in raising a weight of one pound through a distance of one foot, or more generally the exertion of a pressure of one pound through the distance of one foot. If 20 pounds be raised 50 ft., the amount of work performed is represented by $20 \times 50 = 1{,}000$ foot-pounds.

Sometimes for convenience other units of work are used, but they are all formed on the same basis and expressed in a similar manner. For example, the work performed in raising one ton one inch is sometimes called one inch-ton, and it is equal to 2,240 inch-pounds or $\dfrac{2240}{12}$ foot-pounds. The work of lifting one ton one foot is one foot-ton, and so on. It will be seen that the different terms used are self-explanatory and are convertible one to another. The foot-pound is, however, the general unit, the others only being employed for convenience in special cases.

Power, horse-power.—In the conception of work and energy no question of time enters. When, however, we consider also the time taken to perform so much work, we are considering *power.* Just as the term *work* necessarily involves distance, so does the term power involve time as well as distance. *Power* may be defined as the *rate at which work is done*. The natural unit of power would be the power of doing work at the rate of one foot-pound per minute, but it is too small to be convenient in engineering. The unit of power adopted is the power of doing work at the rate of 33,000 foot-pounds per minute. This unit of power is termed a *horse-power*.

Efficiency.—In every machine there are always certain causes acting that produce waste of work, so that the whole work done by the machine is not usefully employed, some of it being exerted in overcoming the friction of the mechanism, and some wasted in various other ways. The fraction representing the ratio that the useful work done bears to the total energy exerted on the machine is called the *Efficiency of the machine* ; or

$$\text{Efficiency} = \frac{\text{Useful work done}}{\text{Total energy expended}}$$

In the propelling apparatus of a vessel, in which the useful work is measured by its effect in giving speed to the ship, there are four successive stages, in each of which a portion of the initial energy is wasted, and these four stages all tend to decrease the total efficiency.

In the first place, only a portion of the heat of combustion of the coal is communicated to the water in the boiler, the remainder being wasted in various ways. The fraction of the total heat that is transmitted to the water in the boiler is, in ordinary cases, not more than from $\frac{6}{10}$ to $\frac{7}{10}$. This fraction is called the *Efficiency of the boiler*.

Secondly. The steam, after leaving the boiler, exerts energy on the piston of the engine ; but, in consequence of the narrow limits of temperature between which the engine is worked, this energy represents only a small fraction of the total heat contained in the steam. The fraction varies very considerably, depending on the type of engine, its steam pressure, rate of expansion, &c.—say from $\frac{1}{5}$ to $\frac{1}{20}$. In large modern *marine* engines it may be taken as from $\frac{1}{5}$ to $\frac{1}{9}$. This fraction, representing the ratio of the energy exerted by the steam to the total amount of heat expended on it, is called the *Efficiency of the steam.*

Thirdly. In the engine itself, a part of the energy exerted by the steam on the pistons is wasted in overcoming the friction of the working parts of the machinery, and in working the pumps, &c. The remainder appears as useful work in driving the propeller. The fraction, representing the ratio that this useful work bears to the total energy exerted by the pistons, is called the *Efficiency of the mechanism* Its value is from $\frac{8}{10}$ to $\frac{8\frac{1}{2}}{10}$, the former being more general.

Fourthly. The propeller, in addition to driving the ship, expends some of the energy transmitted to it in agitating and churning the water in which it acts, and the work thus performed is wasted ; the only useful work being that employed in overcoming the resistance of the ship and driving her through the water. The ratio of this useful work to the total energy expended by the propeller is called the *Efficiency of the propeller.* It may be taken as averaging from $\frac{5}{10}$ to $\frac{6}{10}$.

The resultant *Efficiency of the marine steam-engine or the whole propelling apparatus* is made up of the four efficiencies just stated, and is given by the product of the four factors representing respectively the efficiencies of the boiler, the steam, the mechanism, and the propeller. Any improvement in the efficiency of the marine steam-engine, and, consequently, in the economy of its performance, is therefore due to an increase in one or more of these elements, and we shall deal with these several points, and in each case describe the efforts that have been made to increase the efficiency.

The efficiency of the marine steam-engine will be seen to be very low. Taking the best case indicated by our figures, viz. that of an engine which has the maximum efficiency in each of the four components of the resultant efficiency, the efficiency would be :—

$$\frac{7}{10} \times \frac{1}{5} \times \frac{8\frac{1}{2}}{10} \times \frac{6}{10} = \frac{357}{5000} = \cdot071.$$

The highest efficiency now attainable is, therefore, a little over 7 per cent. with the marine steam-engine, and is generally less—say nearer 5 or 6 per cent.

Further information respecting this is given under the respective headings in greater detail.

CHAPTER III.

HEAT AND ITS EFFECT ON WATER.

IN order to comprehend the principles on which the construction and performance of the steam-engine depend, and the object of the various improvements that have from time to time been introduced, it is necessary that the true nature and properties of heat should be known. We will, therefore, as concisely as possible, state the principal points relative to this subject, in order that the succeeding chapters may be clearly understood.

Temperature.—The temperature of a body may be defined as the extent to which it may be capable of communicating sensible heat, or heat that may be felt, to other adjacent bodies.

When two bodies of different temperatures are placed in contact with each other, it is a well-known fact that the hotter body becomes cooler and the colder body hotter, till at length the two bodies become of the same temperature, after which no change in the temperature takes place. This is caused by the passage of heat from the hotter to the colder body, and shows clearly that heat is something that can be transferred from one body to another, so as to diminish the amount of heat in the former body and increase it in the latter.

Effect of and nature of heat.—When heat is added to or abstracted from a body, one of the two following effects is produced : either the temperature of the body is altered, or its state is changed. For example, if heat be added to water under the atmospheric pressure, the temperature is increased until it reaches 212° Fahr. After this the addition of heat does not further increase the temperature, but causes the water to evaporate and become steam—that is, it changes the condition from that of a liquid to that of a gas. Again, if heat be abstracted from water, the temperature is reduced till it reaches 32° Fahr., after which the diminution of heat does not further decrease the temperature, but changes the condition of the water from the liquid to the solid state, forming ice. The quantities of heat passing from one body to another can thus be estimated by the effects produced, so that it is clear that heat is something that can be both transferred and measured.

The true nature of heat has been determined by experiments on friction. It is a matter of common observation that the work expended in friction is apparently lost—that is, it appears no longer in the form of mechanical work ; but at every place where friction occurs, heat is developed, and the greater the friction the greater is the amount of heat produced. Experiments have shown that the amount of heat generated by friction is exactly equivalent to the amount of work lost, and we therefore infer that heat is of the same nature as mechanical work—that is, it is one of the forms of energy.

British thermal unit.—The unit by which heat is measured is called a thermal unit, and in British measurements represents the quantity of heat necessary to raise one pound of water at its maximum density, which corresponds to a temperature of about 39° Fahr., through one degree Fahr.

Joule's equivalent.—The honour of determining the exact relation between heat and mechanical work belongs to Mr. Joule, who proved, by an elaborate series of careful experiments on the friction of oil, water, mercury, and other substances, that one thermal unit is equal to 772 foot-pounds of mechanical work [1]—that is, that the quantity of heat necessary to raise the temperature of one pound of water at its maximum density, one degree Fahr., can be made to perform work equal to the raising of 772 lbs. one foot high. In honour of the discoverer this important constant, 772, expressing the relation between heat and mechanical work, is called Joule's equivalent, and is frequently denoted by the letter J.

The convertibility of heat and work, in a definite ratio, is expressed in the following statement, generally known as the mechanical theory of heat, viz. : Heat and mechanical energy are mutually convertible, and heat requires for its production, and produces by its disappearance, mechanical energy in the proportion of 772 foot-pounds for each unit of heat. This statement forms also the *first law of the science of thermo-dynamics.*

Communication of heat.—Heat may be communicated from one body to another in three different ways, viz., by radiation, conduction, and convection.

Radiation.—Radiant heat is given off from hot bodies in straight lines, and the rays of heat are subject to the same laws as the rays of light. As far as the generation of steam is concerned the useful radiation is confined to the furnace, the crowns and sides of which, intercepting the rays of heat from the burning fuel, become themselves heated, and the heat passes through them to the water in the boiler. A considerable amount of heat is given off by radiation from burning coal, and it is very important, therefore, to intercept this, and to insure that as far as possible the whole of the heat diffused in this way should be transmitted, either directly or indirectly, to the water in the boiler, and not wasted on the external air or other bodies.

Radiation is an important item to be considered with reference to the economical employment of steam, for it always causes a certain loss of heat, and unless proper precautions are taken this loss may become very considerable.

The surfaces of the boilers, steam-pipes, cylinders, &c., when the engines are at work, are very much hotter than the surrounding bodies, and consequently, in order that loss of heat by radiation may be avoided as far as possible, all those surfaces should be clothed with some non-conducting material. Hair-felt has been largely employed for this purpose, and this is usually kept in its place by an outer

---

[1] Subsequent experiment appears to show that the exact value is somewhat (nearly 1 per cent.) higher than this—viz., 778.

covering of canvas, wood, or sheet-iron. Preparations of cork and other non-conducting materials have also been used. These substances, however, when applied to very hot surfaces, are in danger of being burnt away, and various incombustible non-conductors, such as asbestos, silicate cotton, fossil meal, &c., are now used. The efficient clothing of the hot surfaces is of great importance, and if it be neglected the economical working of the machinery may be seriously impaired.

Conduction.—The second way in which heat may be transferred from one body to another is by conduction. There are two kinds of conduction, called respectively internal and external conduction. The conduction that takes place between the contiguous particles of one continuous body is called internal conduction. The term external conduction is used when heat passes through the points of contact of two distinct bodies.

In boiler plates and flues the resistance offered to heat entering and leaving the surfaces of the plates is in general so much greater than the resistance offered to its passage through the body of the plate, that the nature and thickness of the plate have little effect on the rate of conduction through it, so that the rate depends on the difference of temperature of the fluids on the two sides of the plate.

The following approximate rule was given by Rankine for the rate of conduction through boiler plates and flues, but its accuracy is some-what doubtful :—

$$q = \frac{(T_1 - T_2)^2}{a},$$

where q = rate of conduction through the plate, in thermal units per square foot of surface per hour ;

T_1 and T_2 = the temperatures on the opposite sides of the plate ;

and a = a constant, which is in ordinary cases between 160 and 200.

Convection.—The third method of transfer of heat is by convection. This is the way in which gases and liquids are heated. Conduction, in the true sense of the word, is very slow in liquids, and almost, if not wholly, inappreciable in gases. When heat is applied to the bottom of a vessel containing a fluid, the particles in contact with the bottom are first heated, and become less dense and therefore rise through the superincumbent mass of fluid, allowing cooler particles to take their place, which become themselves heated, and rise and circulate through the mass in a similar manner.

It is essential that circulation and mixture of all the particles of a fluid should take place to cause the temperature to be uniform throughout the mass. In order that heat may be efficiently transmitted through boiler plates and flues, each of the fluids in contact with them—viz. the water on the one side, and the heated gases on the other—should have free circulation, so that the particles in contact with the plates should not be considerably different in temperature from those at some distance from the plates. Boilers are sometimes fitted with circulating plates to set up currents in the water, and with bafflers and bridges in the flues to break up the currents of hot gas and form eddies, in order to promote circulation and mixture in the respective fluids.

In order to render the transfer of heat from one fluid to another through a plate most efficient, the general motion of the two fluids should be in opposite directions to each other, so that the hottest parts of the two fluids are opposed, and the least difference of temperature differs as little as possible from the greatest difference. Consequently, in a boiler, in order that the best results may be obtained, the feed-pipes and circulating plates should be so arranged that the general motion given to the water should be as far as possible in the opposite direction to that of the hot gases on their way to the funnel. For the same reason, the action of a surface condenser is most efficient when the cold water, for condensing the steam, enters the condenser at the end at which the condensed water leaves it, so that the entering steam will be opposed to the water which has been heated to some extent by its passage through the condenser.

Application of heat to water.—We will now consider the effects produced by the application of heat to water. At first the temperature of the water is raised. The particles of water in contact with the heating surface, which in a marine boiler consists of the plates of furnace, combustion chamber, and tubes, become heated, and rise and circulate through the mass of water, their places being taken by cooler particles, till at length the whole of the water is raised to the boiling point by the convection of heat.

Sensible heat.—The heat added to the water up to the temperature at which boiling occurs is generally called sensible heat, its effect being simply to change the temperature, and not the state, of the water, and its amount may be calculated by means of the thermometer.

Latent heat.—After this, in order to convert the boiling water into steam, a large quantity of heat has to be expended which does not produce any increase in the temperature. This heat is known as *latent heat*.

During the period when heat was considered as a kind of substance called *caloric*, it was supposed that the quantity of heat required for evaporation became hidden or latent in some way during the change from the liquid to the gaseous state, and that it again became sensible or tangible on the reverse process being performed. We now, however, know that heat is not a substance, but simply one of several forms of mechanical energy, and the development of the science of thermo-dynamics has shown that this amount of heat, instead of being lost or hidden, is simply expended, principally in performing the work of overcoming the molecular cohesion of the particles of water which resists the change of state, and also in overcoming the resistance of external bodies to the change of volume which ensues. Work is therefore done in changing the water from a liquid into a gas, and this is stored up as mechanical energy, which can be yielded back again either as work, or heat, when the gas returns to the original state of water.

The term *latent heat* has been retained for the sake of convenience, but it must be understood as an expression that means simply *the quantity of heat that must be added to or subtracted from a body in a given state, to change it into another state without altering its temperature.*

Boiling point.—The boiling point, or the temperature of ebullition of any liquid, may be defined as that stage in the addition of heat to the liquid at which the pressure on it is just overcome by the pressure of vapour due to the temperature.

The temperature of the boiling point depends on the *pressure* under which the liquid is evaporated. The greater the pressure the higher is the temperature at which the liquid boils.

Pressure in lbs. per square inch by gauge	Pressure in lbs. per square inch absolute	Temperature of boiling point Fahrenheit	Latent heat in B.T.Us.	Sensible heat from 32° F., B.T.Us.	Total heat from 32° F., B.T.Us.	Volume of 1 lb. of steam in cubic feet	Weight of 1 cubic foot of steam in lbs.	Increase of pressure in lbs. per sq. in. for difference of 1° F.	Increase of temperature in degrees Fahr. for increase of 1 lb. pressure
1	2	3	4	5	6	7	8	9	10
−4·7	10·	193·24	979·0	161·91	1140·91	37·84	·0264	·250	3·991
0	14·7	212·00	965·7	180·90	1146·60	26·36	·0380	·398	2·510
15	29·7	249·65	938·9	219·15	1158·05	13·62	·07343	·542	1·846
20	34·7	258·88	932·3	228·55	1160·86	11·78	·08492	·644	1·554
25	39·7	266·65	926·8	236·47	1163·30	10·371	·09641	·693	1·440
30	44·7	273·87	921·7	243·86	1165·50	9·280	·10777	·758	1·320
35	49·7	280·47	917·0	250·60	1167·50	8·396	·11908	·824	1·210
40	54·7	286·54	912·6	256·76	1169·36	7·677	·13028	·888	1·128
45	59·7	292·18	908·5	262·56	1171·07	7·080	·14143	·948	1·056
50	64·7	297·46	904·6	268·07	1172·66	6·557	·15258	1·029	·972
55	69·7	302·32	901·2	273·00	1174·20	6·108	·16354	1·046	·956
60	74·7	307·10	897·7	277·89	1175·60	5·729	·17447	1·131	·888
65	79·7	311·54	894·5	282·44	1176·95	5·393	·18539	1·183	·844
70	84·7	315·76	891·5	286·78	1178·24	5·096	·19632	1·242	·804
75	89·7	319·78	888·6	290·90	1179·45	4·825	·20724	1·295	·772
80	94·7	323·64	885·8	294·89	1180·62	4·587	·21801	1·351	·740
85	99·7	327·34	883·1	298·64	1181·74	4·371	·22876	1·408	·710
90	104·7	330·89	880·5	302·37	1182·84	4·171	·23951	1·457	·686
95	109·7	334·32	878·0	305·90	1183·89	3·996	·25026	1·520	·658
100	114·7	337·61	875·6	309·28	1184·87	3·836	·26091	1·597	·626
110	124·7	343·87	871·1	315·73	1186·78	3·543	·28221	1·698	·589
120	134·7	349·76	866·8	321·86	1188·64	3·296	·30351	1·795	·557
130	144·7	355·33	862·7	327·63	1190·34	3·077	·32470	1·905	·525
140	154·7	360·58	858·9	333·08	1191·94	2·893	·34577	1·996	·501
150	164·7	365·59	855·2	338·28	1193·47	2·726	·36684	2·096	·477
160	174·7	370·36	851·7	343·22	1194·92	2·577	·38791	2·183	·458
170	184·7	374·94	848·3	347·98	1196·29	2·448	·40871	2·288	·437
180	194·7	379·31	845·1	352·54	1197·61	2·330	·42951	2·381	·420
190	204·7	383·51	842·0	356·86	1198·90	2·222	·45006	2·463	·406
200	214·7	387·57	839·0	361·14	1200·14	2·126	·47062	2·558	·391
210	224·7	391·48	836·1	365·23	1201·33	2·036	·49118	2·653	·377
220	234·7	395·25	833·3	369·16	1202·48	1·954	·51174	2·732	·366
230	244·7	398·91	830·6	372·96	1203·59	1·879	·53230	2·825	·354
240	254·7	402·45	827·9	376·65	1204·58	1·809	·55279	2·907	·344
250	264·7	405·89	825·4	380·21	1205·64	1·744	·57319	2·994	·334
260	274·7	409·23	823·0	383·68	1206·68	1·685	·59358	3·077	·325
270	284·7	412·48	820·6	387·11	1207·71	1·629	·61399	3·165	·316
280	294·7	415·64	818·2	390·46	1208·67	1·576	·63440	3·247	·308
290	304·7	418·72	815·9	393·75	1209·61	1·528	·65485	3·322	·301
300	314·7	421·73	813·6	396·88	1210·54	1·481	·67516	3·401	·294
310	324·7	424·67	811·4	399·99	1211·45	1·438	·69545	3·484	·287
320	334·7	427·54	809·2	403·10	1212·34	1·398	·71574	3·571	·280
330	344·7	430·34	807·1	406·10	1213·18	1·359	·73605	3·650	·274
340	354·7	433·08	805·0	409·01	1213·98	1·322	·75636	3·731	·268
350	364·7	435·76	802·9	411·84	1214·77	1·288	·77662		

The foregoing table gives the boiling temperatures of fresh water for various pressures, ascertained from the experiments of M. Regnault.

The temperature depends on the *total or absolute pressure*, i.e. the pressure including that of the atmosphere, so that in ascertaining the temperature corresponding to any given pressure, as shown on an ordinary pressure gauge, the atmospheric pressure must be added.

To obtain the latent heat corresponding to any pressure intermediate to those given above, it will be sufficient for practical purposes to use the method of interpolation, thus : to ascertain the latent heat corresponding to 106 lbs. by gauge we have :—Latent heat for 100 lbs. $= 875 \cdot 6$ B.T.U. Difference for 10 lbs. $= 4 \cdot 5$ ∴ Difference for 6 lbs. $= \frac{6}{10} \times 4 \cdot 5 = 2 \cdot 7$ ∴ Latent heat at 106 lbs. $= 872 \cdot 9$ B.T.U. Similar methods may be used for intermediate values in columns 5 to 8. Intermediate values for corresponding pressures and temperatures may be obtained by the use of columns 9 and 10.

To meet the cases of pressures below atmospheric pressure the following table has been prepared showing the temperature corresponding to various amounts of vacuum. It will be found useful in dealing with questions concerning condensers :—

Vacuum measured in inches of Mercury	Absolute pressure in inches of Mercury	Absolute pressure in lbs. per square inch	Temperature of boiling point in degrees Fahrenheit	Latent heat of evaporation in B.T.Us.	Sensible heat of evaporation from 32° F. in B.T.Us.	Total heat of evaporation from 32° F. in B.T.Us.
Gauge						
$29\frac{1}{2}$	$\frac{1}{2}$	·245	59·1	1072·8	27·1	1100·0
29	1	·490	79·3	1058·8	47·3	1106·1
$28\frac{1}{2}$	$1\frac{1}{2}$	·735	92·0	1049·9	60·1	1110·0
28	2	·980	101·4	1044·4	69·5	1112·8
27	3	1·470	115·3	1033·7	83·4	1117·1
26	4	1·96	125·6	1026·5	93·8	1120·3
25	5	2·45	134·0	1020·6	102·2	1122·8
24	6	2·94	141·0	1015·7	109·3	1125·0
23	7	3·43	147·0	1011·5	115·3	1126·8
22	8	3·92	152·3	1007·8	120·5	1128·4
21	9	4·41	157·0	1004·5	125·4	1129·8
20	10	4·90	161·5	1001·3	129·9	1131·2
19	11	5·39	165·6	998·4	134·1	1132·4
18	12	5·88	169·2	995·9	137·7	1133·5
17	13	6·37	172·8	993·4	140·3	1134·6
16	14	6·86	176·0	991·1	144·5	1135·6
15	15	7·35	179·1	988·8	147·7	1136·5
14	16	7·84	182·0	986·9	150·6	1137·4
12	18	8·82	187·4	983·1	156·0	1139·1
10	20	9·80	192·3	979·6	161·0	1140·6
5	25	12·25	203·0	972·1	171·8	1143·9
0	30	14·70	212·0	965·7	180·9	1146·6

14·7 lbs. = atmospheric pressure = 30 inches of mercury.

The boiling point of a liquid is also affected by its *density*. Solid matter dissolved in the liquid, as, for example, salt in water, resists ebullition and increases the temperature at which the liquid boils.

Ordinary sea-water contains about $\frac{1}{32}$ or $\frac{1}{33}$ part of solid matter, and this raises the temperature of the boiling point by 1·2° Fahr., so that the boiling point of sea-water under the atmospheric pressure, instead of being 212° Fahr., is 213·2° Fahr.   The density of the water in marine boilers in ordinary work is generally not allowed to exceed three to four times that of sea-water, and at this density the boiling point at atmospheric pressure would be about 216° Fahr.

Total heat and latent heat of evaporation.—The *total heat of evaporation* is the sum of the sensible heat and latent heat of evaporation, and is defined as the quantity of heat necessary to raise one pound of water from the freezing point, 32° Fahr., to a particular temperature, and to evaporate it at that temperature.

If H represent the total heat of evaporation, L the latent heat of evaporation, and S the sensible heat, we have

$$H = L + S.$$

The *latent heat of evaporation* of a pound of steam in thermal units at any given temperature of evaporation, T, is given by the following approximate formula :—

$$L = 966 - 0·7\,(T - 212)$$

Though the latent heat diminishes considerably as the temperature of evaporation is increased, the increase of temperature, or, in other words, the increase of sensible heat, is greater than the decrease of the latent heat, so that the *total heat of evaporation* is gradually increased. This is shown in column 6 of table.

The table also gives approximately, in thermal units, the latent, sensible, and total heat of evaporation of one pound of steam up to a pressure of 350 lbs. per square inch above the atmosphere, which is not exceeded by the highest pressure used at present in marine boilers, whether cylindrical or water-tube.   The volume of one pound of steam and the weight of one cubic foot have also been added for each pressure.

The *total heat of evaporation*, at any temperature T, may be calculated from the following formula [1] :—

$$\begin{aligned}
H &= L + S \\
  &= 966 - 0·7\,(T - 212) + (T - 32) \\
  &= 1082 + 0·3T
\end{aligned}$$

This formula shows very clearly that the rate of increase in the total heat of evaporation, as the temperature of evaporation is raised, is about $\frac{3}{10}$ of a thermal unit for each degree of rise of temperature.

Evaporation of water under constant pressure.—The different stages in the evaporation of water just discussed may be summarised in the following manner :—

Suppose one pound of water, at a temperature of 32° Fahr., to be

---

[1] These formulæ assume the specific heat of water to be constant, which assumption is sufficiently accurate for the purpose of this book.   It is found, however, that the specific heat gradually increases, so that at a temperature of 400° F., it is about 4 per cent. greater than it is at 39° F. ; allowing for this, more accurate formulæ are

$$L = 966 - ·71\,(T - 212)\ \text{and}\ H = 1082 + ·305\,T.$$

contained in a cylinder A B, open at the top, in which a piston c works steam-tight, loaded with a certain weight. The pressure on the water, indicated by arrows, consists of the weight of the piston, the weights added, and the atmospheric pressure. This pressure is represented by P pounds per square inch on the piston.

In Fig. 13 three stages in the process of applying heat to the bottom of the cylinder are shown.

Practically no movement of the piston occurs until the temperature of evaporation is attained, which temperature will depend on the amount of the pressure P produced by the piston on the water. This part of the process, viz. the raising of the temperature from the freezing to the boiling point, is shown in Stage 1.

From this point the *temperature* remains constant, and steam is given off at the constant pressure P pounds per square inch, which causes the piston to gradually rise, as shown in the two figures of Stage 2, the piston continuing to rise during the addition of heat, as more and more of the water is evaporated, until the whole of the water is turned into steam. The first sketch for Stage 2 represents the condition of affairs when only a portion of the water has been evaporated ; the second sketch for this stage represents the final condition, when all the water has just been evaporated. During the whole of this stage the temperature remains constant at that corresponding to the pressure of evaporation P.

If, after all the water is evaporated, more heat be applied to the steam in the cylinder, the pressure P on the piston remaining the same, the volume will continue to increase still further, while the temperature also will again increase, and both volume and temperature would increase without limit if sufficient heat be applied. The steam in this case is said to be superheated, and is indicated in Stage 3.

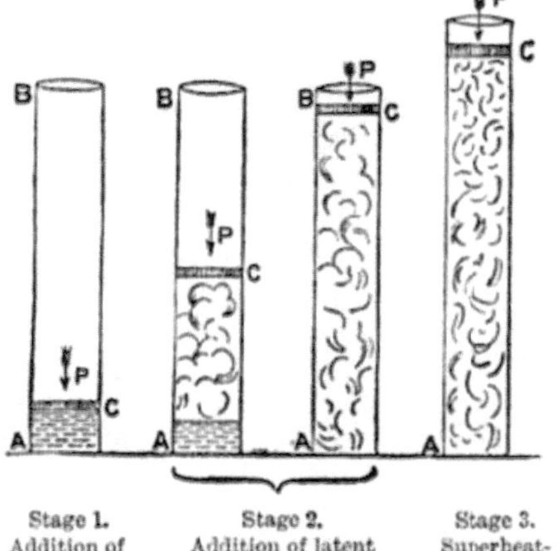

Stage 1.
Addition of sensible heat. Rising temperature.

Stage 2.
Addition of latent heat. Steam saturated. Constant temperature.

Stage 3.
Superheating. Rising temperature.

Fig. 13.

In Stage 1, therefore, we have increase of temperature without any practical increase of volume ; in Stage 2, increase of volume without increase of temperature ; in Stage 3 we have increase of both temperature and volume.

For a complete theory of the steam-engine a thorough knowledge of all these stages would be required, but the properties of steam in the last stage, viz. when heated without being in contact with water, have not yet been fully ascertained, and in investigations on the action of superheated steam it is generally assumed that its properties are sensibly those of a perfect gas. This assumption appears to be correct, provided the steam be considerably superheated, but not for moderate degrees of superheating.

Steam for marine engines which has been superheated by the direct application of heat is not now generally used since high pressures have been introduced. As, however, the formation of steam which has been superheated to a certain extent indirectly by the action of the mechanism is common, accurate information as to its behaviour when in this condition seems desirable.

Extensive experiments have however been made, giving almost all necessary information with reference to the other stages, which are those that most concern us in this treatise.

Evaporation of steam at constant volume.—An important modification in the conditions under which the steam is generated in the above example will now be considered. It has been pointed out that the piston in the cylinder illustrated above, is free to move and allow the steam to gradually expand in volume as the water is evaporated, but we will now suppose that this is not the case, and that the piston is fixed in the cylinder at a certain distance from the water, so that whatever steam is formed from the water has to occupy the same constant volume, as shown in Fig. 14. Suppose further that only the water occupies the space A C, so that there is no pressure therein. If heat be now applied to the water, instead of the formation of steam taking place only when a certain temperature is reached, as in our first case, steam immediately commences to be formed, and *both the temperature and the pressure* gradually increase as more of the water is evaporated, although the temperature and pressure are still connected by the same law as before.

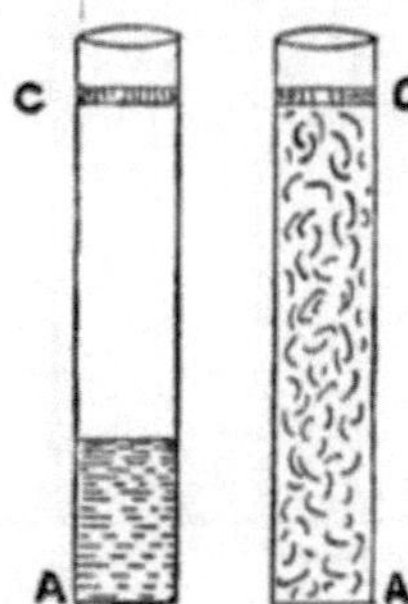

Fig. 14.

The pressure and temperature of the steam when all the water has just been evaporated can be ascertained from our knowledge of the weight of water, and the known volume of the steam, for the weight of steam is the same as that of the water from which it was formed, so that its volume per pound can be calculated, whence from column 7 of table, page 26, its pressure and temperature can be ascertained.

It will be seen at once that this can occur in practice when steam is being raised in a boiler, from cold water, with the stop-valves and other outlets shut, except that instead of there not being any pressure on the water prior to the application of heat, there is the pressure of the atmosphere. In this case the temperature of the water will gradually rise, but no steam will be formed, and the pressure will not increase till the temperature reaches that corresponding to the atmospheric pressure—viz. 212° F.—when steam commences to be given off, and both temperature and pressure rise. In our practical illustration, also, the evaporation does not continue till all the water is evaporated, as the amount of water is so large compared with the volume of the boiler that the desired pressure is attained when only a small portion of the water has been evaporated.

To ascertain exactly the expenditure of heat necessary to accomplish this raising of steam pressure, we see that the whole weight of water has been raised to the final temperature and a small portion of it evaporated. In an ordinary cylindrical boiler, however, the volume of water is generally from ·65 to ·75 times the whole internal volume of the boiler, so that the amount of heat expended in formation of steam is comparatively very small.

In all such cases of raising steam from cold water, or of raising steam pressure from one point to another, the expenditure of heat in thermal units may, for all practical purposes, be taken as $W (T_1 - T_2)$, where

$$W = \text{weight of water in pounds.}$$
$$T_1 = \text{final temperature of water.}$$
$$T_2 = \text{initial temperature of water.}$$

The correction due to neglecting the formation of steam will not exceed about 1 per cent., even at high pressures, with the proportions common in the usual marine boilers.

CHAPTER IV.

COMBUSTION AND ECONOMY OF FUEL—BOILER EFFICIENCY.

In this chapter the processes through which fuel passes during combustion will be considered, and the precautions necessary to insure economy in the process.

Owing to the extent of its occurrence in nature and being always easily obtainable, the common fuel for boilers practically consists of coal. Mineral oil has been tried in the past and the results were originally not good, but its use is now being revived with greater success. Both these fuels consist essentially of

Carbon,

Hydrogen,

and Oxygen,

and of these, the heating elements are hydrogen and carbon. Sulphur is sometimes present in small quantities, but its heating effect is small.

The presence of oxygen is considered to detract from the value of a fuel, as the oxygen is generally regarded as being already combined with its proportion of hydrogen in the form of water (H_2O). As these gases combine in the proportion of $1 : 8$ by weight, this virtually reduces the amount of hydrogen available for combustion by one-eighth of the weight of the oxygen present.

Combustion.—Combustion is simply a *rapid chemical union of oxygen with the hydrogen and carbon* in the fuel, heat being evolved during the process. When burning fuel in the furnace of a boiler, the main object to be effected is to obtain this heat and utilise it for the generation of steam. On account of the almost universal adoption of coal as a fuel, its combustion will be considered somewhat at length. In the first place a certain temperature is required for ignition, so that it is necessary to apply heat to start the process, but the subsequent chemical action produces the necessary temperature to continue the combustion.

There are two distinct stages in the combustion of coal, viz. the formation and combustion of the gases, and the combustion of the solid residue. The gaseous constituents of coal are not given off *during* the combustion, as the distillation of the gases is an entirely distinct operation from the combustion of the gases or solid residue.

Consider the combustion of bituminous coal, which is the most difficult to burn economically in furnaces on account of the inefficiency of the ordinary arrangements for consuming the gaseous products.

When coal is thrown on a bright fire, it at first absorbs heat from the fire to liberate the gaseous constituents. These are the same as the coal gas generated in retorts and used for lighting purposes, and consist principally of light carburetted hydrogen gas (fire-damp or marsh gas), represented by the chemical symbol CH_4, and heavy carburetted hydrogen gas (olefiant gas), denoted by the formula C_2H_4. Until all the gases are separated from the solid part of the fuel no combustion takes place, and the coal remains in an unburnt and comparatively cool state, so that, unless proper precautions are taken to consume the gases, they may be a source of loss instead of gain, because heat is abstracted from the fire to effect their liberation.

On the application of heat the hydrogen and carbon are separated ; and by providing an adequate supply of oxygen by means of atmospheric air each enters independently into combination with oxygen, forming steam and carbonic acid gas. From the combining equivalents of hydrogen, carbon, and oxygen, we find that each volume of light carburetted hydrogen gas will require two volumes of oxygen for its combustion, and each volume of the olefiant gas three volumes of oxygen. Thus, between two and three volumes of oxygen will be required for the complete combustion of each volume of the gas formed in the furnace ; and as the oxygen in atmospheric air amounts to only one-fifth of its bulk, between ten and fifteen volumes of air will be required for each volume of gas.

Air required for combustion of gases.—One ton of bituminous coal is estimated to produce about 10,000 cubic feet of gas ; therefore 100,000 to 150,000 cubic feet of air must actually combine with the gases produced from each ton of coal to effect their complete combustion. To insure thorough mingling of the air with the gas, in order to effect perfect combustion, it is found that from one and a half times to twice the quantity of air theoretically necessary must be admitted ; so that a minimum of 150,000 to a maximum of 300,000 cubic feet of air might be required for the combustion of the gases alone produced from one ton of bituminous coal, and it may be taken that not less than 200,000 cubic feet are necessary. All this air should, if the fires are thick, be admitted above the bars, as, if it were allowed to pass through the burning coal on the grate, it would be deprived of a great portion of its oxygen, and its value for burning the gas be depreciated.

Combustion of the solid carbon.— We come now to the coke or carbon that remains on the bars after the gases have been disposed of. The air for its combustion must pass between the bars and through the fuel. At first air is in excess and the union of oxygen with the carbon is complete, and carbonic acid gas (CO_2) is formed ; but if the layer of coal is thick relatively to the quantity of air passing through it, much of this gas as it rises through the fire takes up more carbon, forming carbonic oxide gas (CO), and unless arrangements are made to consume this gas by adding additional oxygen, a large quantity of heat will be wasted, the products of combustion passing off as carbonic oxide, by which less than one-third the heat is produced that would be yielded if the combustion were complete and the products passed off in the form of carbonic acid. It is therefore necessary, especially with thick fires, to admit air above the fuel, for the complete combustion of the carbon, in addition to that referred to already as necessary for the combustion of the gases.

Stoking.—The question of firing or stoking will now be considered a little in detail. Coal can easily be thrown through the fire doors, but skill is necessary to place it on those parts of the grate which require it. This is one of the chief requirements of good stoking, viz. to produce a fire of fairly uniform thickness over its whole area. If any depressions occur, the resistance to the passage of air is reduced so that the air flows through this part in greater volume and the coal is rapidly burned away and the bars may soon become bare.

With thin fires no doubt sufficient air for complete combustion may pass through the fuel, in which case we are independent of the air supply above it. More air also passes through a thin fire and so increases the rate of combustion and power of the boiler, unless carried to extreme limits.

With thick firing, although the doors are opened less frequently, thus causing less labour, large volumes of gases are suddenly produced, for which there is generally not sufficient air for combustion, and an undue lowering of temperature is caused, which may also prevent ignition. This is especially the case in most water-tube boilers, where the time for the gases to mingle with air and burn before reaching the tubes is small. On the whole, the plan giving the best results with usual arrangements is to ' fire lightly, fire quickly, and fire often ' ; and as this involves the greatest expenditure of manual labour on the part of the stokers, constant watchfulness on the part of persons in charge will be required to see it fully carried out. With large grates, such as most water-tube boilers are provided with, the two halves of the grate should be fired alternately at equal intervals, so that the gases liberated from the coal thrown on one half the grate are kept up in temperature for ignition and combustion, by the glowing carbon of the other half. For similar reasons the furnaces of tank boilers leading into the same combustion chamber should never be fired at the same time, but at intervals of four or five minutes.

Total quantity of air required.—The quantity of air necessary for the combustion of the carbonaceous portions of a ton of coal can be estimated as follows. Every 6 lbs. of carbon requires, in order to form carbonic acid gas (CO_2), 16 lbs. of oxygen. The volume of air necessary to supply this would be about 900 cubic feet. Assuming 80 per cent. of carbon in the coal, about 240,000 cubic feet of air are required *theoretically* for the combustion of the solid residue of each ton of coal after the gases have been distilled.

Increasing this from one and a half times to double the amount, as in the case of the gas, to insure perfect mingling, we get from 360,000 to 480,000 cubic feet, which, added to the 200,000 cubic feet required for the gas, make a total of 560,000 to 680,000 cubic feet, which enormous volume of air is necessary for the complete combustion of each ton of coal.

The following formula is given by Rankine for the weight of air theoretically necessary for the complete combustion of each pound of fuel :—

$$A = 12 \left\{ C + 3 \left(H - \frac{O}{8} \right) \right\}$$

where A = lbs. of air required per lb. of fuel ; and C, H, and O are the fractions of carbon, hydrogen, and oxygen respectively contained in the fuel.

This formula is obtained from the following considerations. The average composition of air by weight is practically 77 parts of nitrogen and a few other constituents, and 23 of oxygen ; and hence to obtain 1 lb. of oxygen, $\frac{100}{23}$ lbs. of air are required. From their atomic weights, it is seen that for complete combustion 1 lb. of carbon would require $\frac{32}{12}$ lbs. of oxygen, or $\frac{32}{12} \times \frac{100}{23} = 11\cdot6$ lb. of air ; and 1 lb. of hydrogen would want three times this quantity. Further, the effect of the oxygen in a fuel has already been explained (see p. 32), and thus the expression

$$A = 11\cdot6 \left\{ C + 3 \left(H - \frac{O}{8} \right) \right\}$$

is eventually obtained ; and in Rankine's formula quoted, the number 11·6 is replaced by the approximation 12.

By experience in actual cases it is found that where the draught is produced by artificial means, such as a fan, this theoretical quantity must be increased by one-half ; and in cases of natural or ordinary chimney draught it must be doubled in order to insure perfect mingling.

In practice it is not necessary to calculate with exactness the quantity of air required, and it is sufficient for all practical purposes to take 12 lbs. of air as the quantity chemically necessary for the combustion of each pound of coal. With natural draught, therefore, 24 lbs. of air must be supplied for each pound of coal to insure perfect admixture and combustion. With artificial draught 18 lbs. of air would probably be sufficient for each pound of coal. This forms, therefore, one advantage of accelerated draught, the temperature of the fire being thereby less decreased, so that the radiation of heat from the burning fuel is greater, and the loss from the heat carried off by the nitrogen in the air less.

Fire-grate.—The carbon being a solid body requires only a definite space, and since its combustion depends on the amount of air supplied to it, and not on the space it occupies, the area of the grate will depend on the draught employed. In locomotive and other boilers with forced draught the rate of combustion is often as high as from 80 to 90 lbs. of coal per square foot of grate per hour, whilst in those marine boilers with draught due only to the heated gases in the funnel, the rate is generally not more than from 20 to 25 lbs. per square foot of grate per hour.

It is essential for economy that the length of grate should be kept within such limits that it may be kept well and uniformly covered with coal. With very long grates there is danger that the back parts will not be properly covered, so that volumes of cold air rush in, cooling the gases, tubes, &c., and causing a considerable waste of heat.

Combustion chamber.—In the combustion chamber the gases are combined, and consequently allowance has to be made for their expansion ; the space above or beyond the fuel should therefore be made as large as possible. During the last few years the tendency has been to increase the combustion chambers of the tank boilers even at the expense of the loss of a certain amount of tube-heating surface, and this is found generally to increase the economical performance of the boilers. The combustion chambers of large single-ended tank boilers were often not more than 15 to 18 inches deep from the backs of the chambers to the tube-plates, but in the later examples they are seldom less than from 22 to 30 inches deep, and in many cases even larger. One method of construction that has the practical effect of increasing this size is to lead the furnaces into a common combustion chamber. By firing the furnaces alternately, the gas given off has the whole volume of the common combustion chamber of the furnaces in which to expand, as well as the heat from the adjacent furnaces to prevent the gases from falling below the temperature of ignition.

As regards the influence of combustion chamber space on the efficiency of a boiler, an interesting experiment was carried out on a marine boiler at Devonport by shortening the tubes one foot and adding to the width of combustion chamber by this amount. It was found that the efficiency of the boiler remained exactly as before the change, the greater volume for combustion, and the increased combustion-chamber surface making up for the loss of a much greater area of tube surface. A limit would, however, soon be reached, beyond which this reduction of tube surface could not be made without loss of efficiency.

It should always be borne in mind that no amount of heat can combine the gases unless air be supplied ; but, on the other hand, if the gases are not kept up to a certain temperature, called *the temperature of ignition*, the oxygen of the air will not chemically unite with them and cause combustion to take place.

In the water-tube boilers introduced into the Navy, it has not always been found possible to arrange for a corresponding combustion chamber to the tank boiler, although in some cases a comparatively large tube surface is arranged, so as to absorb the heat from the gases ; yet it is possible that this extent of surface, encroaching on and causing the absence of sufficient space for combustion, may have such a cooling effect on the gases as to reduce them to a temperature below the igniting point, and so sometimes do harm. The most economical forms of these boilers have been where some attempt has been made to provide a space to serve the purpose of a combustion chamber.

Total heat of combustion of carbon and hydrogen.—The total amount of heat produced by the complete combustion of 1 lb. of carbon is found by experiment to be 14,500 thermal units, and this is sufficient to convert 15 lbs. of water at a temperature of 212° Fahr. into steam of the same temperature. This is spoken of shortly as the evaporation of 15 lbs. of water 'from and at 212° Fahr.' If the carbon be only imperfectly burned, so that carbonic oxide instead of carbonic acid is produced, the amount of heat generated is only 4,400 thermal units, which is less than one-third of the heat yielded by complete combustion. The evaporative power of hydrogen is 4·28 times as great as that of carbon, viz. 62,032 thermal units per pound.

Total heat of combustion of fuels generally.—There are two methods of ascertaining the calorific value of actual fuels, first by burning samples of them in the calorimeter, and secondly by chemically analysing them, and calculating the heating value of the separate components. The first plan is now, with our improved instruments, the more accurate and reliable, and is generally carried out, when exact knowledge is important, by means of the bomb calorimeter of Messrs. Berthelot and Vieille. In this instrument, which is very simple, the powdered fuel is burned by pure oxygen under pressure in an iron vessel under water. The ignition is caused electrically, and the rise of temperature of the water gives the heating value of the fuel. Thomson's calorimeter is also used for this purpose, but the necessary corrections are more numerous than with the preceding.

The method based on the chemical analysis is not very reliable, and many formulæ have been devised in the endeavour to represent the result in terms of the chemical composition. The principal assumption made is that the value of the elements as existing in the fuel is the same as if they existed in the separate and uncombined condition, and that no heat is absorbed in the separation of the carbon and hydrogen of the hydro-carbons. A certain amount of heat is certainly absorbed in this separation, but its amount depending on the components actually existing in the coal is unknown. In the absence of exact formulæ, the calorific value may be approximately represented by one of the oldest of the formulæ, which gives generally somewhat too large a result, viz. :—

$$h = 14{,}500 \left\{ C + 4 \cdot 28 \left(H - \frac{O}{8} \right) \right\}$$

where h=total heat of combustion of the fuel in thermal units, and C, H, and O are the fractional parts of carbon, hydrogen, and oxygen respectively contained in it.

The expression $\left(H - \dfrac{O}{8} \right)$ is obtained, as previously explained, by deducting the amount of hydrogen already assumed to be combined with oxygen. The expression in the large bracket is the equivalent weight of pure carbon.

Evaporative power.—To convert 1 lb. of water at a temperature of 212° Fahr. into steam of the same temperature, 966 thermal units are required ; therefore, by dividing the total heat of combustion by 966, we get the number of pounds of water that each pound of fuel is theoretically capable of converting into steam from and at 212° Fahr. This is called *the evaporative power of the coal*, and is equal to

$$\frac{h}{966} = 15 \left\{ C + 4 \cdot 28 \left(H - \frac{O}{8} \right) \right\}$$

If, for example, we apply this formula to a bituminous coal, containing, say, 80 per cent. by weight of carbon, 5 per cent. of hydrogen, 5·5 per cent. of oxygen, and 9·5 per cent. of ash, &c., which latter has no evaporative power, we shall find that the total heat of combustion of 1 lb. of this coal is 14,268 thermal units, and this is theoretically capable of evaporating 14·77 lbs. of water. Again, if we take 1 lb. of Welsh steam coal, containing, say, 90 per cent. of carbon, 4 per cent. of hydrogen, and 4 per cent. of oxygen, we find that it is theoretically capable of evaporating 15·75 lbs. of water. Therefore, if all the heat produced by the complete combustion of the coal could be utilised in the boiler, about 15 lbs. of water should generally be evaporated for each pound of coal burned. In practice, however, we fall far short of this. The best Welsh coal burnt in ordinary furnaces under the best conditions only evaporates from 10 to 12 lbs. of water from and at 212° Fahr. per lb. of coal, and in general practice in marine boilers is less than this, and often considerably less.

Sources of waste.—The difference between the *available* evaporative power and its *theoretical* evaporative power is due mainly to the following causes :—

1. Waste of unburnt fuel in the solid state.
2. Waste of unburnt fuel in the smoky and gaseous states.
3. Loss of heat by the hot gas leaving by the funnel.
4. Waste by external radiation and conduction.

The waste of unburnt fuel in the solid state generally arises from brittleness in the fuel, and considerable air spaces between the firebars ; the coal breaking into small pieces and falling between the bars into the ashpits. This loss may be reduced by firing evenly, disturbing the fires as little as possible, and taking care to burn all the small coal and cinders that may fall into the ashpits. With careless stoking the loss from this cause may be very considerable, but with the best firing and management it has been found by experiment to vary from 1 per cent. to 3 or 4 per cent.

The waste resulting from the escape of uncombined gases from the funnel can be prevented by providing a sufficient supply of air to the furnaces, admitted in a suitable place, and by good stoking. It is difficult to obtain perfect combustion of the gases with a moderate admission of air in any case, as the fires are so close to the tubes that the gases have to be distilled, mixed with air, and consumed in a short period and often in a confined space.

With care, however, the loss from this cause ought not to be of any magnitude. In six ships experimented on by the Institute of Mechanical Engineers, this loss, as measured by the presence of carbonic oxide, was nothing in four of the ships, and 1·3 per cent. and 3·6 per cent. respectively in two others.

With improper stoking, however, and bad arrangements for air admission, the loss from this cause will be considerably greater than these figures indicate.

Smoke.—The arrangements fitted to furnace-doors and other parts for the supply of air to the furnaces above the fuel, for the gases, should always be used to assist in rendering the combustion complete.

It may, however, be a grave error to infer that when the *emission of smoke* has been prevented the desired end has been attained. If the combustion be complete, no smoke will be emitted, because the carbonic acid gas formed is invisible. But carbonic oxide gas also is invisible, and if the combustion be imperfect and the products pass off in this form, no smoke will be visible, but the heat produced will be less than one-third of that yielded by complete combustion.

It should therefore be clearly understood that the absence of smoke is not necessarily a sign of economy. The great object to be attained is economy of fuel by rendering the combustion perfect, and the prevention of smoke will then follow as a natural consequence. It appears to be immaterial where the air is admitted, if it completely mixes with the gases before the latter are cooled below the temperature of ignition. It should not be admitted in volumes but in small jets, and this is done by causing the air to pass through perforated plates into the furnaces or combustion chamber, where it mixes with the hot gases, or, as in the Belleville boilers, by pumping jets of compressed air into the space immediately above the fire.

An efficient practical plan appears to be the fitting of suitable openings in the furnace door or frame, so that in the furnace of an ordinary cylindrical or water-tank boiler the air has to pass over the fuel. This allows more space and time for the mingling of the air with the gases, heating the former and preventing its cooling the gases below their igniting temperature, so that there is an increased chance of their complete combustion.

Mechanical stoking.—The maximum economy of coal can only be obtained by keeping a continuous supply on the fires and introducing a regular quantity of air for its combustion. The more continuous the supply of fuel the more certainly can it be properly consumed, but a continuous supply cannot be kept up while hand stoking is a necessity. The furnace door is wide open for some seconds during firing, allowing cold air to enter, and a large quantity of coal is thrown on the fire. The generation of gas is then large and sudden, and it is often not entirely burnt, whereas if the supply of fuel were regular the distillation of the gases would be gradual, and they would easily be burnt.

It would be a great improvement if mechanical stoking arrangements suitable for marine boilers could be designed ; but the problem is a difficult one, and not any have been sufficiently satisfactory to warrant adoption, so that we are still dependent on the care and skill of the stoker, qualities frequently difficult to obtain. One of the advantages of the use of liquid fuel consists in the ease with which a regular and continuous supply can be provided. See page 55.

Losses by hot gases leaving funnel—Funnel draught.—The third and principal cause of waste of heat is that due to the hot gases passing up the funnel. We will consider first the subject of draught. The draught of boilers with funnel only, is produced by the difference in weight between the hot gases in the funnel and that of an equal column of the external air, the adoption of any system of accelerated draught being equivalent to an increase in the length of the funnel.

Let $T_1 =$ temperature of the air,

and $T_2 =$ „   „   gases in the funnel.

It is easily proved that the weight of the gases discharged from the funnel per second is a maximum when

$$\frac{T_2 + 461}{T_1 + 461} = \frac{25}{12}$$

At the ordinary atmospheric temperatures this formula would give about 600° Fahr., or about that of melting lead, as the temperature of funnel gases that gives the most powerful funnel draught. If the temperature be increased beyond this amount, although the velocity of the gas in the funnel would increase, yet its volume would increase in a greater ratio, and consequently the weight of the gases discharged —that is, the draught—would be decreased.

The elevation of temperature of the products of combustion of coal of good quality, assuming the draught to be produced only by a funnel, so that double the quantity of air chemically necessary is supplied, and assuming that the combustion is completed before any heat is abstracted, would be 2,400° to 2,500° Fahr., and as the maximum draught is produced with a temperature of about 600° Fahr. it appears that it is never necessary to expend more than one-fourth of the total heat of combustion, for the purpose of creating a draught by the funnel.

If the draught be accelerated and the arrangements such that one and a half times the air chemically necessary is sufficient, the elevation of temperature on the same assumption would be about 3,200° Fahr., while in this case also no elevation of temperature above that of the external air is necessary for the gases in the chimney. We see, therefore, that with accelerated draught or forced combustion the boilers are for a double reason capable of greater economy than if with funnel draught only.

With funnel draught only if the funnel is large enough in area to give sufficient draught with a less funnel temperature than 600° Fahr., the temperature can be reduced economically below this point by additional heating surface, but it is never advantageous to increase it. With accelerated draught the only limit to the reduction of funnel temperature, and therefore the waste from this cause, is that imposed by the extra weight and cost of the additional heating surface required, whether this take the form of additional boiler-heating surface, feed-water heaters in the uptakes as in the Belleville economiser and others, or air-heating appliances in the uptakes, as in Howden's, and Ellis & Eaves' systems.

A portion of this waste heat used to be extracted by the old super-heaters,[1] but these were not efficient as heat abstractors, owing to the low specific heat and bad conducting powers of the steam contained in them. The feed-water heaters or economisers are much more efficient as heat abstractors. The heat thus abstracted from the funnel gases is a clear gain, and reduces the amount of this loss, which is always the principal one in boilers.

The loss of heat from this cause increases with the rate of combustion. At the higher rates it is often from 25 to 30 per cent., but much less at lower rates of combustion, when the proportion of heating surface to coal burnt becomes increased, while with extreme forcing the loss may be very much greater than this figure.

Temperatures of gases in the boilers.—It will be interesting to see the distribution of temperature in the interior of a boiler when at work. Some experiments on this point were made recently at Devonport on a marine return tube boiler worked on shore. The boiler had two furnaces and 2¾-inch tubes, 6 ft. 8 in. long, and was burning coal at the rate of 17 lbs. per square foot of grate with funnel draught only. The temperatures were taken by a Le Chatelier thermo-electric pyrometer.

Under these circumstances we saw above that if double the air chemically necessary be admitted, the elevation of temperature of the products, assuming combustion to be completed before any heat is abstracted, would be 2,400° Fahr. This condition is, however, never realised in practice, since the abstraction of heat goes on in the furnace continuously, and the combustion is not entirely completed

[1] See Chapter XIII.

there.   The temperature of the gases in the furnace will, therefore, be less than 2,400° Fahr.   The experiments showed that in the combustion chamber the temperature was 1,576° Fahr. ; in the tubes it varied from 1,302° Fahr. just inside at the combustion chamber end, to 795° Fahr. near the exit ; the temperature in the smoke-box being 740° Fahr.   Fig. 15 shows this graphically.

With severe forcing, as in torpedo boats and destroyers, the funnel temperature is much higher ; 1,444° Fahr. has recently been recorded.

In the 'Powerful's' Belleville boilers, on shore, with clean tubes and fresh water, and with careful stoking so that combustion all occurs below the tubes, conditions favourable to efficiency of heating surface, and burning 24 lbs. of coal per square foot of grate, it was about 650° Fahr. by pyrometer.   With the newer Belleville boiler, with 'economiser' in the uptakes, the temperature on exit from the tubes is only

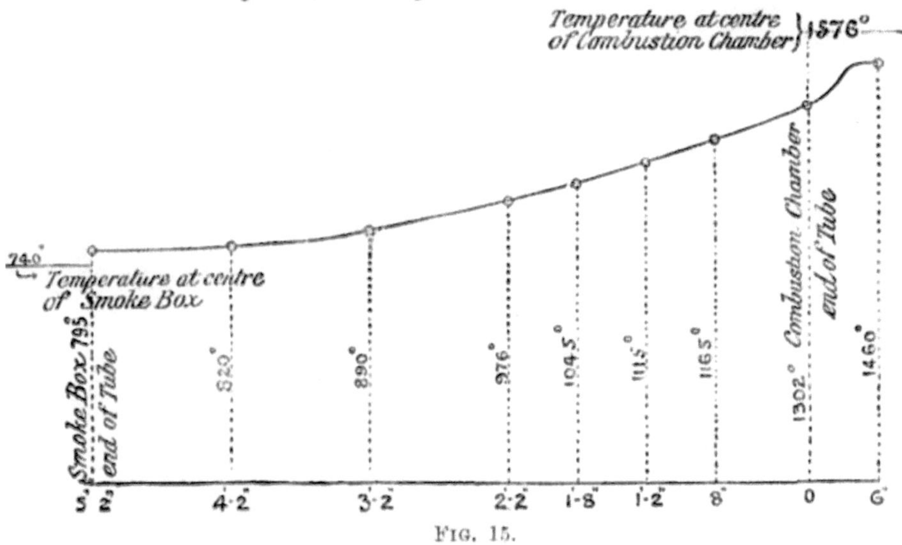

FIG. 15.

about 500° Fahr. with the same rate of combustion and favourable conditions of trial on shore.   Under sea-going conditions, however, the heating surface is less clean and efficient, while the stoking is not so good, so that some combustion probably occurs among the tubes, and these latter temperatures are exceeded.

Radiation and conduction.—The loss by radiation and conduction is taken as the remainder after the three preceding losses have been measured.   The loss by radiation depends largely on the size of the boilers for the power being exerted, or rather the extent of surface for radiation per pound of coal burnt.   This will be smaller, in the same type of boiler, the smaller is the size of the boilers for the power developed.   Although the whole of the surfaces that can be so treated are covered with a lagging of silicate cotton, this serves only to reduce the waste, which is always appreciable and sometimes considerable.   With boilers of ample size for power developed, and with high steam pressure, the loss may rise above 10 per cent. ; but such arrangements could not be regarded as satisfactory.   With well-designed arrangements, well clothed with non-conducting material, the loss from this cause, or the loss not accounted for by either of the three preceding causes, should not exceed 6 per cent.

Efficiency of marine boilers.—The ratio borne by the heat actually transmitted to the water in the boiler, to the total heat developed by the combustion of the fuel is called the *efficiency of the boiler.*

The several causes of waste enumerated above are always at work, so that the total quantity of heat that should be yielded by the complete combustion of the coal, is not available for transmission to the water in the boiler. The total amount of waste depends greatly on the skill exercised in the design of the boiler and the care displayed in its management. In the well designed marine boilers, with careful manipulation of the fires, the waste amounts to 30 per cent. to 40 per cent. of the total heat of combustion of the coal. If the management be careless and unskilful the loss will considerably exceed this. The 30 per cent. would only be attained with the best boiler skilfully managed.

The efficiency of marine boilers of the better class, therefore, varies between 60 and 70 per cent. Below 60 per cent. it would be considered bad, while in the best designed examples, with suitable coal and with good and careful stoking, it rises to 70 per cent.

Having now briefly explained the sources of the various losses, we may give the approximate distribution of heat, under sea-going conditions, in a *good* example of cylindrical marine boiler, supplied with a sufficiency of air and burning about 20 lbs. of coal per square foot of grate, the heating surface being about thirty times the grate. This would be as follows :—

	Per cent.
Absorbed by feed water	68
Wasted in funnel gases	24
Waste by unburnt carbon in ashes	2
Waste by imperfect combustion	0
Balance accounted for by radiation, &c.	6
	100

The first number, 68 per cent., represents the efficiency of the boiler.

Furnace frames and doors.—The furnace frame is generally made double, and an air space arranged between the plates.

In Fig. 16, which shows the door of a Belleville boiler, the door proper has an outer and inner plate, the former being a screen plate with edges open for the admission of air. The door is perforated with holes at the lower part, through which the air is drawn, and the inner plate, which is of cast-iron, is closed at the bottom, and has holes for the discharge of air at the top. When the fires are alight, there is a continuous current of air flowing into the furnace through these plates.

Fig. 17 shows another variety, the air being admitted through holes at the bottom of the wrought-steel door proper, a perforated inner cast-iron plate being fitted to shield the door. The wrought-steel furnace frame which carries the door also has an inner shield plate of cast-iron perforated with holes.

Fig. 18 shows the furnace door of a torpedo-boat destroyer. In

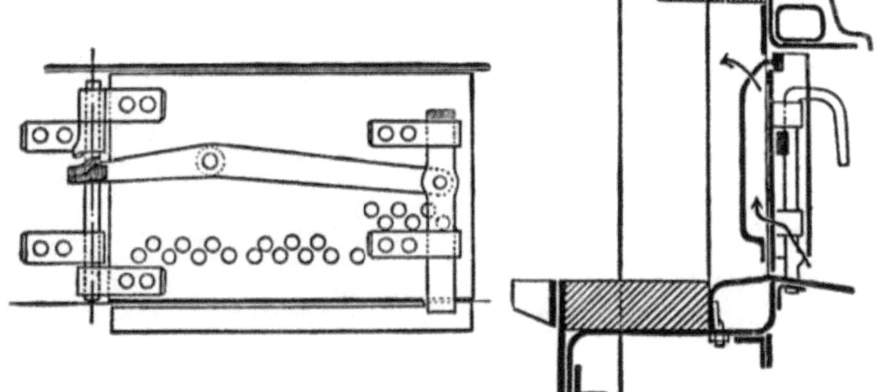

Fig. 16.

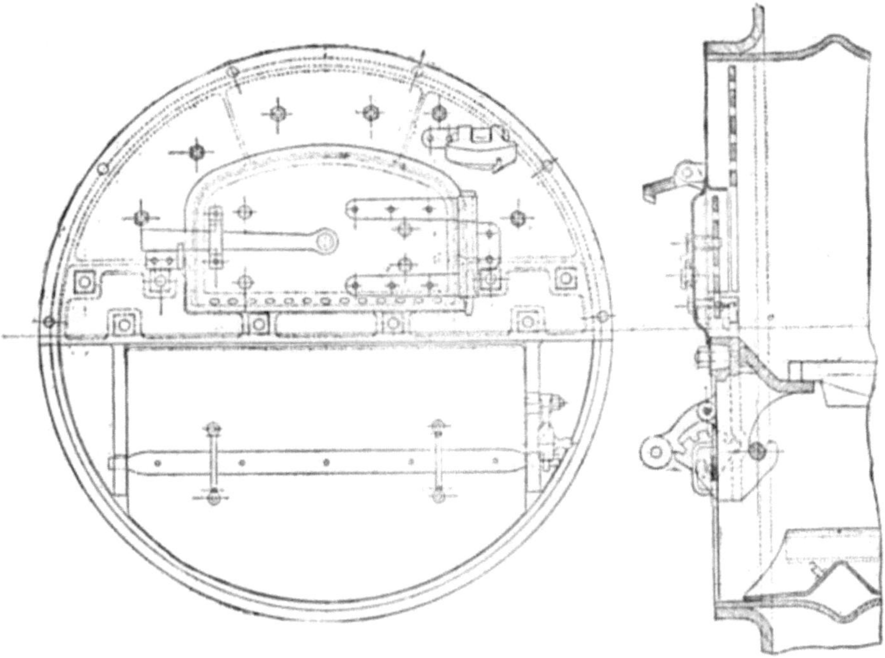

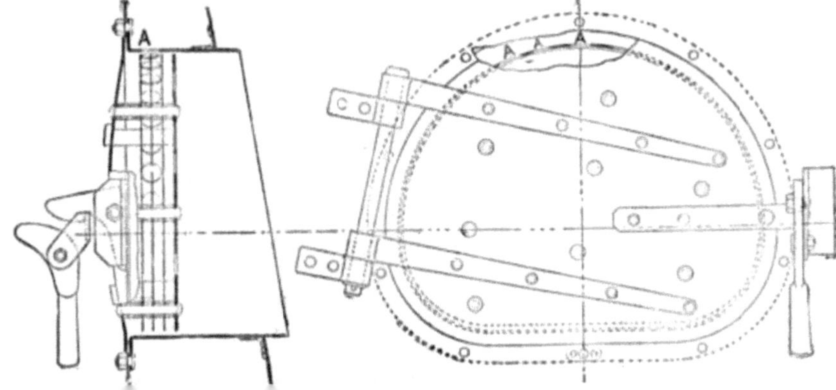

Fig. 17.

such vessels, which are heavily forced, all openings connecting the furnaces and the stokehold must be protected by non-return flaps, so that in case of a tube giving way no flame will enter the stokehold.   In this case, therefore, the furnace doors are not perforated, but a supply of air is obtained by connecting the tube between fire-door and fire, with the ashpits, a series of holes A (about sixteen in number one-inch diameter) being made in this tube at the upper part, through which the air is forced by the pressure in the ashpit.   The door has a series of three or four screen plates lightened with holes, and the air is discharged from the holes into the space between these plates, and is thus warmed and discharged to the fires.   This door is a 'self-closing' one, so that, in the event of any casualty happening in the furnace, requiring the stoker to leave the stokehold during the operation of firing, the furnace doors close themselves, and prevent flames entering the stokehold.   To effect this, the furnace door is swung on an axis inclined to the vertical, and the lower part of the axis is also shifted out from the front of the boiler. The door, when so fitted, will quickly close by its own weight if released when open.

CHAPTER V.

METHODS OF ACCELERATING THE RATE OF COMBUSTION OF FUEL.

Accelerated draught generally.—The question of weight and space occupied by the machinery on board ship is one of great importance. With natural draught only, the rate of combustion per square foot of fire-grate in marine boilers is comparatively slow, even under the most favourable circumstances, as the height of the funnel is necessarily limited, and if the natural draught were alone depended on, the boilers would in many cases require more space than could be allotted to them, especially in warships. It is therefore necessary that methods should be adopted to increase the rate of combustion in the fires, and consequently the generative powers of the boilers, in order to obtain the required power in a limited space.

Steam blast.—An old plan adopted for forcing the draught in marine boilers was by admitting a jet of steam from the boilers at the base of the funnel ; this is usually known as the 'steam blast.' It can be very readily applied, and the rate of combustion can thus be increased by about 25 per cent. ; but it is a very extravagant way of obtaining increased power, and in these days of high-pressure steam, quite inadmissible, owing to the loss of fresh water involved. As an example of the expense of this means of producing draught, it may be mentioned that when burning 30 lbs. of coal per square foot of grate by the aid of the steam blast, the steam used by the blast is 10 per cent. of the total steam produced.

A modified form of this plan is in general daily use in the railway locomotives, but it is peculiarly adapted to the conditions under which they have to work. In these no attempt is made to condense the steam after its utilisation in the cylinders, and it is exhausted at a comparatively high pressure from them to the funnel direct, thus causing the blast ; special arrangements are made to provide the necessary supply of fresh feed-water. Hence the steam used for blast purposes would otherwise do no useful work, and in this way a simple, and under the circumstances efficient, means of accelerating the draught is obtained.

Principal plans.—The principal other plans tried are :—

1. Creating draught by admission of steam in a closed ashpit.

2. Admitting jets of compressed air into the base of the funnel in a similar manner to the steam jet.

3. Fitting a centrifugal fan in the uptake to draw off the products of combustion.

4. Blowing the air into closed ashpits.

5. Closing the stokehold and keeping it filled with compressed air.

Air jets in funnel.—The admission of compressed air to the base of the chimney was tried to some extent in France, but when the success of torpedo boats fitted with closed stokeholds was demonstrated, competitive trials were made in that country with various systems, viz. with air jets in the funnel, using exhausting fans in the uptakes, and using fans in a closed stokehold. The expense of production of draught was found to be in favour of the closed stokeholds, and the latter were then definitely adopted in the large vessels, although it does not appear that the evaporative power of the fuel with the three systems was ascertained, it being assumed apparently that the effect of a certain draught—whether produced by stokehold pressure, or air, or fan suction in the funnel—was the same. A small installation has recently (1895) been fitted in the 'Wild Swan,' to assist in maintaining the power under adverse conditions of draught, but reports received show that no benefit is derived from it, while the consumption is sensibly increased. This system has, therefore, had practically no application of importance.

Fans in uptake or induced draught.—The fitting of a centrifugal exhaust fan in the funnel, through which the whole of the gases from the boiler must pass, has been tried in the Royal Navy in the 'Gossamer' with locomotive boilers, and many experiments were carried out in that vessel. It has since been applied to the battleships 'Magnificent' and 'Illustrious' and gunboat 'Torch.' The arrangement consists essentially of a single fan in the uptake of each boiler of considerably larger dimensions than required with closed stokeholds. A second gunboat, the 'Alert,' with 'closed stokehold' fittings, but in other respects exactly similar to the 'Torch,' was built at the same time, and this has enabled comparative tests of long duration to be carried out. These tests have shown no economy in favour of induced draught as has been claimed, while the fans and fittings sometimes become overheated to an extent which causes these appliances to fail. The advantage of the open stokehold, however, remains.

Closed ashpits.—The fourth plan, viz. blowing air into closed ashpits, is an efficient method of increasing the power of boilers ; but it necessitates closed ashpits, as the pressure in the furnaces is greater than that in the stokehold, and unless proper precautions be taken before opening the furnace doors at the time of firing, the flame may be blown into the stokehold, with possibly dangerous consequences.

This plan is often adopted in small steamboats in the Royal Navy, as it is a simple means of increasing the draught. It has also been fitted in many vessels of the American and other navies, and many ships of the mercantile marine. As the air for combustion does not pass through the stokeholds, special arrangements are provided to supply air for the men engaged there. This system of forced draught is generally preferred in vessels of the mercantile marine, and the arrangements are generally such that the air supply to the ashpits is automatically closed by the operation of opening the furnace door. As the pressure over the fires is rather greater than that in the stokehold, it is necessary, in order to secure admission of air through the fire-doors, that the latter should be surrounded by a chamber in connection with the ashpit, so that the required pressure of air will be obtained.

Closed stokeholds.—The fifth plan, by which the stokeholds are made airtight and filled with slightly compressed air by means of blowing fans, has been generally fitted in vessels of the Royal Navy where forced draught has been required. This system was first adopted by the designers of torpedo boats, and very high powers were obtained from their boilers when worked under air pressure. In these original boats only one boiler was fitted, so that the application of the system was more simple than in the case of vessels containing a number of boilers.

The latest method of applying this system in the Royal Navy is shown in Figs. 77 and 78. The stokeholds are enclosed for the purpose of being placed under air pressure, by fitting vertical screen plates carried down between and at the ends of the boilers to meet the front boiler bearers. These screen plates are worked around the fronts of the boilers to enclose the smoke-boxes, so as to keep the stokeholds cool, and are carried back sufficiently far at the sides of the boilers to clear the water gauges. In this figure the top of the enclosure is formed by the steel, or protective deck. In many cases, especially of the older vessels, where there is a considerable space between the tops of boilers and the deck, the top of the airtight enclosure is formed by fitting a horizontal ceiling, extending from the coal bunker bulkhead to the front of the boiler, at about the level of the top of the boiler, as illustrated in Figs. 19 and 20. The stokeholds are thus made into closed airtight chambers of comparatively small dimensions. The screens are shown in thick lines.

Débris deck.—The airtight ceilings of the stokeholds, when fitted separately, usually form portions of the 'débris' or 'splinter' deck generally fitted over the openings in the machinery department to protect the steam pipes and fittings from injury from fragments of shot, shell, or other débris. This débris deck then serves for carrying the fans for producing air pressure in the stokeholds.

Air-locks.—In order to provide for passage to and from the stokeholds when under pressure, air-locks are fitted. These consist of small airtight chambers fitted with two-hinged doors opening against the air pressure, as shown in Fig. 78, and also in Figs. 19 and 20. In passing through, one door only is open at a time, which makes it possible to enter or leave the stokehold without allowing much air to escape, and so reduce the pressure in the stokehold. Air-locks are necessary at all places at which communication is made between the compartments under pressure and any other part of the ship.

In the stokeholds of most of the fast cruisers no special horizontal ceilings are required to be fitted, as the deck of the ship answers the purpose. All that is necessary is to carry vertical screen plates around the boilers from the deck to the boiler bearers, so as to isolate the stokeholds. The other fittings are similar to those in the armour-clad ships, modified in detail as required to suit the different arrangements of the ships.

Advantages of closed stokeholds.—Forced draught in general possesses the important advantage for warships that a great reduction can be made in the space and weight required for the boilers; the extra power necessary for full-speed working, instead of being obtained by the provision of additional boilers, which would occupy much space and weight, although but seldom required, is provided by

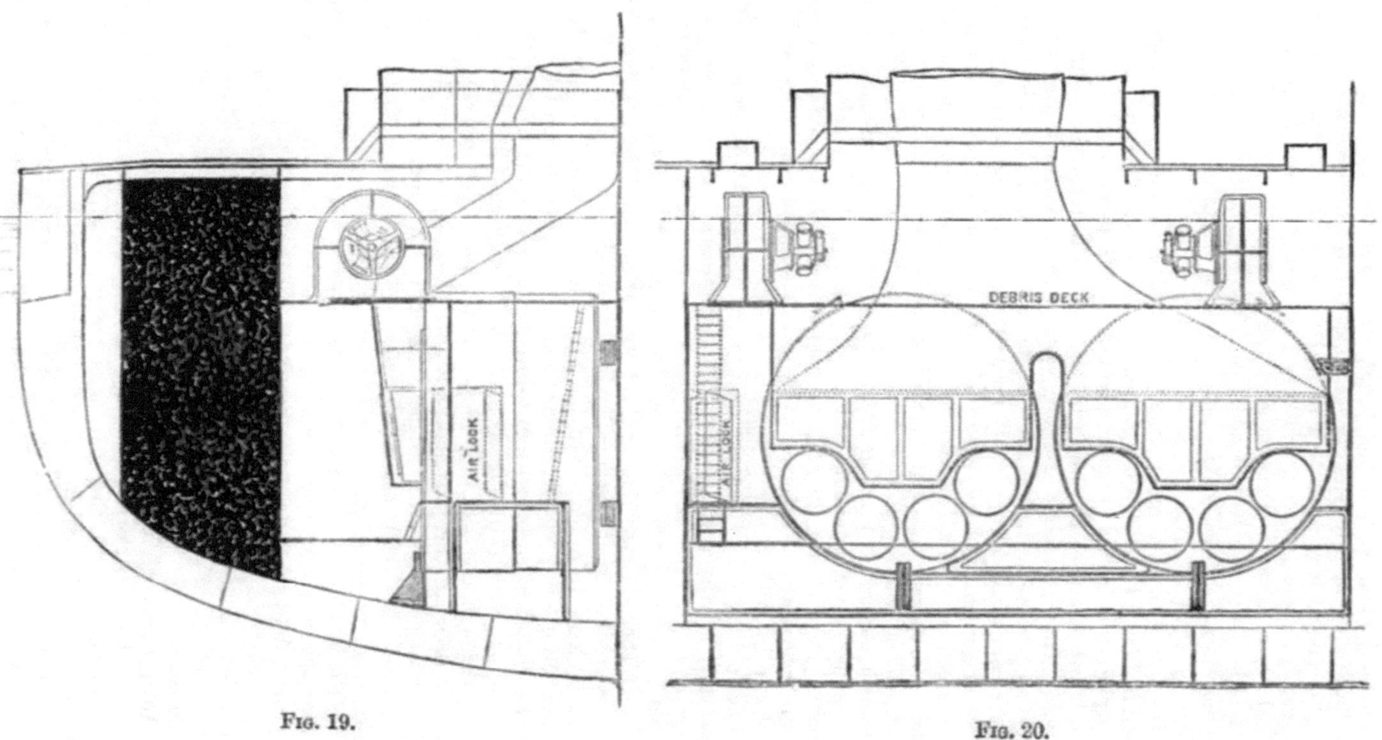

Fig. 19.   Fig. 20.

the addition of fans and screens, which are comparatively inexpensive and involve very little additional space and weight.

The openings in the deck for the boiler rooms may be reduced to the minimum required for the supply of air to the fans, for the funnels, and for convenient access to the boiler rooms. The supply of air to the boiler rooms being entirely provided by the fans, the power of the ship is practically independent of the wind, which is a matter of importance, especially in the Tropics, and the power developed can be easily regulated by the speed at which the fans are driven.

The first ships in the Royal Navy to which this system was applied were the sloop 'Satellite' and the turret ship 'Conqueror' in 1882. During the four hours' full-power trial of the 'Satellite' with natural draught, 10·15 I.H.P. were developed per square foot of fire-grate. With an air pressure in the stokeholds equal to $1\frac{1}{4}$ to 2 inches of water, 16·9 I.H.P. per square foot of firegrate were obtained, being an increase of 66·5 per cent. In the 'Conqueror,' also, the gain in power with a mean air pressure of $1\frac{3}{4}$ inches over that obtained with natural draught was 68·6 per cent.

Large numbers of vessels have since been fitted with boilers on this system, and where not carried to extreme limits it has given satisfaction. As an example of the results obtained, that of the 'Sanspareil' may be mentioned. This vessel was tried in 1888, and with a grate surface of 722 square feet and total heating surface of 19,980 square feet, developed 14,483 I.H.P. for four hours with 2 inches of air pressure, or 20 I.H.P. per square foot of grate surface.

Since this period, however, experience has shown the desirability of reducing the amount to which the boilers are forced, and the last Admiralty specifications for water-tank boilers provide a total heating surface of not less than 2·5 square feet per I.H.P. at natural draught power, and 12 to $12\frac{1}{2}$ I.H.P. per square foot of grate, while the forced draught power is limited to 20 per cent. beyond the natural draught power.

Air heating systems.—It was seen on page 40 that the amount of heat passing up the funnel and wasted is very considerable, and various plans are in operation to reduce it. The most extensively used consists in heating the air passing to the furnaces for combustion, by the escaping hot gases. This is effected by fitting in the uptakes of the boilers a series of thin tubes, through or around which the air for combustion is made to pass, and on the other side of which are the hot gases on their way to the funnel.

The combination of this system with the closed ashpit method of producing the draught and other modifications of detail, is known as Howden's system. The combination of air heating with the induced draught caused by fitting fans in the uptake, produces Ellis & Eaves' system, introduced and developed by Messrs. Brown, of Sheffield.

Howden's system.—The development of the air-heating principle in this country is due principally to Mr. Howden, of Glasgow. The air-heating appliances in his system consist of a considerable number of thin vertical tubes arranged in a chamber immediately over the smoke-box, and through which tubes the escaping hot gases pass. The air for combustion is delivered by the fans through a pipe, enters this chamber at the middle, and proceeds past these tubes on either side,

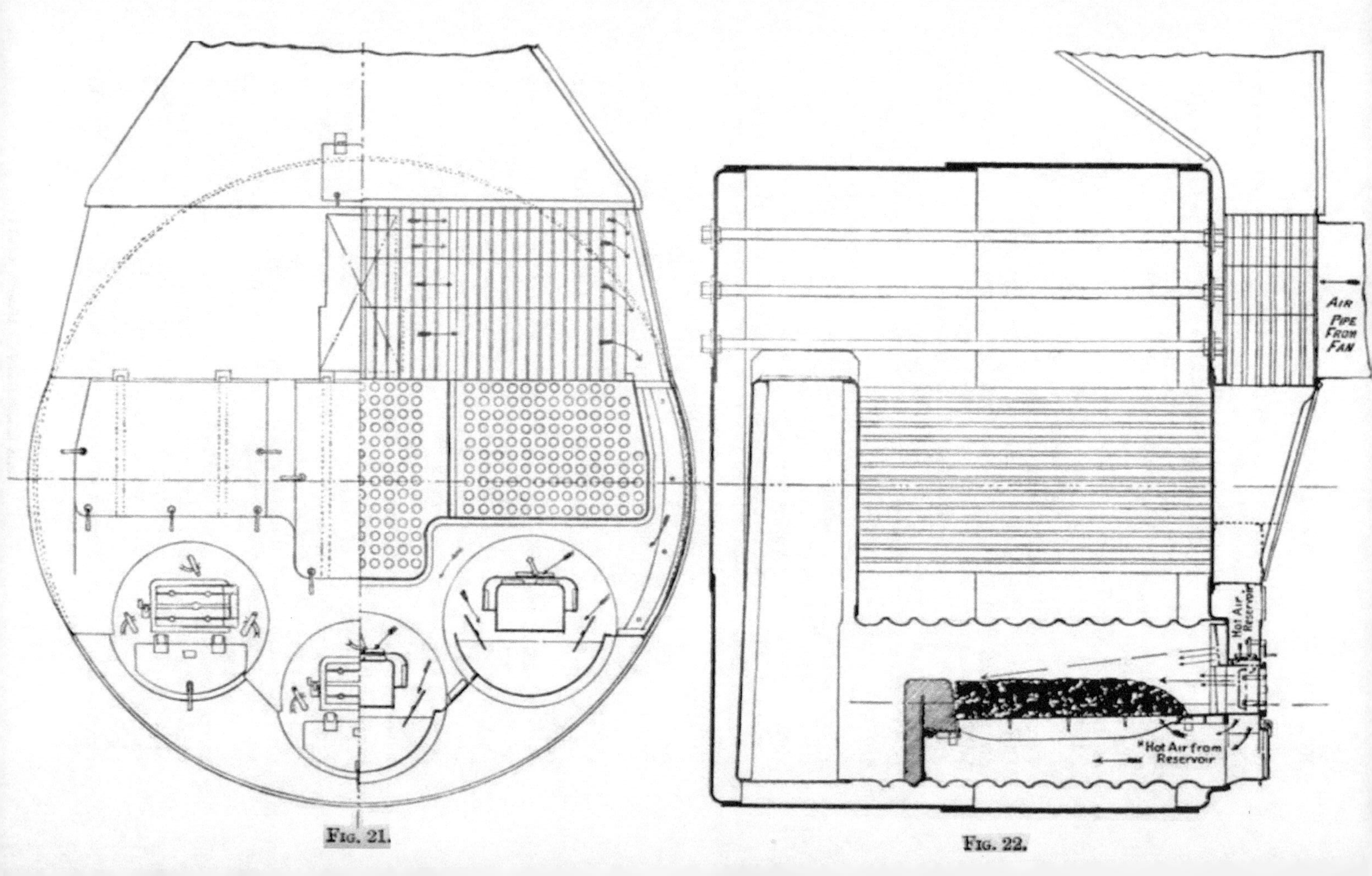

FIG. 21.

FIG. 22.

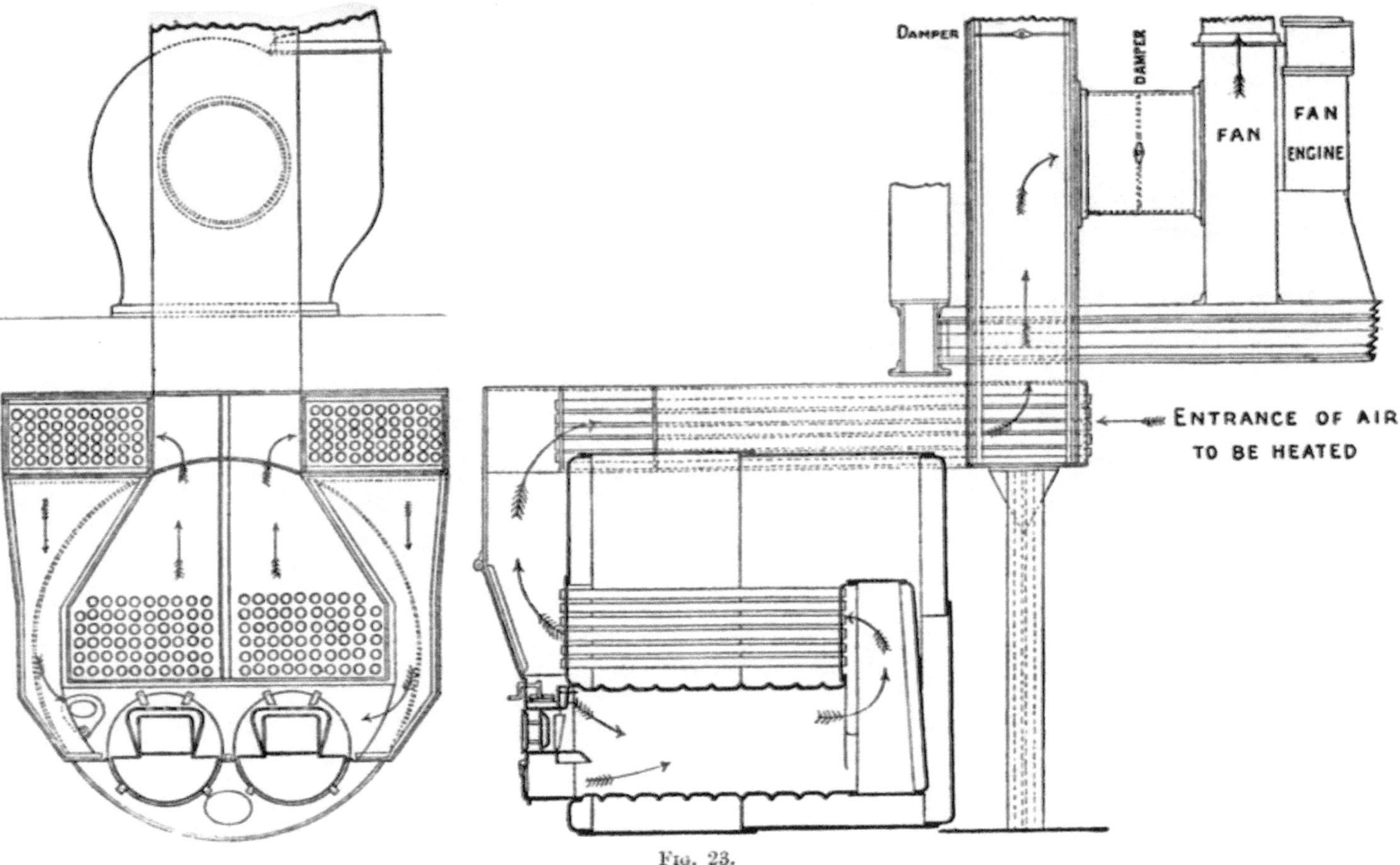

Fig. 23.

gradually increasing in temperature by contact with them, and being delivered through channels formed on either side of the smoke-box to closed spaces in connection with the ashpit, and also in the furnace frame. Valves are fitted to admit a certain proportion of this heated air under pressure to the ashpit, and also a certain proportion to the furnaces over the fires, the proportions being ascertained from experience. The front of the ashpit is closed as in the closed ashpit system. The details of the apparatus are shown in Figs. 21 and 22. Special strips of twisted plate are also placed in each boiler tube, called 'retarders,' which cause the gases traversing these tubes to take a spiral course and be retained in contact with the boiler tubes for a longer period than they otherwise would. Mr. Howden's grate is a very short one, so that the ratio of heating surface to fire-grate is considerably more than usual. Howden's system is fitted in a very large number of vessels of the mercantile marine, and also in several ships of the American Navy, satisfactory results being obtained.

Ellis & Eaves' system.—This combination of draught by exhaust fans in the uptakes with air-heating appliances was introduced at a later period than the Howden system. In this plan the air-heating tubes are arranged in nests of horizontal tubes of considerable length on top of the boiler. Unlike Mr. Howden's arrangement, the escaping hot gases are passed along on the outsides of the tubes on their way to the fan in the uptake, while the air for combustion enters the ends of the tubes from the open stokehold and passes through them (see Fig. 23). The heated air is conducted, as before, by channels at the sides of the smoke-boxes to the ashpits, and also to spaces around the furnace frames. A certain amount of air is admitted above the fires as well as through the ashpits. The front of the ashpit is closed, as in the last system mentioned. This plan has been fitted to several vessels of the mercantile marine, and satisfactory results have been reported.

With the fittings as arranged by Messrs. Brown, and also in large numbers of boilers not working on this system, a special form of boiler tube is used, known as the 'Serve' tube (Fig. 23a). It consists of an ordinary tube with the addition of several internal projecting ribs, which conduct an additional quantity of heat from the escaping gases to the surrounding water. These tubes add to the efficiency of a boiler, but the weight of tubes is about double that of an ordinary plain tube.

Fig. 23a.

CHAPTER VI.

PETROLEUM AS FUEL.

Petroleum fuel.—During the last few years a more or less successful attempt has been made to adopt petroleum as a fuel for marine boilers. The automatic and uniform supply of fuel to furnaces appears from many abortive trials of mechanical stokers to be recognised as impracticable with coal, but is easily carried out with oil fuel, such as petroleum. The natural petroleum is distilled, and gives off at first some very inflammable vapours, which are allowed to escape ; at a higher temperature, the oils used for lamps come over ; at still higher temperatures, the mineral oils used for lubrication are obtained. The residue is called 'astatki,' and is a heavy viscous oil amounting to about one-sixth that of the original petroleum, which by its considerable weight and evaporative power, the comparatively high temperatures below which it does not give off any vapour or burst into flame, and the little danger there is in its preservation and handling, is the most suitable for employment as liquid fuel in marine boilers. Many other oils have, however, been tried, such as blast furnace oil, tar oil, &c.

Petroleum consists practically only of carbon and hydrogen, so that its calorific value is very great. One analysis gives 85 per cent. carbon, 13 per cent. hydrogen, and 2 per cent. oxygen, giving a calorific value of about 20,000 British thermal units per pound, or at least one-third more than the best Welsh coal, the exact increase being doubtful. Some trials have indicated that for an equal value as regards production of steam it occupies only one-half the space required for coal. The specific gravity is ·9.

The first attempts at burning liquid fuel, about the year 1875, were to run it in the liquid form in channels formed in the grate, but the combustion was slow, irregular, and produced much smoke.

The means now employed with much greater success consist in securing an intimate mixture of air with the oil, by injecting it through an orifice under pressure, and to reduce this stream of petroleum to a finely-divided condition of oil spray, by breaking up the issuing jet of oil by means of a similar jet of steam or compressed air under a rather greater pressure, which jet of steam or compressed air may be either oblique or concentric with the oil jet, generally the latter. The resultant petroleum spray mixes intimately with the air, of which a sufficient supply is also admitted, and when the relative discharge of the two jets is properly regulated, it burns with a clear, smokeless flame. Pumps are furnished to draw the oil from the bunkers into a reservoir, and to discharge it to the nozzles at the boilers.

Petroleum burners.—A large variety of designs for these have been tried. Most of the varieties consist of nozzles with two or three holes or annular spaces, from one of which the petroleum flows out under pressure, and to another the pulverising steam or air is admitted at a higher pressure; the third annular orifice or hole, sometimes fitted at the nozzle, supplies the air necessary for combustion. If not thus supplied, the air for combustion is admitted by suitable orifices in the front of the furnace. The burners are sometimes fitted as two long straight orifices, with directions at right angles, one of which supplies the petroleum and the other the steam or compressed air. The horizontal steam jet blows transversely across the petroleum jet, as in a blowpipe.

Means are fitted for regulating the amount of petroleum and steam supplied to suit various rates of combustion, but the adjustment of the various supplies requires considerable care and attention, so that it is often recommended to design the proportions of the nozzles for a given rate of burning, and to provide for increase of power by additional nozzles, which may be started or shut off. By this plan the range of adjustment of each nozzle is either much limited or absent altogether.

Mr. Holden, of the Great Eastern Railway, has been successful in applying liquid fuel to many locomotives, and his arrangements are being fitted to half the boilers of the torpedo-boat destroyer 'Surly' for trial. The air is admitted through a central pipe, steam is supplied through an annular space outside it, while the oil to be burned is admitted to another annular space outside the latter. The speciality in Holden's burner, shown in Figs. 24 to 26, lies in the fact that the steam is not only admitted inside the burner to spray the oil, but is also admitted to a pipe B bent in the form of a ring A near the mouth of the burner, with small holes from which the steam rushes, and is directed on the issuing jet of petroleum and steam, which assists in pulverising it and mixing it with the air for combustion. Fig. 24 is a vertical section, while Fig. 26 is a horizontal section, showing how the steam is supplied to the pipe B and ring A. Fig. 25 shows a horizontal section through the burner.

Furnace arrangements for liquid fuel.—Should the long column of flame formed by the burning petroleum meet any comparatively cold body, such as a boiler plate or tube, before its combustion is complete, the further combustion is prevented. In boilers, therefore, with but little space for combustion prior to meeting any comparatively cold surfaces or entry among the tubes, brickwork screens are arranged for baffling the flame and providing a red hot surface, against which it impinges and assists the combustion. A layer of incandescent cinders and lime is sometimes fitted on the fire-grate.

Pulverising medium.—Compressed air appears to be the better medium for pulverising the petroleum jet in marine boilers, since less steam is used through the interposition of the compressor, and in consequence the loss of fresh water to be made up by the evaporators is not materially increased. There is also no risk of the flame being extinguished by water carried over with the steam. Allowing for the expenditure in the evaporator, the amount of steam used in the nozzle direct would be $3\frac{1}{2}$ to 4 times the expenditure of steam for supplying air by means of a compressor. Actual trial only can determine the relative convenience of the two plans. The amount of steam required to be used in the nozzle may be taken on the average as $\frac{1}{2}$ lb. per lb. of petroleum.

There is the same difficulty in the two cases as regards starting the combustion, unless an auxiliary supply of steam is available until steam is raised in the boilers. If this auxiliary supply is not available, a hand pump for compressing air for the nozzles, or a trough with burning petroleum may be used.

Advantages of petroleum fuel.—The advantages are : Superior evaporation, and therefore reduction in weight of fuel to be carried, or increase in steaming power for a given weight.

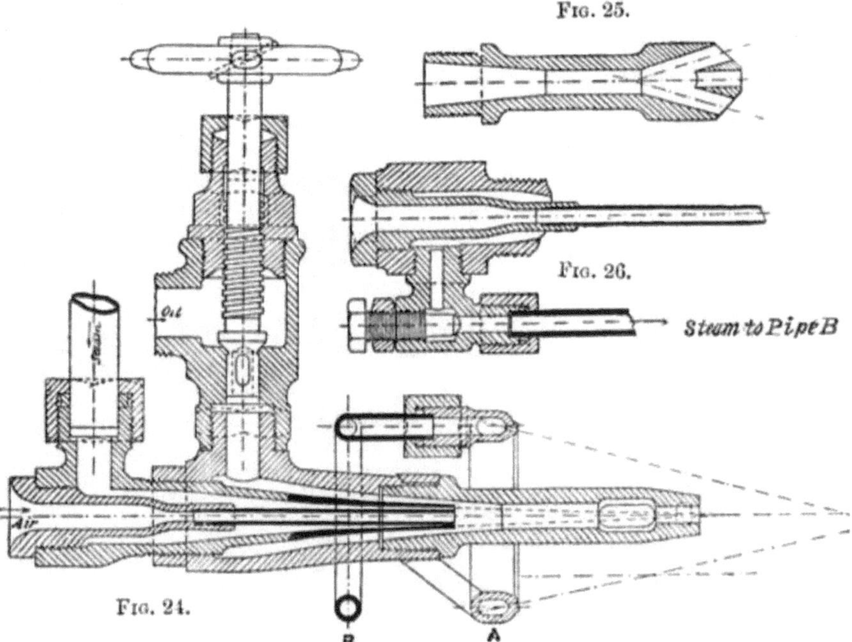

Less space occupied by the fuel for a given weight, and simplification of means of shipping it into the bunkers.

Reduction of stokehold staff, owing to the absence of hand labour in trimming and stoking, which is very exhausting, especially in tropical climates.

Less stokehold space required.

Regularity of combustion, and no reduction of power due to cleaning fires, the fires being always clean and in the same condition.

Absence of coal dust and ashes. Also, with proper regulation of nozzles, an entire absence of smoke, which is especially important in warships.

No variations of temperature due to opening fire-doors when coaling or cleaning, hence increased durability of boilers. With highly pressed boilers, as for torpedo boats and destroyers, there would be increased safety due to this.

Greater control over the expenditure of fuel, and fires put in and out very readily. Waste of steam at safety valves – or a short supply of steam—is easily avoided.

Disadvantages.—On the other hand, the principal objection to its use is the limited supply, especially in the form of the residue known as 'astatki,' which is the most suitable for use in boilers. Even if the more imflammable products of petroleum are used, which are less safely handled than this residue, the supply is still limited. Vessels proceeding on long voyages could not at present replenish their bunkers. The risk of the generation of inflammable gases would be rather greater, while in warships there would also be the possible loss of the fuel in the event of injury to the bunker containing it. If steam be used for the pulverising nozzles, this necessitates a considerable addition to the evaporating plant ; but the fact that special means are necessary in order to raise steam and start the fires can hardly be regarded as a serious objection to its use.

Combustion of coal and petroleum combined.—The combination of coal and petroleum as fuel is also being tried, especially in Italy and France. The furnaces in this case are fitted as for coal, a couple of nozzles for petroleum being also added in the front above the fire for injecting petroleum over the incandescent coal. This application is intended for large vessels, in which the abolition of coal and complete substitution of petroleum is not contemplated.

The advantages claimed for war vessels lie in the power of rapidly augmenting the combustion and increasing the production of steam, also of maintaining the steam-producing power when the fires have clinkered, and postponing the necessity of cleaning them.

Liquid fuel experiments in the Royal Navy.—Trials are being made on the Normand boilers of H.M.S. 'Surly' to ascertain the value of liquid petroleum residues as fuel for this type of vessel.

Holden's burners have been used, and both compressed air and steam have been tried for pulverising the liquid fuel. Compressed air was found unsuitable owing to the size of the compressors required, and steam only has been used for the later trials, an extra evaporating plant having been supplied to make up the steam used. Various modifications have been tried, as regards arrangement of brickwork, number and arrangement of burners, and pressure of steam for pulverising. The experiments at present appear to show that the water-tube type of boiler, which is very successful under forced draught with Welsh coal, is not suitable for the rapid combustion of liquid fuel. When burnt in combination with coal, only ·8 of the full power of the boiler could be maintained, and burning oil alone, injected against brickwork baffles, not more than ·3 of the full boiler power has yet been obtained. Further trials with other burners and different oil fuels are now in progress, as the advantages of oil fuel are recognised, provided it can be burnt in sufficient quantity without increasing the weight and size of boilers which will develop a given power with coal fuel.

CHAPTER VII.

ARRANGEMENT AND EFFICIENCY OF BOILERS—WATER TANK BOILERS.

In this chapter and the succeeding, we will consider the different types of marine boilers in general use, and their efficiencies.

It is obvious that the evaporative power of a boiler must depend largely on the efficiency of its heating surface. The duty of the heating surface is to transmit the heat from the products of combustion to the water in the boiler, and the more of this available heat is transmitted, the greater will be the production of steam. The efficiency of the boiler clearly also depends on the completeness of the combustion as well as on the efficiency with which the heat is transmitted.

The efficiency of the heating surface is the ratio between the quantity of heat transmitted to the water in the boiler, to that available for transmission. The *efficiency of combustion* is the ratio between the quantity of heat available for transmission, and the amount that would be yielded by the complete combustion of the fuel.

The *efficiency of the boiler* is the ratio between the heat transmitted to the water and the total quantity of heat that would be yielded by the complete combustion of the fuel. $\therefore$ The efficiency of the boiler = efficiency of combustion $\times$ efficiency of the heating surface. The efficiency of combustion is dealt with in Chapter IV. The efficiency of the heating surface will be dealt with now.

Efficiency of heating surface. — The conditions on which the efficiency of the heating surface depend are :—

1. Its extent, nature, and condition as to cleanliness.
2. Its position and arrangement.
3. The difference of temperature between the fluids in contact with the two faces.
4. The time allowed for the transmission of heat.
5. The nature of the medium for transmitting heat and the manner in which the heat is transmitted, whether from flame, incandescent fuel, or heated gas.

In comparing the evaporative powers of boilers it is not sufficient to estimate simply the total heating surface, consisting, as it does generally, of furnaces, combustion chambers, tubes, &c., for the powers of transmission of these surfaces differ greatly.

In an experiment made by placing a hot substance in the interior of a cubical metallic box submerged in water, it was found that the upper face generated steam more than twice as fast as the vertical sides, per unit of area, whilst the lower face yielded none. The poor efficiency of the sides was due to the difficulty with which steam separates from vertical surfaces to give place to fresh particles of water, so that a thin film of non-conducting steam is formed in contact with the plates. By slightly inclining the box, the rate of evaporation of the elevated side was increased, whilst from the depressed side the steam escaped so slowly as to lead to an overheating of the metal.

In an ordinary cylindrical boiler the furnaces above the fire-bars form the most efficient heating surface, next come the tops of the combustion chambers, then the sides and ends, and lastly the tubes, omitting the heating effect of the smoke-box tube plate which is very small.

Use of tubes for heating surface.—By the use in boilers of small tubes, through which the heated gases have to pass, a large amount of heating surface can be obtained in a small space, and this arrangement is necessary, though heating surface in this form is comparatively inefficient.

If we consider the case of an ordinary multitubular boiler, with horizontal tubes through which the gases pass, only the upper halves of the tubes can be considered as effective heating surface, owing to the difficulty with which the steam can detach itself from the lower halves, and also in consequence of the soot, &c., deposited inside the tubes. The direction of the tubes in this type of boiler is the same as that of the currents of hot gases on their way to the funnel, instead of being normal to it, as it should be in order to extract the maximum amount of heat from the gases. Flame cannot pass through long tubes of small diameter, and consequently the useful combustion of the gases cannot extend much beyond the combustion chamber. If the combustion has not then been completed the flame is extinguished within a few inches from the entrances of the tubes, and the gases pass through unconsumed, possibly to burst into flame in the uptake or funnel.

In horizontal tubes the first few inches of length are the most efficient. In coming in contact with the first unit of length, the gases part with some of their heat and proceed at a continually diminishing temperature, as they pass along the tubes, so that only a comparatively small evaporative power can be expected from the exit ends of long tubes, and this is confirmed by experiment.

Experiments on steam producing power of heating surface.—In 1830, Stephenson found that in a locomotive boiler open to the atmosphere, with the fire-box separated from the barrel, one square foot of fire-box was equal to three square feet of tube surface. In 1840, experiments were made by dividing the barrel of a locomotive boiler into six compartments, that next the fire-box being six inches and the others twelve inches long. These experiments showed that the first six inches of tube surface were equal, area for area, to the fire-box surface, the second compartment was only one-third as effective, whilst in the remaining compartments the rate of evaporation was small.

In 1864 further trials were made on a multitubular boiler five feet long, the tubes being divided into six parts by plates. The compartment next the fire-box was only one inch long, the second ten inches, and the four remaining were each twelve inches in length. The following quantities of water were found to have been evaporated after three hours' work :—

Compartment No. 1 (1 inch long) . . . 46 ozs.
        ,,   2 (10   ,,   ) . . . 47 ,,
        ,,   3 (12   ,,   ) . . . 30 ,,
        ,,   4 (,,   ,,   ) . . . 22 ,,
        ,,   5 (,,   ,,   ) . . . 18 ,,
        ,,   6 (,,   ,,   ) . . . 17 ,,

The high rate of evaporation in the first compartment, which was only one inch long, was no doubt due to the action of the tube plate, but a comparison of the second compartment with the others shows how the evaporative value of the tubes diminished as the gases passed from the combustion chamber to the smoke-box, and gradually gave up their heat and became of less temperature.

Although the exit ends of the tubes are less powerful in steam-producing power than the inlet ends, they still add appreciably to the power of a boiler within the limits of length adopted in practice. In the Devonport experiments on the distribution of temperature inside a marine boiler, the gradual fall of temperature of gases between the two ends of a tube is shown, also the fact that even at the exit end the temperature is still considerably higher than that of the water (Fig. 15).

The steam-producing power of any section of the tube depends really on the difference of temperatures between its inside and outside surfaces, which temperatures are generally unknown. The temperature of the water on one side is however known, as was also, in the experiments referred to, the temperature of the hot gas inside the tube. The steam-producing power will be proportional in some way to the difference between the temperatures of the gas on one side and the water on the other, and this difference even at the end of the tube is, it will be seen by reference to the figure, still considerable.

Diameter of tubes.—For coal that burns with a long flame, the diameter of the tubes should be large, so as to allow the flame to pass as far along the tubes as possible. But for coke and anthracite coal, if the hydrocarbons and carbonic oxide can be burnt before they reach the tubes, they may be made of small diameter, so as to increase the surface and facilitate the action of the hot gases on it.

As a general rule the ratio of length to diameter of tube in marine boilers rarely exceeds 35 to 1, and the area through the tubes should be about one-seventh the grate area. In locomotive boilers the ratio of length to diameter of tubes is often as great as 50 to 1.

For a given description of boiler the evaporative efficiency will depend mainly on the ratio between the quantity of coal burned, and the extent of heating surface to transmit the heat of combustion to the water.

Rankine's formula for efficiency.—Rankine has given the following approximate formula for calculating the efficiency of a boiler :—

Let E be the theoretical evaporative power of the coal.

    E′ ,, its available evaporative power.

    S ,, the number of square feet of heating surface per square foot of fire-grate.

    F ,, the number of pounds of coal burnt per square foot of fire-grate per hour.

Then the efficiency of the boiler is

$$\frac{E^1}{E} = \frac{BS}{S+AF}$$

Where B and A are constants to be determined by experiment.

The fraction on the right-hand side of the equation, if B be omitted, represents the efficiency of the heating surface itself. B is a fractional multiplier to allow for miscellaneous losses of heat whose value is found by experiment. A is a constant to be found empirically, and is probably proportional approximately to the square of the quantity of air supplied per pound of coal.

Rankine gives the following values for the constants A and B, deduced from the practical performances of a number of boilers.

	B	A
I. The convection taking place in the best manner, either by introducing the feed-water at the coldest part of the boiler, and making it travel gradually to the hottest; or by heating the feed-water in a set of tubes placed in the uptake. Draught produced by the chimney only	1·0	0·5
II. Ordinary convection and chimney draught only . . .	$\frac{11}{12}$	0·5
III. Best convection and forced draught	1·0	0·3
IV. Ordinary convection and forced draught	$\frac{19}{20}$	0·3

When there is a superheater or feed-water heater its surface must be included in computing S.

This formula is framed on the assumption that the losses from imperfect combustion and excess of air are inappreciable, and that the construction and management of the furnaces are the best possible. If this be not the case, the coefficients A and B must be modified to suit the altered circumstances.

Case II., viz. that of ordinary convection and chimney draught, is that of the majority of marine boilers. Rankine gives the value of B in this case as $\frac{11}{12}$, and this appears to agree very well with the actual results of the performances of the high rectangular boilers working with steam pressure of about 30 pounds per square inch. Mr. Robert Wilson gives $\frac{5}{6}$ as the value of B, which seems to approximate more closely to the performances of cylindrical marine boilers. The formula is of little value however.

Low-pressure boilers.—The first boilers fitted to work marine engines were of the rectangular, or 'box' form; an example of this type is shown in Figs. 27 and 28, which represent the most general type of marine boiler for steam pressures not exceeding from 30 to 40 lbs. per square inch above the atmosphere. This form is now entirely obsolete for new vessels, not being suitable for high pressures, as in these boilers the stresses are resisted principally by the action of straight iron stay-rods. For pressures above 30 or 40 lbs. per square inch, these would have to be so numerous and closely spaced, that the boilers would be excessively heavy, and the internal parts inaccessible.

The furnaces were made with flat sides, and arrangements could be made to keep their crowns sufficiently high above the bars to allow

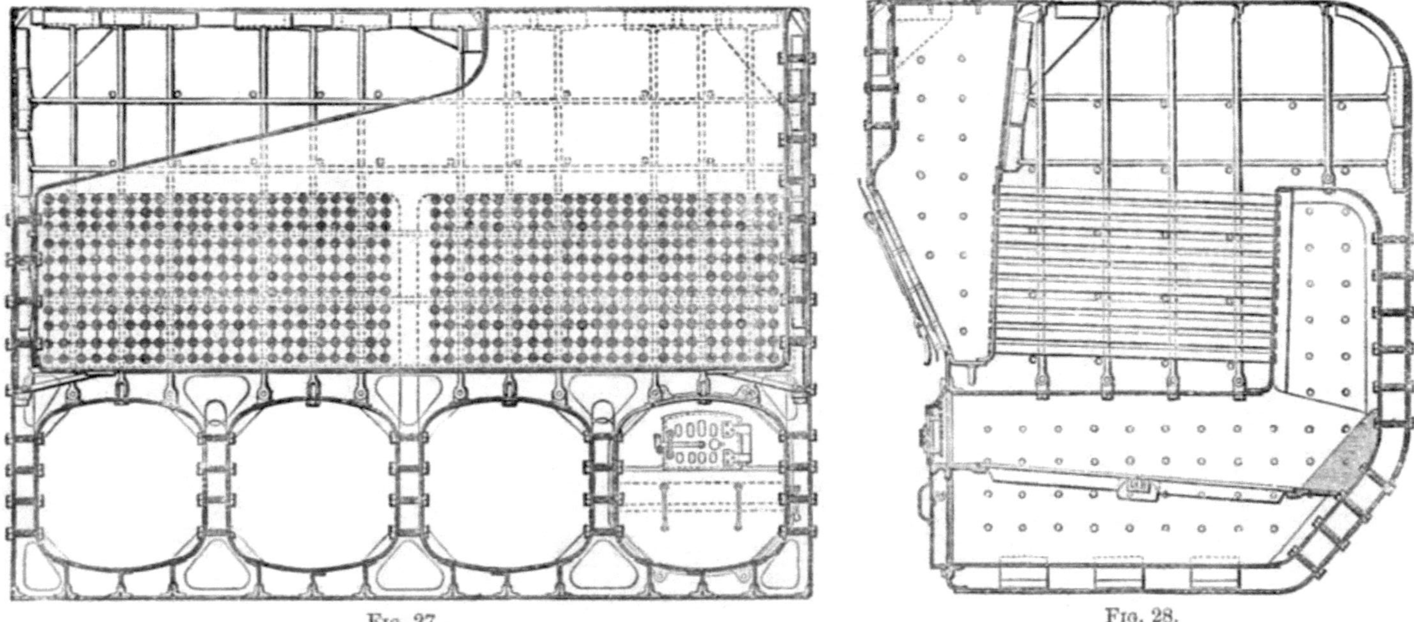

Fig. 27.

Fig. 28.

the gases to mingle freely with the air, whilst the bottoms of the ash-pits could be kept low enough to permit an ample supply of air to pass through the fires for combustion. Good results were obtained from these boilers, and this was due to a great extent to the very roomy furnaces and combustion chambers with which they were fitted. The furnaces were usually arranged in pairs, each pair having a common combustion chamber, as shown in the diagrams. The object of this is pointed out in Chapter IV., under the heading combustion chamber.

From the combustion chamber the smoke and gases pass through tubes, arranged over the furnaces, to an uptake in the front of the boiler, in which they all unite, and are conveyed to the funnel.

Many boilers of this type were fitted with superheaters, which are described in Chapter XIII. The heat added to the steam in the super-heater from the hot gases on their way to the funnel would otherwise have been wasted, and there can be little doubt that much of the saving that has resulted from superheating steam has been due to the partial utilisation of the waste heat in the escaping gases.

The plates in these boilers were thin, the necessary strength being obtained by suitable staying. The area of the stays was made sufficient to resist the action of the whole of the steam pressure, and care was taken to place them sufficiently close together to prevent any appreciable buckling of the plates between the stays when under pressure.

If we take an average of the performances of the best examples of boilers of this type we find that, at full power, about 30 lbs. of coal were burnt per hour, and 10 indicated horse-power developed, per square foot of fire-grate. With boilers fitted with superheaters and the engines with surface condensers, as was usually the case, the con-sumption of feed-water per hour may be taken at about 26 lbs. per indicated horse-power.

Therefore the quantity of water evaporated per pound of coal was equal to

$$\frac{10 \times 26}{30} = 8\cdot7 \text{ lbs.}$$

Taking the theoretical evaporative power of the coal as 14·5 lbs. from 100° Fahr. at 275° Fahr., which is the temperature corre-sponding to a pressure of 30 lbs. per square inch above the atmosphere, this gives as the actual efficiency of the boiler,

$$\frac{8\cdot7}{14\cdot5} = 0\cdot6$$

These boilers had about 30 square feet of total heating surface per square foot of fire-grate, so that their efficiency calculated by Rankine's formula would be

$$\frac{E'}{E} = \frac{BS}{S+AF}$$
$$= \frac{\frac{11}{12} \times 30}{30 + \frac{30}{2}} = \frac{11}{18} = 0\cdot61$$

In this case, therefore, the results of the actual performance agree with those calculated by Rankine's formula.

For higher pressures of steam the rectangular, or 'box' boilers had to be abandoned, and boilers with cylindrical shells and furnaces substituted for them.

High-pressure boilers.—These may be divided into two classes, high or 'return-tube' boilers, and low or 'through-tube' boilers. High boilers are generally used where they can be conveniently arranged for, but the low boilers are fitted in war vessels of small depth of hold to keep them below the steel deck or water line for protection from shot, &c. These boilers are rather inferior to the low-pressure boiler in economy of generation of steam and in the amount of coal capable of being burnt per square foot of grate with the same draught. Figs. 29 and 30 show the general arrangement of a large example of the high type of cylindrical marine boiler used for pressures of 150 lbs. to 180 lbs. per square inch. In the diagram, which represents a four-furnace boiler of about sixteen feet diameter, each pair of furnaces has a separate combustion chamber, which is the most general arrangement in these boilers.

The end plates above the tubes and combustion chamber and below the furnaces are supported by long bar stays passing through the plates with nuts inside, and nuts and stiffening washers outside. The large stiffening washers are riveted to the plate as shown in Fig. 29. The front plate and tube plate between furnaces and tubes are similarly stayed.

The sketch indicates the construction of all the parts in detail. The top of the combustion chamber is stayed by 'dog stays,' and supporting bolts screwed through the combustion chamber plate from below. The bottom of the girder is kept well clear of the top plate to facilitate cleaning and circulation of water. In this boiler every alternate tube in half the horizontal rows is a stay tube (Fig. 35), and these stay the front tube plate to the front of the boiler, while the sides and back of the combustion chamber are stayed to the shell and back of the boiler by short stays screwed through both plates and nutted. The zinc slabs for preventing corrosion are also indicated at various parts of the boiler.

The comparatively low evaporative power and economy in these boilers is mainly due to the form of the furnace. In the low-pressure boilers, with furnaces of approximately rectangular forms, the necessary distance above and below the fire-bars could generally be obtained whatever the width of the furnace may be. But in the high-pressure boilers, in which the furnaces are cylindrical, the height above and depth below the bars, are entirely dependent on the diameter of the furnace, and it is difficult, in most cases, to keep the crown of the furnace sufficiently high above the fires, or to make the ashpit large enough to allow an ample supply of air to the fires. The smaller their diameter, and the greater their length, the greater is the difficulty of securing a proper measure of efficiency.

In these boilers the front itself forms the outer tube plate, and the smoke-box and uptake form an entirely external fitting instead of being partly built in the boiler, as in the case of the earlier low-pressure boilers.

Another feature which tends to reduce the efficiency of cylindrical boilers is the often restricted area of water surface and volume of steam chest, which renders them more liable to priming. *Priming* is the

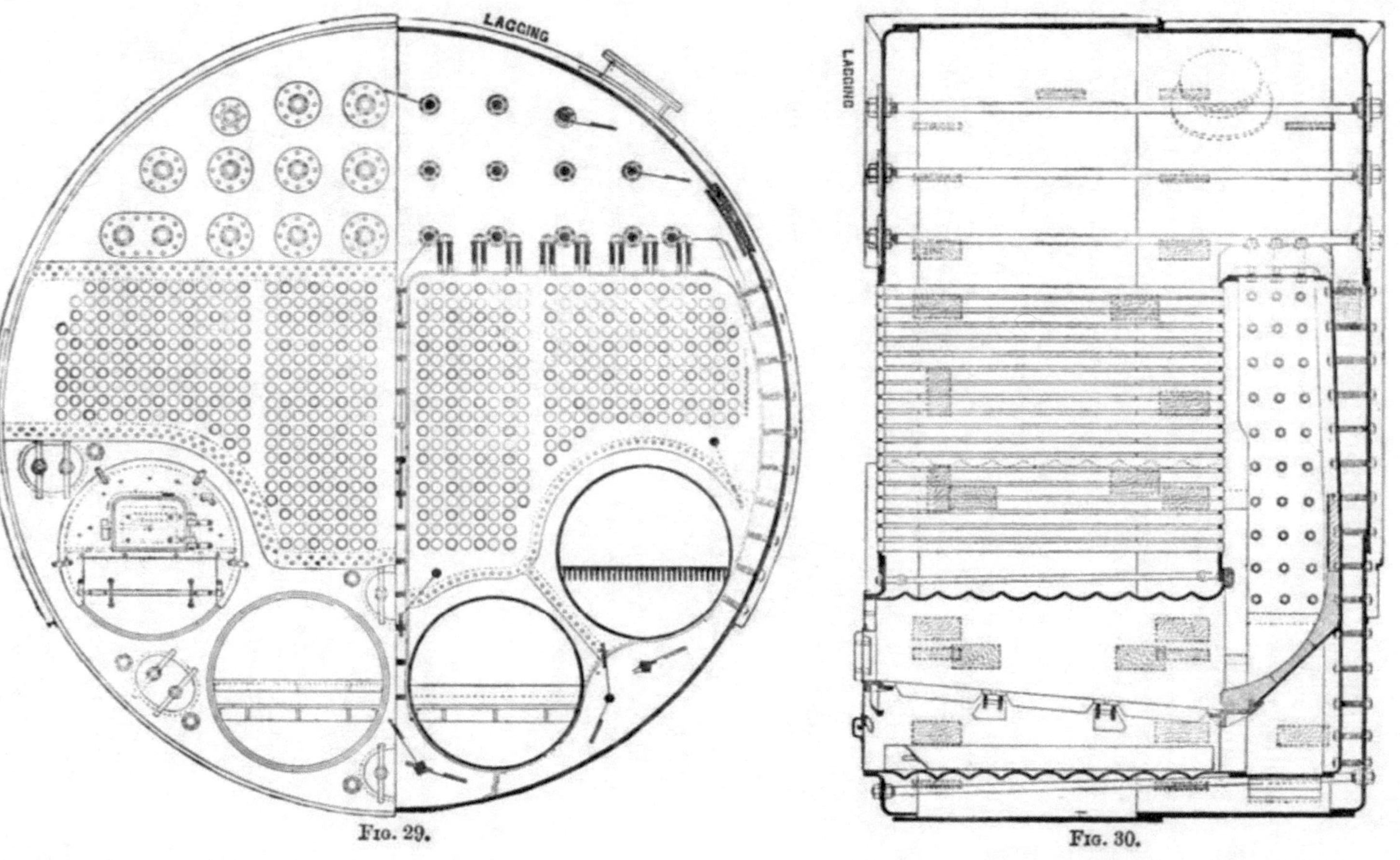

LACCING
LACCING
Fig. 29.
Fig. 30.

name given to the passage of water, with the steam, from the boilers to the engines, which sometimes takes place, and which is liable to produce serious results, reducing the power of the engines, and causing severe stresses on the cylinders, &c., and when it is excessive it may lead to overheating of the boiler plates and tubes, by withdrawing a large quantity of water from the boilers. To avoid this, the depth of the steam chest should, if possible, be at least one-quarter the diameter of the boiler.

Furnace bridges.—The bridge of brickwork at the end of the fire-bars, to limit the extent of the fire, is supported by an iron casting and inclined plate, and the brickwork extends for some little distance up the back of combustion chamber to take the first impact of the flame. The joint of the combustion chamber tube plate with the furnace is gene-rally also protected by a brick lining, as shown in Fig. 30.

Fig. 31 shows another plan of building up this bridge without using any bricks of special shapes, but only the usual square pattern trimmed as required.

The bridges of the older boilers were pro-vided with means for admitting air behind the bridge into the combustion chamber, but this was found not to be efficient for its purpose under usual sea-going conditions, and is not now fitted.

Attachment of tubes.   Tube ferrules.—The ordinary tubes in boilers are passed moderately tightly into the tube plate holes, and are then rolled or expanded by a roller drift which makes the ends steam and water tight. The stay tubes are screwed into both plates and then similarly expanded by the roller drift to make them tight. Figs. 35 and 36 show the stay tube and plain tube respectively. The diameter of the smoke-box ends of the tubes is made slightly larger than that of the fire-box end to facilitate their entry and removal.

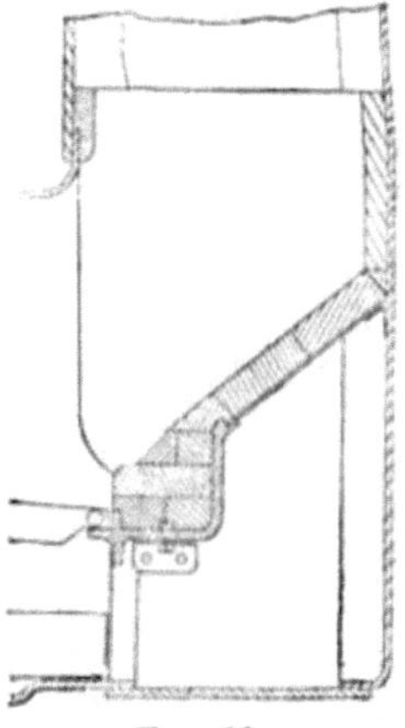

FIG. 31.

When the tubes are much worn at the fire-box end, they are often supported by inserting and *rolling* into them short pieces of tube termed ferrules. In the Royal Navy all the fire-box ends of the tubes are fitted with the Admiralty ‘cap ferrule,’ shown in black in Figs. 35 and 36. This ferrule is in contact with the tube, only at some distance away from the plate, and the cap of the ferrule shields the tube plate from the impact of the hot gases, and conducts the heat to that part of the tube away from the joint, where it is transmitted to the water without doing any harm. These ferrules have been very suc-cessful in the prevention of leaky tube ends, and in lengthening the lives of the tubes. The cap ferrule is simply driven in tightly.

Low type of high-pressure boiler.—The low type of cylindrical boiler, shown in Figs. 32 to 34, is fitted on board ships of the smaller classes, such as sloops, gun-vessels, &c., and also where, in larger vessels, there is not sufficient room below the vessel's protective deck to enable the high type of boiler to be fitted. Boilers of this type in the Navy have generally given higher evaporative powers than those just described.

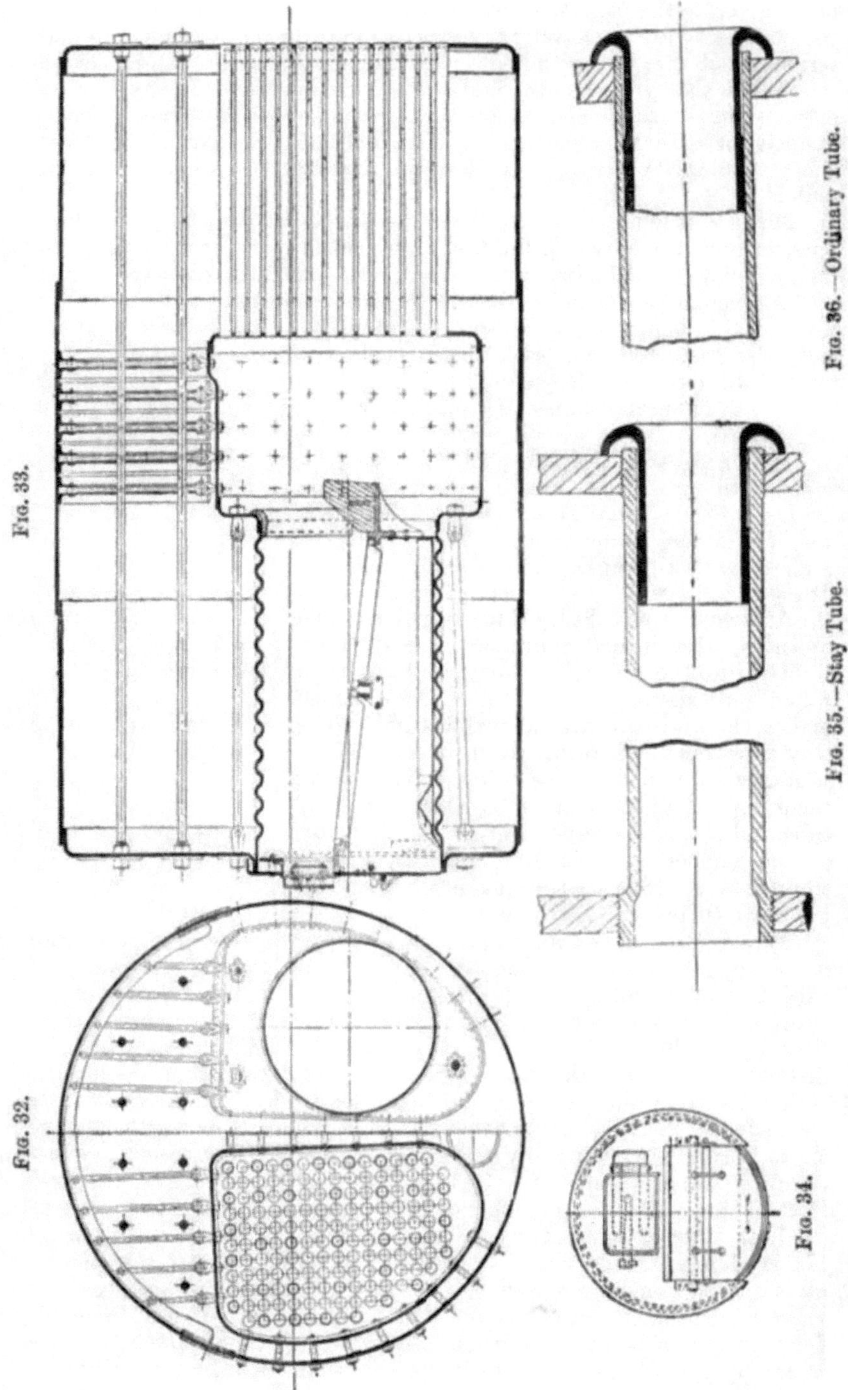
Fig. 33.
Fig. 32.
Fig. 34.
Fig. 36.—Ordinary Tube.
Fig. 35.—Stay Tube.

The sketches show a low boiler with two furnaces, but in many vessels three furnace boilers of this type have been fitted, and in a few cases four and even five furnaces.

In the large majority of such boilers the furnaces discharge into a common combustion chamber, and such boilers have generally given very good results. The more recent examples supplied for the Navy have been fitted with a divided combustion chamber as recommended by the Admiralty Committee of 1892, so that each furnace has a separate combustion chamber. Fig. 32 shows such a boiler.

In this type it will be seen that the combustion chamber is wide, and that the tubes, instead of returning above the furnaces to the uptake at the front of the boiler as in the high type, are continued along the boiler at about the same level as the furnaces, to the uptake which is situated at the other end of the boiler. The path of the gases to the funnel is thus more direct than with the high type. This type is sometimes known as the 'through-tube type.'

The early examples of this boiler were provided with two fittings which are not supplied to the later examples for the Royal Navy. One of these was a hanging brick bridge in the middle of the combustion chamber, extending from the top to about two-thirds the depth of the combustion chamber, to insure the lower rows of tubes conducting more of the hot gases to the funnel than they probably otherwise would, and thus promote efficiency. Trials showed, however, there was little difference between the efficiency with and without this fitting, and as it is troublesome in practice, on account of frequent renewal, it is not now supplied. The other fitting was the ash-tube, which was, in cases where there was no central furnace, low down in the boiler, fitted below the tubes between the two tube plates, for the purpose of more readily clearing the combustion chamber of ashes, &c. These tubes gave trouble by corrosion and consequent weakness, and were really not required.

Double-ended boilers.—Figs. 37 and 38 show a double-ended boiler. This is a common type for mercantile steamers, and is also fitted in a considerable number of ships of the Royal Navy. It is practically equivalent to two single-ended boilers placed back to back, but lighter for equal power, because the weight of the end plates and of much water in the spaces at the backs of the combustion chambers, is saved.

The arrangements fitted to such boilers as regards combustion chambers have been very varied. In some cases in the Royal Navy, with 'four furnaces at each end, the whole eight furnaces have been led into one large common combustion chamber. Others have had the combustion chamber divided into four parts by central longitudinal and transverse water spaces, so that each end of the boiler supplies two separate combustion chambers, there being four altogether. This type is illustrated, and is equivalent to two boilers similar to those of Figs. 29 and 30, placed back to back and united. Other examples have had the combustion chambers divided into two parts by a transverse vertical water division, the four furnaces at each end having a common combustion chamber. The most general arrangement, however, is to have three furnaces at each end, and three combustion chambers formed by longitudinal water spaces, each opposite pair of

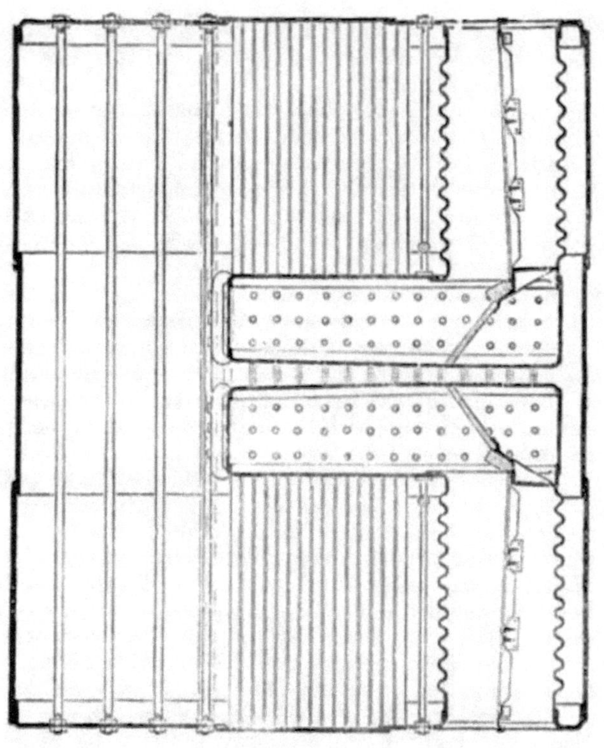

Fig. 38.

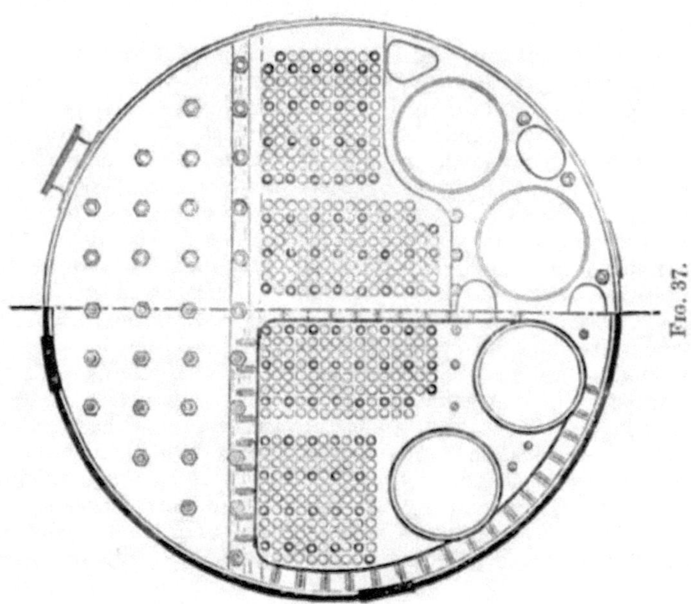

Fig. 37.

furnaces leading to one common combustion chamber. This type of boiler is very common, and has been found, on the whole, to be a convenient and satisfactory arrangement. Several boilers, with three furnaces at each end, have been fitted in the Royal Navy with one large combustion chamber ; while again others have had six separate chambers, one to each furnace.

Varieties of furnace tubes.—The early cylindrical boilers had plain furnaces, stiffened at intervals by Adamson joints, such as shown in

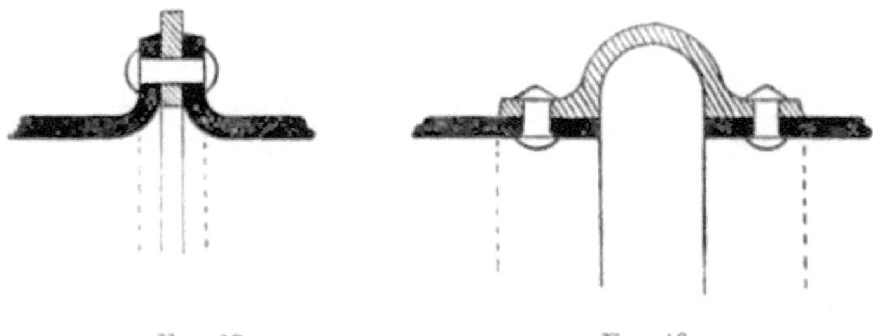

FIG. 39.   FIG. 40.

Fig. 39, Bowling rings, indicated by Fig. 40, and other devices. These were sufficient for moderately low pressures, such as 60 lbs., without requiring an excessive thickness of furnace plates. Beyond this pressure, however, it became desirable to adopt a stronger form to avoid excessive thickness. Fox's corrugated furnace (Fig. 41) was then for many years almost universally employed for marine furnaces. They were much stronger to resist compressive stress, and enabled the higher pressures to be carried without increase of thickness of plate.

Fig. 42 shows the Purves flue manufactured by John Brown & Co., while Fig. 43 shows a later variety of furnace known as Morrison's 'Suspension' furnace.

Marine locomotive boilers.—Figs. 44 and 45 illustrate the locomotive type of boiler which has been used for marine purposes in torpedo boats, &c., in which the working pressures of steam have been

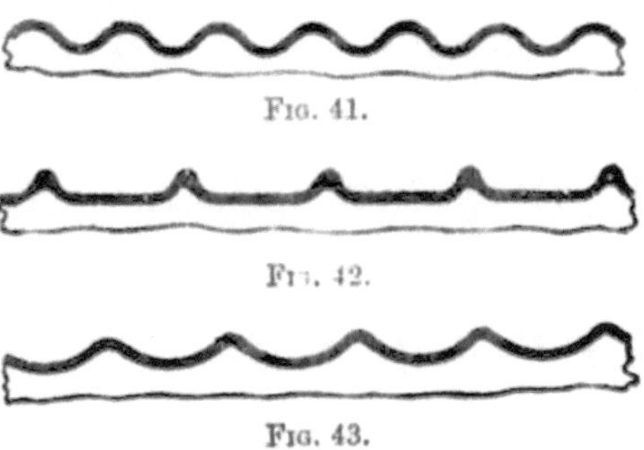

FIG. 41.

FIG. 42.

FIG. 43.

from 120 lbs. to 180 lbs. per square inch. In this type of boiler there is a broad and practically rectangular fire-box at one end, the crown of which is strengthened by means of stays to the roof of the boiler, as shown. The example illustrated is by Yarrow & Co.

The air for the combustion of the coal is supplied from underneath, and there is considerable space and height above the fires to allow for the combustion of the gases. The barrel of the boiler beyond the furnace is cylindrical, and contains the tubes which lead to a smoke-box at the opposite end of the boiler. In the cases in which these boilers have been employed the stokeholds have been closed, and kept under a pressure of air, equal sometimes to 4 inches or 5 inches of water, by means of blowing fans, the rate of combustion of coal per

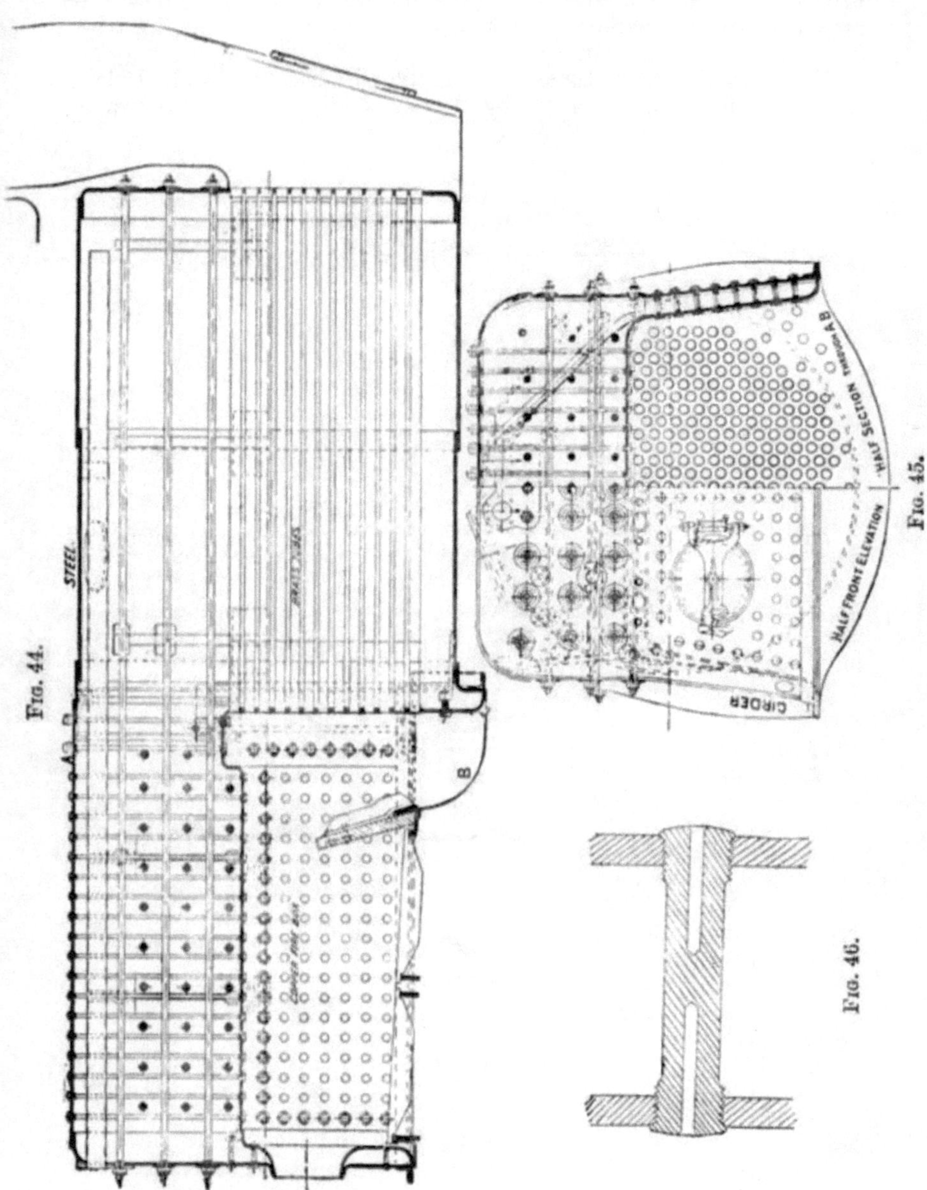

square foot of grate being from 80 to 90 lbs. per hour, occasionally reaching 100 lbs.

The fire-box and tube plate are joined to the rectangular shell around them at the lower part, and the bottom of the furnace is open or 'dry bottomed,' and contains the fire-bars. The tubes are 2 in. diameter in the body, reduced to $1\frac{3}{4}$ in. for about 9 inches of length at the furnace end and closely spaced, so that the water spaces of the boiler are small, and the weight of the boiler for a given amount of heating surface is correspondingly reduced. All parts of such boilers, except the barrel, require to be closely stayed. The water spaces round the furnace contain large numbers of short screwed stays, either riveted or nutted at the ends. Copper stays are often used and these are riveted into place. As such stays are liable to crack inside the water space, small holes are drilled in the stay (Fig. 46) to detect this defect by the leakage through the hole. The furnace roof is stayed by long

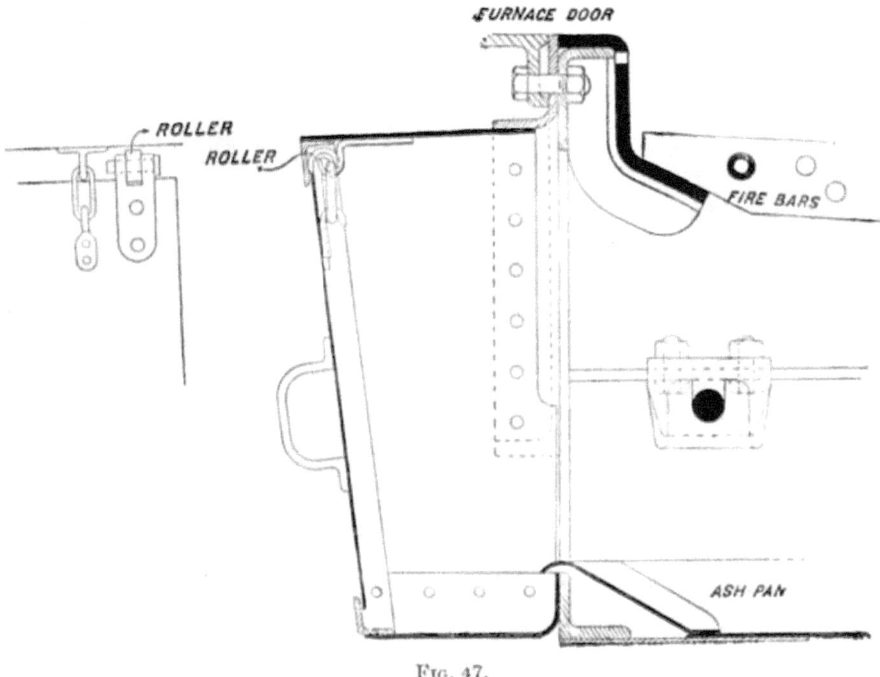

Fig. 47.

stays to the roof of the boiler, and the two ends of the boiler are stayed to each other by long bar stays.

The interior of the boiler, owing to the presence of so many closely-pitched stays, is not accessible for cleaning, so that the use of fresh water with such boilers is essential.

A large amount of heating and grate surface is obtained in these boilers on a limited weight and space, but after a few hours' working at full speed the tubes become choked at the mouths with scoriæ and ash, so that the power then rapidly falls.

A similar boiler, with modifications, has been fitted in many torpedo gunboats. In these the water spaces at the sides of the fire-box have been continued round the bottom below the ashpit, and the boiler is then called a 'wet-bottom' boiler. The air for combustion in this case enters through the front of the ashpit. In many recent cases the furnace has been divided into two parts by a complete longitudinal water space extending to the tube plate, which is then fitted as two separate plates. The object of these extra water spaces has been to improve the circulation of the water round the fire-box where the heat is most intense, and much weight has thus been added to the boilers, but it is doubtful, after experience, whether any advantage commensurate with the additional weight and cost has been gained.

Automatic safety air inlets.—Locomotive boilers are invariably worked under forced draught, and safety arrangements are provided to prevent injury to the persons in the stokehold in the event of any accident to the fire-box, or any considerable leakage of tubes. Two such arrangements are fitted ; (*a*) consists of forming a 'protection box' in the front of the ashpit, through which all the air for the fires

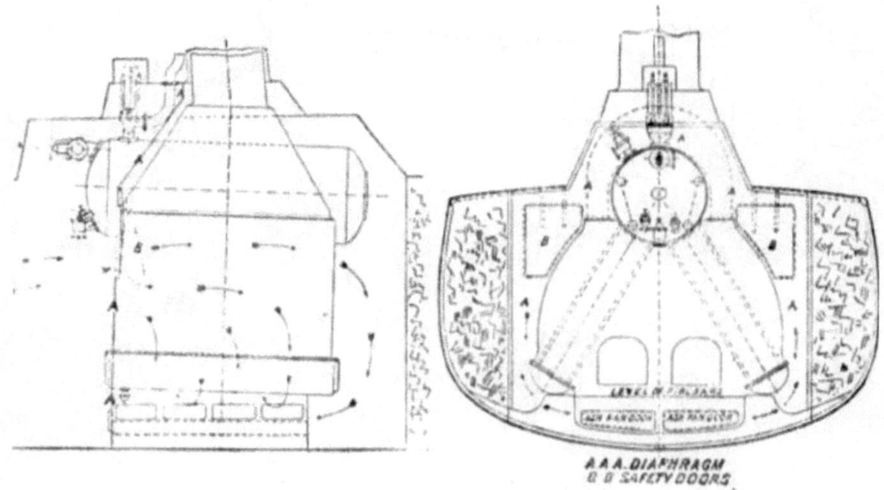

Fig. 43.

has to pass, as shown in Fig. 47. The inlet doors for the protection box are light, hinged or hung at the top, and open inwards. The pressure of air in the stokehold keeps these doors open for the admission of air, but in case of any steam being discharged into the furnace and attempting to enter the stokehold, the protection box doors act as non-return valves, close, and confine the steam and flame to the ashpit, whence it escapes up the funnel.

(*b*) In the second plan the ashpit door is bolted up when under way, a screen or light bulkhead is fitted round the boiler at each end, and non return air flaps are fitted in the screen adjacent to the stokehold, opening from the stokehold into the space between the screens, as shown in Fig. 48. This space is in free communication with the ashpit, so that while air enters through the flaps when the pressure of air opens them, and proceeds thence to the ashpit and fires, the flaps would close and prevent any steam or flame issuing into the stokehold if discharged from the furnace. The front of the ashpit is only unbolted for the removal of ashes. This plan (*b*) is evidently only applicable with dry-bottom boilers.

In both torpedo boats and torpedo gunboats, however, the locomotive boiler has now been abandoned in favour of the water-tube boiler described in the next chapter.

CHAPTER VIII.

WATER-TUBE OR TUBULOUS BOILERS.

THE previously described boilers, having the water outside the tubes and contained in an outer shell or so-called tank, are technically called 'water-tank' boilers, to distinguish them from the class known as 'water-tube' boilers described below.

'Water-tube' boilers are those in which the flame and water in the older form of boiler are interchanged, so that the water being evaporated is contained inside the tubes, and the hot gases outside them. The hot gases outside the tubes are confined and led to the funnel by a casing fitted for the purpose.

The desire to obtain boilers having the capacity of safely generating steam of higher pressures than had been previously used, combined with lightness of construction, and having the tube ends favourably situated for resisting leakage, has led engineers for many years to seek for a satisfactory water-tube boiler.

History of water-tube boilers.—The earlier examples of the water-tube boiler fitted in the mercantile marine, commencing on the Clyde about 1857, were not successful ; they generally failed owing to rapid corrosion of the tubes, combined in some cases with incrustation due to saline deposits on the water side of the tubes, from the salt water which either leaked through condensers or was admitted to supply the waste of feed-water. This incrustation was usually not readily accessible for removal.

Most of these early water-tube boilers were eventually removed and replaced by the cylindrical multitubular boilers previously described, the pressure of steam being correspondingly reduced.

Later on, about 1870-75, with higher pressures, renewed attempts were made in Great Britain to obtain such boilers, but they were again unsuccessful, and for some years after this, the attempt in this country was practically abandoned. Mr. Loftus Perkins was perhaps the most successful, and the Perkins boiler and engine, with pressures of 300 to 500 lbs. per square inch, attracted considerable attention. Other of these early boilers were the Rowan, Howard, and Root types.

In France an important application of such a boiler was made in 1879, by the fitting of Belleville boilers to a despatch vessel which was employed on actual sea service to a considerable extent, and her boilers were reported to have given satisfaction, so that from this time there was a gradual extension of the use of this type in the French Navy. A cruiser launched in 1885 was the next vessel fitted with these boilers, followed in 1889 by the cruiser 'Alger,' of 8,000 I.H.P., and two torpedo gunboats.

Soon after this two steamers of the Messageries Maritimes Company were fitted with Belleville boilers, and as the result of the experience this company has fitted similar boilers to all their new vessels, including their largest and fastest mail steamers.

A considerable number of vessels of the French Navy have also been fitted with water-tube boilers of the Niclausse, and also of the Lagrafel and D'Allest types, and some of these have also been supplied to the French mercantile marine.

In England, in 1882, a mission steamer, and in 1885, No. 100 second-class torpedo boat, were fitted with Thornycroft water-tube boilers ; and the same type was fitted in three first-class torpedo boats for the Indian Government in 1888 ; in the torpedo gunboat 'Speedy,' of 4,500 I.H.P., tried in 1893 ; and in several foreign vessels.

In 1893, Belleville boilers were ordered to replace the defective locomotive boilers of 'Sharpshooter.' It being recognised that these boilers had passed out of the experimental stage, it was subsequently decided to fit the 'Powerful' and 'Terrible,' large cruisers each of 25,000 I.H.P., with them, and subsequently all large new vessels for the British Navy have similar boilers, including (up to 1899) 27 cruisers of 10,000 to 30,000 I.H.P., and 16 battleships of 13,500 to 21,000 I.H.P., besides gunboats and other vessels. Figs. 49 to 57 show these boilers.

In England the Babcock and Wilcox water-tube boiler, previously fitted in some small vessels, was fitted and tried in 1893 in the s.s. 'Nero,' and some other mercantile vessels have since been fitted with this type. They have also been fitted to H.M.S. 'Sheldrake,' which vessel passed through all her contract trials satisfactorily, and also in several vessels of the U.S. Navy, the performance of which during the war with Spain was very satisfactory.

Comparison with locomotive type.—As regards the use of those varieties of water-tube boilers which give the greatest power for their weight and the space occupied, a very considerable extension took place in Great Britain in 1893 by the demand for the class of small vessels of great speed known as 'torpedo-boat destroyers.' Many varieties have since that date been fitted and tried in such vessels with satisfactory results, and they have now entirely superseded the locomotive type, which had previously been mostly used for such purposes. An example of the results obtained in sister vessels with locomotive and water-tube boilers may be given in the trials of 'Havock' and 'Hornet,' built and engined by Messrs. Yarrow & Co., the 'Havock' with locomotive boilers having copper fire-boxes similar to that illustrated in Fig. 44, and the 'Hornet' with water-tube boilers similar to Figs. 65 and 66.

Ship	Type of boiler	I.H.P.	Speed in knots	Weight of boilers, mountings, brickwork, and water, tons	Grate surface sq. ft.	Heating surface, sq. ft.
'Havock'	Locomotive	3,497	26 18	53	100	5,010
'Hornet'	{ Yarrow's water tube }	3,884	27·6	44·8	172·8	8,216

Having now briefly described the history of the revival of water-tube boilers in recent years, we will proceed to the detailed consideration of these boilers, their advantages lying in their lightness for the power generated, the capacity of raising steam quickly owing to the small quantity of water carried, and their comparative freedom from leaky tubes, the joints being more protected from the direct impact of flame.

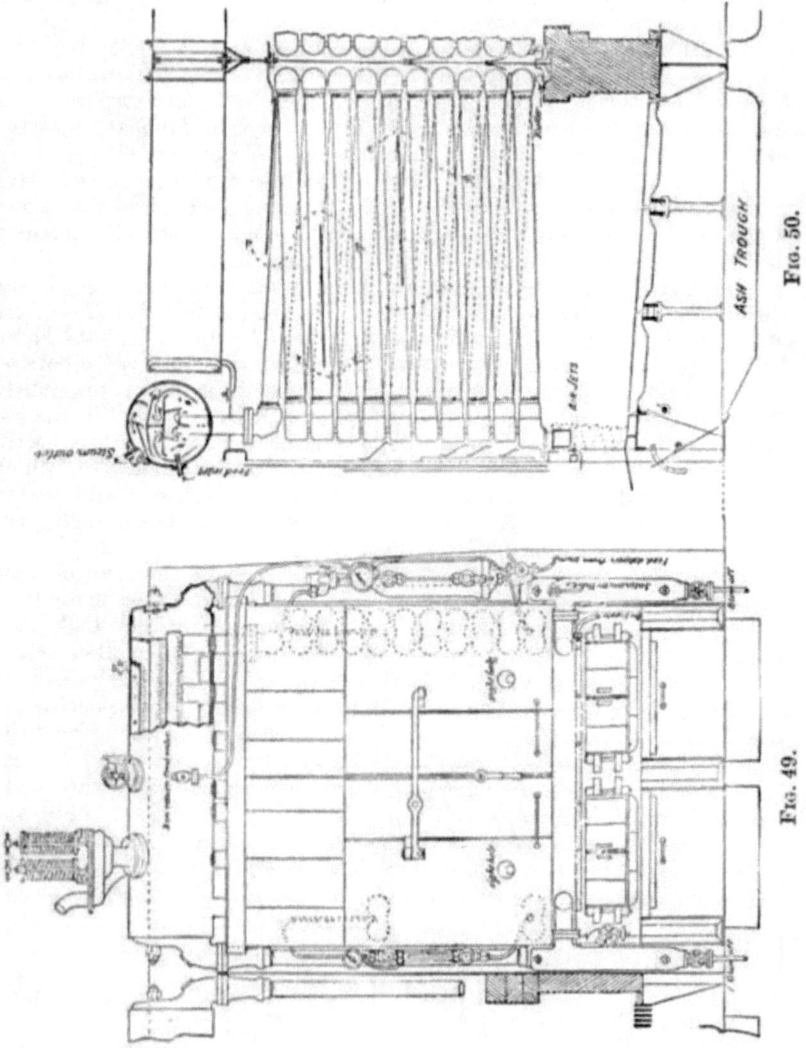

The Belleville boiler.—This type of water-tube boiler is shown in Figs. 49 and 50, and is of more extensive use on board large ships than any other. It consists essentially of a top steam cylinder and a lower water chamber, with a series of straight zigzagged tubes of comparatively large diameter connecting them. There is an external return water pipe on each side, connecting the ends of the top steam chamber with the lower water chamber. The zigzag generating tubes are inclosed in a sheet-iron or steel casing, which confines the flame and gases generated from the combustion of the coal on the fire-bars. These fire-bars are situated at the lower part of the casing, about two feet below the lowest of the tubes. A series of *baffle plates* are secured at intervals among the tubes, to insure that as far as possible the gases should traverse the whole of the surface of the tubes, before passing off to the chimney, in order to obtain the full value of the whole of the heating surface.

The generating tubes are arranged in vertical groups, technically termed 'elements,' in such a manner as to form a kind of flattened spiral. In the boilers of this type at first fitted in the Royal Navy each element consists of twenty straight tubes of $4\frac{1}{2}$ inches external diameter, and about 7 ft. 6 in. long, arranged in this manner, the ends of the tubes being connected together by being screwed into malleable cast-iron boxes, which latter form the turns of the spiral (see Figs. 51 and 52). The inclination of the tubes is about $2\frac{1}{2}°$ to the horizontal.

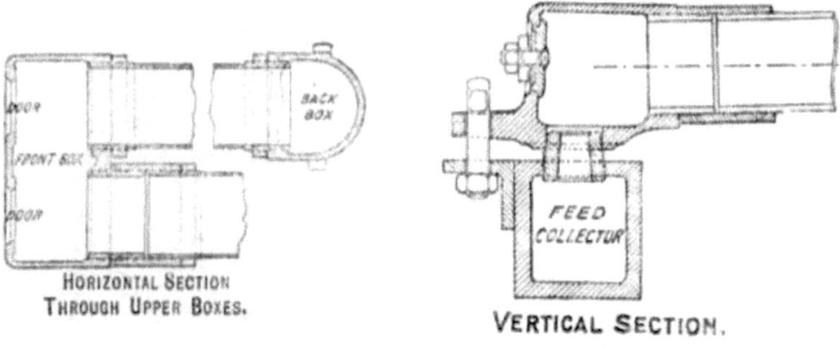

HORIZONTAL SECTION
THROUGH UPPER BOXES.

VERTICAL SECTION.

Fig. 51.   Fig. 52.

The connections are made in such a manner that the whole twenty tubes form one continuous passage for steam and water from the bottom to the top, so that the water, after having passed through any tube, has to traverse a short distance horizontally through the end boxes, to obtain access to the next tube in its ascent.

The front boxes have hand holes opposite each tube so large in diameter that a light can be passed along to the end of the tube, which enables the condition of the interior to be seen, and its cleaning effected. The malleable boxes are so shaped as to allow access from the front for brushes or scrapers to the outside of the tubes. Both inside and outside of the tubes are therefore very accessible for thorough cleaning and inspection from the stokehold floor. A steam-tube sweeping apparatus is also provided for use when under steam.

The front of the lowest part of each element is connected to the water chamber, and the front of the top of each element is connected to the steam collector. The connection between the element and the water chamber is made by means of a coned nipple secured by a single bolt (see Fig. 52). The inlet orifice through the nipple is reduced considerably below the area of the tube, to insure that the central elements shall obtain their fair share of the water brought by the return tubes. The amount of reduction necessary is found by experiment, by the insertion of small pipes in the top tubes with cocks outside, and observing the proportion of steam to water discharged from them.

A safety arrangement is fitted to each element in the shape of two fusible plugs of lead, which are driven into small holes bored in the front of the boxes. They are fitted, one at the lower part of the element and one near the upper part, to give warning should there be any obstruction to the free entry of water or any failure of the feed-water supply.

A series of 7 to 10 elements are placed side by side inside the casing. The flame or gases traversing the spaces between the tubes generate steam inside them, and cause a circulation of steam and water from the lower water chamber through the tubes, and the mixture is discharged into the top steam collector from the tops of the elements. In this steam collector a series of baffle plates and other means are fitted for separating the steam from the water, the steam being drawn off through the stop-valve, and the water flowing along the bottom of the collector to the return water pipes on each side, and thence again to the elements.

The feed-water is admitted through a small non-return valve at the middle of the top collector, through a small orifice, at a considerably higher pressure than that of the steam in the boiler ; it then falls to the bottom of the collector, and flows with the other returning water to the return water pipes. This water at the bottom of the collector is, owing to the admission of feed-water, colder than the steam, and the tops of the elements are carried up to a distance of about eight inches above the bottom of the collector to prevent this colder water entering the element and interfering with the continuous discharge of steam therefrom. In technical language, the tubes are therefore not 'drowned.'

Before entering the lower water chamber from the return pipe the water passes a non-return valve to a sediment collector at the bottom

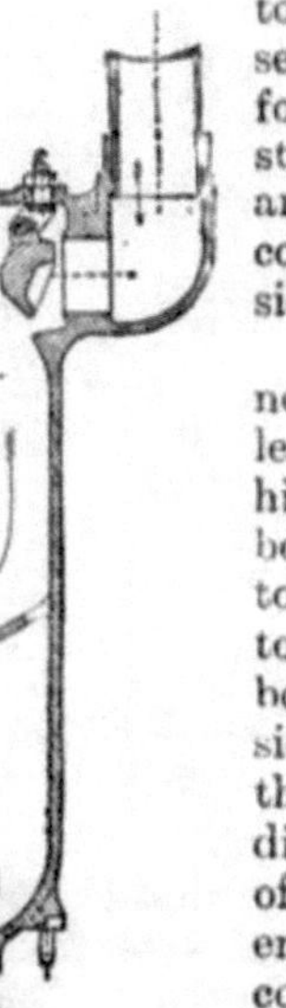

Fig. 53.

of each return pipe, shown in Fig. 53. This non-return valve is important, and should be kept in proper order. It prevents the water leaving the element and ascending the return tube when the vessel is rolling, and regulates the direction of the circulation currents, especially when steam is being raised. The resistance to the motion of the water caused by the whole of the tubes is considerable, and on raising steam there is often a tendency for the heated water of the lower tube to flow into the return pipe, so causing reversal and confusion of the currents. Glass models show the existence of this tendency, and it is prevented by the non-return valve described.

The sediment chamber has a division plate, and the lowest part forms a fairly large space in which the velocity of the water is not great, so that nearly all the grease, lime, or other solid ingredients settle to the bottom and do not enter the generating tubes. The bottom of the sediment chamber is provided with a blow-off valve, the deposits being blown away about once a watch.

The impurities which may be contained in the feed-water are two in number : first, any grease carried over from the engines which may escape the feed-water filters ; and secondly, the lime and other salts, due to the leakage of salt water through the condenser tubes, or, in cases of emergency, by the admission of sea-water to make up losses.

The deliberate admission of sea-water for feed-water make-up should only be resorted to in cases of emergency, such as the failure of the fresh-water appliances at a time when a continuation of steaming is imperative, but the admission of sea-water due to leaky condenser tubes is to a small extent often met with, and the presence of a small quantity of grease must also be anticipated. The arrangements described keep these impurities out of the generating tubes of the boilers, where they would be a source of danger.

As the feed-water is admitted into the steam space below the baffle plates, its temperature is considerably raised by contact with the steam and the other water flowing to the return pipes. By the time it reaches the sediment collector, its temperature has been so raised that it becomes incapable of holding the lime and magnesia salts in solution. They are precipitated in a powdery and largely non-adherent form, and gradually settle to the bottom of the sediment chamber, whence they can be blown out.

Grease is more difficult to deposit in the sediment chamber than lime. In order to facilitate its deposition, a lime box is provided in the engine room in which a certain quantity of lime is placed, and a small stream of water is admitted to it at a high pressure from the feed-pipes to stir up the lime and facilitate the admixture of lime and water. It is then conducted to the feed-tank. The grease contained in the feed-water adheres to the particles of lime thus admitted, and acquires sufficient density and mass to settle at the bottom of the sediment chamber. In practice, very little lime or grease should be found in any of the boiler tubes, even when a considerable quantity of sea-water feed make-up has been used, provided the arrangements fitted are properly used. Practically all that enters is found in the lowest row of tubes.

Belleville automatic feed gear.—A very important part of the Belleville boiler is the automatic feed apparatus, by means of which the water in the gauge glass is maintained at its working level. The working of a boiler of this kind would be practically impossible without this apparatus or some equivalent.

In the first place, the feed discharge pipes and valves are so proportioned as to require a considerably higher pressure in the feed discharge pipe than exists in the boiler. For a boiler pressure of 250 lbs. per square inch, the pressure delivered by the feed pumps on exit from the latter should be about 450 lbs., which with the usual arrangements is found to give sufficient pressure at the boiler, allowing for the losses due to the pipes and valves between the pumps and the feed-valve on the steam collector of the boiler.

The automatic feed regulating apparatus (Figs. 54 and 55) consists of a chamber connected at the top and bottom with the elements of the boiler, and to which one of the gauge glasses is attached. This

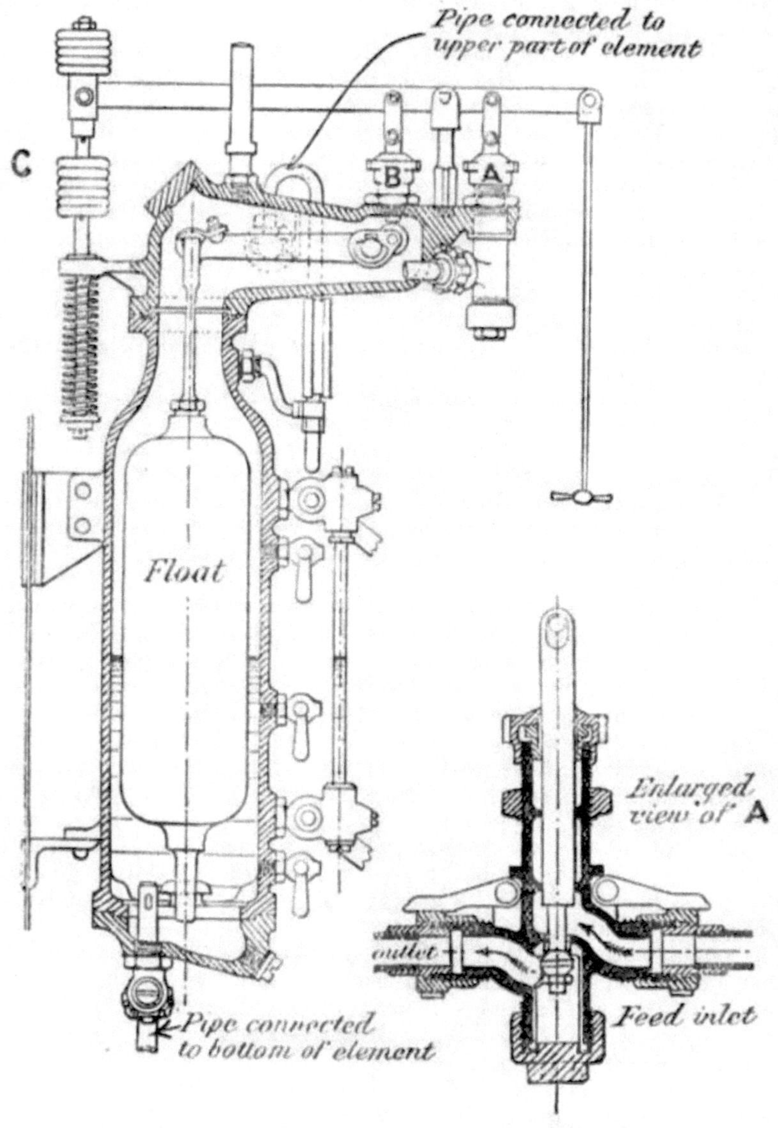

Fig. 54.   Fig. 55.

chamber contains a hollow float. The feed-pipe is carried to the side of the chamber, and a valve and spindle A is placed on it at this part, connected with the float by a system of levers and weights in such a manner that as the water level rises and lifts the float, the external weights at the end of the lever close the valve. The admission of feed-water to the boiler then stops until the water level in the chamber falls sufficiently to enable the float to descend and again raise the weights and thus open the valve. The feed-water is led from this valve to the non-return valve at the steam collector of the boiler. It should be noted that there is no connection between the feed-pipes and the regulating chamber, although the feed-valve at A is bolted to this chamber for convenience.

Particular care is taken as regards accuracy of the fitting of the various parts of this gear, knife edges being fitted for all bearings to reduce the friction to a minimum, but even when this is done the float, before it can open the valve, has to overcome the friction of the rods at A and B, working through steam and watertight glands respectively, and when closing the valve the weights have also to overcome this friction. As the float has to be made of substantial strength to withstand the external water pressure, it is not light enough to be waterborne with about half its volume immersed, as it should do to enable proper feed regulation to take place in each direction. To lighten the float, as it were, and enable it to float freely with about half its length immersed, the weights C are added outside the apparatus. They have the effect of altering the position at which the float and connections are water-borne. Most of the external weights are fixtures, but a small number at the upper part are portable, for use as explained below. Great care is exercised in packing the glands of the rods of this apparatus, so as to reduce the friction as much as possible. A special form of anti-friction packing is used, composed of about 40 per cent. of tin with a little antimony, 46 per cent. of lead, 10 per cent. of graphite, and 4 per cent. of mineral oil.

Amount of water carried. Action when stopping or starting.— Experiment has shown that at ordinary rates of evaporation sufficient water is present when the water in the glass is about midway between the two points of attachment of the gauge. The middle of the water gauge is therefore placed at this point, and the mechanism so arranged that the water level at ordinary rates of evaporation is kept approximately at $\frac{1}{2}$ to $\frac{3}{4}$ glass. It should be noted that, unlike the water-tank boiler, the height of the column of water in the gauge glass does not simply indicate the amount necessary to balance the statical pressure of a similar column of water in the boiler, for there is an appreciable difference of pressure between the top and bottom connections of the element, where the gauge connections are, due to the force necessary to cause the flow of water and steam through the element. The height of the water in the gauge glass therefore indicates the weight of the water between the points of attachment plus the pressure necessary to cause the flow of water and steam, and as this latter increases with the rate of combustion, the height necessary in the gauge glass to carry the same quantity of water in the boiler increases with the rate of evaporation.

At the higher rates of evaporation therefore, more water should be carried in the gauge glass, and to enable this to be done a few portable weights are supplied on the feed regulator, by removing which, the float sinks lower in the water so that a higher level is required in order to shut the feed-valve. If the evaporation be suddenly stopped the mixture of steam and water subsides, and the level shown by the glass gauge will fall until it corresponds with this. As, however, any lowering of water level causes the feed-valve to open wide, and thus reduce the pressure in the feed discharge pipe, the feed-pump immediately increases speed, and pumps the water level back again to the shutting-off point, at about ½ to ⅔ glass. This lowering of level on stopping is to be expected, and does not indicate any defect. The feed-pumps will continue to work till the water level is restored.

Conversely, when getting under way quickly, as the feed-pumps will have pumped the water level back to about ½ or ⅔ glass, whereas when at work the quantity required is much less than is contained in the boiler under these circumstances, the excess of water is passed into the steam pipe to be caught at the separator, or if the increase of speed be made slowly, it is gradually evaporated, the feed inlet-valve closing while this is happening. We thus explain the usual phenomena with these boilers—i.e. feed-pumps working rapidly when slowing down, and either working slowly or stopping when the speed is being quickly increased.

Gas-mixing appliances.—The space between the fire and the lowest tubes is not large, so that unless complete combustion of gases takes place within a short distance of the fire their combustion will take

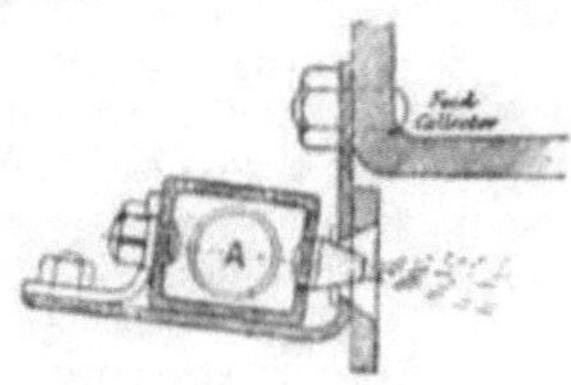

Fig. 56.

place above the lowest tubes, and much heat will pass off to the funnel, which, had the combustion taken place lower, would have been abstracted by the water in the tubes. With a properly regulated and thin fire which passes the proper amount of air there is less likelihood of this, but it has been found that the forcing of air in small streams under pressure above the fire has a beneficial effect in thoroughly mixing the gases, and so accelerating their combustion. It should be observed that the apparatus is simply a gas-mixing one, and not for forcing the rate of combustion of the coal.

The arrangement consists of a square air-pipe A, Fig. 56, about 10 or 12 inches above the fire-bars, into which air is forced in small jets by an air compressor at a pressure of 5 to 15 lbs. per square inch. A series of nozzles about $\frac{3}{16}$-inch diameter, slightly inclined downwards, discharge the air among the gases above the fire with such force as to reach all parts of the furnace and thoroughly mix the gases with the oxygen. In the front casing are sight holes, two or three in number (see Fig. 49), with sliding covers, which can be moved on one side to enable the condition of the fire to be inspected and the admission of air regulated, so as to obtain the best result, which, with experience, the person in charge is able to do.

Facility for repairs.—Pipes are screwed into the steam collector to the height previously explained, as shown in Figs. 49 and 50, and the top of the elements are secured to them by flange joints. The bottom of the element is secured to the feed-box or collector by means of a conical joint, shown in detail in Fig. 52, the jointing material consisting of a thin conical nickel ring inserted between the coned nipple and the conical hole in the lower box. The single bolt shown is all that is necessary for satisfactorily making this joint. Should it be found necessary to renew any tube, this can be accomplished by withdrawing the 'element' containing the tube from the boiler.

The bolt which makes the joint with the feed collector at the lower part, and also the four bolts making the flanged joint of the top tube with the steam collector are removed, the front of the element is then lifted sufficiently to allow the lower box to clear the cone of the feed collector, sufficient spring being allowed at the top tube of the element to enable this to be done. The element is then free and can be drawn out into the stokehold to enable the new tube to be fitted.

Economiser type of Belleville boiler.—The preceding description refers to the Belleville boiler as fitted in 'Sharpshooter,' 'Powerful,' 'Terrible,' and four other cruisers, but the later vessels building for the British Navy are provided with a modified and improved variety described as the 'economiser' type. In this type the boiler is divided into two parts, viz. (*a*) a lower part consisting of elements of exactly the same construction and with the same fittings as in the previously-described boiler, except that the height is considerably reduced, each element containing fourteen tubes, and sometimes only twelve, instead of twenty—this part is called the 'generator'; and (*b*) a series of smaller elements termed the 'economiser,' placed 4 or 5 feet above the top tube of the generator, in the boiler uptake, and through which the feed-water is first discharged and raised in temperature before being admitted to the steam collector.

The space between the generator and the economiser acts as a combustion chamber, in which any unconsumed gases that may have passed the lower parts of the boiler are provided with additional air to assist their combustion, and given room to expand, prior to traversing the spaces between the economiser tubes and giving up heat to the feed-water contained therein.

The economiser generally consists of one or two less number of elements than contained in the generator, but of smaller diameter, viz. $2\frac{3}{4}$ inches instead of $4\frac{1}{2}$ inches, as in the generator. The number of tubes in each economiser element varies from 12 to 20, depending on the height available. The length of the economiser is less than that of the generator portion, and in most boilers building is about 6 ft. The economiser is formed similarly to the lower elements, and consists of straight zigzagged tubes screwed into malleable cast-iron end boxes.

The sketch, Fig. 57, shows a boiler with the elements in the generator each seven pairs of tubes high, each economiser consisting of elements nine pairs of tubes high, a considerable space being allowed between the generator and economiser. In this arrangement the feed-water proceeds from the pump to the valve A at the feed regulator chamber, exactly as previously described, but on leaving this valve, instead of entering the steam collector direct, it proceeds through a non-return valve to the pipe B, called the 'cold water collector,' at the bottom of the economiser, and then enters the element through an orifice in each lower front box, and is pumped upwards to and fro through the elements and abstracts heat from the gases. It issues into a pipe C, called the 'hot water collector,' at the top of the elements, and is thence led to the non-return valve D on the steam collector. The fronts of the economiser tubes are fitted

Feed outlet from economiser
C
To Funnel
K
Feed inlet to Economiser
B
Steam Outlet
Feed inlet to Boiler after leaving economiser
D
P
Air Inlet
COMBUSTION CHAMBER
Baffle
Automatic Feed Regulator
A
Baffle
Baffle
SIMILAR BOILER HERE AT BACK OF OTHER.
Mud Box & Side
Air Inlet
ASH & WATER TROUGH

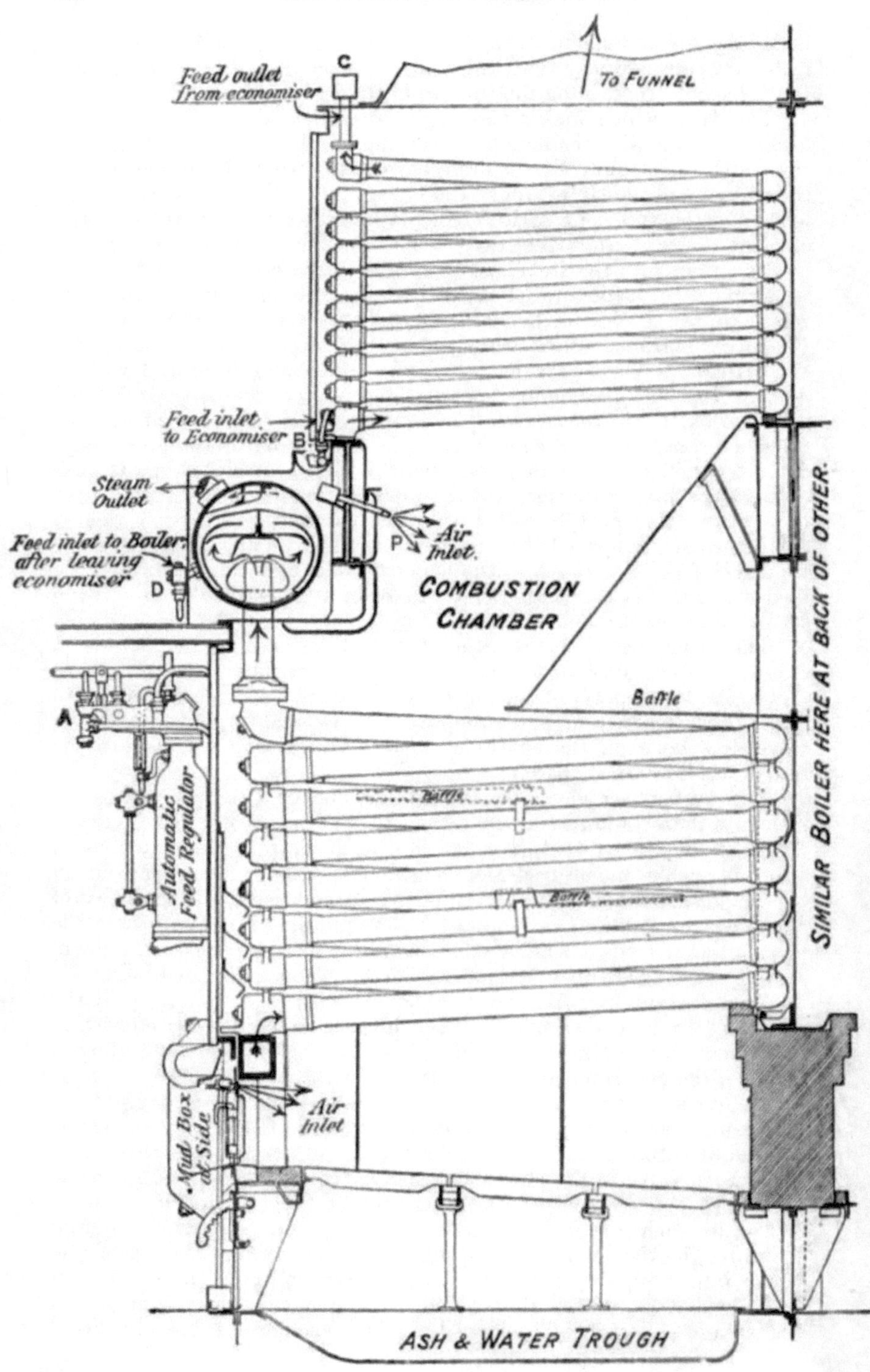

Fig. 57.

with cleaning doors, and the economiser casing is provided with doors at the front for access to the tubes.

A few small nozzles P are supplied with compressed air from the furnace air pumps, and inject air into the combustion chamber space to supplement that admitted by the gas-mixing jets above the fire. A small safety-valve is fitted on the discharge pipe from the economiser.

Very high results have been obtained with this modified type of Belleville boiler, as will be seen from the following table, giving the results of trials made by Admiralty officers on one boiler erected on shore. Good Welsh hand-picked coal was used, and a large separator fitted to ascertain if any water was carried over with the steam.

EVAPORATION TRIALS OF BELLEVILLE BOILERS WITH ECONOMISERS

Coal burnt per sq ft. grate in lbs.	18·5	24·5	31	37
Ratio of heating surface in generator to grate	21	21	21	21
Ratio of heating surface in economiser to grate	11·7	11·7	11·7	11·7
Ratio of total heating surface to grate	32·7	32·7	32·7	32·7
Duration of trial in hours	8	8	4	4
Actual evaporation of water into lbs. of dry steam per lb. of coal	9·94	9·62	9·33	9·17
Equivalent evaporation from and at 212° F.	12·0	11·6	11·2	11·0
Actual evaporation of water into dry steam in lbs. per sq. ft. of total heating surface	5·63	7·23	8·84	10·4
Steam produced in lbs. per sq. ft. of grate	183·9	235·7	289·2	339·3
Temperature of feed, Fahr	68°	68°	68°	68°
Steam pressure in boiler, lbs. per sq. in.	205	215	220	230
Temperature of feed leaving economiser, Fahr.	226	250	300	330
Temperature at base of funnel, Fahr.	394	518	650	750
,, between generator and economiser, Fahr.	860	1,112	1,300	1,560
Vacuum at base of funnel, inches of water	·46	·62	·8	1·12

The Thornycroft boiler ('Speedy' type), Fig. 58, consists essentially of a central upper steam cylinder A, and two smaller lower water cylinders B, these latter being fitted about the level of the fire-bars. A series of steam generating tubes of small diameter are fitted between the upper cylinder and each of the lower water cylinders. They are secured at each end by being simply rolled into the cylinder plating by means of the roller expander, the parts of the cylinders into which they are rolled being made thick enough for this purpose. These tubes form practically the whole of the heating surface of the boiler, and the inner row on each side is curved in such a manner that they are close together at the top and form the roof of the furnace or combustion chamber. Each of these two rows is made into a wall of tubes, through which the gases cannot penetrate except through orifices left for this purpose at the bottom of the tubes. This is effected by bending the tubes just above the lower cylinder and fitting each alternate tube into the space between its neighbours, so that it forms a closed wall, except for the spaces E F at the bottom. It will be seen that the curvature of the tubes allows considerable freedom of expansion.

The outer row on each side is similarly made into a wall of tubes through which the gases cannot escape except through openings G H

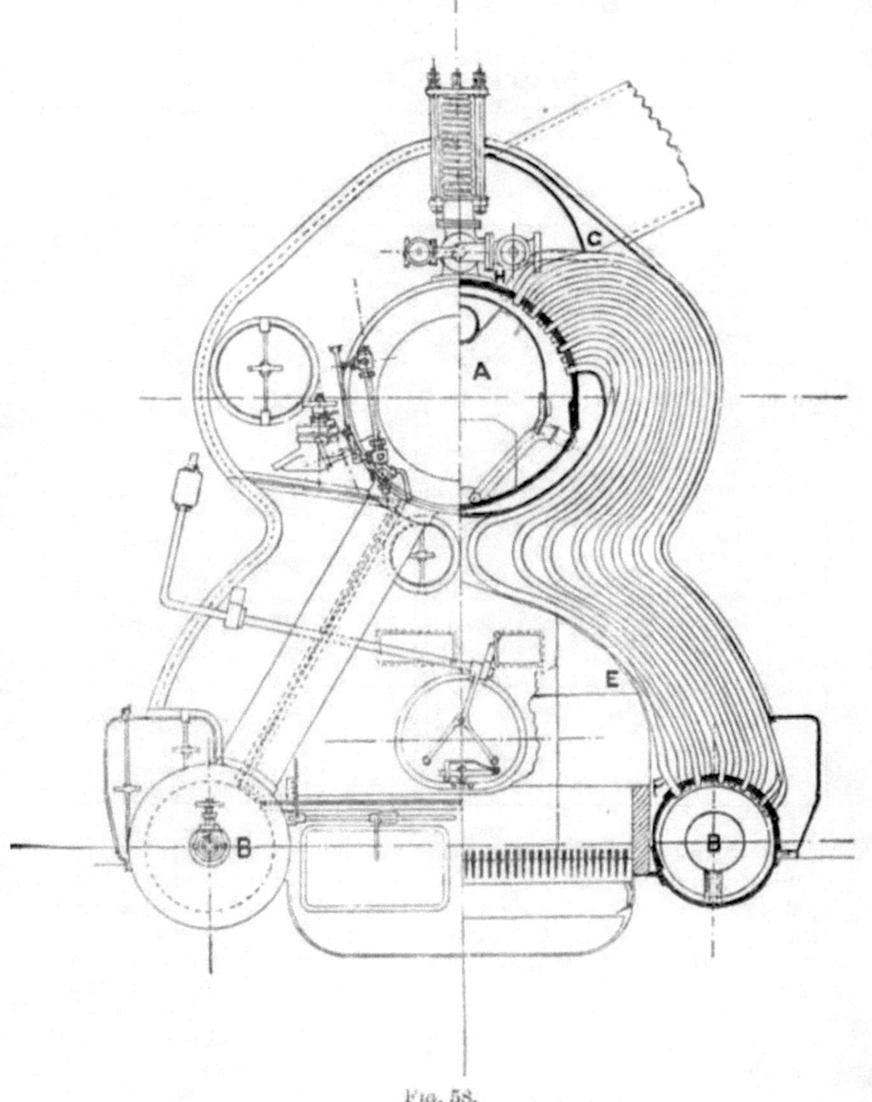

Fig. 58.

left for this purpose at the top. The gases, therefore, generated in the furnace enter among the tubes through the opening left at the bottom of the inner walls of tubes ; they ascend, traversing the whole of the tube surface between the inner and outer walls, and emerge on their way to the funnel through the openings near the top, left in the outer wall of tubes. The whole of the generating tubes are so curved as to enter the top collector above the water level ; there is therefore no possibility of any water being returned to the lower water chambers by means of these tubes, so that special return water tubes are essential. These return water tubes, two in number, are fitted at one end of the boiler ; they are of large diameter, and connect the top cylinder with each of the lower water chambers outside the smoke casing of the boiler.

The flame and gases traversing the tubes, and emerging at the top on their way to the funnel, cause a rapid circulation of water upwards through the tubes, and some portion is evaporated into steam. The steam and water emerge at the tube ends against a baffle plate or shield, which guides the water being discharged down to the water surface at the bottom of the collector, and prevents the entry of spray into the internal steam pipe which runs along the cylinder at the top immediately below the baffle plate to draw off the steam produced. A light steel casing is fitted over the tubes on the outside, and the ends of the boiler are formed by flat casings, and in the vicinity of the fire-bars a brick lining is fitted, forming a boundary for the fire. The feed-water is admitted about the centre of the top cylinder. The tubes in the ' Speedy's ' boiler are ·128 inches thick for $1\frac{1}{4}$ inch diameter (external) and ·104 inches for $1\frac{1}{8}$ inch diameter (external).

The trials of the ' Speedy ' were successfully completed, and on actual service good reports were received on the behaviour of her boilers until the tubes became so corroded and worn as to require renewal, which occurred about four years after being first commissioned. The large ratio of heating surface to grate, viz. 85, no doubt accounts for their economy. The trials showed that these boilers could not be worked at high power with much salt water in them without considerable priming—in fact, this feature is common to all the various types of small-tube boilers. Special care is therefore necessary by frequent examinations to insure that the glands of the condenser tubes are properly packed and adjusted to prevent leakage.

Thornycroft (Daring) type.—The length of the ' Speedy's ' boilers to allow for return tubes is considerable, the tubes are not very accessible, and the height of the furnace is not great, so that when the demand for torpedo-boat destroyers came, in order to meet their special requirements as regards lightness, also to give an improved furnace and greater means of access to the tubes, a modified type of boiler was designed, known as the Thornycroft (Daring) type (Figs. 59 and 60).

This type obtains two furnaces in each boiler and a greater amount of fire-grate in the available space. It consists of an upper cylinder A similar to that of the preceding type, into which the upper ends of the generating tubes are rolled. Vertically below this is the principal lower cylinder B, to which the lower ends of the majority of the tubes are attached. Two smaller water cylinders, D, are arranged on each side of the principal lower cylinder, and the furnaces are situated between them. Three rows of generating tubes connect the upper cylinder to each of the small water cylinders and form the outside boundaries of the furnaces, the inner boundaries being made by the tubes connecting the upper cylinder with the principal lower one. Of

SIGHT DOOR
SIGHT DOOR
A
F
C
SOOT DOOR
G
AIR DOOR
SIGHT DOOR
B
H
D

Fig. 59.

A
MAIN FEED
G
G
G
G
H

Fig. 60.

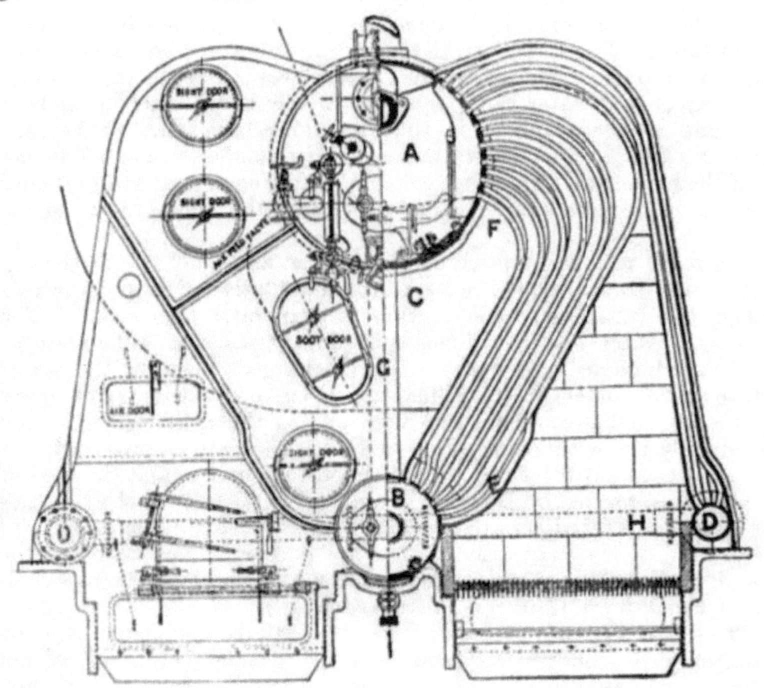

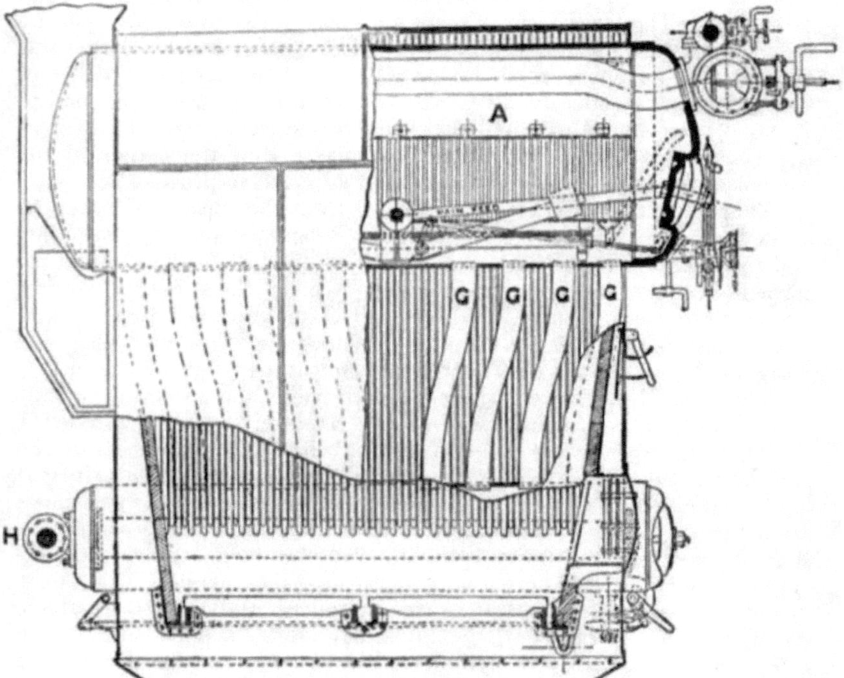

the three rows connected to the small water cylinder, the outside two touch each other, and so form a water wall which confines the flames and gases. The main body of the tubes are so curved as to leave a considerable space, C, between the two groups on each side ; the gases are discharged into this space, which forms the uptake of the boiler.

The inner and outer rows of tubes of each centre group are formed as walls of tubes, except at the lower part of the furnace side and upper part of the uptake side, where spaces are left for the entry and exit of gases. The gases, after leaving the fire, enter through the spaces E, at

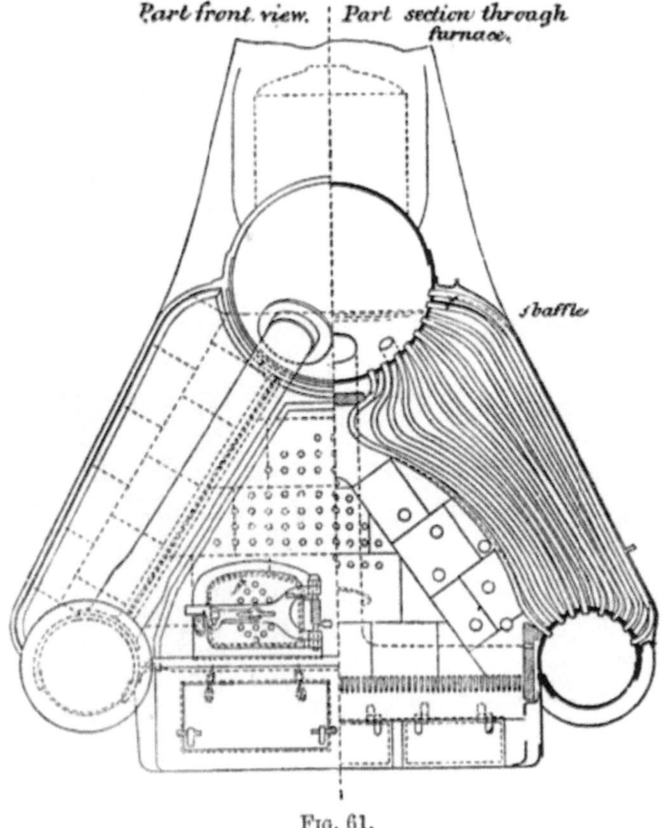

Fig. 61.

the bottom of the outer row, pass up between the walls among the tubes, and emerge through the spaces F at the top of the inner rows to the uptake space C, between the two centre groups of tubes. They proceed along this space to the end of the boiler and thence to the funnel.

Provision is made for the return of water to the lower chamber by fitting a series of vertical return pipes G between the bottom of the upper chamber and the top of the lower cylinder. These return tubes therefore pass through the flue of the boiler and abstract a certain amount of heat from the gases before they escape from the boiler.

As the result of experience, a different kind of baffle plate to that used in the 'Speedy' for the separation of the steam and water is fitted in the steam collector. It consists of a series of gratings, through which the steam and water has to pass before it obtains access to the internal steam pipe.

The small outside water chambers, D, are connected by means of horizontal pipes, H, at the ends, with the central lower chamber, so that by this means they obtain their share of the water brought down by the return pipes. The generating tubes are of steel, $1\frac{1}{8}$ and $1\frac{1}{4}$ inches external diameter and ·104 inch thick.

It will be noticed that all the tubes in the Thornycroft boiler of both types discharge their water and steam above the water line.

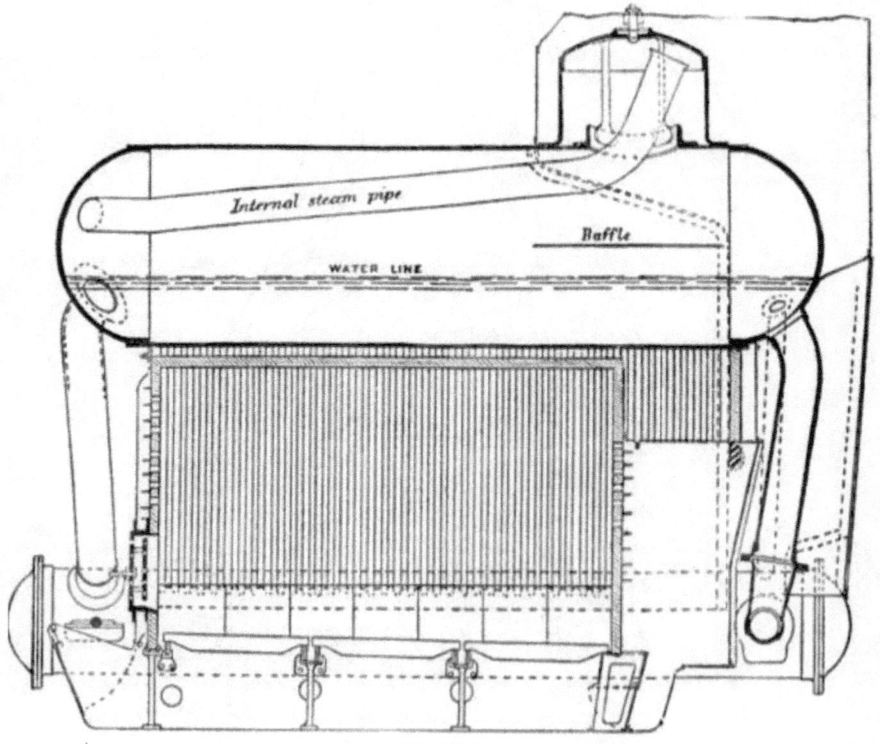

Fig. 62.

This situation of the upper ends of the tubes in relation to the water line is spoken of as being 'not drowned,' to distinguish it from other boilers in which the upper ends are below the water line or 'drowned.' Certain advantages are claimed by Mr. Thornycroft for his arrangement, principally that of steady circulation undisturbed by sudden collapse of steam bubbles on exit from the tube, or any tendency of water to return through the heating tubes. Unfortunately, however, the tubes above the water line appear specially liable to corrosion.

Normand boiler.—The next most extensive experience has been obtained in the British Navy with the Normand type, with more or less modification fitted in a considerable number of torpedo-boat destroyers by Messrs. Laird Bros. and the Clydebank Engineering Company, and this type of boiler has given satisfaction in all cases where the boiler tubes have been made of steel.

In the Normand type, a drawing of which is shown in Figs. 61 and 62, there is the usual top cylinder with two lower water chambers. Large external return water tubes are also fitted at each end. The tubes enter the top chamber mostly below the water level, but a few of them discharge above this level. The two outer rows of tubes on each side are formed into a wall of tubes, as in the Thornycroft type. The furnace does not extend the full length of the boiler, and in its vicinity the tubes are arched upwards so as to leave space for a combustion chamber, whereas beyond the furnace, where there is no necessity for so arching them, they are of much less curvature, and as no combustion chamber is required at this part a larger number of tubes are fitted. It will be noticed that all the tubes adjacent to the fire have a considerable amount of curvature, while even at the ends beyond the furnace, where the heat is less intense, the tubes have also a certain amount of bending, which allows for expansion when heated.

The gases proceed from the fire among the tubes, as shown by the arrow on Fig 63, which shows a half section through the tubes, and traverse the length of the boiler to the uptake end, where they pass below a brick deflecting plate to the space around those tubes that are less bent. They then rise on each side in the smoke casing, unite, and proceed to the funnel. A large steam dome is provided to which the steam pipe is led.

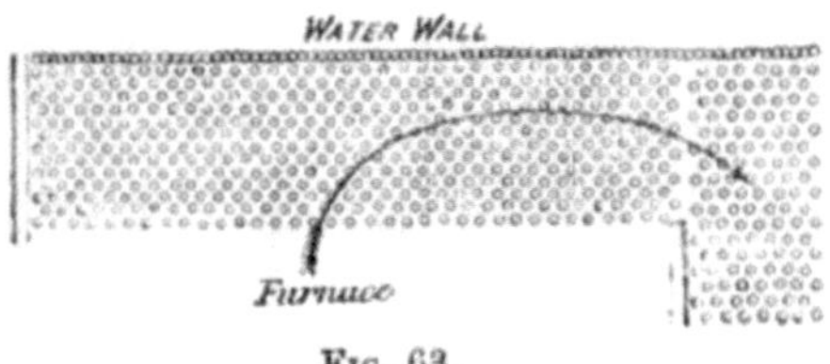

FIG. 63.

In this boiler provision is made for the admission of air above the fire by means of a small air casing at the front and back, and a series of small holes about one inch in diameter leading through the brickwork to the space above the fire. This casing is connected with the air supply below the ashpit, and serves the double purpose of keeping the front and back of the boiler cool and sending a supply of warm air through the holes into the space among the gases above the fire. A series of steel pins project into this air space from the brick lining, and the air in passing these pins absorbs heat from them as well as from the surface of the steel casing. As the holes in the brickwork and steel casing must correspond to insure the passage of air in this manner, the bricks have to be well secured to the casing.

Normand ' Brazen ' type.—The Clydebank Company in their later destroyers have introduced important modifications in this type of boiler. This modified boiler, called the ' Brazen ' type, was originally designed for a vessel of this name. The modifications consist of arranging additional partial walls of tubes in such a manner as to cause the gases to travel backwards among the tubes between the partial walls, before proceeding along the length of the boiler to the flue or uptake at the funnel end.

To form these partial walls a portion of the two inner rows at the front ends, and a portion of the middle rows at the back ends, are bent

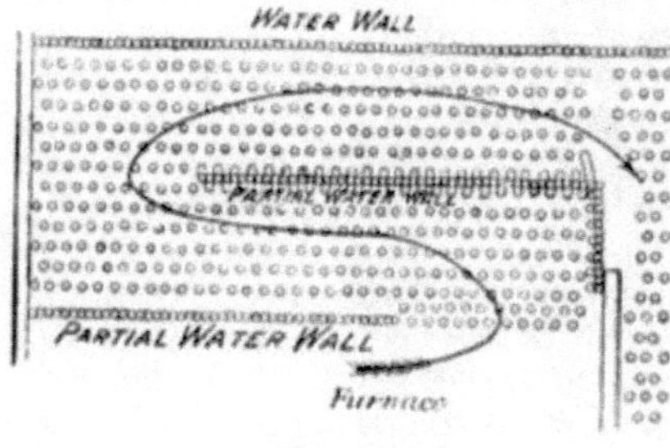

FIG. 64.

so as to be close together, thus forming the partial walls of tubes, in such a manner that the gases enter among the tubes at the back ends, return to the front end around the middle wall, and thence to the uptake at the back (see Fig. 64, which shows a half section through the tubes). The back end of the boiler or uptake end is similar to that of the original Normand boiler. This type of boiler is fitted in several of the torpedo-boat destroyers, and in the 'Pelorus,' a third-class cruiser of 7,000 I.H.P.

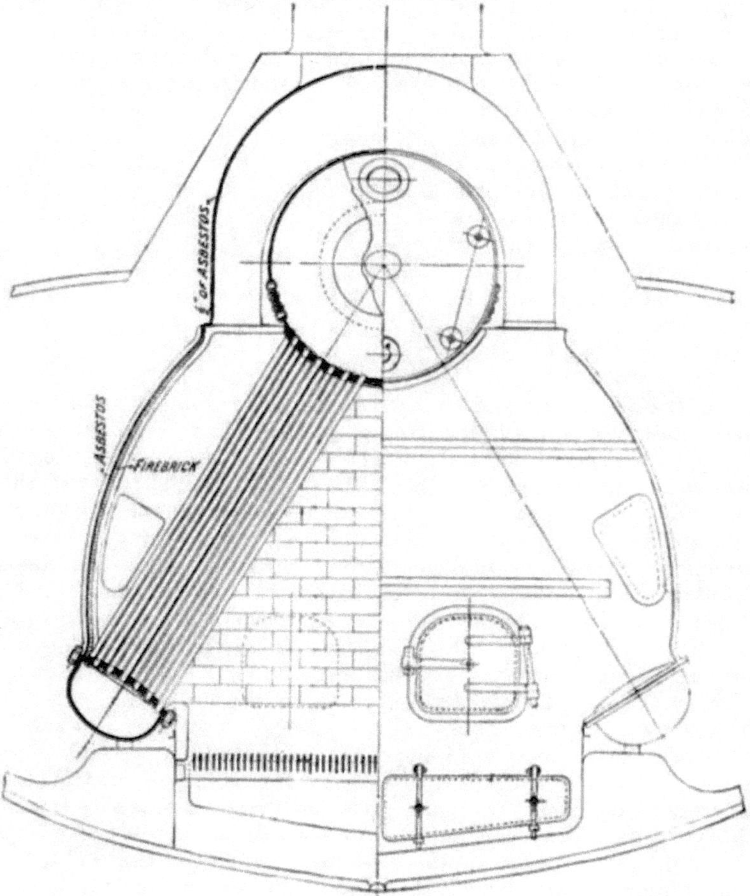

FIG 65

Yarrow boiler.—We come now to the Yarrow boiler (Figs. 65 and 66), which has been fitted in several British torpedo-boat destroyers, and many foreign ones. This boiler consists of a steam drum at the top, in the centre, with flat tube-plates at the lower end on each side, between which and the steam drum are a series of straight tubes which form the heating surface of the boiler. The tubes all deliver their steam to the steam drum below the water line. A small water chamber is

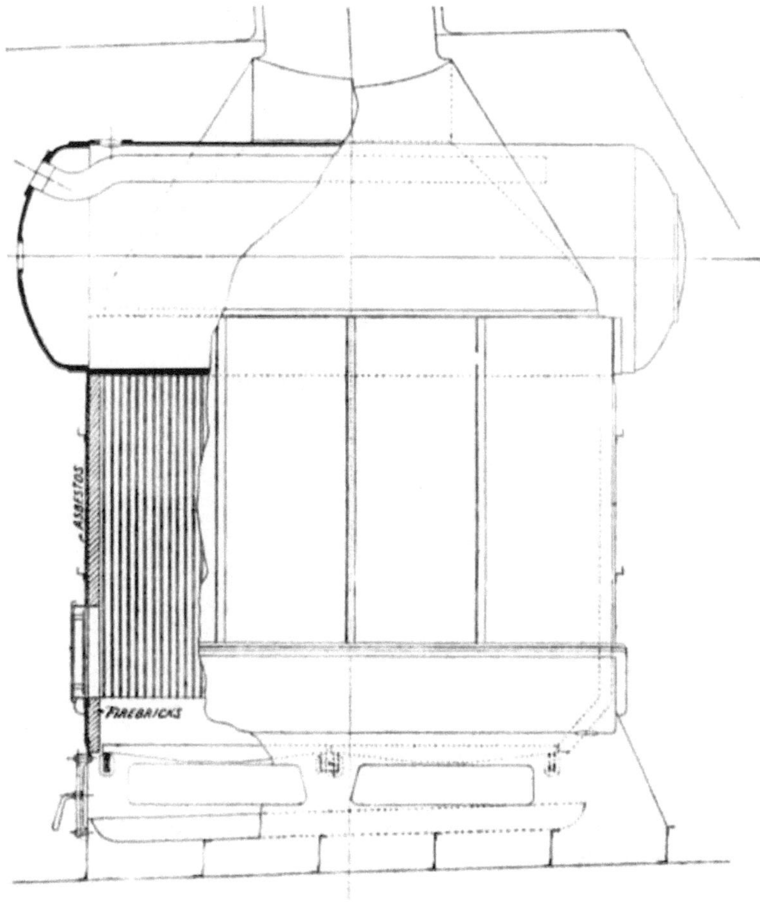

Fig. 66.

bolted to these lower tube-plates. The original boiler of this type fitted in No. 77 torpedo boat had external return water-tubes. In the torpedo-boat destroyer 'Hornet,' however, which was the next vessel fitted with these boilers in our Navy, these external return water tubes were omitted.

The return of water must, therefore, take place down those tubes which are exposed to the least intense heat, and a few are now generally shielded from the fire at the ends by means of a diaphragm plate fitted between the tubes, to facilitate the return flow of water from the steam drum to the lower water chambers. Some of these boilers have also had small return tubes fitted at each end, which also act as stays to the boiler. The 'Hornet' with Yarrow boilers was the first torpedo-boat destroyer with water-tube boilers to complete her trials.

In the latest variety a diaphragm is fitted along the lower water chambers to enable the feed water to be passed up through the rows of tubes farthest away from the fire, by which an improvement in economy results similar to that with the economiser type of Belleville boiler.

Blechynden boiler.—Another type of boiler similar in general

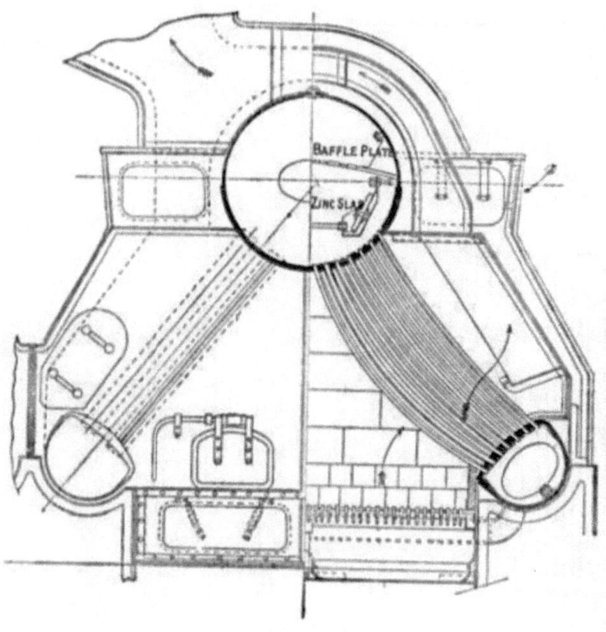

Fig. 67.

arrangement to the Yarrow type is the Blechynden boiler, Fig. 67. It consists of an upper steam drum of considerable diameter, and two lower water chambers larger in size than those in the Yarrow boiler. At the top of the steam drum are a series of holes about $2\frac{1}{2}$ inches in diameter, fitted on each side of the centre line in the first boilers of this design. The sketch shows the later form of this boiler in which there is only one series of holes, at the centre line. The intention of these holes is to facilitate the replacement of tubes should any become damaged or otherwise require withdrawal. The tubes are slightly curved to a large radius (30 feet and 50 feet respectively, depending on their position) which enables the holes at the top to be made much smaller than would otherwise be necessary The first boilers of this type contained two outer rows on each side formed into walls of tubes by

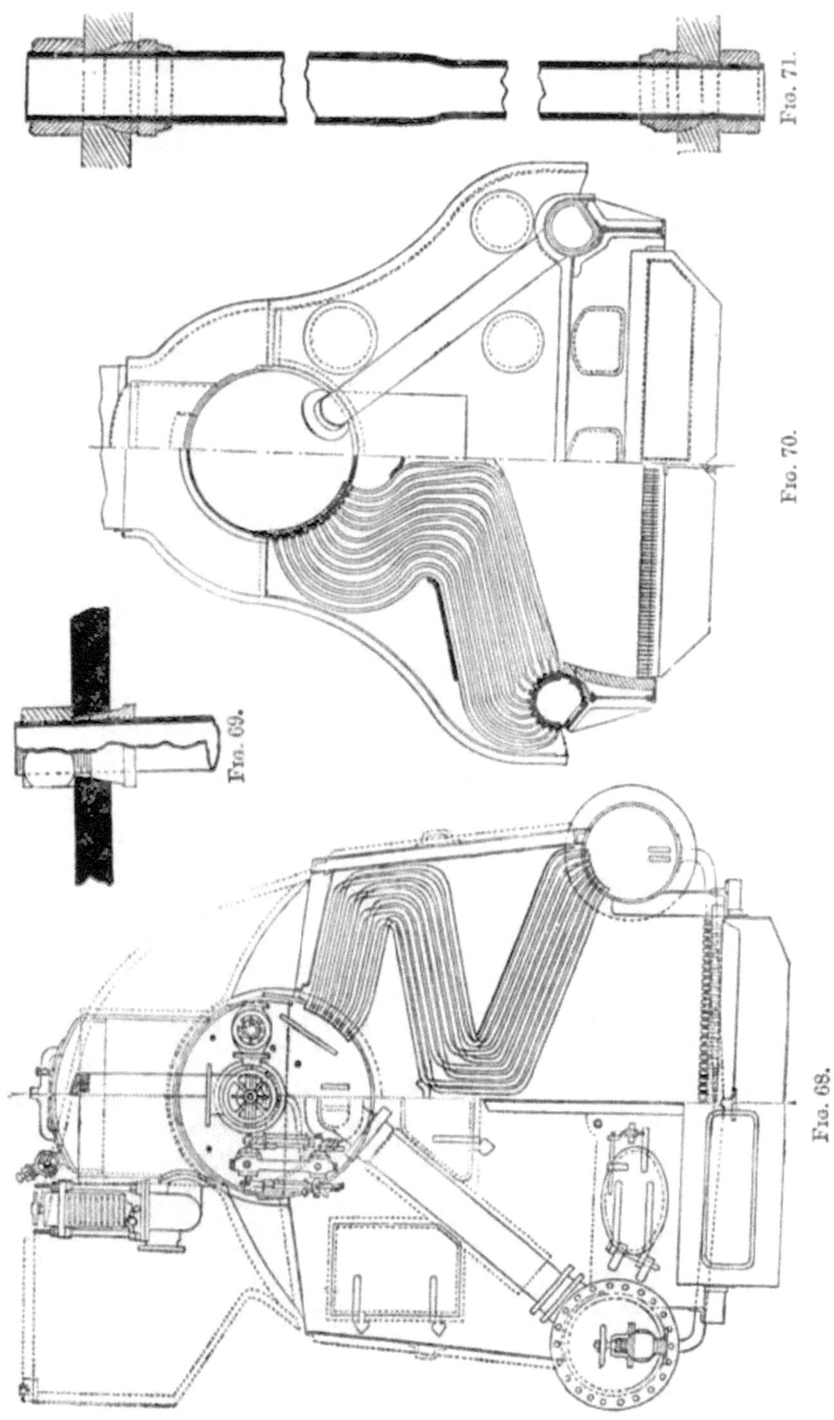
Fig. 71.
Fig. 70.
Fig. 69.
Fig. 68.

being bent in the usual way, so as to be close together except at the top, where spaces are left between them for the exit of the gases. The later variety shown in the sketch does not contain this feature. The tubes all discharge their steam and water below the water line. Four $3\frac{1}{4}$-inch return tubes are fitted at each end between the steam drum and the bottom collector for the return of water.

Du Temple boiler.—This is of the same general character as Thornycroft's, except that the generating tubes discharge into the steam collector below the water line. It is shown in Fig. 68, and its special feature consists in the attachment of the tubes to the steam and water chambers by joints formed by cones and nuts (see Fig. 69), which enable the tubes to be readily dismantled when required. Most of the Du Temple boilers have square water chambers, with covers bolted on, and giving ready access to the lower ends of the tubes. These boilers are fitted in H.M.S. 'Spanker,' and in a large number of vessels of the torpedo boat type in France. The lower water chambers of the 'Spanker's' boilers are, however, made cylindrical with end doors, and not with bolted covers. The lower ends of the tubes are of smaller diameter than the upper parts, to increase the area for the passage of gases when leaving the fires. This was one of the earliest of modern water-tube boilers.

Reed's boiler.—This boiler, shown in Fig. 70, is much like the Du Temple boiler, and consists of the usual top collector and two lower water chambers, with generating tubes between them, considerably bent. It has large external return tubes at each end. The special feature consists in the attachment of the tubes, which is effected by means of screwed connections at each end, with nuts inside the chambers, as shown on the large scale sketch, showing one of the tubes, Fig. 71. The connection of the tubes is much the same as in the 'Du Temple' type, the difference being that the nipples are of a spherical shape instead of being coned. The generating tubes are $1\frac{1}{16}$ inches outside diameter, reduced at the bottom to $\frac{3}{4}$-inch, which allows extra space for the entry of the gases among the tubes and gives sufficient space for the lower nuts.

Diaphragms are fitted where shown in the drawing to insure the gases traversing the bulk of the heating surface before they proceed to the funnel. An air casing is fitted round the boiler, through which air is delivered to the back of the ashpit, thus serving the double purpose of keeping the outside of the boiler cool and warming the air supplied to the ashpits.

Babcock & Wilcox boiler.—One of the best known water-tube boilers on land in England and America is the Babcock & Wilcox, one of which was fitted and tried in the s.s. 'Nero' in 1893.

In this boiler (Figs. 72 and 73) the generating tubes are fitted between a number of headers, or narrow sinuous vertical water chambers of square section, each pair of which (one at the front and one at the back) is united by tubes inclined at an angle of about 1 in 4. The tubes are expanded, and are examined, through doors in the header. The front and back headers are connected by short and long pipes respectively, as shown, to the cylindrical receiver above them, which is kept, when at work, about half full of water. The gases from the fire pass around the tubes and thence to the funnel, and the water circulates up the inclined tubes to the upcast headers, thence by the long top pipe to the receiver, and the downtake headers, back to the generating tubes.

The tubes are expanded into the headers by ordinary roller expanders. The bottoms of the headers are connected by horizontal square pipes, between which run the lowest of the boiler tubes. The tube connecting the lower ends of the downtake headers is connected to a sediment chamber at each end, and to this the blow-out apparatus is fitted. There are return tubes at the ends leading to the bottom of the headers. The details of boilers of this type vary very considerably. In some varieties there are additional vertical tubes, forming the casing of the boiler, and placed on each side.

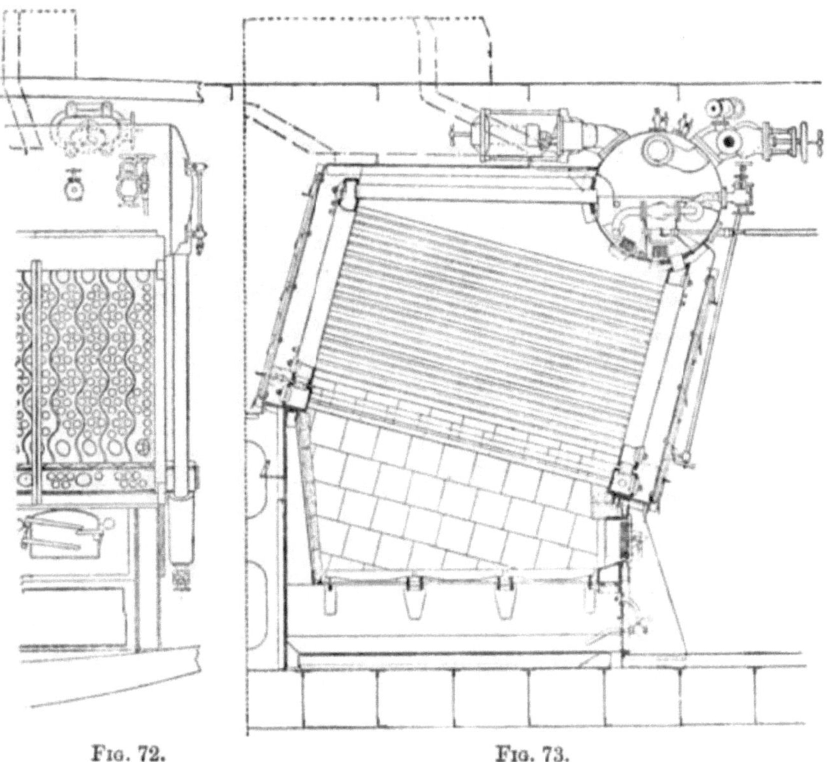

Fig. 72.   Fig. 73.

A series of tubes are also fitted in the 'Nero's' boiler, in the uptake above the generating tubes, through which the feed-water is pumped on its way to the boiler, forming thus a feed-water heater. The Babcock & Wilcox boiler is fitted in H.M.S. 'Sheldrake' for trial.

Niclausse boiler.—This is illustrated in Figs. 74 and 75, and has been fitted in a considerable number of vessels in foreign navies, and consists of a series of slightly inclined double tubes, one inside the other, attached at the front end in such a manner that the colder water flows down the inside tube, and returns to the front between the two tubes when heated by the action of the fire and hot gases on the larger outside tube. An arrangement of diaphragms is fitted at the front ends of the tubes which completely separates the down-coming water from the ascending currents of hot water and steam, as shown in section at the upper part of Fig. 75. Each vertical row of tubes is attached at the front to a separate square pipe or header, making the currents of each series quite independent of the others.

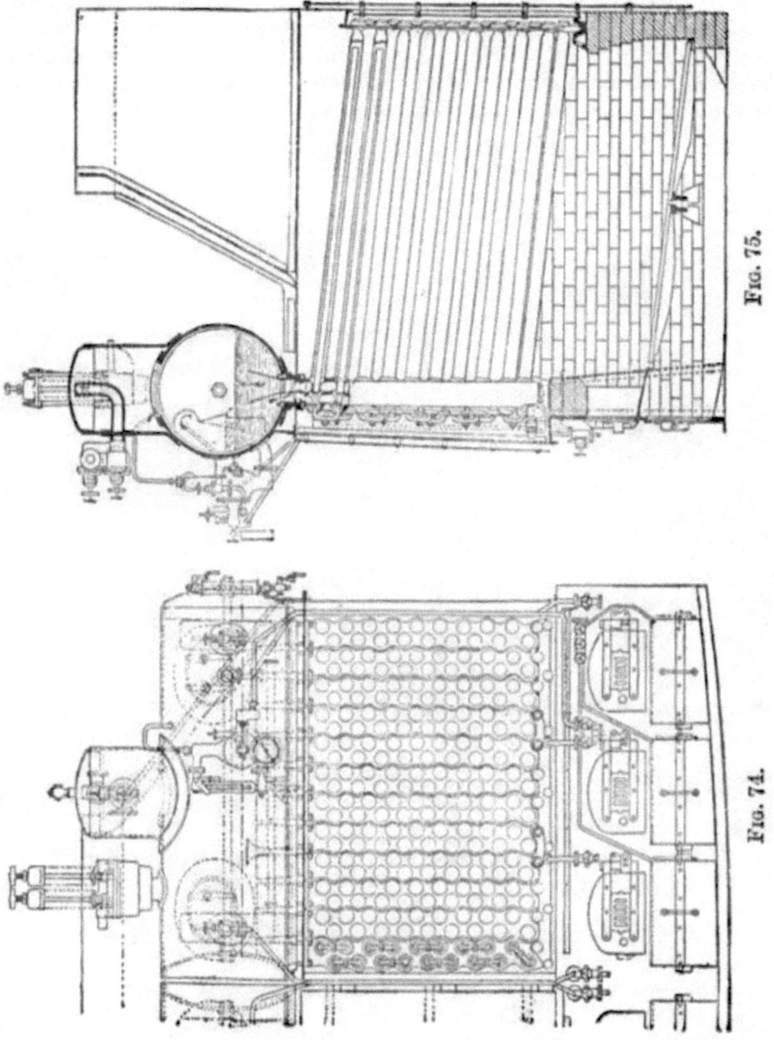

FIG. 75.

FIG. 74.

There are a series of such headers placed side by side, and they all lead into a top collector, fitted with a diaphragm and arrangements for keeping the entering feed-water and descending currents separate from the currents of hot water and steam ascending from the headers. The back ends of the tubes are supported by being allowed to rest in holes formed in a suitable plate or wall.

A remarkable feature in this boiler is the means of attachment of the tubes to the headers, which is by coned surfaces on the tubes, bearing on similar coned surfaces in the headers. Outside dogs keep these coned surfaces in contact, as shown by the two tubes in section, Fig. 75. This joint appears to give no trouble by leakage, or in any other way, and when the water has been run down, a tube can be withdrawn for examination and replaced again in a few minutes. The headers are connected at the bottom by a blow-out pipe, but since each tube slopes downward from the header and at the lower part is separate from all other tubes, the boiler cannot be emptied of water except by removing all the tubes. It is being tried in H.M.S. 'Seagull.'

The ' Mosher ' boiler, fitted in some United States torpedo boats, is similar in principle to the Thornycroft, a section being shown in Fig. 76. It consists of two upper steam drums fitted vertically over two smaller water drums, and connected by a considerable number of small diameter tubes. As in the Thornycroft boiler, the generating tubes enter the steam collector at the upper part only, and return of water from this collector to the water chamber is provided for either by external return tubes, as in diagram, or by the outer rows of tubes entering the steam collector at the bottom. The end tubes are curved downwards and fitted close together, and form a wall where the furnace ends, as shown at A.

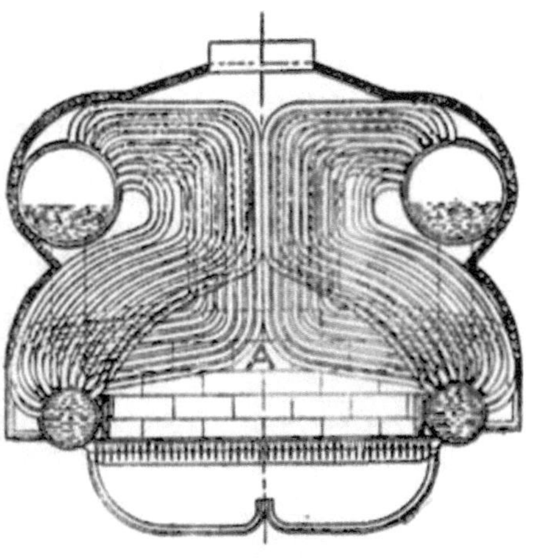

Fig. 76.

The Ward boiler, fitted in the United States 'Monterey,' has a circular casing, and consists of a set of vertical headers arranged in a radial row on one side the centre, receiving the feed-water through orifices at the bottom. A similar series of headers is fitted on the opposite side, but at a slightly higher level. The two series of headers are connected by small, slightly inclined semicircular tubes, and the water circulates from the lower headers through these tubes to the higher headers, the steam leaving at the top of the latter, and the water returning from the bottom to the lower headers. The fire bars are below, and the flame and gases travel upwards among the tubes to the funnel.

Other boilers.—There are many other water-tube boilers, but space will not permit of further descriptions. In this country the Fleming & Ferguson, Weir, White, Mumford, and other boilers are used, and in America the 'Towne.' In Germany the 'Durr' boiler is used, which consists of the same arrangement of tubes as in the Niclausse, except that the connections at the front, instead of being in the form of separate headers, consist of continuous vertical sheets or walls.

CHAPTER IX.

BOILER MOUNTINGS AND BOILER-ROOM FITTINGS.

Smoke-box.—The gases emerging from the boiler tubes are received by a structure of steel plates bolted to the end of the boiler for this purpose, and termed the smoke-box, in the front of which a series of hinged doors are fitted, so that by opening these doors the ends of the tubes are accessible for sweeping or repair. The smoke-box doors are generally on vertical hinges, and are fastened by two or more clips. The front of the smoke-box slopes away from the boiler as it proceeds upwards, so that the area increases with the volume of the products discharged from the tubes.

Funnel and uptake.—The hot gases after leaving the smoke-boxes are conveyed from the different boilers, through passages called the uptakes, as shown in sketches Figs. 77 and 78.

The uptakes are therefore the parts between the funnel and the smoke-boxes, and they are rectangular in section, and should be fitted with plates separating the uptakes of the several smoke-boxes, carried a sufficient height to cause the gases to be moving in approximately the same direction when they mingle together, so as to avoid loss from confusion of currents.

The smoke-boxes, uptakes, and funnel are surrounded by an outer casing, forming an air space which prevents the heat radiated from being excessive. This outer casing A is carried continuously from the lowest part of the uptakes to the top of the funnel, and is fitted with a hood a little distance from the top to prevent the entry of rain inside the casing, as shown at H in Fig. 77.

The funnel is carried between the various decks inside a hatch C fitted for this purpose, called the 'funnel hatch.' An additional air screen B is fitted to the uptakes and lower part of the funnel for carrying off the heated air from the top of the boiler room. This casing is carried a sufficient height above the upper deck to prevent inconvenience to people in the vicinity from the hot air discharged.

The area of the funnel in marine boilers is usually from one-seventh to one-eighth the area of the fire-grate.

Funnel dampers.—Hinged dampers are generally fitted in the uptakes of water-tank boilers to enable each boiler to be shut off when not at work, and also for use when cleaning fires. In the example illustrated there is one combustion chamber to each two furnaces, so that one damper is fitted to the uptake space from each two furnaces. These dampers are generally fitted so that there are no means of closing them permanently, and if released they should move to the open position. These dampers are shown at D D in the uptake section, Fig. 77.

Telescopic funnels.—Many of the old masted ships of the Royal Navy are fitted with telescopic funnels, so that when proceeding under sail alone they can be lowered to clear the spars necessary for working the sails, but this fitting is now practically obsolete.

Funnel stays.—The funnels are stayed by wire ropes carried from the top of the funnel to the ship's sides, usually called the funnel stays or guys. These are fitted with adjusting screws to regulate the strains, and should be slackened before raising steam to allow for the expansion of the funnel as it becomes heated. In modern vessels, funnels of from 90 to 100 feet high from the furnaces are common, and in such cases an additional set of funnel stays are fitted to the outer casing about 15 feet below the top of the funnel as an additional precaution in case of rolling. Gantling blocks are fitted at the top of the funnel with chains to facilitate painting.

Funnel cover.—When the ship is in harbour, or any funnels are not being used, portable covers are fitted on the top of the funnel to prevent rain water coming down and corroding the uptakes, &c. The covers are kept a little above the top, so as to allow sufficient space for the escape of the smoke from the small fires used for airing and warming the boilers, and small derricks are fitted to the top of the funnel and a ladderway inside to facilitate their removal and replacement. In many ships, hinged dampers, worked from the deck, are fitted. A sketch of this is given in Figs. 79 and 80. In this case suitable drain pipes are fitted to carry off the rain water.

Ventilation.—The ventilation of the stokehold, when natural draught only is used, is obtained by a suitable arrangement of screens to separate the downcast from the upcast currents of air, so that the streams of air, attempting to move in different directions, may not destroy each other and render the circulation stagnant. This may be the case if no divisional plates were fitted.

Two points have to be considered : first, the supply of a sufficient quantity of air for the fires ; and secondly, the removal of the hot air and provision of fresh air for respiration, and for the reduction of the temperature of the stokehold, in order that the men may work as comfortably as possible.

In the Royal Navy closed stokeholds and blowing fans have been fitted for many years, wherever ordinary cylindrical boilers have been used, to enable the boilers to be worked with forced draught. By these means the ventilation of the stokehold is much simplified, and an ample supply of fresh air can be obtained under all circumstances. The details of this arrangement are described in Chapter V.

Ash-tube.—In all vessels there is at least one tube fitted for the purpose of raising ashes from the stokehold to the deck to be thrown overboard. These ash-tubes or shoots are often utilised as ventilators. The lowest ends are either carried low down permanently or made telescopic, so that they may be lowered to within four feet from the stokehold plates, to prevent accident. In closed stokeholds the ash-tubes have to be specially fitted to prevent loss of air when raising ashes under forced draught. Two methods of effecting this are shown. In Fig. 81 the ash-buckets are carried up and down in a frame or cage which works practically airtight in the tube. Fig. 82 shows a more simple plan which is equally efficient. An iron plate, P, of sufficient

H
HOOD
HOOD
A B C
ASH TUBE
COFFER DAM
COFFER DAM
Doors in casing all round Hatchway
E ARMOUR BARS
BULKHEAD BETWEEN STOKEHOLDS
D
D
FUNNEL
FLOOR
DOUBLE BOTTOM

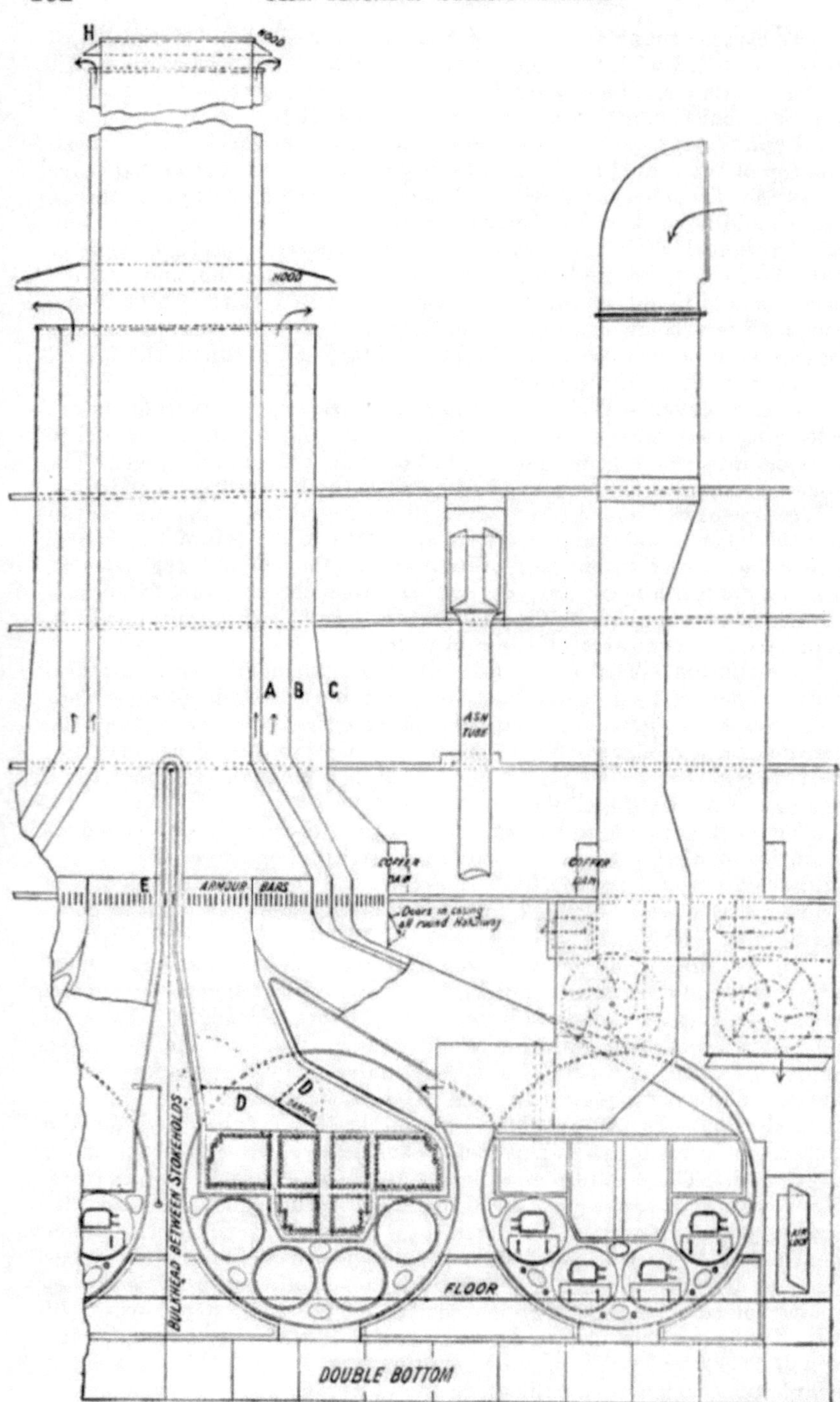

Fig. 77.

COFFER DAM
ARMOUR DECK
E
AMMUNITION PASSAGE
WING SPACE
COAL BUNKER
ASH TUBE
AIR SCREEN
MIDDLE LINE BULKHEAD
Holes in casing for ventilation
FLOOR

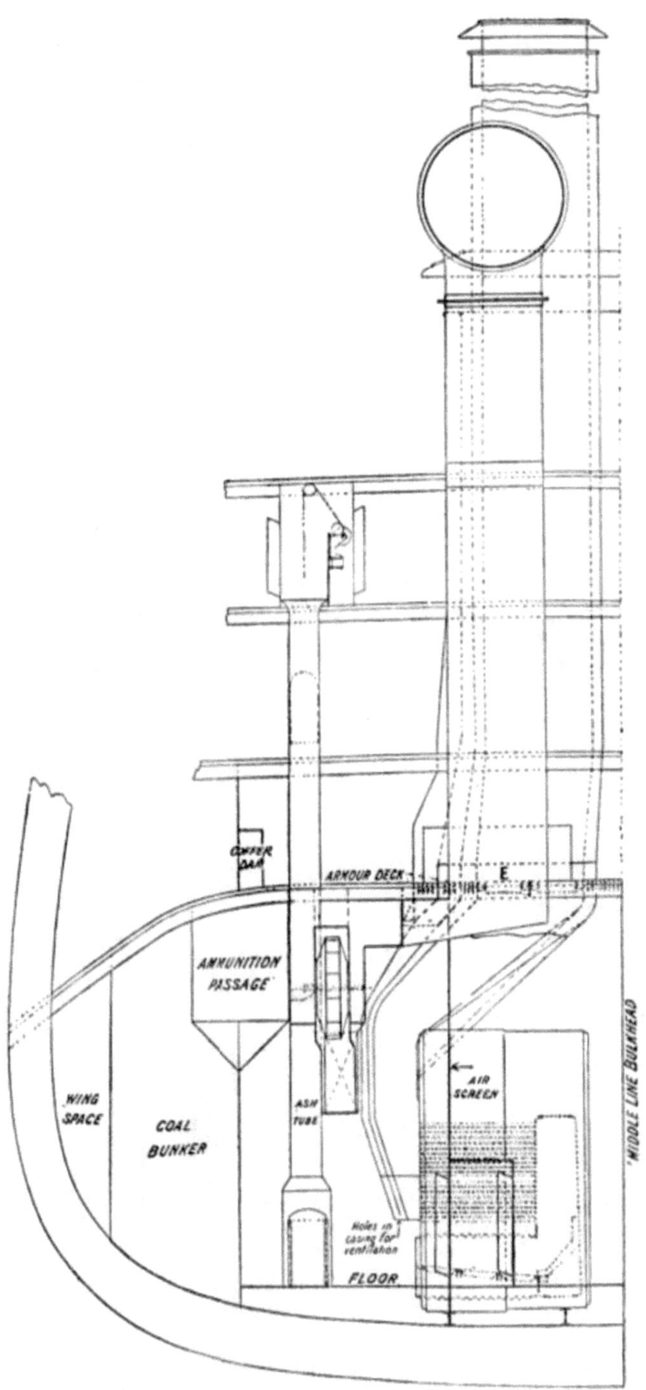

Fig. 78.

weight to resist the air pressure in the stokehold is carried loosely on the bucket chain, and acts as a valve when the bucket is at the bottom of the shoot, enabling the door to be opened and buckets to be taken out and put in as required.

A small steam-engine is provided for raising the ashes, automatic

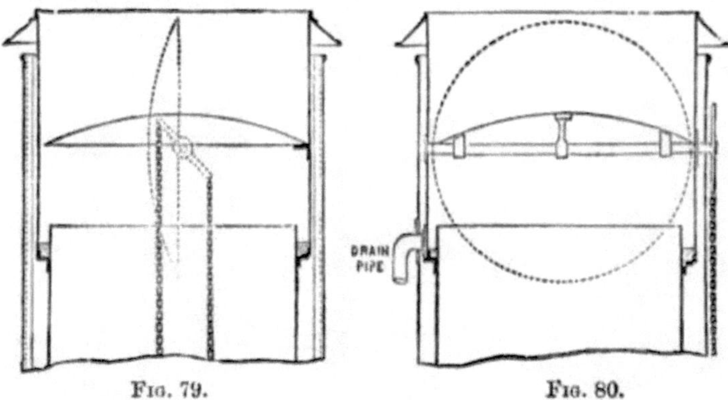

Fig. 79.   Fig. 80.

gear being provided, so that the engine is stopped when the ash-bucket is raised to the proper height. A gong, voice pipe, or other means of signalling from stokehold to deck is also fitted.

Armour gratings.—In all war vessels with protective decks, the machinery hatches, such as funnel hatch, the funnel itself, the air down-takes, engine room hatches, &c., are fitted with deep iron or steel *armour bars* to protect the parts below from danger from shot or shell, and the newer vessels are also provided with *splinter nets* of steel wire spread a short distance below the bars to stop the smaller pieces of *débris*. The armour bars at the base of the funnel are shown at E in Figs. 77 and 78. The plates at the sides of the funnel are carried

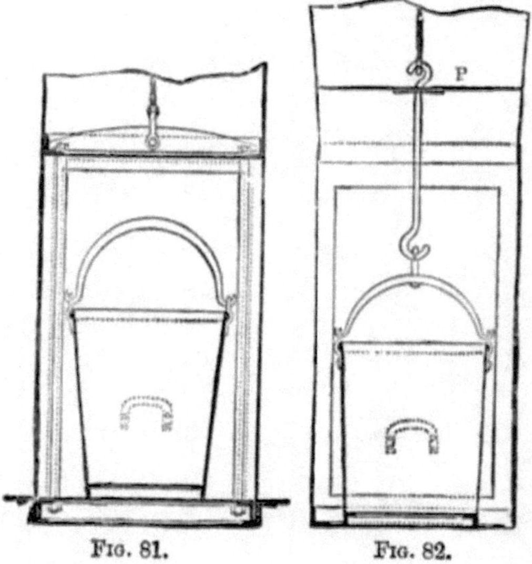

Fig. 81.   Fig. 82.

across and secured to the ship by angle irons, so that the uptakes are relieved of the weight of the funnel and armour gratings, which are supported by the sides of the hatchway.

Arrangement of boiler mountings.—Before describing the boiler mountings in detail, it will be desirable to show their usual position and arrangement. The details of the various mountings will be found described below. Figs. 83 and 84 show the principal mountings on a

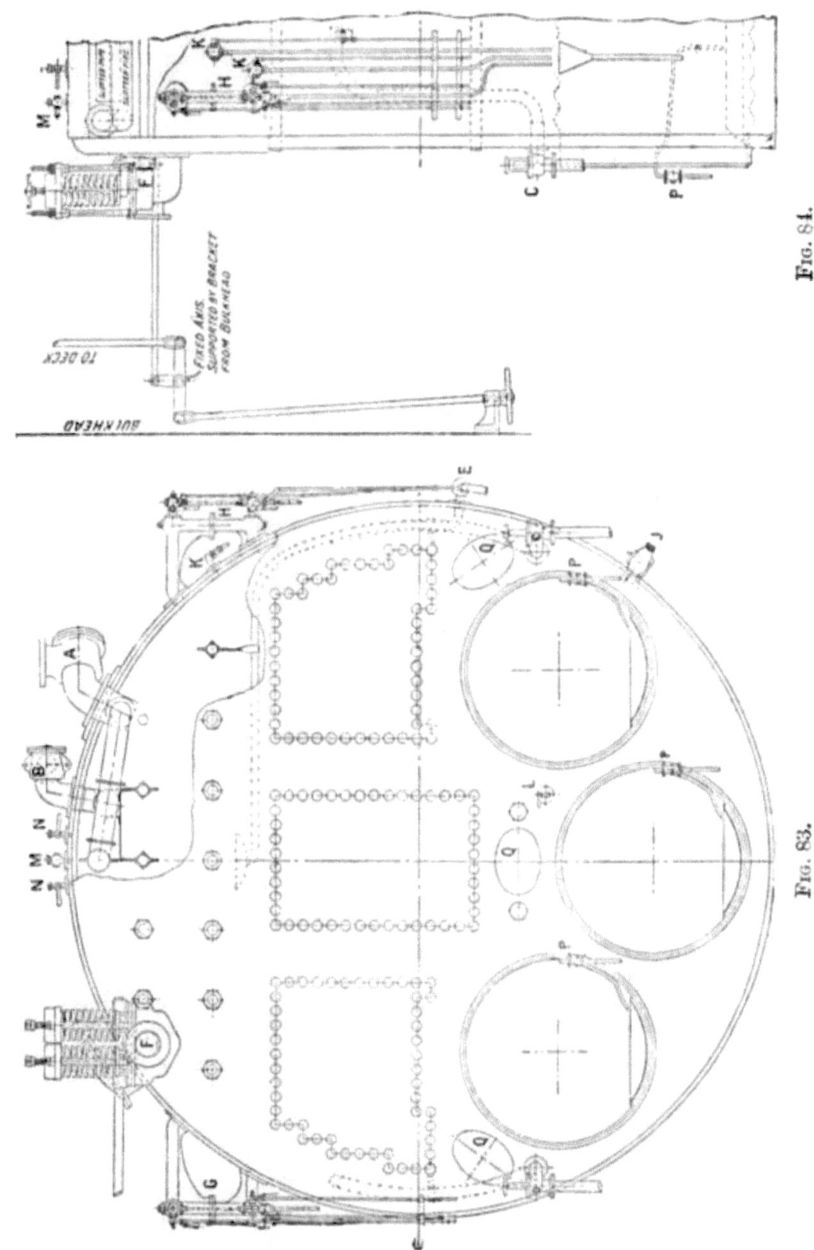

cylindrical marine boiler. A and B are respectively the main and auxiliary steam stop-valves, C and D are the main and auxiliary feed-valves, the main feed being on the right-hand side ; E the surface blow-off, with internal pipe, as shown, leading to a trough near the surface ; F are the safety valves, with rod for raising valves by hand, and behind the safety valves is the top manhole, through which access to the interior of the boiler is obtained, the lower manholes being indicated at Q ; G and H are the two stand-pipes, on which are fitted the glass water-gauges ; J the valve with hose connection for running off water ; K are the test cocks ; L the hydrometer cock ; M is an air cock on top of the boiler shell ; N cocks leading to the boiler pressure gauges ; while P P are the cocks leading water to the ashpans. The side view, Fig. 84, shows the independent lifting gear, enabling the safety valves to be raised either from the deck or the stokehold. This view shows rods for working the gauge and test cocks, which otherwise cannot be reached from the stokehold floor, and the lead of internal feed-pipes. In both views a portion of the top of the boiler is removed to show the internal steam pipes and the method of supporting them.

All valves, cocks, and other boiler mountings are made with spigots passing into the plates to prevent corrosion.

Safety valves.—If all exit from a boiler were closed, and heat continuously applied, the pressure would continue to increase until at length the boiler must of necessity explode. This is prevented by safety valves, which are designed and fitted so that when the pressure in the boiler exceeds the safe working pressure, they open and let the excess steam pass off into the atmosphere, and thus prevent danger.

Sketches of safety valves loaded with springs are shown in Figs. 85 and 86. The safety-valve boxes are fitted to suitable orifices at or near the top, and directly on the boiler, and distinct from the stop-valve box, internal steam pipe, or any other possible obstruction, and the valves are kept on their seats by springs of sufficient force to just resist the maximum working pressure. When the steam pressure exceeds this, it opens the valves and the steam escapes to the atmosphere through an orifice in the box, to which the waste steam pipe leading to the atmosphere is connected. The springs are placed outside the box to prevent corrosion.

Weighted valves were used with the first safety valves fitted. They were loaded by lead weights placed directly on the spindle above the valve. These valves for marine boilers had many disadvantages. The oscillation of the weights due to the rolling of the ship caused the valves and seats to grind away and become leaky. The reduction of the direct load on the valve by the heeling of the ship also caused waste of steam, and there were other disadvantages. They had, however, the advantage that when they began to open they did not require any increase of pressure to open them still further, as is the case with spring-loaded valves.

The more a spring is compressed the greater is the pressure required to compress it still further ; and, within the limit of elasticity of the spring, the pressure required to compress it a certain distance increases directly as the amount of compression. By employing springs of ample length and diameter so as to obtain sufficient flexibility no difficulty is experienced from this cause, so that spring-loaded safety valves are in general use for marine purposes.

The safety valves should always be fitted in a vertical position or nearly so, wherever this can be arranged. It is undesirable to place them horizontally. The guide feathers or spindle on the valve are always made with a certain amount of clearance to prevent their sticking, and horizontal valves tend to drop from the central position, so as not to find their true seating, and so allow steam to leak past them.

The breadth of the face need not be more than from one-twelfth to one-eighth of an inch. With conical valves the seatings should be narrow, and fitted so as to be quite tight at the bottom of the cone ; otherwise the actual area on which the steam pressure acts will be greater than the nominal area of the valve, so that steam will be

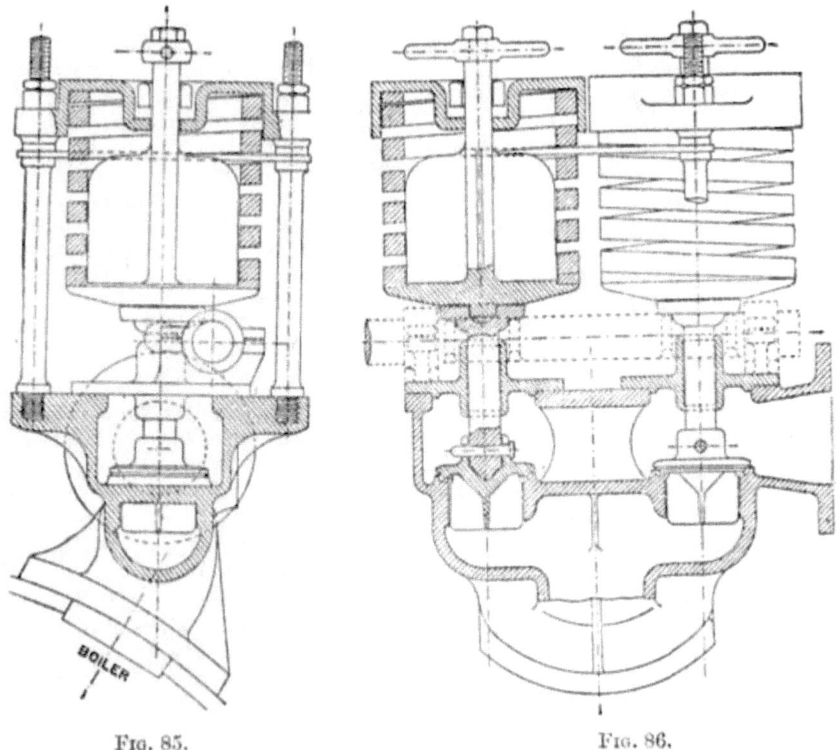

FIG. 85.   FIG. 86.

wasted, as the valves will lift before the steam attains the proper working pressure.

Area of safety valves.—It has been proved by experiment that when the absolute pressure of the medium into which the steam enters on passing the orifice is not more than one-half the initial absolute pressure of the steam, the velocity of issue, and therefore the weight of steam discharged per minute, is constant, so that the moderate pressure in the waste steam pipe when blowing off may be neglected in calculating the area of valves.

The requisite safety-valve area for each boiler should be divided between two or more valves, and not concentrated in one. The area for discharge of the steam depends on its periphery and lift, so that when two or more valves are used, the lift required to liberate the steam is reduced because the periphery is increased. The division of the safety-valve area has also the advantage of reducing the danger from the valves sticking, as the probabilities are against all the valves becoming inoperative at the same time ; and if one become set fast, the others would still act to free the boiler of undue pressure, when necessary.

The total area allowed for safety valves for the higher pressures may be reduced, because the rate of efflux of steam increases with the pressure, so that the safety-valve area should depend on the pressure of steam.

The area of the safety valves is often calculated from the grate surface only, but it should really be based on the *quantity of steam* the boiler is capable of producing when worked at full power, and not on the grate area, because the rate of combustion varies considerably under different circumstances. This is rendered especially necessary by the introduction of accelerated draught, which has largely increased the generative powers of boilers. The steam-producing power of the boilers may be represented approximately by the maximum I.H.P. developed, and we have seen that the rate of efflux of the steam will vary as the absolute pressure. If P represents the *absolute* working pressure of steam, the total area of safety valves required may be calculated from the formula

$$\text{area} = 3\frac{\text{I.H.P.}}{\text{P.}}$$

This formula is obtained by taking the rate of flow of the steam through the orifice, in pounds per minute, to be three-fourths the absolute pressure in pounds, and assuming the valve to lift one twenty-fourth of its diameter when blowing off the steam necessary to give the designed horse-power.

Accumulation of pressure.—The face of a safety valve should be so arranged in relation to the lip or body of the valve, that by the reaction of the escaping steam the pressure may be kept up when the valve lifts. The amount of accumulation of pressure when blowing off depends very much on small features of design in the safety valves, and by utilising the reaction of the escaping steam on projecting lips or by contracted orifices just beyond the valve seat, the accumulation may be reduced to very small dimensions, as the area on which the pressure acts is increased when the valves commence to blow. The object is to make the safety valve lift a considerable amount when it commences to blow, and to ensure its closing when the pressure has fallen about 4 or 5 lbs. below the safety-valve load. The sketches, Figs. 87 to 89, show three forms of safety valve with the arrangement for adding to the lift when it commences to open.

Safety valves of water-tank boilers are required by the Board of Trade to be tested with the boiler under full steam and full firing for about twenty minutes, with feed- and stop-valves shut off, and in this case the accumulation of pressure should not in any case exceed 10 per cent. of the loaded pressure. In the most recent Admiralty vessels this excess is limited to 7 per cent. with the stop-valve shut, but feeding the boiler with water in the usual manner.

Safety-valve springs.—In the Admiralty service all safety-valve springs have to undergo tests as to their strength and elasticity. The compression with the working load is first noted, and the spring is then further compressed through a distance equal to one-quarter the diameter of the valve, and if on the removal of the load the spring does not regain its original length it is rejected. The Admiralty practice is to make the amount of compression to give the working load equal to the diameter of the valve.

Lift of safety valves. Lifting gear.—Gear is always fitted so that the safety valves may be lifted by hand, and the amount of hand-lifting allowed is one-fourth the diameter of the valve. When this lift is attained stops come into operation to prevent further lifting. It must not be thought, however, when at work and blowing off even large volumes of steam from the boilers that the valves lift to this extent.

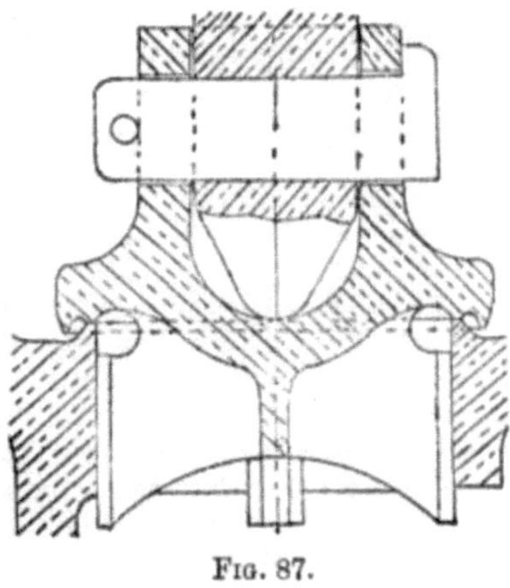

Fig. 87.

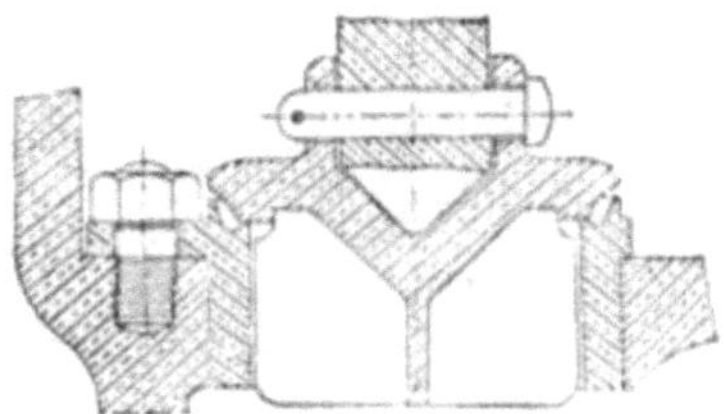

Fig. 88.

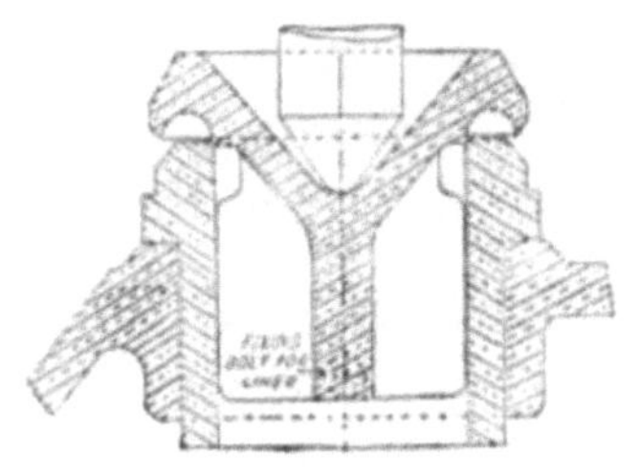

Fig. 89.

The actual lift when blowing off the full quantity of steam does not exceed about one twenty-fourth the diameter of the valve, or with the usual dimensions about one-eighth of an inch, so that the actual increase of load due to the extra compression of the springs should be small.

A washer or ferrule should be placed under the compressing screw, so that the spring cannot be compressed more than sufficient to give the maximum working load on the boilers, also a nut on the valve spindle, which prevents the extension of the springs beyond a small amount when being removed for examination, and so facilitates this operation.

The gear used for lifting the safety valves is shown in Fig. 84. It usually consists of levers acting either under the valves themselves or under collars on the valve spindles, these levers being worked by screw gear from the boiler room, and in the Royal Navy generally from the deck as well. The two sets of gear work independently of each other, and are so fitted that the valves may be lifted from either position without moving the gear at the other position. It is also arranged that neither lifting gear impedes the automatic action of the valve in any way when acted on by the steam pressure in the boiler, as shown in the figure. All the joints in the safety valve easing gear should either be fitted with gun-metal bushes, or the joint pins should be of gun-metal, to prevent the gear rusting and setting fast. When separate seatings fitted into the valve chest are used, they should be so arranged that they cannot lift with the valve, as in this case there would be no outlet for steam. To keep the seatings from working loose, they are carefully secured by bolts or pins, as shown in Figs. 88 and 89.

Pressure gauges.—The steam pressure in the boiler—or, more strictly speaking, the excess of the pressure in the boiler above that of the atmosphere—is usually indicated by Bourdon's pressure gauges.

Fig. 90 shows their general construction and arrangement. A is attached to a cock on a small pipe connected to the boiler with a cock N (Fig. 83) at the junction. B B is a curved metallic tube, of elliptical section, as shown to enlarged scale at c, Fig. 91, which is closed at one end and open to the steam pressure through A at the other. The greatest breadth of the section of the tube is perpendicular to the plane in which the tube is curved. The closed end of the tube is connected by a sector D to a small pinion on the axis of the index finger E F, which points to a graduated arc. When the pressure inside the tube is greater than the external pressure, the tube straightens itself, and this causes the sector to act on the pointer and indicate the pressure.

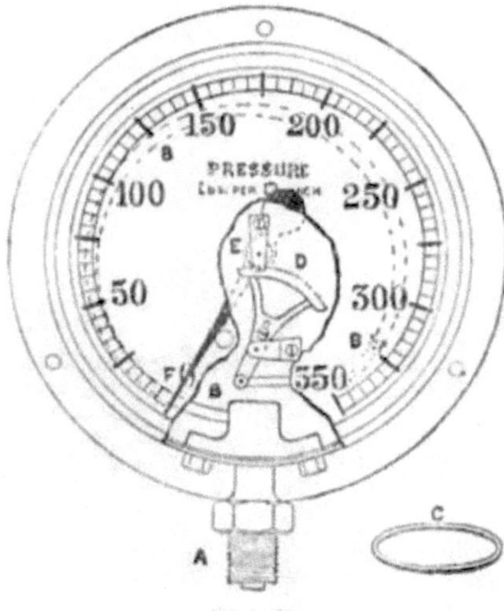

Fig. 90.   Fig. 91.

The graduation of these gauges is obtained by comparison with a mercurial gauge, into which mercury can be pumped to sufficient heights to obtain the necessary indications on the Bourdon gauge.

In the Royal Navy each boiler is always fitted with two pressure gauges, in order to provide for the case of one gauge getting out of order, and to be a check on each other. With double-ended boilers two pressure gauges are fitted at the working end of the boiler—i.e. at the end on which the feed-valves are placed and where the person in charge would generally be—and a third pressure gauge is fitted at the other end. One gauge on each boiler is graduated to rather more than the hydraulic test pressure, to enable it to be used when testing the boiler at regular stated intervals.

Water gauges.—The level of the water in the boiler is indicated by a glass tube fitted between two asbestos packed cocks, one in connection with the steam space and the other with the water space of the boiler, while a drain cock and pipe are supplied for the bottom of the glass to enable it to be blown through and cleared. The general arrangement is shown in Fig. 92. In most cases in the mercantile marine these gauge cocks are fitted on a brass pipe, known as a steady or stand pipe, the top of which is connected to the steam chest, the bottom being connected by an outside pipe to the lower part of the boiler, where there is but little disturbance of the water. Cocks are fitted at the top and bottom, where these pipes join the boiler shell (see Figs. 94 and 95).

Sometimes, however, the gauge cocks are bolted direct to the fronts of the boilers themselves, which is the usual plan in the Navy in the case of low boilers, in which the front of the boiler is clear of the uptakes, and room can be found. The only difficulties met with in this position arise from the tendency of any grease or light impurities floating at the water line, to enter the glass and dirty it, and when such boilers are forced much, unsteady indications are sometimes obtained, due to violent ebullition near the gauge orifice. With large return tube boilers, where the uptakes cover most of the front of the boilers, so that the glasses have to be fitted on the circular shell, the usual practice in the Royal Navy is to fit the gauge glass cocks on a brass casting, forming a short steady pipe, having a hole of comparatively large diameter (two inches), so that there is little or no danger of its becoming choked. This forms a convenient method of attachment to the shell, and the intervention of the stand pipe causes the indications to be comparatively free from disturbance due to rapid ebullition at the water surface. A sketch of this attachment is given in Fig. 93. On this system no cocks are required in the steady pipe, which is an advantage, as these may, by being inadvertently closed, be a source of danger. If the lower cock is bolted directly to the boiler shell and an internal pipe led down into the water space, a branch from this should be carried up open ended into the steam space as well as down into the lower part of the boiler, otherwise the indications will be unreliable ; but in general it is better to dispense with internal pipes.

A small screw plug is fitted to each of the two cocks, opposite the hole making connection with the boiler or stand pipe, to enable a wire to be passed in to clear them when necessary. Two sets of water gauges are fitted to each boiler in ships of the Royal Navy ; while in double-ended boilers, three are fitted, two at the working end and one at the other end.

The general practice in water-tank boilers is to fix the hole in the lower gauge cock at a small distance above the level of the highest part of the heating surface, so that when the water is just disappearing from the glass its level is from three to four inches above the highest part of the heating surface. The total length of the gauge glasses used in H.M. service for large boilers is 14, 16, or 18 inches, external diameter $\frac{3}{4}$ inch, and thickness $\frac{1}{8}$ inch. Allowing for the part of the length of the glass tube in the glands of the cocks, the depth of the water over the highest part of the heating surface when the glass is half full will be found to be 10 to 11 inches. For small boilers, as for pinnaces, cutters, &c., the gauge glasses are only $\frac{7}{16}$ to $\frac{1}{2}$ inch in diameter and $\frac{3}{32}$ inch thick, and shorter than the preceding lengths. The water side of the gauge mounting contains a small ball which, if the glass breaks, is forced up by the escaping water and stops the orifice, thus greatly reducing the amount of water escaping. In the

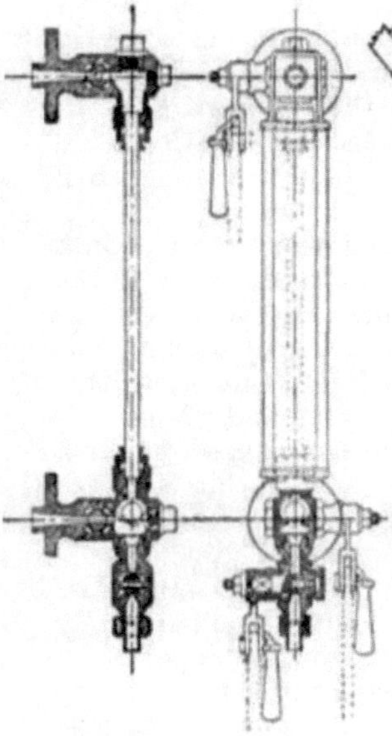

Fig. 92.

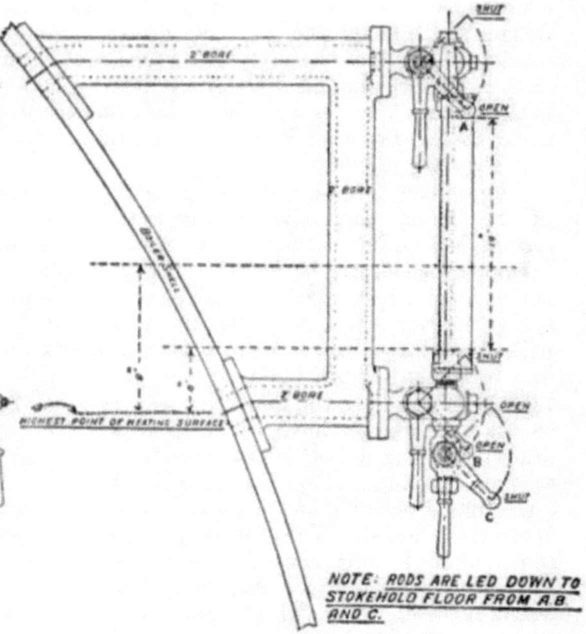

NOTE: RODS ARE LED DOWN TO
STOKEHOLD FLOOR FROM A.B
AND C.

Fig. 93.

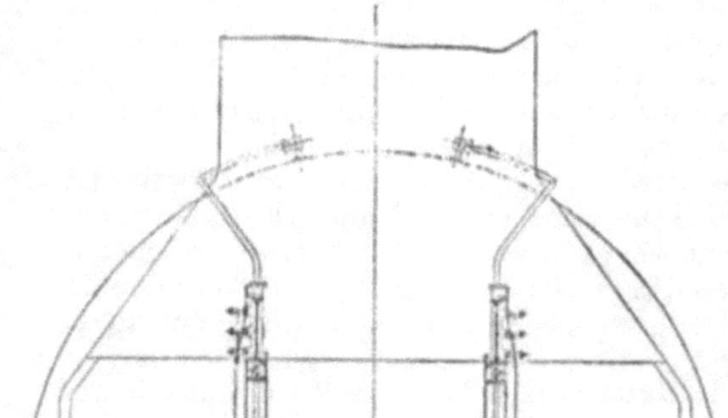

Fig. 94.

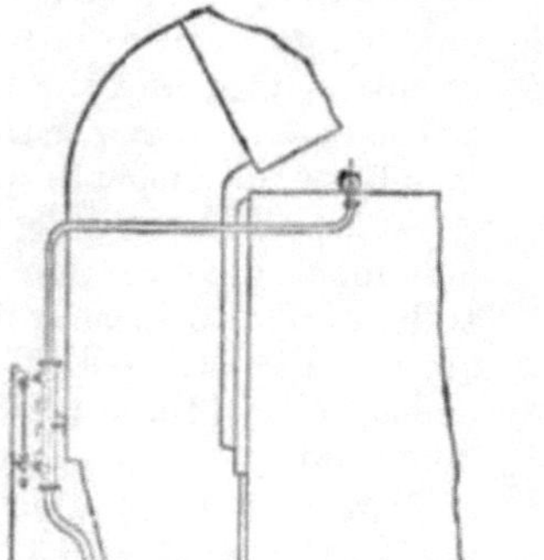

Fig. 95.

mercantile marine the glasses are larger in diameter, usually $\frac{3}{4}$ inch. Klinger's water gauges are described at the end of this chapter.

Effect of list on the boilers.—When the vessel has a list the relation between the level of the water in the glass gauge and the amount of water above the highest part of the heating surface undergoes an important and considerable change, and one that should be carefully ascertained in every steam vessel. The effect is to bring part of any heating surface much nearer the water line, and if the list is of the considerable amount, in a large boiler the heating surface will be left bare of water even when the gauge glass may be full. Fig. 96 shows a boiler placed with tubes fore and aft in the ship, and the lines drawn indicate that with a list of 7° even when one of the glasses is full, the wing combustion chamber is uncovered. Evidently in this case the other glass only should be worked with.

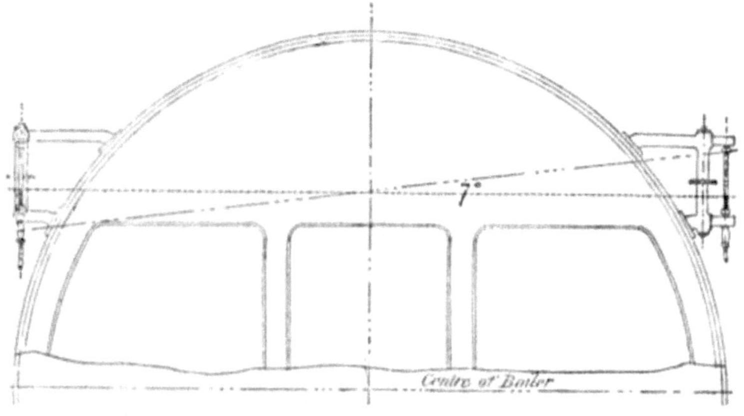

Fig. 96.

Fig. 97 shows a boiler with tubes placed athwartship. In this case the combustion chamber becomes uncovered with a list of $9\frac{1}{2}$°, even when the gauge glasses are full of water, although the combustion chamber is sloped away to reduce this angle. In this case, as both gauge glasses are affected alike, the boiler becomes practically unworkable. These sketches show actual examples in naval vessels.

Great importance is therefore attached to a proper understanding of the procedure necessary for working the boilers in the event of a permanent list, especially in naval vessels, where it may occur owing to a compartment on one side being flooded during an action. The best course to pursue should be considered by the engineers of each vessel.

Many water-tube boilers also are affected by a list in the vessel, the Belleville and Niclausse for example. In the former, when the tubes are placed athwartship, as the inclination of the tubes to the horizontal is only $2\frac{1}{2}$°, a list interferes with the circulation of water and a wedge is supplied for use under these circumstances, so as to keep the automatic feed-valve always open a minimum amount to insure a sufficiency of water. When the tubes are placed fore and aft, as in the great majority of British warships, this is unnecessary. In the Niclausse boiler also, a list in one direction interferes with the flow of water down the internal supply tube of the boiler when placed athwartships.

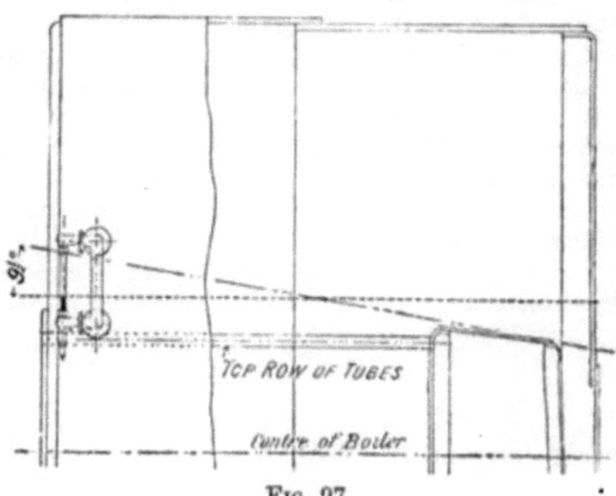

Fig. 97.

Test cocks.—On the front or shell of the boiler, small cocks, called test cocks, generally two in number, are usually fitted, and shown at κ in Figs. 83 and 84. The orifice of the lower of these cocks is about two inches above the highest part of the heating surface, and that of the upper cock twelve inches above the highest part of the heating surface. The use of these cocks is to enable the level of the water to be ascertained approximately in case of accident to or derangement of the glass gauges. When working by these cocks it is clear that if, on

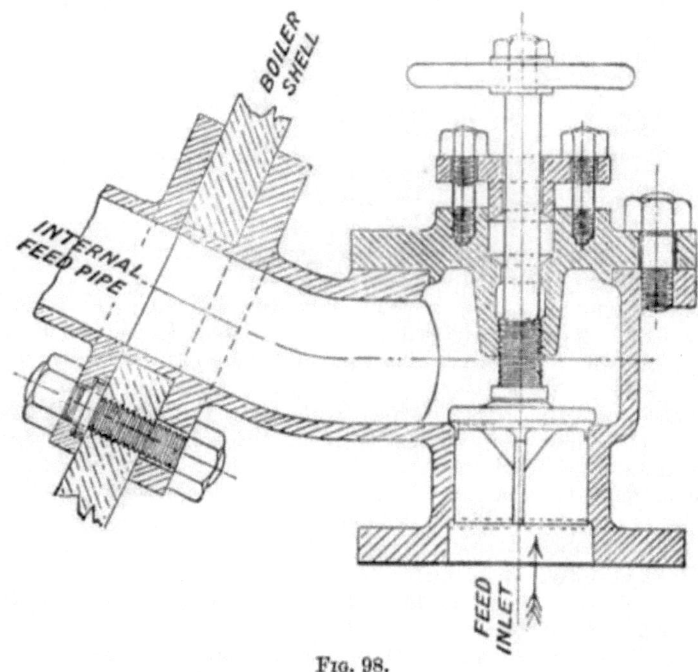

Fig. 98.

opening the upper cock, steam only issues, the water is not too high in the boiler ; and as long as water can be drawn from the lower cock the water-level is not dangerously low.   These test cocks should evidently be fitted without internal pipes.

Feed-valves.—These are the valves through which the feed-water is admitted to the boilers.   They are screw-down non-return valves,

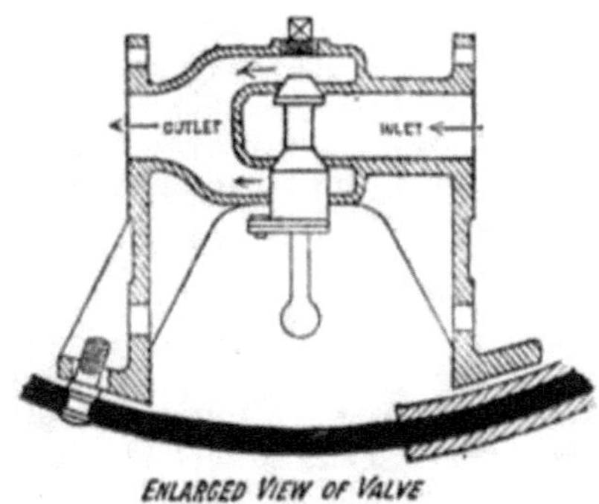

Fig. 99.

which may be kept closed, or their lift regulated, as shown in Fig. 98. There is no connection between the valve and the screwed spindle, the latter simply limiting the lift of the valve or pressing against it when closed.   These valves are made non-return, so that in case of the feed-pumps ceasing action from accident or other cause, the water in the boiler may not be forced back through the pipes by the steam pressure.   An additional valve is fitted in the delivery pipe of each feed-pump for completely shutting off the pump from the feed-pipes and so enabling any examinations and adjustments to be made.

Two feed-valves are generally fitted to each boiler, one, called the main feed-valve, being in connection with the main feed-pumps, and the other, called the auxiliary feed-valve, connected with the auxiliary or donkey feed-pumps.   In the Royal Navy the main feed-valve is placed on the right-hand side of the boiler, while the auxiliary feed-valve is placed on the left.

Automatic feed apparatus.—The feed-regulating apparatus for

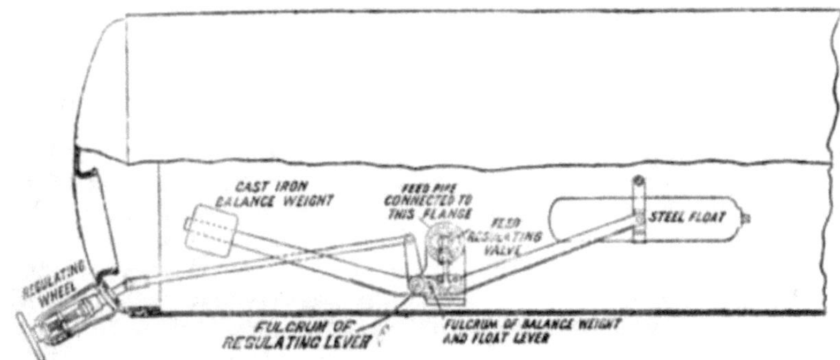

Fig. 100.

Belleville boilers is described in Chapter VIII.   Similar apparatus is now generally fitted to all water-tube boilers, and its use has been extended in several cases to water-tank boilers.   Two forms of such apparatus are illustrated.   Figs. 99 and 100 show the apparatus fitted by Messrs. Thornycroft, while Fig. 101 shows that by Messrs. Laird.

They are very similar in principle, consisting of a hollow float, rising or falling with the water level and actuating a balanced feed-valve, so that when the proper water level is reached, the valve is closed, and water ceases to enter and vice versa.   A detail of Thornycroft's feed-valve is shown in Fig. 99.   It is a double beat valve, while that of Messrs. Laird is a circular piston valve.   In Fig. 100 the external wheel raises or lowers the fulcrum on which the float lever turns, thus enabling the water level to be adjusted.   The external handle in Fig. 101 enables the valve to be moved to and fro in case it sticks.

Surface and bottom blow-out valves.—Blow-out valves are fitted to enable the grease, scum, and other impurities on the water surface, or any dirty water, to be discharged overboard.   The usual practice for many years was to fit two screw-down valves as blow-out valves, one, the *surface blow-out or scum valve*, dealing with the water near the water line, and the other, the *bottom blow-out*, dealing with the water at the bottom of the boiler.   From the surface blow-out valve, which is always fitted at a convenient height for access, a pipe is carried inside to the central part of the boiler, where it terminates in an open pan placed a little below the water level.   When the valve is opened the grease and impurities are discharged through the surface blow-out valve into a pipe led to a sea valve at the bottom of the vessel and thence overboard.   The bottom blow-out valve was, in the days of low-pressure steam, the means of filling the boilers with sea-water, and of

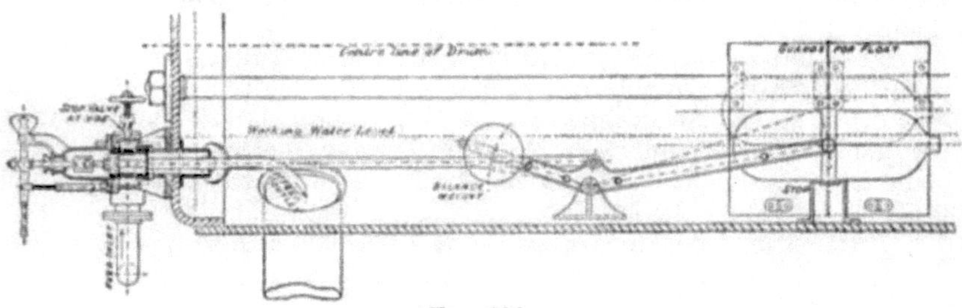

Fig. 101.

brining the boilers when they were fed with salt water, or, in later examples, when salt water was used to make up losses of feed-water. It is an ordinary screw-down valve fitted near the bottom of the boiler with short internal pipe leading to the lowest part.   It was at this part that the densest water accumulated, and the heavy deposits from sea-water were found.   These were blown away into the sea by means of the bottom blow-out valve.   The pipes from surface and bottom blow-out valves led into a common pipe carried to a sea valve, there being one such pipe to each boiler, led independently to a guard cock attached to the sea valve.   To avoid accident from leaving the blow-out open, a guard is fitted on this cock (Fig. 102), to prevent the spanner from being removed without first closing it ; so that when the spanner is off, it is certain that the cock must be shut.

With the more extended use of fresh water for boilers the bottom blow-out cock has become of minor importance, and as with the higher pressures of steam they are liable to leak and waste fresh water they have not been fitted to naval boilers for some years past.   It should be noted that the Belleville water-tube boilers form an exception to this, as with these boilers a bottom blow-out valve is fitted to the sediment collector of each boiler.   In modern boilers in the Royal Navy, in lieu of the old blow-out valve, a valve is fitted with a nozzle and hose connection, so that when there is no pressure in the boiler a hose can be connected and water run into the reserve fresh-water tanks, as, for example, when the boilers have been kept full of fresh water, and it is desired to reduce it to working height to enable steam to be raised.

Asbestos packed cocks.—For various purposes cocks are more convenient than valves, the boiler gauge cocks for example, and when such cocks are subject to high pressures, and have at the same time to be not too tight to be readily workable, they generally give trouble by leakage. A device for overcoming this, known as an asbestos-packed cock, is shown in Fig. 102, in which it will be seen that not only are the top

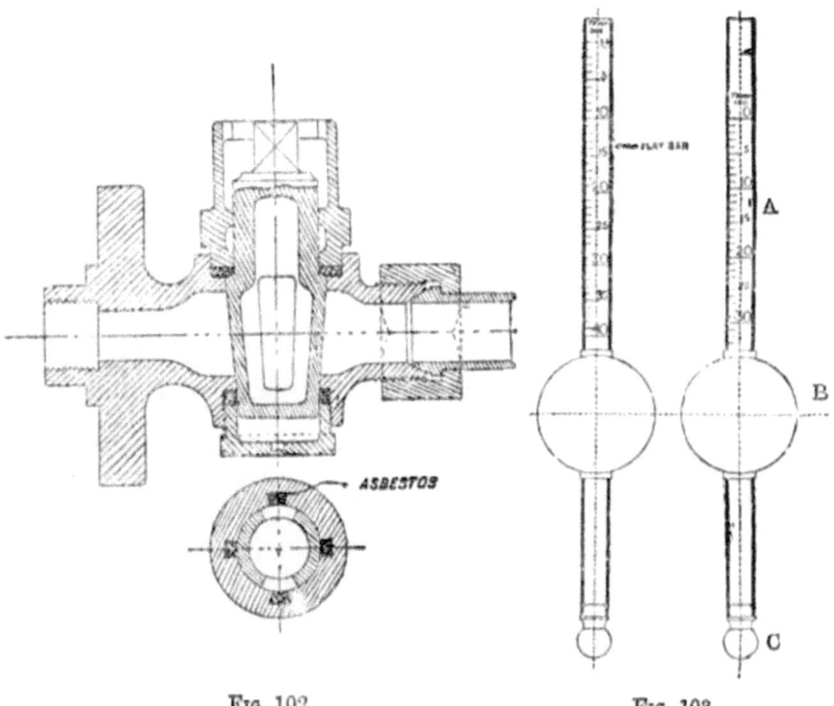

Fig. 102.   Fig. 103.

and bottom glands packed with asbestos, but longitudinal grooves are formed in the shell, as shown, also packed with asbestos, on which the faces of the plug work. The example shown is a blow-out cock for boilers, the guard which prevents the handle being removed except when the valve is shut, being shown in the figure.

Hydrometer. Hydrometer cock.—The density of the water in the boiler, evaporator, or other part is given by the hydrometer, an instrument of the form shown in Fig. 103, made either of glass or metal. It has a slender stem A, and two bulbs ; the larger one, B, containing only air, gives buoyancy, and the smaller one, C, loaded, keeps the instrument vertical in a liquid.

When any body floats freely, the weight of the liquid displaced is equal to the weight of the body, so that the higher the density of the liquid the less depth will the body sink in it.

Sea water contains $\frac{1}{32}$ part of solid matter, so that hydrometers are often graduated to show densities of 0, $\frac{1}{32}$, $\frac{2}{32}$, and so on—a density of $\frac{2}{32}$ representing the presence of solid matter equal to twice that contained in sea-water. The usual naval hydrometer is graduated in degrees, each degree representing the presence of one-tenth the solid matter in sea-water. Ten degrees, therefore, represent the density of sea-water, or $\frac{1}{32}$ part of solid matter; zero will represent fresh water; and 40 degrees represents a density caused by the presence of four times the solid matter in sea-water.

As the density of water depends on its temperature, a thermometer is really required as well as a hydrometer in order to determine the density with great exactness; but in practice, boiler hydrometers are graduated to suit a temperature of 200° Fahr., which is about the temperature of the water a few seconds after being drawn off for testing. This plan has been found to be sufficiently accurate for the purpose, and is now generally adopted, as it avoids the complication involved in the use of two instruments. The water is drawn off from the *hydrometer cock* (L, Fig. 83), fitted for this purpose, into a long pot called the hydrometer pot, into which the hydrometer is inserted.

The brass naval hydrometer has an additional graduation suitable for a temperature of 100° Fahr. placed on the reverse side of the stem, which can be used for taking the density of the feed-water, &c. Care should be taken that the temperature in this case does not differ much from 100°. The two graduations are shown in the figure, and by comparing them it will be seen how important the effect of temperature is, the two scales differing by about 10°.

Ordinary boiler stop or communication-valves.—These valves are for the purpose of regulating the passage of steam from the boilers to the engines, and to enable any boilers not in use to be shut off from the steam pipes. One of these valves is fitted to each boiler, and connected to the main steam pipe. Its general form and construction are shown in Fig. 104. It is fixed so that the pressure of the steam in the boiler may be inside the valve, which is worked by means of a screw, the spindle passing to the outside of the valve-box through a steam-tight stuffing box and gland as shown. A stop is fitted to prevent the valve turning round when being screwed up.

Self-closing stop-valves.—In warships, in order to lessen the damage resulting from accident to a boiler, as, for example, its being pierced by a shot, the boiler stop-valves are made self-closing. This form of valve is shown in Fig. 105. The valve is simply a non-return valve, the action of the screw outside being only to either keep the valve closed on its seat, or to regulate the amount of opening. In the event of the pressure in any boiler falling from rupture or any other cause, the pressure in the steam pipes would close the valve and isolate the boiler, thus not only minimising the damage, but also the loss of boiler power.

With the ordinary stop-valve, if a hole were made in any boiler, the whole of the boilers in connection would be rendered useless, until the stop-valve of the injured boiler could be closed by hand, which, in all probability, would not be until the steam from all the boilers had discharged itself through the damaged one, increasing the extent of the disaster, and rendering the ship for the time helpless. Self-acting valves might therefore be of great value in a warship in action.

Valves of this description should always be placed in a horizontal

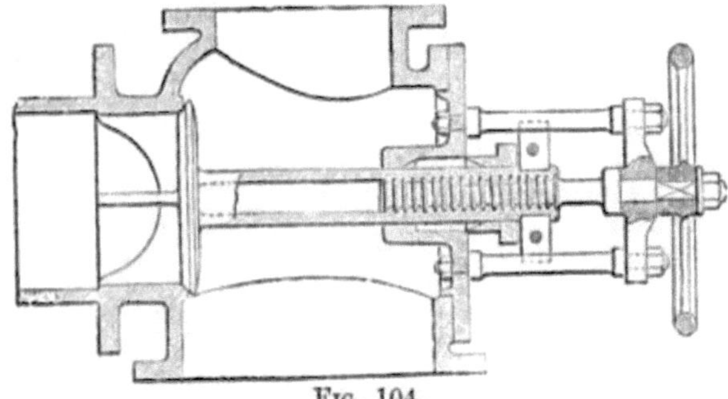

Fig. 104.

position, as when placed vertically, the pulsations of the steam cause them to work up and down on their seatings with violence, and in some cases the valves have been broken from this action.

The continuation of the valve spindle is provided with a cross handle so that the valve can be turned on its seat, and this handle also

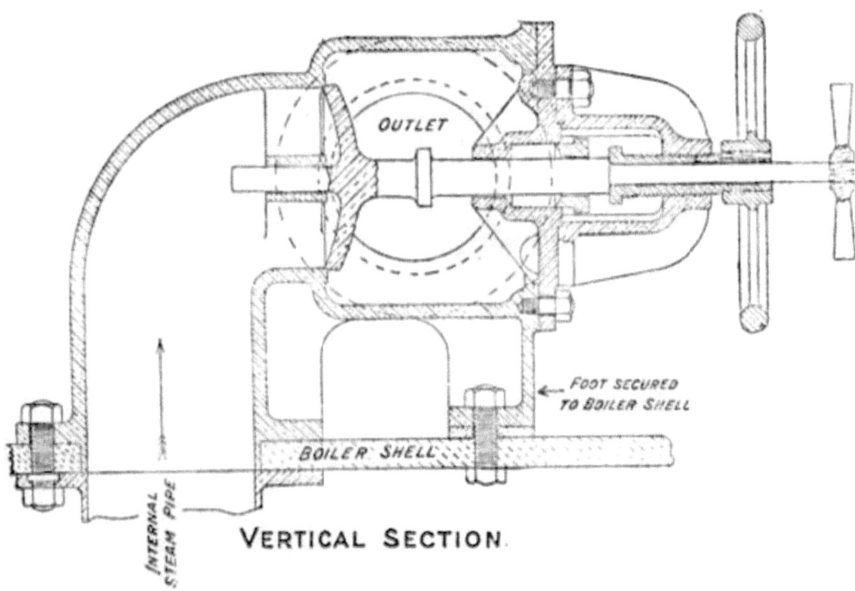

Fig. 105.

enables the valve to be pulled open after the screw has been worked back when opening the valve. This should always be done, as otherwise the friction of the glands will keep the valve closed till the excess pressure inside is sufficient to overcome this friction, when the valve would often open with violence.

Internal steam pipes.—The stop-valves have attached to them thin brass pipes, which are carried inside across the steam chest close to the top of the boiler, and are called the internal steam pipes. They are closed at the end, but have narrow slits cut at the top, which allow the steam to enter the pipe and pass through the stop-valve to the engines. The object of this fitting is to prevent priming as far as possible, or the passage of water through the stop-valves with the steam. By spreading the area of collection of steam, the evaporation is rendered more uniform, and the tendency to priming from the rush of the steam to a single orifice is obviated. A drain hole is fitted in the pipe to prevent accumulation of water.

From the stop-valves on the different boilers steam pipes are carried, which unite at the end of the stokehold in one main steam pipe, through which the steam passes to the engines.

Bulkhead self-closing stop-valves.—In ships of the Royal Navy that have more than one boiler room, the steam pipe from each boiler room is carried independently to the engine-room bulkhead, and at the end of each pipe another self-closing valve is fitted, called the 'bulkhead self-closing valve,' so that in the event of any steam pipe being damaged on the boiler side of this valve, only the boilers in connection with that steam pipe would be put out of action, the others remaining efficient. These bulkhead valves perform for each stokehold the same functions that the boiler self-closing valves perform for each boiler, and are constructed similarly to Fig. 105.

Arrangement of main steam pipes.—The general arrangement of the main steam pipes of vessels in the Royal Navy having several boiler rooms and two engine rooms is shown in Figs. 106 to 108. In each boiler room the steam from each boiler leads through the boiler self-closing valves A into a common pipe which is led to the engine-room bulkhead, where the bulkhead self-closing valve B is fitted. An entirely separate pipe from each boiler room is led to the engine-room bulkhead. On the engine-room side of these bulkhead valves, the steam pipes lead into one common athwartship pipe, of reduced size, communicating with each set of engines. On each branch from this athwartship steam pipe to the main engines an ordinary screw-down stop-valve C is fitted in large vessels, which may be opened or closed by hand from the engine room and also at some position entirely outside the engine room, on one of the ship's decks, by the gear shown in Fig. 107.

This valve is intended for use in case of any accident in the engine rooms causing an escape of steam. Under these circumstances if the discharge of steam is so great as to force the engine-room staff to leave the engine room, they can proceed to the deck position and shut off the steam from the engines.

In the more recent naval engines another stop-valve D is fitted in the athwartship steam pipe at the middle line, worked from either side of the bulkhead, so that in case of any injury to the athwartship pipe the steam can be confined to one side of the ship if necessary, and thus enable one set of engines to be worked.

At the end of the branch steam pipes on each side is the regulating valve E, for the main engines, described in Chapter XV., and fitted close to the high-pressure valve casing.

The additional screw-down valve C is fitted to close with the steam

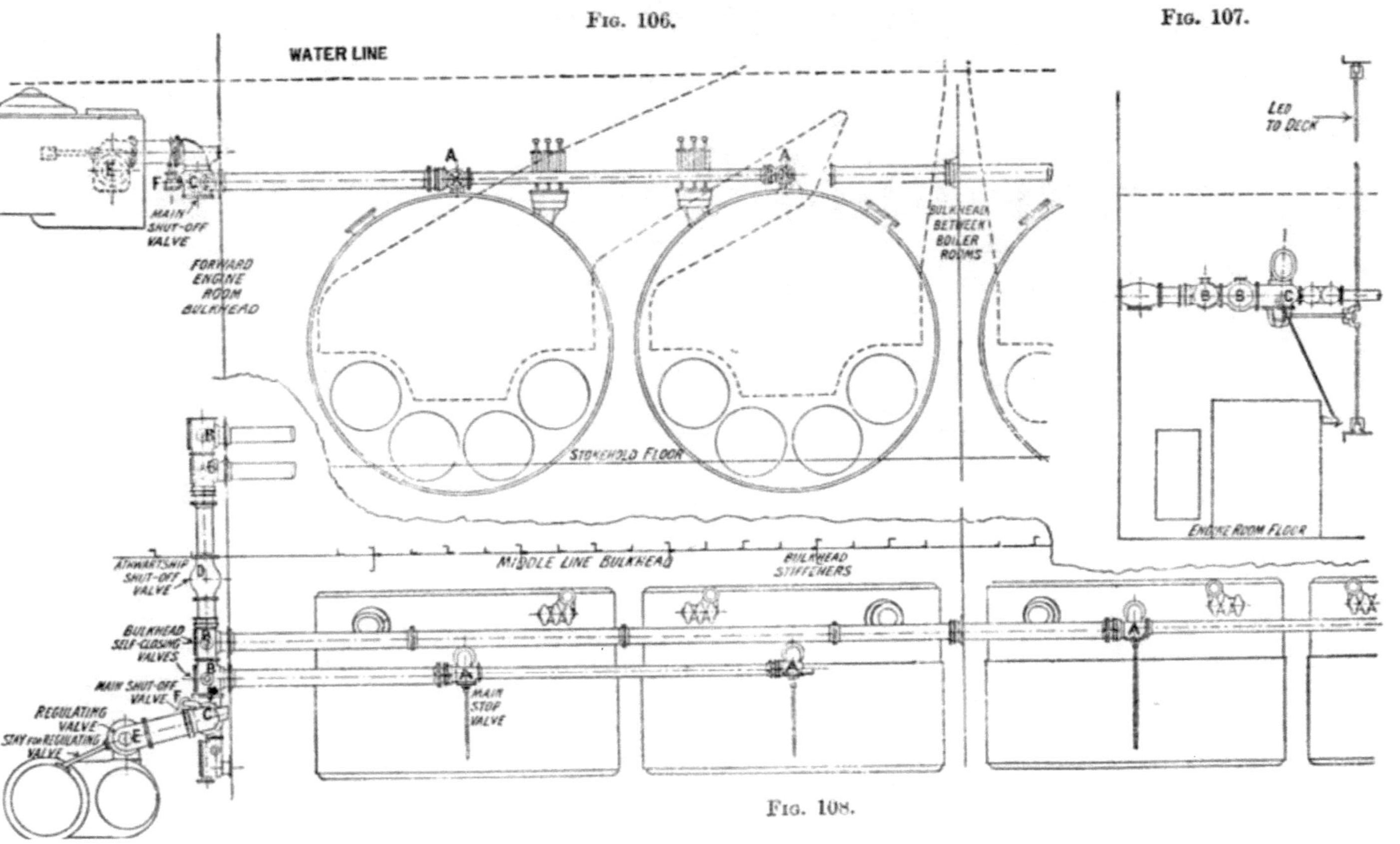

FIG. 106.
FIG. 107.
WATER LINE
LED TO DECK
A
BULKHEAD BETWEEN BOILER ROOMS
MAIN SHUT-OFF VALVE
FORWARD ENGINE ROOM BULKHEAD
STOKEHOLD FLOOR
ENGINE ROOM FLOOR
ATHWARTSHIP SHUT-OFF VALVE
MIDDLE LINE BULKHEAD
BULKHEAD STIFFENERS
BULKHEAD SELF-CLOSING VALVES
MAIN SHUT-OFF VALVE
REGULATING VALVE
STAY FOR REGULATING VALVE
MAIN STOP VALVE
FIG. 108.

pressure to ensure tightness when closed, and to facilitate opening this valve, a small pass-valve F is fitted, by means of which the pressure on each side can be equalised, and moving the valve against the steam pressure is facilitated.

Expansion joints.—As the steam pipes are subject to considerable increase of temperature when they contain steam, they necessarily expand and lengthen, and provision has to be made to enable this expansion to take place without bringing undue strains on any part. In small pipes this can be arranged by bending them sufficiently, so that the pipe at the bend is sufficiently elastic to allow for this elongation and contraction. In large pipes expansion joints have to be fitted which enable one end of the steam pipe to slide in and out of the adjacent pipe as changes of length take place. Fig. 109 shows the usual type of expansion joint formed by a stuffing-box and gland. Care must be taken when such expansion joints are fitted in pipes having a bend, that the un-balanced force is provided for either by struts or safety stays, otherwise the bent part of the pipe may be drawn out of the other. The expansion joints in the arrangement of Fig. 108 are indicated, one being fitted adjacent to each of the boiler stop valves A, and others elsewhere.

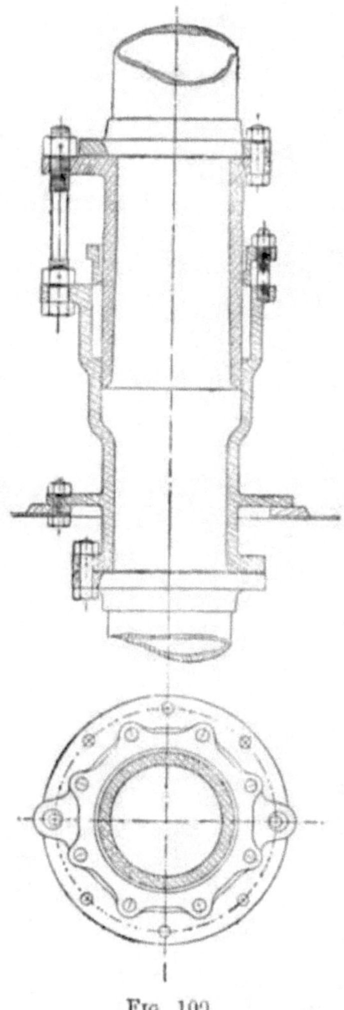

Fig. 109.

Separator.—Before reaching the engines the steam often passes through a separator similar to that shown in Fig. 110. The object is to provide an additional safeguard against priming, by preventing any water in the steam pipes from entering the cylinders. It is divided from the top to nearly the bottom by a diaphragm, D, the steam entering on one side and leaving on the other. Any water that reaches the separator is mostly left at the bottom, only the steam passing on to the cylinders. A drain-cock or valve is fitted, so that the water may be discharged by hand into the hot-well or feed-tank, and returned to the boiler. A non-return valve is fitted at the end of the pipe. The level of water is shown by a glass gauge G.

Automatic separator.—In the fast-running engines of the torpedo-boat destroyer type with water-tube boilers, water is occasionally passed into the steam pipes with the steam which, if it entered the cylinders, owing to the great speed and light construction of the engines, would probably do considerable damage before being passed through. In the recent vessels of this class, separators with automatic blow-out apparatus are fitted, so that when any quantity of water accumulates in the bottom of the separator by priming or other means, a float is raised, which by a system of levers opens an orifice of considerable area for drainage, so that the water is very quickly got rid of.

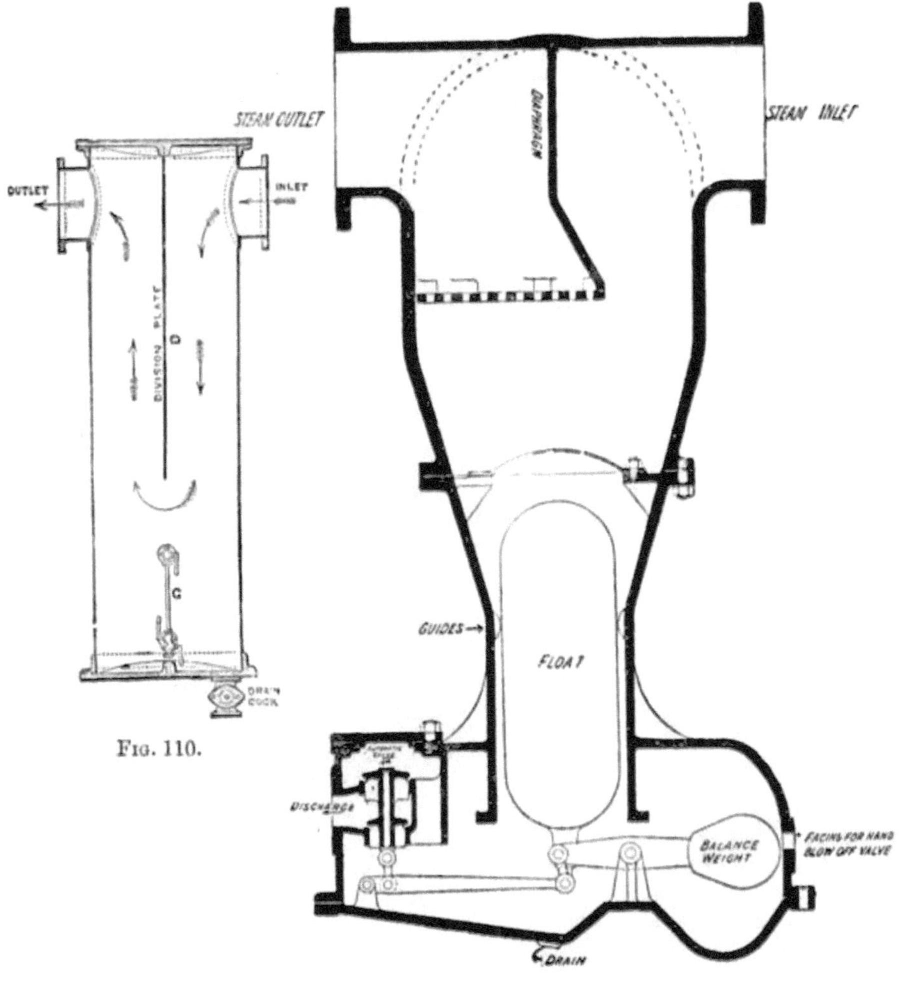

Fig. 110.

Fig. 111.

With such machinery the old separator with hand-blow-out apparatus is of little or no value. Fig. 111 shows an example fitted in the most recent thirty-knot destroyers. It is a gun-metal casting, provided with the usual diaphragm, while hand-blow-off apparatus is fitted in addition to the automatic arrangement.

Belleville separator.—Figs. 112 to 115 show the arrangement and details of the automatic separator placed in the main steam pipes when Belleville water-tube boilers are fitted. This apparatus, which is found very efficient in practice, consists of a cylindrical separator shown in Fig. 115, with steam inlet at the top and outlet at the side, the division plate between them being of circular form, with closed ends and an opening at the side, as shown by the horizontal section (Fig. 114), so that the steam has to traverse the circular casing before reaching the outlet. A dash plate is fitted below the circular diaphragm, and the water accumulates at the bottom, where an automatic valve worked by steam is fitted, as shown in Fig. 112 at c. To the side of the separator, near the bottom, the steam-tight casting D is bolted, having the double valves and float attached, as shown in Fig. 113.

When there is little water in the separator the float and valves are in the position shown in Fig. 113, the steam valve E being open, and the exhaust valve F shut, so that steam pressure is supplied through the branch B above the valve C, which keeps it tightly shut, as the area acted on by the steam pressure through the branch B is greater than the area of the valve C. When the water rises in the separator it lifts the float G, which actuates the valves E and F, closing E and opening F, which puts the space above the valve in connection with the exhaust, so that the pressure is immediately reduced and the steam pressure below the valve C forces it open, and the water in the separator is blown out. A hand-blow-off cock is fitted also the stop-cock, A, to enable the automatic apparatus to be shut off when required.

As considerable quantities of hot water may be rapidly blown out, the discharge is generally led to the upper part of the tube space of the main condenser, so that the hot water may be cooled before it reaches the feed-tank, otherwise the action of the feed-pumps may be interfered with. To limit the velocity of discharge, the orifice below the valve C, through which the water has to pass, is considerably smaller than the valve.

Auxiliary steam pipes.—Most marine boilers, in addition to the main stop-valves and steam pipes, are fitted with an auxiliary steam service, consisting of small stop-valves, B, Fig. 83, similar in construction to the main valves, leading into a set of steam pipes, which may be used for the auxiliary engines, distilling purposes, &c. These fittings prevent the necessity of filling the whole range of steam pipes with steam when one boiler is in use for distilling or other auxiliary purposes, so that the main valves and pipes are only used for the actual working of the main engines.

The auxiliary steam valves on the boilers have been dispensed with in many ships, especially in those with large numbers of water-tube boilers, branches being led from the main steam pipes to supply the auxiliary steam pipes leading to the auxiliary engines. This arrangement lessens the number of holes required to be cut in the shells of the boilers, and simplifies the arrangement, although when steam is always in one or other of the main steam pipes for long periods in harbour the joints require more care and attention to keep them efficient.

Steam-pipe drains. Steam traps.—The steam and exhaust pipes must be fitted with means of efficiently draining them from water.

Small drain pipes are fitted, which, in important cases, are led to steam traps which automatically drain the steam-pipes, &c., of water.

The action of the trap is as follows (see Fig. 116).   The water condensed in the pipes, &c., enters through the inlet orifice A, and fills the

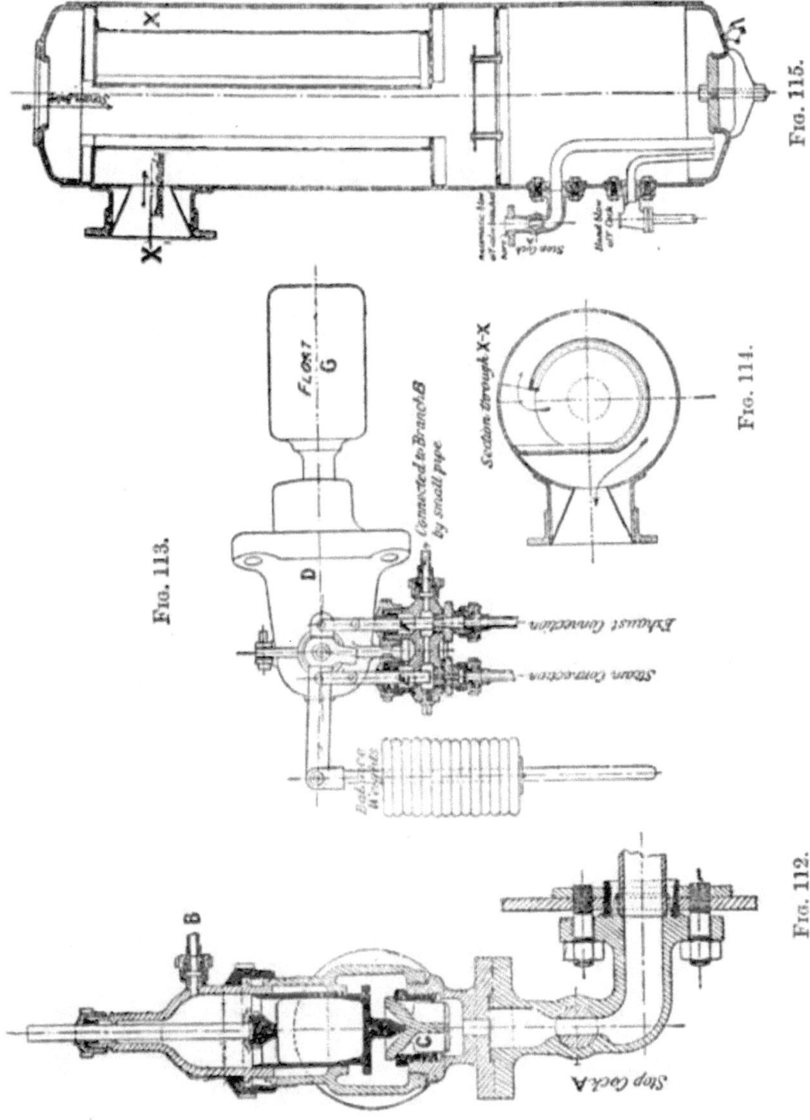

annular space G outside the pan until it reaches the level P Q.   The water then overflows into the pan and gradually fills it.   When the level of the water in the pan reaches a certain height, the pan drops, thus opening the valve D, and the water is forced out by the steam

pressure through the orifice F and the outlet passage B to the drain
system.   When the water level in the pan falls to about X Y, the pressure of the water outside it lifts the pan and keeps the valve closed

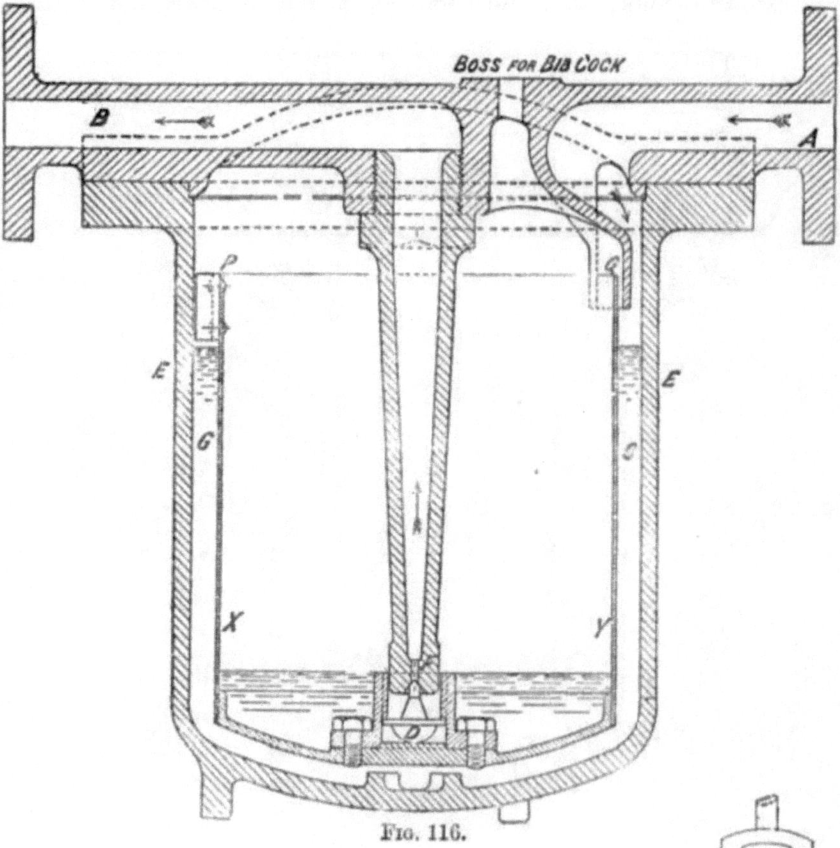

Fig. 116.

until the pan is nearly filled with water, when it is again
opened, this action being repeated so long as A is open to
steam.   A small bib cock is fitted on the cover to ascertain
whether the trap is in working order.

Klinger's water gauge mounting.—The usual round thin
gauge glasses give trouble with high-pressure steam, owing
to frequent fractures, while the water level
is often indistinct. Klinger's glass, designed
to obviate these defects, gives promise of
success.   It consists of a thick flat glass,
with smooth front and serrated back, shown
in section Fig. 116a.   A and B, the front
and back of the mounting, are bolted together with the glass and packing, shown
by thick lines, between them.   The serrations, when clean,
cause the water to appear black, as in Fig. 116b.

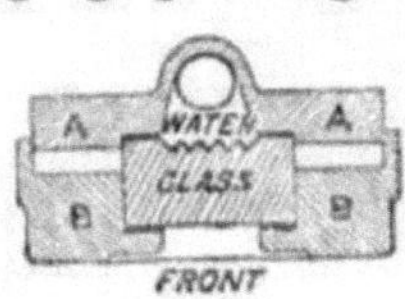

Fig. 116a.

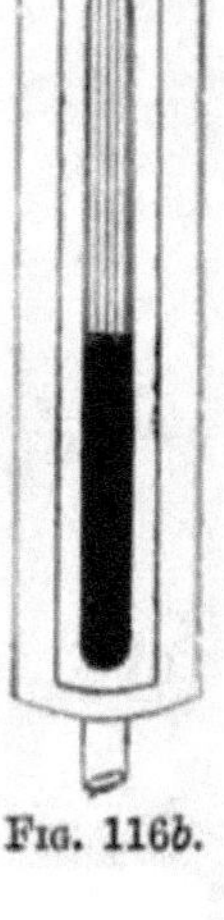

Fig. 116b.

CHAPTER X.

CORROSION AND PRESERVATION OF BOILERS.

THE question of the durability of boilers is one of the greatest importance as regards the continued efficiency of steamships, and much attention has therefore to be paid to it. The evidence given before an Admiralty Committee on Boilers by leading engineers and chemists showed the great variety of opinions and practice relative to this subject common at that time (see Appendix A, p. 118, of the Committee's Report, published in 1877). This Committee's Reports and further Admiralty experiments cleared up many obscure points, and the methods of treatment subsequently adopted have materially increased the durability of boilers.

The question is one specially important to officers in command ; and the leading principles should be clearly understood, enabling the captain and the engineer officer to work together to attain the desired end. Although the care and preservation of the boilers is mostly professional, and in the province of the engineer, many points in their management must be controlled by the captain, and their durability will depend also on his appreciation of the points involved, and knowledge of the subject.

The efficiency of a warship in the present day may be measured largely by that of her machinery, so that if the boilers are injured the evil cannot be estimated by the depreciation in their value alone, as the efficiency of the ship for the purpose for which she is designed is decreased, which is a much more important consideration. Whilst it is important that by proper care and precaution the boilers should be enabled to retain the original working pressures for as lengthened a period as possible, a certain amount of reduction of pressure is always permitted, as they become worn, in order to lengthen their lives, so as to avoid the expense of new boilers and the loss of the vessel's services while new boilers are being fitted.

Within certain limits the initial pressure may be reduced without any very great loss of power for ordinary work, although the consumption of coal will be increased, the increased expenditure of coal being more than compensated for by the ship being kept efficient for probably years longer than would otherwise be the case.

Influence of surface condensation. Early theories as to corrosion.—The introduction of surface condensation at first considerably decreased the durability of boilers, and brought the subject prominently into notice. A special corrosive action was found to take place in boilers supplied with water from surface condensers, and extraordinary cases of rapid decay occurred.

As the tubes in the surface condensers were generally made of copper, it was at first supposed that galvanic action would account for the decay of the boilers, either by the copper condenser tubes and the iron boiler plates forming a great battery, or by the tallow used for lubrication forming fatty acids on decomposition by the heat, and carrying into the boilers particles of copper dissolved from the condenser tubes or feed-pipes. The fact, however, that the condenser tubes and feed-pipes themselves generally appeared to suffer little or no deterioration after considerable periods of work, effectually disposed of this hypothesis.

Although slight traces of copper were found in the specimens of deposit taken from boilers, it was quite insufficient to account for the action produced, and it was also found by experiment that water, even when condensed by tinned or electro-plated tubes, still acted powerfully on the iron, which clearly showed that the action was not due to the contact of the water with the copper condenser tubes.

Influence of vegetable or animal oils. Saponification.—The general opinion of the chemists was that the main causes of the rapid decay of the earlier boilers fed with water from surface condensers were, that the fatty acids evolved by the action known as *saponification* from the heated tallow and vegetable oils at that time used for internal lubrication, were carried into the boilers by the feed-water, and acted directly as corrosive agents on the iron of the boiler plates and stays, and destroyed them. This action was intensified with the superheated steam then used.

Tallow is a compound of fatty acids, chiefly stearic, with glycerine, and when boiled in a solution of soda it is decomposed into stearic acid and glycerine, of which the former unites with the soda, forming a soap, the glycerine remaining free. A similar decomposition takes place when tallow is boiled alone at high pressures, but as no soda is present, the acid remains free ; and though these fatty acids are feeble in comparison with mineral acids such as sulphuric, hydrochloric, &c., yet they slowly attack iron and other metals.

The remedy for this is the employment of hydrocarbon or mineral oils for the lubrication of the interior of the cylinders, slides, &c., instead of tallow or oils of vegetable or animal origin, as these mineral oils are not subject to decomposition so as to produce fatty acids. The use of mineral oils for the internal lubrication of engines with surface condensers is now general.

Irregularity of corrosion.—One remarkable feature of this corrosive action was its irregularity. Whilst the boilers of some ships were completely worn out in a very short time, the boilers of other ships employed on the same service, and treated apparently in a similar manner, showed no unusual corrosion. Even in the same boiler some plates have been found to be seriously corroded whilst adjoining ones have been unaffected.

The most serious decay showed itself in the form of *pitting* or local corrosion, deep pits being formed in the plates. This has been attributed to the presence of slag, or to irregularity in the structure of the material, the softer parts being the more readily attacked.

The irregularity of the action was also explained by the fact that clean surfaces would be attacked more readily, and that all parts covered with a thin film of oxide or scale would be protected. Caustic lime or soda was suggested to be put into the boilers from time to time to neutralise the acids in the water.

Influence of workmanship.—Unless skill and care be exercised in the manufacture of any structure its intended strength and durability will be decreased. In boiler work great care should be exercised to insure that the holes in the plates at the joints are *fair* before the rivet is put in. If they are found to be not exactly true they should be made so by the use of a rimer, and not be drifted, by which the plate may be actually broken in manufacture, for it is obvious that in such a case durability cannot be expected. Sometimes a smaller rivet has been used in order to get it in and hide the fault. The worst feature of these defects is, that they cannot generally be discovered when the boiler is made, and only show themselves after the boiler has been subjected to the stress of actual work, when it is very difficult for them to be effectually rectified.

In good boiler work the rivet holes in the plates are now always drilled. When the plates are drilled together they should be taken apart before being riveted, to allow the burr or sharp edge to be taken off from the holes.

Another point to be secured is to get the joints properly closed, so that little caulking is necessary. In good boiler-making, the joint should be tight without caulking; and if it be not fairly tight no amount of caulking will permanently remedy it, though it may conceal the defect for the time. Excessive caulking is very injurious, and is probably one of the most fruitful causes of the *grooving* that sometimes occurs along the rivet-seams. It also tends to raise the edge of the upper plate and cause looseness at the joint. The edges of the plates should be planed with a bevel of about $75°$, and the only caulking required should be a little along the thinner edge of the bevel.

Use of wrought-iron.—Wrought-iron was at first universally employed for all parts of boilers, and it was supposed that the irregular manner in which corrosion showed itself in iron boilers might be accounted for by the manner in which the plates were made.

From the methods of manufacture of iron plates homogeneity cannot be expected. The slag in the puddle-bars is squeezed out to a greater or less degree according to the amount of work performed on the iron, but it is impossible to be certain that it has been altogether eliminated, and, if not, laminations and blisters in the plate are the result.

Steel plates.—With steel the case is quite different, as it can be cast in an ingot of sufficient size to form the plate, so that no welding is required, and the ingot has only to be hammered and rolled to form the finished plate, the structure of which should therefore be homogeneous.

For some years, however, steel was looked upon with suspicion and regarded as unreliable for boilers; but the steel now used for this purpose, although containing sufficient carbon to enable it to be fused to insure homogeneity, cannot be hardened, and may be worked with more freedom than iron. The use of mild steel made by the Siemens-Martin process now general for boiler work, has considerably helped to solve the boiler corrosion question. It is less costly and stronger than iron, and therefore boilers may be more cheaply and lightly made. The plates can also be rolled of larger size than with iron, which simplifies construction.

Marine boilers are now made entirely of steel, except the tubes, which are usually of iron in the mercantile marine. In the Navy the tubes are also of steel. The furnaces and internal parts that have to be welded or flanged are made from steel plates of specially soft quality.

Present causes of corrosion in boilers.—The specially severe corrosion which occurred when vegetable or animal oils were used for cylinder lubrication has been entirely obviated by the use of mineral oils for such internal parts.

The principal cause of corrosion in boilers at the present time is the oxidation of the plates, which results from contact with *moisture and air*, either carried in with the feed-water when at work, or existing in the atmosphere when the boilers are empty. This action, it should be understood, requires the simultaneous presence of both air and moisture, for neither dry air, nor fresh water thoroughly deprived of air, have any chemical action on steel or iron. Air dissolved in water is especially energetic, and the action is increased by the presence of various chlorides, such as those of magnesium and sodium.

There are other minor causes of corrosion ; for example, sea-water, even when entirely deprived of air, if it be heated, has some action on steel and iron. It is stated that at the high temperatures now common in boilers, the chloride of magnesium contained in it is decomposed by the heat and gives off hydrochloric acid, the evolution of acid being accelerated with increase of density. This, however, requires confirmation. Sea-water should, if possible, never be admitted.

Another probable minor cause of corrosion in boilers is galvanic action originating in slight differences in the material used in their construction.

Prevention of corrosion when at work.—The admission of air into the boilers is prevented as much as possible, when the boilers are at work, by the separate feed or hot-well tanks described in Chapter XX., with ample surface and other means for the escape of air, and by the fitting of independent feed-pumps, which can be so regulated in speed as to be always fully supplied with water, and never to empty the feed-tank, and so suck in and discharge air into the boilers. The necessity for the complete exclusion of sea-water has already been pointed out ; the waste of feed-water should be made good by the evaporators now always fitted together with a reserve of fresh water in tanks. Mineral oils which consist of hydro-carbon only, should be exclusively used for lubrication of all internal parts, air pump rods, and the piston and slide rods which enter the steam spaces of cylinders. Should, however, the boiler water be found by the litmus test to show traces of acidity, it should be neutralised by the admission of lime or soda into the feed-water.

Zinc protectors.—After all these items are attended to there remains an efficient precautionary means of protection consisting in the suspension of slabs of zinc in various parts of the boilers, both below the water-line and in the steam space, in the manner indicated in Fig. 117. If there be any galvanic action the zinc slabs will be attacked instead of the material of the boiler itself. It is important in fixing these zinc slabs that they should be in actual *bright metallic contact* with the material of the boiler and well distributed, so that every portion of the boiler surface is protected. The uniform distribution of zinc slabs over the surface of the boiler is indicated by the positions shown in Figs. 29 and 30, representing the usual arrangement. When properly fitted they undoubtedly produce a beneficial effect, although whether the corrosive action they prevent is entirely galvanic or partly chemical is not fully determined. Zinc being a strongly electro-positive metal, it causes the steel of the boiler to become electro-negative, and induces any corrosive agents to attack itself, leaving the steel uninjured. This action requires the presence of an exciting liquid, so that the zincs have no preservative action when the boilers are empty. It is doubtful whether absolutely pure fresh water is sufficient to induce this action. The zincs fitted in the steam space are for use when the boilers are filled with water.

Procedure if corrosion is discovered.—When the foregoing precautions are attended to, the decay of boilers on service is not very great, but if oxidation is seen to be occurring at any part it will probably be owing to the nearest zinc being too far away from it, requiring re-arrangement of or additional slabs, or from decay of the zinc, or failure of the metallic connections. As a further precaution the affected part should be carefully cleaned with strong soda solution, and all rust scraped off, and, provided it is not a heating surface, the clean surface coated with a thin coating of Port-land cement, which is a substance impervious to moisture.

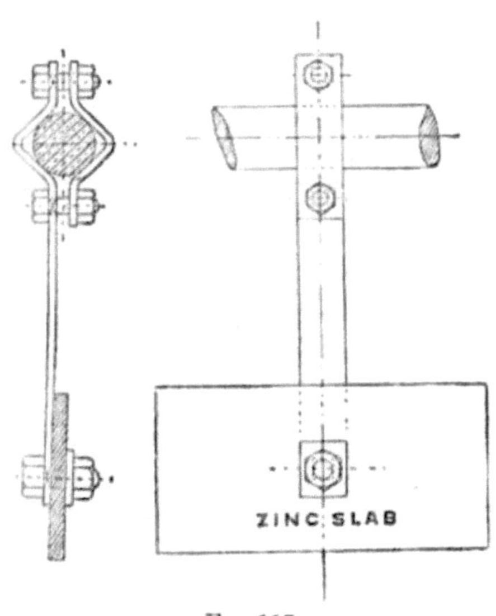

Fig. 117.

Corrosion is sometimes produced by using certain shore waters. All shore waters contain air and other gases dissolved in them, and these being set free when the water is heated will act on the boiler. Some waters contain a considerable amount of matter in suspension, and this will be deposited on the surfaces, and by retaining moisture and keeping the surfaces damp when the water is run off, may cause corrosion. Some shore waters, particularly in volcanic regions, have pronounced acid properties, and should therefore be avoided.

Boiler tubes, being thinner than the other parts of a boiler, require renewing more often ; the average life of steel tubes, with careful treatment, is about eight years, but is often less.

Effect of intermittent working.—The work of warships is, from its variety and intermittent action, with consequent repeated expansion and contraction, more trying to the boilers than the steady and continuous steaming usual in the ships of the mercantile marine.

Warships on ordinary service only steam at slow speeds, the engines developing, say, from one-fifth to one-twentieth their full power. Only a portion of the boilers is required at one time, and if any are kept empty, unless great care be exercised, moisture will get into them, through the cocks and valves, and this moisture, if atmospheric air be present, is one of the most fruitful causes of corrosion.

General preservation when at work.—Changes of temperature should take place as seldom and gradually as possible. Unless in cases of emergency, steam should be raised slowly, to allow the different parts of the boilers to gradually expand and prevent local straining. Banking fires should be resorted to as rarely as possible, to prevent change of temperature. Any saving of coal that may be gained by frequently banking fires is paid for at the expense of the boilers themselves.

Injury may be done by drawing fires when steaming is over, as large volumes of cold air rush through the boilers, and the sudden contraction that ensues frequently causes leaks, and damages the boilers. If possible, sufficient notice as to the probable length of time that steam will be required should be given, to allow the fires to burn down ; and when the engines are done with, the boilers should be closed up and allowed to cool, so that they contract gradually and prevent undue strains on any part. The furnaces should be cleared out after all has become cool.

In cases where bottom blow out arrangements are fitted, the water should never be emptied by the steam pressure, unless on an emergency, but allowed to remain until cool and then run or pumped out. This is a more tedious process, but the efficiency of the boilers is the first point to be considered.

Cleanliness.—As regards the preservation of boilers, their cleanliness is of the first importance. As little oil as possible for internal lubrication should be used, as this, when admitted to the boilers, is deposited on the heating surfaces in the form of a highly non-conducting substance, which often leads to the overheating and absolute failure of the plates and tube ends. Consequent overheating due to such greasy deposits is a fruitful source of wear in boilers.

Much of this oil will float on the surface of the water, so that a slight occasional use of the surface blow-out is desirable. When boilers are intended to be completely emptied, the surface water should always first be blown out, as otherwise the oil floating there, on its descent through the boiler when emptying, will be deposited on the boiler surfaces.

To reduce the amount of oil entering the boiler, modern ships are now always fitted with filters, through which the feed-water has to pass, and which prevents most of the grease from entering the boilers (see Chapter XXVIII.).

In most tank boilers it is impossible to thoroughly clean the tube plates without drawing the plain tubes. The tubes, being arranged in vertical rows, allow of narrow scrapers being worked vertically between them, and in this way these parts of the boiler can be fairly well cleaned, but it is impossible to thoroughly clean the horizontal spaces between the tubes. As a general rule, each boiler should have many of the tubes withdrawn for cleaning purposes about once in two years, if the conditions of the service on which the ship is employed permit ; but the vessel need not be laid up at all for this, as the tubes can be drawn in regular rotation, dealing with a nest at a time.

Care is required in drawing boiler tubes to avoid damaging many of them during the operation, but when properly carried out with steel tubes not more than 5 per cent. need be spoilt. Before replacing the tubes, the ends should be annealed and dressed.

Preservation of boilers when not at work.—Boilers not in use, in store, or on board ships for a lengthened period, may deteriorate very rapidly if proper precautions be not taken, and to prevent this they are, when kept empty, carefully dried, and perforated trays containing burning charcoal or coke are placed in them, the boilers being then immediately closed and hermetically sealed, to prevent access of air. The glowing carbon will absorb most of the oxygen of the air in the boiler, and no internal decay will ensue. This is the best method of preservation. Another plan after drying is to insert about $\frac{3}{4}$ cwt. of quicklime per furnace in shallow trays, also a tray of burning coal, well coked, and then close up. The quicklime absorbs any moisture.

If steam is required to be raised in any of the boilers, it will generally be best to keep the empty boilers open and dry, and raised above the temperature of the surrounding atmosphere by fires in the ashpits, but great care is necessary to ensure that leakage past the steam stop and feed valves of boilers not in use does not occur and the boilers become damp. Special care is also required to guard against leakage past the sea valves, which must be kept in good order.

If danger of leakage through the sea valves is feared, or if otherwise desirable, the following system may be used if there is no risk of water freezing. The boilers may be quite filled with a fresh water solution of carbonate of soda, containing about one pound of soda crystals to 100 lbs. of water, by putting on a slight pressure, and allowing the air to escape through a small cock at the highest part. If possible the water should be heated to expel the air. After using this method the boilers must be emptied and washed out before steam is raised.

Corrosion of water-tube boilers.—In such boilers experience up to the present shows that cleanliness of the surfaces and tubes is the most important element in their preservation. All foreign matter should be kept out of the boilers, and the system adopted in repairing and cleaning should be arranged so as to avoid the possibility of anything being left in them which might fall into and choke the tubes or obstruct the circulation of water. When a tube fails quickly the cause is generally found to be overheating, due to the circulation being obstructed by the presence of foreign matter in the tube, or to the presence of some saline lime or greasy deposits on the surfaces, obstructing the passage of the heat from the tube to the water. As it is impracticable in many water-tube boilers to clean off deposits of lime when once formed, sea-water, and also shore water containing lime salts, should be carefully excluded. Zinc slabs have been found to exert considerable protective action in water-tube boilers in which fresh and even distilled water has been generally used, and the good contact and renewal of these fittings should therefore be carefully attended to.

CHAPTER XI.

EFFICIENCY OF THE STEAM.

The total amount of energy in the form of heat transferred to the water in the boiler in order to convert it into steam is not given out as mechanical energy at the engine, but only a small portion of it—say, in ordinary cases, from one-twentieth to one-fifth, according to the type of engine. The ratio which the energy exerted by the steam bears to the total amount of energy in the form of heat expended in its generation is called *the efficiency of the steam.*

It was pointed out in Chapter III. that the total heat of evaporation of steam slowly increased as the temperature of evaporation was raised. In other words, the expenditure of heat necessary to produce a given weight of steam from water supplied to the boiler at a given temperature, increases when the pressure and temperature of the steam are increased. The rate of increase in the total heat of evaporation is, however, very slow. For example, the expenditure of heat required to produce a given weight of steam at the pressure of 10 atmospheres is only 1·04 times that necessary to produce an equal weight of steam at the atmospheric pressure, the temperature of the feed-water in each case being 100° Fahr.

Since the difference between the amounts of heat required to produce a given weight of steam at different pressures is so small, the problem of obtaining the greatest possible quantity of work from a given expenditure of *heat,* is reduced practically to the simpler one of obtaining the greatest amount of work from a given weight of *steam,* the difference in the total heat of evaporation at various pressures being so slight that it may be neglected in approximate calculations.

The indicator diagram.—Before dealing further with the question of the efficiency of steam, it will be necessary to explain the diagram known as the indicator diagram, by which the action of steam in the cylinder is best represented. The term 'indicator diagram' is derived from the instrument used in obtaining it in practice.[1]

This diagram is the geometrical representation of the pressure of steam in the cylinder at various points in the stroke of the piston. The diagram, Fig. 118, is a *theoretical indicator diagram* in which the horizontal ordinates represent volumes, and the vertical ordinates pressures. Its area may be calculated from geometrical principles, so that the diagram may be used in theoretical investigations on the power and efficiency of the engines. For a cylinder of given diameter, the volume may be represented by the length of the stroke of the piston.

In Fig. 118, let o p represent the stroke of the piston of the engine,

---

[1] See Chapter XXVI.

and o A the *absolute* pressure of the steam during its admission. The initial pressure of the steam in the cylinder is never quite so great as that in the boiler, because a portion of the energy of the steam has to be exerted in overcoming the resistance of the stop-valves, steam pipes, ports, passages, &c. In ordinary cases of marine engines working at full power the reduction of pressure due to this cause may be taken to be about one-tenth of the absolute pressure of the steam in the boilers, but under certain circumstances, which will be explained later,[1] the reduction may considerably exceed even this amount.

During admission the steam passes into the cylinder at this reduced initial pressure, and this part of the action of the steam is shown by the line A B, which is commonly known as the '*steam line*' of the diagram. At B, when the piston has traversed the part o N of its stroke, the whole stroke being represented by o P, the admission of steam to the cylinder is cut off by the closing of the steam ports by the valve.

The expansion of the steam in the cylinder now commences, and the piston is pressed forward by the expansive force of the steam, the pressure continually diminishing as the piston moves onward to the end of the stroke and increases the volume occupied by the steam. This part of the action is represented by the '*expansion curve*' B C.

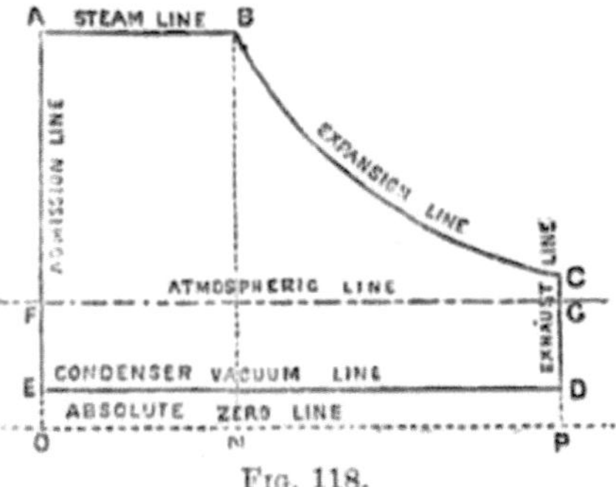

Fig. 118.

The *ratio of expansion* is the ratio between the final volume of the expanding steam, and its volume at the instant of cut-off. In our example $\frac{O\ P}{O\ N}$ is the ratio of expansion.

The laws according to which the pressure of steam diminishes during its expansion vary according to the conditions under which the expansion takes place, and the initial state of the steam.[2] For elementary purposes, however, it is sufficient to assume the simple approximate law that the *absolute* pressure will vary inversely as the volume—i.e. when the volume is doubled, the *absolute* pressure falls to one-half, when it is trebled to one-third, and so on.

When the piston arrives at the end of its stroke and the expansion is finished, the communication with the receiver or condenser is opened, the steam escapes, and the pressure falls to P D, the constant back pressure which acts against the piston during the whole of the return stroke. Fig. 118 is the diagram of a condensing engine, and in this case the line D E is technically called the '*vacuum line*' of the diagram. o P is the '*zero line*,' or line of no pressure, from which all absolute pressures are measured. F G is called the '*atmospheric line*,' o F representing the pressure of the atmosphere.

It is important to remember that in all investigations on the action

<hr>

[1] See Chapter XXVI.   [2] See Chapter XII.

of steam, the *absolute pressures*, or the pressures measured from the zero line must be taken, and not the pressures indicated by ordinary pressure gauges, which simply represent the excess of the steam pressure above that of the atmosphere.

Area of the indicator diagram.—*Mechanical work* is produced by the exertion of a force through a space, and the mean value of the force multiplied by the space through which it acts, gives the amount of mechanical work done. In the case of a steam-engine the space is represented by the distance through which the piston travels in a given time, and the force is the excess of the average forward pressure exerted by the steam on one side of the piston, during its admission and expansion, above the average back pressure it exerts on the other side of the piston whilst being discharged from the cylinder.

It is easy to see that the area of the diagram A B C D E represents on some proper scale the work done by the steam on one side of the piston during the double stroke described above.

The greater, therefore, the area of this diagram obtained from a given weight of steam, the greater will be the efficiency of the steam.

The area may evidently be increased in two ways, namely (1) by reducing the back pressure—i.e. by lowering the line E D—or (2) by increasing the mean height of the upper part of the diagram obtained from the same weight of steam used ; (1) is effected by means of the condensation of steam and (2) by means of its expansion.

Increase of efficiency due to condensation.—We will now consider the increase of efficiency of the steam due to the application of the principle of condensation.

In the non-condensing engine (often called by the misleading term ' high-pressure engine ') the steam, after having done its work in the cylinder, escapes to the atmosphere, and the back pressure is not less than from 3 to 4 lbs. per square inch above the atmosphere, corresponding to an absolute pressure of from 18 to 19 lbs. per square inch. or a temperature of about 224° Fahr., and with contracted exhaust passages and quick-moving engines it is sometimes much higher. When a condenser is used so that a partial vacuum is formed in the cylinder behind the piston, the back pressure is only 3 to 4 lbs. *absolute*, corresponding to a temperature of 140° Fahr. to 150° Fahr. In this case, where the back pressure is less than that of the atmosphere, the difference between the back and atmospheric pressures is technically called the ' *vacuum in the cylinder.*' The amount of vacuum in a cylinder or condenser is generally measured in inches of mercury.

Imagine two engines, one condensing, the other non-condensing, working with steam of 60 lbs. per square inch above the atmosphere, or 75 lbs. absolute, the initial pressure and ratio of expansion being the same in each case. Then the steam line, until the end of the forward stroke, would be the same both in the condensing and non-condensing engines, the only difference in the two cases being in the position of the line of back pressure.

The indicator diagrams, Fig. 119, represent the action of the steam in the two engines under consideration, the corners of the diagrams being here rounded off as is the case in actual diagrams, due to the gradual opening and closing of the ports by the slide valve, instead of the sudden opening and closing assumed in theoretical diagrams

In the non-condensing engine the back pressure line D E, Fig. 119, will be about 3 or 4 lbs. above the atmospheric line H K. In the condensing engine the pressure at the end of the stroke falls considerably below the atmospheric pressure, and the back pressure will only be 3 to 4 lbs. absolute, or, say, 12 to 11 lbs. below the atmospheric line, as shown by the line F G, so that by the application of the condenser the work done by the same weight of steam is increased by an amount represented by the area E D F G.

The forward pressure would be the same in each case, but in the non-condensing engine this would be resisted by a back pressure of 18 to 19 lbs. per square inch ; whereas with the condenser, the pressure resisting the forward motion would be only 3 to 4 lbs. absolute. It is clear that, in a non-condensing engine, the cut-off should never be early enough to cause the pressure of steam to fall below that of the atmosphere before the completion of the stroke ; for this would necessitate the latter part of the stroke being performed by the expenditure of work accumulated in the moving parts during the earlier part of the stroke, and would probably cause difficulty in starting, and prevent smoothness and regularity in working.

It is evident that an equal quantity of steam would be used by both engines, because the absolute pressure of the steam N M just before release, which represents the steam used, is the same both in the condensing and the non-condensing diagrams.

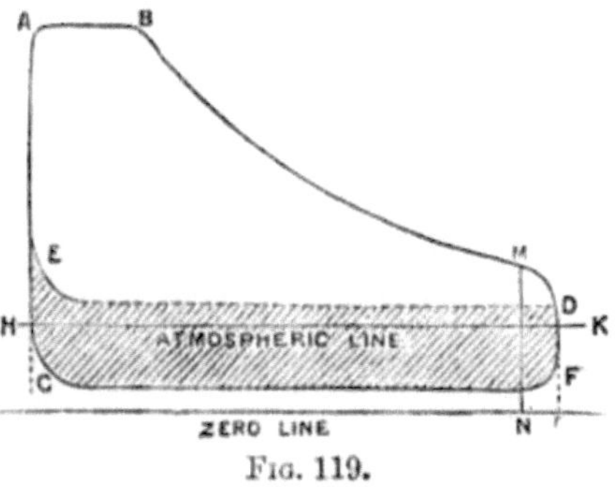

FIG. 119.

Application of formula for maximum efficiency.—A very important theorem and formula of the science of thermo-dynamics will enable this increase of efficiency to be shown. It is as follows, viz. :—

The greatest possible efficiency of any heat engine depends on the difference between the initial and final temperatures at which it is worked, and is represented by the formula—

$$\text{Maximum efficiency} = \frac{T_1 - T_2}{T_1} = \frac{t_1 - t_2}{t_1 + 461}$$

where T_1 = initial absolute temperature = $t_1 + 461$

T_2 = final absolute temperature = $t_2 + 461$

t_1 = initial temperature in degrees Fahr.

and t_2 = final temperature in degrees Fahr.

We will apply this formula to the cases of the two engines above referred to. The temperature corresponding to 75 lbs. pressure absolute is 307° Fahr., while the corresponding temperature for 18 to 19 lbs. pressure is about 224°, and for 3 to 4 lbs. 150° Fahr.

The non-condensing engine would therefore be working between the limits 307° and 224°, whilst the limits in the case of the condensing engine would be 307° and 150°. The relative maximum efficiency of the condensing to that of the non-condensing engine would therefore be—

$$\frac{307 - 150}{307 - 224} = \frac{157}{83}$$

or nearly two to one, so that the efficiency of the steam could be nearly doubled by the addition of a suitable condenser. It should be noticed from the form of the equation that the relative gain is much greater at low pressures than at high pressures.

The following table given by Professor Cotterill shows the calculated consumptions of steam per hour if the engine were perfect, both in the case of a condensing and of a non-condensing engine, and clearly shows the gain in efficiency due to the condensation, and also that the percentage of gain is greater at low than at high pressures.

Pounds of Steam per I.H.P. per hour.

Initial pressure in atmospheres	Condensing	Non-condensing	t_1 in degrees Fahr.
	lbs.	lbs.	
2	11·2	50·4	249°
4	9·2	24·8	291°
6	8·3	18·9	318°
8	7·7	15·9	340°

In the condensing engine it was assumed that the feed-water was taken from the condenser at a temperature of 100° Fahr., and in the non-condensing engine that the exhaust steam had been used to raise the temperature of the feed-water to about 212° Fahr.

CHAPTER XII.

EXPANSION OF STEAM.

WE will now consider the increase in the efficiency of the steam obtained by utilising its property of expansion, the second of the two means of increasing efficiency referred to in the last chapter.

Referring again to an indicator diagram, Fig. 120, it will be seen that the pressure represented by the mean height of the line A B C can be divided into two distinct parts ; first, the pressure during admission while the steam is passing from the steam pipes into the cylinder, represented by the height of A B, and second, the diminishing pressure during the expansion of the steam when its flow into the cylinder has been cut off, this diminishing pressure being represented by the expansion curve B C. It is clear therefore that, as there is no further expenditure of steam during this part of the stroke, the amount of work done during expansion is so much gain, and the amount of work obtained from a given weight of steam, and hence the efficiency of the steam, is increased.

Limit of useful expansion.—It is clear from the diagram that energy would continue to be exerted by the steam whilst its forward pressure was greater than the back pressure P D, so that in order to get the greatest possible quantity of energy exerted by the steam, the expansion should be such that the forward pressure becomes so far reduced as to be just equal to the back pressure ; i.e. the cut-off should be so early, that the expansion curve will, at the end of the stroke, just fall to the back pressure line D E, as indicated by the dotted curve in the diagram, so that there is no sudden fall of pressure on exhaust.

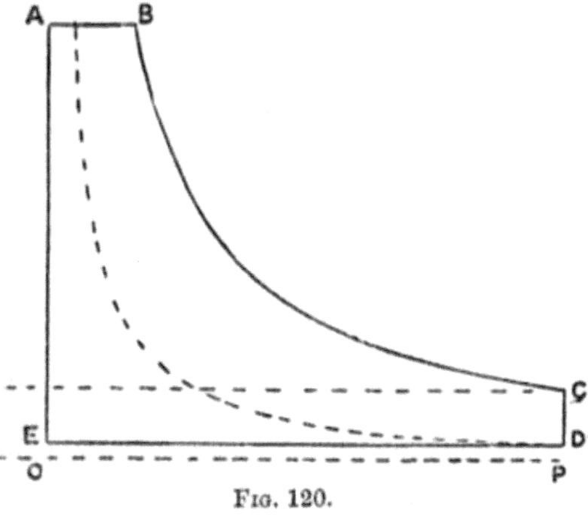

FIG. 120.

In a steam-engine a portion of the work obtained from the steam is expended in overcoming the friction of the working parts of the machinery, so that even theoretically, in order to obtain the greatest possible amount of *useful work* from a given quantity of steam, the expansion should only be carried out until the pressure in the cylinder is so reduced as to be just equal to the back pressure, *plus* a pressure equivalent to the friction of the mechanism.

In practice it is not possible to carry out the expansion, efficiently, to so great an extent as this, and it must only be taken as a theoretical statement of what might be the case if the steam were expanded in a perfectly non-conducting cylinder, and as the condition to which we must endeavour to approximate as closely as possible, by suitable appliances to existing engines.

Illustration of gain by expansion.—By inspection of an indicator diagram it will be obvious that this increase of efficiency due to expanding steam becomes greater as the initial pressure and amount of expansion are increased. This is illustrated in a simple manner by means of a theoretical indicator diagram, in which the pressure is assumed to vary inversely as the volume occupied by the steam, and a cylinder in which different pressures of steam can be admitted and any desired cut-off obtained, the back pressure being constant.

Suppose steam of 25 lbs. absolute pressure per square inch be admitted to this cylinder throughout the entire stroke, represented by G F, Fig. 121, and let O G be the constant back pressure, then the indicator diagram will be N E F G, and the rectangle G E will represent the work done. Next suppose steam of 50 lbs. absolute admitted and cut off at half stroke, the remainder of the stroke being completed by the expansion of the steam. The pressure then at the end of the stroke will be 25 lbs., so that the quantity of steam used is the same as before, since in each case we have used a cylinder full of steam of 25 lbs. pressure. The indicator diagram will be K D E F G, so that, subtracting the common area G E, the increase of area representing additional work done is K D E N, and similarly for higher pressures.

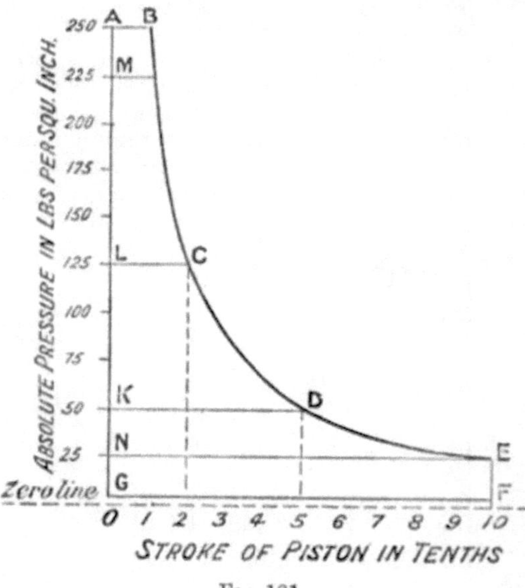

Fig. 121.

The theoretical diagrams for two higher pressures—viz. 125 lbs. initial pressure with cut-off at $\frac{2}{10}$ stroke or ratio of expansion of 5, and 250 lbs. with cut-off at $\frac{1}{10}$ stroke, or ratio of expansion of 10—have also been drawn on the same figure for comparison. It will be seen that as the initial pressure and ratio of expansion are increased, the greater is the gain in the area of the diagram, so that it is clear that theoretically the greater the pressure and number of expansions, the greater is the efficiency—i.e. the greater the amount of work obtained from a given weight of steam.

It should be noticed, however, that the higher the initial pressure becomes, the smaller is the gain by a given increase of pressure ; for example, compare the gain by increasing from 25 lbs. to 50 lbs. represented by K D E N with the gain by increasing from 225 lbs. to 250 lbs. represented by the much smaller area M B.

General conclusions.—By examining the formula for maximum efficiency of the theoretical heat engine,

$$\text{Maximum efficiency} = \frac{t_1 - t_2}{t_1 + 461}$$

the increase in maximum efficiency due to increase of pressure may also be seen, for this expression may be written

$$1 - \frac{t_2 + 461}{t_1 + 461}$$

which becomes greater as t_1 is increased and therefore also as the pressure is increased.

It was shown in the last chapter that the lower the back pressure the greater was the efficiency, so we learn that the higher the mean forward pressure obtained from a given weight of steam, and the lower the back pressure, the greater is the efficiency of the steam.

The initial temperature and pressure of the steam are limited by considerations of the strength and safety of the boilers, cylinders, and other parts exposed to steam pressure, and also the continued efficiency of all working parts exposed to these high temperatures.

In Watt's time, workmanship and knowledge of the strength of materials were not in such an advanced state as at the present, so that most engineers of that time were necessarily very cautious in the adoption of high pressures, and relied more on obtaining a low back pressure. As experience was gained, the pressures at which boilers were worked were gradually increased, and of late years the advances in that direction have been great, and there has been much gain in economy from the high pressures and rates of expansion now in general use.

In the preceding explanation the expansion of the steam is supposed to be in accordance with the hyperbolic law, which is approximately the case in practice, and a table showing the gain per cent. at various rates of expansion can easily be deduced on this assumption. There are other possible curves of expansion of steam, however, depending on its treatment during expansion (see later in this chapter).

Numerical results for gain by expansion.—The following table has been calculated on the assumption that the expansion curve is a certain curve, which will be explained later, called a 'saturation' curve—i.e. it represents the steam as always in a state of saturation whatever the pressure may be. This curve always falls slightly below the hyperbolic curve. On this assumption it shows how the amount of work done by one pound of steam is augmented as the initial pressure and ratio of expansion are increased. Since the total heat of steam is practically the same at all temperatures, the increase in the performance of work may be taken to represent very nearly the theoretical increase in efficiency due to the increased expansion.

The pressure in each case at the end of the expansion is supposed to be the same, viz. 10 lbs. per square inch absolute, and the back pressure 3 lbs. per square inch absolute.

Initial absolute pressure	Relative volume [1]	Specific volume [1] in cub. ft.	Ratio of expansion	Mean absolute pressure in lbs. per sq. in.	Mean effective pressure in lbs. per sq. in.	Relative indicated horse-power
10	2368	37·8	1·0	10·0	7·0	100
20	1231	19·7	1·9	17·2	14·2	289
40	643	10·3	3·7	24·5	21·5	538
60	434	7·0	5·4	29·0	26·0	716
80	338	5·4	7·0	33·3	30·3	901
100	270	4·4	8·6	36·2	33·2	1033
150	184	2·96	12·7	39·6	36·6	1195
200	142	2·27	16·6	42·5	39·5	1340
250	114	1·83	20·6	44·8	41·8	1459
300	96	1·54	24·5	46·4	43·4	1544

[1] See definitions later in this chapter.

It will be seen that by increasing the initial pressure of the steam from 20 to 80 lbs. per square inch absolute, the work done per pound of steam is increased more than three times, whilst at 100 lbs. pressure it is three and a half times, and at 200 lbs. nearly five times as great as at 20 lbs. pressure absolute—or, say, 5 lbs. above the atmospheric pressure, which was the ordinary working pressure in the early days of steam navigation—the heat required to produce the steam being but little different in each case.

Comparison of throttling and expansive working with simple engines.—The economy due to the expansive working of steam in simple engines used to be practically illustrated by taking indicator diagrams when working expansively and throttled respectively. First, a diagram was taken working expansively, noting the revolutions per minute the engines were making. Secondly, the expansion gear was put out of operation, or the link motion put into full gear, and then the throttle valve partially closed until the revolutions were the same as before. The two diagrams were found to be as shown in Fig. 122. The revolutions being the same, the work done will be the same, and consequently the areas of the two diagrams must be equal. The expansion diagram is represented by the full lines, and the throttled diagram by the dotted lines.

The quantity of steam used is represented by its pressure at the

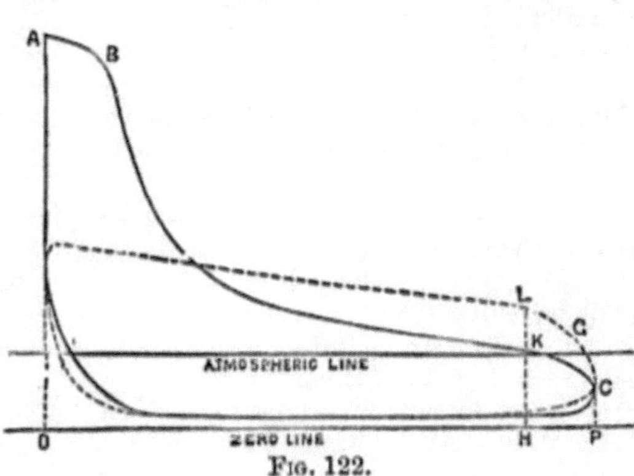

Fig. 122.

end of the stroke, when the cylinder may be considered to be full of steam at its final pressure, and we therefore see that the amount of steam required to perform a given quantity of work when used expansively is less than when it is throttled and no expansion employed. If we take any point, H, of the stroke just before release commences, it will be seen that the quantities of steam required when working expansively and throttled, will be approximately proportional to the absolute pressures H K and H L, respectively. As less steam is used when working expansively the vacuum will be better, unless the quantity of condensing water is increased when working throttled, which would augment the work done by the pumps, and thus further decrease the efficiency of the engine.

Experiments showing the gain in economy by using high-pressure steam and expansion in a simple engine.—Among many such experiments and tests, a careful series made on the engines of the United States ships 'Bache' and 'Dexter,' with cylinders of from 25 inches to 26 inches diameter, and 2 feet to 3 feet stroke, showed the gain in economy that follows the use of high-pressure steam worked expansively, as compared with steam at a lower pressure worked at a reduced rate of expansion.

In the case of the 'Bache,' the most efficient rate of expansion with the steam of about 80 lbs. pressure when the cylinders were jacketed was about five times. Above this expansion the consumption of feed-water per I.H.P. per hour increased. The trials showed that within the limits that would occur in practice, in case of reduced power being required, the initial pressure should not be reduced and the steam worked at a less rate of expansion, but that the original pressure should be maintained with the higher grade of expansion.

In two expansion trials, with about 81 lbs. pressure, the expenditure of feed-water was 24 lbs. per I.H.P. per hour with $8\frac{1}{2}$ expansions, and 27 lbs. with $12\frac{1}{2}$ expansions, whilst when the initial pressure was reduced to 30 lbs. per square inch, and the expansions to $2\frac{1}{2}$, the consumption of feed-water rose to 34 lbs. per I.H.P. per hour (see columns 0, 2, and 3 of table in Chapter XIII.).

The results from the 'Dexter,' with cylinders not jacketed, were very similar.

Reduced power working.—These results are important with regard to the machinery of warships, which on ordinary service is generally worked at reduced power. It is clear from the figures given, that with engines of the kind experimented on, *it is desirable, for the sake of economy, to work expansively to the greatest extent practicable.*

These results were obtained in simple engines with moderate steam pressures, and although there is reason to believe that the fall in economy when working throttled, as compared with working at a higher rate of expansion and pressure, is not so great with triple-expansion engines as indicated in these experiments, it is still appreciable ; so that within ordinary limits, in all engines, the reductions of power should be obtained by linking-up, keeping the steam pressure as high as possible.

The boiler pressure should therefore not be higher than corresponds to the pressure which can be carried in the cylinders, and throttling should be avoided as much as possible, as it unnecessarily strains the boilers and steam pipes.

When working at reduced powers, the linking-up or other expansion gear should be set to the highest grade at which it can be worked with the regulating valve wide open, or nearly so, and the pressure of steam then kept as high as possible in the slide casings. This statement, however, requires the qualification that the boiler pressure should never be kept lower than that necessary for handling the engines readily, so as to be prepared for the emergency of stopping and starting the engines.

Practical limit to amount of economical expansion.—It will be noticed from the figures given for the actual trial of the 'Bache' that beyond a certain amount of expansion, the consumption of steam increases, which shows that there is a practical limit to the attainment of the economy which the theoretical diagram indicates. The reason for this will be explained later.[1]

James Watt, and expansion.—Though it is only in comparatively recent years that much attention has been devoted to the development of high rates of expansion of steam in order to attain economical working, we find that in 1769, James Watt indicated the gain that would ensue from the utilisation of the expansive power of steam, and published a body of principles expressing the conditions necessary for the efficient and economical working of the steam-engine. It is remarkable to note how sound these conclusions were.

It will be interesting to state Watt's principles in his own words. He says :—

My method of lessening the consumption of steam and consequently of fuel in fire engines consists of the following principles :—

First.—That vessel in which the powers of steam are to be employed to work the engine, which is called the cylinder in common fire engines, and which I call the steam vessel, must, during the whole time the engine is at work, be kept as hot as the steam that enters it, first by enclosing it in a case of wood or other material that conducts heat slowly ; secondly, by surrounding it with steam or other heated bodies ; and thirdly, by suffering neither water nor any other substance colder than the steam to enter or touch it during that time.

Secondly.—In engines that are to be worked wholly or partially by the condensation of steam, the steam is to be condensed in vessels distinct from the steam vessels or cylinders, though occasionally communicating with them. These vessels I call condensers, and whilst the engine is working, these condensers ought to be kept as cold as the air in the neighbourhood of the engines, by the application of water or other cold bodies.

Thirdly.—Whatever air or other elastic vapour is not condensed by the cold of the condenser, and may impede the working of the engine, is to be drawn out of the steam vessels or the condensers by means of pumps wrought by the engines themselves or otherwise.

Fourthly.—I intend in many cases to employ the expansive force of steam to press on the pistons, or whatever may be used instead of them, in the same manner as the pressure of the atmosphere is now employed in ordinary fire engines. In cases where cold water cannot be had in plenty, the engines may be wrought by this force of steam only by discharging the steam into the air after it has done its office.

Lastly.—Instead of using water to render the pistons and other parts of

[1] See under 'Liquefaction in Cylinders' in this chapter.

the engine air and steamtight, I employ oils, wax, resinous bodies, fat of animals, quicksilver, and other metals in their fluid state.

During the same year (1769) Watt invented the cutting off of the admission of steam, so as to make it work expansively, but he did not use it till 1776, and only published it in 1782, when he patented it together with his invention of the double-acting engine.

Before proceeding further it will be necessary to define a few terms that will often recur, as it is important that their meanings should be clearly understood.

Relative volume.—By relative volume is meant the ratio of the volume of the steam produced to that of the water from which it was generated.

Specific volume.—The specific volume of steam is the volume, in cubic feet, of one pound of steam at any given pressure.

Saturated steam.—In all gases the density, pressure, and temperature are connected together by certain fixed laws, so that if any two of them be known, the third can be determined. In the case of steam, or any other vapour, in contact with the liquid from which it is generated, there is, for each temperature, a corresponding density, which is the greatest density the vapour can have without its being partially, or wholly, condensed into the liquid form. Consequently for each temperature there is a maximum pressure which the vapour can exert.

A vapour which is at the maximum density and pressure corresponding to its temperature is called '*saturated vapour*.' It is then just at the point of condensation, and any increase of pressure or decrease of temperature will cause some of the vapour to be condensed. Steam, therefore, at any given pressure is said to be *saturated* when it is at its maximum density consistent with its remaining as vapour. Saturated steam is often called *dry steam*, because it is pure steam without any admixture of liquid water.

Formulæ connecting pressure and temperature.—The relations between the pressure and temperature of saturated vapour are very complicated, and, for all practical purposes, the required results are best taken from tables showing the properties of steam (Chapter III.). Many formulæ have been suggested to represent these relations, but most of them are only of theoretical interest. All the most accurate formulæ are of logarithmic form. The best formula to use in the absence of tables is the following :—

$$\log p = 5 \frac{t - 212}{t + 367} + \log 14\cdot7$$

where p = absolute pressure in pounds per square inch
and t = temperature in degrees Fahrenheit.

This represents the experimental results with fair accuracy.

For theoretical work the following formulæ, which are more exact in form, are most useful.

Suppose t the temperature of the boiling-point on Fahrenheit's scale,

T the absolute temperature of the boiling point, $= t + 461$, and p = absolute pressure of the steam in pounds per square inch,

Then,

$$\log p = A - \frac{B}{T} - \frac{C}{T_2} \quad \text{(Rankine's formula)}$$

$$\log p = a - \frac{b}{T} - c \log T \quad \text{(Dupré's formula),}$$

A, B, C and a, b, c, being constants.

The preceding two formulæ are complex in character, and their calculation would be tedious, but they are of great use in theoretical investigations, the latter being the more accurate.

For practical purposes the following roughly approximate formula may be used :—

$$p = \left(\frac{t + 40}{147}\right)^5$$

t = temperature of boiling-point in degrees Fahrenheit, p = absolute pressure in pounds per square inch.

This is nearly correct for absolute pressures between 6 and 60 pounds per square inch, while for pressures near that of the atmosphere the index becomes 5·5 instead of 5, and for high pressures the index becomes 4·5. This formula is very useful as showing in a form which can be easily appreciated the very small increase of temperature which takes place as the pressure of saturated steam is increased.

Formulæ connecting pressure and volume.—The density of a vapour is measured by the space occupied by a given weight, and the volume of one pound of saturated steam as obtained by direct experiment, may be calculated by the approximate empirical formula given by Fairbairn :—

$$v = {\cdot}41 + \frac{389}{p + {\cdot}35}$$

where v = volume of one pound in cubic feet, or *specific volume*, and p = absolute pressure in pounds per square inch.

This formula gives results too large when the pressure of 100 lbs. is exceeded.

The formula may be written :—

$$(p + {\cdot}35)\,(v - {\cdot}41) = 389$$

which indicates an easy way of forming the curve representing the relation between p and v, viz. by determining one point on it by calculation, and drawing an hyperbola through this point with axes distant ·41 cubic feet to the right, and ·35 lbs. per square inch below the original axes. The hyperbola referred to the original axes will be the required curve (see Fig. 123).

The volume of one pound of saturated steam, at any given absolute pressure, may also be calculated from the formula,[1]

$$p\,v^{\frac{17}{16}} = 475$$

where v = volume in cubic feet

and p = absolute pressure in pounds per square inch.

Superheated steam.—If the steam be removed from contact with the water from which it is generated, and additional heat be applied, the pressure being kept constant, its volume and temperature increase,

[1] A more accurate formula is $p\,v^{1\cdot046} = 479$.

as pointed out in Chapter III., and the steam becomes *superheated* ; that is, it contains more heat than that necessary to keep it in a state of saturation at the given pressure. The properties of superheated steam tend to approach those of a perfect gas, and the greater the amount of superheating, the greater does this resemblance become. Our present knowledge of steam in this condition is, however, not great.

Moist or wet steam.—If heat be abstracted from saturated steam, the pressure being kept constant, a portion of the steam liquefies, and the steam becomes *supersaturated* or *moist steam.*

Expansion generally.—We will now consider more particularly the subject of expansion, the laws to which air and steam conform during expansion, and the case of steam expanding in the cylinders of a steam-engine. If the vessel or chamber in which any gas is confined be enlarged or contracted, the gas will still completely fill the vessel, but at an altered pressure.

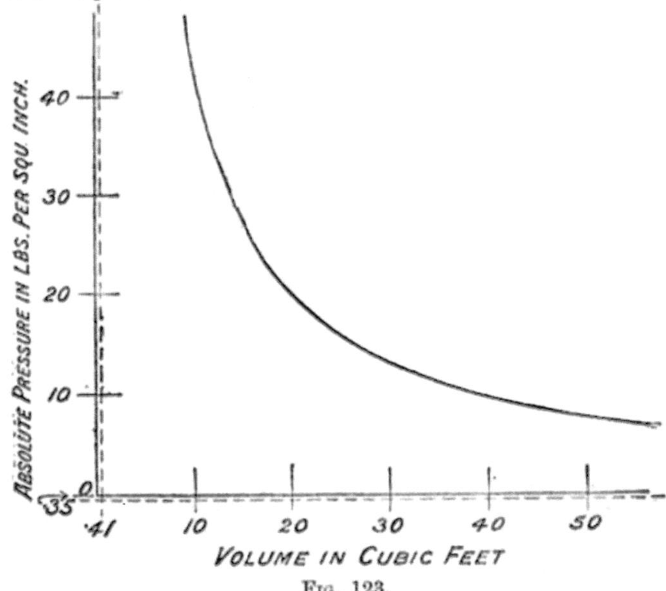

Fig. 123.

Expansion of a perfect gas.—During the process of expansion of a perfect gas, of which atmospheric air may be taken as a type, the pressures and volumes are connected by the law that their product is always proportional to the absolute temperature, or if

p = the pressure,
v = the volume of one pound of the gas,
and T = its absolute temperature,
then $p\,v = c\,T$, where c is a constant quantity.

If the temperature remain constant, the alteration of pressure will bein inverse ratio to the alteration of volume. For example, if two cubic feet of air at 10 lbs. pressure were compressed into a volume of 1 cubic foot, and the temperature were unaltered, its pressure would be increased to 20 lbs. per square inch. If it were allowed to expand into a volume of 4 cubic feet, its pressure would be reduced to 5 lbs. per square inch, and so on. This law is generally expressed by saying that if the temperature remain constant, the pressure varies inversely as the volume, or that the product of the pressure and volume of a perfect gas is constant. Therefore, in this case, $p \times v =$ constant.

Geometrical representation.—This may be shown graphically by means of the ordinates of a rectangular hyperbola referred to its asymptotes as axes, this curve representing the law of expansion of air and other perfect gases; the horizontal distances or abscissæ representing the volumes, and the vertical distances, or ordinates, the pressures. In Fig. 124, o x and o y are two axes drawn at right angles to each other, o

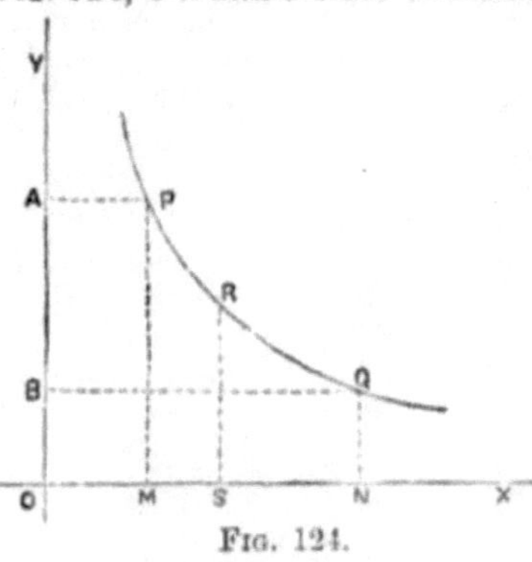

Fig. 124.

being the origin of co-ordinates. Let p m represent the pressure of the gas when its volume is represented by o m, and q n the pressure corresponding to the volume o n. Then, by hypothesis, o m × m p = o n × n q = constant, or $p v$ = constant. The curve passing through a series of such points will therefore be represented by an equation of the form $x y = c$, which is that of a rectangular hyperbola, to which the asymptotes are axes, the ordinates representing pressures and the abscissæ volumes. The pressure corresponding to any other volume, o s, is found by drawing the vertical ordinate through s, cutting the curve in r, the line r s representing the required pressure. The work done by the gas in expanding from the volume o m to the volume o n is represented by the area of the figure p q n m.

Expansion of steam.—The laws followed by steam during expansion are different from those just described of a perfect gas, though the general character of the expansion curve is similar.

Free expansion.—There is an important difference to be noted between the free expansion of steam—that is, its expansion without the performance of any mechanical work—and its ordinary expansion in the cylinders of a steam-engine, in which during expansion it exerts pressure on the piston and performs work. It is very necessary that this difference should be borne in mind in considering the expansive action of steam in an engine.

Imagine one pound of saturated steam at any given pressure to be confined in a cylinder behind a piston, both the cylinder and piston being made of non-conducting materials. Suppose the piston to be very rapidly moved by an *external* force, so that the volume of the steam is increased without its having performed any work on the piston. Then it is evident that as no heat has been either added to, or abstracted from, the steam during the process, the total amount of heat in it is the same at the end of the expansion as it was at the beginning. But, as was pointed out in Chapter III., the total heat of saturated steam increases slowly with its pressure, so that, since the steam was saturated at its original pressure, the total amount of heat in the steam is more than sufficient to keep it in a state of saturation at the reduced pressure at the end of the expansion, so that the steam will be to some extent superheated.

To take a numerical example, suppose one pound of saturated steam at a pressure of two atmospheres to be allowed to expand, without doing any mechanical work, to a pressure of one atmosphere. The total heat in one pound of saturated steam at the pressure of two atmospheres is 1157 thermal units. Since the steam expands without doing any external work, the whole of this heat is retained in the steam when its pressure has been reduced by expansion to one atmosphere. But the total heat necessary to keep a pound of steam at a pressure of one atmosphere in a state of saturation is only 1146 thermal units,[1] and the difference, or 11 thermal units, must have been expended in superheating the steam.

The phenomenon of *free expansion*, or expansion without the performance of mechanical work, is one that often occurs in triple expansion and other stage expansion engines on the admission of steam to the receivers or reservoirs between the cylinders. Taking a triple expansion engine, the final pressure in the high-pressure cylinder is generally somewhat higher, and in many cases considerably higher, than the initial pressure in the intermediate cylinder, so that when the steam escapes from the high-pressure cylinder to the intermediate receiver, its volume is suddenly increased without any external work being done; and the difference between the amount of heat in the steam at the end of the stroke in the high-pressure cylinder and that necessary to keep it in a state of saturation at the reduced pressure is expended in superheating it, if it were saturated on release, or in drying it, if, as is usually the case, it be moist on release.

Work done during expansion.—When, however, steam during its expansion *performs mechanical work*, the conditions of the case are very different from those just discussed. We will in the first place assume that the expansion takes place in a perfectly non-conducting cylinder, so that heat is neither added to nor subtracted from the steam during the operation. Until the true nature of heat was first determined, it had been supposed that when steam was expanded in this way, the total amount of heat in it was the same at the end as it was at the beginning of the expansion. It was, however, always found that water collected in the cylinders, but this was supposed to be due to priming, or the carrying of spray from the boilers to the cylinders, which explanation was often found to be unsatisfactory.

The real cause of the presence of this water in the cylinders was, however, readily explained when the principles of thermo-dynamics became understood. It was then seen that the mechanical work done by the steam during the expansion was due to the fact that a portion of the energy that had been stored in the steam in the form of heat had become transformed into mechanical work, and appeared no longer in the form of heat, so that the total quantity of heat contained in the steam had been diminished. The abstraction of the amount of heat thus changed into mechanical work was sufficient not only to

---

[1] See Chapter III.

lower the temperature of the steam to that corresponding to its reduced pressure, but also to cause some of it to liquefy and become water.

For example, suppose one pound of *saturated* steam at an absolute pressure of 60 lbs. per square inch, to expand in a non-conducting cylinder, without addition or subtraction of heat,[1] pressing a piston before it, till its pressure fell to $3\frac{1}{2}$ lbs. per square inch absolute,

Then, in round numbers,

	ft.-lbs.
Total heat in one pound of steam at 60 lbs. pressure (absolute)	904,000
Work performed during expansion	157,000
Difference—or heat remaining in the steam at end of the expansion	747,000
Heat necessary to keep one pound of steam saturated at a pressure of $3\frac{1}{2}$ lbs. (absolute)	870,000
Deficiency	123,000

The heat equivalent of this amount of work is $\frac{123,000}{772}$ thermal units = about 160. Knowing, then, the latent heat of the steam, the amount that must liquefy is readily obtained. We see, therefore, that a considerable quantity of steam must become liquefied during the expansion.

Liquefaction in cylinders.—In the preceding case, in which the steam has been supposed to expand in a non-conducting cylinder, the water of liquefaction would simply be carried to the condenser at the end of each stroke and no *waste* of heat would ensue. Unfortunately, however, we have to deal in practice with very different conditions, as the cylinders and pistons are necessarily made of conducting materials, by which we shall see the loss from liquefaction in the cylinders becomes very great.

Considering a low-pressure cylinder for the sake of illustration, the hot steam enters the cylinder after it has been open to the condenser for a whole stroke, and when the temperature of the metal to a certain depth below its internal surface may be supposed to approximate to that of the steam passing to the condenser, say from 140° to 150° Fahr. It is therefore evident that a quantity of the entering steam will be condensed on these cool surfaces, and the heat given up by this condensed steam will be expended in raising the temperature of the cylinder, cylinder cover, piston, &c.

As the steam expands, a further portion of it liquefies, due to the work done, and probably exists in the form of spray, or collects on the surfaces of the cylinders, &c. Consequently, when the pressure of the steam has fallen, and its temperature is below that of the metal of the cylinder with its film of condensed steam, this film of water immediately commences to evaporate, as its temperature is higher than that due to the pressure of steam in contact with it, and it will evaporate till its temperature corresponds to that of the expanding steam. It also abstracts heat from the metallic surfaces, tending also to reduce them to the same temperature.

During the period of exhaust, when the steam pressure has fallen to, say, 2 to 3 lbs. absolute, under which pressure water boils at about 140° to 150° Fahr., evaporation of the film of water becomes much more

---

[1] Termed adiabatic expansion. (See later.)

rapid, and further heat is also abstracted from the metallic surfaces. The heat abstracted originally from the entering steam by this agency goes direct to the condenser, and not only does no useful work, but increases the back pressure on the piston to an extent sensibly felt in many unjacketed engines. The cylinder being now in this comparatively cool state, fresh steam enters, and condensation again takes place, with deposition of a film of water, and again raising the temperature of the cylinder surfaces.

This process goes on at every stroke, and the great loss that generally arises from liquefaction in the cylinders of a steam-engine is therefore due to the fact that the water in the cylinder, existing probably as a film on the surfaces, acts as an equaliser of temperature, lowering the initial and raising the final temperatures and pressures, and thus decreasing the efficiency of the steam. The effect is the same as if, during each stroke, a certain portion of the steam passed direct from the boiler to the condenser, without performing any work whatever.

The action of any water remaining in the clearance spaces and pockets is also similar, and also occasions a direct transfer of heat to the exhaust.

Experiments on liquefaction at various rates of expansion in simple engines with unjacketed cylinders.—In some experiments made by Mr. Isherwood, of the United States Navy, it was found that with an expansion of only four times, the amount of steam wasted as described above was more than that performing work, so that the expenditure of heat was more than doubled. The experiments were made on simple engines with unjacketed cylinders, having a piston speed of about 224 feet per minute supplied with saturated, or perhaps rather moist steam. Comparing the actual water used, by measurement, with that shown by the indicator diagrams, the results were that the amount of steam wasted by condensation, clearance, and leakage was 15 per cent. with a ratio of expansion of 1·07, rising to 46 per cent. with an expansion of $2\frac{1}{2}$ times, and to 61 per cent. with a ratio of expansion of 4.

In the United States vessel 'Michigan,' with a steam pressure of 20 lbs., the least consumption of steam per I.H.P. per hour was 32·67 lbs. with a cut-off $\frac{4}{9}$; it did not differ much for cut-offs between $\frac{1}{4}$ and $\frac{7}{10}$, while with greater expansion the consumption rapidly increased, till with a cut-off of about $\frac{1}{11}$ it had risen to 46 lbs. per I.H.P. Mr. Isherwood inferred from these trials, having regard to the effect on the size of the cylinders, that the best point of cut-off for naval vessels of this type was about $\frac{7}{10}$, the consumption then being 34·8 lbs. per I.H.P. per hour.

Cutting off earlier than at $\frac{4}{9}$ of the stroke resulted in loss instead of gain, so that we see how serious was the limitation imposed by practical considerations on the attainment of the theoretical advantage due to expansion.

Owing to the low piston speed and small size of the engine, these cases were unfavourable as regards liquefaction, as both items are powerful factors in increasing the losses due to this, but the experiments, however, show how great the losses by liquefaction become when no provision is made to prevent or reduce them.

As showing the influence of steam pressure on these results another experiment by Mr. Isherwood, on a vessel using steam at the higher pressures of from 40 to 50 lbs., may be mentioned. In this case the most economical point of cut-off was at ·38 stroke, 30·3 lbs. of steam being used per I.H.P. per hour, but there was little difference in economy up to a cut-off of ·56 stroke, which gave a consumption of 30·62 lbs. per I.H.P. At an earlier cut-off than ·38 there was again a loss. With the higher pressure, therefore, we see that expansion could be carried economically to a greater extent.

At still higher pressures the loss from liquefaction remains very considerable unless its effects be counteracted.

Non-conducting materials required for efficient expansion.—The highest theoretical efficiency in the expansive working of the steam can only be realised if the cylinders and pistons are made of perfectly non-conducting materials. It is not sufficient to cover the exterior of the cylinders with such non-conducting materials, which only prevent the passage of heat from the steam to the atmosphere and not the complex action which goes on in the cylinder by the abstraction of heat from the steam during the admission, which heat is again given out to the steam during the exhaust. In this process it is only necessary that the metal of the cylinder should be cooled for a very small distance below the surface, which is probably what happens in practice.

Influence of size of engine.—Small engines with unjacketed cylinders are less economical than large ones. This is easily seen when we consider that the smaller the diameter of cylinder, the greater is the ratio of the surface of the cylinder, &c., which is alternately heated and cooled, to the volume of steam contained in the cylinder, so that the amount of liquefaction is proportionately increased, and the quantity of heat taken up by the metal of the cylinder during admission and given out during exhaust will be proportionately greater.

To take a simple case for illustration. In a cylinder one foot in diameter and one foot long the area of the cylinder surface is 3·1416 square feet, and the area of the piston and cylinder cover 1·5708 square feet, making a total surface of 4·7124 square feet. The volume of the cylinder is ·7854 cubic foot, so that the ratio of surface to volume is 6 to 1. In other words, there are six square feet of heating and cooling surface to one cubic foot of steam used. Now suppose the diameter of the cylinder to be doubled, the stroke remaining the same. In this case the volume is increased in the ratio of 4 to 1, the cylinder containing 3·1416 cubic feet of steam. The areas of the piston and cylinder cover are also increased in the ratio of 4 to 1, but the internal surface of the cylinder is only increased in the ratio of 2 to 1, and the total surface is 12·5664 square feet. In this case, then, there are only 4 square feet of surface for each cubic foot of steam instead of 6 square feet, as in the previous example. We conclude, therefore, that with unjacketed cylinders the percentage of loss from liquefaction will be less in large engines than in small ones, and consequently that large engines are more economical than small ones per unit of power developed, when the cylinders are unjacketed.

Adiabatic expansion of steam.—The law which steam follows when expanded in a non-conducting cylinder *without gain or loss of heat* is represented approximately by the equation

$$p\,v^{\frac{10}{9}} = \text{constant.}$$

The curve representing this is called the *adiabatic curve*, and for the same point of cut-off it falls considerably below the hyperbola.

Zeuner gives the following equation to represent it, viz. :—

$$p\,v^{\left(1\cdot035\,+\,\frac{x}{10}\right)} = \text{constant.}$$

where x is the initial dryness fraction of the steam.

The smaller x is—that is, the more moisture the steam contains—the nearer will the expansion curve of the steam approximate to the hyperbola.

When the steam is quite dry $x = 1$, and the equation to the curve becomes

$$p\,v^{1\cdot135} = \text{constant,}$$

which does not differ much from the previous formula

$$p\,v^{\frac{10}{9}} = \text{constant.}$$

Zeuner's equation does not hold good for cases in which the steam contains more than 30 per cent. of moisture, i.e. for values of x below ·7.

Comparison of various expansion curves of steam.—It will be interesting to compare the three expansion curves we have now referred to—viz. the hyperbola, the saturation curve, and the adiabatic curve, representing the expansion of the volume A B of steam to the final volume O P. The three curves will be relatively as shown in Fig. 125.

B C, the hyperbola, lies above the others, B D is the saturation curve, and B E, the lowest, is the adiabatic curve.

As we saw previously, a considerable amount of steam

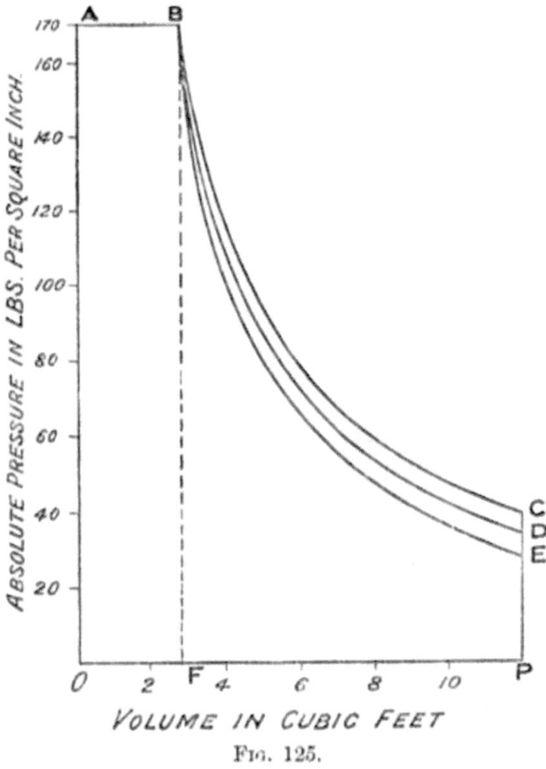

Fig. 125.

must be liquefied when steam expands adiabatically doing external work. This liquefaction of a certain volume of steam reduces the pressure as the expansion proceeds, which explains the falling away of the curve B E from the curve B D, which represents always the same weight of dry saturated steam. The difference D E represents the final fall of pressure.

If steam expands according to the saturation curve B D, then clearly heat must be added to the expanding steam by a steam jacket or other means to bring about this result. As, however, there is more heat in steam of high pressure than in that of low pressure, the amount of heat to be added will be less than that equal to the external work done, by the difference between the total heats of the steam in its initial and final conditions.

If the amount of heat added to the steam when expanding exceeds that referred to above for the curve B D, the steam will become super-heated if it be initially dry, but the transfer to the steam of such an amount of heat as to superheat it, is very improbable in practice. If the steam initially contains a certain amount of water, which is the usual condition in practice, a portion of the moisture will be evaporated. In each case a rise of pressure ensues beyond the satura-tion curve, while if the supply of heat is sufficient, the curve will approximate to the hyperbola B C, which represents the expansion of a perfect gas at a constant temperature.

The amount of heat necessary to be added to steam during expan-sion to maintain the hyperbolic curve can be calculated from the amount of work done during expansion—i.e. the area B C P F in Fig. 125, and the difference between the total heats of the fluid before and after expansion.

It will be found that considerable differences in the amount of heat supplied will make very small differences in the form of the expansion curve, and this renders it difficult to analyse the performances of engines from the indicator diagram. The result is, however, that for practical purposes the expansion curve can be assumed to be the ordinary hyperbola, by which all calculations of pressure and power are much facilitated.

Construction of various curves of expansion.—The hyperbolic curve is readily drawn by the geometrical rule previously described. The saturation curve can be most readily drawn from a table of properties of steam, as given in Chapter III. The adiabatic curve may be constructed either by calculation, or more simply by utilising the fact that the horizontal distances of this curve from the saturation curve are equal to that of the latter from the hyperbola.

CHAPTER XIII.

METHODS OF INCREASING THE EXPANSIVE EFFICIENCY OF STEAM.

THE methods which are or have been adopted for preventing or reducing the loss by the liquefaction of steam in the cylinders of a steam-engine, and thus increasing its expansive efficiency, are :—

1. Surrounding the cylinder with a casing or jacket kept full of steam of high temperature, i.e. ' steam-jacketing.'

2. Superheating the steam before it is admitted to the cylinder.

3. Dividing the expansion of steam into stages, as in compound engines (either double, triple, or quadruple expansion).

Steam-jacketing.—The steam jacket was invented by James Watt, but it is not certain that he properly understood the principles of its action, and most engineers at that period, arguing from the erroneous theory of caloric, which was then generally accepted, deemed it unnecessary and discontinued its use, and it was considered to be sufficient to clothe the cylinders carefully with non-conducting materials to prevent loss from radiation.

The use of the steam jacket was, however, retained in a few special cases, such as the pumping engines for the Cornish mines, and in such engines the economy properly due to high rates of expansion was realised. These engines were for many years famous as being the most economical in the country.

In almost all other engines of the period under review, and certainly in all marine engines, steam jackets were not fitted. The result was that little or no practical advantage ensued if the steam were expanded more than from two to three times, and this became an article of faith amongst engineers in general, for its truth in the case of unjacketed cylinders was manifested, not only by experiments, but also by every-day experience in the working of engines.

When, however, the true nature of the action of expansion in a steam cylinder was discovered, and it was ascertained that the work of the engine was performed by the abstraction of heat from the steam and its conversion into mechanical work during expansion, which caused a portion of the steam to liquefy, it was seen to be necessary, in order to increase the efficiency of the steam, to make provision for the addition of heat to the steam during its expansion.

The reintroduction of steam jackets has therefore taken place, and they are now fitted to most modern engines. Experience has shown their value as regards the economical use of high-pressure steam, although, as will be seen later, their usefulness becomes less as the size and speed of the engine increases.

Action of the steam jacket.—The effect of the jacket is to reduce the changes of temperature of the metal of the cylinder that take place in the unjacketed engine. The heat added to the steam expanding in the cylinder should be just sufficient to prevent any appreciable quantity of it becoming liquid, and under these conditions the expansion diagram should be a curve representing the successive pressures and corresponding volumes of a given weight of saturated steam.

The work done by the steam necessarily causes liquefaction to take place somewhere in jacketed as well as in unjacketed engines ; but in the former case, if the steam jacket is able to supply sufficient heat to the expanding steam, this liquefaction takes place in the jacket, where it produces no subsequent bad effect, and the condensed steam is simply collected and returned again to the boiler, and no *waste* of heat ensues in consequence. It was pointed out in Chapter XII. that the liquefaction due to the work done did not constitute in itself a loss of work, but that it leads indirectly to a loss of efficiency, from its action in equalising the initial and final temperatures ; and, consequently, it is in the reduction of this action that the efficiency of the steam jacket lies.

The preceding remarks explain the theory of the economy due to steam jackets, but in practical cases they are not so efficient as to warrant the assumption that liquefaction is prevented entirely. On the contrary, even with jackets, there is usually considerable liquefaction, but the liquefaction is reduced by proper jacketing and economy of steam generally obtained.

Moisture in steam considerably increases its power of conduction of heat. By means of the steam jacket the steam is kept drier, so as to be a bad conductor of heat, and the moisture it contains, though probably sufficient to lubricate the piston, is thus prevented from increasing to such an extent as to carry away any considerable amounts of heat from the metal of the cylinder and piston to the condenser.

Extent of steam-jacketing.—Steam jackets were at first fitted to the barrels of cylinders only ; they were then added to the covers and ends, and in some cases arrangements were made, by fitting hollow piston-rods and telescopic steam pipes, to admit steam to the interior of the piston, thus causing the steam during its expansion to be entirely surrounded with a hot steam jacket. There is, however, more advantage to be derived from jacketing the barrels than from jacketing the ends or the piston, because the friction of the piston keeps the surface of the cylinder barrel comparatively clean, whilst the surfaces of the ends and piston soon become covered with a deposit which interferes with the passage of heat through them to the steam. The arrangements for admitting steam to the interior of the piston are also, necessarily, of a somewhat complicated character, so that pistons are now seldom or never jacketed. The ends and covers are also generally unjacketed. In the Royal Navy only the cylinder barrels are steam-jacketed in modern vessels.

Experiments to prove the economy due to steam-jacketing.—Many experiments have been made from time to time to ascertain the gain in economy due to the use of the steam jacket. The late Mr. John Penn made some experiments on this subject, but although the working pressure was only 7 lbs. per square inch, when the cylinders were jacketed with steam of this pressure, the gain was considerable and the economy increased as the pressure in the jacket was increased.

Some valuable quantitative experiments to ascertain the efficiency of steam jackets and other information were made by Mr. Emery on the cylinders of the 'Bache,' and they deserve careful study. The results are given in the following tables. In these trials the respective ratios of expansion, both with and without the jacket in use, were practically the same in many trials, so that the results represented very fairly the economy due to the use of the steam jacket.

Columns 1 to 6 give the results when the engine was worked as a simple expansion engine, with steam pressure of 80 lbs., and the most economical results were obtained, both with and without the jacket in use, when the ratio of expansion was about five times. Above this amount of expansion the consumption of steam increased considerably even when the jackets were used, while without the jackets in use the consumption increased with much greater rapidity. When the jacket was not in operation 26·25 lbs. of feed-water were required per I.H.P. per hour, whilst when the jacket was used only 23·15 lbs. were required, showing at the most economical point of cut-off a saving of 11·77 per cent. by the application of the steam jacket.

At the higher rates of expansion the percentage of saving due to the jacket was much greater, being, when the rate of expansion was about eight times, 18·67 per cent., while at about twelve it was 22·7 per cent.

When the engine was worked as a compound engine, the amount of feed-water required per I.H.P. per hour was practically the same from a total rate of expansion of 5·7 up to a total rate of 9·2, the most economical results being obtained with between 6 and 7 expansions. Below 5·7 expansions there was a loss, as compared with 6 or 7 expansions, while at 16·8 expansions there was a considerable loss (see Columns 7 and 11). For about the same expansion of $6\frac{1}{2}$ to 7, the consumption of feed-water when the jacket was not used was 23·03 lbs., whilst when the jacket was used only 20·33 lbs. were required, per I.H.P. per hour, showing in this case a saving of 11·75 per cent. (see Columns 9 and 13). Again, for the rate of expansion of 5·6 to 5·7 the saving indicated in Columns 8 and 12 is rather greater than this.

Experiments of the Institution of Mechanical Engineers, &c.—The Institution of Mechanical Engineers has recently made valuable inquiries on this question, their results showing that from 10 per cent. to 17 per cent. was saved by the steam jacket in double or triple expansion engines, and about 20 per cent. in simple engines. In many cases a comparatively small quantity of steam liquefied in the jacket caused a very large saving of total steam. For instance, in one experiment on a small engine, a condensation in the jackets of 7 per cent. of total steam effected a saving of 25 per cent. in total steam used.

Professor O. Reynolds has also recorded experiments made with a small experimental triple expansion engine, showing that the liquefaction amounted to 40 per cent., even when the expansion was split up into three stages, and that the steam was rendered nearly dry on exhausting to the condenser by steam-jacketing all cylinders with boiler pressure steam.

On the other hand, recent experiments made with and without steam in jackets on H.M.S. 'Argonaut' must be mentioned. These

| — | | Working as simple engines | | | | | | | Working as compound engines | | | | | | | |
| | | Jacket in use | | | | Jacket not in use | | | L.P. jacket in use | | | | | L.P. jacket not in use | | |
		0[1]	1	2	3	4	5	6	7	8	9	10	11	12	13	14
1. Duration of trial	hrs.	1·88	2·11	1·68	2·1	2·05	1·98	1·80	2·0	1·98	1·93	2·06	1·73	2·13	2·06	1·83
2. Pressure in boilers	lbs.	30·8	79·5	81·0	80·8	78·1	79·6	81·0	79·0	80·1	80·2	80·3	81·3	80·3	80·28	82·0
3. Total ratio of expansion		2·2	5·1	8·6	12·6	5·3	7·6	11·8	4·2	5·7	6·9	9·2	16·8	5·6	6·6	9·1
4. Vacuum in condensers	ins.	24·0	25·5	25·3	24·6	24·2	23·8	24·0	26·5	26·5	26·5	26·5	24·5	24·6	24·3	24·0
5. Revolutions per minute		45·3	53·8	46·2	39·9	47·0	44·9	37·3	60·6	56·3	53·2	48·2	38·9	49·2	47·7	42·6
6. Indicated horse-power		66·7	116·0	74·6	54·8	89·1	71·8	47·2	134·5	110·5	99·2	77·5	46·4	85·8	77·0	55·9
7. Water used per indicated horse-power per hour by measurement	lbs.	34·03	23·15	24·09	27·11	26·25	29·62	35·07	21·17	20·37	20·33	20·71	25·1	23·21	23·03	23·76
8. Ditto estimated from indicator diagrams	lbs.	24·04	16·25	15·58	16·42	17·35	17·76	21·03	16·2	15·25	14·77	15·76	18·5	12·34	12·31	12·7
9. Percentage of water used accounted for by indicator diagrams of low-pressure cylinder		70·7	70·2	64·6	60·5	66·1	59·9	59·9	76·6	74·9	72·6	76·1	73·8	53·2	53·4	53·4

[1] Note that this trial was made with low-pressure steam of about 30 lbs. All the remaining trials were with steam pressure of about 80 lbs.

experiments showed but little difference between the two methods of working ; in fact, the water consumption with steam in jackets was slightly greater than without steam in jackets, but in this case the jacket pressures used did not much exceed the initial pressure in cylinders while the engine is large and of high speed.

Jacket steam pressure.—From the explanation given of the action of steam jackets, it appears that for high efficiency they should, if practicable, be filled with steam of a considerably higher temperature than that being admitted to the cylinder, for as there must be some difference in temperature between the inside and the outside of the cylinder to cause heat to flow to the inside surface, the temperature of the inside surface of the cylinder would be otherwise less than that of the entering steam.   Unfortunately, however, practical difficulties are met with if the jacket pressure is high compared with the initial pressure, and several cases of scoring of cylinder liners in the Royal Navy have been attributed to this cause.   It seems undesirable to pass the steam, *on its way* to the cylinder, through the jacket, because in this case it would be partially condensed before admission to the cylinder, and its efficiency consequently reduced by the presence of water, although it is sometimes considered that the rush of steam past the jacket surface would increase the capacity of the latter for receiving heat by sweeping away any film of condensed steam which prevents the ready passage of heat.

Influence of size on economy.—Calculation shows that the jacket area is comparatively less in large than in small engines, for whilst the volumes of the cylinders increase as the square of the diameter, the area of the jacket surface only increases directly as the diameter.   The percentage of saving from the use of the jacket may, therefore, reasonably be expected to be greater in small than in large engines.

Influence of speed.—Similarly, as regards speed, it will be readily admitted that with low speeds the cylinder will have sufficient time in which to abstract heat from the steam and give it up again during exhaust.   When, however, the speed becomes very great, the changes between steam and exhaust are so rapid that there is not sufficient time for the cylinder walls to exercise their full deleterious effect.   This no doubt accounts for the fair amount of economy obtained in the cylinders of the fast-running torpedo-boat destroyers.   We conclude, therefore, that steam jackets become less efficient in action as the size and speed of the engine increase.   Trials by the late Mr. Willans confirm this conclusion as regards speed.

The arrangements of steam pipes and drain pipes fitted for steam jackets include a drain pipe from the lowest part of the steam jacket, led to a collector near the lower platform fitted with a glass water gauge, by means of which the amount of condensed water present can be seen and regulated, and any accumulation blown off into the feed-tank or condenser, or steam traps may be fitted for this purpose.

Amount of heat transmitted by the jacket.—The amount of heat transmitted from an ordinary steam jacket to the cylinder steam is, in practical examples, generally not sufficient to altogether prevent liquefaction in the cylinders.

Supposing even that the jacket were maintained at a much higher temperature than the steam entering the cylinder, it is known that dry steam is a very bad conductor of heat, so that when the steam has received sufficient heat to make it dry, or nearly so, it will receive additional heat very slowly, so that superheating due to the action of the jacket does not occur in practice.

Superheated steam.—Another method for preventing liquefaction in the cylinder, which was used with steam of low pressure, was to superheat the steam before its admission. It was pointed out in Chapter III. that when the steam was kept in contact with the water from which it was generated, the temperature was dependent on the pressure, but when heat was added to the steam, in a separate chamber, the pressure being kept constant, the volume and temperature were increased and the steam became superheated—that is, it received more heat than was necessary to keep it in a state of saturation.

The usual method of superheating low-pressure steam was to cause it to pass, on its way to the engines, through or around tubes placed in the uptakes of the boilers, the other surfaces of the tubes being in contact with the hot gases escaping from the furnaces.

The superheaters were however, cumbrous, and troublesome to keep in an efficient condition, and their decay was rapid.

Economy due to superheaters.—Much of the economy which resulted from their use was due to the fact that, in addition to increasing the efficiency of the steam, they also increased the efficiency of the boiler by extracting some of the waste heat passing off into the atmosphere in the uptake gases.

In the old boilers worked with steam pressures of 30 lbs. per square inch and under, considerable gain in economy resulted from the use of superheated steam, for to steam of such pressures a large quantity of heat could be added without increasing the temperature to a dangerous extent. In any case, however, in which a superheater is applied, it may be expected to increase the efficiency of the steam, even if the steam at the engine be not superheated ; for long steam pipes, insufficiency of lagging or clothing, or priming in the boilers, tends to cause the steam to enter the cylinders in a moist condition, which reduces its efficiency. The superheater in this case would at least dry the steam, and the additional heat added would tend to prevent its falling below the temperature of saturation during its passage through the steam pipes, &c.

The late Mr. John Penn found that a saving of fuel of about 20 per cent. was effected by superheating steam of 20 lbs. pressure per square inch above the atmosphere, to the extent of 100° Fahr. The temperature of saturated steam at this pressure is 259° Fahr., so that in his experiments the initial temperature of the steam was only 359° Fahr., which was not found too high.

As a simple illustration of the relation between saturated and superheated steam, it may be noted that steam of 30 lbs. pressure, above the atmosphere, corresponding temperature 274°, if superheated to the extent of 66° Fahr., falls to saturation when expanded without gain or loss of heat, in the ratio of about 2 to 3, or, more accurately, when cut off in the cylinder is at ·65 of the stroke. It is evident, in such cases, in order that a moderate amount of expansion should be efficiently carried out without the use of an excessive degree of superheating, that steam jackets should be fitted as well as superheaters, otherwise in simple engines the economy of working which follows the absence of liquefaction will not be fully realised.   Most of the old marine engines made to work with steam of 30 lbs. pressure were therefore fitted both with steam jackets and superheaters, and they formed the most economical type in use before the introduction of compound engines and higher pressure steam.

For higher pressures, the gain resulting from superheating is not only less, but the difficulty of largely increasing the temperature of the steam, which is then considerable, increases, and the practical difficulty of dealing with such high temperatures, in association with dryness, becomes greater.

Causes of abandonment of superheaters.—When the temperature of the superheated steam was above a certain point, its effect on the engines was found to be injurious.   The internal lubricants became burnt, so that the valves and pistons, working dry, were found to grind the cylinder and slide-faces, and soon caused leakage ; also, the packing in the stuffing-boxes was soon destroyed.   With more modern engines, also, where internal lubrication is either not used or reduced to a minimum, extreme dryness of the working surfaces must be avoided as much as possible.

It is not so much the high temperature that causes trouble, as the extreme dryness which results when such high temperatures are obtained by superheating.   For example, but little extra difficulty will be found with the working parts, for an increase of temperature obtained by increase of steam pressure, while if the same increase be obtained by superheating, the absence of the lubricating effect of the moisture usually contained in the steam causes difficulty with the working parts.   For these reasons, and also on account of the rapid corrosion previously referred to, superheaters have not been fitted in modern high-pressure marine engines.

Recent and future practice.— There is a tendency now, however, to revive the practice of superheating, in view of the admitted economy, especially on land engines, as no other improvement at present known is calculated to afford such a certain gain as regards economy.   In some experiments made on land during the last few years, satisfactory results from the use of superheaters in the uptakes have been obtained, the steam being superheated to the extent of about 80° Fahr. and a saving of about 20 per cent. reported.   This amount of saving is probably rather over-estimated, but it may be taken as not less than 15 per cent. with a superheating of 100° Fahr. above the saturation temperature.   In the writer's opinion, superheating to this extent is quite possible, for although difficulties exist, they are probably not now insurmountable, and the practice is worthy of further trial.

CHAPTER XIV.

COMPOUND OR STAGE EXPANSION ENGINES.

WE have referred to steam-jacketing, and in a lesser degree to super-heating, as tending to prevent liquefaction in engine cylinders, but they are far from doing so entirely, in ordinary engines, and in order to realise the full benefits of a high ratio of expansion, the system of dividing the expansion into stages, carried out in two or more separate and successive cylinders, must be adopted. Engines of this description are generally called '*compound or stage expansion engines.*'

Invention and abandonment of compound engines.—This system was invented as far back as 1781, but was, however, soon abandoned, for it is principally adapted for high pressures, which were not then in use ; but when the fact was fully accepted that in order to make long voyages remunerative, the pressures and rates of expansion of steam must be increased so as to reduce the expenditure of coal, the question of the stresses brought on the framing and shafting of the engine by working the steam at a high rate of expansion in a single cylinder became one of great importance ; as, in large engines especially, the variation of pressure during the stroke would be so great that the maximum stresses produced would probably be dangerous to the structure unless it were made excessively strong. Attention was again directed to the employment of the compound engine, in which the high-pressure steam acts on a small piston only, and a reduced pressure on the large piston, which reduces the maximum stresses on the framing, &c , and makes the turning moments more uniform.

Re-introduction of system. Causes of advantages.—With the increase of pressure the system was re-introduced, and the economy resulting was so decided that its application for marine purposes soon became universal. As the working pressures increased additional stages in the expansion became desirable, and this led to the *triple* and *quadruple expansion* engines now so extensively used. The principle is simply an extension of James Watt's idea of keeping the steam vessel or cylinder as warm as possible and the condenser as cool as possible. With simple condensing engines, the cylinder into which the boiler steam is admitted is also open to the condenser for nearly the whole period of the return stroke of the piston, so that its temperature, or at least that of a certain layer of thickness of the internal surface, together with any water remaining in the cylinder, may be supposed to be considerably cooled during this part of the stroke, to be again raised in temperature by the liquefaction of the entering steam, thereby causing a considerable loss due to the direct transfer of heat to the condenser, without the performance of any work, as previously explained.

This loss by liquefaction is greater, the greater is the difference between the initial and final temperatures, so that with increased pressures and temperatures, the difference or range of temperature in the cylinder becomes greater, and the loss from this cause when expanding to the full extent in a single cylinder is proportionately increased. If, however, we divide the expansion into two or more stages, the cylinder into which the high-pressure steam is admitted is never open to the condenser, and its temperature is never reduced below that of the intermediate receiver ; also, the steam condensed and evaporated in the first cylinder re-appears as working steam in the second cylinder, instead of passing straight to the condenser. The useful work done by it is one source of the economy of stage expansion engines. The loss from liquefaction in the second cylinder is also reduced, in consequence of the smaller range of temperature between admission and exhaust in that cylinder.

Another way in which the adoption of stage expansion engines has increased the efficiency of the steam, is by reducing the clearance spaces into which the boiler steam is admitted. These clearance spaces are much smaller in the high-pressure cylinder of a compound engine than they would be had the whole expansion taken place in one large cylinder. At each stroke of the engine this space has to be filled, while no work is being done by the piston, so that the loss of efficiency due to the waste of steam by clearance spaces is much less in the compound engine than in the simple engine. On the other hand, the compound or stage expansion engine has losses of efficiency, due to sudden expansion and wire-drawing between the cylinders, which do not exist in the simple engine, but these losses are of much smaller magnitude than the gains just described, so that to obtain the highest economy from high-pressure steam the stage expansion engine is essential.

We have only referred in this chapter to the effect on the efficiency of steam by the use of compound or stage expansion engines, but, as will appear later, this type of engine has other advantages.

Trials of double compound versus simple engines with the same steam pressure and ratio of expansion.—The experiments made by Mr. Emery on the engines of the 'Bache' gave valuable information as to the comparative efficiencies of the two systems, and the results tabulated in Chapter XIII should be carefully studied in this connection.

On reference to the table it will be seen that the consumption of water per I.H.P. per hour was always considerably less in the compound than in the simple expansion engine when working at about the same rate of expansion. This is the case when the cylinders are jacketed, as well as when they are not jacketed.

From Columns 1 and 8 with steam jacket in use, it is seen that with an expansion of between five and six times, which proved to be the most economical rate for each type of engine, the feed-water used per I.H.P. per hour was in the simple engine 23·15 lbs., whilst in the compound engine it was only 20·36 lbs., showing in this case a gain in economy at 80 lbs. steam pressure by the use of the compound engine of rather over 12 per cent. At the higher rates of expansion the percentage of economy due to the compound engines was still higher.

The consumption of feed-water for the power developed was, both in the compound and in the simple engine, considerably greater at the high rates of expansion shown in Columns 3 and 11 than at the lower rates.

In each case, therefore, the efficiency of the steam was considerably reduced when the rate of expansion was increased beyond a certain point.

Tri-compound or triple expansion engines.—For steam pressures above 120 lbs. to 130 lbs. per square inch, which are now generally used, it has been found desirable to extend the compound system by dividing the expansion into three stages, so as to reduce the range of temperature in each cylinder, and still further limit the effects of liquefaction. The triple expansion type is now the most common one for modern marine engines, and the gain in economy by its use over the previous double compound engines fitted is well established. The saving of fuel with a triple expansion engine of 150 lbs. to 160 lbs. pressure may be taken as about 20 per cent. compared with the compound engine of about 90 lbs. pressure.

The consumption of good fuel with the most successful triple expansion engines, where the engines are designed principally with a view to economy only, as in many vessels of the mercantile marine, is reported to be from $1\frac{1}{3}$ lbs. to $1\frac{1}{2}$ lbs. per I.H.P. per hour. The average of 28 steamers collected by Mr. Blechynden in 1891 gave 1·52 lbs. as the average consumption per I.H.P. with steam pressure averaging 158 lbs. per square inch at 64 revolutions per minute.

Experiments on double versus triple compound engines.—A valuable series of experiments was made on six steamships by a committee of

—	Double compound, cylinders not jacketed			Triple compound, more or less jacketed. (See line 9)		
Name of vessel . . .	Fusi Yama 1	Colchester 2	Ville de Douvres 3	Meteor 4	Tartar 5	Iona 6
1. Duration of trial hrs.	14	11	9	17	10	16
2. Pressure in boilers lbs.	71	95	120	160	158	179
3. Total ratio of expansion	6·1	6·1	5·7	10·6	15·7	19
4. Condenser vacuum ins.	25	25	$20\frac{1}{2}$	$24\frac{1}{2}$	26	$27\frac{3}{4}$
5. Revolutions per minute .	55·6	86·5	36·8	71·8	70	61·1
6. I.H.P.	371	990	2977	1994	1087	645
7. Actual water used per I.H.P. per hour lbs. by measurement	21·17	21·73	20·77	14·98	19·83 [1]	13·35
8. Percentage of water used, accounted for by indicator diagrams of L.P. cylinder	70·8	52·7	72·5	75·3	60·3	59·1
9. Particulars of cylinder jackets	None	None	None	All	I. & L. only	H. only

[1] Probably included priming water.

the Institute of Mechanical Engineers which reported in 1892. A few particulars of these trials, which included double and triple compound engines, are shown on the last page. The double compound engines were not steam-jacketed, and the reader should compare the results of these trials given in Columns 1 and 2, with 71 and 95 lbs. of steam respectively, with the corresponding trials without jackets in the 'Bache,' with 80 lbs. pressure, given in Columns 12, 13, and 14 of the table in Chapter XIII. It will be seen that the feed-water used in these recent trials was rather less than in the 'Bache.'

The great efficiency of the 'Iona' should be noticed, due to her high steam pressure of 180 lbs. and expansion of 19 times. Her consumption of 13·35 lbs. of water per I.H.P. per hour is about the lowest well authenticated result with a large marine engine.

The conclusion to be drawn from these interesting experiments is that a substantial gain in economy is obtained by the triple expansion engines with higher steam pressures, which is shown by the consumptions of feed-water for the various vessels indicated on line 7.

General conclusions.—It will appear from the observations made in the preceding chapters :—

1. That economy is increased by the use of higher steam pressures, and expanding the steam, provided the expansion is not excessive.

2. That the amount of expansion required with high-pressure steam can be carried out most efficiently and economically in stage expansion engines, so that the variations of pressure and temperature in each cylinder are comparatively small.

3. That it is desirable with high pressures and ratios of expansion to surround the cylinder with a jacket filled with steam of high temperature to add to the efficiency of the expansion. These jackets have an important effect in small and slow-moving engines, but become less effective as size and speed are increased.

4. That additional efficiency of the steam would result from the use of superheaters, so that renewed efforts to overcome the practical difficulties attending their use appear desirable.

CHAPTER XV.

REGULATING AND EXPANSION VALVES AND GEAR.

Regulating valve.—The steam, after leaving the separator, when this is fitted, arrives at the regulating valve for the engines. The object of this valve is to regulate the supply of steam to the engines, so that the speed may be varied as required.

The regulating valve, as originally fitted, consisted simply of a flat plate or disc in the pipe, having a central spindle passing through to the outside of the pipe, by means of which it could be turned so as to either close or open the passage as required. This is called a 'throttle valve,' but it is now seldom fitted, as it is difficult to keep even approximately tight with high-pressure steam, and it does not admit of sufficiently exact regulation of the speed of the engines.

Flat valves, called 'gridiron valves,' were next used. They consisted of a number of bars with open spaces between them, sliding on a corresponding seating.

As pressures increased, however, their friction became too great, and they were superseded by the 'double beat' or equilibrium valve, now used for regulating purposes.

Equilibrium or double-beat valve.—A sketch of the double-beat regulating valve is shown in Fig. 126. It consists of two valves on the same spindle ; the steam pressure acts on the top of one valve and on the bottom of the other, so that the valve is nearly in equilibrium, and little force is required to move it from its seat. The larger diameter of the lower valve in the arrangement shown must obviously be somewhat less than the smaller diameter of the upper valve, to enable the valve to be put in its place. The amount of opening for a certain height of lift is practically double that for the same lift of an ordinary single conical valve of the same diameter.

Manœuvring valve.—Owing to the frequent small changes of speed of engines required in war vessels, when steaming in the company of other vessels, due to the necessity of 'keeping station,' it has been found necessary in these ships to fit a special small valve. This valve is shown at A, in Fig. 126, and it admits steam from one side to the other of the regulating valve. It is found that the latter is so large that a small change in its opening makes a considerable alteration in the speed of the engine when steaming slowly, and small changes of speed are very difficult to obtain by its means.

By means of the small manœuvring valve, however, these necessarily small changes in the speed of the engine to meet the requirements of station keeping are secured. The valve fitted is generally an ordinary screw-down valve.

These regulating and manœuvring valves are worked by screw gearing, so that the speed of the engine may be adjusted with more exactness than is possible with an arrangement of levers. There is also much less back-lash with such gearing than with levers. The wheels leading to the gearing of the regulating and manœuvring valves are placed in convenient situations close to the starting position.

Expansion valves.—Although of little or no importance now for marine purposes, the arrangements fitted in most simple engines, and in some of the early compound engines, to secure economy by using the steam more expansively than could be advantageously effected by the ordinary slide-valves, are worthy of notice. To secure high rates of expansion, separate valves, usually called 'expansion valves,' were fitted for the purpose of cutting off the admission of the steam at a sufficiently early part of the stroke. The sole office of these valves was to

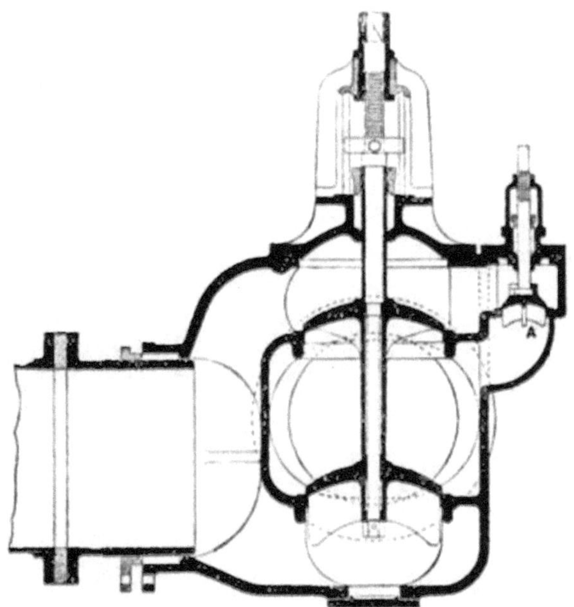

Fig. 126.

stop the admission of steam at the required point at each stroke, and they had nothing further to do with the distribution of the steam, the remaining operations being effected by the slide-valves.

Some early compound engines also had separate expansion valves fitted to the low-pressure cylinder in order to regulate the distribution of work between the two cylinders.

These valves were usually of the gridiron type, a portion of one such valve being shown in Fig. 127. The steam enters the expansion valve casing, and when the valve is in such a position that the ports are open, the steam passes into the slide-valve casing underneath. When the valve is in its middle position all the ports are wide open. A great number of ports are desirable, so that the amount of opening may be considerably affected by a small motion of the valve, and the cut-off, therefore, sharper and more effective.

Expansion gear.—Expansion valves are worked by eccentrics on the crank-shaft, and the extent of the travel of the valve is regulated by a link, fitted with a sliding block attached to the expansion valve rod. The gear should be so arranged that when the engines are not being worked expansively the motion of the valve should, if possible, be reduced to zero, the valve remaining in its central position, with all the ports wide open, or the motion reduced to such an extent that it has no appreciable effect on the passage of the steam, so that the handling of the engines, going astern, &c., is not affected. By altering the position of the block in the link so as to increase the travel of the valve the point of cut-off is made earlier. The greater the travel the higher will be the rate of expansion.

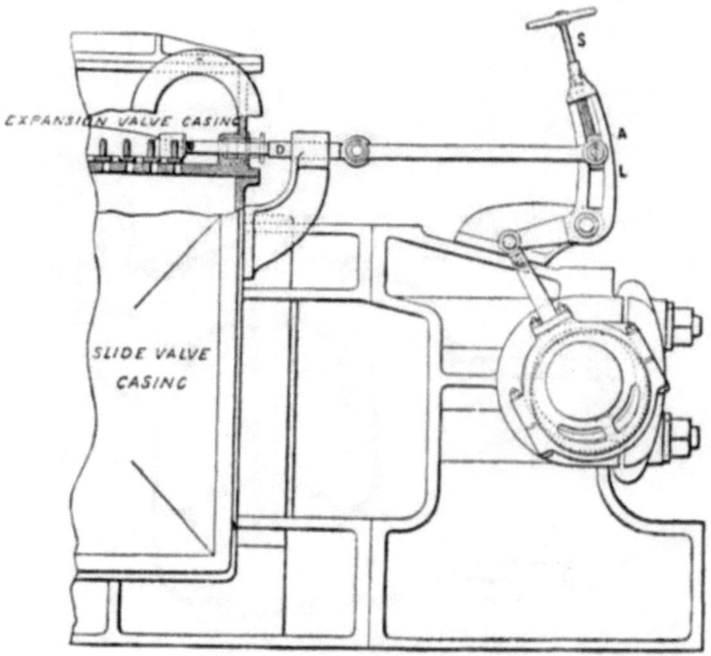

Fig. 127.

Fig. 127 shows the arrangement of expansion gear for a valve of this description as fitted to an old horizontal engine, and the method of its action can be easily seen from the diagram. By altering the position of the block A on the vibrating lever L by means of the screw s, the travel of the expansion valve is altered, and the point of cut-off of the steam regulated as may be required.

Increase of clearance volume.—With an expansion valve such as described above, it will be seen that the clearance between the expansion valve and the main slide-valve was considerable, and when the clearance between the main slide-valve and piston was also added, the total clearance space to be filled with fresh steam at each stroke was so great as to neutralise much of the advantage due to the use of an expansion valve. The actual amount of expansion was consequently much less than that indicated by the fraction of the cut-off.

Expansion valve on back of main slide.—To overcome this defect the gridiron valve was sometimes fitted to work on ports formed in the back of the main slide-valve, as shown in Fig. 128, the expansion valve being worked as before by a separate eccentric, and the cut-off regulated by the amount of travel of the expansion valve.

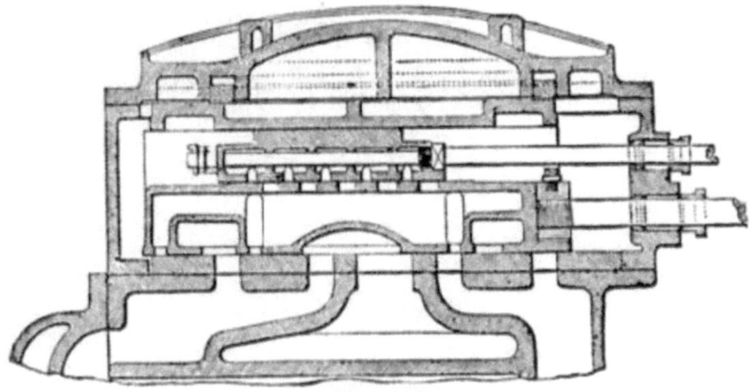

FIG. 128.

Another plan of fitting an expansion valve on the back of the main slide-valve is shown in Fig. 129. In this case the expansion valve was constructed of two separate but similar parts, connected together by a right- and left-handed screw, by means of which their distance from each other might be varied. In this arrangement the travel of the valve was constant, and the point of cut-off was regulated by the distance between the two plates that formed the valve, which could be varied as required by moving the wheel in connection.

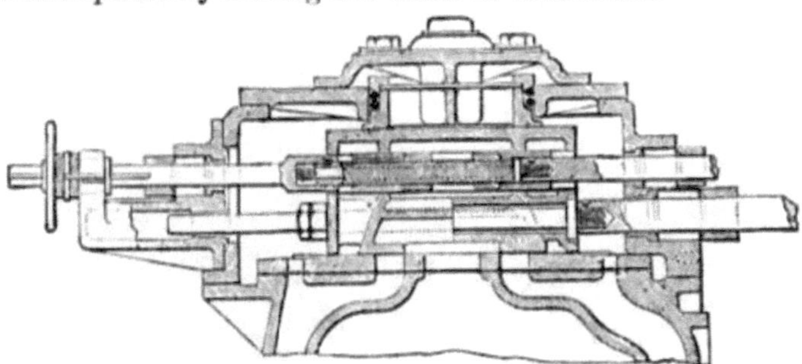

FIG. 129.

So far as the distribution of the steam is concerned these valves, which worked directly on the backs of the main slides, had a great advantage over the expansion valves working in separate casings, as the clearance space that had to be filled with steam at each stroke was much diminished. It was, however, often found difficult to properly lubricate the working surfaces, especially in large engines, and the valves wore away rapidly, causing excessive stresses on the gear from the great friction, and for this reason the most commonly employed expansion valve was that working in a separate casing, as in Fig. 127, which gave less trouble.

Reasons for abandonment of separate expansion valves.—The separate expansion valves when fitted were always troublesome to maintain in proper order. As steam pressures increased and larger ratios of cylinder were fitted in compound engines, the necessity for such valves passed away. It was found that most of the expansion capable of being usefully carried out could be obtained with the cut-off of the ordinary slide-valve in association with the stage expansion system, so that for a steam pressure of 90 lbs. the expansion valves were abandoned. The usual ratio of H.P. to L.P. cylinder-volumes with this pressure was 1 to 4, so that a fair amount of expansion was

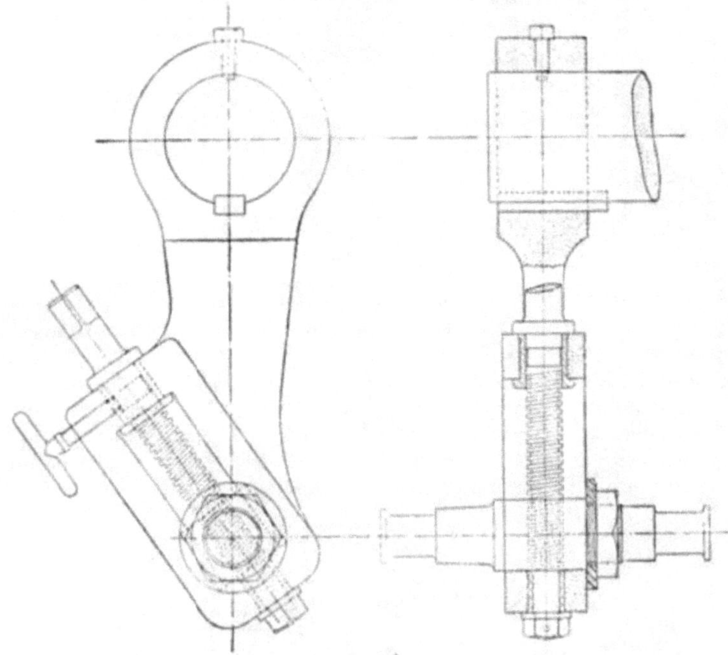

Fig. 130.

obtainable within the limits of cut-off which could be given efficiently with the ordinary slide-valve.

With the modern triple and quadruple expansion engines there is still less necessity for separate expansion valves, and they are not fitted, as all the expansion required is obtainable by means of the link motion.

Independent linking-up gear.—All modern engines in the Royal Navy which are intended to work with considerable variations in the total power are provided with means for independently linking up the slide gears of the various cylinders. This gear enables the cut-off in any cylinder to be made earlier than that corresponding to the position of the main reversing gear. This latter gear, when moved by the starting-engine or wheel, alters the cut-off in the various cylinders to the same extent, but the independent linking-up gear enables various alterations of cut-off to be made in any cylinder, so that the total power at any speed may be more equally divided between the various cylinders, and any other desirable adjustments made.   The effect of these changes on the distribution of power in the various cylinders is explained in Chapter XXVI.

To enable this to be effected, the reversing arms attached to the weigh-shaft are fitted with slots and sliding blocks to which the suspension rods leading to the links are attached.   By moving these blocks the links are altered in position.   As the alteration of the blocks takes some time, the angle of the slot is so arranged that in the astern position the slot is approximately perpendicular to the suspension rods, so that the position of the block in the slot does not affect the link in the astern position.   This being so, the engines may be reversed without making any alterations in the independent linking-up gear.   A sketch of this fitting is shown in Fig. 130.   A nut and washer are provided on one side of the block pin, which when tightened up secure it in position.   This nut is slacked back before any alterations in the position of the block are made.

CHAPTER XVI.

SLIDE-VALVES AND FITTINGS.

Slide-jacket.—The steam, after passing the regulating valve, enters the slide-jacket or casing, which is simply a rectangular or cylindrical box bolted to the cylinder, in which the slide-valve works. This slide casing is either cast in one with the cylinder, or bolted to it.

Slide-valve.—The distribution of steam in each of the steam cylinders of an engine, involving the processes of admission, expansion, and finally exhaust into the receiver pipes of the succeeding cylinder or the condenser as the case may be, is now effected by the agency of a single valve, called the 'slide-valve.' The slide-valve is one of the most important parts of the engine, and on the skill and care exercised in its design and fitting, the satisfactory working of the machinery will greatly depend.

A section of an ordinary single-ported slide-valve is shown in Fig. 131.

In the cylinder face there are three passages, called 'ports,' marked respectively A, B, and C. A and B are the *steam* passages or ports, one leading to each end of the cylinder, and C is the *exhaust* port leading to the condenser. s is the slide-valve, which is rectangular in plan, and the hollow space, D, in its centre is called the *exhaust cavity* of the valve. The valve is shown in its central position, and it will be seen that it not only closes the steam ports, but overlaps the edges for some distance on the steam side. The object of this will be explained later.

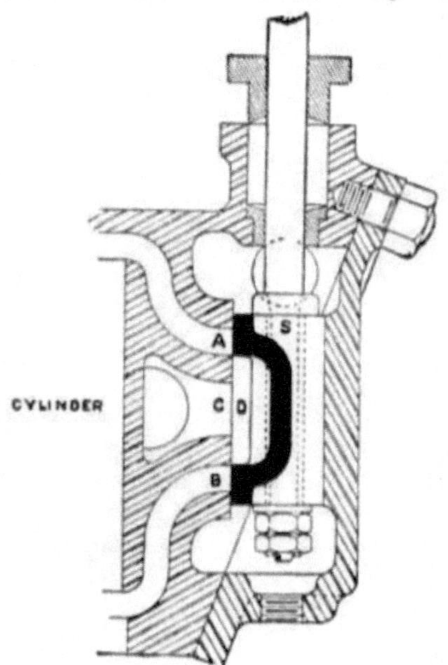

Fig. 131.

The slide-valve has a flat face, and it works steamtight on the corresponding flat face of the cylinder. The casing around it is supplied with steam, while the exhaust cavity is connected either to the condenser, the reservoir, or the atmosphere, depending on the type of engine.

Action of the slide-valve.—We will examine first the motion of such a valve and the distribution of steam in the cylinder during one revolution of the engine, noting the movements of the piston at the same time.

We will assume the piston to be just commencing its stroke, it being always arranged that the slide-valve shall then have uncovered the steam port by a certain distance called the '*lead*,' this condition being represented in Fig. 132. Steam enters through the port A and pushes the piston in the direction of the arrow, the valve moving also in the same direction. The other port, B, is open on the inside edge, and exhausts the steam on the side E of the piston to the exhaust pipe shown in the exhaust cavity C. When the piston and valve have travelled a certain distance in the direction indicated, the valve reaches the end of its travel and is for an instant at rest, the piston, however, continuing to move in the same direction as shown in Fig. 133. The exhaust port, B, is now wide open, but the valve and

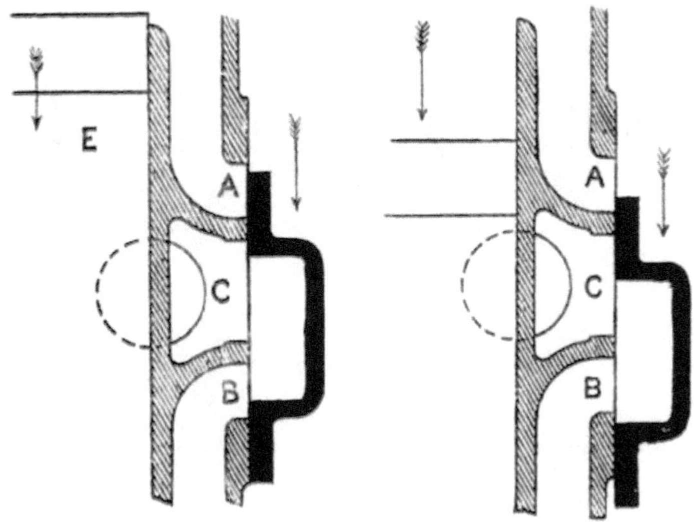

Fig. 132.   Fig. 133.

ports are generally arranged so that the ports are never wide open to the steam, so that A is not wide open. The reason for this will be explained later.

The valve now commences its return stroke, the piston and valve travelling in opposite directions, the next important phase being shown in Fig. 134, when the admission of steam to the cylinder is stopped by the steam edge of the valve closing the port A. This is called the *instant of 'cut-off*,' and the remainder of the piston's motion in the direction of the arrow is caused by the expansion of the steam previously admitted. It will be noticed that the port B is still open to exhaust. The piston and valve now proceed still further in opposite directions until the piston has travelled nearly the whole of its stroke and the valve reaches the middle of its travel, as in Fig. 135. In this position the two inner or exhaust edges coincide with the inner edges of the port.

Two important operations now occur. On the side E of the piston the steam or vapour which had previously been passing out through the port B into the exhaust pipe is now confined by the closing of the port, and as the piston proceeds further in the same direction the steam still remaining in the end E of the cylinder is compressed, and its pressure will gradually increase as the piston gets nearer the end

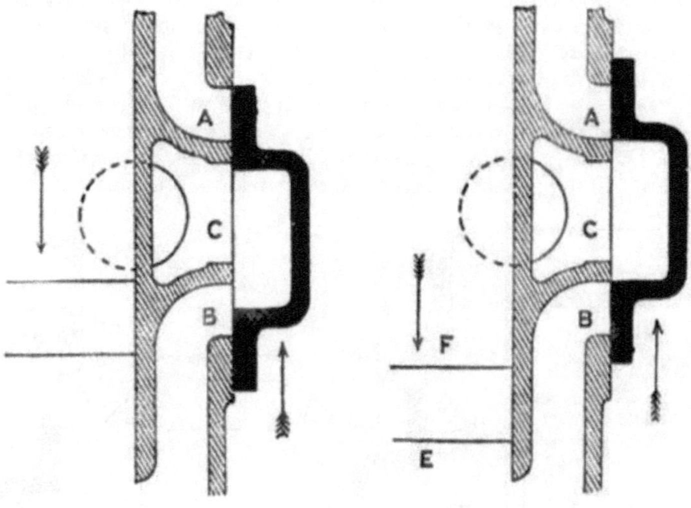

Fig. 134.   Fig. 135.

of its stroke. This is called the *instant of 'compression.'* Its effect is to provide an elastic cushion of steam to absorb the momentum of the piston and parts attached, and bring them to rest gently before the opposite stroke is commenced, thus avoiding shocks, and assisting the entering steam to start the piston on its return stroke. It has also an important effect as regards efficiency of the steam, as by its means the clearance spaces are filled with compressed steam, and a smaller quantity of steam from the steam pipe is thus required for each stroke. See Chapter XXVI.

On the other side, F, of the piston another important operation also occurs, for the valve is still travelling in the direction of the arrow, and the inner edge of the valve now commences to open the port A to the exhaust pipe, and the steam which has previously been driving the piston forward by its expansive force now rushes off to the condenser, and the pressure on the side F is suddenly reduced. This is called the *instant of 'release.'* It will be noted that with the valve as shown, having both its exhaust edges exactly corresponding to the exhaust edges of the cylinder ports at the same time, the operations of 'exhaust' on one side of the piston and 'compression' on the other occur at the same instant. If, as is often the case, these edges do not correspond exactly, the exhaust and compression will occur at different instants.

As the piston travels still further towards the end of its stroke, the valve proceeds in the direction of the arrow, and rapidly uncovers the port A to the exhaust pipe, and also the compression on the side E proceeds till just before the piston reaches the end of its stroke, when the steam edge of the valve reaches the edge of the port B and commences to admit steam. This is termed the *instant of ' admission '* (Fig. 136). The pressure on the side E then rises to the full steam pressure, and the small remaining part of the piston's stroke is completed against this steam pressure, which continues the action of the compressed steam in bringing the piston gradually to rest prior to the commencement of the return stroke.

When the stroke of the piston is completed, as in Fig. 137, the valve is again open to steam by an amount equal to the 'lead,' and the operations described above are repeated on the opposite side of the piston, while the latter performs the return stroke, until the piston and valve are again in the same position as in Fig. 132. The steam is thus

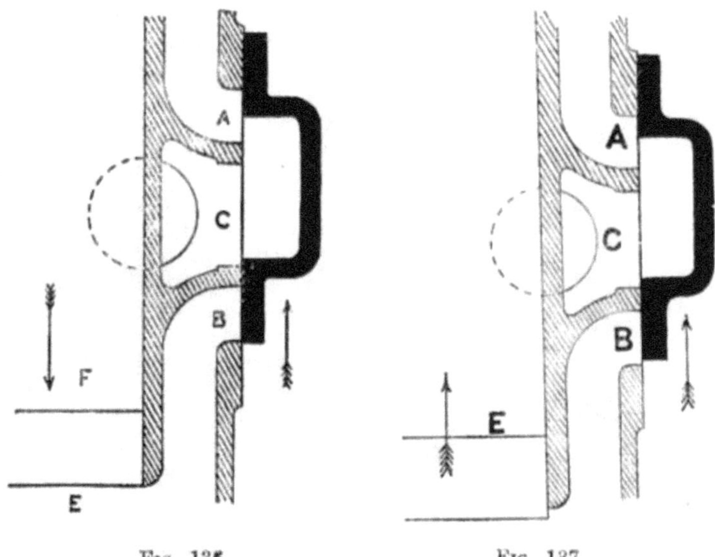

FIG. 136.   FIG. 137.

admitted to, and exhausted from, the opposite ends of the cylinder, and a motion of the piston to and fro in the cylinder caused, and this reciprocating motion of the piston is communicated to the crank-shaft of the engine by the mechanism described in Chapter XXI, the shaft being thus continuously rotated so long as steam is supplied to the cylinder. The effect of arranging the slide-valve with 'lead' is to considerably increase the opening to steam when the piston is commencing its stroke, so as to assist in avoiding any considerable fall of pressure due to contraction of the steam inlet at this period. It also, as explained above, allows steam to be admitted just prior to the completion of the stroke, and thus helps in bringing the piston gradually to rest and avoiding shocks at the end of the stroke.

It should be clearly noticed that the points of admission and cut-off are determined by the steam edge of the valve, and those of release and compression, by the exhaust edge.

In considering the motion of the slide-valve the student will find it a very instructive exercise to draw to scale a section of the cylinder ports as shown in the diagrams, and make a cardboard model of the section of the slide-valve, so that it may be worked over the cylinder ports as desired.

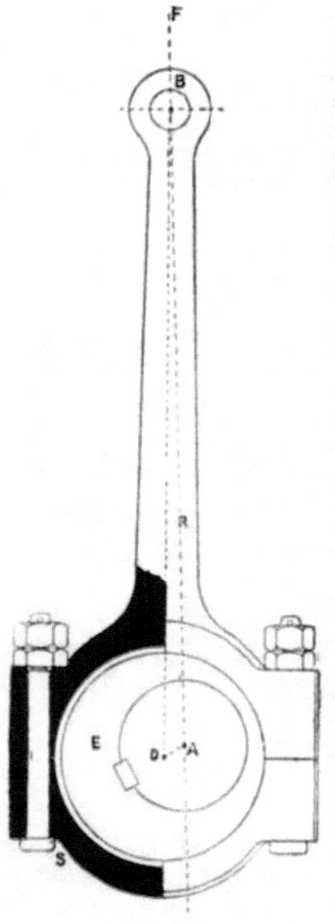

Fig. 138.

Motion of the slide-valve, eccentric, and eccentric rod.—The motion of the slide-valve to and fro, causing the reciprocating motion of the piston, is generally produced by means of an eccentric and rod, sketches of a small example of which are given in Fig. 138. A circular cast-iron sheave, E, has bored in it, eccentrically with its own circumference, a hole of the same diameter as the crank-shaft. This eccentric sheave is keyed firmly on the shaft, so as to revolve with it. The centre of the eccentric is indicated at D, while A is the centre of the shaft, which remains fixed, and about which centre the shaft, carrying with it the eccentric, rotates. On the circumference of the eccentric there works a ring, S, called the eccentric strap, to which the eccentric rod, R, is attached. The end, B, of the eccentric rod is connected by a joint to the slide-valve rod. In large marine engines this connection is not made direct, but through the agency of a 'link,' as explained in Chapter XVII.

When the shaft revolves, carrying the sheave with it, as the end B of the eccentric rod is prevented from moving except along the line A F, the sheave must slide in the strap and sway the latter to and fro, thus producing a reciprocating motion in the end B, of the eccentric rod, and consequently in the slide-valve itself, to which it is connected.

The extent of the travel of the end B of the rod along the line A F is evidently equal to twice A D ; i.e. twice the distance between the centres of the crank-shaft and eccentric sheave. This distance A D is called the '*eccentric radius*' or '*eccentric arm*,' or '*throw of eccentric.*'

Eccentric and rod equivalent to crank and connecting rod.—This motion is evidently the same as that outlined in Fig. 139, where the eccentric sheave and shaft are replaced by a solid plate revolving about the point C. The eccentric rod E D is evidently always normal to the circumference of the revolving plate, and therefore *always points to its centre*, P. As C P is a constant distance, the motion is thus equivalent to that which would ensue were the point E connected to C by means of a revolving crank, C P, and a connecting rod of length E P. The eccentric and rod are therefore clearly equivalent in action to that of a small crank and a connecting rod, and are adopted in cases where, from the smallness of the travel, it is inexpedient to obtain the motion by the direct intervention of a crank.

It is important, in examining the action of the slide-valve, to carefully consider this motion. It will be seen that the longer the connecting rod, P E, the more nearly does its direction become parallel to the line of motion, C E, of the end of the connecting rod. When this length becomes infinitely great the direction of P D becomes parallel to C E. The motion is then equivalent to that obtained by the eccentric acting against a flat bar, A B (Fig. 140), at the end of a sliding rod, s, which

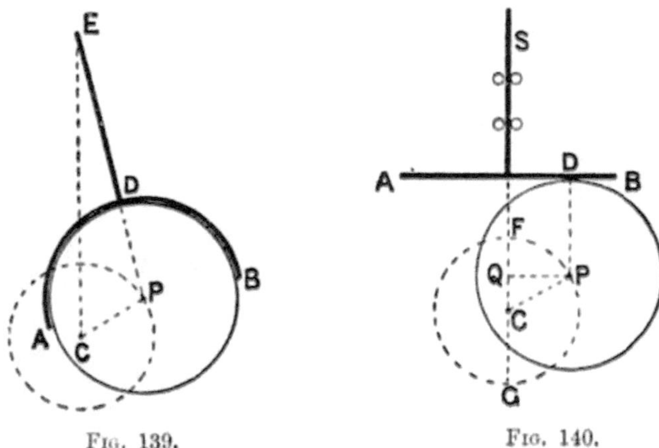

Fig. 139. Fig. 140.

is kept moving in a vertical straight line, S C, by suitable guides. The point of contact, D, of the bar with the cam, will always be vertically above the centre, P, and the vertical motion of the bar is then exactly the same as that of the point P, and therefore also of the point Q, the foot of the perpendicular drawn from P on the line C E.

Harmonic motion.—As the length of the eccentric rod in well-designed gears is large compared with that of the eccentric radius, its influence in causing a deviation from the motion illustrated in Fig. 140 is not very great, and for most practical purposes the motion of an ordinary slide-valve may be assumed to be as shown in the last-mentioned Figure, and its geometrical representation and examination is thereby much facilitated. If the point P is made to revolve uniformly about the centre C, the motion of the point Q along the line G F is described geometrically as an exact 'harmonic' motion. It will be seen that its velocity reaches a maximum when passing the centre, C, while near the ends of the stroke the velocity gradually lessens, till it becomes zero when the point P arrives at F and G the ends of the stroke. Q is then for an instant at rest while its motion is being reversed.

The slide-valve is therefore at the centre of its stroke when the eccentric arm makes an angle of 90° with the line of motion, and further, as C Q = C P cosine P C Q, the distance of the slide-valve from its central position is equal to the eccentric radius multiplied by the cosine of the angle this radius makes with the line of motion of the end of the rod, or line of dead centres.

Geometrical representation.—This motion is capable of simple geometrical representation as follows. We have seen that when the eccentric radius is at C P, the slide-valve is distant C Q from the centre of its stroke. Suppose we mark off along C P a distance C Q' = C Q. If we do this for all positions of C P, and draw a curve through all the points such as Q', we obtain two circles with diameters C F and C G (see Fig. 141, in which for clearness the circle F G has been enlarged). This is easily proved, for if F Q' be joined the two triangles C Q P and C Q' F are equal in all respects, therefore the angle F Q' C, which is

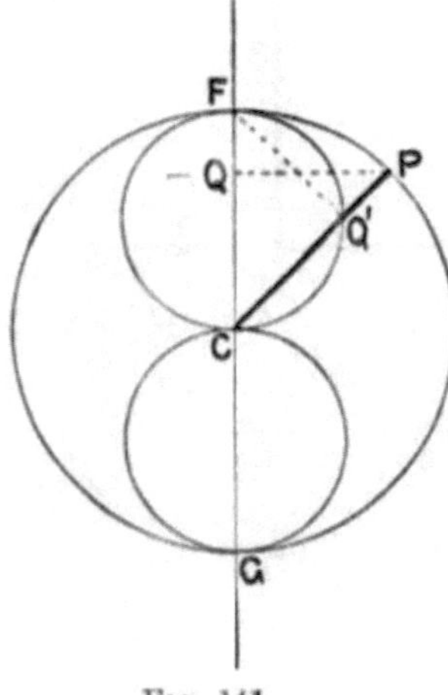

equal to the angle P Q C, must be a right angle ; hence the point Q' must lie on a circle with C F as diameter. These circles are such, therefore, that if any position of *eccentric radius* such as C P be drawn, the part C Q' intercepted

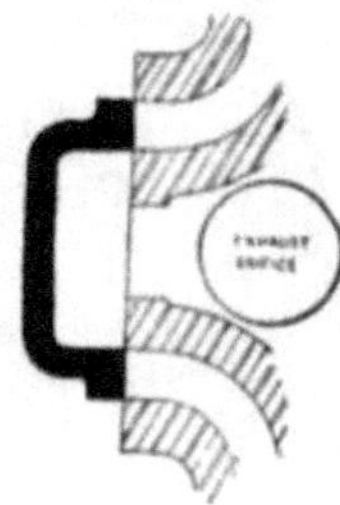

Fig. 141.Fig. 142.

by the circle gives us the distance the slide-valve has moved from its central position when the *eccentric radius* is in the position C P. The diameter of each of these circles is the half travel of the slide-valve.

Slide-valve without lap or lead.—The most simple form of the slide-valve is a single-ported valve, without either lap or lead, as shown in Fig. 142. It is clear that any slide-valve must be long enough to cover both ports on the steam side at the same time, or otherwise the steam would pass to both sides of the piston at once, and no motion would ensue. In the present example the valve is just of sufficient length to exactly cover both the ports.

In the figure the valve is shown in the centre of its stroke, just closing both steam ports, while at this instant the eccentric radius must be perpendicular to the line of motion.[1] The piston is clearly at the commencement of its stroke, and the crank on its dead point. We see, therefore, that in such a case the eccentric must be fixed on the shaft in such a position as to make an angle of 90° with the crank. As the

[1] See top of this page.

crank and eccentric revolve, the valve begins to admit steam to one side of the piston, and to place the other side in connection with the condenser through the exhaust passages, so that the steam behind the piston may escape. The amount of opening continues to increase, till the piston arrives at half-stroke, when the steam port is wide open. After this it begins to close, but does not shut completely till the piston arrives at the end of its stroke.

With this arrangement, the valve begins to open the ports, both to the steam pipe and condenser, at the beginning of the stroke ; the ports continue open to a greater or less extent during the whole period of the stroke, and there is no expansion.

Reversibility with single fixed eccentric.—This simple form of slide-valve is one very commonly used for small auxiliary engines, for by a simple arrangement it can be made reversible, although it has only *one fixed eccentric*. To enable this to be seen Fig. 143 has been drawn, showing the valve after it has performed a part of its stroke downwards from the middle position, while below it is shown the corresponding position of eccentric radius and crank. If, as is commonly the case, the space A is in connection with the steam pipe, and B in connection with the exhaust, the steam would in this position enter the top of the cylinder, causing the piston to descend, and the motion of the crank to be as indicated by the arrow in full lines. Conversely, if the space B be supplied with steam, while A is connected with the exhaust pipe, steam will enter the bottom of the cylinder through the inner edge of the lower port, and the piston will be forced upwards, and motion will ensue in the opposite direction, viz., that indicated by the dotted arrow. The last-mentioned arrangement of steam and exhaust supply to the valve is sometimes arranged for permanently ; but in the case more immediately under consideration, viz., that in which reversibility is required by means of a simple arrangement, a device is adopted by which the steam and exhaust pipes can be placed in connection with A

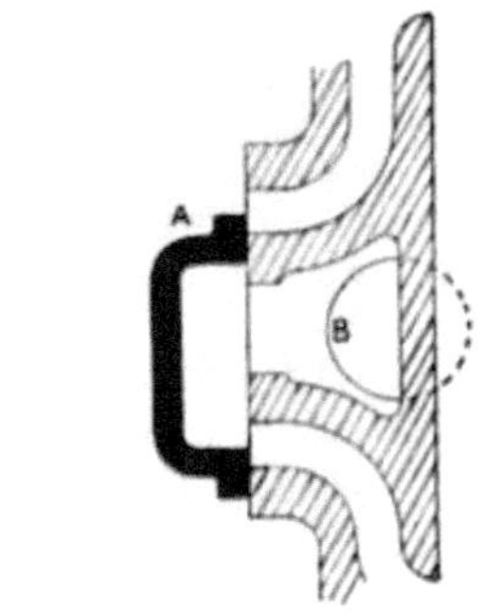

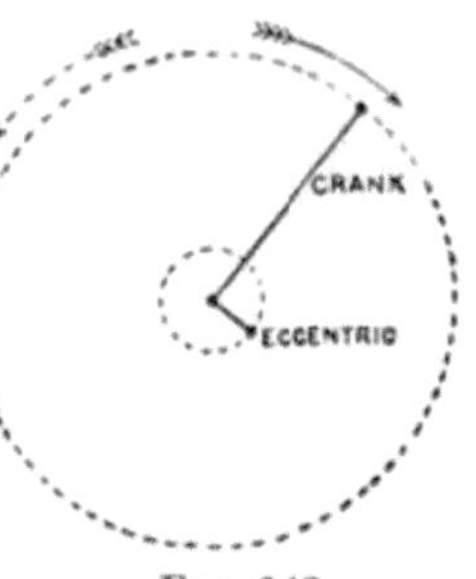

Fig. 143.

and B respectively, or interchanged as desired, and by this means the engine is made to run in either direction.

The apparatus by means of which this interchange of steam and exhaust is effected is described elsewhere.[1] It will be seen, therefore, that with a valve of this description the eccentric radius is fixed at 90° in advance of the engine crank when the steam is supplied to the outside edges of the valve, while it is 90° behind the engine crank when the steam is supplied to the inside edges of the valve. All reversible engines with a single eccentric to each cylinder are fitted

---

[1] See Chapter XVII.

with valves of this character, such as steering engines, capstan engines, starting engines, turning engines, &c. These valves are generally of the piston type.

It may be mentioned in passing that as the slide-valves are practically always open at each end of the cylinder, either to steam or exhaust, drain-cocks are often omitted from these engines, the accumulated water being forced by the piston into the exhaust pipe on starting the engine.

Having described the elementary slide-valve, we proceed now to consider the most usual type of slide-valve in more detail, first explaining a few definitions.

Lead.—In ordinary engines, to facilitate their working, the slide-valves are arranged so that they may open both to steam and exhaust shortly before the end of the stroke. This is done by advancing the position of the eccentric arm with respect to the crank, so that all the motions of the valve may be earlier.

If this be done with the valve shown in Figs. 142 and 143, it will be seen that although the valve opens just before the end of the stroke, yet it does not produce expansive working of the steam, as the ports are still open either to steam or exhaust for the whole duration of a stroke.

The lead of the valve is defined as the length of opening of port to steam at the *beginning of the stroke of the piston.*

Lap.—It is found in practice that, in order to produce smooth and economical working, it is necessary to provide means for cutting off the admission of the steam before the end of the stroke. This is accomplished by giving the valve *lap* or *cover*, or, in other words, by lengthening the valve so as to make it more than exactly cover the ports when in its middle position, as shown in Fig. 144, in which one end only of the valve is shown. P represents the steam port of the cylinder, and s the section of the slide-valve.

The side of the steam port of the cylinder at which the steam enters is called the induction or steam side, and the side at which it begins to exhaust the eduction or exhaust side. Similar names are given to the corresponding edges of the slide-valve itself. For example, in Fig. 144, assuming steam to be supplied to the outside of the valve, c is the induction or steam side, and D the eduction or exhaust side of the cylinder port, and A the induction and B the eduction edge of the slide-valve.

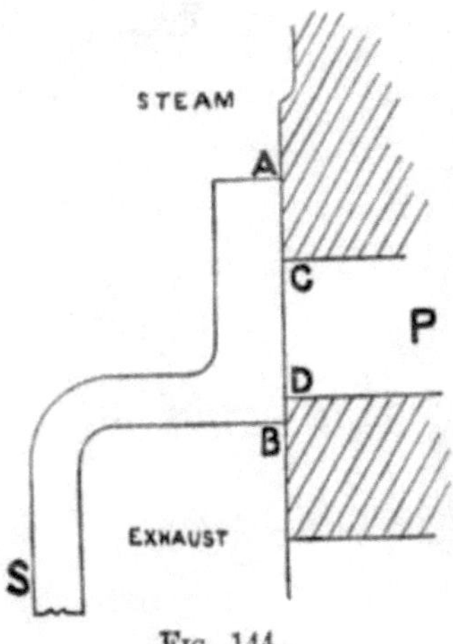

Fig. 144.

The lap or cover of a slide-valve is the extent to which the edge of the valve overlaps the adjoining edge of the cylinder port *when the valve is in the middle of its stroke.* For example, A c is the lap on the steam or induction side and B D the lap on the exhaust or eduction side of the slide-valve. The lap on the steam side is generally called the outside lap, and that on the exhaust side the inside lap of the valve.

The lap on the exhaust side when fitted is always small, and is often absent altogether, as it is important that the communication with the condenser should be as free as possible. In many cases, especially in fast-running engines, *negative lap* on the exhaust side is fitted to increase the length of time the cylinder is open to the condenser during each stroke. In Fig. 145 B D is the amount of negative inside lap.

Giving outside lap to the valve will, in the first place, necessitate an increased travel, to obtain the same amount of opening for the steam ; for it is clear that the valve must travel through a distance equal to its outside lap before it begins to open the steam port at all. Secondly, in order to give the necessary lead at the beginning of the stroke, the eccentric will have to be still further advanced with respect to the crank than in the case of a valve without lap, and consequently all the movements of the valve will be earlier than before. The effect of lap on the exhaust side or inside lap will be to close the communication with the condenser earlier than would otherwise be the case, so that a larger quantity of steam would be confined in the cylinder, and compressed behind the piston, until the end of the stroke.

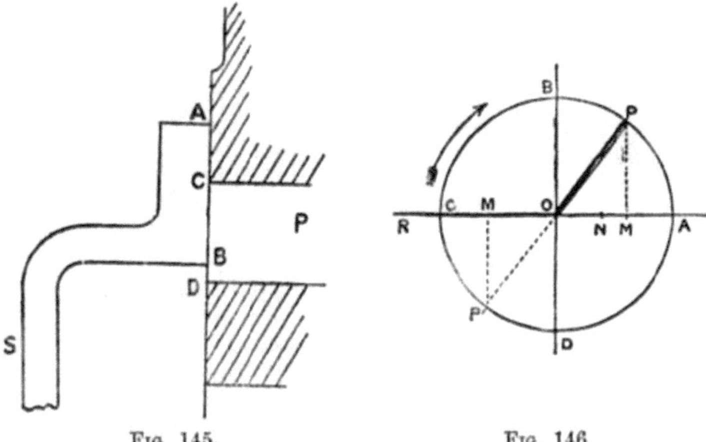

Fig. 145.Fig. 146.

Angular advance of the eccentric.—In a slide-valve without lap or lead we saw that the eccentric arm was at right angles with the crank [1] ; but in the ordinary slide-valve with lap and lead, the action of which was described on page 173, it is necessary, in order to give the valve the required lead at the beginning of the stroke, to considerably advance the eccentric beyond this position, and the amount it requires to be moved is termed the ' *angular advance of the eccentric.*'

In ordinary engines, therefore, in which the slide-valves work parallel to the pistons, the angular advance is the angle between the eccentric radius and a perpendicular to the crank arm. To meet the exceptional cases in which the slide-valves do not work parallel to the pistons, the term may be defined as follows :—When the crank is on the dead centre, the angle at which the eccentric radius stands in advance of the position that will bring the valve to its mid stroke is called the ' angular

<hr>

[1] See p. 178.

advance of the eccentric.'   These definitions apply to all cases, whether the steam be taken on the inside or outside edges of the valve.

The angular advance of the eccentric may be obtained, approximately, as follows :— Draw a circle, A B C D, Fig. 146, with the length of the eccentric arm as radius.   Let A R be the line of motion of the piston, and O R the position of the crank when on the dead centre.   If steam is taken on the *outside* edges of the valve, set off *away* from the crank, O M = the outside lap, plus the lead.   Draw M P vertically, cutting the circle in P.   Then O P will be the approximate position of the eccentric radius when the engine crank is on the dead centre, and the angle B O P will be the angular advance of the eccentric.   This follows from the fact that when the crank is on the dead centre the valve is distant from its middle position by an amount equal to the lap plus lead.

If, however, steam is taken on the inside edges of the valve—as is often the case, especially with piston valves—the lap plus lead must be marked off in the opposite direction, viz. *towards* the crank, and O P' will then be the position of the eccentric, and D O P' the angle of advance. O D is then the eccentric position if without lap or lead, and, to provide this, the eccentric arm is 'advanced' from O D to O P'.

Opening of the steam port.— The opening of the port to steam, at any instant, is equal to the distance the valve has moved

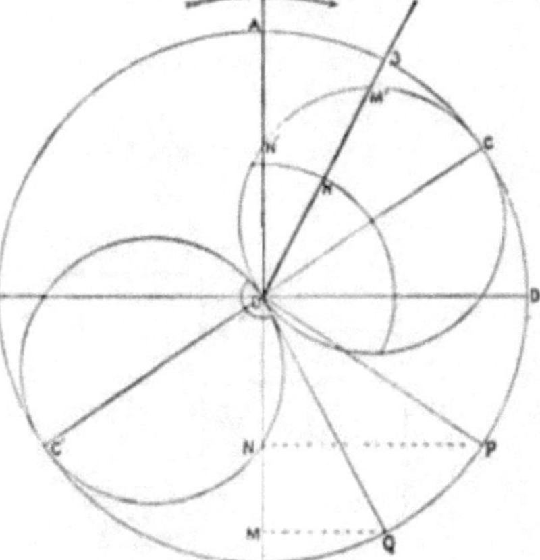

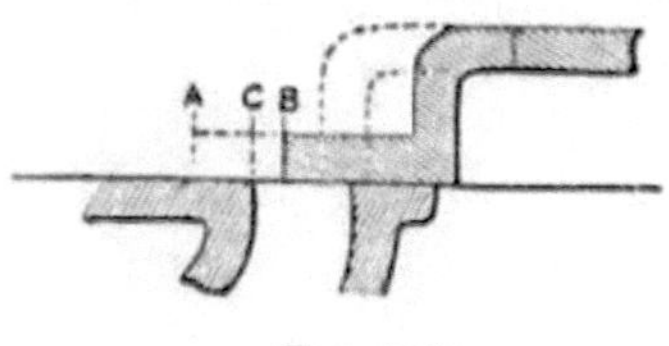

Fig. 147.   Fig. 148.

from its central position, minus the lap of the valve.   Let the dotted lines in Fig. 147 represent the valve in its central position, and the full lines its position at any given instant.   Then A B is the distance the valve has travelled from the middle position, and A C is the outside lap.

Therefore Opening of port = B C = A B − A C

= movement of valve from middle position − outside lap. . . (1).

Zeuner's valve diagram.—The simple diagram (Fig. 141) gave for each position of *eccentric radius* the distance of the slide-valve from its middle position, but what is generally required is a diagram giving the position of the slide-valve for each position of the *crank arm* and piston.

Suppose the crank on the dead centre in the direction O A, Fig. 148, and the eccentric radius in the direction and equal to O P, then P O D is the angle of advance, and the valve in this position is distant O N from its central position.   Set off O N' along O A equal to O N.   Next, suppose the crank has moved to O B, then the eccentric radius has moved to O Q such that angle A O B = angle P O Q, and O M is the distance of the valve from middle position. Set off O M' along O B equal to O M. If this is done for all positions it will be found that all the points such as N', M', &c., lie on two circles with diameters O C and O C', which are each equal to the half travel of the valve, and make an angle with the line of dead centres measured in the direction of motion of the crank equal to 90° minus the angle of advance. We now have a diagram which gives for each position of the *crank*, the distance of the slide-valve from its central position.

If now a circle be drawn with centre O and radius O H equal to the outside lap, the amount of opening of steam port for any position of crank, such as O B, must be given by the part H M'. This follows from equation (1) above, since O M' is the movement of the valve from middle position. From these circles we are enabled to completely analyse the motion of the slide-valve. The construction is due to Zeuner.

The complete Zeuner's diagram is given in Fig. 149, and this should be carefully studied. To avoid complication it is drawn for one side of the piston only, viz. the top side, and all dimensions such as lap, lead, &c., are also for the top of the valve.[1]   The upper circle is termed the 'steam circle' and the lower the 'exhaust circle.'

Now admission and cut-off of the steam occur when the valve is distant from its middle position by an amount equal to the outside lap, i.e. the intersections of the lap circle with the valve circles give the positions of the crank when admission and cut-off occur. Similarly *on the other side of the middle position of the valve*, as release and compression occur when the valve is distant from its mid position by an amount equal to the inside lap, the positions of crank at release and compression are given by drawing an arc of a circle with centre O and radius equal to the inside lap, and the intersection of this arc with the opposite circle gives the positions of the crank at release and compression. O P is the position of the crank at release, and O M the position when compression takes place.

If, as is often the case, the inside lap be negative, the intersection of the inside lap circle with the other circle, O G C, must be taken to obtain the positions at release and compression. The lines O P and O M will then lie on the other side of the perpendicular O N.

For any position of crank O S we see that T S is the amount of opening of valve to steam. The intercepts on the shaded area of the top circle all represent steam openings. Therefore F G is the lead. From the position O B to O C we see that the opening to steam continuously increases, at first quickly, and finally slowly, while from O C to O D the valve is closing at first slowly, and finally rapidly.

Similarly on the exhaust circle the intercepts on the shaded area represent exhaust openings. As, however, the valve is fully open to exhaust when it has travelled a distance from the centre equal to inside lap + the width of the port, we must draw an arc H K on the exhaust circle with this as radius to give the outside limit of the width of opening. Between O H and O K the valve is fully open to exhaust, from O P to O H it gradually opens, and from O K to O M it gradually closes.

The angle C O Y is the angle of advance. A line drawn through

---

[1] They are often different for the two ends of the valve.

o perpendicular to c c′ gives the positions of crank when the valve is in its middle position.

There are some useful geometrical facts to be observed in this diagram, attention to which will facilitate the solution of problems. Join D B, then this line is a tangent to the cut-off circle. Also draw A L perpendicular to D B, then A L = F G = lead.

Again, if O N be perpendicular to c o c′, a perpendicular from N on

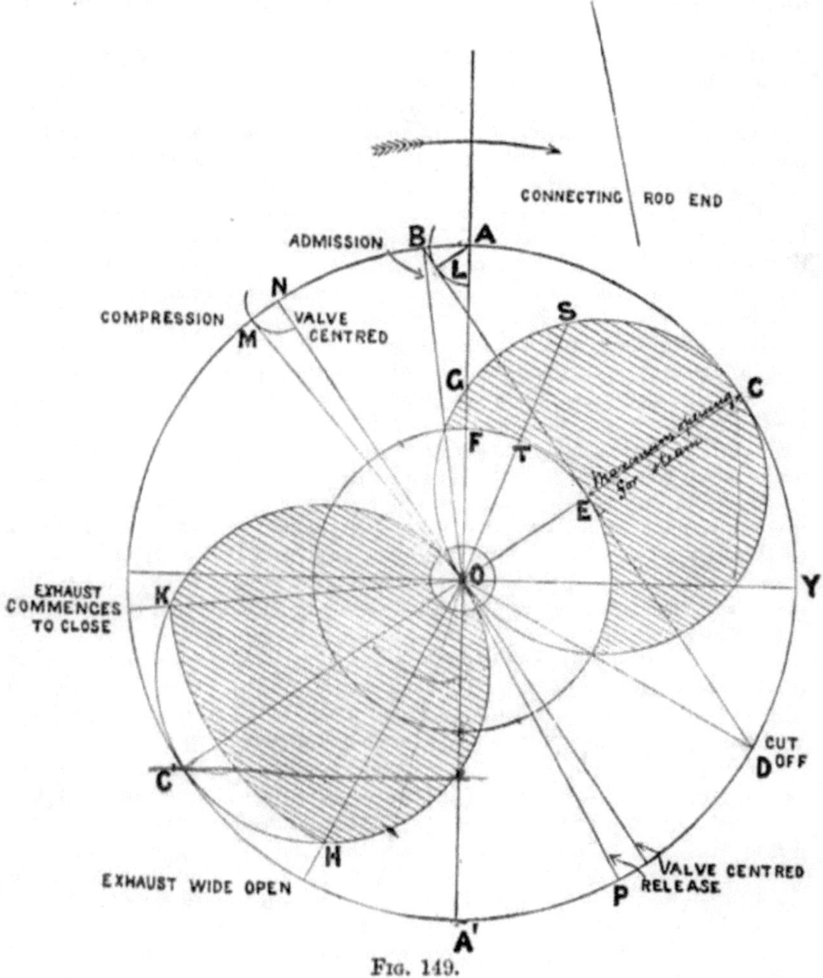

Fig. 149.

o M the compression line, will be equal to the inside lap. These propositions can be easily proved.

The latter fact is generally used for ascertaining more accurately the inside lap from the position of release or compression, or *vice versâ*, as the liability to error is less, it being sometimes difficult to determine the exact point of intersection of the compression line with the exhaust circle.

If now we let A A′ represent on some other convenient scale the stroke of the piston, the mean indicator diagram to be expected can be drawn, neglecting the obliquity of the connecting-rod, by ascertaining by projection on a vertical line the positions of the piston corresponding to points of admission, cut-off, release, and compression.

As regards the diagram for the bottom of the piston, the steam circle for top of piston becomes the exhaust circle for the bottom, and *vice versâ.*

If the inside and outside laps are the same for bottom as for top, the same lap circles would be continued to the opposite circles to give the corresponding points for the bottom of the piston. Often, however, they are different, when, of course, the correct radii must be used.

An elementary knowledge of geometry will, by the application of this diagram, lead to the solution of most of the problems relating to the motion of slide-valves. By varying some of the points the alteration in the others may easily be found, and by assuming certain elements the remainder may be determined.

Position of piston.—As we have stated, the influence of the length of the eccentric rod may be neglected in considering the motion of the slide-valve, unless this length be much shorter than is usual in practice as compared with the eccentric radius. The connecting-rod is, however, always much shorter relatively to the crank-arm, and it must always be taken account of in considering the distribution of steam by the slide-valve. The motion of the piston is evidently the same as that of the crosshead at the end of the connecting-rod. Suppose X′ P X, Fig. 150, to be the path of the crank-pin, and let O P and O Q be two positions of crank-pin at equal angles with the line of dead centres. When the crank is at P and Q respectively, the position of the crosshead is found by drawing from these points as centres, arcs with radius equal to the connecting-rod, cutting the line of centres.

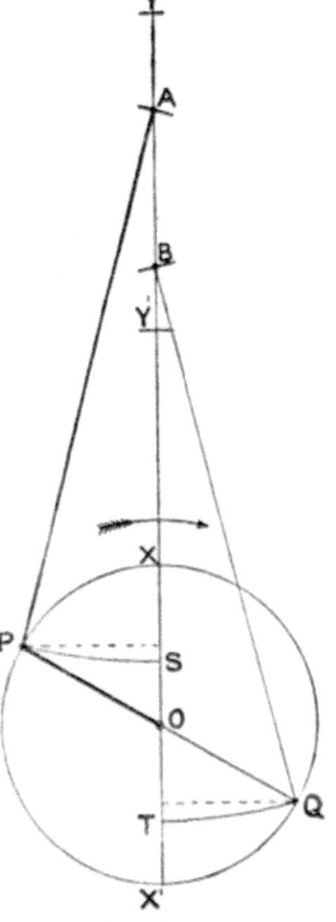

Fig. 150.

Suppose A and B be the positions thus found, and let Y and Y′ be the ends of the stroke of the crosshead. With centres A and B draw arcs P S and Q T; then X S and X′ T will be the distances of the piston from the ends of its stroke. This is easily seen since S A = P A = X Y ∴ S X = A Y.

Suppose, for example, Q and P are the positions of the crank at cut-off on the down stroke and up stroke respectively, then it will be seen that the piston on the down stroke has at the point of cut-off travelled a distance X T, which is greater than the distance X′ S which has been travelled on the up stroke. For the same position of crank at cut-off, therefore, more steam will be admitted to the cylinder on the down stroke than on the up stroke. The piston, except when on a dead centre, is, in fact, owing to the influence of the connecting-rod, always nearer the crank-shaft end of the stroke than it would be if the connecting-rod were infinitely long. In the latter case, the distances travelled during the up stroke and down stroke would be equal, and would be represented by the feet of the perpendiculars from P and Q respectively, as shown by the dotted lines.

Having obtained in Fig. 149 the positions of the crank for the various operations of the slide-valve, the positions of the piston can be obtained by drawing arcs, such as P S and Q T of Fig. 150, and this is necessary before the fraction of stroke performed at cut-off, &c. can be given. The geometrical method described below may also be used.

The following table shows the relative fractions of the stroke traversed for the particular, but very common, case in marine engines, of the connecting-rod being equal in length to four times that of the crank :—

Down Stroke or Outward Stroke		Up Stroke or Inward Stroke	
Angle of Crank	Distance travelled	Distance travelled	Angle of Crank
0	0	1·0	180
10	·009	·991	170
20	·037	·963	160
30	·082	·918	150
40	·143	·857	140
50	·215	·785	130
60	·297	·703	120
70	·384	·616	110
80	·474	·526	100
83	·500	·500	97
90	·562	·438	90
100	·647	·353	80
110	·726	·274	70
120	·797	203	60
130	·868	·132	50
140	·914	·086	40
150	·948	·052	30
160	·977	·023	20
170	·994	·006	10
180	1·000	0	0

It will be noticed that to bring the piston to its mid stroke the crank has to travel through only 83° on the down stroke, while on the up stroke this is not effected till the crank has traversed 97°.

Geometrical representation.—This is well represented graphically by another diagram [1] :—

Suppose in Fig. 151 that $o\ o_1 =$ the length of crank-arm,

$o_1\ A =$ the length of connecting-rod ;

with centre o and radius $o\ A$ describe a circle, and with centre o_1 and radius $o_1\ A$ describe another circle. If $o\ R$ be any position of the crank, $s\ R$ the intercept between these circles will be the distance travelled by the piston. By joining $o_1\ s$ it is easily seen that as $o_1\ s =$

[1] Due to Müller.

connecting-rod length, the triangle o o₁ s is an exact reproduction of the relative positions of the crank, connecting-rod, and line of motion of piston when the crank has turned through the angle o₁ o s, so that o s is the distance of the crosshead from the centre of the shaft.

The difference o R – o S = s R must therefore be the distance the piston has travelled from the top of the stroke.

By drawing another cir le with centre o and radius = o B, we get T R = B C = full stroke, so that T S will be the distance of the piston from the other end of the stroke, and if o R be the position of the crank on the up stroke, T S will be the distance it has travelled from the bottom position

For any position of the crank, therefore, we have the exact position of the piston given by the point s, the outside intercept s R giving the distance from the top of the stroke, and the inside intercept the distance from the bottom of the stroke.

The diagram may conveniently be superimposed on Zeuner's valve diagram to such a scale as to be clear of the latter, as shown in Fig. 152, and by this diagram the exact position of the piston and valve for any po-i-tion of crank can be accurately studied.

The lap circles are drawn for the *top* of the piston, so that, for example, when the

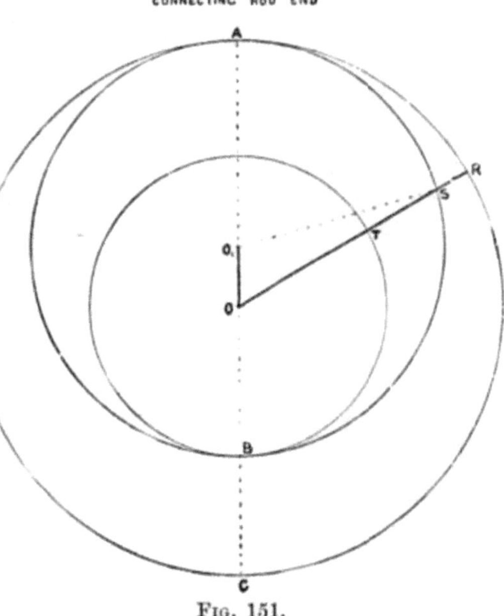

Fig. 151.

crank has turned to o D cut-off takes place, and the piston has then travelled through the distance s R of its stroke, the fraction of cut-off being $\frac{s\,R}{T\,R}$. Again compression takes place when the crank is at o M, and the piston has then travelled a distance, P Q, from the bottom of its stroke. Similar lap circles should be also drawn for the bottom of the piston, but this is omitted on the diagram for clearness.

It will be seen, therefore, that if the outside lap be the same at each end, the position of piston at cut-off will be later, and therefore the power exerted will be greater in the stroke towards the crank than stroke from the crank, and this is aggravated in vertical engines by the weight of the reciprocating parts, which act in the same direction.

For this reason, therefore, in large vertical engines the outside lap on the top side is made greater than that on the bottom in order to rectify the inequality. This is often done by simply shifting the valve a small distance upwards along its rod, which also increases the lead and the inside lap at the bottom end, which gives more cushioning at this end, thus counteracting the descending weight of the piston, rods, &c.

Double- and treble-ported slide-valves.—When the cylinders are large, it is found that the single-ported slide-valve shown in Fig. 131 would necessitate a very great travel, which would be inconvenient in practice, and cause much extra work. To meet this difficulty, double-ported valves, and sometimes treble-ported ones, have been introduced. Sketches of a double-ported valve are given in Figs. 153 and 154, Fig. 154 being a cross section through the dotted line at B E. These valves are fitted to all large marine engines. Their action in the distribution of the steam is the same as that of the single-ported valves, but the details of their construction are different. The steam passage at each end of the cylinder, instead of terminating in a single port in the cylinder face, is divided into two parts, each being one-half the width necessary for a single port ; so that the travel of the slide-valve, to admit a given quantity of steam, is only one-half of that required for the ordinary valve.

In the single-ported slide-valve the steam is only admitted at the ends, and enters the cylinder when the valve has moved a sufficient distance to allow the steam to pass from the outside of the valve to the steam port of the cylinder. The outside edges of the double-ported valve act in a similar manner, but, in addition, there is what is practically an inner valve, to which steam is admitted through the passages A A, formed in the body of the valve itself, the steam entering these passages at the sides of the slide-valve. The inner steam ports are at the face of the valve in the passages A A, and D D D D are the steam ports in the cylinder, two of which lead to each end ; E is the exhaust port in the cylinder leading to the condenser or reservoir, and B B B the exhaust passages in the slide-valve. The exhaust steam from the outer ports reaches the exhaust cavity in the cylinder by passing through the triangular exhaust passage formed in the valve, as shown by the arrows. This exhaust passage is marked B in the lower view. In the cases in which the cylinder has three steam ports at each end, the travel of the valve is still further reduced for a given area of opening.

Length of the eccentric rod.—For theoretical purposes the length of the eccentric rod is understood to mean the length measured from the centre of the eccentric strap to the centre line of the link. This must clearly be equal to the distance from the centre of the crank-shaft to the centre of the pin at the end of the slide-rod, when the valve is in the middle of its stroke.

Position of eccentric.—If the motion of the valve be considered, it will be clearly seen that its half-travel, or the throw of the eccentric, is equal to the lap of the valve, added to the maximum opening of the port to steam, which represents the extreme distance that the valve moves from its central position in either direction. Slide-valves are usually arranged so as to only partially open the cylinder port to steam, say two-thirds to three-fourths, but to open it wide to exhaust.

The position of the eccentric is best ascertained by the slide-valve diagram shown in Fig. 149, from which the most suitable

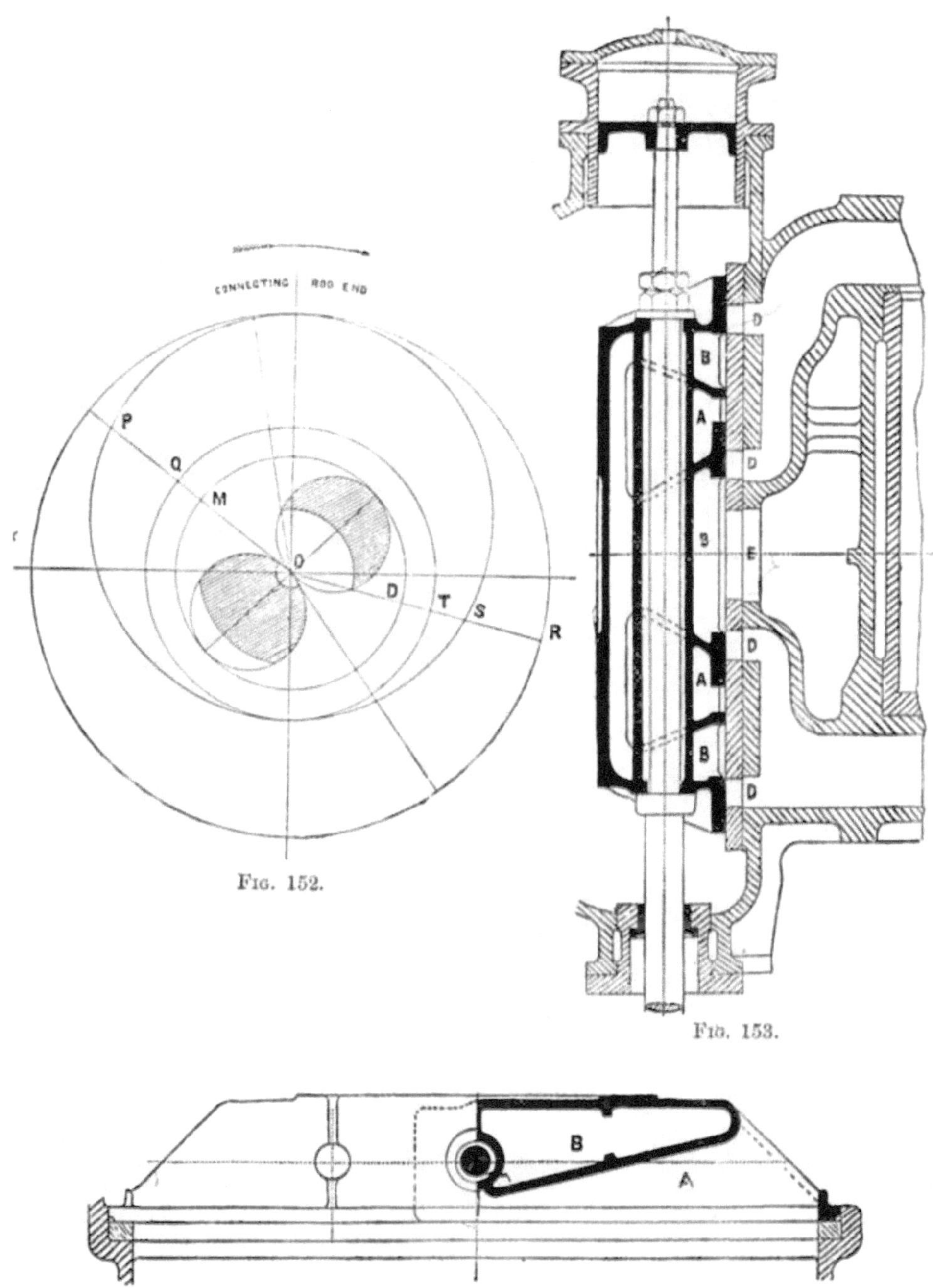

Fig. 152.

Fig. 153.

Fig. 154.

angle of advance can be determined with exactness. The approximate position is, however, frequently ascertained practically by drawing on the end of the shaft a circle with the throw of the eccentric as radius, and setting off from its centre, distances equal to the lap and required lead of the valve, as shown in Fig. 146. The eccentric is then secured in this position, temporarily, by means of a set screw.

Setting slide-valves.—The fixing of the slide-valve in its proper position on the slide-rod, to insure, by its reciprocating action, the correct distribution of the steam in the cylinder, is a comparatively simple process, but one on which the efficient working of the engine will materially depend. This operation is called technically *setting the slide-valve*, and is performed practically as described below.

The whole of the rods and gear are coupled together, the crank-arm is placed on its *dead centre*, and the slide-valve, by means of screws and nuts on the slide-rod, is fixed in the proper position to give the required *lead* for the corresponding end of the cylinder. By the expression *dead centre*, or *dead point*, is meant that position of the crank when it is in a line with the piston-rod, so that the pressure of the steam on the piston exerts no turning moment on the crank-shaft, but produces only a direct thrust, subjecting the shaft to bending action only.

The shaft is then turned round until the crank is on the opposite dead point, and the lead given by the slide-valve for that end of the cylinder measured. If, as is frequently the case on first trial, the amounts of lead at the opposite ends of the cylinder are different to that required, the position of the slide-valve on the rod must be adjusted, by means of the nuts and screws previously mentioned, until the *leads at the opposite ends are either equal or differ by the designed amounts*. When this is the case the slide-valve should be securely fixed on the rod, so that its position may not alter.

If it be desired to increase or decrease the lead at *both ends* of the cylinder at the same time, this must be done by the alteration of the angular advance of the eccentric on the shaft, and not by interfering with the position of the slide-valve.

If the centres of the slide-valve, when the crank is on each of the dead points in succession, be marked on a batten, the centre of the distance between the two points thus found will give the central point of the stroke of the valve, which should correspond with the middle of the exhaust port.

In vertical engines, for the reasons previously explained, the lead at the lower end of the valve is generally made somewhat greater than that at the upper side, and more exhaust lap is allowed. In this case, of course, the valve is correctly set on the rod, when the difference between the two leads corresponds with the designed amount. Should the lead be too great or too small at both ends, the eccentric must be moved to alter this.

The lead at the end nearest the eccentric rod may generally be allowed to be slightly in excess of that at the other end, to allow for adjustment of the eccentric straps as they wear, which tends to draw the valve forward, and correct the original deviation from the exact position.

Relief packing-rings for flat slide-valves.—The pressure of the steam at the back of a large flat slide-valve would, unless special provision be made to prevent it, cause great friction between the working faces of the valve and cylinder, and bring severe stresses on the working parts of the slide-gear, probably grinding the faces themselves and quickly wearing them away. To lessen the pressure between the working faces, and thus prevent these injurious results, relief or equilibrium rings are fitted for the backs of the valves, as shown in Fig. 155. These rings are sometimes fitted on the back of the valve, but are generally fitted on the slide-casing cover, and are pressed out by the action of suitable springs, so as to work steamtight on a true surface planed either on the back of the slide-valve or on the inside of the slide-jacket cover, depending on the situation of the ring, thus reducing the area on which the steam pressure can act. The space inside the packing-ring is connected to the condenser or the receiver of the succeeding engine, so that, if any leakage of steam should occur, it would not accumulate and produce pressure on the back of the valve inside the relief ring. In triple expansion engines the back of the low-pressure slide-valve is always placed in communication with the condenser, the back of the intermediate valve, if flat, being connected either with the low-pressure receiver or the condenser depending on the area of ring fitted. When flat valves are used for the high-pressure cylinder, its connection is made to one of the receivers.

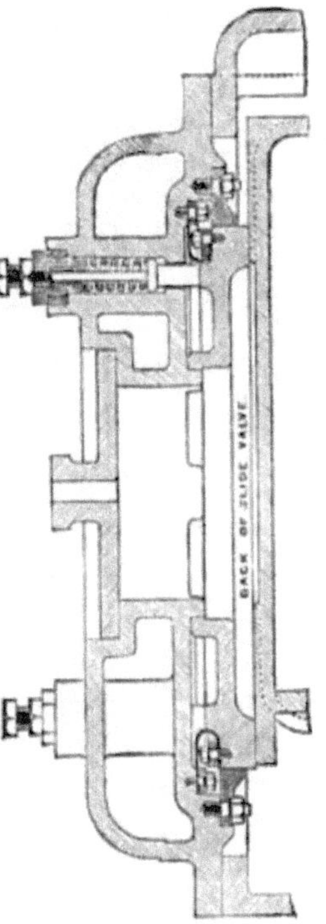

Fig. 155.

These relief rings remove a considerable pressure from the slide-valves, the area being never made large enough to prevent there being always sufficient excess of pressure to keep the slide-valve steamtight on the cylinder face under ordinary working conditions.

The connection should be made by leading a pipe from the slide-cover, in the space enclosed by the relief ring, to the receiver or condenser, as the case may be ; this being preferable to drilling a hole in the back of the slide-valve to connect the hollow space inside the packing-ring with the exhaust port of the cylinder.

A cock should be provided in the pipe leading from the back of the slide-valve, and a small cock to open the space inside the ring to the atmosphere. By this means the efficiency of the relief arrangements can be tested by closing the cock in the pipe and noticing the amount of leakage as shown by the cock in connection with the atmosphere. A pressure-gauge should always be fitted to indicate the pressure inside the relief ring, so that the difference in pressure between this space and that of the slide casing can be always seen. For high steam pressures special care is necessary in this respect.

The relief rings are now generally fitted in the slide-cover, the back of the valve itself being a plane surface on which the ring slides, which arrangement possesses the advantage of enabling the packing-rings to be adjusted at any time from the outside, whether the engines are working or not, which cannot be done if the ring is fitted on the slide-valve.

Details of various relief rings.—The details of these relief rings vary considerably, but the principle is the same in all.

Fig. 155 shows the plan adopted by Messrs. Humphrys, Tennant & Co., in which steam is prevented from passing the back of the relief ring by means of a copper spring ring, which keeps the back of the relief ring steamtight. Details of this ring are shown on an enlarged scale in Fig. 156. Stops are fitted at each end of the ring to prevent the

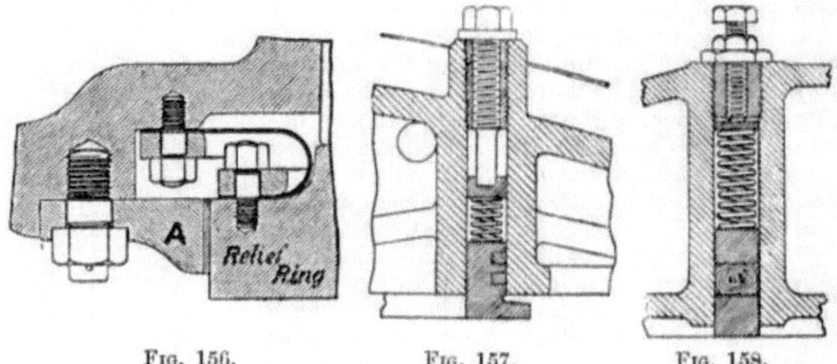

Fig. 156.   Fig. 157.   Fig. 158.

friction of the valve on the relief ring straining the copper ring. These stops are shown at A.

Other plans of relief ring are also shown, in which different methods of preventing leakage past the back of the relief ring are used. In Fig. 157 this consists of small *Ramsbottom rings*. In Fig. 158 a turn of soft packing is used as shown. Fig. 159 shows a ring working on the valve casing known as *Church's relief ring*.

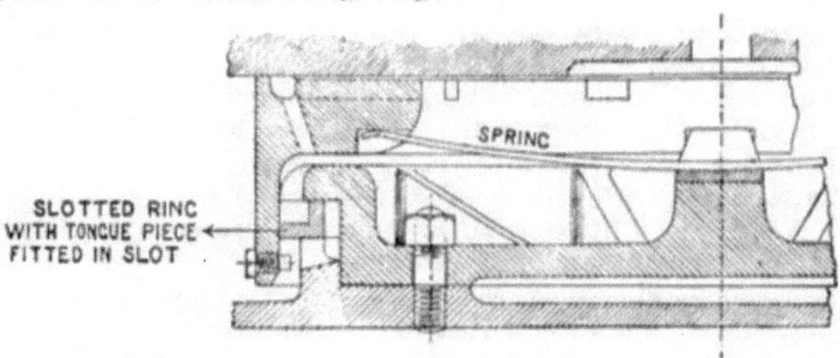

Fig. 159.

A series of spiral springs is generally fitted in recesses, pressing the relief ring against the back of the slide-valve. In two or more of these recesses the springs are omitted and stop pins fitted, a sketch of one being given in Fig. 160. These are so fixed that their points are about $\frac{1}{32}$ inch clear of the relief ring, and they prevent the slide-valve from leaving the cylinder face by more than this distance. A washer should be fitted, so that these cannot be inadvertently screwed up beyond their correct positions. In Fig. 159, showing one form of Churen's ring, a flat spring is used for pressing it against the valve-casing cover.

Unfortunately, however, relief rings for the back of flat slide-valves do not behave in an entirely satisfactory manner. They are troublesome to make efficient when new, and are difficult of accurate adjustment, and it is often found that they do not remain efficient for long periods, especially with the higher pressures.

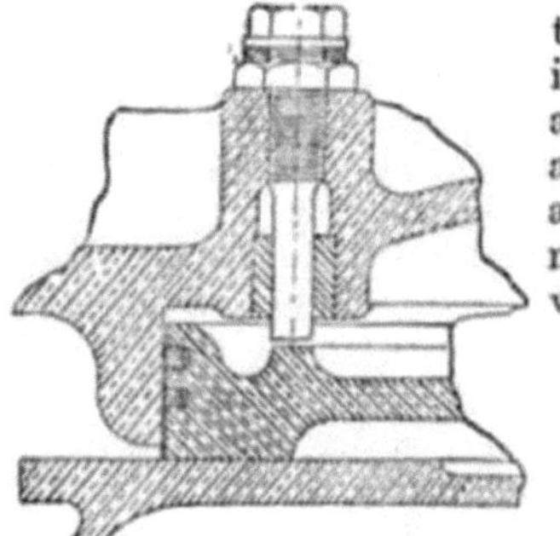

FIG. 160.

Piston slide-valves. To overcome this defect, the slide-valves of the high and usually the intermediate cylinders of engines using high-pressure steam are fitted with cylindrical or piston slide-valves, instead of flat slide-valves, so that the steam does not cause any pressure between the rubbing faces, and no relief arrangements are necessary. The valve is formed by two pistons connected together, which work in cylindrical chambers that contain the steam ports, and are generally kept steam-tight by spring rings in the usual manner. The face of each of the pistons corresponds to the bars of the single ported flat slide-valve, and is of the same length, i.e. it is just long enough to cover the steam ports and allow the necessary lap.

These valves are single-ported, as double-ported piston-valves

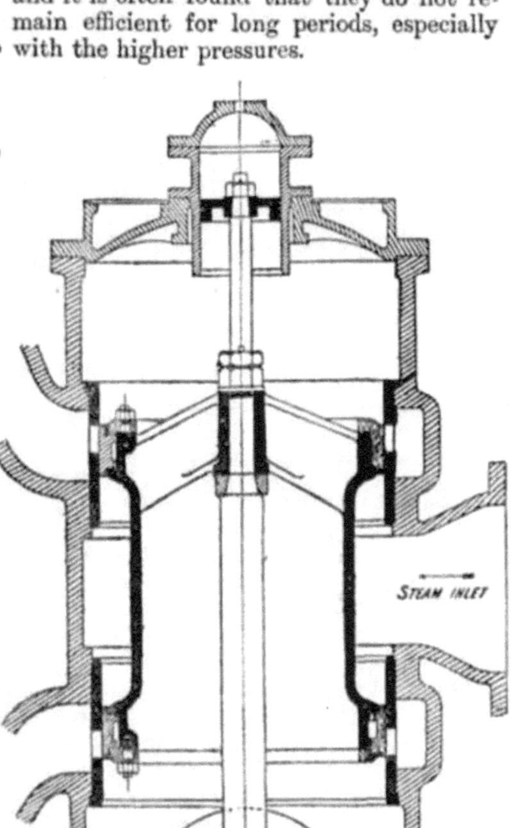

FIG 161.

would be very complicated, and are unnecessary, owing to the considerable length of port secured by the cylindrical form.

The face of the circular slide-valve may be imagined to be formed from a flat valve face by curving the latter into the circular form. The steam is either admitted to the spaces on the outside of the two pistons with the exhaust space between them, or *vice versâ*. In the form shown in Fig. 161 the steam is admitted to the space between the two pistons around the tube that connects them together, while the exhaust takes place at the outer ends of the pistons, and the exhaust steam from the opposite ends of the valve-chest is in communication through the tube that connects the two pistons together. In Fig. 162, which

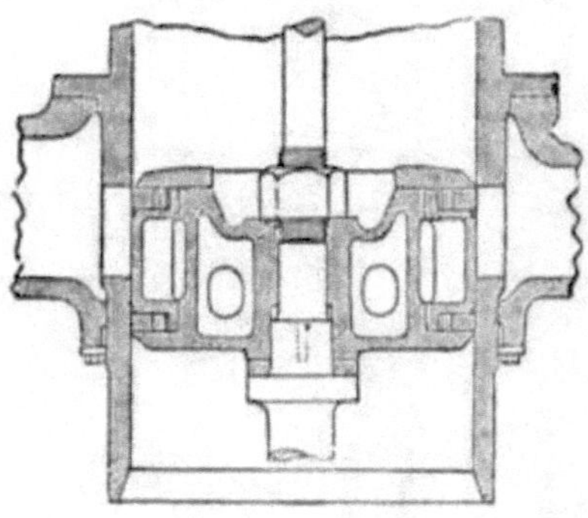

Fig. 162.

shows the lower half of a piston-valve at the centre of its stroke, a steam pipe connecting the two ends is carried outside the cylinder. The steam is admitted to the cylinder from the outsides of the valves, the exhaust taking place on the inside. The steam ports are formed in separate cylindrical faces secured to the cylinder ports, as shown, and the openings are stayed with bars, that run diagonally across and serve also as guides for the piston-valves, and prevent the packing-rings springing out into the ports.

Balance pistons, &c.—In vertical engines the weight of the slide-valve, rod, and link-gear will all be taken by the eccentric and its strap, unless means are fitted to prevent this. With large slide-valves in vertical engines balance pistons are therefore fitted to take the weight of valves and gear off the links and eccentrics. Small cylinders with pistons are fitted on top of the slide casing immediately over the slide-valve, as shown in Figs. 153 and 161. The lower side of the balance piston is in connection with the slide casing, the steam pressure in which acts on the balance piston, the area of which is so arranged that the total steam pressure is sufficient to balance the weight of the gear.

The top of the balance cylinder is connected by a pipe with the exhaust steam from the cylinder.

With piston slide-valves the balancing can be effected by making the diameter of one end of the valve a little greater than that of the other, so that the steam pressure acting on the excess area balances the weight of valves and gear.

Momentum cylinder.—With very fast-running engines the momentum of the moving slide-valves brings considerable forces to bear on the eccentrics and link motion, so that it is important to reduce the weight of the valves to the lowest point consistent with strength. In fast-running engines of torpedo boats and destroyers the valves are often of gunmetal, or similar composition, to effect this object ; but even when all is done that can be in this direction, the momentum forces at speeds of, say, 400 revolutions per minute are very considerable. A simple momentum cylinder is often fitted above the slide-valve to neutralise this. This consists of a small piston and cylinder, with arrangements for compressing a certain volume of steam or air at the end of each stroke of the valve, to absorb the forces due to the velocity of the valves and bring them gradually to rest without strain.

Joy's assistant cylinder.—Sometimes arrangements are supplied with vertical slide-valves, not only to support the weight of the valve, but to also relieve the eccentrics and link-gear of most of the work required to move the valve to and fro.   One such arrangement is Joy's assistant cylinder, Fig. 163.

This consists of a small cylinder and steam-piston attached to the valve-spindle.   The cylinder has a central inlet for steam, A, and two exhaust ports, B, one for each end, leading to a common exhaust pipe, and the piston is so constructed that by its motion the operations of steam admission, cut-off, release, and compression are performed on each side of the piston. The apparatus is, therefore, a small engine which exercises a force on the valve to move it up or down, and cushions steam at each end to absorb the momentum forces.   These assistant cylinders give diagrams similar to that of an ordinary engine ; they exert from 15 to 25 I.H.P. each for the sizes fitted in marine engines, and the amount of power developed can be adjusted by means of a valve on the steam-pipe.   If the main valve be linked in, the assistant cylinder is also automatically similarly affected.

Eccentrics and rods for large marine engines.—Eccentric sheaves for large marine engines are of cast-iron, and are generally made in two

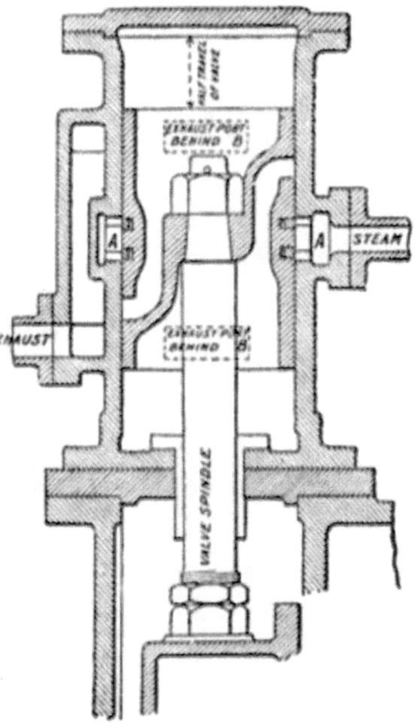

Fig. 163.

parts, owing to the couplings, &c., preventing their being put on the shaft in one piece.   The parts are firmly secured together by bolts.   The rod is of wrought-iron or steel, and generally has a T end, by means of which it is secured to the eccentric strap by studs and nuts.

The two halves of the eccentric strap were for many years made of gunmetal.   In some examples the eccentric strap, as well as the rod, is made of wrought-iron or steel, one-half of the strap being forged solid with the rod, with gunmetal liners fitted to the strap to form the rubbing surfaces.

In the most recent practice the strap is of forged or cast-steel, lined with white metal, which forms the rubbing surface working on the cast-iron sheave.   This combination of metals has been found to give excellent results, and it is now specified by the Admiralty.

Fig. 164 shows the details of a modern eccentric sheave, strap, and rod, the sheave being lined with white metal. In some examples, in order to reduce the diameter of the eccentric sheave, the smaller of the two parts is made of wrought-steel, which enables the least thickness

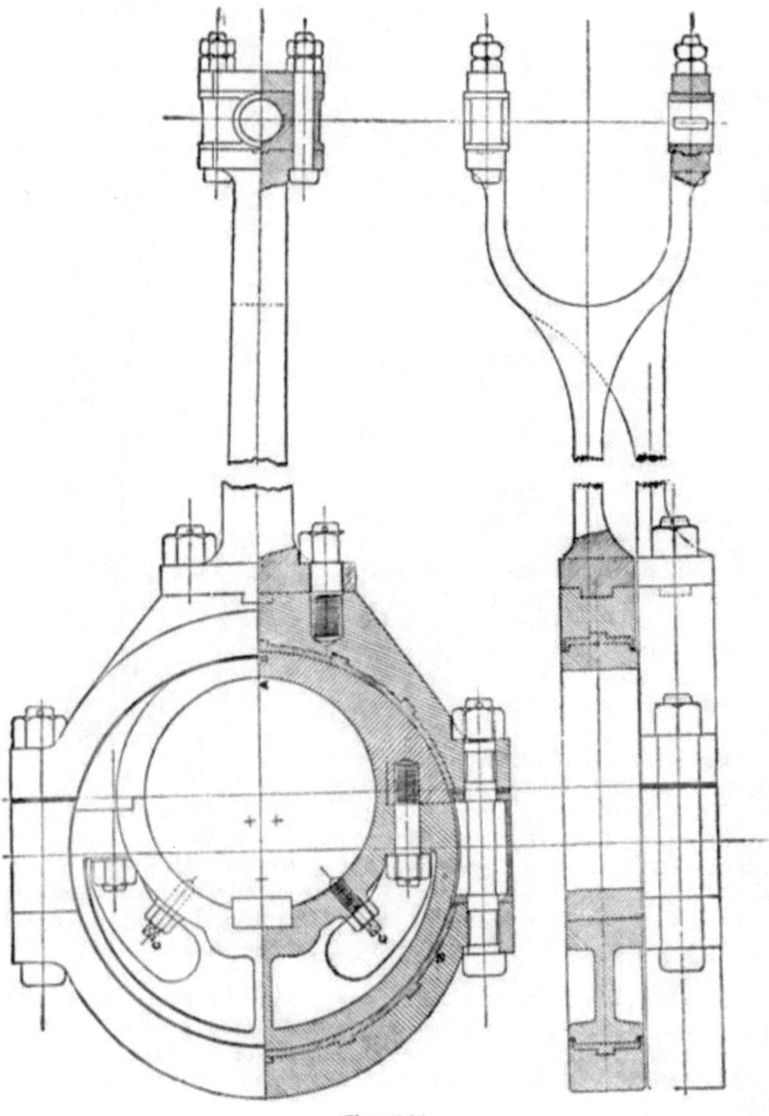

Fig. 164

of the sheave around the shaft at A B to be diminished. Set screws, C, are fitted for purposes of adjustment before the key is fitted.

CHAPTER XVII.

STARTING AND REVERSING ARRANGEMENTS.

ALL marine engines must be arranged so as to be capable of being worked in opposite directions, in order that the ship may be driven either ahead or astern. It is necessary, therefore, that suitable reversing gear should be fitted to enable the slide-valves to be placed in the proper positions to produce revolution of the crank-shaft in either direction.

Loose eccentric.—In the earlier paddle-wheel steamers this was accomplished by means of a single eccentric, fitted *loosely* on the shaft,

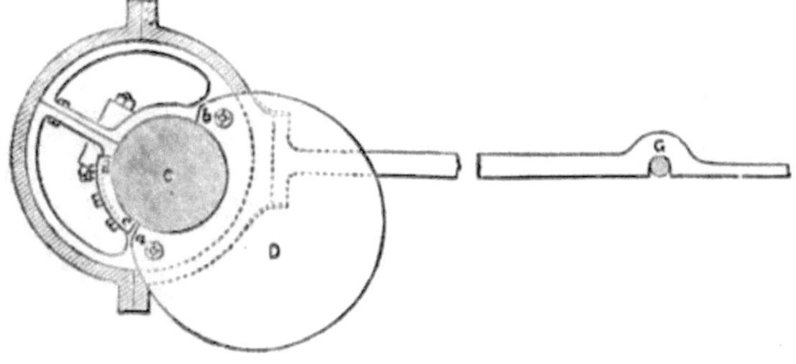

Fig. 165.

and driven by stops fixed in suitable positions on it, to give either ahead or astern motion as required. A sketch of this arrangement is given in Fig. 165.

This loose eccentric is balanced by means of the disc D, to prevent it falling away from its position when the slide-valve is moved by hand. The eccentric rod is attached to the slide-valve rod by means of the gab G at its end, which fits over a corresponding pin on the end of the slide-rod. In starting or reversing these engines the gab G is disconnected from the slide-rod, and the slide-valves worked by hand to start the crank-shaft revolving in the proper direction, or reverse its motion as the case may be, and cause the stop for the proper motion to come in contact with the eccentric, and drive it in the required direction. The gab end then drops over the pin and continues the motion.

In Fig. 166, let O R represent the position of the crank on the dead point. Then, from what has been previously explained about the motion of the slide-valve, if steam be taken at the outside edges of the valve, and the eccentric radius be in the position O P, the crank will revolve in the direction A B C, whilst if the eccentric arm be in the position shown by the dotted line O Q, the motion of the crank will be in the opposite direction A Q C. The stops on the crank-shaft must, therefore, be so arranged as to bring the eccentric pulley to the position O P, or to the position O Q, according as the engine is to be driven ahead or astern.

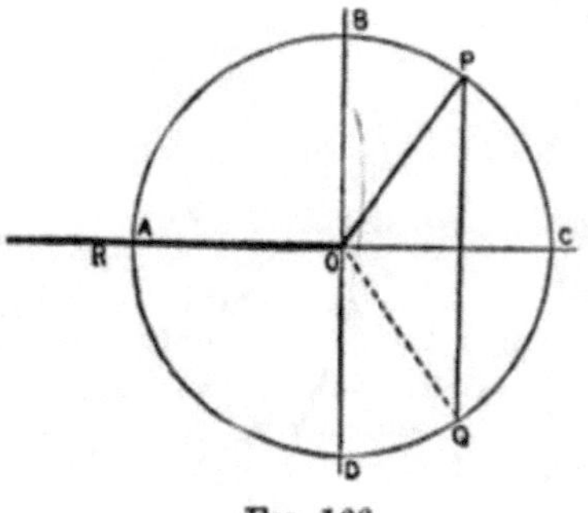

Fig. 166.

The manner in which this is accomplished is shown in Fig. 165. On the crank-shaft, C, is fixed a stop $c\,d$, extending a sufficient distance round its circumference, and the ends of D, the balancing disc on the eccentric, are arranged to form corresponding stops, a and b. When, therefore, the top of the shaft revolves from right to left, the edge c comes in contact with a, and the eccentric and shaft revolve together so long as the motion continues in this direction; but as soon as the engine is reversed, the stops become detached, and after about a quarter revolution the edge d comes in contact with b, and the engine works in the reverse direction.

Link motion.—The reversing of modern marine engines is usually effected by means of the 'link motion,' which was invented by Stephenson. It is simple in construction, and not only can the engines be reversed by it, but it provides for a considerable range of expansive working of the steam, without the interposition of any other gear.

The general construction and arrangement of this gear are shown in Fig. 167. On the crank-shaft C there are keyed two eccentrics, one

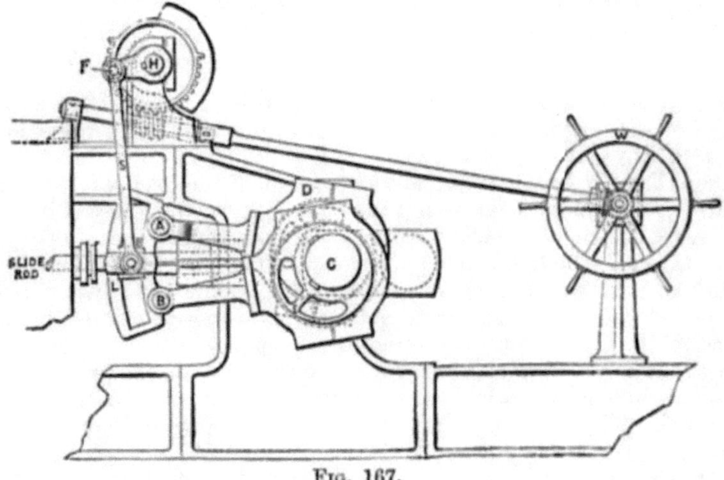

Fig. 167.

in the position to give ahead motion and the other in the position for astern motion. The eccentric rods are of equal length, and their ends are attached by working joints to the opposite ends of a curved link L, with a slot in the centre, which slides over a brass block B, to which the end of the slide-valve rod is attached. This gear forms a ready means of throwing either of the eccentrics into gear as desired, and at the same time throwing the other out of gear.

It will be seen that when the link is moved from its middle position, so as to bring the pin A in a line with the slide-valve rod, the motion of the valve will be governed by the eccentric D, while the other simply swings the link without affecting the motion of the slide-rod. If, on the other hand, the link be moved to the other side, so as to bring the end of the eccentric rod B in a line with the slide-rod, the eccentric E will govern the motion of the slide-valve, the other eccentric having no effect, and the engine will work in the reverse direction. When the link is in the central position the motion of the valve is considerably reduced, and the distribution of the steam is such that no revolution of the engine could ensue.

The centre of the link is commonly called its 'dead point.' If the link be placed in such a position that the sliding block B is between the centre and the ahead end of the link, the ahead eccentric exercises the greatest influence over the motion of the valve, so that the engine continues to work in the ahead direction; but the astern eccentric has now some effect in modifying the motion of the valve, the result being that the travel of the slide-valve will be less than when the link is at its extreme position, and all the operations of the valve will be earlier than when in full gear, as if the valve were now being worked by an eccentric with greater angle of advance and smaller throw. The steam is therefore cut off earlier and worked expansively.

The operation of working expansively by means of the link motion is technically called 'linking up' in horizontal engines, or 'linking in' for vertical engines, or, generally, 'shortening the link.'

Varieties of links. — There are three varieties of links used : (*a*) the slotted link, (*b*) the solid-bar link, and (*c*) the double-bar link.

The *slotted link* consists of a curved bar with a slot cut in it (Fig. 168), in which slot the link block is fitted. This link block is attached to the slide-rod by a pin about which an oscillating motion of the block occurs. Two projections are formed on the link on one side, with eyes to which the ends of the two eccentric rods are attached. This is the original form of Stephenson's link, and is still commonly used in small engines. The centre of the eccentric-rod end cannot in this form be made to coincide with the centre line of the link block, and the motion is not so regular or the means of adjustment so good as in plan (*c*), which is now the general plan used for large vertical engines.

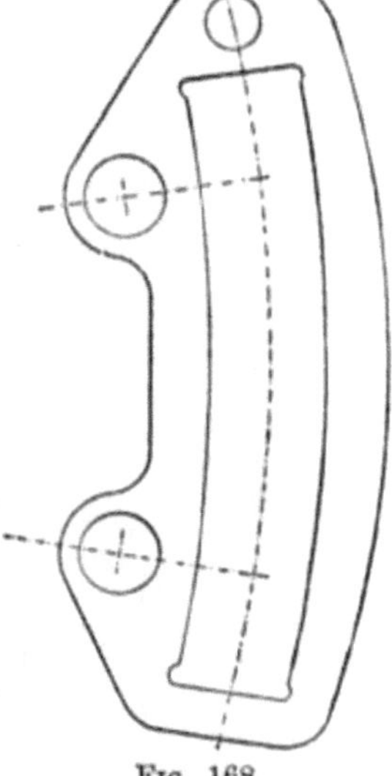

Fig. 168.

The *solid-bar link* (Figs. 169 and 170) is always fitted by Messrs. Humphrys, Tennant & Co., and consists of a simple curved rectangular bar, with eyes formed at each end for the attachment of the eccentric rods. The solid bar passes through the block, which consists of two segmental pieces of gunmetal, cylindrical on the outside, and which

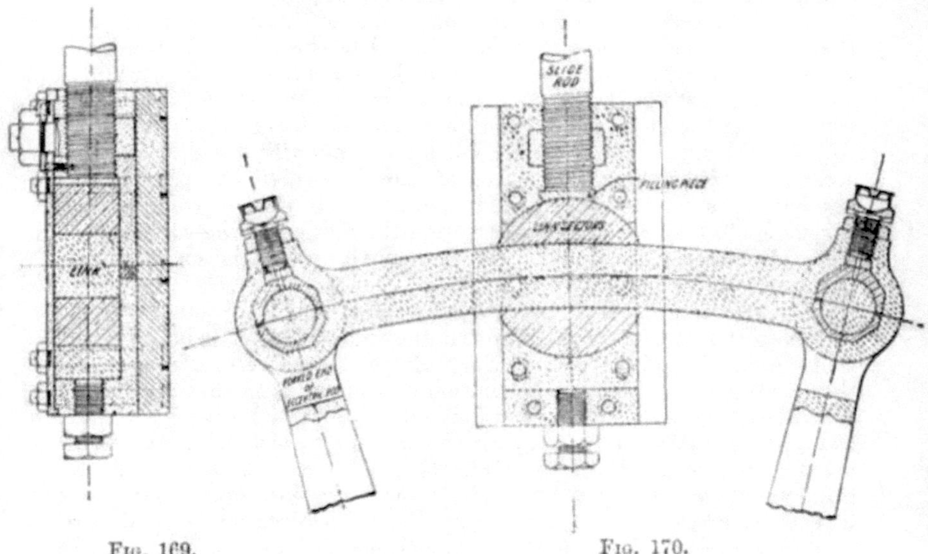

FIG. 169.　　　　　　　　　　　　FIG. 170.

have an oscillating motion in its bearing when at work. This variety also has the advantage of being easily adjusted in all parts. The end of the eccentric rod cannot be brought in line with the slide-rod, and even in full gear the motion is one with a 'shortened link.' The sketches show in detail the construction and means of adjustment of all parts.

The most general plan is the *double-bar link* (Figs. 171 and 172) consisting of a pair of curved steel bars joined together at the ends,

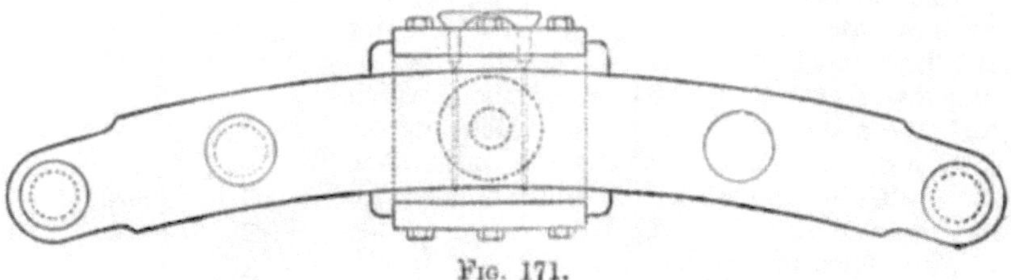

FIG. 171.

and kept a certain distance apart by distance pieces. Projecting pins are formed on the link bars, two on each side, for the attachment of the eccentric rods. The ends of the eccentric rods are forked, and contain each two adjustable bearings which embrace the pins on each side of the link. The link block consists of a steel or iron pin sliding between the bars, with top and bottom projections each side, which embrace the link bars. The link bars slide through these projections, and adjustable gunmetal liners are fitted as working surfaces between the link block projections and the link bars. All parts are capable of ready adjustment, and when the link is in full gear the centre of the

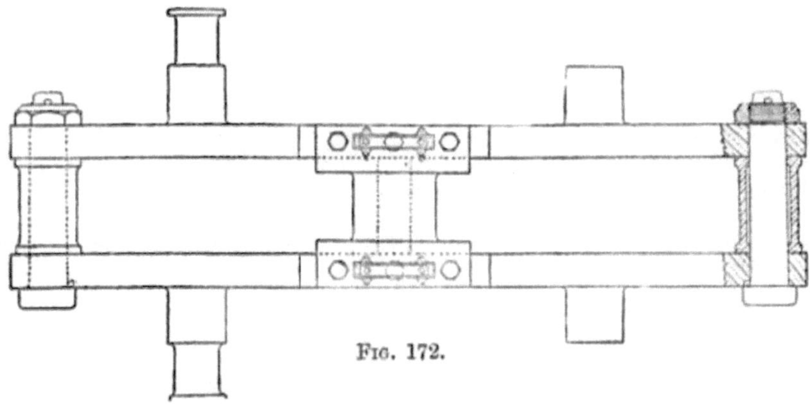

FIG. 172.

eccentric rod end coincides with that of the link block. Detailed sketches of the link block and its lubrication arrangements are given in Figs. 173 and 174.

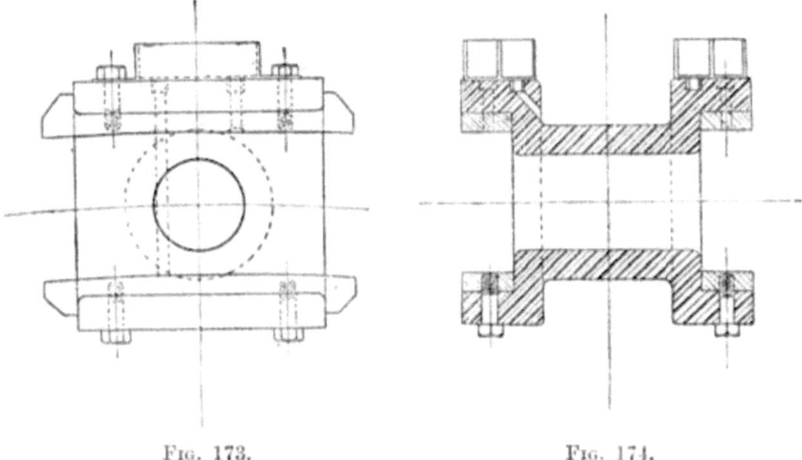

FIG. 173.

FIG. 174.

These different arrangements of link motion, however, only differ in the details of construction, the principles involved being the same in all.

For detailed construction of the eccentric sheave, strap, and rod see end of preceding chapter.

Curvature of link.—If the link were used simply for reversing the engines, its amount of curvature would not be of importance, or it may even be straight ; but as it is required to be used for working expansively, its shape must be such that when the block is in any intermediate position the centre of the travel of the valve will be always constant, otherwise the distribution of steam between the two ends of the cylinder would be interfered with. To effect this quite accurately the link should be a parabola of large focal distance, but an approximation sufficiently close for practical purposes is obtained by making it a circular arc of radius equal to the length of eccentric rod—i.e. the length between centre of eccentric sheave and centre of pin at end of rod.

Open rods and crossed rods.—If the eccentric rods are so placed that when the crank is pointing *towards* the link in cases where steam is taken on the *inside* edges of the valve, and pointing *away* from the link in cases where steam is taken on the *outside* edges of the valve, the rods are not crossed, the gear is said to have '*open rods.*' If, when the crank is so placed, the rods cross one another, the gear is said to have '*crossed rods.*' Figs. 175 and 176 show open and crossed rods respectively for the case in which steam is taken on the outside edges of the valve.

The motion produced on the slide-valve when the link block E is at any intermediate position, F, of the link may be found geometrically as follows. Connect the points A and B by an arc of a circle of radius $= \frac{1}{2} \frac{\mathrm{A\,B}}{\mathrm{C\,D}} \cdot \mathrm{A\,C}.$ For open rods this arc should be concave, and with crossed rods convex, to the centre O. If this arc be divided at the point G, in the same ratio that the point F divides the link, the motion of the slide-valve will be very nearly the same as if it were worked, direct, by an eccentric arm O G, having an angle of advance equal to the

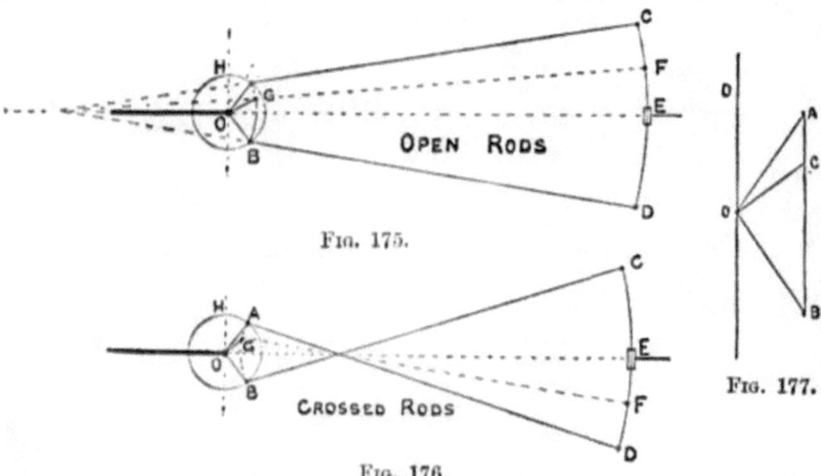

angle H O G. O G is called the '*virtual eccentric radius,*' and H O G the '*virtual angle of advance.*'

A simple approximation to the motion of the valve for any position of the block in the link, when the rods are long, may be made as follows. Let O, Fig. 177, represent the centre of the shaft, O A the ahead, and O B the astern eccentric radius. In full gear, O A is the throw of the eccentric, and the angle D O A is equal to the angular advance. For any intermediate position, divide the line A B at C in the same ratio that the block divides the link ; then the motion of the valve will be due, approximately, to an eccentric arm O C, set at an angle of advance equal to the angle D O C.

By drawing Zeuner's valve circle for the linked-in positions we see that all the operations are earlier, also that with open rods the lead greatly increases as we link in, while with crossed rods it slightly diminishes and may become negative. The objection to crossed rods is that the travel diminishes so considerably when linking up, causing wire-drawing, and for this reason they are not so common as open rods.

Starting gear.—The link is suspended generally at its centre or ahead end, as shown in Figs. 178 and 167, by the suspending rod s ; and during the working of the engines it oscillates about the pin F at the end of the suspending rod.

The object of the starting gear is to move the link into the proper position, to bring the correct eccentric into action for the required

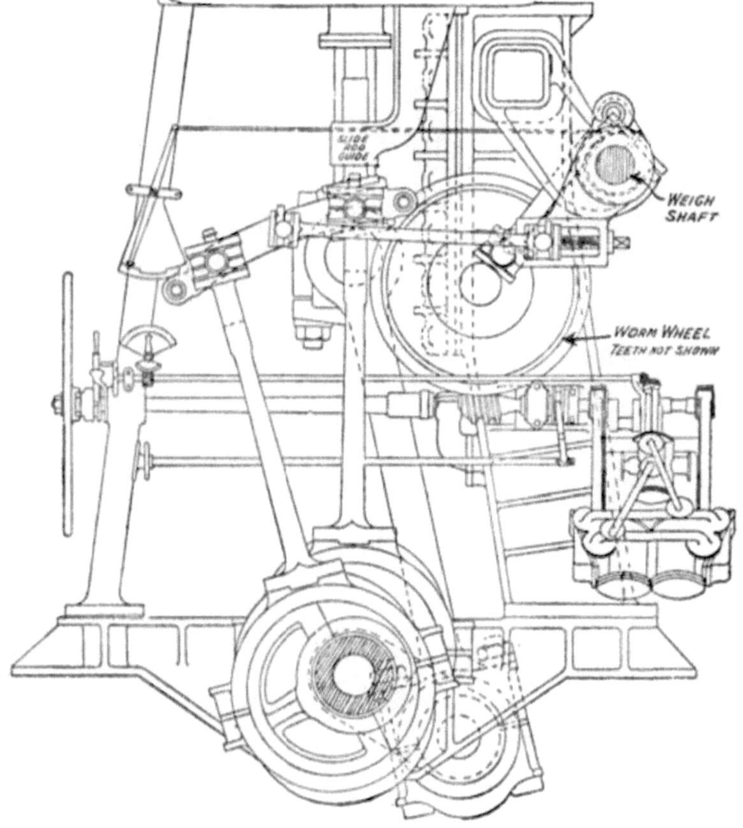

Fig. 178.

motion, and this is done in small engines, in which little force is required to move the slide-valves, by means of a simple lever.

In engines in which the slide-valves are large and require considerable force to move them, the starting gear is worked by steam as well as by manual power. The use of steam saves labour and considerably facilitates the handling of the engines. Steam-starting gear is now generally fitted to all marine engines, except very small ones. This also prevents the necessity of crowding the starting platform with men to stand by the starting gear, and renders it possible for the engines to be reversed quickly in case of emergency, with only the engineer of the watch in the engine room, without waiting for the assistance necessary with hand-starting gear.

Steam-starting gear fitted in H.M. Navy.—Fig. 178 shows a general arrangement of starting gear of the type used in the Royal Navy. The reversing and starting arrangement consists of a weigh-shaft running along the upper part of the engine columns on which are keyed a series of reversing levers, one to each link, which are attached to the latter by suspension rods, so that the operation of reversing or starting consists in moving this weigh-shaft through a certain angle. An additional lever is fixed on the weigh-shaft near the starting engine, and by means of this lever the starting engine actuates the weigh-shaft and moves the links to and fro. The engine is generally an ordinary double-cylinder reversible steam-engine which works a worm geared to a worm-wheel. To a point in this worm-wheel, the lever above referred to is attached by means of a rod. The angle through which the reversing lever and weigh-shaft turns between the extreme positions of ahead and astern is clearly governed by the diameter of the circle traversed by the pin on the worm-wheel, and the proportions are so arranged that the extreme travel is only just sufficient to move the links to the required positions. The worm-wheel is capable of continuous circular motion, and if the reversing engine is allowed to travel beyond the proper position no harm is done, and the links are only brought back again a small distance.

This is often spoken of as an 'all round' reversing gear, and with it the starting engines were often made non-reversible, and the worm-wheel allowed to travel round until the required position is reached. A longer time is thus taken to manipulate the engines. In the Royal Navy, however, where quick manœuvring is essential, they should always be reversible. This continuous motion reversing gear is also very useful for safely and quickly warming up the engines, for as soon as steam is available, if the reversing engine be kept slowly revolving in the same direction, the links are kept moving up and down and a small amount of steam passes safely through the engines.

To reduce the rapidity of the motion a double worm arrangement is often fitted, in which the engine is not connected directly to the main worm-shaft, but to a smaller worm, working a worm-wheel fixed on the main worm-shaft.

A hand wheel is fitted for use when steam is not available, or should any accident derange the starting engine, two clutches being fitted as shown, so that either the hand wheel or the starting engine can be used independently.

In cases in which a rotary engine is employed for starting purposes and the 'all round' arrangement is not fitted, there is a possibility of the engine running beyond the extreme working position, and either jamming the screw or other gear used, or straining the link motion. In such cases automatic stopping gear is necessary for the starting engine.

The steam for working the starting engine should be taken from a branch on the main steam pipe and not from the auxiliary steam service, the branch being on the boiler side of the regulating valve of the main engines.

Mercantile marine starting engine.—The general type of starting

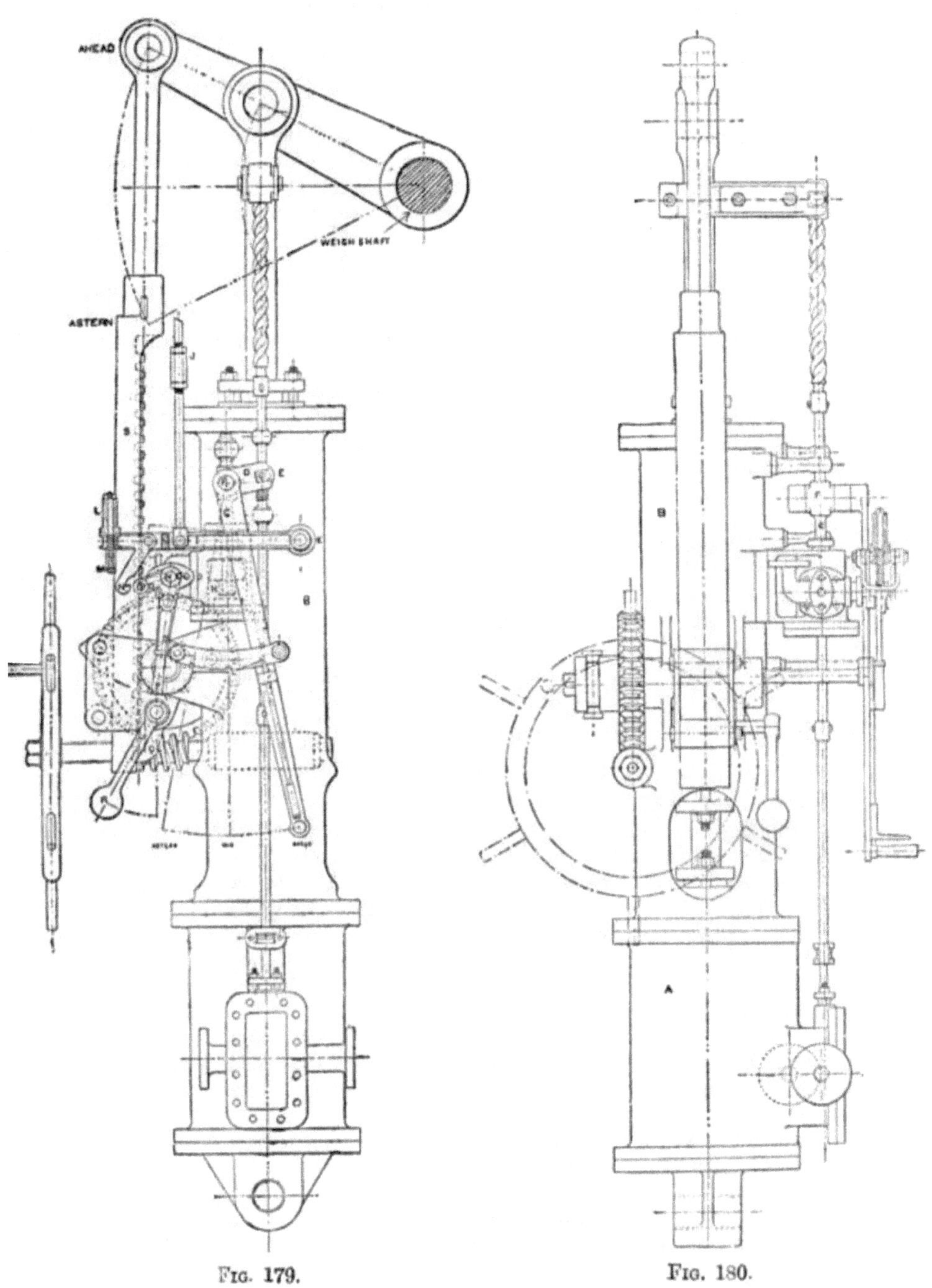

Fig. 179.

Fig. 180.

engine fitted in the mercantile marine consists of a direct-acting steam-engine with hydraulic cylinder brake, the piston-rod of which acts on the end of the weigh-shaft lever, pulling it to and fro, and thus moving the links and stopping or reversing the engine.

One of the most extensively used of such gears is that designed by Messrs. Brown Bros. & Co. Sketches of this reversing gear, similar in principle to that supplied by this firm to many vessels, are given in Figs. 179 and 180.

The reversing engine is attached to the bed-plate or column of the marine engine by the oscillating joint formed on the lower end of the steam cylinder A. In this cylinder a piston and rod are fitted, the latter being continued through the top and attached to a metallic-packed piston, working in the hydraulic cataract cylinder B, which is filled with water to steady the motion of the engine. The rod passes through a metallic-packed stuffing-box on the steam cylinder, and through stuffing-boxes at each end of the hydraulic cylinder, and its upper extremity is attached to the weigh-shaft lever which actuates the links of the main engine.

The starting engine is handled by the long lever indicated, working in a quadrant, which is notched for the positions ahead or astern, or any intermediate expansion necessary. On moving this lever in either direction it moves the valve-rod of the steam cylinder A, and admits steam to one side of it, and thus actuates the weigh-shaft and the link motion. A horizontal arm with coarse spiral nut is attached to the piston-rod, working on a coarse spiral thread cut on a prolongation of the valve spindle of the cylinder A, the motion of the reversing engine, with the arm and spiral-nut, causes the valve spindle to revolve, screwing it back to the shut position through the nut E (Fig. 179), which is operated upon by the reversing lever.

The oscillation of the engine is so small that any practical length of copper pipe for steam or exhaust usually met with in marine engines is sufficient to give the requisite amount of elasticity without stuffing-boxes.

The independent hand gear with locking arrangement is also shown in the figures. The locking device Q is fitted with a balance weight R, and engages the teeth of a rack. When working with shortened links, the reversing valve is left slightly open to keep a strain upon the pawl, so that the links are held firmly. At the same time the engine is ready for immediate reversal astern. Any motion in that direction causes the pawl to fall out. The rack s is actuated in the usual way by a pinion attached to a worm-wheel shaft, which in its turn is operated upon by the worm and wheel driven by the hand wheel as shown.

In many recent engines Messrs. Brown's automatic emergency governor has been fitted, in view of some serious casualties which have occurred through the racing of marine engines to a dangerous extent, caused by broken shafts or propellers.

Brown's governor gear.—The governor arrangement is shown in the drawings, and acts as follows :—

The reversing lever is in this case attached to a *movable* fulcrum F attached to a piston working in the small additional steam cylinder H. This fulcrum is *fixed* in cases where no governor gear is fitted. The cylinder is connected to the cock c, which admits steam to the bottom of the piston when the engines are working at safe speed. The end of the reversing lever D works the starting engine valve gear at E. Another lever I is reciprocated about three inches by the rod J, attached to the indicator gear, air-pump levers, or other parts of the engines. This lever works on a fixed fulcrum K, and carries a small weight L supported on a spiral spring in the box M, adjusted to act at an unsafe speed. This weight has a groove into which the upper end of the bell-crank lever N gears, while the lower end is ready on emergency to engage and turn the lever of the cock c.

When the engines are working at their normal speed the spring is so set that the weight L (which compresses the spring at each stroke of the engine in virtue of its momentum) shall not cause the lower end of the lever N to approach too near the lever o. Should the engines exceed a safe speed the momentum of the weight will compress the spring, so as to cause the hook N to engage the lever on the cock, turning steam above the piston of cylinder H, and exhausting it from the bottom, pulling the fulcrum F down, carrying with it the starting-engine valve-rod E, which turns steam on the top of the piston of starting engine A, and so moves the links into or near mid-gear.

The motion of the main engines is thus arrested simultaneously in all the cylinders, more rapidly than by closing the stop-valve, however quickly the latter may be effected. When this action has taken place the piston of the governor cylinder can be returned to its normal position by the handle P, when necessary to restart the engines. As the links are only moved to mid-gear, the apparatus forms an efficient governor without completely stopping the engines, as the momentum of the ship causes them to revolve slowly, when the attention of the engineer on watch is at once attracted. Being always in motion and in sight, it is not open to the objection frequently made of governors, that they are liable to be found out of order when wanted.

Differential reversing valve.—Steam-starting engines are made reversible, sometimes by fitting them with double eccentrics and link motion, but more generally by fitting them with a special reversing valve, called a '*differential valve*,' shown in Fig. 181, which illustrates one form of starting engine fitted with automatic stopping-gear.

The engine in this case is fitted with a single fixed eccentric ; and as this must be capable of working the starting engine in either direction, it must be keyed on the shaft at right angles to the crank (see page 178)—that is, the eccentric has no angular advance, and consequently the slide-valve must be without either lap or lead.

The reversing valve, or differential valve, is shown at K, and is of similar construction to an ordinary slide-valve, but it has suitably arranged ports, and is worked by hand by means of a lever. It may be either an ordinary slide-valve, as there shown, or, more generally, a cylindrical valve, the action of which, however, is precisely similar to that of a flat valve. The space A outside the reversing valve K is kept supplied with steam, while the hollow of this valve is in connection with the exhaust. The valve K, as drawn, is in its middle position, and the reversing engine is stopped. If, now, the reversing valve K be lowered by moving the handle to the right, steam flows from A through the upper port to the outer edges of the cylindrical slide-valve, while the inner edges of this slide-valve have free communication with the exhaust through the lower port of the reversing valve, and the engine then rotates.

If the reversing valve K be now raised, the upper port of the reversing valve is cut off from the steam space A, and placed instead in connection with the exhaust through the hollow of the reversing valve, while the lower port of the reversing valve is opened to the steam supply space A, instead of being, as before, in connection with the exhaust. The inner edges of the cylindrical slide-valve are now

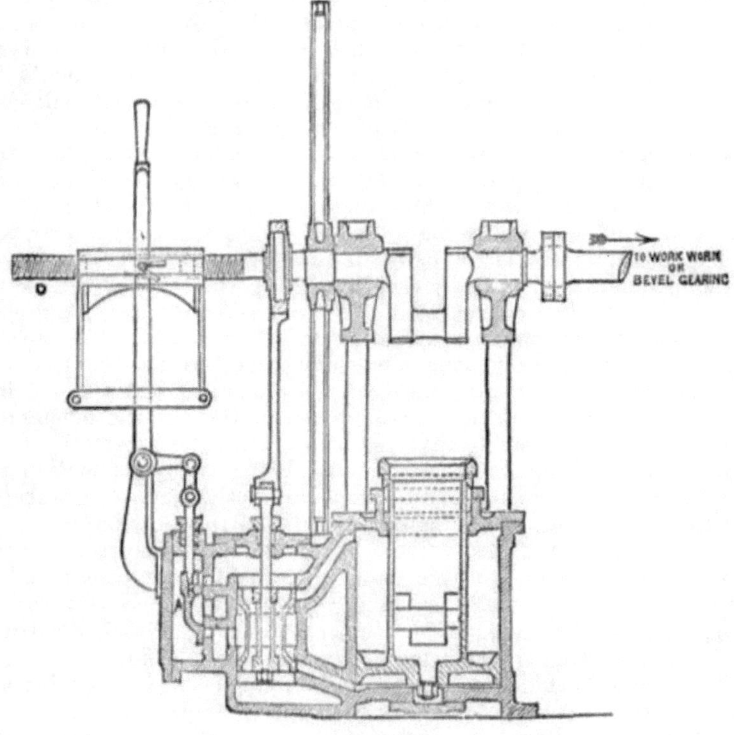

Fig. 181.

supplied with steam, while the outer edges are in connection with the exhaust, so that the steam and exhaust spaces of the engine slide-valve are interchanged, and the steam pressure is transferred from one side of the piston to the other, consequently the engine now moves in the reverse direction.

It should be observed that steam and exhaust are always on the same side of the reversing valve K, but changes at the engine slide-valve. The steam and exhaust supply to the reversing valve K are not shown on the drawing. In the particular example illustrated the shaft of the engine is screwed at D, and works a nut which actuates a frame at the reversing handle. When the latter is moved the revolution of the starting engine works the frame along, and brings the reversing handle back again to the vertical position, thus stopping the engine.

If flat slide-valves are fitted to the engine provision must be made to prevent them from being forced off the cylinder face, when the steam pressure is acting inside the valve and the outside is connected with the exhaust. Owing to the absence of lap on the slide-valve this arrangement is not economical in the distribution of steam, but it is very convenient, and is largely adopted in small engines, such as starting, steering, turning, turret, capstan, boat-hoisting engines, &c., in which economy is not of the first importance.

Radial valve gears.—Many different arrangements of gear for working the slide-valves have been designed to supersede the link-motion. Several of them produce a good distribution of steam at all points of cut-off, and have been often used in recent engines. In most of these slide-valve gears the motion of the valve is obtained by compounding two motions, one in the direction of motion of the piston and the other at right angles to it. By suitably proportioning the various parts and adjusting their positions relative to each other, any degree of expansion may be obtained with uniform lead at all points of cut-off, or the direction of motion of the engines reversed as may be desired.

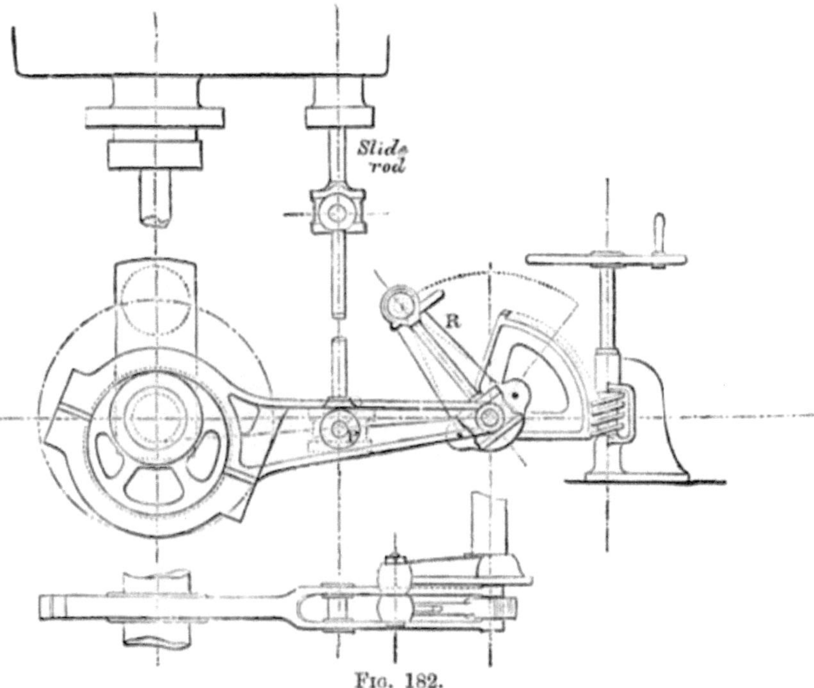

Fig. 182.

Marshall's valve gear.—This arrangement of slide-valve gear, which has been fitted by Messrs. Hawthorn, Leslie & Co. to a large number of marine engines, is illustrated in Fig. 182. In this system only one eccentric is used, the end of the eccentric rod being attached

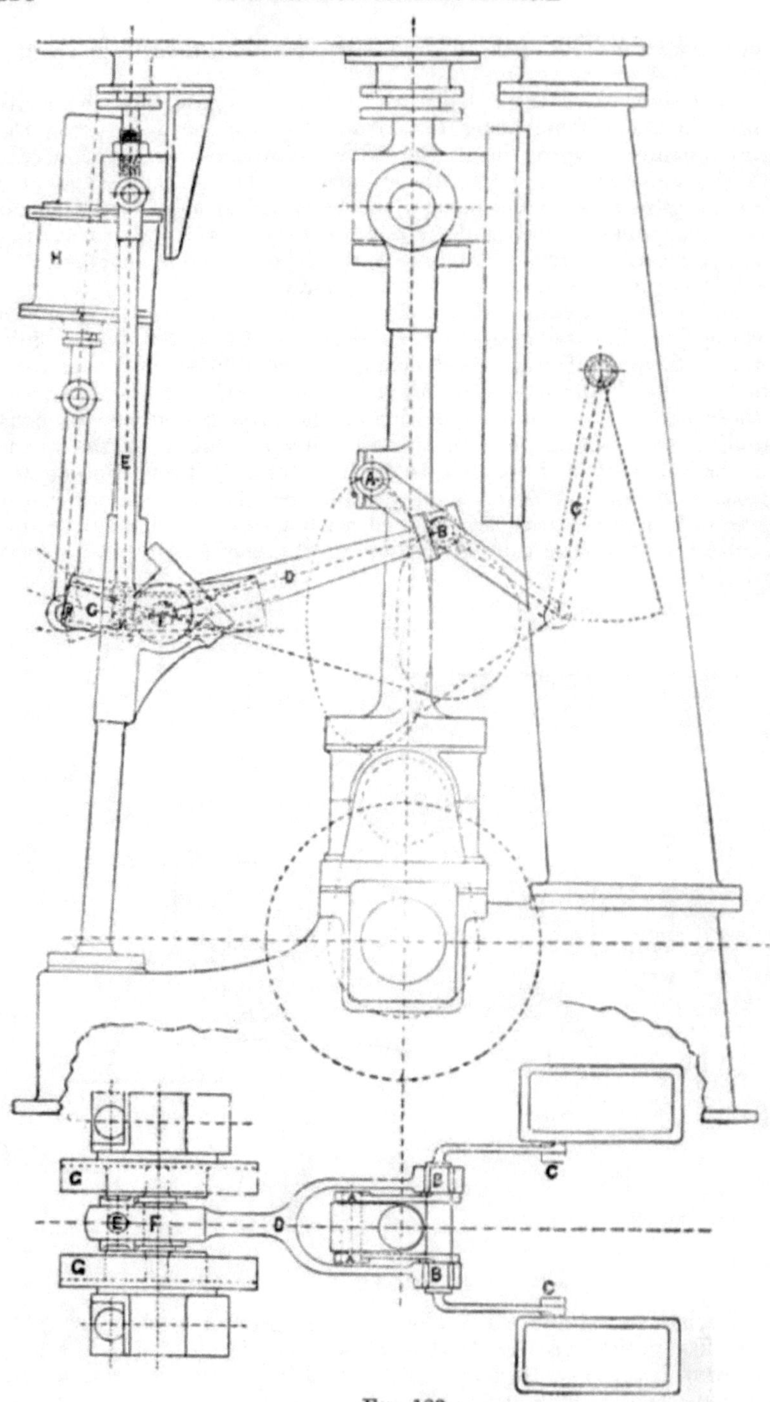

Fig. 183.

to a rod hung from a pin on the reversing shaft lever, R, by which it is constrained to move in an arc of a circle inclined to the centre line. To an intermediate point, P, in the eccentric rod a connecting link is attached which communicates the necessary motion to the slide-valve rod. By adjusting the position of the reversing lever, R, any desired degree of expansion can be obtained, or the engines reversed as required.

Joy's valve gear.—Fig. 183 shows an elevation and plan of the latest arrangement of Joy's valve gear applied to a vertical engine. In this gear eccentrics are dispensed with, and the movements of the slide-valve obtained from the connecting rod. The vibrating link B, jointed to the connecting rod at A, has one end constrained to move horizontally by the action of the radius rod C. One end of another rod, D, works on a pin in the vibrating link B, near the other end is a fulcrum carried by a pin F attached to sliding blocks on each side working in sectors G, which are carried by the reversing shaft, the centre line of the sector passing through the centre of the reversing shaft. From D the motion is communicated to the slide-valve rod by means of the link E, attached to a point K in the rod D beyond the fulcrum F.

The forward or backward movement of the engine is governed by inclining the sector on one or the other side of the horizontal centre line, and the amount of expansion depends on the amount of the inclination, the exactly central or horizontal position being 'mid-gear.' The reversing arm F R moves these sectors to the required position, and its extremity R is connected to the starting engine H. The paths of the point A in the connecting rod, and also of the point B in the vibrating link, as the engine revolves, are indicated by dotted lines, as are also the extreme positions of the sector centre lines for ahead and astern working respectively. The gear as drawn is in the stop position. By this gear a constant lead is secured for all linked-up positions, since when the piston is at the top or bottom of the stroke the pin F coincides with the centre of the reversing shaft, so that in this position any movement of the sectors does not affect the position of the slide-valve. The up and down motion of the point B therefore gives a constant movement of the valve equal to the *lap plus the lead*, while the horizontal motion sliding the block to and fro in the sectors adds the amount required for steam opening, this amount increasing with the angle of the sector to the horizontal.

This gear has been fitted to a large number of locomotive and marine engines. Where applied it will be seen that the slide-valves are in front of the engines, which shortens the length of the engines considerably. With the ordinary slide-valve the intervention of an intermediate shaft is necessary to work the valves in this position.

CHAPTER XVIII.

ARRANGEMENT OF THE CYLINDERS OF COMPOUND, TRIPLE AND QUADRUPLE EXPANSION ENGINES.

THE type used for modern engines in the mercantile and Royal navies is either the triple or quadruple expansion engine, by which with high-pressure steam considerable advantage is gained over the earlier types of engines as regards economy, in reduction of heavy stresses on the machinery, and in other respects.

We will first describe the reasons for the superiority of the old compound over the simple engine, and the arrangement of cylinders in the former, as this will explain the similar reasons which, with increased steam pressure, subsequently led to the abandonment of the compound type and the introduction of triple, and also large numbers of quadruple expansion engines.　Only one quadruple expansion engine above the steam pinnace size has so far been fitted in the Navy, viz. that of No. 90 first class torpedo boat, but their use in the mercantile marine is gradually extending.

The principal difference between the mechanism of the old simple expansion engines and that of triple expansion and other stage expansion engines is in the arrangement of the cylinders, the other parts being generally the same.　In the simple expansion engine the steam enters each cylinder direct from the boilers, and at the end of each stroke is exhausted direct into the condenser.　In the compound engine the steam from the boilers is only admitted direct to the smaller or high-pressure cylinder, and at the end of the stroke in that cylinder, instead of passing direct to the condenser, the steam enters a larger cylinder, called the 'low-pressure cylinder,' in which the expansion is completed, after which the steam passes as before to the condenser.

As will have been gathered from Chapter XIV., the compound engine has now been generally superseded by the triple expansion engine, in which the steam from the boilers is admitted to the high-pressure cylinder, from whence it is led to a larger cylinder called the 'intermediate-pressure cylinder,' in which it expands further and performs more work.　On being exhausted from the intermediate cylinder, it is conducted, as in the previous case, to a still larger cylinder, called the 'low-pressure cylinder,' in which its expansion is completed, and on being discharged from this cylinder it proceeds to the condenser.

Two-cylinder compound engines.—Two principal types of two-cylinder compound engines used to be fitted.　The type shown in Fig. 184, generally known as the 'tandem' type, has certain advantages and was largely adopted, especially for engines of large power. Two pairs of cylinders were fitted, so that large powers were obtained without introducing castings of extraordinary complexity. It was also the readiest form to which a simple engine could be converted.

This sketch shows the cylinders of a horizontal tandem compound engine with return connecting rods, numerous examples of which are still running in the Navy. In this type of engine a defect was that the clearance spaces in the high-pressure cylinders were very great, which decreased the expansive efficiency and caused considerable waste of steam.

The simpler and more usual arrangement was that with the high-

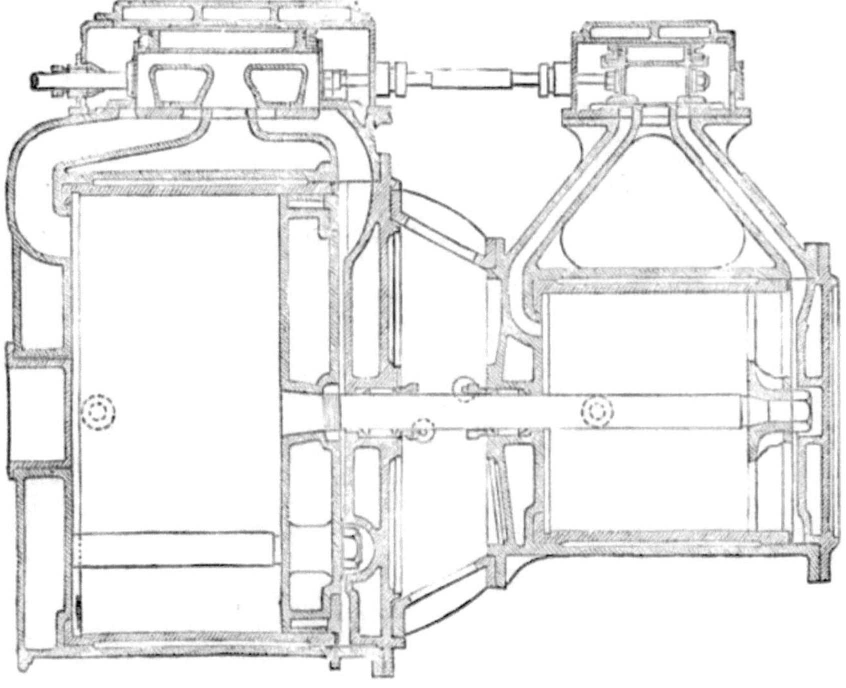

Fig. 184.

and low-pressure cylinders placed side by side, the pistons acting on cranks at right angles to each other.

Three-cylinder compound engines.—The ordinary three-cylinder compound engine is simply a modification of the type just described, but instead of a single low-pressure cylinder, two cylinders are used, the steam on exhausting from the high-pressure cylinder to the receiver being conducted to two low-pressure cylinders.

The three-cylinder type of compound engine was used when the power was so great that the employment of a single low-pressure cylinder would be inexpedient on account of its unwieldy dimensions, so that the division of the work between two low-pressure cylinders is preferable. The angles at which the cranks of three-cylinder compound engines were placed with respect to each other were very varied. In the majority of cases they were set at equal angles of 120°, but various other arrangements of cranks were common, depending on the opinion of the makers as regards regularity of twisting moments, and distribution of steam. It is, however, doubtful if any of these variations possessed any practical advantage over that of placing the cranks at equal angles with each other.

Definition of the term 'receiver.'—By the term 'receiver' is to be understood in the case of a compound engine the whole of the space between the high-pressure piston when at the end of its stroke, and the back of the low-pressure slide-valve or valves, comprising the volumes of the steam and exhaust passages of the high-pressure cylinder, the exhaust pipes from the high-pressure cylinder to the low-pressure valve casings, and the low-pressure valve casings themselves.

In the case of a triple expansion engine, the space between the high-pressure piston at the end of its stroke and the intermediate slide-valve is called the 'intermediate receiver,' and that between the intermediate piston at the end of its stroke and the low-pressure slide-valve the 'low-pressure receiver.'

Capacity of receivers.—Large reservoirs or receivers for the steam between the cylinders were usually fitted to the first compound engines, but experience proved that they were not required, all that was found necessary being a comparatively large exhaust pipe from the eduction orifice of the high-pressure cylinder to the steam inlet of the low-pressure cylinder, the volume of the exhaust passage and pipe from the high-pressure cylinder and the low-pressure valve casing being sufficient to allow for the compression that takes place between the release from the high-pressure cylinder and admission to the low-pressure cylinder. Similar remarks apply to the receivers of triple and quadruple expansion engines, and the volumes of these spaces which are necessary for other reasons are found to be sufficient for receivers. Most modern engines are made in this way.

The capacity of the receivers is immaterial so far as the total power of the engines is concerned, its effect being shown on the back pressure line of the diagram from the preceding engine, which becomes more nearly straight, and on the admission line of the diagram from the succeeding engine, which becomes more nearly parallel, to the atmospheric line as the volume of the receiver is increased.

Influence of size of cylinder on the power of stage expansion engines.—The power of any stage expansion engine, *working at any given rate of expansion*, depends entirely on the dimensions of its low-pressure cylinders, and is not affected by the size of the high-pressure cylinder, which must only be regarded as carrying out one stage in the expansion. The capacity of the low-pressure cylinder or cylinders of such an engine requires to be the same as that of the whole of the cylinders of a simple expansion engine of the same power working at the same initial pressure of steam and total ratio of expansion. Neglecting for the moment the complicating effects of clearance and compression, this will be easily seen from the consideration that since the initial pressures and the ratios of expansion are the same, the final pressures and volumes must be identical in the two cases. In the simple engine the whole of the steam at the end of the expansion fills all the cylinders, whilst in the compound engine it is contained by the low-pressure cylinders only. Consequently the capacity of the low-pressure cylinders of the compound engine must be equal to the capacity of all the cylinders of the simple expansion engine.

Mechanical advantages of compound and triple expansion engines.—A great advantage of the stage expansion engine, so far as its mechanism is concerned, is the facility with which it allows high rates of expansion of steam to be carried out without bringing excessive stresses on the framing. As an example, if we consider the cases of two engines working at the same number of revolutions, one simple, the other compound, each supplied with steam of 60 lbs. initial pressure, and developing 2,100 I.H.P. with a total rate of expansion of 8 times, we shall find that whilst the maximum turning moment in the case of the compound engine is 960 inch-tons, it would be 1,250 inch-tons in the engine with simple expansion, or more than 30 per cent. greater. the mean moment and therefore the horse-power being the same in the two engines.

In consequence of the greater uniformity of twisting moment, the shafting and framing may be made lighter in the compound than in the simple engine, and much greater steadiness of motion may be obtained, and more efficient action of the propeller in the water expected. The great variations of pressure to which the shafts of simple engines are exposed when worked at high rates of expansion appear to produce the same effect on the material that vibration does, viz. to cause the structure to become crystalline. Several cases of broken shafts in engines of this class were attributed to the excessive intermittent stresses brought on them.

In the compound engine, although the steam is expanded 8 times when developing full power, it can be expanded still more when working at reduced powers, whereas in the non-compound engine, the steam being expanded in a single cylinder, it cannot be expanded much more than 8 times, whatever the reduction in the power may be. This results from the necessary mechanical arrangements, and is altogether independent of any loss of efficiency that would ensue from liquefaction, &c., when attempting to carry out a high rate of expansion in a single cylinder.

The superiority of the stage expansion engine is further demonstrated as the engine becomes worn. When the slides and pistons begin to leak, the loss in the simple engine is much greater than in the compound, in consequence of the greater difference of pressure in the former.

The steam leaking past the piston in the simple engine goes direct to the condenser without doing any useful work, whilst in the compound engine the steam leaking past the high-pressure piston does useful work in the low-pressure cylinder before passing to the condenser, and the amount of leakage in the low-pressure cylinder is reduced on account of the considerably smaller difference of pressure on the two sides of the piston in that cylinder.

Use of expansion valves and independent expansion fittings.—Since the cylinders of triple expansion and compound engines provide in themselves for a considerable amount of expansion, special cut-off or expansion valves are now dispensed with, thus reducing the complexity and number of parts, as compared with the simple engine, in which expansion valves, suitable for early cut-off, are a necessity when high-pressure steam is used.

Many of the early compound engines, however, were fitted with expansion valves on the high-pressure cylinder, and some had expansion valves on the low-pressure cylinder also, in order to regulate the proportionate amount of work done by the two cylinders and equalise the stresses on the machinery. Without this valve, or some equivalent, at very low powers, as in warships on ordinary service, the work done in the low-pressure cylinder becomes very small. By setting the low-pressure expansion valve to an early cut-off, the pressure in the receiver, which forms the back pressure in the high-pressure cylinder, would be increased, so that the work done in that cylinder would be diminished and that in the low-pressure increased, and the power would consequently be more equally divided between the two cylinders.

Separate expansion valves are not now fitted to the cylinders, but to allow of adjustment in the points of cut-off, the reversing arms of the engines are now fitted with sliding blocks to enable the slide-valves to be linked up independently of the high-pressure valve, so as to vary the amount of expansion (see Chapter XV.).

Triple expansion engines generally.—The arguments which prove the superiority of the ordinary compound engine over the simple expansion engine when the working steam pressures were increased from 30 to 60 lbs. per square inch, also explain the superiority of the triple expansion engine over the compound engine for steam pressures above 120 lbs. per square inch. The principal gain in each case is the increased economy due to the greater amount of expansion conveniently obtained, and the reduction of the variation in temperature of the cylinders, which decreases the loss from liquefaction. Further, as previously mentioned, there is a more regular turning moment on the shafting, and a great reduction of maximum stresses on the engine and framework.

Some of the forms in which the triple expansion system has been carried out are illustrated in Figs. 185 to 195.

The arrangement shown in Fig. 185, has the high-pressure and intermediate pistons on the same rod, with the low-pressure acting on a separate crank at right angles to the other. Though convenient in some cases, this cannot be considered altogether satisfactory, as the stresses on the crank-pins would be very unequal.

In Fig. 186, each of the cylinders is fitted over a separate crank, the high, intermediate, and low-pressure cylinders being arranged in succession. This is the usual arrangement of triple expansion engines of moderate power both in the Royal Navy and mercantile marine. The cranks are arranged at equal angles with each other, although other arrangements have sometimes been fitted. The direction of revolution when going ahead may be either with the high pressure in advance of the intermediate, or the reverse.

Four-cylinder triple expansion engines.—For large powers, especially with quick-running engines, the low-pressure cylinder becomes so large as to require to be divided into two parts, although this generally necessitates four cranks, and an increase in the length of the engine room. We thus get the four-cylinder triple expansion engine fitted in H.M.S. 'Powerful' and 'Terrible' of 25,000 I.H.P., also in all subsequent battleships and cruisers where the horse-power exceeds 10,000, as shown in Fig. 187.

Fig. 188 shows another form suitable

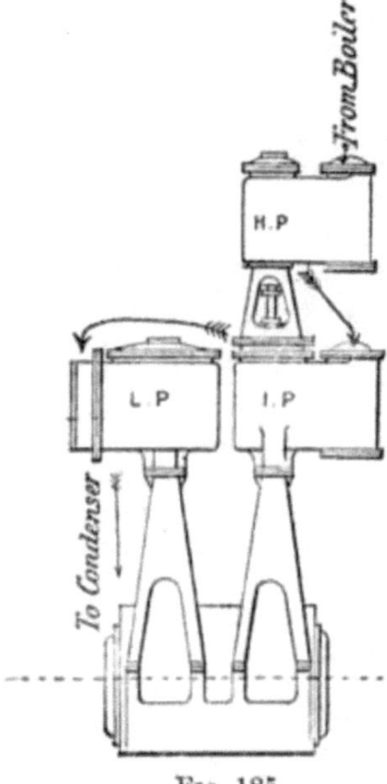

FIG. 185.

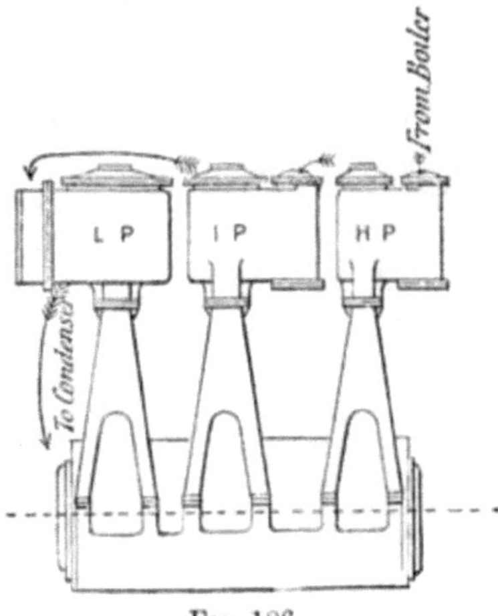

FIG. 186.

for high powers, which can be fitted in cases where a considerable height is available for the machinery, as is often the case in the mercantile marine. This does not require a great length of engine room, and produces fairly uniform strains on the shafting, the high and interme-diate-pressure cylinders being above the two low-pressure cylinders.

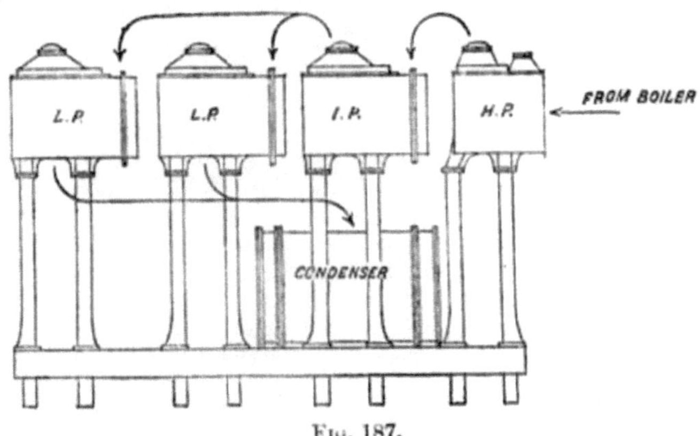

FIG. 187.

As previously pointed out, the relative positions of the cylinders do not affect the distribution of the steam, and are settled entirely by practical considerations. The four-cylinder triple expansion engine is now the most usual type for large triple expansion engines, and may be taken as the standard type of modern marine engine now being fitted in the Royal Navy, and a common type for the high power vessels of the mercantile marine. The proportions and relative situation of the four cylinders and the arrangement of the slide casings and other details differ considerably.

Usual arrangement of triple expansion engines.—A vertical and horizontal section through the cylinders and slide-valves of the most usual type of large triple expansion engine is given in Figs. 189 to 192. In this example it will be seen that circular slide-valves are fitted for the high-pressure and intermediate cylinders, and flat valves for the low-pressure cylinders. In this respect engines by various makers differ from one another.

The arrangement as drawn represents that being fitted in the majority of new naval engines. In this service some few examples have flat slide-valves fitted on the high-pressure cylinder also, while in

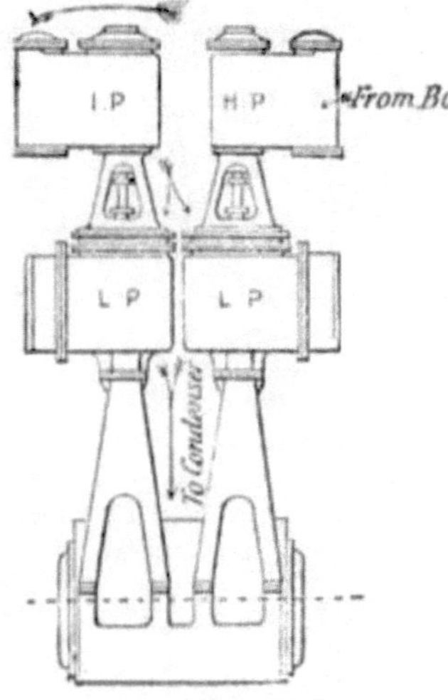

Fig. 188.

some of the earlier examples circular slide-valves have been fitted for all three cylinders. The Admiralty now specify that flat valves shall be fitted in the low-pressure cylinder and circular slides on the high pressure, the type fitted on the intermediate-pressure cylinder being also circular with the higher pressures of steam. Some circular slide-valves fitted were found difficult to keep steam-tight and allowed direct passage of steam to the exhaust side of the valve, and this is most objectionable in the low-pressure cylinder. Also, in this cylinder as the pressure forcing a flat valve against the cylinder face is not great there is no objection to its use.

Ratio of cylinders.—In the mercantile marine the ratio of low-pressure to high-pressure cylinder-volumes with triple expansion engines generally varies from 6 at 140 lbs. steam pressure, to 7 at 160 lbs. pressure, and $7\frac{1}{2}$ at 180 lbs., and rather an earlier cut-off in the high-pressure cylinder is arranged for than is usual in the Navy. In the Navy smaller ratios of cylinders are fitted for the following reasons. In the first place the naval engine seldom works at full power, this being reserved for special occasions, while the mercantile vessel generally works at near full power. The greater part of the steaming in the Navy is performed at only a small fraction, say, on the average, about one tenth the full power.

It is also of great importance to keep the weight and space occupied by the machinery as small as possible, as very large powers are provided. To reduce the weight, therefore, the size of cylinders and amount of expansion allowed at full power is limited, as the economy at the highest power is not so important as that at lower powers. Limiting the size of the cylinders conduces to greater economy at low powers,

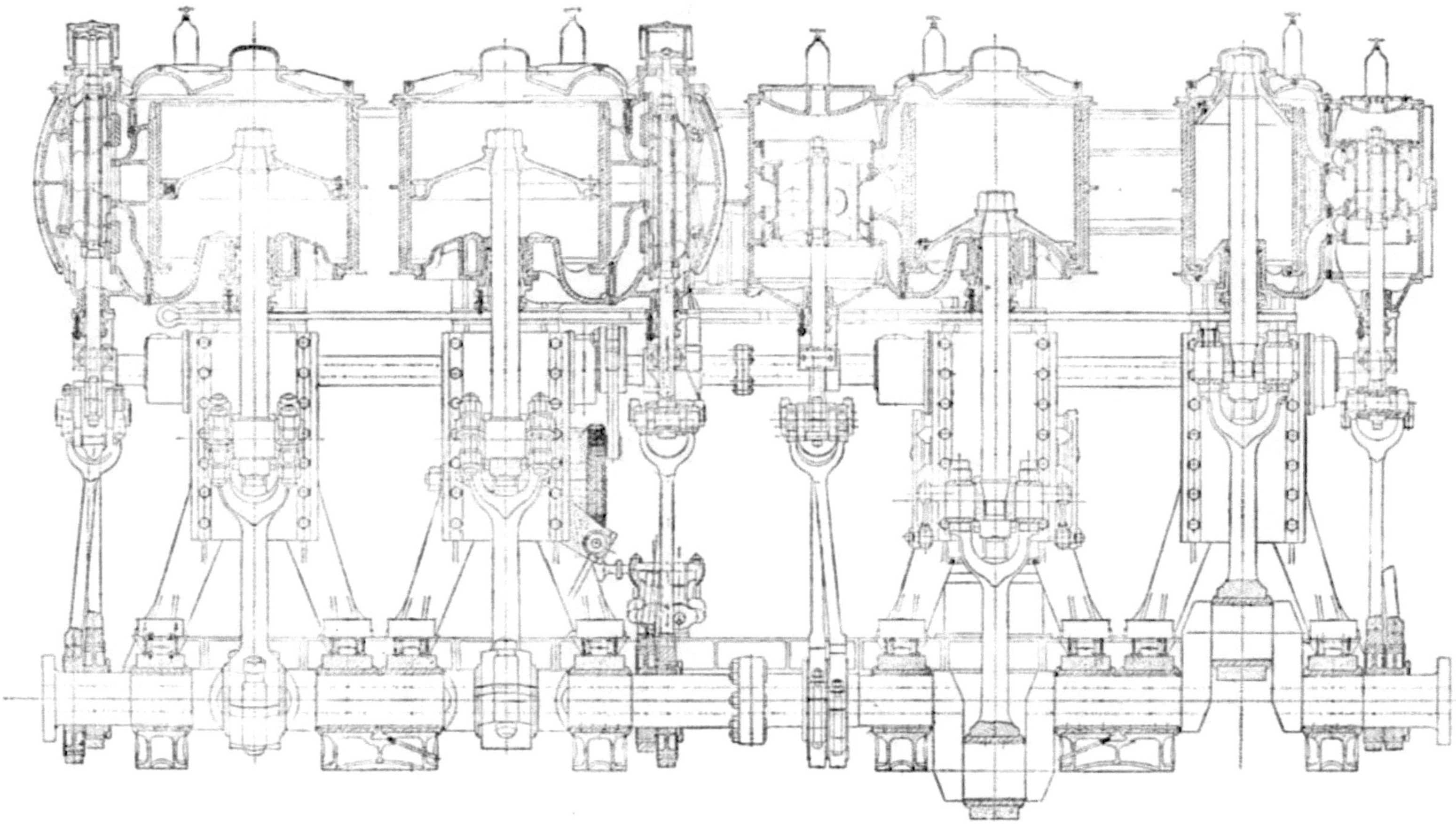

Fig. 189.

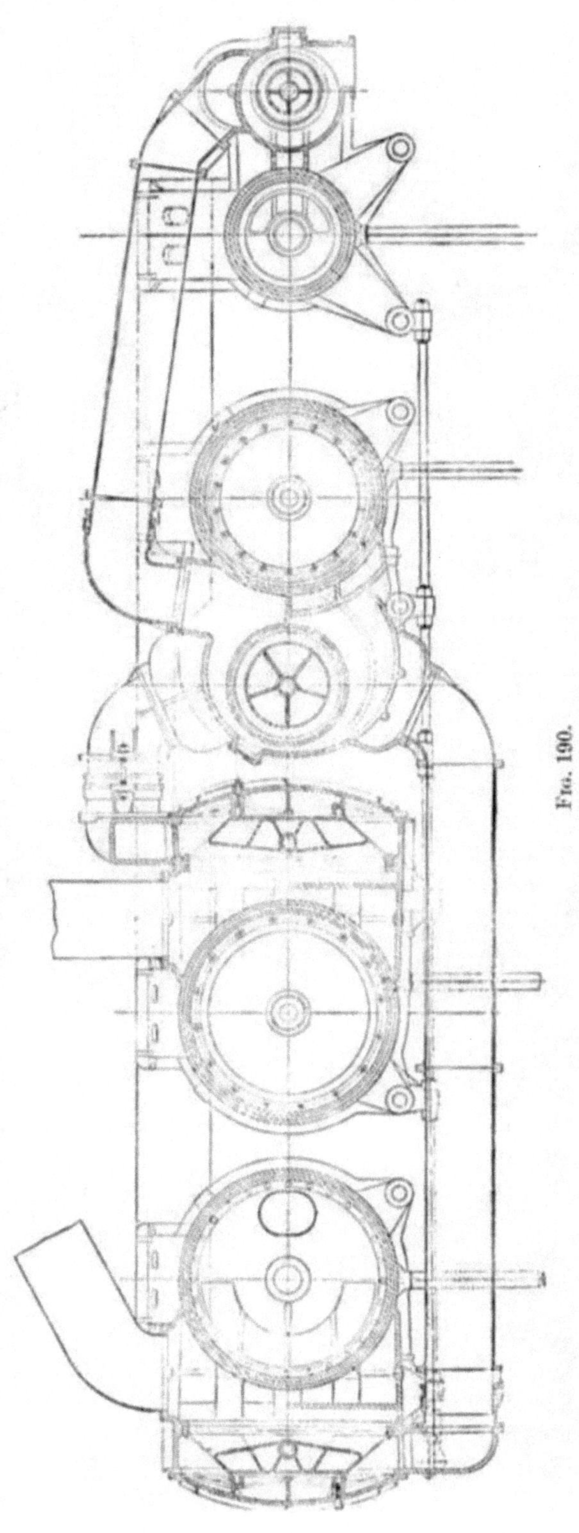

as with large cylinders and considerable expansion at full power the limit of economical expansion is very soon reached when the power is reduced, while with the smaller cylinders and less ratio of expansion at full power, there is a greater range for the utilisation of the maximum amount of expansion combined with an unreduced pressure of steam.

The ratios of cylinder-volumes adopted in the Navy for 155 lbs. steam pressure are usually $1 : 2\frac{1}{4} : 4{\cdot}84$ to 5 for H.P. : I.P. : L.P. ; for 210 lbs. it is $1 : 2{\cdot}4 : 5{\cdot}7$; while for 250 lbs. it is $1 : 2{\cdot}6 : 7$. In the mercantile marine it is about $1 : 2{\cdot}7 : 7$ at 160 lbs. pressure.

Arrangements of cylinders and cranks in four-crank triple expansion engines. — In arranging the cylinders and cranks of these engines the designer has a considerable range of choice, so that actual engines show a great variety in this respect. The usual plan is to arrange the two after cranks opposite each other in the end view, the two forward being also opposite but at right angles to the after ones. This is indicated in Fig. 193 for the

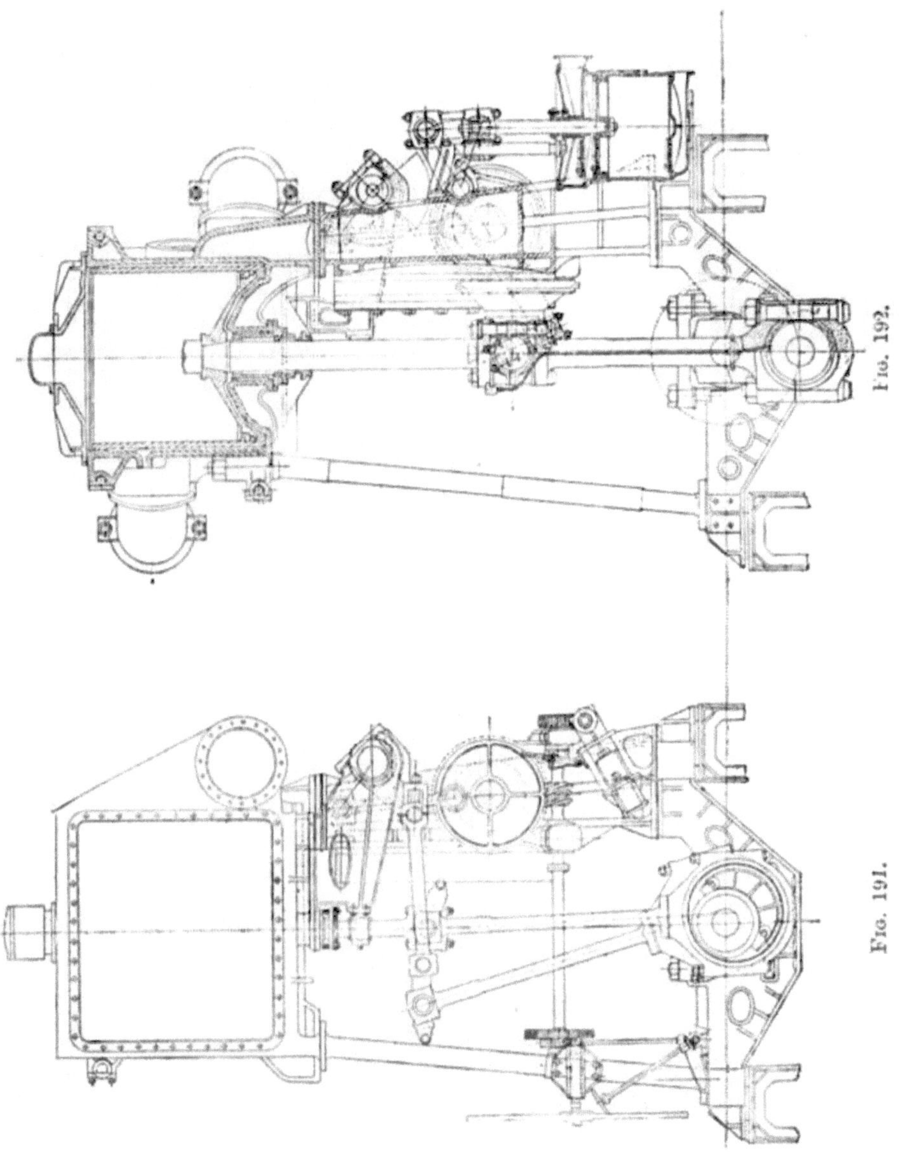

Fig. 192.

Fig. 191.

arrangement of cylinders shown in Fig. 190. Another plan is to place the two after cranks at right angles, with the forward ones opposite, as in Fig. 194. In a few examples the three-cylinder triple expansion arrangement has been repeated, the two low pressure cranks being placed at the same point in the circle, and the high-pressure and intermediate at angles of 120° with them. The two first-mentioned plans were tried in the 'Powerful' and 'Terrible' respectively. The second plan gives a more uniform turning moment on the crank shaft, and favours starting the engines, while the first plan reduces the magnitude of the reciprocating forces which cause vibration of the vessel.

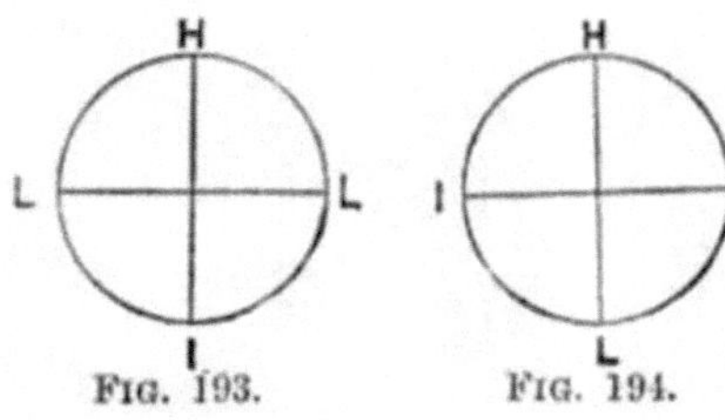

Fig. 193. Fig. 194.

In the 'Terrible' the vibration was so considerable at certain speeds that the cranks were altered and a series of experiments carried out with different settings of cranks. The 'Powerful' arrangement, Fig. 193, was found much superior to that at first fitted in 'Terrible,' Fig. 194, while with two other arrangements tried, viz. Figs. 194a and 194b, the vibration was much further reduced. Fig. 194a was found to be difficult to start in certain positions, so that Fig. 194b was adopted with satisfactory results, and represents the setting of cranks now in the vessel.

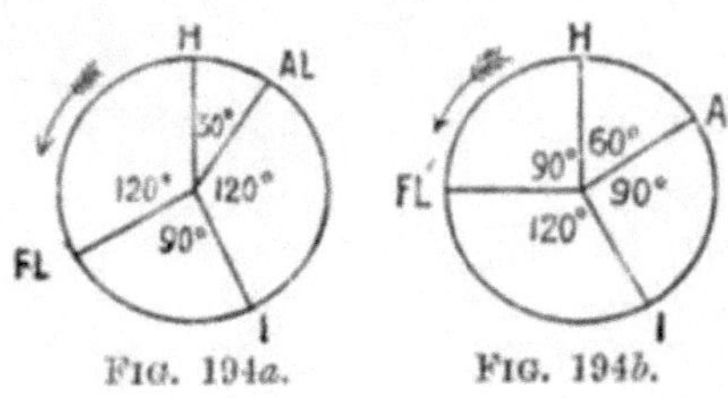

Fig. 194a. Fig. 194b.

In the arrangement of cylinders and slide-valves in the fore and aft direction, also, there are many varieties. Fig. 187 shows the

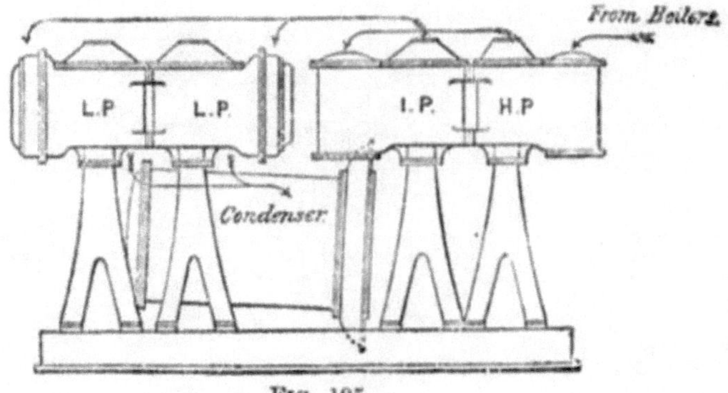

Fig. 195.

arrangement of H.M.S. 'Powerful' and others, while Fig. 195 shows a later arrangement in many large recent vessels of the Royal Navy, adopted when the importance of reducing vibration forces was realised. The two end cylinders are brought as near together as possible, with valve gears outside, while the forward pair of engines is served similarly. As each end pair acts on cranks practically opposite one another, the rocking moments tending to set up vibration are thus reduced. In many recent cases the two low-pressure cylinders are placed forward and aft respectively, the valve gears being outside ; the centres of each end

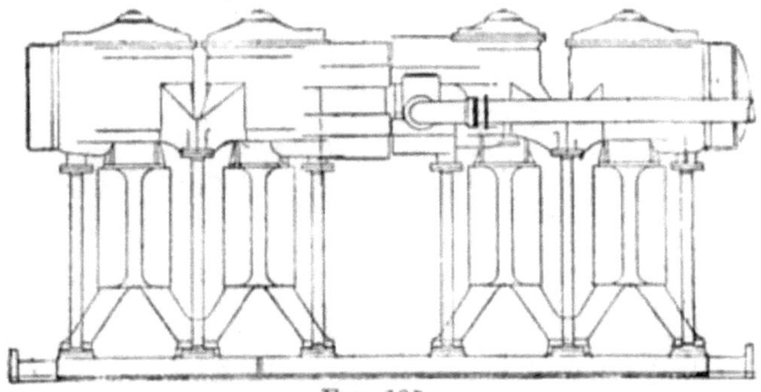

Fig. 195a.

pair of cylinders are thus brought rather closer together than with the

Fig 196.

preceding plan, while the cranks are similarly arranged, *i.e.*, the H.P. and forward L.P. cranks would be opposite or nearly so, while the I.P. and aft L.P. would be practically opposite but at right angles to the forward pair. These two arrangements are probably on the whole the best for four-cylinder triple expansion engines. In some designs for new American battleships the two L.P. cylinders are placed together in the middle, the H.P. and I.P. cylinders being at the forward and after ends respectively. There are also other arrangements, but the remainder do not possess any importance. In many vessels with divided L.P. cylinders the L.P. reciprocating parts are made much lighter than those of the H.P. and I.P. to correspond with the smaller amount of work done.

Quadruple expansion engines.—In the mercantile marine a considerable number of quadruple expansion engines have been fitted, by

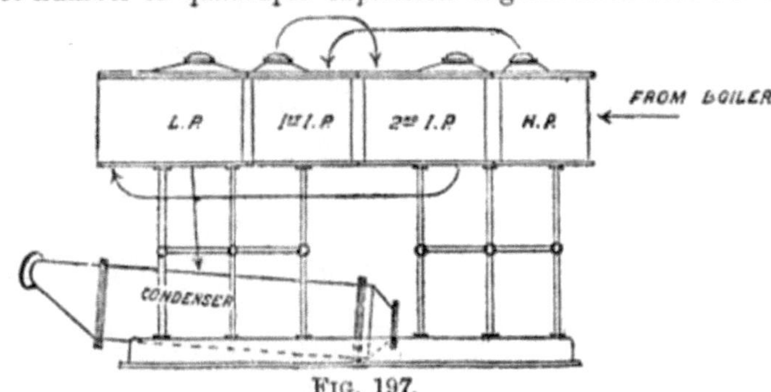

Fig. 197.

which the expansion of the steam is split up into an additional stage and further economy obtained. The steam pressure is now generally 200 lbs.

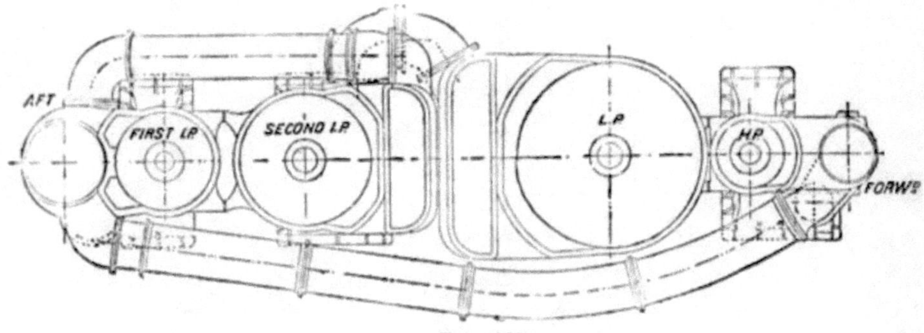

FIG. 198.

per square inch, with ratio of cylinder-volumes about $1 : 2\frac{1}{8} : 4\frac{1}{4} : 8\frac{1}{2}$, for the high-pressure, first intermediate, second intermediate, and low-pressure respectively, and the cut-off of steam about 70 per cent. in the high-pressure cylinder at maximum power.

Fig. 196 shows an arrangement sometimes fitted where fore and aft space is important, and there is sufficient head room. Fig. 197 shows that of No. 90 torpedo boat, the only vessel in the Royal Navy fitted with quadruple expansion engines. The relative arrangement of cylinders, slide-valves, and cranks in quadruple expansion engines varies still more than in the four-crank triple expansion engine, and in this case, again, the low-pressure

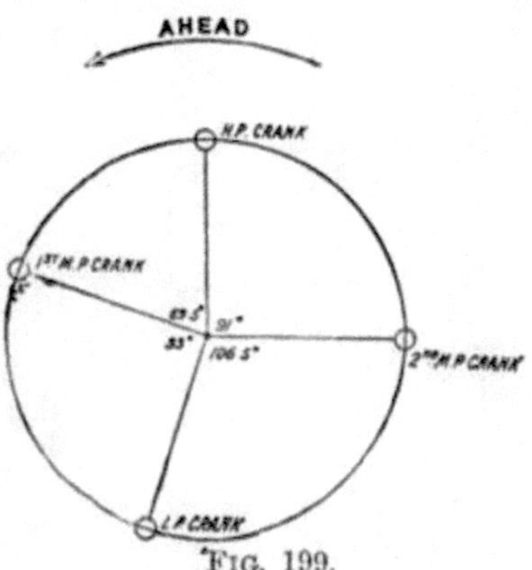

FIG. 199.

cylinder has been sometimes divided into two parts, and five cylinders and cranks fitted, as in the s.s. 'Inchmona,' a vessel working at 250 lbs. pressure.

Fig. 198 shows an arrangement of cylinders, and Fig. 199 the angles of cranks in a large mail steamer, designed with the special object of reducing the forces causing vibration. The H.P. cylinder is forward, and the first intermediate aft, the others following in sequence. The weights of the smaller pistons are usually increased beyond the ordinary amount, while the cranks are shifted from the normal right-angled positions by amounts given by calculation, to assist this object. This arrangement is known as the Yarrow, Schlick, and Tweedy system, and is also applied to four-cylinder triple expansion engines.

CHAPTER XIX.

DETAILS OF CYLINDERS AND ENGINE-ROOM FITTINGS IN CONNECTION.

WE now describe the details of the cylinders and fittings.

Figs. 200 to 203 show sections of two cylinders, with pistons, slide-valves, &c., complete, and from these sketches the general form and arrangement may be understood.

The structure of a large cylinder is composed of three separate principal parts, viz. (*a*) the cylinder casting, or shell containing in one casting the outer framework of the barrel, the cylinder bottom, and on one side the passages or ports through which the steam is admitted to and discharged from the cylinder ; (*b*) the cylinder liner, which is bored to a true cylinder and forms the steamtight surface on which the piston actually works ; (*c*) the cylinder cover, which closes the open end of the cylinder and completes the steamtightness at this part.

The cylinder shell.—From an examination of the sketches it will be seen that this casting is of a complicated nature, and to insure a sound and satisfactory casting, a brand of cast-iron is used which is suitable for running freely in the moulds prepared. This brand of cast-iron, although very suitable for this purpose, is too soft to be used for the rubbing surfaces, so that these latter are separate, and are constructed of a harder variety of cast-iron, and owing to the simple form of these rubbing surfaces, no difficulty is experienced in satisfactorily casting them in the harder metal. These rubbing surfaces are the cylinder liner on which the piston works, and the cylinder slide face on which the slide-valve works. Owing to its complicated form it is not possible to make the cylinder with ports in steel.

The cylinder slide face A should be arranged as near as possible to the cylinder barrel, consistent with obtaining sufficient area for the inlet of steam through the steam ports B, and for free exhaust through the exhaust port C.

On the bottom of the cylinder are cast the feet which are secured to the columns on which the cylinder is supported.

The lower or crank end of the cylinder being usually cast with it, forms a part of the cylinder itself, and in the centre of this end there is a hole, which allows the boring bar to be passed through, for the purpose of boring out the internal surface. This hole is afterwards closed by a door or plug, which is jointed so as to be steamtight, and which carries the piston-rod stuffing-box and gland. In large cylinders, where there is sufficient room between the piston-rod stuffing-box and the cylinder barrel, a manhole and cover, D, are fitted to the bottom of

Fig. 200.

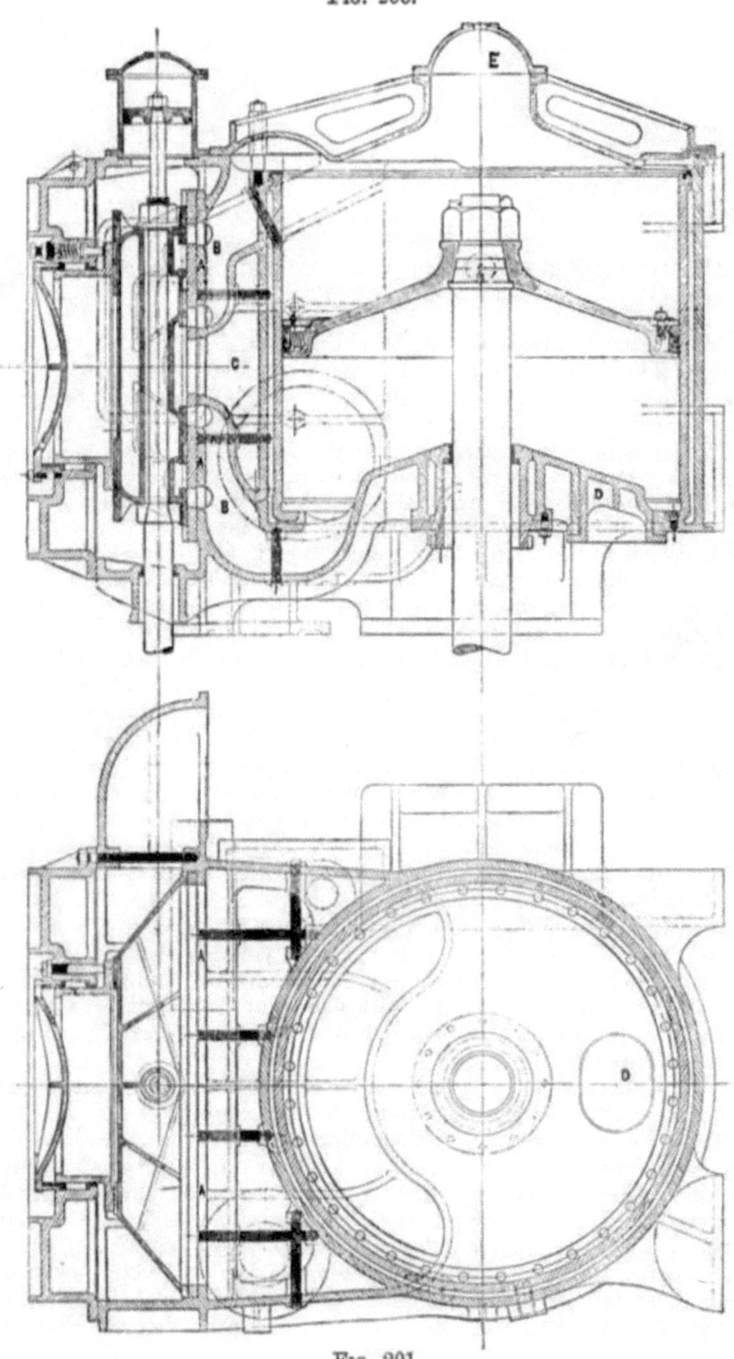

Fig. 201.

the cylinder, to enable examination to be made without removing the cylinder cover and piston.

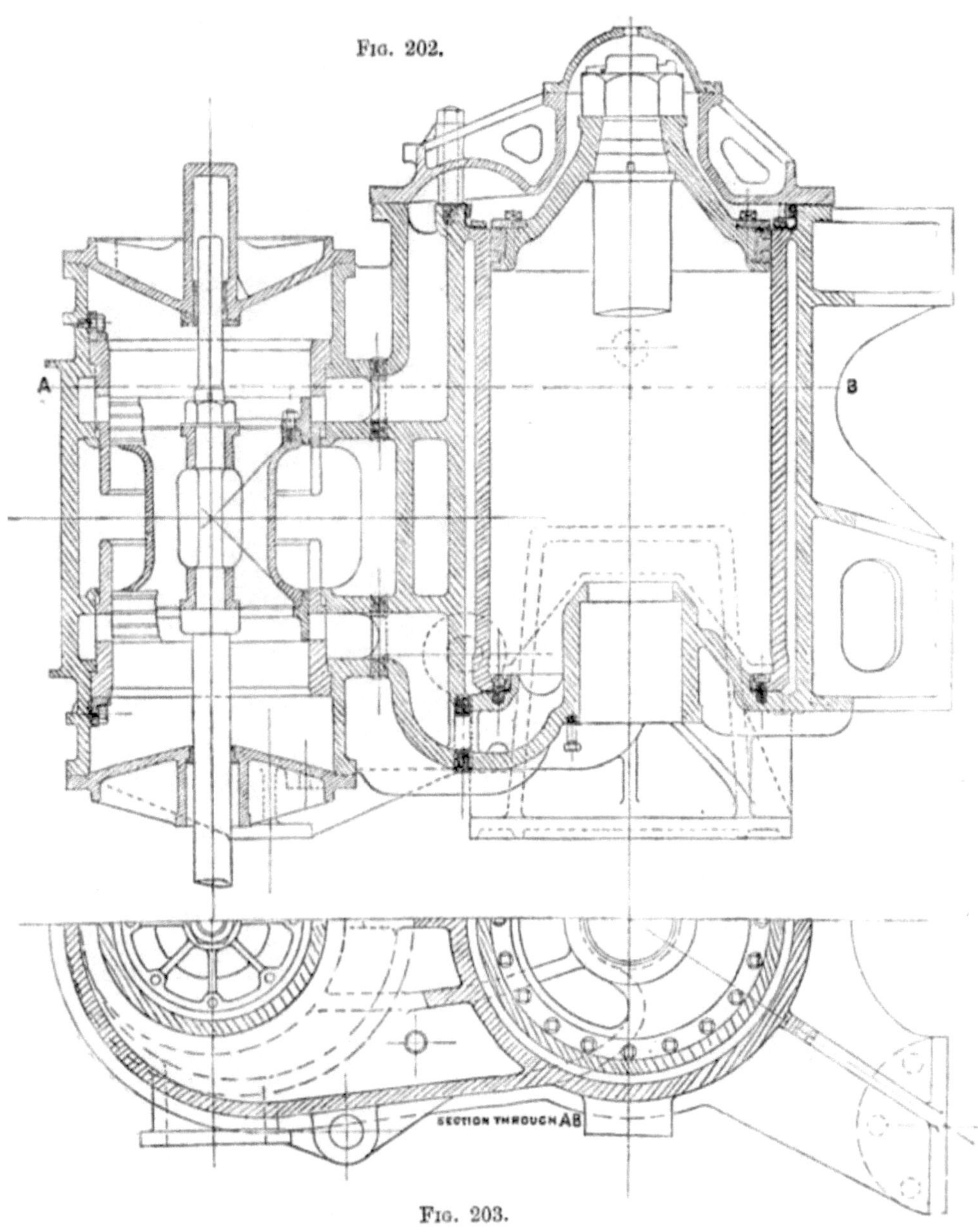

FIG. 202.

FIG. 203.

Cylinder cover.—The top or open end of the cylinder is fitted with a cover, which is sometimes round, but more often forms a continuation of the upper steam port, as shown in Figs. 200 and 202. This cover is also fitted with a manhole, E, and door in the centre in order to avoid repeatedly breaking the large joint between the cover and cylinder for examination purposes. This cylinder cover is generally made of cast-steel and formed of a single wall of metal stiffened by deep radial ribs.

The cylinder end and cover were at one time cast hollow, the space between the two plates being kept full of steam when the engine is at work, and forming part of the steam-jacket, but this is generally not now so fitted. The general construction of the cylinder end is now as shown in the sketch, in which the end has only one wall of metal, but is stiffened by numerous radial ribs.

Where piston-valves are used the construction of the steam ports is different, and this is shown in Figs. 202 and 203, which gives details on a larger scale of the H.P. cylinder of the same engine, the low-pressure of which is shown in Figs. 200 and 201. In both these examples the cylinder ports are supported and strengthened by numerous ribs and screwed stays.

Cylinder liner.—The working barrel is secured by a flange at the bottom end, fitted with bolts which are generally recessed into the flange. In the Royal Navy, in consequence of some cases having occurred in which these bolts have slacked back, they are secured from turning. Fig. 204 shows the head of the bolt slightly hammered out into a groove formed in the recess for this purpose. The cylinder cover end is left free to allow for expansion. The joint is kept steamtight, by fitting either a small stuffing-box as shown, packed with asbestos or other material; or a copper ring, of the section shown in Fig. 205, which also allows the necessary expansion. This latter plan is con-sidered preferable, a permanent and lasting joint being the result. The space between the liner and cylinder is usually from $\frac{3}{4}$ to $1\frac{1}{4}$ inch in depth, and is generally kept filled with steam, thus forming the steam-jacket, and also permitting of the gradual warming of the cylinders when raising steam prior to starting.

There are many advantages resulting from this method of con-struction. It very much reduces the complexity of the casting for a jacketed cylinder. In many cases in which cylinders have been made with the inner and outer barrels in one casting, the unequal contraction of the metal in cooling has caused excessive strains on parts of the material, which developed into cracks by the working of the engines and gave much trouble and anxiety.

With the separate liner or barrel, it is also more easy to insure that the working surface should consist of hard and sound material, so that the friction may be decreased and the durability of the cylinder increased, and when the working surfaces of the cylinder become much worn, the liner may be renewed at a comparatively small cost. In many cases the working barrels of cylinders have been made of forged steel, sometimes hydraulically compressed; but recent practice has been to fit hard close-grained cast-iron for these working barrels.

Cylinder face.—The face, on which the slide-valve works, is now generally cast separate from the cylinder, as shown in Fig. 200, and secured by a number of bolts with countersunk headed gun-metal or naval brass screws, which are recessed to some depth below the working surface. These recesses act as small oil-cups or reservoirs, and assist the lubrication. The advantage of this arrangement is that good sound hard metal can be insured for the working faces, and in case of wear, the face can be easily renewed. The faces are made of hard close-grained cast-iron. Phosphor-bronze was tried for these faces some years ago, but it was found to be inferior to good cast-iron.

Clothing or 'lagging' of cylinders.—In addition to the steam-jacket, which is fitted to nearly all large modern engines, it is necessary that the outside surfaces of cylinders and slide-jackets should be carefully covered or clothed with non-conducting material to prevent radiation. Where the temperature is great the non-conducting material is one that is also incombustible, to avoid the charring which would otherwise occur. The high-pressure and intermediate cylinders are generally lagged in this manner, but in some cases a thin foundation of incombustible material, such as sheet asbestos, is fitted next to the hot surface, and the necessary thickness made up with other non-conducting material, not incombustible. The clothing material is usually kept in place by an outer covering of wood, or sheet steel or iron, the sheet material being preferred, as it lasts longer and can be more readily taken off without damage when necessary for any purpose.

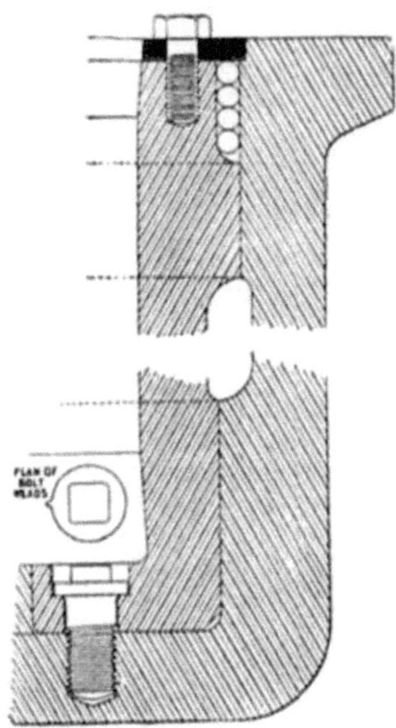

Fig. 204.

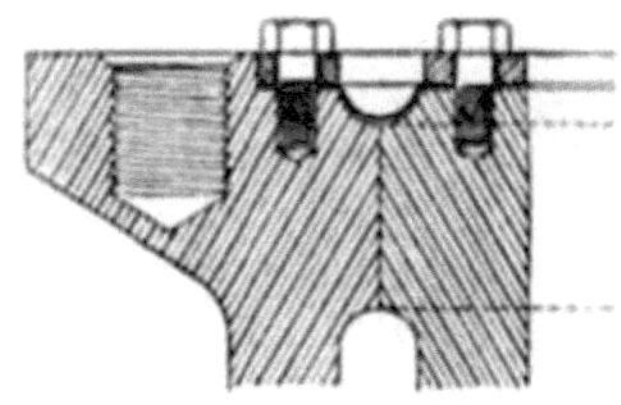

Fig. 205.

Pistons.—The piston is the agent by which the energy exerted by the steam is transmitted to the mechanism of the engine. It was for many years made of cast-iron of hollow form, and stiffened by internal ribs, which was a strong construction. This old form is shown in Fig. 184, but it is now generally made of cast-steel, and its usual construction is as shown in section in Figs. 206 and 207, which give details of two pistons of a triple expansion engine. By this use of cast-steel for pistons a saving of weight of about 40 per cent., as compared with cast-iron, has been effected, for pistons of cast-steel, on account of superior strength, are made of a single thickness, and of conical or dished form to give stiffness.

The piston consists of three principal parts, viz. the piston body,

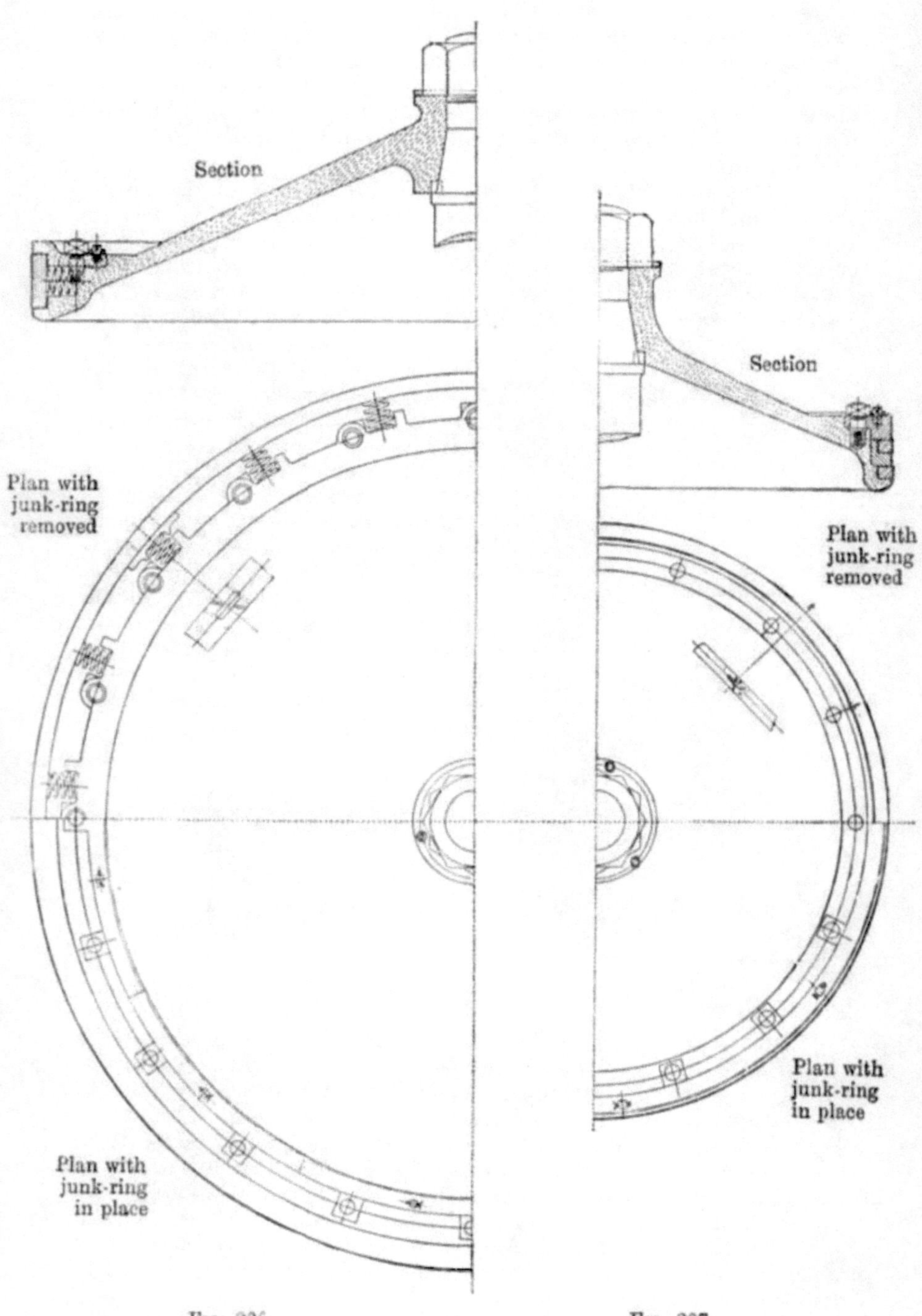

Fig. 206.   Fig. 207.

the packing-ring which works on the cylinder barrel, and the junk-ring which secures the packing-ring in position.

The piston should work steamtight in the cylinder in order to prevent leakage from one side to the other, which causes waste of steam and needlessly increases the back pressure. It should also be quite rigid in resisting any tendency to deformation due to the steam pressure acting alternately on its faces, and it should also move in the cylinder with as little friction and wear of rubbing surfaces as possible. Its attachment to the rod should be of the firmest possible description.

Packing-ring.—In nearly all old marine engines, and also in the low-pressure pistons of stage-expansion engines, the steamtightness is accomplished by means of a metallic *packing-ring* of considerable depth, sometimes called the *spring-ring*, which is kept pressed against the surface of the cylinder by the action of steel springs. Some makers use springs similar in form to coach-springs, as in Fig. 208 ; others use complete circular springs of various forms to press the packing-ring against the cylinder ; and in other cases spiral springs are fitted in recesses in the body of the piston. This latter plan is shown in Fig. 206, and is now preferred and specified for engines of the Royal Navy, as the pressure exerted by the springs against the packing-ring, which forces the latter against the cylinder barrel, can be regulated and adjusted as required, and is always known. With coach-springs it is always a very variable and uncertain amount. The spiral springs are compressed so as to exert a pressure of about 2 lbs. per square inch of the bearing surface of the packing-ring.

In order to allow the ring to naturally tend to spring tightly against the cylinder or liner, it is made of slightly larger diameter than the latter ; a piece is then cut obliquely out of the circumference, and the ring closed to fit the barrel, so that the effort of the ring to regain its original diameter helps to keep it tight against the cylinder.

Tongue-piece.—To prevent the passage of steam from one side of the packing-ring to the other through the oblique cut, shown at *a b* (Fig. 209), a groove, *c d*, is cut in the adjoining edge, and a gunmetal plate, A, is fitted behind the joint, with a tongue-piece to fit tightly in this groove. The plate is secured to one end of the metallic packing-ring rigidly, and to the other by bolts in elongated holes, so that, as wear occurs the ring expands, and still keeps steamtight on the cylinder surface. This construction applies principally to broad packing-rings, but narrow rings are sometimes fitted similarly, as shown in Fig. 207.

In many cases, in order to prevent excessive pressure on the cylinder, should steam obtain access to the back of the packing-ring, the tongue-piece is so fitted as to prevent the ring from increasing in diameter beyond a certain amount ; but recent experience in the Royal Navy is in favour of forming small projections on the packing-rings, as shown at B in Fig. 208*a*, fitting in corresponding recesses, which prevent the rings from increasing in diameter more than a small amount. Fig. 208*a* shows a common construction for the rings of H.P. pistons.

Junk-ring.—One edge of the packing-ring is in contact with a rim on the piston, and it is kept in its place by an annular plate called the '*junk-ring*,' firmly bolted to the other side of the piston (see Figs. 206 and 208). The edges of the packing-ring, and the faces of the piston and junk-ring in contact, are carefully fitted together so that the joints may be steamtight. The origin of the term 'junk-ring' may be traced to the time before metallic packing was introduced, when the pistons were packed with hemp gasket or junk packing, and the office of the junk-ring was to keep this packing in place, and press it against the cylinder, to keep the piston steamtight.

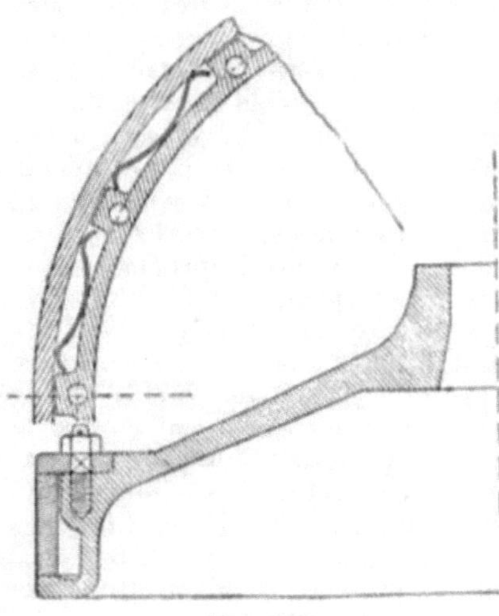

FIG. 208.

The figures last mentioned show the arrangement of the springs, &c., and the method of attaching the junk-ring to the piston. When the pistons were of cast-iron, brass nuts were let into the body of the piston, into which the junk-ring bolts were screwed, as the junk-rings have to be frequently taken off for the examination of the springs, and if the bolts were screwed into the body of a cast-iron piston they would soon become slack. With the separate brass nuts defects are less likely to occur, and can be readily made good by the fitting of new nuts and bolts. With steel pistons these recessed nuts are not usually fitted, but either steel studs are fitted in the piston with gunmetal nuts, or the junk-ring bolts are made of naval brass or some similar material, so that they will not rust fast in the piston body, and when worn can be readily renewed. For horizontal engines the springs are not continued all round the piston, but solid blocks, termed 'cod pieces,' are substituted for them at the bottom, for about one-fourth of the circumference, to assist in support-

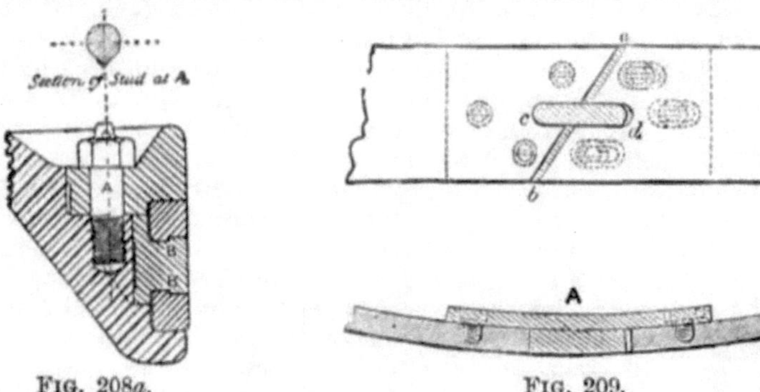

FIG. 208a.   FIG. 209.

ing the weight of the piston, while in some vertical engines similar blocks are fitted, instead of springs, on each side of the piston to resist the forces caused by the rolling of the vessel, which tend to cause the piston to press on one side of the cylinder barrel.

Special piston packings.—Large numbers of patent piston packings have been devised, many of which have split packing-rings, which aim at causing the springs not only to press against the cylinder barrel, but also to press against the faces of the junk-ring and piston, and prevent steam passing to the back of the spring ring. One of them (Lockwood and Carlisle's) is shown in Fig. 210. It consists of a split packing-ring, containing a compound spring constructed as shown. The helical parts of this compound spring press the spring ring against the cylinder, while the remaining portions press the two halves of the packing-ring against the junk-ring and piston flange respectively, so as to keep those joints steamtight. The junk-ring compresses the springs about $\frac{3}{16}$ inch.

With steam of very high pressure, should the junk-ring be badly

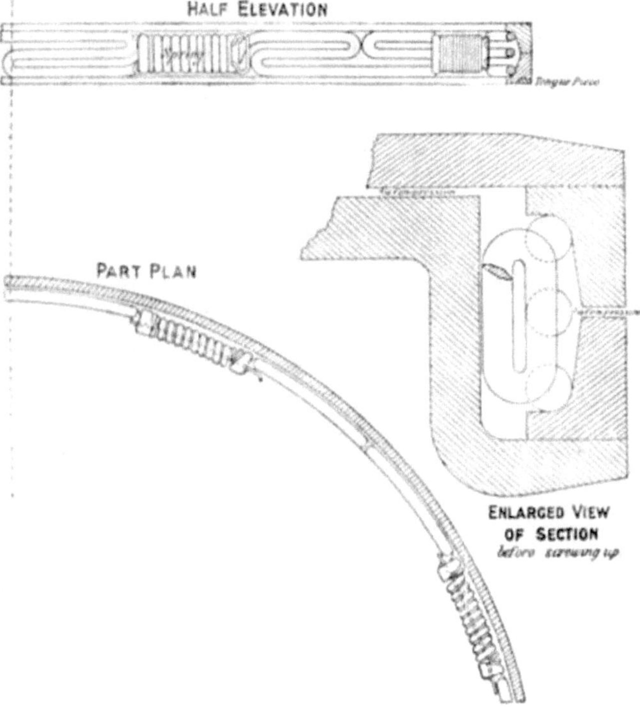

Fig 210.

fitted or worn at the edges, so that steam is allowed to pass to the back of the packing-ring, a great pressure acts, forcing it against the cylinder barrel, causing excessive friction and wear. Careful attention should therefore be paid to this part of the engine. With high-pressure steam the packing-rings of the high-pressure cylinder, instead of being of the broad single-ring type, are generally small square rings of cast-iron or special bronze without springs behind them, as in Figs. 207 and 208a. These large rings cannot be sprung into position, so that a carrier frame and junk-ring are necessary as before.

Guard-ring.—To prevent the possibility of any of the junk-ring bolts or nuts slacking back, a guard-ring is generally fitted to the heads of the bolts or nuts to prevent their turning after they have been screwed up tight. This guard-ring is secured by square-necked studs, with nuts and split pins. Sometimes, however, the nuts of junk-ring studs are prevented from slacking back by stout split pins, the studs being square-necked. The former method is preferable as being less liable to be left out of place.

Ramsbottom rings.—In many small pistons, such as those for auxiliary engines, &c., two or more small rings, cut at one part of the circumference, are used instead of a single packing-ring. In this case the piston is solid, and neither junk-ring nor springs are required. Grooves are cut in the circumference of the piston into which the rings are sprung, the joints not being placed in the same line. These are known as Ramsbottom rings. The piston of the steam cylinder in Fig. 362 is fitted in this way.

Piston-rod.—The piston-rod is made of wrought-steel, and, except in the few special cases where it is secured by a flange, passes through the piston and is secured by a nut on the opposite side. The part in the piston is usually coned to allow it to be drawn up tightly, and fitted with a stop to prevent the piston turning. It is, however, sometimes made parallel, with a collar on the rod, to take the thrust of the piston. To some steel pistons the piston-rod is attached by means of a flange, as shown in Fig. 211.

Sketches of piston-rods of different kinds are given in Figs. 212 to 215. The attachment of the piston to the rod should be very secure, and the rod should be very carefully fitted to the hole in the piston. A substantial pin or cotter is sometimes fitted through the end of the rod to prevent the nut unscrewing, and in this case the pin or cotter should be recessed into the nut as in Fig. 212. The most usual method is, however, to fit a plate around the nut, secured to the piston by studs with square necks, and having nuts secured by split pins. This plate is shown in Figs. 214 and 215. Considerable racking strains come on this part, especially if water should at any time accumulate in the cylinder, when a considerable bending moment acts, tending to bend the rod near the lower surface of the piston. For this reason it is undesirable that any diminution of section should be permitted at this part, and any collar desired should therefore preferably be obtained by an enlarged diameter.

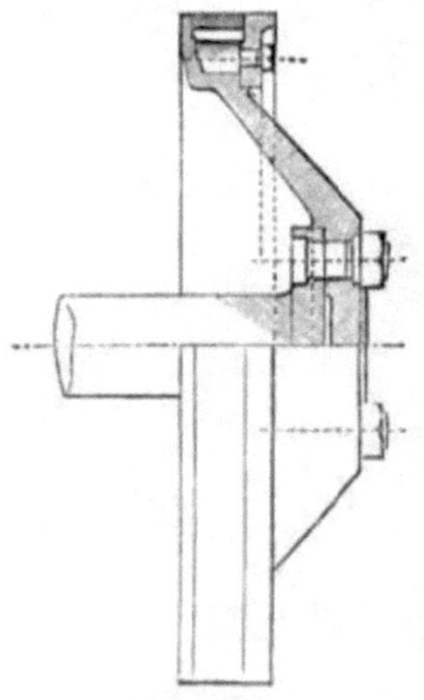

Fig. 211.

Either a substantial collar or a sufficiently steep cone should be fitted, and in some cases both are found. In the latter case, sometimes both collar and cone are very carefully fitted to bear on the rod together, or a small space is left between the collar and the piston to enable the former to come into operation should there be any yielding of the cone in the piston when at work. The removal of the piston-rod from the piston is often very difficult, and to facilitate this operation, when required, special fittings are generally provided for forcing it out. Two plans of effecting this are shown by dotted lines in Figs. 213 and 215, which show the portable fittings. Fig. 213 is an example from a torpedo boat destroyer.

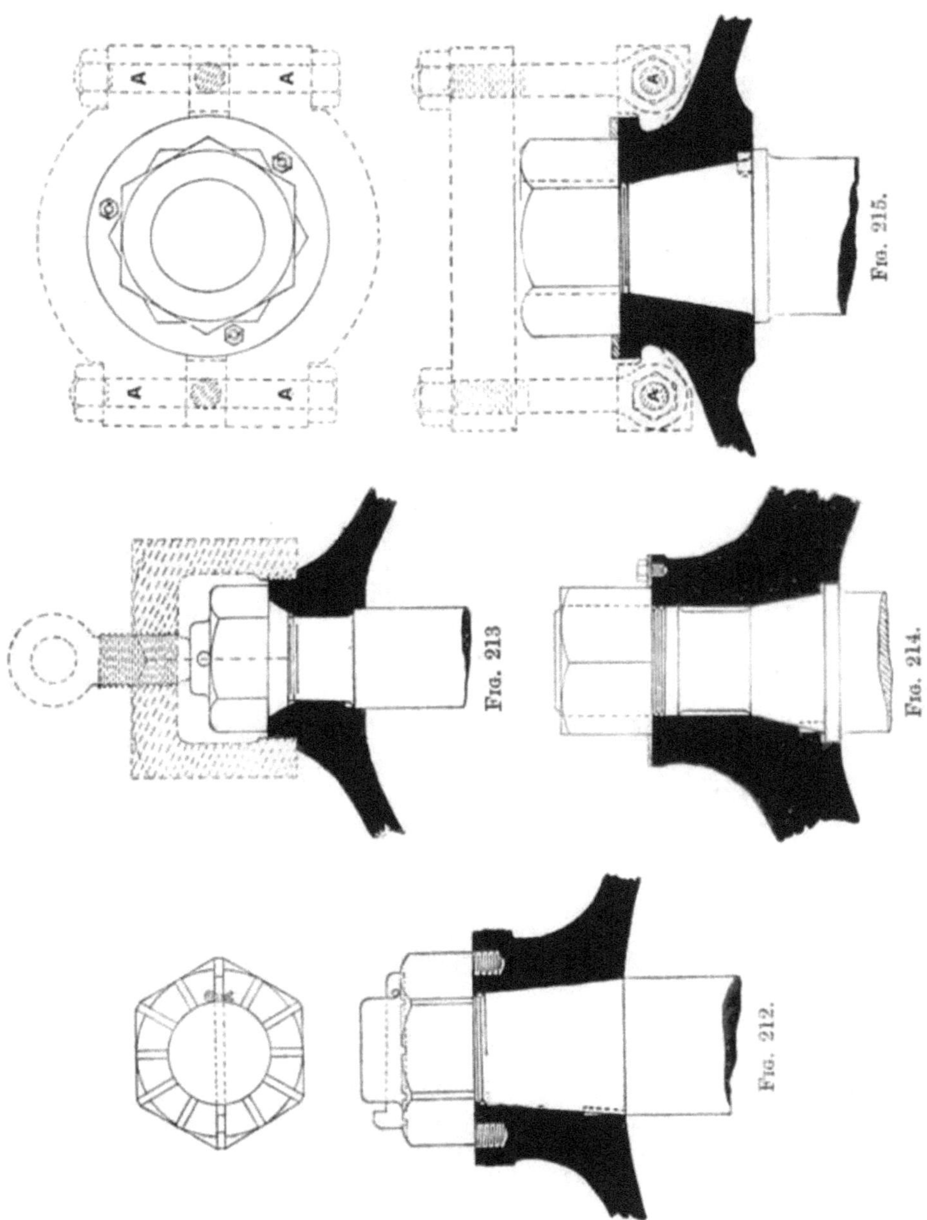

Supporting the weight of horizontal pistons.—Large horizontal engines are now obsolete, but when they were used means were provided to support the weight of the pistons, to prevent the wearing of the cylinder and metallic packing-ring at the bottom.

This was effected by a tail-rod or trunk at the cylinder-cover end of the piston, continued through a stuffing-box in the cover, with a block fitted on the end of it working on a suitable guide, so that the only pressure between the working surfaces of the piston and cylinder might be that due to the springs of the metallic packing-ring.

With vertical engines tail-rods fitted as continuations of the piston-rods, and working through stuffing-boxes in the cylinder covers, are often fitted in the mercantile marine, but in the Navy experience has indicated that they are unnecessary and may be objectionable, and they are not now fitted.

Stuffing-boxes.—The holes in the ends of the cylinder through which the piston-rods pass are fitted with stuffing-boxes, which, while they keep the cylinder ends steamtight, permit the reciprocating motion of the rods to take place. Stuffing-boxes are necessary in all cases in

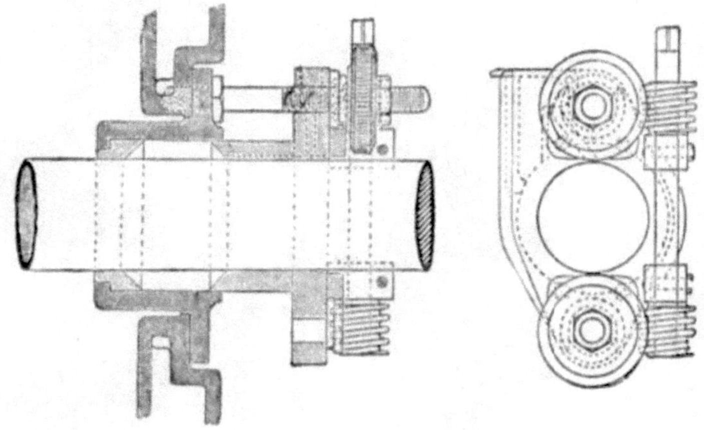

Fig. 216.

which a rod that must be free to move is brought through the end of any chamber that has to be kept steam or watertight. This includes all piston- and pump-rods passing through the ends of steam or water cylinders, the slide and other valve-rods, and all similar fittings.

A general arrangement of a stuffing-box for ordinary purposes is shown in Fig. 216. This view shows a stuffing-box for a rod working horizontally, and consists of an annular space around the rod, which space is filled with material of an elastic nature, generally known by the name of *packing*. The inner end of the stuffing-box is fitted with a brass *neck bush*, and the gland by which the packing is pressed against the rod, so as to keep it steamtight without unduly increasing the friction, is either of brass or of cast-iron faced with brass.

For the packing, gasket made by interweaving strands of hemp or cotton to form a rope may be used for pump-rods, stern glands, &c., but elastic core packing, which consists of a core of indiarubber, round which canvas or asbestos is tightly coiled, is sometimes used for such purposes. For steam rods asbestos fibre is generally used, except when the steam pressure and temperature are high, in which case this wears too rapidly.

Metallic packing for stuffing-boxes.—For high steam pressures, metallic packings of various kinds are now fitted, and are essential for continued efficiency. There are many varieties, and one which gives satisfaction is shown in Fig. 217. It consists of alternate rings of white metal A, and gunmetal B, with wedge-shaped sections, carefully fitted and scraped together. The white metal is in contact with the moving rod. These metallic packings bear the contact with, and

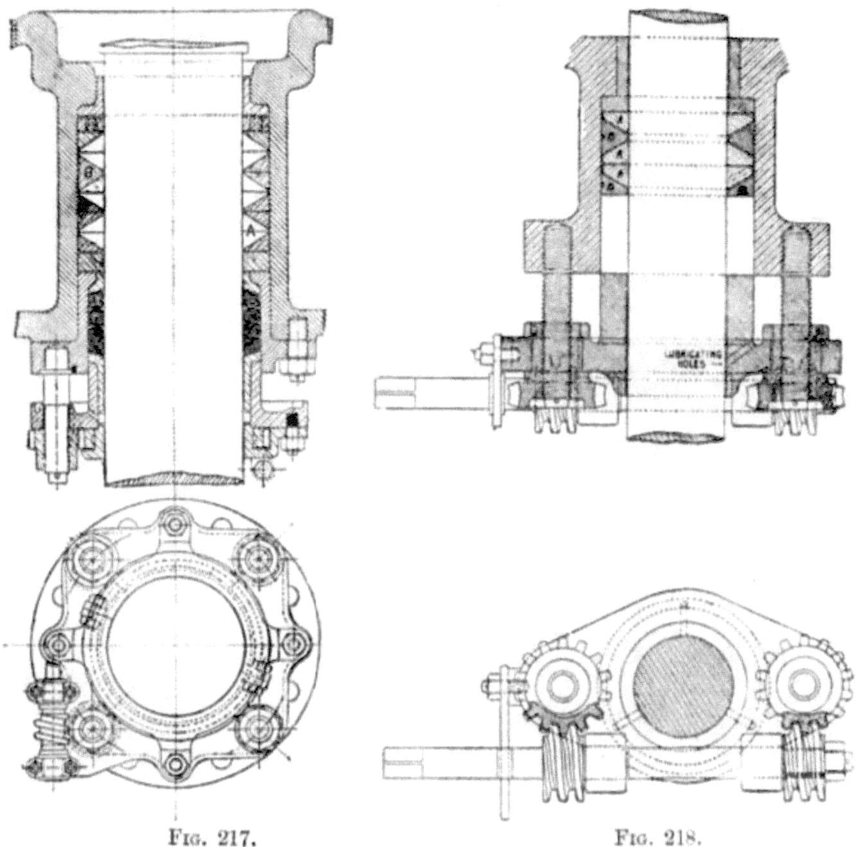

FIG. 217.
FIG. 218.

impact of the steam, without being soon destroyed, as soft packings are in such positions, but they generally require to be supplemented by a few turns of soft packing, which is then removed from the destructive action of the high-pressure steam, and stops any small leakage of steam which passes the metallic packing.

For large rods, soft packing is fitted in entirely separate stuffing-boxes, as shown in Fig. 217, while for smaller rods it is fitted either in this manner or with the soft packing bearing on the metallic packing, as shown in Fig. 218. All piston rods of any size in the Royal Navy, and many slide-rods are fitted as in Fig. 217, while small rods are fitted as in Fig. 218.

In the type shown in Fig. 217, where there is no means of adjustment for the metallic packing when under way, springs are fitted as shown, so that any slackness developed by wear in working may be taken up, so as to prevent movements of the packing in its gland.

Screwing-up gear.—The nuts of the piston-rod, slide-rod, and other principal glands are fitted with toothed or worm gearing, so that they may be screwed up or slacked uniformly, and adjusted with safety when the engines are at work. Arrangements of this kind are shown in the preceding sketches, where it will be seen that for each of the glands the screwing-up gear is fitted to the gland bearing on the soft packing, and is arranged to be screwed up with a right-hand motion.

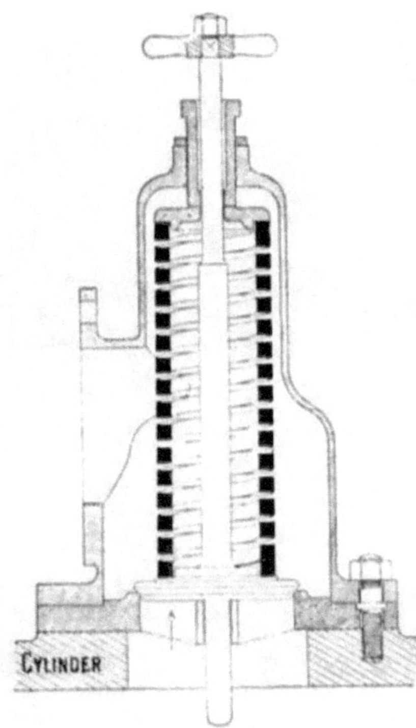

Fig. 219.

Cylinder escape valves.—It is necessary that escape or safety valves should be fitted on the cylinders, so that in case of water accumulating from priming or condensation during the working of the engines, means of escape will be provided, to prevent excessive stresses being brought on the cylinders. These valves are generally ordinary conical valves, kept in their places by springs loaded a little above the maximum working steam pressure in the cylinder, and long enough to allow the valve to open a considerable amount without unduly increasing the load. Cylinder escape valves should be fitted with suitable guards and pipes to lead away the hot water and prevent the danger of people being scalded by its sudden escape. Fig. 219 shows such a valve. Provision is made for adjusting the compression of the spring and locking it in this position, and for turning the valve on its face. The guard and branch for conveying away water are shown in the sketch. The pipe attached is led to the bilge, but with its end in such a position that any water discharged can be readily seen.

The top of the high-pressure cylinder and the bottoms of all the main cylinders are usually fitted with escape valves, but they are often omitted from the tops of the intermediate and low-pressure cylinders, and occasionally from the high pressure. It is desirable, however, especially when the starting valves admit steam to the cylinders direct, that escape valves should be fitted on the top of all the cylinders, and this is the usual practice.

Cylinder relief or drain cocks.—In addition to the escape valves, small relief or drain cocks, worked by levers from the starting position, are fitted at the lower ends of the cylinders, by means of which they can be cleared of water. They are generally fitted to discharge into the condensers when under way. In the Navy the high and intermediate-pressure drains are led to the auxiliary condenser, and the low-pressure to the main condenser. A branch pipe from a switch cock is also fitted to enable the water to be drained to the bilge when the engines are not working, and when starting. These drains were formerly led to the feed-tank, but owing to their noise, and for other reasons, this is not now generally done.

The levers for working the cylinder relief cocks should be led to a position close to the starting wheel or lever, and the handles should be in the same consecutive order as their corresponding cylinders to prevent mistakes. Where pipes from different cylinders or slide casings are led into a common pipe, non-return valves are generally fitted.

Slide jacket drains.—Cocks are also fitted for draining water from the lower parts of the various slide jackets, and these should be capable of being worked from the lower platform to insure rapid opening when required.

Indicator cock.—This is a three-way cock connected by pipes to either end of the cylinder, and having on the exit orifice a screwed socket to which the indicator may be attached. The hole in the plug of the cock is right-angled, so that the indicator may be put into connection with each end of the cylinder in turn, and the diagrams showing the work done on the opposite sides of the piston thus taken on a single card. A small hole in the shell of the additional cock fitted on the indicator enables the indicator piston to be put in communication with the atmosphere, to enable the atmospheric line to be drawn on the diagram.[1]

Auxiliary starting or pass-valves.—To facilitate the handling of the engines, in which steam of boiler pressure is admitted to one cylinder only, small auxiliary starting valves or pass-valves are fitted to the cylinders, worked by hand levers at the starting position. These valves take their steam from the main steam pipe, and they provide the means of admitting steam, by hand, to the cylinders. The valve fitted for this purpose may be one of two kinds, viz. auxiliary starting valves or pass-valves.

Auxiliary starting valves are those which admit steam direct to the top or bottom of the cylinders—i.e. between the slide-valve and piston. By moving the lever in one direction steam is admitted to the top of the piston, and by moving it in the reverse direction steam passes to the bottom of the piston. The levers are preferred to be so arranged that they move in the same direction as the steam admitted tends to move the piston, so that if, on looking at the crank, it is seen that it is required to descend to move in the correct direction, the auxiliary starting valve lever would be moved downwards. With the three-crank triple expansion engines, these starting valves would be fitted on the intermediate and low-pressure cylinders, starting valves on these

[1] See Chapter XXVI.

two cylinders being sufficient to enable the engines to be started when the high-pressure slide-valve is closed to the admission of steam.

Pass-valves are those by means of which steam is admitted to the receiver spaces, and not to the cylinders direct. They are fitted to the intermediate receiver, and also to the low-pressure receiver, either two entirely separate valves and levers being fitted, or one valve and lever, the motion of which in one direction admits steam to the I.P. receiver or steam space of I.P. slide-valve, while motion in the reverse direction admits steam to the L.P. receiver or steam space of slide-valve. By one of these means steam is admitted to the receiver required, and the steam proceeds to the top or bottom of the piston depending on the position of the slide-valve. Should the slide-valve of that engine be in such a position that neither port is open to steam, the pass-valve will not be able to operate on the piston, and steam to the other receiver must be admitted. Care must be taken in the design of the engines that the cut-off in the cylinders is sufficiently late that, when either crank is at or near the dead centre, one of the other slide-valves is always open to steam both for ahead or astern working.

Pass-valves require no mental consideration as to which direction the piston should be moved ; but, on the other hand, they are rather slower in their action, as the steam has to fill the receiver as well as the cylinder space on one side of the piston, and at the same time that it increases the forward pressure on one piston it increases the back pressure on the preceding but smaller piston. On account of their simplicity in use and their freedom from error they are generally preferred. Fig. 221 shows such an arrangement, one valve and lever only being used, the motion of which in one direction admits steam to the I P receiver, while motion in the other admits steam to the L P receiver. A detail of A, the pass-valve itself, is shown in Fig. 220.

Receiver safety valves and pressure gauges.—The intermediate and low-pressure receivers convey steam to the respective cylinders, and as each of the latter is constructed and tested for a working pressure of steam much lower than that in its preceding cylinder, safety valves are fitted on each receiver to give warning should the pressure in the cylinder by any means exceed the proper amount. Such an excess of pressure would occur probably if the slide valve of the preceding engine were to get off from the cylinder face, and in starting the engines. These safety valves discharge their steam into the engine room, and so give warning to those in charge.

The pressure in these receivers is shown at the starting platform by pressure gauges, which are always fitted, and connected to the high-pressure, intermediate, and low-pressure *slide jackets.* With the ratio of cylinders used in the Royal Navy, for a steam pressure of 150 lbs., the safety valves on the intermediate and low-pressure receivers are loaded to 80 lbs. and 30 lbs. respectively, and for a steam pressure of 250 lbs. at the engines the loads are 130 lbs. and 45 lbs. respectively.

Steam cylinder jacket fittings.—To fill the jacket spaces around the cylinder barrels with steam, a steam pipe is led to a stop-valve on the main steam pipe. Before entering these spaces, in the case of the intermediate and low-pressure cylinders, the steam passes through *reducing valves*, by means of which the pressure, and therefore temperature, in the jacket can be regulated to that suitable for the working pressures in the cylinders. Small *safety valves* are also fitted to the intermediate and low-pressure cylinder jackets to insure the desired pressure not being exceeded. These safety valves blow of into the engine room, and so attract attention when the proper pressure is being exceeded, either by failure of the reducing valve or other cause. Steam of boiler pressure can generally be admitted to the high-pressure jacket, but sometimes the steam supply is taken from the high-pressure slide casing so that the jacket pressure can never be above the

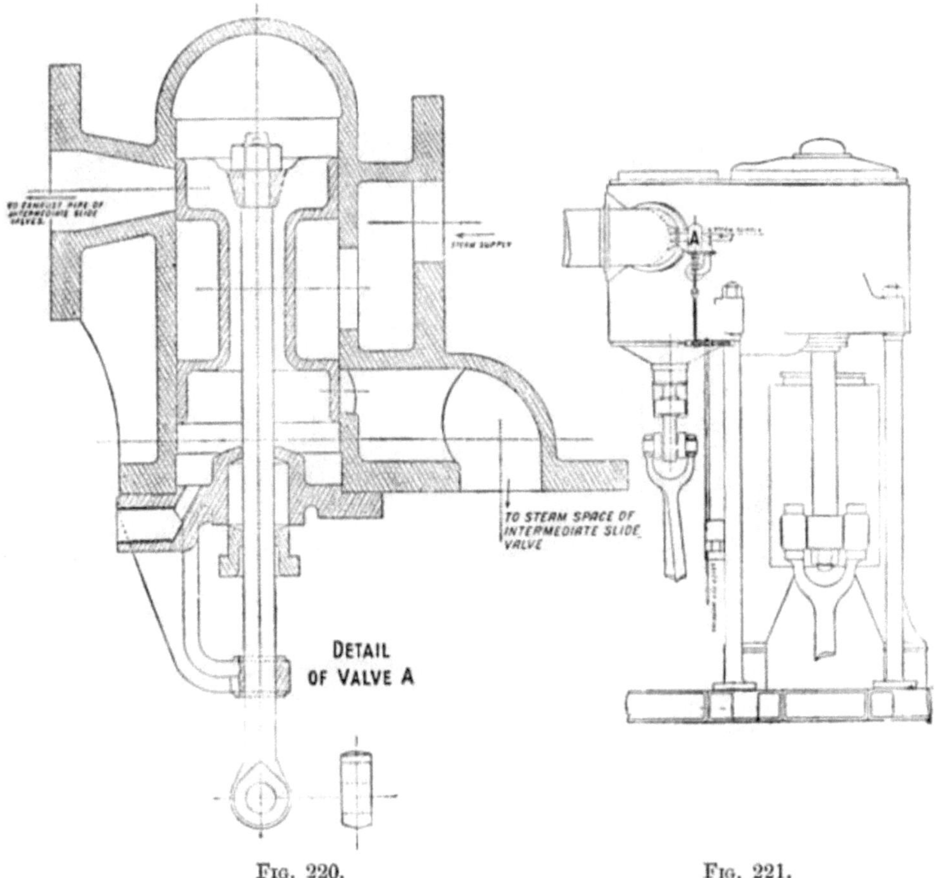

Fig. 220.   Fig. 221.

initial pressure in the cylinder. In the other jackets the reducing valves are adjusted so that the pressure is a little in excess of the maximum working pressure in the corresponding cylinders.

With steam of 150 lbs. boiler pressure, for example, the steam-jacket pressures in intermediate and low-pressure cylinders would be about 80 lbs. and 30 lbs. respectively. In the naval engines now building with 250 lbs. working pressure, it is 130 lbs. and 45 lbs. respectively. *Gauges* are fitted to indicate the pressure in each of the cylinder jackets.

To keep these steam jackets free of water, *drains* are led from their lower parts to the auxiliary condenser, or main condenser when an auxiliary condenser is not fitted. In the Navy in order to facilitate the adjustment of the drain-valves to the required amount so as just to remove the water of condensation, each of the drain-pipes is led to a water collector in sight of the starting platform. These collectors have glass water gauges and regulating drain-valves to enable the adjustment to be accurately made. The drain-valve should be so regulated that the collector remains always about half full of water, and when this is so we know that the cylinder jacket is properly drained and that no steam is being blown through the valve to waste.

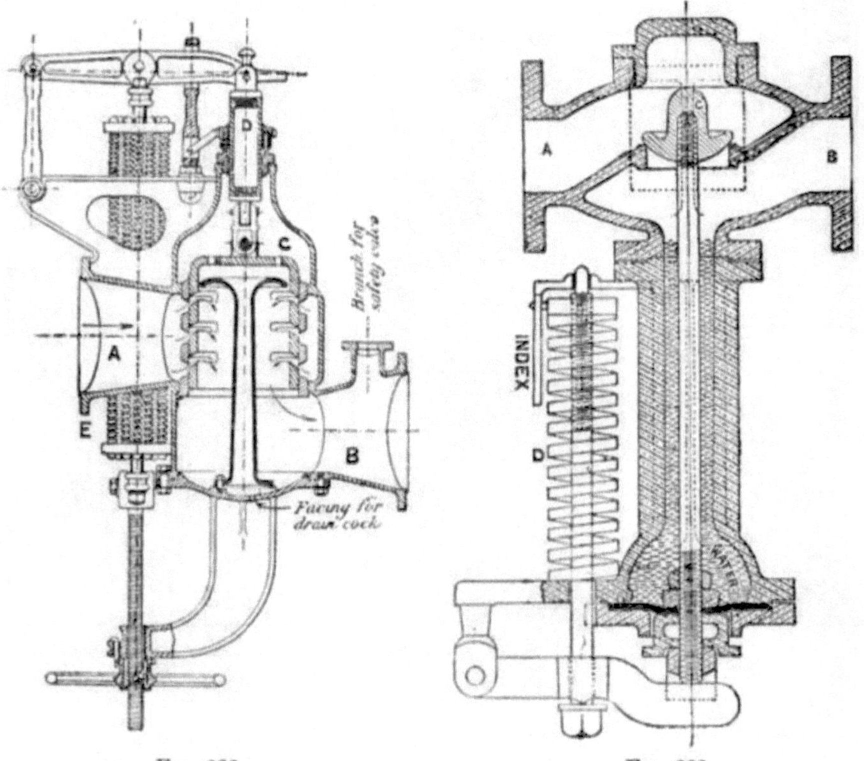

Fig. 222.　　　Fig. 223.

Reducing valves.—The reducing valves previously mentioned are fitted for several purposes. They are necessary for insuring that the pressure of steam supplied for some purposes, from a source at higher pressure, does not exceed the amount it may be safe or desirable to use, as, for example, in steam jackets. They are useful in maintaining steadiness of the steam pressure working an engine, although the steam pressure in the boilers may vary, which is important, for example, in the case of dynamo engines. They are also, for similar reasons, used in the Royal Navy for the main engines of vessels fitted with the higher pressures of steam and water tube boilers.

Two common types of reducing valves are illustrated, in both of which the valve remains open till the pressure of steam on the reduced side attains a certain amount regulated by springs, when the valve closes. Fig. 222 shows the Belleville reducing valve fitted between engines and boilers of warships with Belleville boilers, in which cases there is generally a difference of 50 or 60 lbs. pressure between engines and boilers. In this case the tension of the springs E keeps the bell valve C open, but as the steam flows through from A to B, the pressure in B gradually rises, and as all parts of the valve are balanced, as regards pressure, except the area of the plunger D, the reduced steam pressure passing through the two holes at the top of the bell, acts on the area of the plunger, and when this force is sufficient to overcome the tension of the springs acting at the smaller leverage, the plunger D rises and closes the ports of the valve. The valve and seating are an easy fit so that this type of valve will not prevent the passage of small quantities of steam. It is generally used for the main engines where large volumes of steam have to be passed. A small safety valve is fitted on the reduced pressure side as a relief in case of any derangement of the gear. Pressure gauges are also fitted on each side of the reducing valve, placed in positions visible from the starting platform when fitted for the main engines.

Fig. 223 shows another example, Auld's, in which the balancing of the valve and the closing force are entirely differently provided for. In this example the compression of the spring D, which can be regulated by a nut and screw, keep the valve open. The higher-pressure steam enters at B, and this steam has no effect either in opening or closing the valve C, since the steam pressure on the bottom of the valve is exactly balanced by the pressure on an indiarubber diaphragm at the other end of the casing, over an orifice of exactly the same area as the valve. This indiarubber is shown in black in the figure, and is kept cold by an accumulation of water which condenses above it. The steam pressure in B having no effect, as soon as the pressure in A, acting on the top of the valve, reaches an amount sufficient to compress the spring still further, the valve closes and shuts off the supply of steam.

CHAPTER XX.

CONDENSERS, FEED-WATER FITTINGS, AND UNDER-WATER VALVES.

Composition of sea-water.—Sea-water contains about $\frac{1}{32}$ part of its weight of solid matter, the composition of which varies somewhat with the locality. Common salt or sodic chloride is always by far the principal constituent of the solid matter. Of this $\frac{1}{32}$ part of solid matter the following may be taken as the average composition :—

Sodic chloride or common salt	76	per cent.
Magnesic chloride	10	,,
Magnesic sulphate	6	,,
Calcic sulphate or gypsum	5	,,

The remainder, 3 per cent., consists of small quantities of carbonate of lime and other substances, with a little organic matter.

Formation of scale.—Common salt, however, gives little trouble to the marine engineer, as, unless under extreme circumstances, it remains soluble in water at all temperatures. The density of sea-water may be increased very largely by concentration of the common salt, and its temperature be considerably increased, without any deposit of this material taking place. The principal scale-forming ingredient is the sulphate of lime or calcic sulphate, which is most troublesome when admitted into the boilers. Deposit is also formed by the sulphate of magnesia, although in a less objectionable form. The deposit from sea-water in boilers is very hard and difficult to detach, and consists of about 85 per cent. of sulphate of lime.

While common salt is just as soluble at high temperatures as at low, it is found that as the temperature of the water increases, a point is soon reached at which the sulphates become insoluble in water, and if admitted to a boiler in which the water is at, or above this temperature, they are precipitated in the solid form and remain in the boiler.

At a temperature of 280° to 295° Fahr., corresponding to a pressure of 35 to 45 lbs. of steam by gauge, the sulphate of lime becomes entirely insoluble, and this substance amounts to 5 per cent. of the solid matter contained in sea-water. As the temperature rises the other sulphates become insoluble, until at about 350° Fahr. or 120 lbs. absolute the sea-water is incapable of holding any sulphates in solution, and if any sea-water is admitted *a deposit necessarily takes place.*

These salts are also precipitated by increase of density from the evaporation of the water, even if the temperature remains about

212° Fahr. ; sulphate of calcium is thus deposited at a density of $\frac{3}{32}$. Common salt does not crystallise out till a density of about $\frac{8}{32}$ is reached.

Use of jet-condenser.—In the first marine engines the temperature of the steam was low, and the jet-condenser was used, in which the steam, after leaving the cylinders, enters the condensing chamber, into which a jet of cold sea-water is injected, which condenses the steam by *actual contact and mixing*. The feed-water, which was drawn from the mixed sea-water and condensed steam, was only a little fresher than sea-water (density about $\frac{26}{27}$), consequently a large quantity of sea-water was sent into the boilers, and to prevent gradual increase of density, and consequent deposits of salt and other substances, a portion of the denser boiler-water had to be blown away into the sea, and the loss made up by admitting a larger quantity of the salt feed-water. This was termed *brining* the boiler.

As, however, the *temperature was low* and the density was not allowed to exceed about $\frac{3}{32}$, the salts were held in solution fairly well, so that but little deposit was obtained even from the sulphate of lime, which is the first to be precipitated. The steam pressure of 35 to 45 lbs. or the density of $\frac{3}{32}$ could not be exceeded with salt water feed without deposit of salts, and when the pressures of steam, and consequently the temperatures, were increased, it was found impossible to prevent the deposit, and in fact the process of brining increased it, from the extra salt water necessary. With high pressures, also, the injurious effect of any scale deposited on the heating surfaces is increased, so that sea-water feed for high-pressure boilers is not practicable.

Introduction of surface-condenser.—The jet-condenser had, therefore, to be abandoned, and the surface-condenser was introduced, in which there is no mixture of the steam to be condensed with the cooling sea-water. The sea-water is pumped through or around a number of small tubes ; the other side of these tubes is in connection with the exhaust steam, so that the latter is condensed by the cold surface of the tubes, and the resulting fresh water is pumped away, to be returned to the boilers as feed-water. By its agency fresh feed-water is obtained for the boilers instead of salt water, and it is owing to the application of this system of condensation that the use of high-pressure steam, which was retarded for many years by the use of the jet-condenser, has now become so general.

One advantage of the surface-condenser consists in the fact that the condition of the condensing water is of no importance as regards the feed-water, so that whether it is salt, muddy, acid, or otherwise impure, pure water is obtained for the boilers.

We will briefly describe the arrangement of the old jet-condenser before dealing in detail with the surface-condenser of the modern engine.

Details of jet-injection condenser.—Sketches showing the general form and arrangement of the jet-injection condenser, with horizontal air-pump and solid plunger, are given in Figs. 224 and 225. A is the condensing chamber, into which the exhaust steam from the cylinder enters through B, the eduction pipe. In Fig. 225, c is the sea-injection valve, on the side of the condenser, worked by levers from the starting platform, and in connection with the sea by means of a Kingston valve and sea-cock on the ship's side. It was necessary to admit the water through a series of small holes in the internal injection pipe to facilitate its mixing with the entering steam.

Air-pump of jet-condenser.—It is evident that the sea-water and condensed steam must be pumped away constantly. Also sea-water always contains a certain volume of air in solution, which may be liberated either by boiling it, or reducing the pressure to which it is subjected, and when the sea-water enters the condenser, owing to the reduced pressure and increased temperature, this air is liberated, and unless pumped away regularly, as it is not capable of being condensed,

Fig. 224.

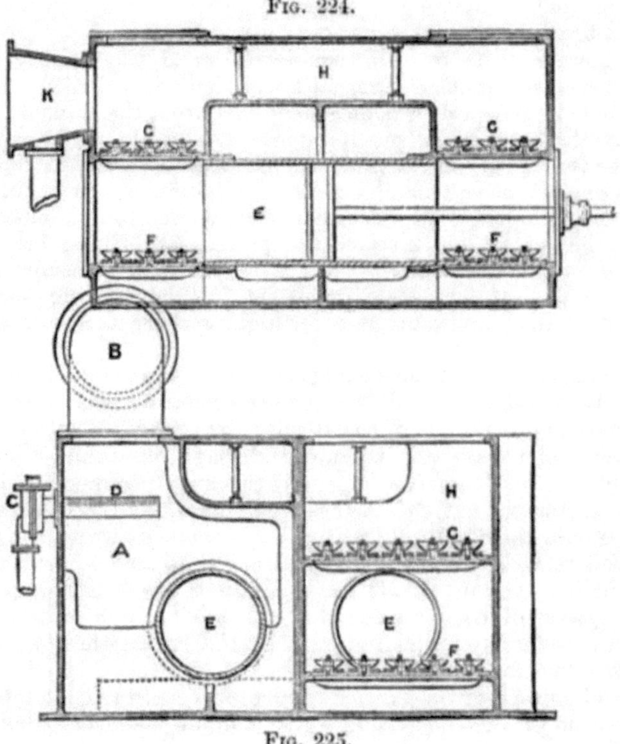

Fig. 225.

it would accumulate and spoil the vacuum. A pump is necessary, therefore, to pump away the air and water, and maintain the vacuum. This pump is called the *air-pump*. It is generally worked direct by a rod attached to the piston of the engine, and is marked E in the figures. By the action of the air-pump, the mixed injection and condensed water, air, vapour, &c., are pumped into a space H, called the hot-well, F F being the suction or foot-valves, and G G the delivery or head-valves, of the air-pump. The air-pump plunger is packed with hemp or cotton gasket, kept pressed against the pump barrel by the action of a suitable gland.

Feed-pumps, discharge pipes, &c.—From the hot-well H, the feed-pumps draw their supply for the boilers. These feed-pumps were usually horizontal plunger pumps worked off the main pistons, and a large pipe K, called the discharge pipe, was led to a self-acting valve on the ship's side, to allow the surplus water, not required by the feed-pumps to supply the boilers, to pass overboard. This valve is called the main discharge valve.

Bilge injection of jet-condenser.—To all jet-condensers an additional injection valve, called the bilge injection valve, was fitted, with inlet pipe leading to the engine-room bilge. In the case of a serious leak in the ship and the bilges becoming flooded with water when the engines were at work, water could by this means be taken from the bilge, instead of from the sea direct, and the air-pump thus utilised for pumping out the ship.

Sea and bilge injection for early surface-condensers.—In the surface-condenser, the cold condensing water is kept flowing past the cooling surfaces by means of a pump called the circulating pump, and in the early surface-condenser, before sufficient experience was

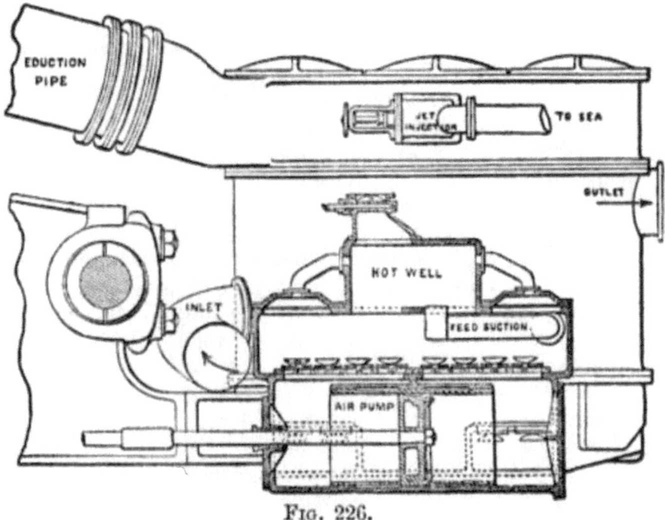

Fig. 226.

obtained of its action, arrangements were made for the admission, if necessary, of sea-water into the steam space of the condenser, thus converting it into a jet-condenser in case of failure of the circulating pump. Fig. 226 shows an elevation of an old surface-condenser showing position of jet-injection valve and section of air-pump. This jet-injection valve was, however, soon abandoned, and is not now fitted.

Arrangements were also made for admitting water from the bilge into the steam space of the condenser, so that the air-pump would assist in pumping water out of the ship. The circulating pumps of such condensers were generally of the reciprocating kind worked off the main pistons, but on the adoption of separate centrifugal circulating pumps for this purpose, described later, which also enabled considerable quantities of water to be pumped from the bilge if required, these bilge injection arrangements were abandoned. The surface-condenser as now fitted therefore contains neither sea nor bilge injection.

The surface-condenser.—This consists of the 'condenser barrel or casing,' generally of cylindrical shape, having a flat plate at each end called 'tube plates.' Between the tube plates are fitted a large number of small thin brass tubes, which are kept cold on one side by sea-water, supplied constantly by the 'circulating pump.' The exhaust steam is conveyed to the upper part of the condenser, and is condensed on the other side of the tubes, the condensed water and any air being withdrawn by the air-pump.

The tubes may be placed either vertically or horizontally. With vertical tubes the steam is generally passed through them, and the water circulated around them, while with the tubes placed horizontally the water is generally circulated through the tubes, and the steam exhausted around them. The exact plan adopted, however, depends principally on convenience of arrangement. If the steam passes inside the tubes, the water being in the space outside, the grease left on the tubes by the steam can be readily cleaned off by passing brushes through them, whilst with steam outside the tubes the only method of effectually cleaning them is by filling the condenser with a solution of potash or other material and boiling it.

Condensers with steam inside the tubes have the disadvantage of holding a larger quantity of water than those in which the water passes through the tubes, and this weight of water has to be added to the total weight of machinery when the engines are at work. The number of joints which are liable to leak and affect the vacuum is also larger with this system, while the condenser casings are in contact with the circulating water, which causes them, when made of cast-iron, to corrode and decay. The system of causing the water to pass through the tubes, the steam being in the space surrounding them, is the more general. Less weight of water is carried, and more definite direction can be given to it to insure contact with the whole of the tube surface, and though the casings are somewhat hotter in consequence of containing steam instead of water, the heat can be prevented from appreciably affecting the engine room by suitable lagging.

Figs. 227 to 230 show two plans of surface-condenser, viz. the horizontal and vertical varieties. Referring to Fig. 228, in which there are two exhaust pipes, the steam enters at the orifices marked A, and is withdrawn, when condensed, through the orifice B by the air-pump. The circulating water enters at C, and is confined by the diaphragm D to the lower half of the tubes, and, having traversed these tubes, it returns through the upper half of the tubes, being finally discharged to the sea through the pipe E. In the vertical condenser, shown in Fig. 230, the same letters apply, the circulating water being forced to traverse the whole of the condensing surface by means of the diaphragm D indicated in sketch. In this type of condenser it is especially important that these directing plates should be fitted, to insure the proper efficiency of the cooling surface.

Details of the condenser.—The condenser casing is in the Navy usually of brass, and is either cast, as in Fig. 230, or built up of brass plates riveted together and stiffened by angles, as in Fig. 228. As this material

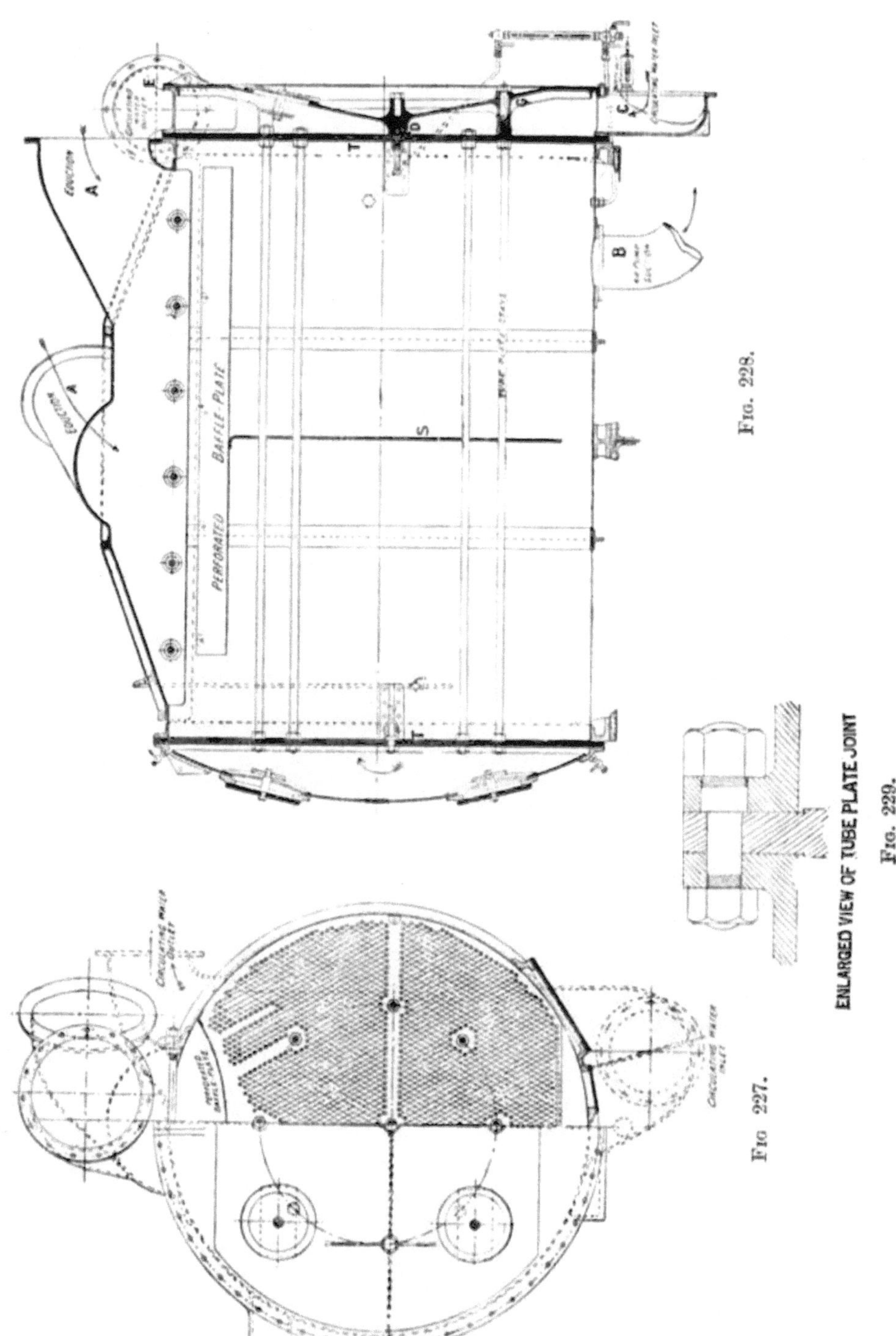
CONDENSED
A
A
CONDENSED
E
D
T
B
C
S
T
PERFORATED
BAFFLE-PLATE
FIG. 228.
CIRCULATING WATER
OUTLET
CIRCULATING WATER
INLET
FIG. 227.
ENLARGED VIEW OF TUBE PLATE JOINT
FIG. 229.

is free from any waste due to corrosion, the casing may thus be made thin and light.   At the ends of the condenser casing are the tube plates T T.   Between these tube plates a large number of small tubes are fitted. For clearness these are omitted in the sketches, but a few are indicated at the top of the section part of Fig. 227.   These tubes are generally

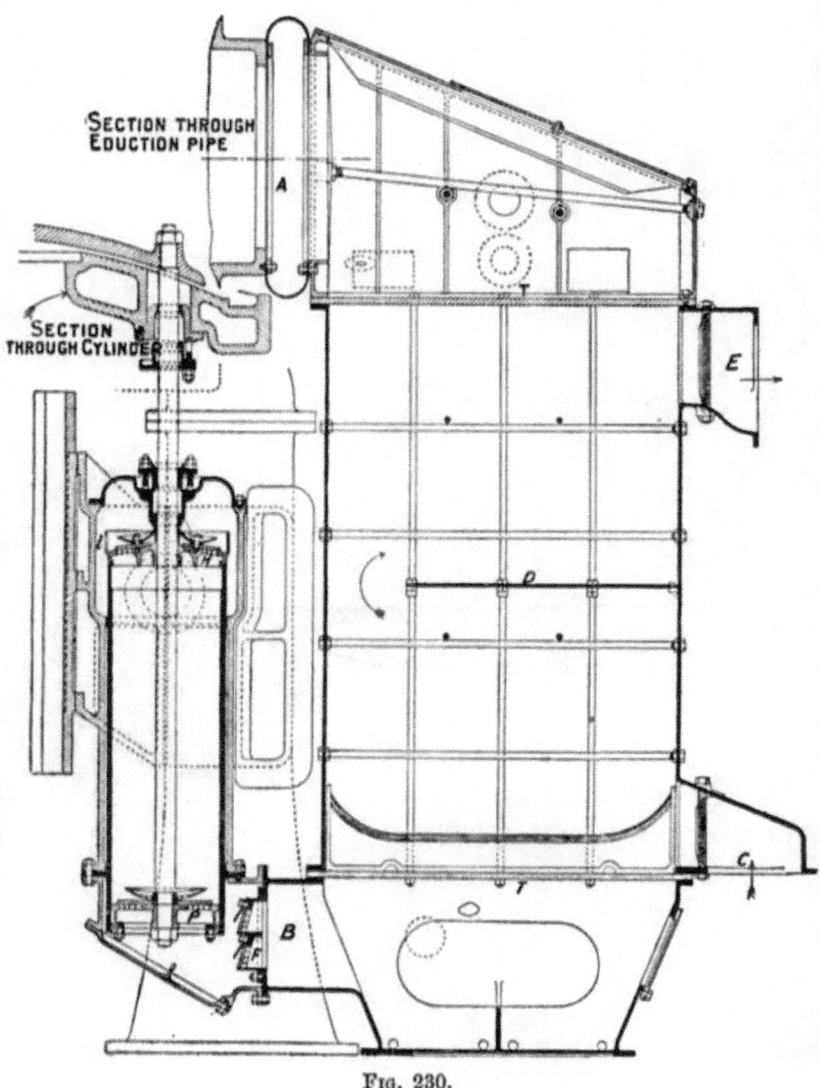

Fig. 230.

$\frac{3}{4}$-inch diameter, and pitched not less than $\frac{3}{4}$ inch apart, to allow sufficient material for the gland.   They are zigzagged so as to occupy as small a volume as possible, and are made of brass, about $\frac{1}{20}$ inch thick, of a composition consisting of not less than 70 per cent. of copper and not less than 1 per cent. of tin, the remainder being zinc. The small quantity of tin is added to prevent galvanic action. The brass for the condenser casing and the tube plates is also made of as near the same composition as possible, or the tube plates are often made of Muntz metal.

The tube plates for large condensers are now made 1 inch thick, in order to provide sufficient depth for insuring a proper watertight attachment for the tubes ; for not only must the tubes be watertight, but they must also be free to expand and contract with the changes of temperature they necessarily undergo. The plan of fitting generally used, and invariably used in the Navy, is to form small screwed stuffing-boxes in the tube plates, and provide screwed ferrules, fitting over the tubes, to tighten tape packings around the tubes at the bottoms of the stuffing-boxes. The ferrules are generally made with small internal projections or flanges at their outer ends, to prevent the possibility of the tubes slipping out of place. This is desirable in all condensers, at each end, but is essential for the lower ends of vertical tubes. These projections are invariably fitted in naval condensers. A sketch of the tube attachment is shown in Fig. 231. Tubes when properly fitted in this manner remain tight for a long time, which is very important, for should leakage occur the sea-water obtains access to the feed-water, is pumped into the boilers, and forms deposits.

The tubes of condensers vary considerably in length up to about 14 to 15 feet, the general length in large condensers being from 8 to 10 feet. With long tubes, diaphragm or supporting plates, s, Fig. 228, are fitted with holes in them to permit the passage of the tubes. These supporting plates prevent bending of the tubes, and disturbance of the stuffing-box joint at the end of the tube. The tube plates are strengthened by a few stay bars secured by nuts at the tube plates as indicated in

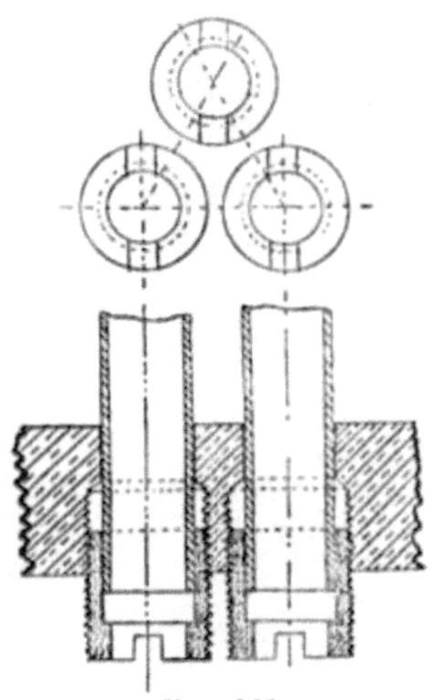

Fig. 231.

sketches, tubes being omitted at intervals to enable them to be fitted.

The condenser covers, G, are attached to the tube plates by bolts fitted so as to be independent of those securing the tube plate to the condenser casing, so that the cover joint may be broken without disturbing the joint between tube plate and condenser barrel. This is often effected by fitting collar bolts, as shown in Fig. 229, in which case it will be seen that any bolt can be renewed without taking off the cover. Doors are fitted in the covers for examination of the glands of condenser tubes, and also on the condenser barrel for examination of the outsides of the tubes.

The area of the condensing surface in surface-condensers was formerly made about the same as that of the heating surface of the tubes in the boilers, but experience shows that considerably less than this is sufficient, and in most modern ships with triple expansion engines the area of cooling surface is only from 1 to 1·25 square feet per I.H.P. ; 1 square foot per I.H.P. at full power has been found in the later warships to be sufficient.   In the torpedo-boat destroyers, where weight is of extreme importance, the area fitted is less than this, and is sometimes as low as ¾ square foot per I.H.P.

Air-pump of surface-condenser.—In surface-condensers the only water that accumulates in the condensing chamber is that from the condensation of the exhaust steam, but a small amount of air is always present, either liberated from the feed-water or due to leakage.   An air-pump is therefore also necessary with surface-condensers, although it can be made very much smaller than that of the old jet-condenser.

The air-pump is of the reciprocating kind, and with vertical engines it is almost invariably fitted as a vertical single-acting bucket pump. With many horizontal engines, where a vertical motion can be conveniently obtained for the air-pump, this vertical variety of pump is also often fitted.   With horizontal engines generally, however, the air-pump is also horizontal, and worked directly off one of the pistons or crossheads. In this case it is generally a double-acting solid piston pump similar to that illustrated in Fig. 232, but the vertical bucket pump is much more efficient.

Vertical air-pump.—The vertical air-pump is illustrated in Figs. 230 and 233.   It consists of a reciprocating bucket or piston, P, fitted with orifices covered by non-return valves, which move in a cylindrical barrel, at each end of which are fitted covers or seatings, F and H, also provided with orifices and non-return valves. These three sets of valves lift vertically, and only allow passage of water or air in the upward direction. The suction pipe B communicates with the bottom of the steam space of the condenser. The valves at the lower end are called 'foot' or 'suction valves,' those in the moving bucket are called the 'bucket valves,' while those at the top are the 'head' or 'discharge valves.' A large door is fitted in the air-pump barrel, so that the bucket and foot-valves can be examined without removal of the head-valves and cover. An air vessel is usually fitted above the head-valves and an escape-valve on the cover, this latter being for use in case an abnormal load is brought on the pump, such as when the engines are inadvertently started too quickly when there is a considerable amount of water in the condenser.

Action of the pump.—During the up stroke of the bucket a partial vacuum is formed between the bucket and the foot-valves, which causes the foot-valves to be opened by the slight excess pressure in the condenser, and water and air to enter the barrel. On this stroke, also, water and air above the bucket is forced out through the head-valves, H, into the discharge pipe, the non-return valves in the bucket being closed by the pressure above them, and preventing return of the water. On the down stroke commencing, the foot- and head-valves close, and the bucket descends through the air and water below it, the bucket valves being forced open and allowing the air and water to pass through to the upper side. On the next up stroke this air and water is discharged, and a fresh supply enters the barrel from the condenser.

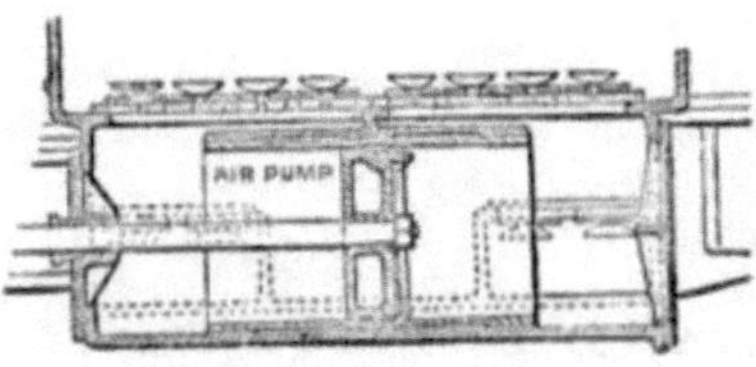

FIG. 232.

Amount of vacuum possible.—It should be noted that there must be an excess pressure in the condenser beyond that in the air-pump barrel, sufficient to lift the foot-valves, so that even with the most efficient air-pump of this construction, a perfect vacuum in the condenser is not

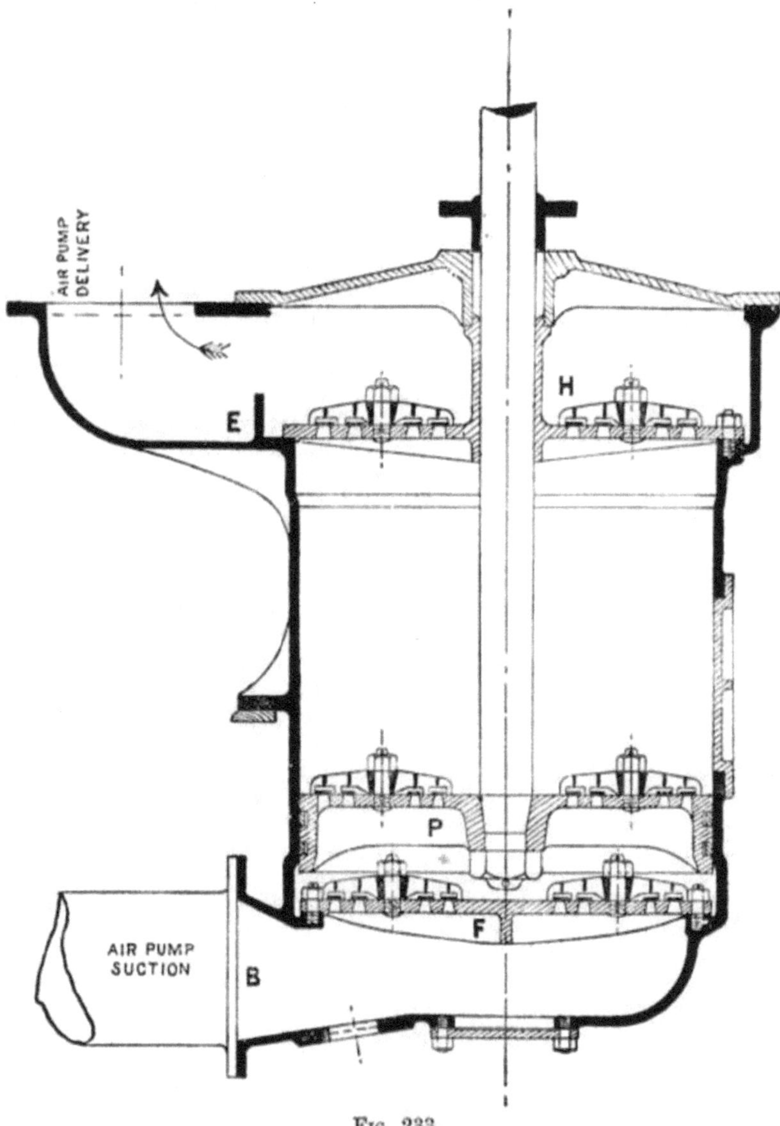

Fig. 233.

possible.   The amount of vacuum possible in the condenser depends on the weight of these foot-valves, and also on the perfection of the vacuum the air-pump creates in its pump barrel, which latter, assuming the air-pump bucket to work airtight in the barrel, depends very greatly on the amount of clearance spaces there are between the bucket and the foot-valves ; the less this clearance is, the greater the vacuum possible, so that the clearance spaces should always be made as small as possible. With the usual construction the clearance spaces in vertical air-pumps are less than in the horizontal ones, as in the former the bucket can be more easily arranged to travel very close to the foot-valves at the bottom of the stroke. Another feature in which the vertical pump is superior to the horizontal exists in the liability of the air-pump rod of the latter to leak and impair the vacuum in the pump, whereas in the vertical pump this is of little importance. Any pockets and spaces in the pump chamber where air may collect should be carefully avoided, for if any accumulation of air exists, a good vacuum cannot be obtained.

When all the parts of the condenser and engine are in good order, the amount of air present is very trifling. On the up stroke of the pump, therefore, we have generally present, above the bucket, water and water vapour. On being compressed, this water vapour returns to the liquid form, so that there is often some shock when the solid water strikes the head-valves and commences to be discharged. To avoid this a small adjustable non-return pet valve is generally fitted to the barrel just below the head-valves, which enables a small quantity of air to be sucked in on the down stroke, which acts as a cushion above the bucket on the up stroke, and so reduces shock. As the bucket also strikes the water suddenly on the down stroke, this pet valve is sometimes fitted a little below the bucket at the top of its stroke, so that a small amount of air is admitted below the bucket to act in a similar manner.

The barrel and bucket of the air-pump and the seatings for the foot- and head-valves are made of gunmetal, and the air-pump rod is made either of the same material, or preferably of some rolled bronze or brass, such as rolled naval brass or manganese bronze.

In the horizontal double-acting air-pump (Fig. 232), where the water only passes through two sets of valves, it is very important that the head-valves should be kept always covered with water, as this improves their action ; the discharge from the air-pump is arranged to insure this. In the vertical bucket-pump this is also desirable, and the sketches show the ledges, l, Fig. 230, and E, Fig. 233, fitted for this purpose.

Air-pump valves.—Air-pump valves are either made of vulcanised indiarubber, or of sheet metal. Indiarubber, if used, has to be specially prepared to resist the action of the mineral oil used for the lubrication of the cylinders and slide-valves, which soon destroys ordinary india-rubber. When used for naval vessels, the indiarubber for air-pump valves contains an amount not exceeding 70 per cent. of oxide of zinc to enable it to resist the action of the oil, while sulphur is present to an amount not exceeding $1\frac{3}{4}$ per cent., the remainder being best caoutchouc, with no other ingredients. Air-pump valves are, however, now generally made of thin sheet metal, of which there are numerous varieties. Many of these give excellent results in practice. They can be made very light, are not affected by grease if occasionally cleaned, and last a very long time.

The orifices covered by the air-pump valves, whether of indiarubber or metal, require to be divided into small spaces by gratings, as in the plan Fig. 237, so that the unsupported area of valve is not too great, while a brass guard secured to the seating by a stud and nut must be fitted to regulate the lift.   Figs. 234 to 236 show various patterns of metal valves, and Figs. 237 and 238 examples of indiarubber valves.   In some examples the seating is a separate casting bolted in position, as in Fig. 238.

Vertical air-pumps are generally worked by rocking levers and links, as shown in Fig. 192, from one of the piston-rod crossheads, generally the low-pressure, arranged so as to reduce the speed by about one-half and keep the speed of the bucket moderate.

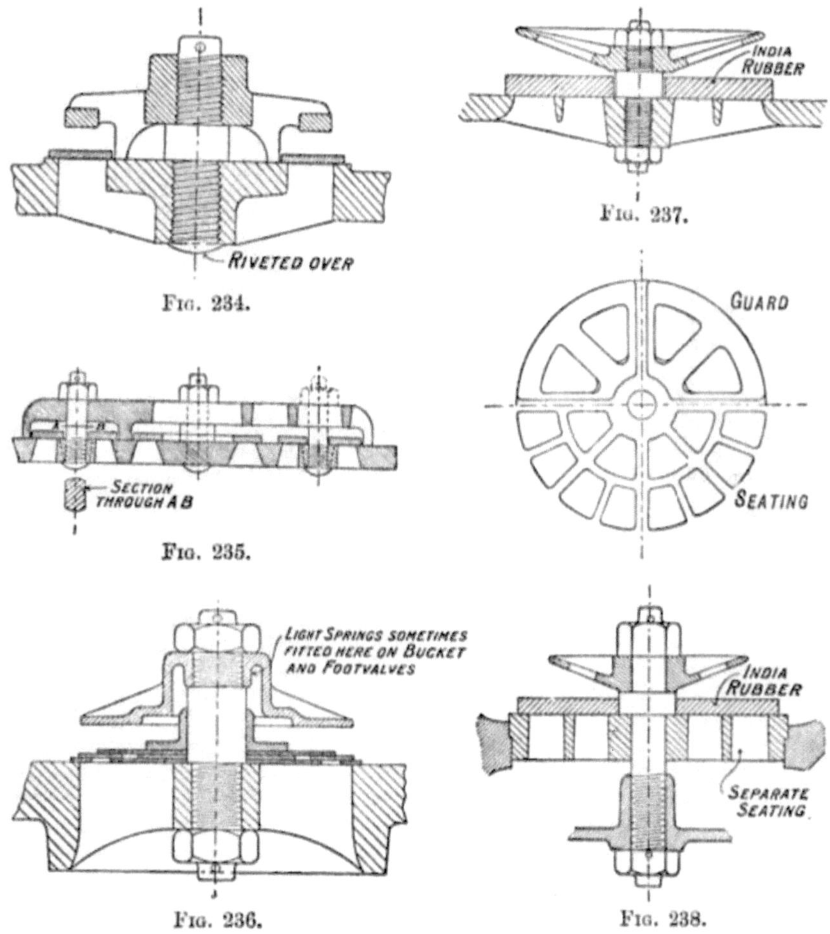

FIG. 234.

FIG. 235.

FIG. 237.

FIG. 236.

FIG. 238.

In the engines by Messrs. Humphrys, Tennant & Co., and occasionally by other firms, the vertical air-pumps are worked as in horizontal engines, from the piston of the engine direct, as shown in Fig. 230, in which case the speed of bucket is of course the same as that of the engine piston.   The attachment to the L.P. piston is also indicated in this sketch.

Independent air-pumps.—In some engines, especially those designed to work at high speeds of revolution, the air-pumps have been detached from the main engines and worked by separate auxiliary engines, the main engines being employed for propelling purposes only. This enables the speed to be regulated independently of the main engines, and a vacuum to be maintained in the condensers whether the main engines are working or not. A pump of this kind to work satisfactorily must be well designed. The type known as the Blake air-pump is described at the end of this chapter.

Feed-tanks.—The air-pump generally discharges its water through a pipe into a tank in the engine room called the 'feed-tank,' from which the feed-pumps draw their water for supplying the boilers. This tank should be of ample capacity, so that the feed-water may have space in which to accumulate when not immediately required for the boilers. Its capacity is generally at least equal to from four to five minutes' supply of feed-water at full power, and it provides a space in which the feed-water is at rest for a time, so that any air contained is more readily liberated, and passes off through a pipe which is open to the atmosphere. An overflow pipe, discharging into the reserve fresh-water tanks, is fitted to the feed-tank, with an internal pipe led to the lower part of the tank, so that if water is discharged from the feed-tank it comes from the bottom of the tank, and any grease floating on the surface of the water does not pass into the reserve fresh-water tanks. A small pipe is fitted to prevent syphoning. An additional overflow pipe with valve is fitted, so that any greasy surface water may be discharged into the bilge, except when a grease filter is fitted, in which case this overflow pipe is often omitted. A glass water gauge and zinc slabs are also fitted, and the feed-tanks of each engine room are connected by a pipe running between the two engine rooms, a shut-off valve being fitted in this pipe, worked from either engine room.

Hot-well tank and pump.—The later naval vessels are fitted with a tank, pump, and grease filter between the air-pump and the feed-tank. It is important that the feed-water should be freed as much as possible from grease prior to entry in the boilers, and it is desirable that any feed-water filters should be fitted to filter the water before admission to the feed-pumps, rather than on the discharge pipes of the feed-pumps. A grease filter between the air-pump and the feed-tank might, when dirty, bring too great a strain on the air-pump, so that, in several recent ships, the air-pump is allowed to discharge into an intermediate tank called the 'hot-well tank,' from which it is discharged by a pump fitted for this purpose called the 'hot-well pump.' This pump takes the feed-water from the hot-well tank, and discharges it through a feed-water filter into the feed-tank, from which tank the feed pumps draw water in the usual manner.

In the event of the feed-water filter becoming clogged up with grease so as to unduly increase the pressure required to be exerted by the hot-well pump to force it through the filter, an escape valve and pipe are generally fitted, so that under these circumstances the water lifts the escape valve and is discharged direct to the feed-tank. An overflow pipe is fitted to the hot-well tank or air-pump discharge pipe, so that in the event of the hot-well pump failing to act, the water will accumulate in the hot-well tank and overflow into the feed-tanks. The hot-well pump is of the ordinary reciprocating variety, **generally** fitted with a float in the hot-well working the steam valve of the pump, so that a constant level is maintained in the hot-well. Details of the feed filters are described in Chapter XXVIII.

Reserve fresh-water tank and feed make-up arrangements.—The practice for many years was to fit a supplementary feed-pipe, consisting of a small pipe connecting the steam and water sides of the condenser, and fitted with a valve, so that any losses of feed-water resulting from leaks, safety valves blowing, &c., could be made up by admitting a quantity of the circulating water to the steam space by this supplementary feed-pipe. With the higher pressures of steam, however, it is found necessary, and is also economical, to prohibit this use of salt-water for auxiliary feed purposes. Arrangements are therefore supplied to enable fresh water to be used under these circumstances.

Reserve fresh-water tanks are supplied, the double bottoms of the vessel being generally utilised for this purpose, and these tanks form a reservoir into which fresh water can be placed from the shore, or into which the distilling apparatus on board can discharge, so that when extra feed-water is required to make up losses, the water in these reserve tanks can be drawn on. Instead of the old pipe and cock between the steam and salt-water sides of the condenser therefore, modern vessels are fitted with a pipe from this reserve tank to the steam space of the condenser, or the air-pump, with a valve conveniently situated for regulating. Losses of feed-water are made up by opening up this connection and admitting the extra fresh water to the condenser whilst the main engines are working. A connection is also made to the auxiliary feed-pump suction, which enables this pump to draw water direct from the reserve tanks.

Zinc slabs are fitted to prevent corrosion, also means for ascertaining the height of water, and air pipes to allow air to escape from the compartment, or to enter, when the tanks are being filled with water or being pumped out. A valve is also fitted so that these tanks can be connected to one of the Downton pumps, and emptied by this means if required.

Advantages of separate circulating pumps.—The cooling water of a surface condenser is generally circulated, i.e. pumped from the sea and returned again to the sea, through the condenser, by means of a *centrifugal pump* worked by an independent auxiliary engine. This plan is universal in the Navy, and is superior to a reciprocating pump worked direct from the engine piston, for with the separate engine the circulating pump can be kept working and the condensers kept cool when the main engines are stopped, whilst in the case of the pump worked off the main engines circulation ceases. In many cases with reciprocating pumps worked from the main engines, it has been necessary to fit suction pipes from the condenser casings to one of the auxiliary pumping engines, to prevent the condensers getting hot before starting the engines. It is also difficult when the pumps are worked by the main engines to vary the amount of circulating water if required, the speed being necessarily the same as that of the main engines. Often at the highest and lowest speeds the pumps do not work so efficiently as at moderate speeds, and the vacuum is consequently decreased. These pumps are also less available for pumping out the ship in case of emergency, as they cannot be worked except when the ship is under way.

The centrifugal circulating pump.—Centrifugal pumps are very useful when large quantities of water have to be pumped with a comparatively small lift, as is the case in marine engine condensers, in which both the inlet and outlet orifices are generally below the surface of the water, and consequently the only work the pump has to do is to overcome the friction of the passages and keep the water in motion. They work very smoothly, have no valves, and have the further advantage that if they should be started before the outlet valve on the ship's side is opened, there is no fear of injury to the condenser, as the pump will only churn the water and not bring great pressures on the passages. When the discharge orifice in centrifugal pumps is not at the highest part of the casing, it is necessary to fit an air-cock at the top to let off the air and prevent accumulation, as the pump must be kept full of water to insure its efficient action, the presence of air interfering with its working.

Figs. 239 and 240 show details of the centrifugal pump and engine for circulating purposes. The pump consists of an impeller, wheel, or fan, revolving inside a casing, B. The impeller generally consists of a central web, A, guiding the incoming water, with two side plates, C C, gradually approaching each other as they near the circumference, and between which run a series of curved vanes, D, from the boss to the circumference. These vanes are curved away from the direction of rotation as they proceed from boss to circumference. The water enters the central part of the impeller from the inlet pipe E, and is thrown by the rapidly revolving vanes D, outwards and around into the casing B, which surrounds the circumference of the wheel. The direction of rotation is indicated by arrows in the sketch. The casing B is of gradually increasing area, and leads to the delivery pipe F, along which the water is forced by the centrifugal action. It thence proceeds to the condenser, where, after traversing the tubes, it is again discharged overboard.

The impeller and casing are made of gunmetal, and the spindle is either cast of gunmetal in one piece with the impeller, or formed separately of forged bronze and keyed to it. This spindle runs in *lignum-vitæ* bearings, which are lubricated with water. The casing is formed in two parts to enable the impeller to be inserted, and the joint should, if possible, be so arranged that the impeller may be examined without disconnecting either the inlet or discharge pipes. In some successful pumps by Gwynne the side plates are entirely omitted.

The circulating pumps take their suction from a large screw-down inlet valve on the bottom of the ship. The discharge is through similar valves on the ship's side.

Under-water valves and fittings.—All holes in the hull of a ship below the water-line for the supply or discharge of condensing water or any other purpose require to be fitted with valves. The old wooden and composite ships were almost always fitted with *Kingston valves*, which are simply conical valves opening outwards, so that the pressure of the water tends to keep them closed. The valves are fitted with long spindles, which are brought inside the ship through stuffing-boxes, to enable the valves to be worked from inboard. They were, however,

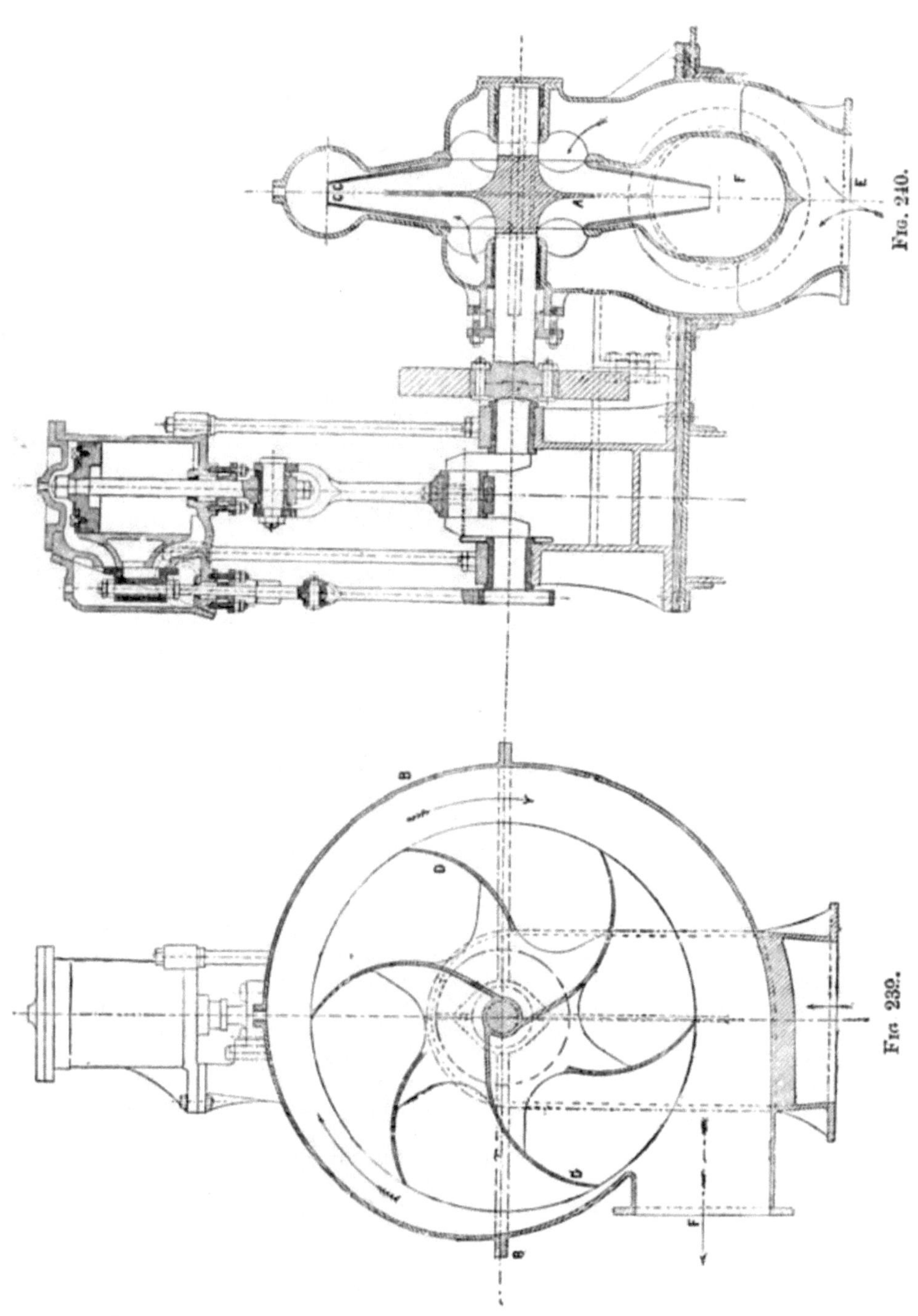

Fig. 240.
Fig. 239.

particularly suitable for wood ships, because they enabled a firm and secure connection to the hull to be conveniently made, as shown in Fig. 241, but were also often fitted to steel vessels. For iron or steel hulls, however, they have no special advantage, and in modern ships the cheaper and lighter ordinary screw-down valves are generally fitted for all the under-water orifices, while another screw-down valve is usually fitted inside the ship in most of the pipes, either at the sea valve or not far from it, for additional security. The Kingston valve is still sometimes fitted for blow-out purposes.

The spindles of all under-water valves in the Royal Navy have to pass a tensile test, equal to half a ton per square inch of area of the valve ; with this limit, however, that the maximum test load is not to exceed twelve tons whatever may be the diameter of the valve.

A sketch of an ordinary sea valve for a steel vessel with a double bottom is given in Fig. 243, which represents the inlet valve for supplying a circulating pump, the valve being fitted at the inner end of a tube between the two bottoms. Gratings of large area are fitted to all sea inlet valves to prevent entry of weeds and other foreign matter. A plan of the grating of Fig. 243 is shown in Fig. 242. The tubes must in sheathed ships all be made of gunmetal to prevent galvanic action, as zinc protectors are then useless. Fig. 244 shows the attachment of such a tube to a sheathed ship, with the means of preventing access of water to the steel outer bottom. In the case of blow-out valves where sudden variations of temperature occur when blowing out, the tube is fixed to the outer bottom, but passes through the inner bottom by means of a stuffing-box, and is not rigidly secured to it, thus allowing for expansion. This is shown in Fig. 245 ; a guard is fitted below the valve to prevent it being lowered too far. The tubes of steel bottom ships are made of steel, where they are large enough in diameter to be properly cleaned and painted, but the smaller ones in which this cannot be done are made of gunmetal. The under-water valve is attached by studs to a thick facing ring, secured for this purpose to the end of the tube, and a spigot is fitted on the valve casing, which enters the tube and protects the end of the tube from wasting away. All gunmetal under-water valves of iron or steel ships are fitted with zinc protecting rings immediately below the valve box or tube and well attached to the steel, to prevent the decay of the hull of the vessel by galvanic action in the neighbourhood of the valve. These zinc protectors are shown in the sketches.

Duplicate centrifugal pumps.—The usual practice in large ships is to fit, for each set of main engines, two centrifugal pumps and engines, each large enough to circulate all the water required for full-power working. This provides for the case of accident to any circulating engine or pump, and doubles the pumping power in the event of a leak. Each pump is fitted with separate sea and bilge suctions, and the valves for changing from sea to bilge suction are arranged to be easily accessible. In some vessels, where weight and space are of importance, one pump only is fitted for each set, the discharge pipes being connected across, so that either pump may, if required, supply both condensers.

Bilge suctions to circulating pumps.—The circulating pump suction pipe leading to the engine-room bilge is provided with a non-return valve

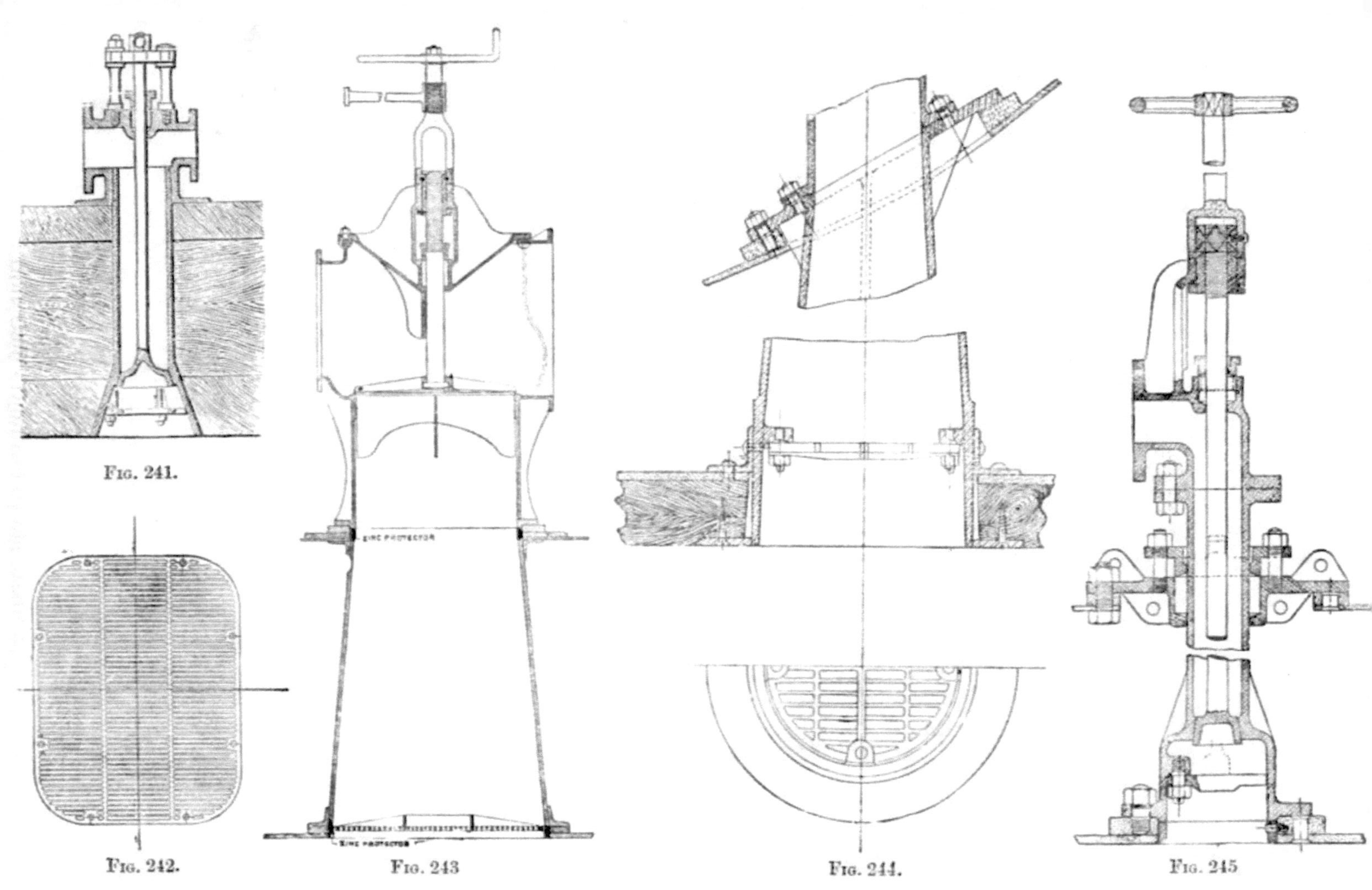

Fig. 241.
Fig. 242.
Fig. 243
Zinc Protector
Fig. 244.
Fig. 245

and strainer at its end, so that, in case of a serious leak, water might be drawn from the bilge and discharged overboard. These centrifugal pumps constitute by far the most powerful pumping appliances on board ship, the amount capable of being pumped out varying with the size of the vessel. In the largest battleships and cruisers, each of the four pumps fitted is capable of discharging about 1,200 tons of water per hour. Figs. 246 and 247 show the arrangement of pipes and valves usually fitted for this service, from which the procedure necessary to alter the pump suction from sea to bilge will be seen.

In this arrangement there is a common screw-down sea suction valve for the two pumps, B B being sluice valves fitted in the sea suction pipe, one to each pump. C C are the two bilge suction screw-down

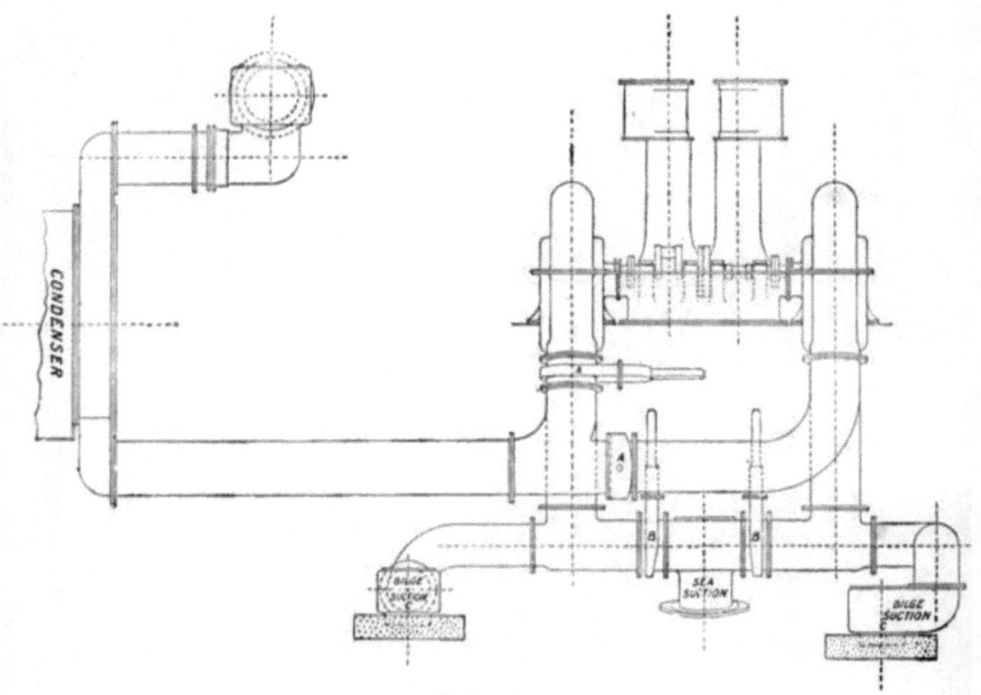

Fig. 246.

non-return valves, and A A are sluice valves fitted in the discharge pipes, one to each pipe. The pumps are not coupled together, but work quite independently, and it will be seen that to enable either pump to draw from the bilge its valve B must be shut, and the bilge suction valve C and the sluice valve A opened. Either bilge suction valve can be examined when the other pump is at work. The valves A and B are closed when it is required to shut off either pump when not at work.

Independent feed and bilge engines.—In many mercantile vessels and all ships of the Royal Navy the feed and bilge pumping engines are fitted as separate engines instead of attaching them to the main engines. Feed pumps when worked by the main engines, especially by high-speed engines, are somewhat spasmodic in their action, and the pressure in the feed-pipes fluctuates more than is desirable. With separate feed engines, their speed is regulated independently of that of the main engines, and is governed solely by the requirements of the boiler, so that the pressure in the feed-pipes is kept more uniform. By this system, too, the speed can be regulated so that the pump always draws a full supply of water, so that the feed-water is supplied to the boilers practically free from air, and this is conducive to their durability.

The feed engines, main and auxiliary, are usually fixed in the stoke-holds, so that the person in charge of each set of boilers has full command of the feeding of his boilers, which is an important feature in ships that are necessarily sub-divided into separate water-tight compartments. The main feed-pumps are fitted to draw from the feed-tanks only, but duplicate sets of pumps are fitted which are arranged to draw both from the feed-tanks, the reserve fresh-water tanks, and from the sea, thus making provision for the event of break-down of any feed-pump.

Vacuum gauge.— The vacuum in the condenser is indicated by a Bourdon gauge, similar in construction to that shown in Fig. 90, called the 'vacuum gauge.' This gauge is graduated to represent inches of mercury, and does not show, directly, the *absolute* pressure in the condenser, but only the difference between this absolute pressure, which acts on the inside of the tube, and the absolute pressure of the atmosphere acting on the outside of the tube. As the actual pressure in the condenser is independent of the atmospheric pressure, the vacuum registered will, therefore, vary almost directly with the atmospheric pressure as recorded by the weather barometer. For example, suppose the constant pressure in the condenser to be represented by four inches of mercury. Then, when the barometer stands at 30·5, the vacuum gauge would register $30·5 - 4 = 26·5$; whilst if the barometer stood at 29·5 the vacuum gauge could only indicate $29·5 - 4 = 25·5$ inches, or one inch lower than in the former case.

This may be readily understood by reference to an indicator diagram,

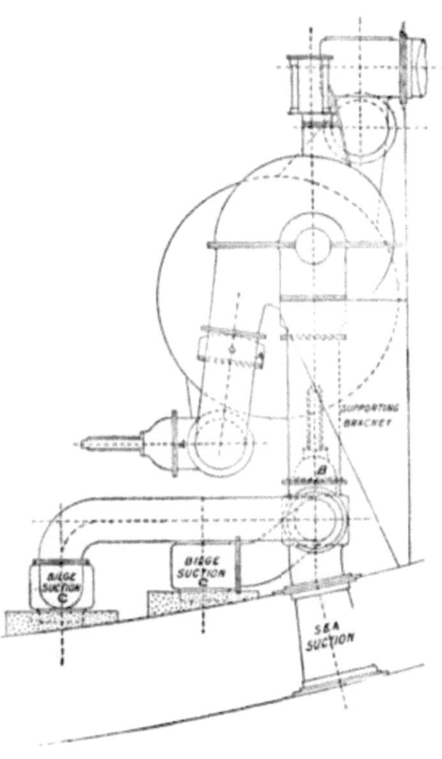

FIG. 247.

Fig. 248. We will assume the actual pressure in the condenser to be the same in each case. If the barometer stand at 30·5, the distance of the zero line o p from the atmospheric line indicated by the full line A A will represent a pressure due to 30·5 inches of mercury. If the barometer stand at 29·5, the atmospheric pressure will be less than before, so that the distance between the zero line, which remains in the same position, and the new atmospheric line indicated by the dotted line B B represents only a pressure due to 29·5 inches of mercury. The back pressure line c c being the same, it is evident that the lower the height of the barometer is, the less will be the vacuum indicated on the diagram below the atmospheric line, and *vice versâ*. It should be observed that this does not affect the area of the diagram, but only the indicated vacuum.

The principal object secured in recording the height of the barometer is the determination of the maximum attainable vacuum in the condenser. To determine this the temperature of the condenser must also be known, and the pressure of steam corresponding to this temperature ascertained by reference to tables, such as given in Chapter III. If this pressure be deducted from the atmospheric pressure given by the height of the barometer, the remainder will be the maximum attainable vacuum with that temperature of condenser. The difference between the vacuum shown on the gauge attached to the condenser and the maximum

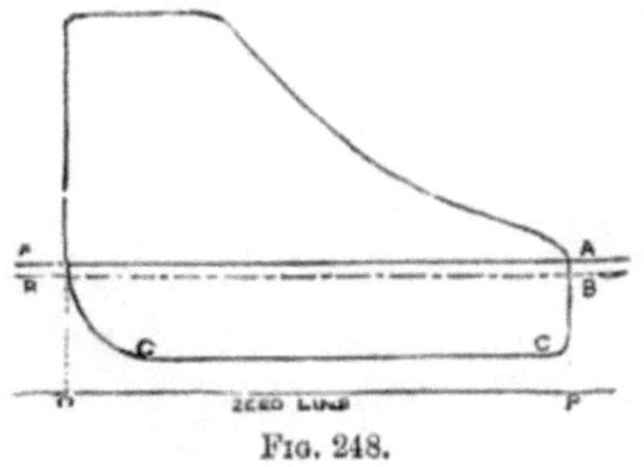

Fig. 248.

attainable will be due to air leaks or other inefficiency in the action of the condenser, air-pumps, &c.

For example, if the temperature of the condenser be 100° Fahr., and the weather barometer stand at 30 inches, which is equivalent to a pressure of 14·7 pounds per square inch, the pressure of vapour due to this temperature of 100° Fahr. = 0·942 pounds per square inch, and therefore the maximum vacuum attainable will be $14·7 - 0·942 = 13·758$ pounds per square inch below the atmospheric pressure, which would be represented by about 28 inches on the gauge. If, therefore, the vacuum in the condenser, as shown by the gauge, be less than this it will be due to the causes mentioned above. If, for example, there is any air set free from the water, it will increase the pressure or reduce the vacuum although the temperature remains unaltered ; hence the desirability of liberating all air from the feed-water before it enters the boiler, as in the feed-tank.

Heat rejected into condenser.—Suppose the steam entering the condenser to have a pressure of 3 to 4 lbs. absolute, corresponding to a temperature of about 150° Fahr. The temperature of the water after condensation may be assumed to be 100° Fahr., which is a good working temperature for the condenser. Then each pound of steam entering the condenser at a temperature of 150° Fahr. is reduced to water at 100° Fahr.

The latent heat of one pound of steam at 150° Fahr. is 1,010 thermal units. So that 1,010 thermal units are liberated, by the condensation to water at 150° Fahr., while in addition the temperature is reduced from 150° to 100°, which represents 50 thermal units. Therefore the total heat given out by the condensation is $1,010 + 50 = 1,060$ thermal units per pound of steam, which is all abstracted by the condensing water.

It should be noticed that this number does not vary much whatever the final temperature of the water, as the latent heat part of the total is very great compared with the sensible heat part.

This quantity of about 1,060 thermal units is called the *heat rejected per pound of steam used*. To ascertain the total 'heat rejected' we must know the number of pounds of steam used per minute. Assuming this to be known, we get by multiplication the 'heat rejected' per minute. The heat imparted in the boiler to the steam will always be found to be greater than the heat rejected, and this represents the quantity of heat which is converted into work and is measured by the heat equivalent of the indicated horse-power.

If H = heat imparted in boiler per minute, R = heat rejected per minute, and I.H.P. = number of horse-power, then

$$H - R = \frac{\text{I.H.P.} \times 33,000}{772}$$

since one thermal unit is equal to 772 foot-pounds of work. In this statement the small loss by radiation is neglected.

Quantity of condensing water required.—We saw above that about 1,060 thermal units were rejected into the condenser per lb. of steam used. Now suppose in a surface condenser that the circulating water is raised in temperature to the extent of 20° to 25° Fahr. by passing through the condenser, then the number of pounds of circulating water per pound of steam condensed must be $\dfrac{1,060}{20 \text{ to } 25} = 53$ lbs. to 42 lbs. For vessels whose service may take them into the Tropics, where the temperature of sea-water in the summer is often 85° Fahr., it is not usual to allow for a greater rise of temperature than 20°, although in colder climates a smaller amount of water with a greater rise in temperature will suffice.

Suppose, next, we are dealing with a jet-condenser, and that the temperature of the injection water is 60° Fahr. In this case the injection water is raised by mixing with the steam to the 100° Fahr.—i.e. a rise of 40° Fahr., so that the quantity of injection water required would be $\dfrac{1,060}{40} = 26\frac{1}{2}$ lbs. per pound of steam. The higher the temperature of the injection water the greater will be the quantity required. As the feed-water for boilers supplied from jet-injection condensers is practically as salt as sea-water itself, frequent blowing out of a portion of the water in the boilers was necessary to prevent undue incrustation on the heating surfaces, and resulted in a considerable waste of heat.

We will now give some calculations respecting the operation of blowing out, which was of great importance in the old jet-condensing days, but is of minor importance now. The principles should, however, be well understood, as they are necessary when investigating the action of evaporators, and even with modern boilers, owing to occasional leakages of the main condenser tubes, the feed-water may have a proportion of sea-water mixed with it, and the effect of this should be considered.

The following calculations are general and will apply to any of the cases just referred to.

Quantity of water to be blown out to maintain constant density.— The proportion necessary to be blown out from an evaporator or boiler to keep the water at any particular density may be calculated thus :—

$$\text{Let } x = \text{quantity of feed-water,}$$
$$\text{,, } y = \text{,, ,, water to be blown out,}$$
$$\text{Then } x - y = \text{,, evaporated.}$$

Suppose the water in the boiler or evaporator to be kept at a density equal to n times that of the feed-water, then the quantity of solid matter blown out is proportional to $n \times y$. The quantity of solid matter pumped in with the feed-water during the same period is proportional to x, and since the density of the water in the boiler or evaporator remains constant, the solid matter blown out must be equal to that pumped in.

Therefore $x \times 1 = y \times n$ and $y = \dfrac{x}{n}$.

Case 1. If the density be kept at twice the density of the feed-water,

$$n = 2, \text{ and } y = \tfrac{1}{2}x.$$

In this case the quantity blown out must be half the total feed-water.

Case 2. Suppose the density in either a boiler working in connection with a jet condenser, or in an evaporator, to be kept at three times that of the feed-water, which in these cases would be sea-water, then

$$n = 3 \text{ and } y = \tfrac{1}{3}x,$$

i.e. the quantity necessary to be blown out to keep the density constant at three times the density of the feed-water is one-third the quantity of feed-water admitted.

Case 3. Suppose we have a modern engine with surface condenser, and that the tubes of the latter are leaking, so that the density of feed-water is 1 on the naval hydrometer—i.e. $\frac{1}{10}$ the density of sea-water— and that the density in the boilers is to be limited to four times that of sea-water ; in this case $n = 40$, and $\frac{1}{40}$ the total feed-water must be blown out.

If the machinery referred to is working at 500 I.H.P. and uses 15 lbs. of steam per I.H.P. per hour, the quantity of feed-water used per hour would be $500 \times 15 = 7,500$ lbs., so that 750 lbs. of sea-water enter the boilers per hour. The quantity of sea-water that must enter to raise the density to four times that of sea-water, is four times the weight of water the boilers contain. Knowing this latter weight, the time it will take to raise the density to any point can be determined by division.

The following calculations are principally given as being important in investigating the efficiency of evaporators. They are of little or no importance as regards boilers with modern machinery.

Heat wasted by blowing out.—

Let T_1 = temperature of the water in the boiler or evaporator ;
„ T_2 =   „   „   feed-water of the boiler, or inlet water to evaporator.

Each pound of water blown out has been raised in temperature from T_2 to T_1, so that the total amount of heat wasted by blowing out is

$$y \ (T_1 - T_2) \text{ thermal units.}$$

The total amount of heat expended on the x lbs. of water admitted to the boiler or evaporator consists of the quantity necessary to raise the whole x lbs. from T_2 to T_1, and also to evaporate $(x - y)$ lbs. at the temperature T'_1, and is therefore equal to

$$x \ (T_1 - T_2) + (x - y) \ \{966 - \cdot 7 \ (T_1 - 212)\}.$$

The proportion of heat wasted is therefore equal to

$$\frac{y \ (T_1 - T_2)}{x \ (T_1 - T_2) + (x - y) \ \{966 - \cdot 7 \ (T_1 - 212)\}},$$

and since $x = n\,y$, the proportion wasted equals

$$\frac{(T_1 - T_2)}{n \ (T_1 - T_2) + (n - 1) \ \{966 - \cdot 7 \ (T_1 - 212)\}},$$

We will now apply this formula to a few cases, selecting first an example of the jet-condenser, representing the practice of many years ago.

Suppose the working pressure in the boiler to have been 30 lbs. per square inch, the density to be kept at 20°, or twice that of sea-water. Temperature of boiler water, $T_1 = 270°$ Fahr., and of feed-water, $T_2 = 100°$ Fahr. Here $n = 2$, and by substitution we find that the proportion of heat wasted

$$= \cdot 1376 \text{ or } 13\tfrac{3}{4} \text{ per cent.}$$

Similarly, if the density be kept at 30°, $n = 3$, and the fraction of total heat wasted $= \cdot 074$, or about $7\tfrac{1}{2}$ per cent. We see, therefore, that the higher the density was kept, the less was the loss of heat by blowing out.

Take next the case of an evaporator receiving sea-water at 50° Fahr., and evaporating it at a pressure of 40 lbs. per square inch, the water being kept at a density equal to three times sea-water by brining. By substitution the loss of heat by the necessary blowing out is 9·3 per cent.

If the formula be applied to Case 3 of the preceding page, it will be found that the waste of heat would be very small should the boilers be worked under these circumstances.

Blake independent air-pump.—This type of air-pump is fitted in many vessels, including several United States warships ; they work at slow speed and give excellent results.

A drawing showing this pump is given in Fig. 248a. It consists of two cylinders and two single-acting vertical air-pumps of usual construction, the rods of the two pumps being connected by a rocking beam so that when one pump is at the top of its stroke the other is at the bottom. The slide-valves of the steam cylinders actuating the pumps, are worked by a separate small auxiliary steam cylinder and

Elevation with auxiliary valve cover removed.
½ Section through valve casing and auxiliary cylinder.
½ Section through main cylinder.
A
D
D
C
MAIN SLIDE CASING.
DISCHARGE
SUCTION

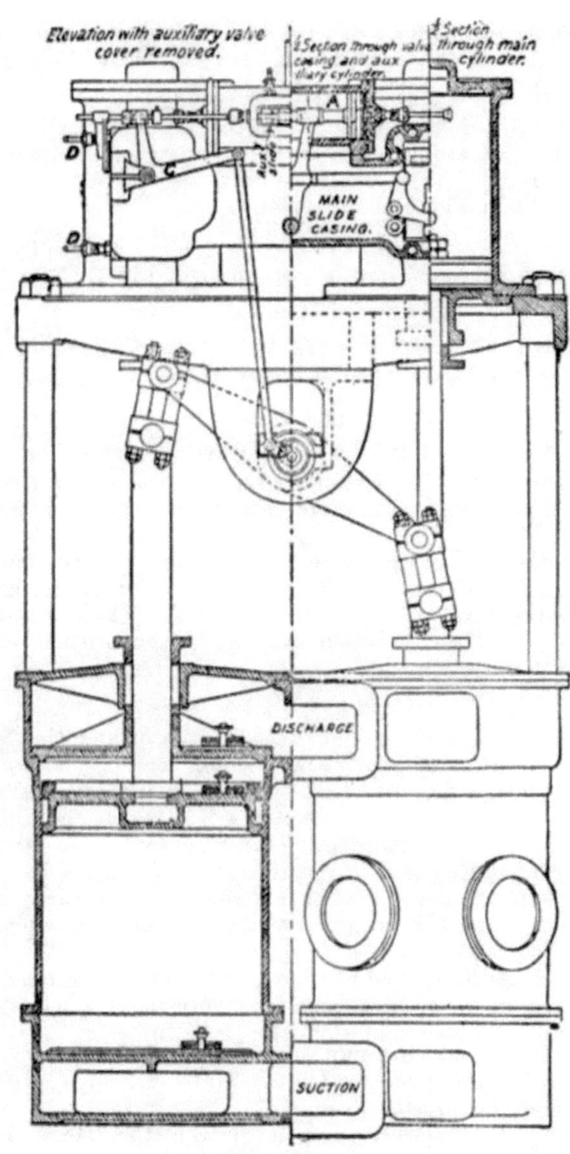

Fig. 248a.

piston A, placed horizontally in front of the two main cylinders. The piston rod of this small cylinder works the two slide-valves of the main cylinders, one on each side, by means of a system of levers working inside the main slide casing and shown below the horizontal cylinder. The slide-valve of the auxiliary cylinder is actuated from the shaft of the rocking beam by the small crank B and bell crank C, adjustable collars being fitted on the auxiliary valve-rod, which enable the travel of the small valve to be regulated so that the pump works with a full stroke of the plunger and at any speed desired. Small cushion valves, D, are also provided on the main cylinders for adjustment purposes. On the trials of some U.S. warships these pumps worked when at full power at fifteen double strokes per minute, maintaining a steady vacuum of 25 inches, the power indicated in their cylinders being only $\frac{1}{800}$ of that of the propelling engines, and the pump plungers sweeping through $\frac{1}{12}$ of the volume swept through by the L.P. pistons.

CHAPTER XXI.

ROTARY MOTION.

Crank and connecting rod.—The mechanism used for the trans-formation of the reciprocating motion of the piston into the rotary motion of the shafting and propeller consists of the connecting rod and crank-shaft, the motion of which may be readily understood by reference to the outline diagrams, Figs. 249 and 250, the direction of rotation being the same in each, as indicated by the circular arrows.

The rotating shaft s, which is carried in suitable bearings, has on it a crank or arm s c, connected to the piston-rod by the connecting rod c B, which has a working joint at each end. The end, B, of the piston-rod is constrained to move in a straight line by the action of a suitable guide G G. It is thus easily seen that the reciprocating motion of the piston is trans-formed, through the medium of the connecting rod B c, into the rotary motion of the crank-shaft s, from which the motion is com-municated to the propeller. The force P acting through the piston-rod, and which we will assume to be constant, is opposed by the resistance offered to the revolu-tion of the crank by the action of the propeller. This produces either thrust or tension in the connecting rod, according as the crank is being pushed or pulled round. The arrows indicate the direc-tions of the forces acting upon the joint B. The resultant of P and Q, as will be readily seen on reference to the diagrams, is always a force pressing on the guide G G for the direction of rotation shown, and is balanced by the equal reaction R of the guide which forms the third force acting on the joint B.

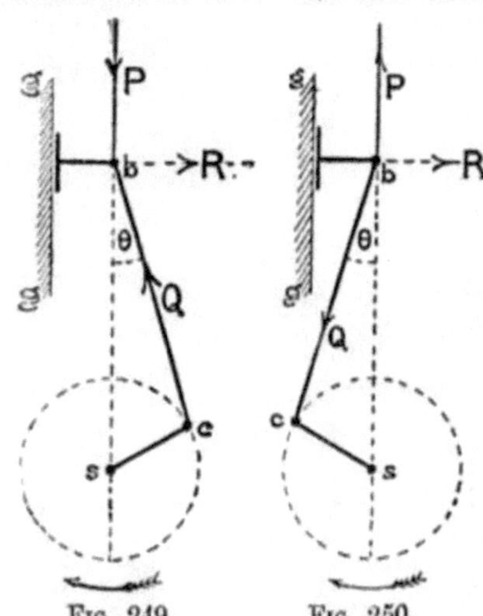

FIG. 249.   FIG. 250.

Forces acting.—By applying the principle of the parallelogram of forces, it will appear that for any angle θ the connecting rod makes with the line of motion we have

$$= Q \cos \theta \quad (1)$$
$$= Q \sin \theta \quad (2)$$

also from (1) $Q = P \sec \theta$, and substituting the value in (2), then $R = P \tan \theta$, also $Q = \sqrt{P^2 + R^2}$.

When the crank is at the dead point the force Q on the connecting rod is obviously equal to the force P, and the pressure R on the guide vanishes, as may be shown by putting $\theta = 0$ in above relations.

Direction of rotation.—The direction of rotation shown in Figs. 249 and 250, which causes the piston-rod head to be always pressed against the guide, is that adopted for ahead working.

If the direction of rotation be reversed, the resultant of the forces P and Q will no longer press on the guide G G, but will act in the opposite direction, and an opposing guide surface will be required to balance this. The guide surface for 'ahead' motion is generally made larger than that for 'astern' motion, as engines rarely have to work astern at full power for any length of time.

In the horizontal trunk engines, which had no piston-rod and no other guide than the cylinder barrel itself, the direction of ahead motion was made the reverse of that indicated above, so that the resultant of the forces P and Q was an upward force, and tended to lift the weight of the piston and trunk, and prevent excessive wear of the cylinder.

No loss involved by using a crank.—It is important to notice that no power is lost by the intervention of the crank, for the force transmitted by the connecting rod to the crank pin can be resolved into two parts : one along the crank, and the other at right angles to it. No motion of the crank pin takes place in the direction of the crank, so that this component does no work. The only work done is by the component at right angles to the crank, which is all usefully employed in rotating it.

It is also necessary to guard against the error of supposing that work is lost in consequence of bringing the masses of the pistons, rods, &c., to rest, and starting them again in motion in the opposite direction twice in every revolution of the engine, and that there is a resultant loss of efficiency in reciprocating engines. Although the pistons, rods, &c., during the first half of the stroke receive acceleration from the steam pressure on the piston, the work thus accumulated is given out by pressure on the crank pin during the retardation, so that nothing is lost, but the distribution only of the work is altered.

Connecting rod.—Figs. 251 and 252 show the form of top and bottom ends most generally employed for connecting rods. On Fig. 251 the connecting rod has a ⊤-shaped bottom end and the brass is spigoted into it ; the top end is forked, with brasses to fit on 'outside' gudgeon pins. In Fig. 252 a 'solid' head is shown, where the brass fits into a semicircular recess cut out from the end of the connecting rod ; the top end here is also forked, but is shown with a gudgeon pin between the jaws, which works in brasses in the end of the piston-rod.

The 'solid' head is on the whole the most efficient, especially for large engines, and it is usually adopted in marine engines.

The brasses of connecting rods are not allowed to butt on each other, but have liners and distance pieces placed between them, so that as they wear the liners can be taken out and filed thinner to allow the bearings to be adjusted, or removed bodily if sufficient wear has taken place. Thin sheet brass or tin plate liners, in addition to the thick cast distance piece or liner, are generally fitted. It is important that the brasses should be screwed hard on to the liners to insure correct working and to prevent straining and bending of the bolts. The bolts of connecting rods are subject to considerable shock at the bottom end of the stroke when the tension comes suddenly on them at the

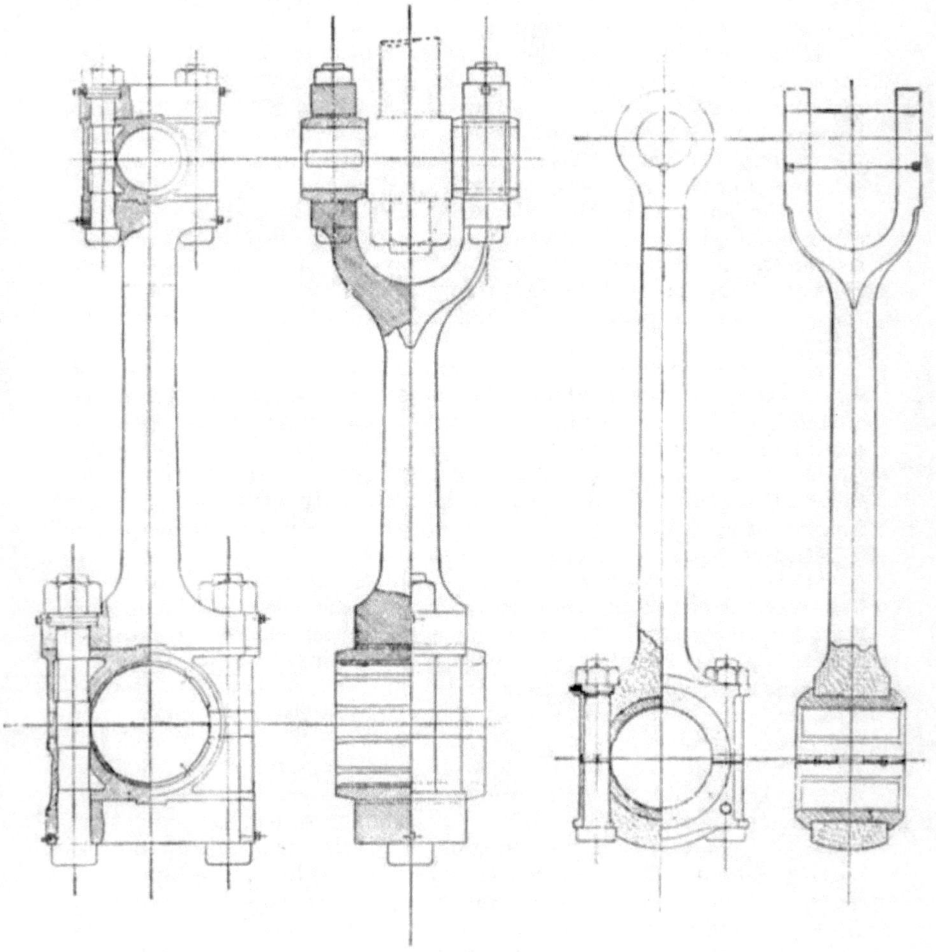

Fig. 251.

Fig. 252.

beginning of the up stroke, and this is much increased if there be any slackness in the bearings. There is no force acting on the bolts during the down stroke. They are, therefore, once in each revolution, alternately stretched by the steam pressure, and returned to their normal condition. This repeated stretching is, unless suitable arrangements are made concentrated on the smallest section below the nut—i.e. the sections at the bottom of the thread which are of small length, so that the bolts tend to break at this point if the stress is high. To prevent this the weakest section is lengthened so that the stretching is not concentrated at one point, but over nearly the whole length of the bolt, which much reduces the liability to fracture. The methods of effecting this are shown in Figs. 253 to 255, the area at the reduced section being made equal to that at the bottom of the thread, while the bearing surfaces are of the full diameter. Fig. 253 is inferior to the others, as there is danger of the hole being drilled too far, and thus weakening the bolt. The same construction is adopted for main bearing bolts.

The nuts on the connecting-rod bolts are secured by means of set-screws, to prevent their slacking back when the engines are at work, and the bolts themselves are secured from turning by stops fitted under the heads, and from falling out when being disconnected, by set-screws screwed into them through the connecting-rod end, as shown in the sketches.

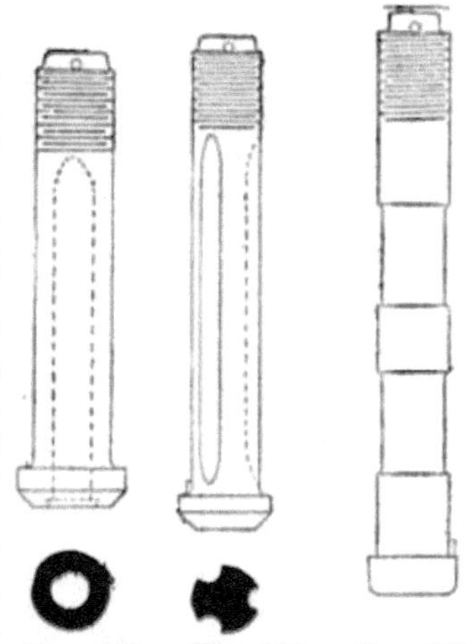

FIG. 253.   FIG. 254.   FIG. 255.

Crank-shafts.—Large crank-shafts are difficult forgings to make satisfactorily, and they are often made in separate pieces, having one crank on each, and joined by flanged couplings, or often, in the case of four-crank engines, a separate part for each pair of cranks. This simplifies the operations of forging and turning, and the several pieces are usually made symmetrical, so as to be interchangeable in case of accident. Fig. 256 represents the three-throw crank-shaft of a naval engine. The crank-shafts of smaller engines are forged in one piece. The various parts of the crank and other main shafting are, in the Navy, always filleted into one another, and are also made hollow, to obtain increased strength for the same weight of material ; and the crank-shafts, arms, and pins are invariably made in one solid forging. The diameter of the hole is about 60 per cent. of the outside diameter.

In the mercantile marine, however, a cheaper construction is common, and gives satisfaction. This consists of 'built up' crank-shafts, the shafts, arms, and pins being separate forgings. This arrangement is shown in Fig. 257, which shows a three-throw crank-shaft in pieces. With this method the crank webs are shrunk on, and a pin is fitted to the shaft and driven in firmly, nearly to the full depth of the web, this pin being fitted part in the shaft and part in the web. A small groove is fitted in the pin to allow air to escape when driving. In some cases the crank-pin is entirely dependent on the shrinkage, but generally a screwed pin is fitted here, as indicated on the drawing. These pins are only shown on one of the pieces of shafting. It will be noticed that the mercantile marine crank-shaft is solid, and not hollow, like the naval shaft.

Centrifugal lubricators.—The usual plan for lubricating the crank-pins of large engines when under way is shown in Fig. 258. The crank-pins being hollow, small holes are bored from the rubbing surface

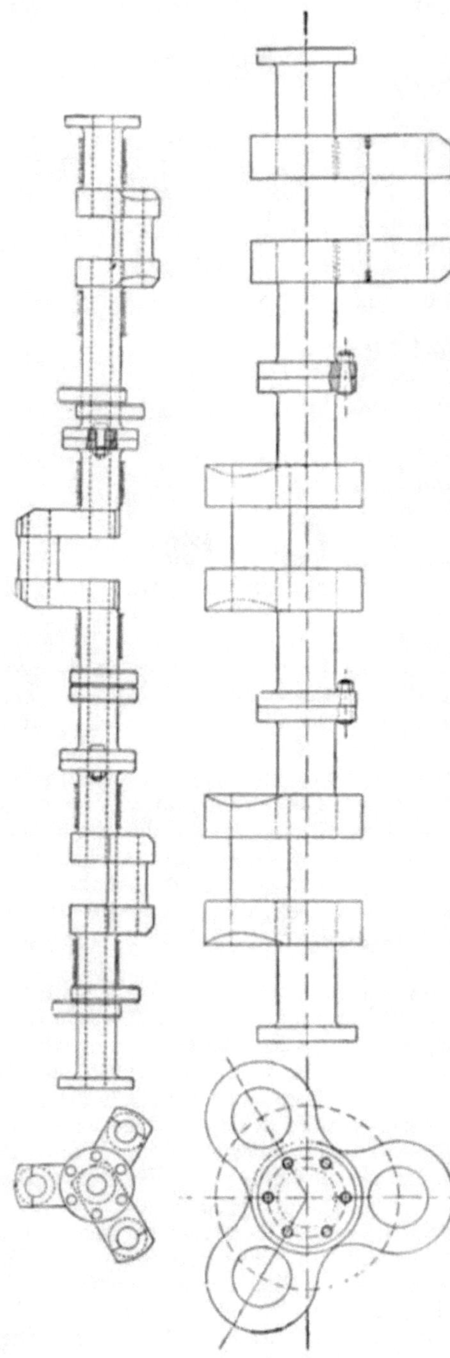

Fig. 257.

to the central space, as shown. An annular lubricator, A, on the crank-shaft is connected to the holes in the crank-pin, and by the revolution of the shaft the oil by centrifugal force flows as far from the centre of the shaft as it can, and makes its way through the small holes to the rubbing surface of the crank-pin. This system has been attended with satisfactory results, and is now applied to all high-speed engines. Many of the ahead eccentrics of the main engines are also similarly fitted with centrifugal lubricators, and the system is also extended to many of the auxiliary engines, which have to work for long periods (see Fig. 240).

Balance weights. — Balance weights were, in horizontal engines, usually fitted on the cranks opposite the crank-pin in order to counterbalance the weights of the crank-arms and connecting-rod heads, but later on this was found practically unnecessary, sufficient uniformity of motion in ordinary practice being obtained without these fittings, while in ordinary vertical engines the sum of the weights of the piston, piston-rod, and connecting rod, which reciprocate, is much greater than any balance weights that could reasonably be fitted. Balance weights are not now fitted except in special cases and on very fast running engines.

In the light quick-running engines of great power fitted in vessels such as torpedo boats and torpedo-boat destroyers, balance weights are often found to be required.

They are then, however, not fitted with the object of securing uniformity
of turning moment on the shaft, but to counteract the forces arising
out of the action of the engine, which cause a bending-moment to be

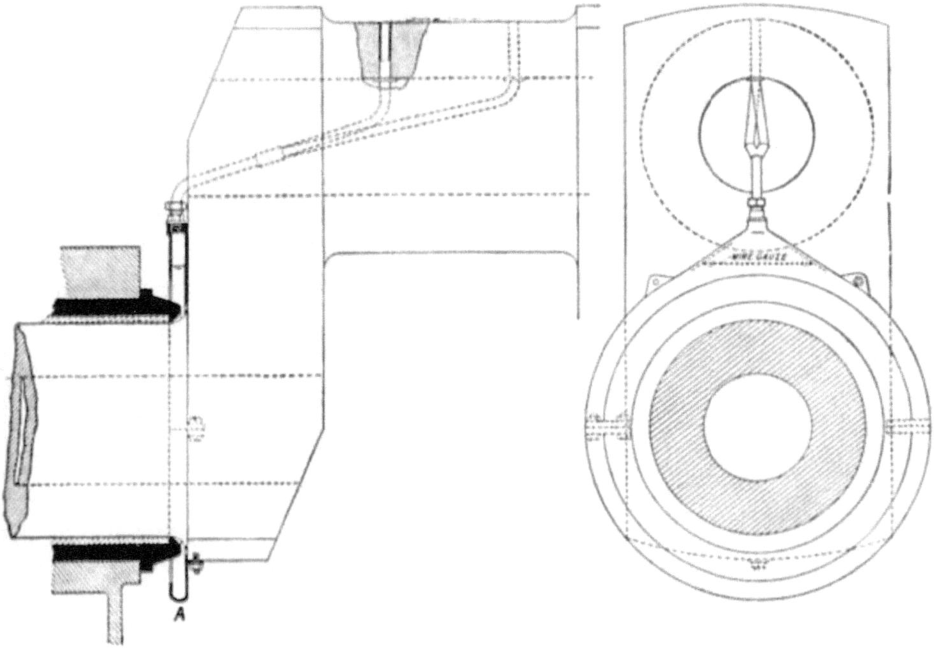

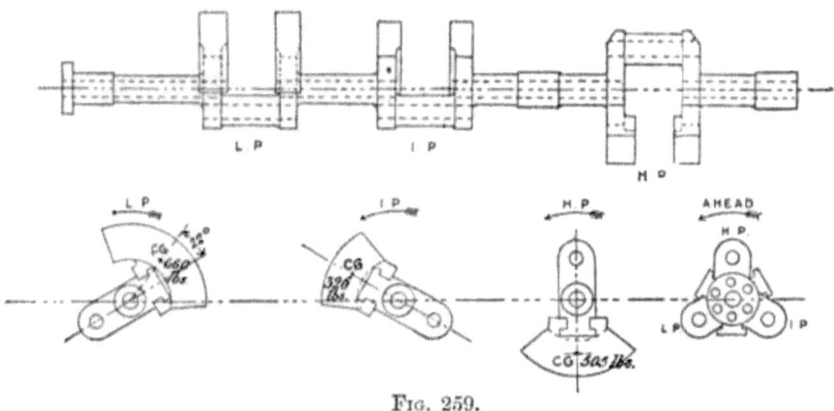

Fig. 258.

exerted on the vessel, and which, repeated with each revolution of the
shaft, often cause excessive vibration in the hulls of such light vessels.

Fig. 259.

It is found that moderate balance weights placed in suitable positions, not necessarily opposite the crank-pins, are very effective in
reducing vibration. Their size and position may be approximately

calculated in cases where they are proved to be required, but are gene rally ascertained by experiment by disconnecting the propeller shaft from the engine and running the latter at various speeds with different arrangements of weights. One such arrangement of balance weights fitted in 'Janus,' exerted a powerful effect in reducing vibration, and is shown in Fig. 259.

Turning wheel and gear.—On the after end of the crank-shaft a large worm-wheel is keyed, which is fitted for the purpose of enabling the

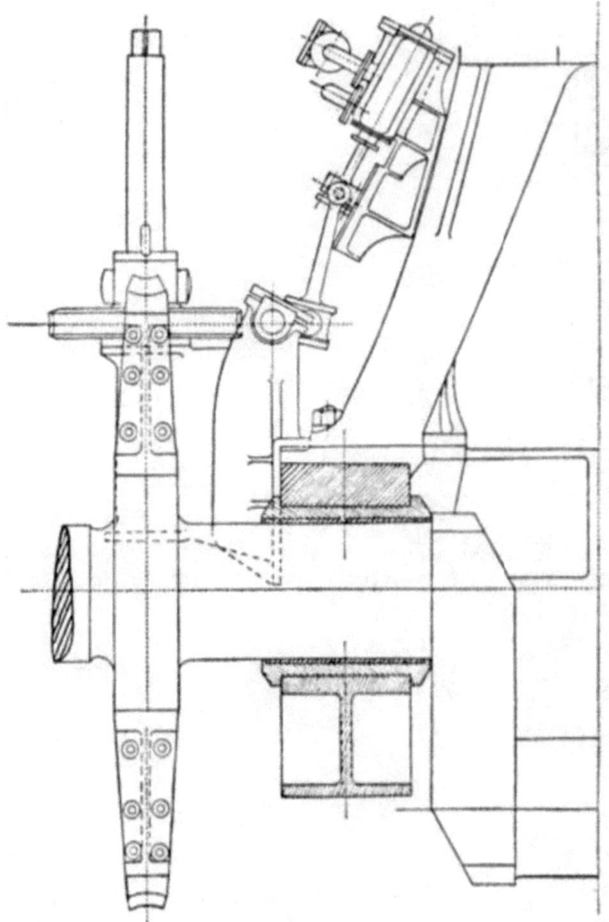

Fig. 260.

engines to be turned when not under steam. The worm is generally worked by a ratchet and lever in small engines. In large engines a small auxiliary engine is fitted to work the worm, so that the engines may be turned more rapidly, when under repair or adjustment.

This gear is so fitted that when steam is not available the worm can also be worked through the ratchet and lever by hand, suitable disconnecting gear being fitted to the engine for use under these circumstances. Arrangements are of course necessary for disconnecting the worm from the worm-wheel when the main engines are required to be used, and in many cases the worm is entirely removed. An arrangement of turning gear is shown in Figs. 260 and 261, the position of the worm when disconnected being indicated by dotted lines. In the

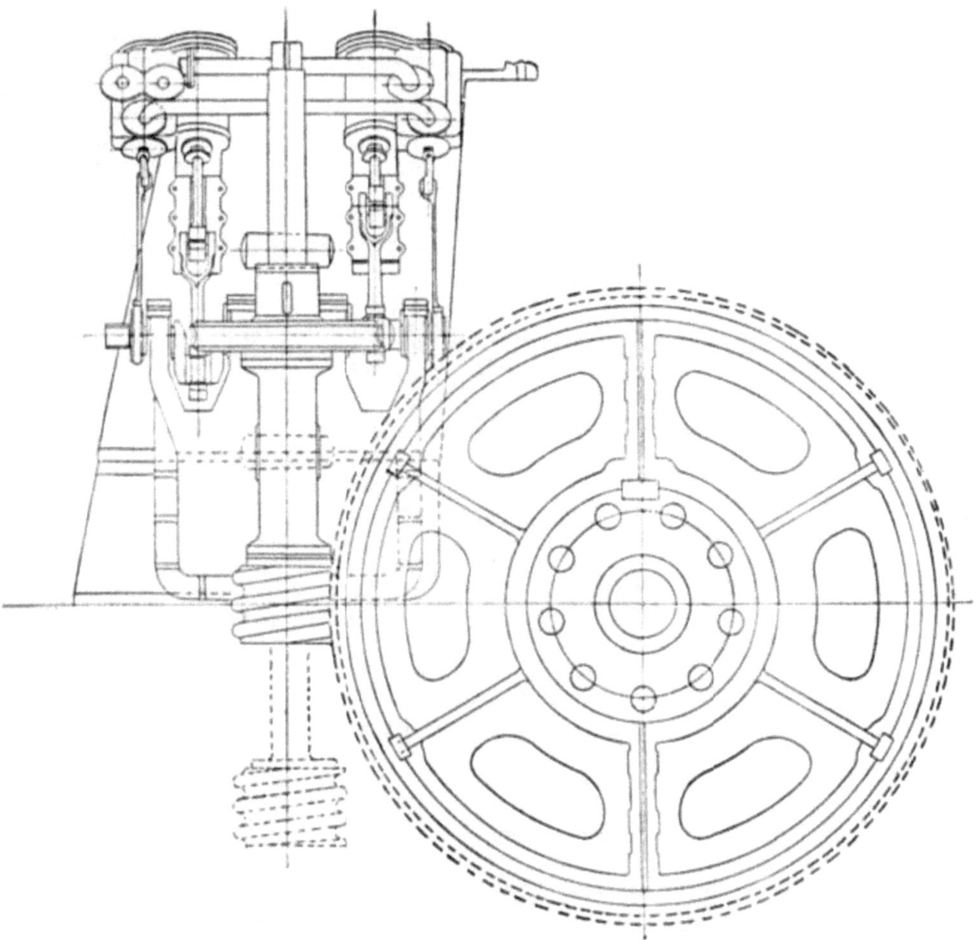

Fig. 261.

Navy it is required that the steam turning engines should be capable of turning the main engines through one complete revolution in eight minutes, when exhausting into the atmosphere. When not under steam the engines should be moved a little daily by the turning gear, to keep them in good order.

Main frames and bearings. Engine bearers.—The engine framing is a rigidly built up structure which holds the working parts in their correct relative position, provides the necessary guides, and the means of attachment of the engine to the ship.   In horizontal engines the main bearings generally form parts of strong cast-iron frames rigidly attached to the cylinders and the engine bearers.   A sketch of one such engine frame is shown in Fig. 262, and the general arrangement of such an engine in Fig. 6.

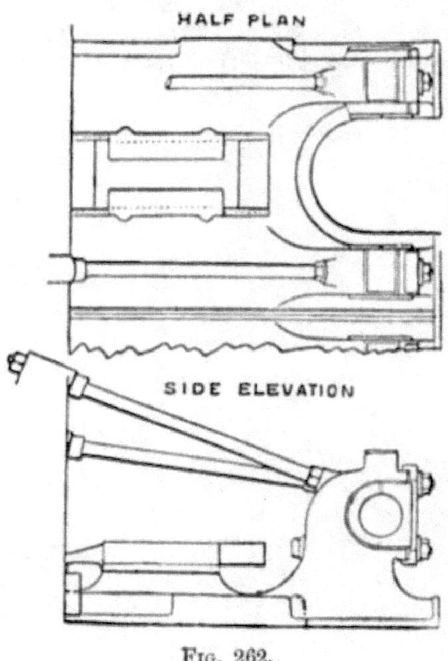

Fig. 262.

In vertical engines the crank-shaft bearings are contained in the *sole* or *foundation plate*, which forms the horizontal bottom part of the framework, and is rigidly secured to the hull of the ship by means of the *engine bearers*, which are a series of strong plate girders built up from the inner bottom of the ship.   These engine bearers are generally of box construction, and their details will be found illustrated in Figs. 11 and 12.   The sole-plate is in one casting in small engines, but in large engines it is constructed of a series of athwartship beams or girders carrying the main bearings of the crank-shaft, and fore and aft girders which rigidly unite these athwartship girders into one rigid structure.   The cylinders are supported by standards or columns, bolted to the sole-plate.   In some vertical engines the condenser forms one of the back standards, and is fixed on the sole-plate, wrought-iron or steel columns being employed for the front supports of the cylinders.

The framing now usually adopted for large engines consists of one of the following two plans :—

(*a*) A substantial cast-iron or steel column, fitted at the back of each cylinder, which carries the crosshead guides, together with two steel pillars at the front of each cylinder.

(*b*) Fitting four cast columns, two to each side of each cylinder.

Plan (*a*) is shown in Figs. 263 and 264.   In this plan the crosshead guide is generally closed, as shown in the enlarged view, Fig. 265. The general arrangement of an engine with this form of guide is shown in Figs. 11 and 12.   Plan (*b*) is shown in Figs. 266 and 267.   In this plan there are two guides on each side of the cylinder, generally of cast-iron, and bolted to the cast columns as shown at G G in the sectional plan, Fig. 267, and the end of the piston-rod is attached to a crosshead with gudgeon pins at each side.   These gudgeon bearings are attached to the slippers, which work in the guides, so that there are two gudgeon bearings to each cylinder.   This plan is very efficient, although not so convenient of access for examination and repair as plan (*a*).   It is, however, superior, in the fact that it provides

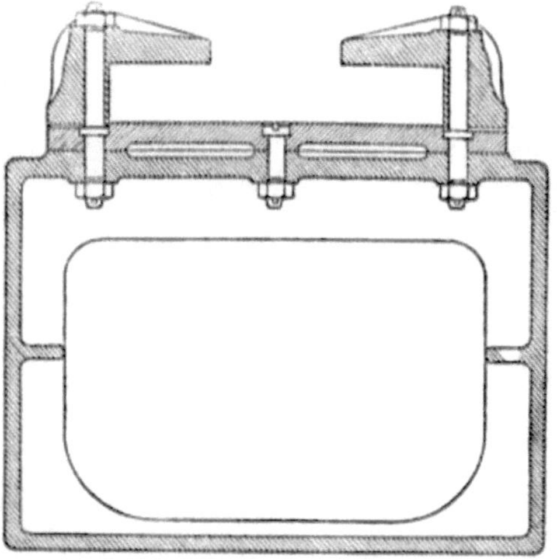

Fig. 265.

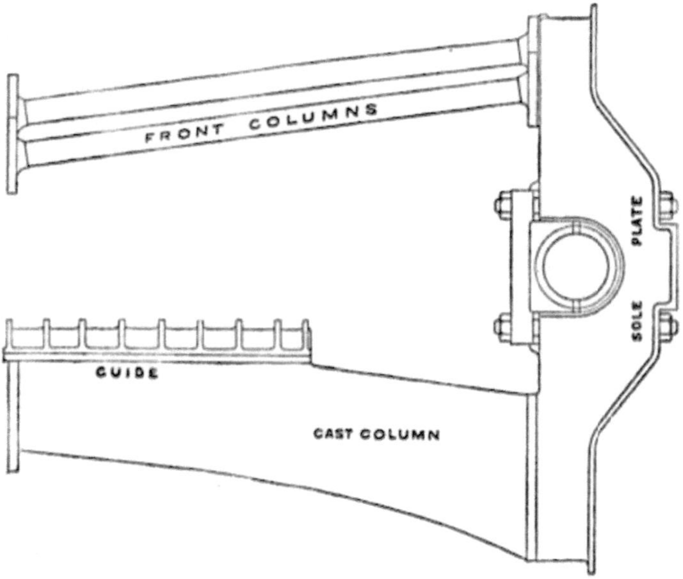

Fig. 264.

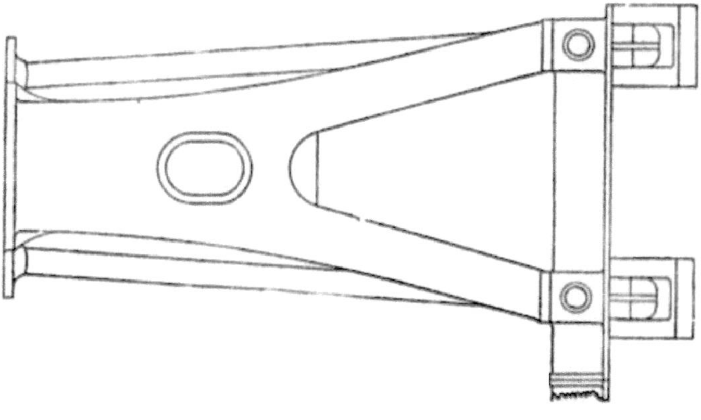

Fig. 263

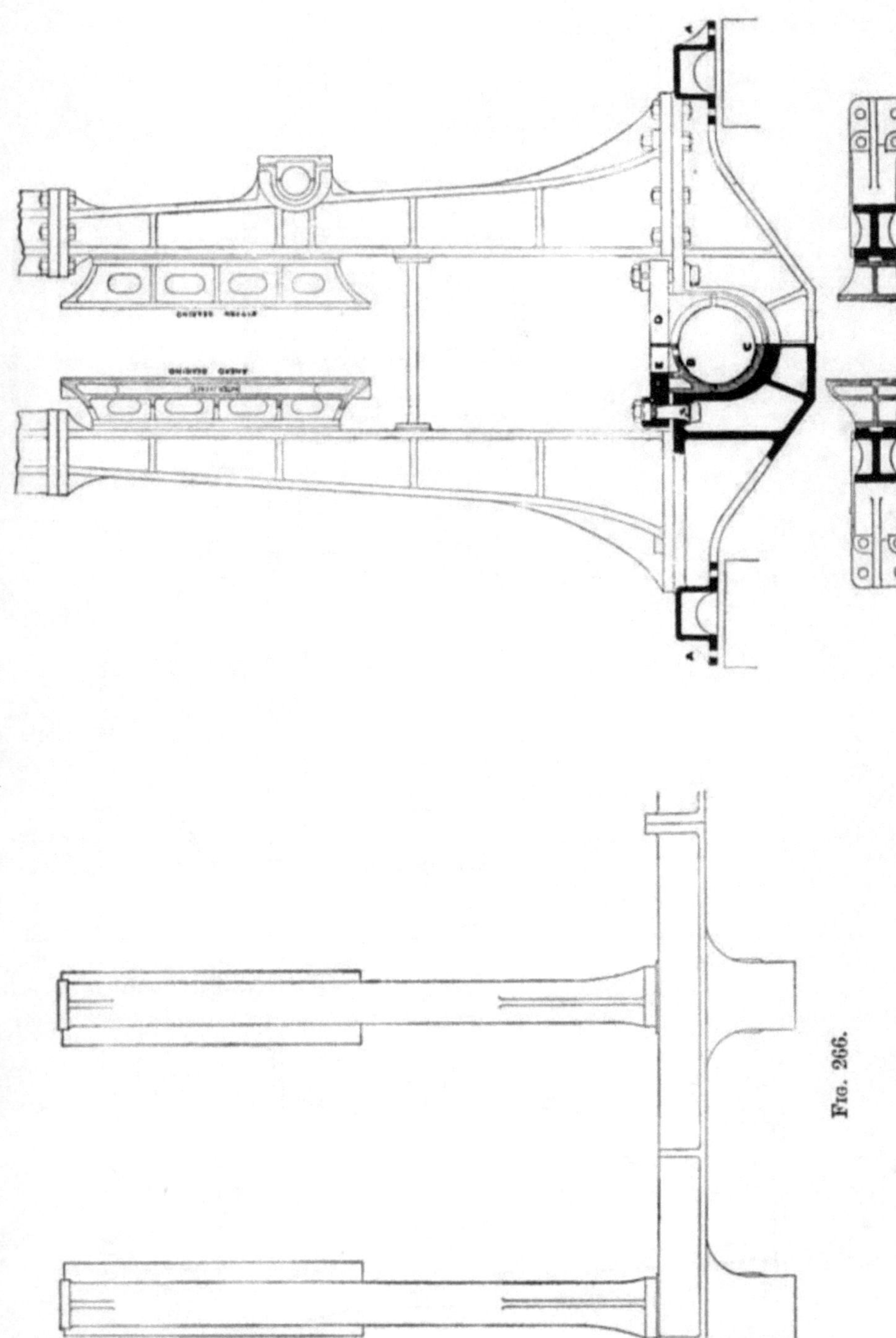

Fig. 267.

Fig. 266.

without difficulty the full area required for astern working, which, with plan (*a*), is more difficult.

In some engines, especially those of the mercantile marine, the front and back cast standards are identical and are one to each cylinder on each side, in which case there would be one gudgeon pin to each cylinder, and one guide at the centre of the cylinder. This plan is indicated by the sketches, Figs. 7 and 8.

In some large warships the framing has been entirely constructed of wrought-iron or steel suitably trussed to give sufficient rigidity, and fitted similarly to the framing of the small high-powered torpedo-boat destroyers described below. It has not often been adopted, however, for such large engines, as the extra expense is not compensated for by the small saving in weight which ensues.

The framing of very light high-powered marine engines, such as those of torpedo boats, torpedo-boat destroyers, and small cruisers, is generally formed of four steel columns attached to each cylinder and bolted at the lower end to the sole-plate and suitably stiffened by cross-stays. A sketch, sufficient to show the general construction of one such arrangement, is shown in Fig. 268.

Crosshead and guide.—The connection between the piston-rod and the connecting rod is made by means of a bearing termed the 'gudgeon pin bearing,' at which part is also fitted the crosshead bearing which works between the guides. There are two principal forms of these crosshead guides. In Figs. 269 and 270 are illustrated what is termed a 'closed' guide bearing which is suitable to the form of engine framing shown in Figs. 263 and 264. Sea-water is circulated at the back of the guide surface to assist in keeping it cool. The astern bearing surface is, as will be seen on the sketch, much less in area than the ahead bearing surface. In the other example (Fig. 271), called an 'open' guide bearing, and which is suitable for the type of framing shown in Fig. 267, the ahead and astern bearing surfaces are often identical. In all guide bearings of any size the ahead bearing surface is always lined with white metal, while in the closed variety the astern surface is now also generally so lined. White metal, which was at one time looked on with suspicion for gudgeon bearings, is now being fitted for such bearings in large engines, and is found to give satisfaction. The part which bears on the guide and carries the white metal, is removable for adjustment and repairs, and is called the *slipper*.

Main bearings.—The brasses in all main bearings should be so fitted as to allow the back or bottom brass to be removed for examination, without taking out the crank-shaft, and without removing the bolts. To effect this the back or bottom brasses are usually made concentric with the shaft, so that when the cap, and the outside or top brass are removed the back or bottom brass may be taken out by revolving the brass round the shaft. The crank-shaft journal revolves within two brasses, B, C (Fig. 267), fitted into each of the transverse sole-plates A A. As the principal forces in a vertical engine acting on the crank-shaft due to the piston are upward and downward, the brasses of the main bearings are placed at the top and bottom of the shaft. In horizontal engines they are placed at the front and back. The top brass B has a flat back on which bears a simple cap D, secured by bolts and nuts, as shown, to the sole-plate A A.   A handhole E in the cap enables the brass B to be felt while the engine is working, to ascertain whether heating of the bearing is taking place.

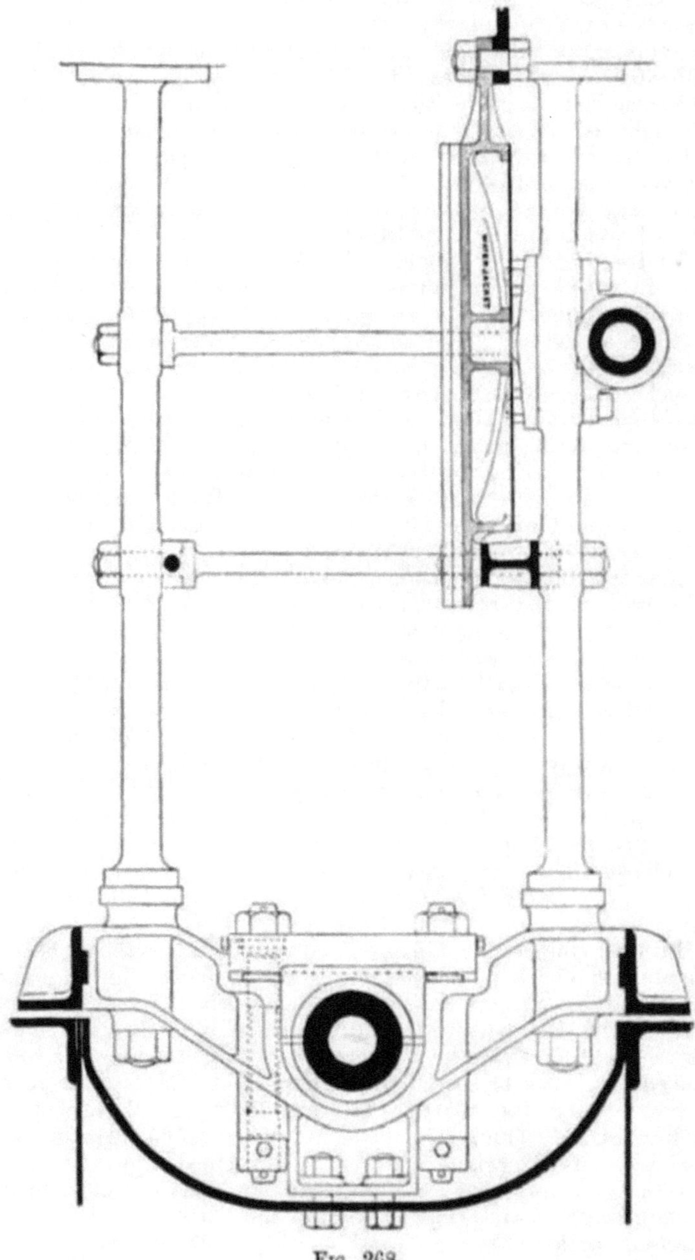

Fig. 268.

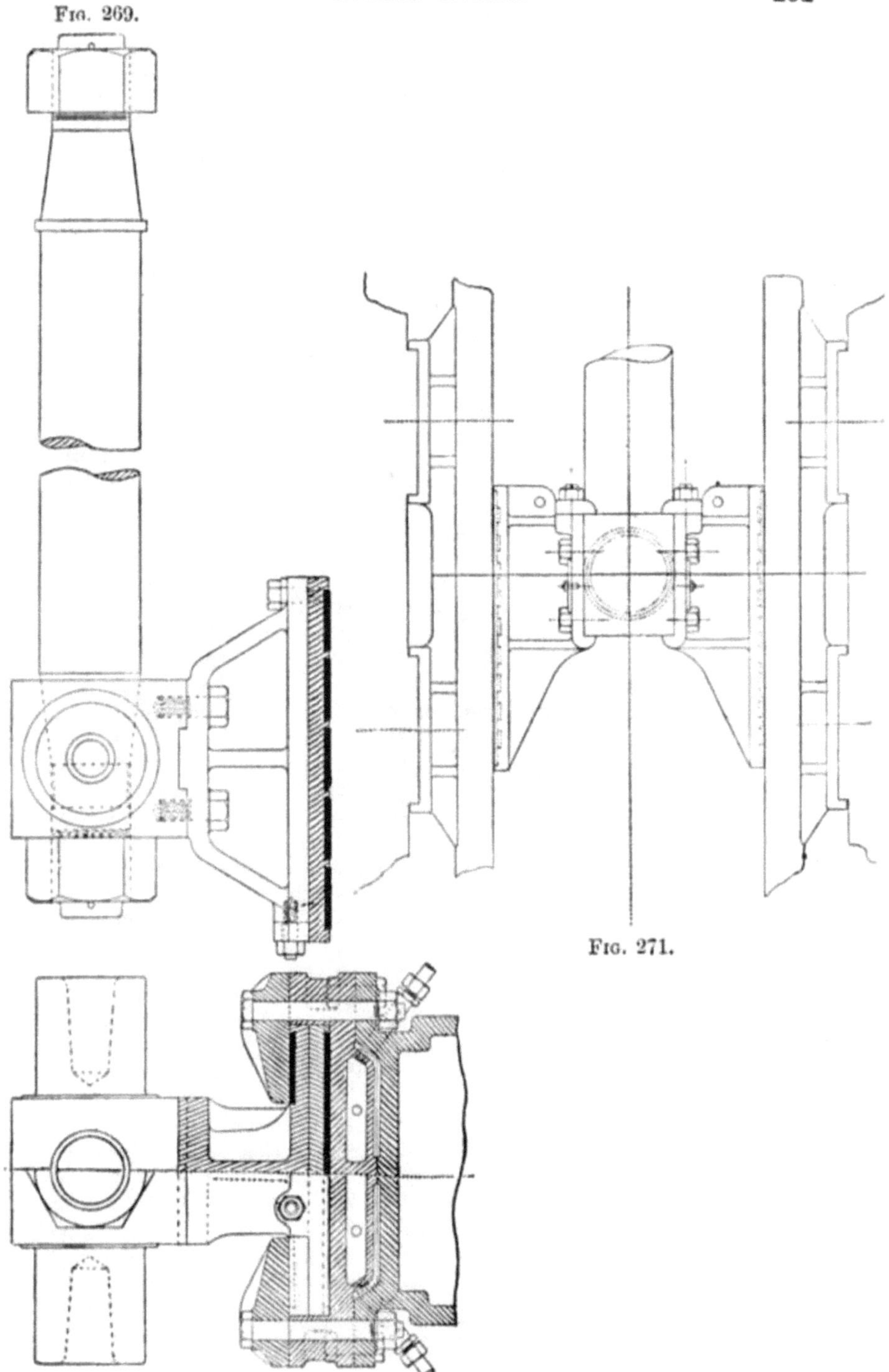

Fig. 269.
Fig. 270.
Fig. 271.

Water service.—The bearing surfaces should be so designed and arranged that, when properly adjusted, the ordinary lubricating arrangements may be sufficient to keep the journals, &c., from heating when the engines are being worked at full power. To provide, however, for the contingency of faulty adjustment, dirt getting into the bearings, or the friction being temporarily increased from any cause, small pipes with stop-cocks are led from one of the sea-valves to each of the principal bearings, to enable cold water to be run on them in case of their overheating. The crosshead guides also are usually hollow on the ahead surface to enable a stream of cold water to be circulated through them when under way.

White metal bearings.—The crank-shaft and crank-pin bearings and many other bearings in marine engines are filled with a soft white metal made of tin, antimony, lead, &c., with copper. The compositions used vary somewhat, but although there are large numbers of patent compositions of a cheaper mixture, none have given such all round satisfaction as Babbits' metal has. This is composed of tin 10 parts, copper 1 part, and antimony 1 part, by weight.

These white metal alloys are soft and plastic, and if they be well lubricated will sustain a great pressure without heating. The white metal is confined by fillets or rims cast on the bearings, to prevent its being squeezed out, the depth of the recesses for the metal being usually about $\frac{3}{8}$-inch. In some cases the white metal is fitted as strips dovetailed into the bearings in the manner adopted for the lignum vitæ bearings for stern-fittings.

Propeller shafting. Plummer blocks.—From the crank-shaft the rotatory motion is communicated to the propeller by means of the screw-shafting, which consists of straight lengths of hollow forged steel shafting, carried in suitable bearings. The size of the screw-shafting between the crank-shaft and the stern tube, where the shafting leaves the vessel. is made smaller than the crank-shaft, since this portion has only to transmit the torsional stress due to turning the propellers, and not to stand any bending stresses such as are brought to bear on the crank-shaft. The bearings of this portion of the screw-shafting have therefore only to carry the weight of the shafting. These bearings are called 'plummer blocks,' they are usually made of cast-iron, and lined with white metal on the lower side to take the weight of the shaft. The upper part does not bear on the shaft. They are fitted with lubricating arrangements, and also a space into which water can be run in case the bearing gets warm. The water and oil boxes should be separate. Fig. 272 shows the general construction.

Shaft couplings.—The different lengths of crank and propeller shafting are secured together by means of ordinary flange couplings, as shown in Fig. 273. The flanges are forged in one with the shaft, and secured together by nuts and bolts which fit the holes in the flanges. The various lengths are, in the Navy, filleted into one another, which keeps them in line. For crank-shaft couplings the number of bolts used depends on the arrangement of the cranks. For instance, with a three-crank engine with cranks at equal angles, if the shaft is in three interchangeable parts, the number of bolts would be six or nine, so that the bolt holes would correspond when a piece of shaft was shifted to a new position or a spare length fitted. Similarly, with cranks at right angles eight or twelve bolts would be used.

The aftermost coupling before the shaft leaves the vessel is a special one. The necessity for this arises from the fact that the length of

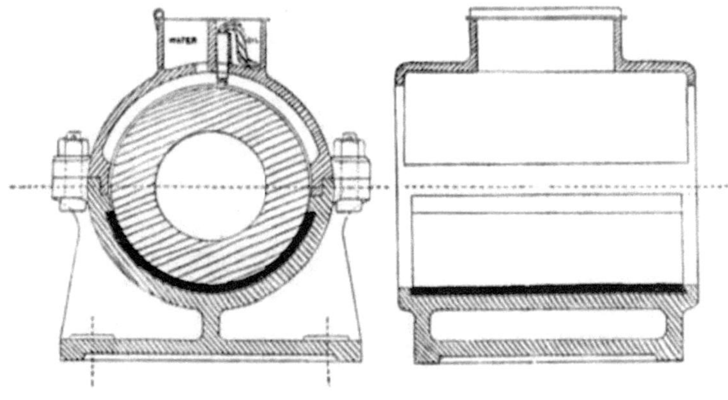

FIG. 272.

shafting in the stern tube has generally to be inserted in its position from outside the ship, owing either to the presence of a coupling at the after end of it, or for greater convenience in avoiding disturbance of internal parts of the vessel when withdrawing it for examination or

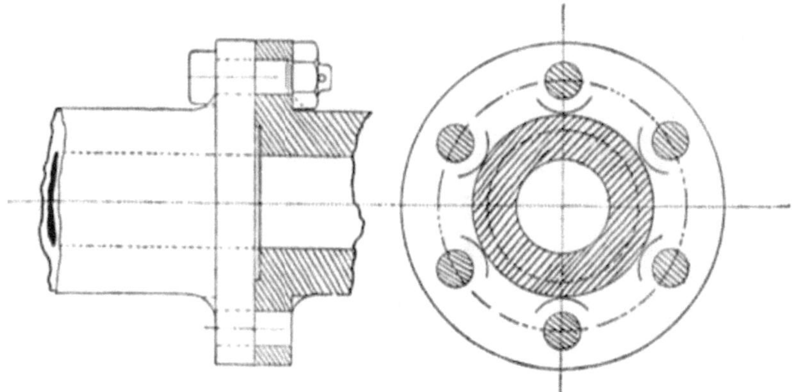

FIG. 273.

repair. To enable the shaft to be passed through the stern tube the forward coupling must therefore be separate and fitted after the shaft is in position. This coupling is often spoken of as a 'loose coupling,' and sketches of two forms of it are given in Figs. 274 and 275. It is found advantageous to make the coupling of wrought-iron if the shaft is of steel. Steel couplings are often found, after a time to be so firmly adhering to the shaft as to necessitate cutting the coupling open to remove it. The turning moment is in each case transmitted by means of three or four keys recessed into the shaft and coupling. The difference in the two plans consists in the means of preventing the stern

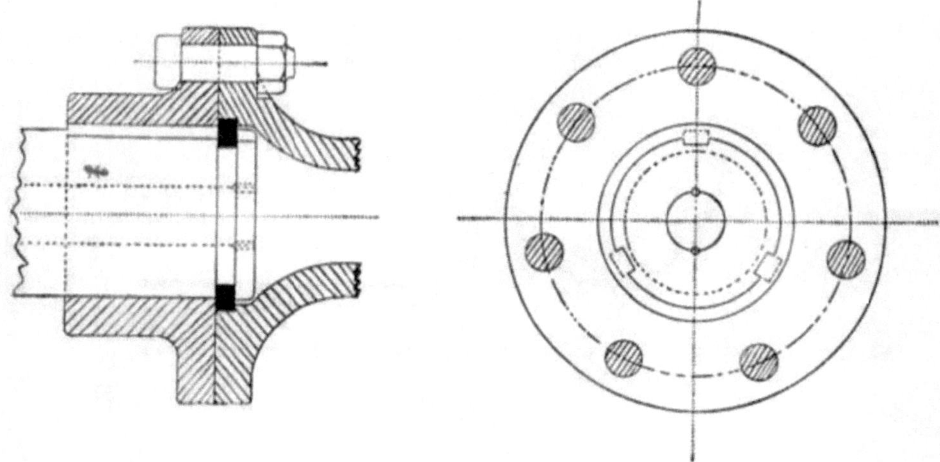

Fig. 274.

shaft from being withdrawn from the coupling when going astern. In Fig. 274 this consists of a recessed ring in halves, shown in the sketch in black. In Fig. 275 the end of the shaft is screwed, and a nut used ; a pin being fitted to prevent the nut unscrewing. The nut or ring bears against the loose coupling and prevents the shaft from

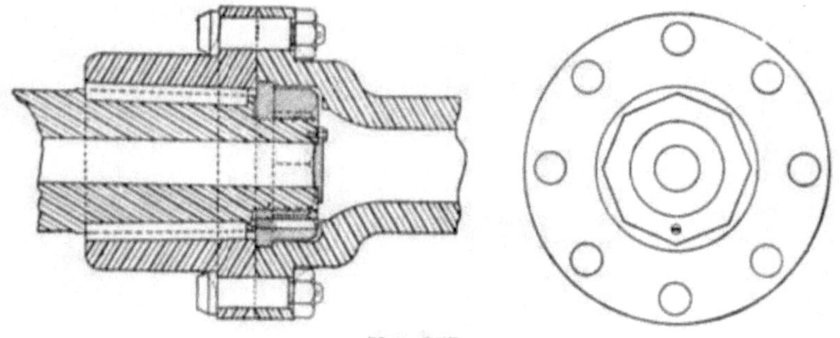

Fig. 275.

being drawn out. In each case a plate or plug is fitted to the hole in the stern shaft to prevent possibility of water passing into the vessel.

Thrust block.—On the foremost length of the propeller-shafting a bearing of special form is usually fitted, to receive the thrust of the propeller and transmit it to the ship. In order to reduce the intensity of the friction, the thrust journal on the shaft is made with several collars, which press on properly fitted thrust surfaces in the bearing, the

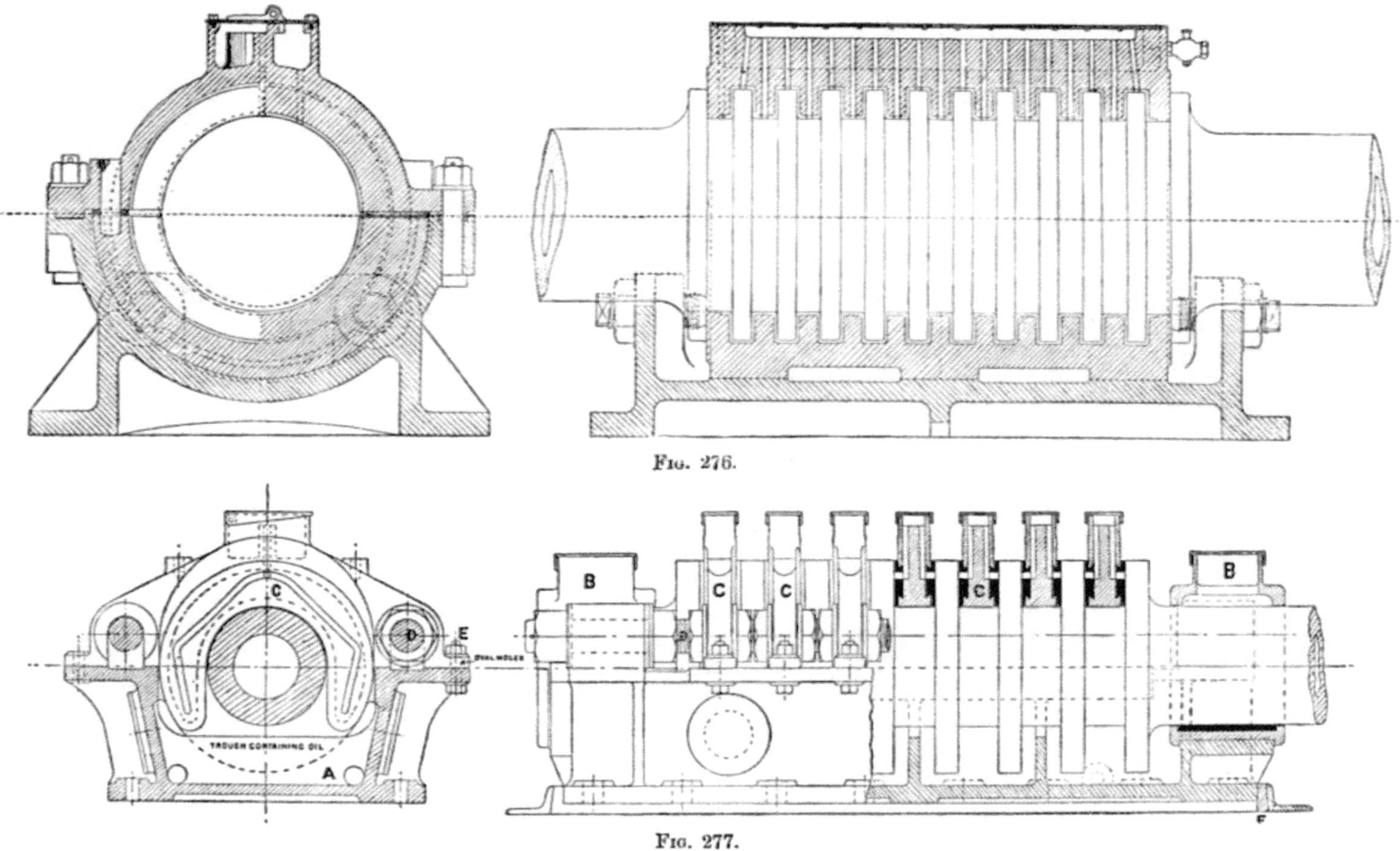

Fig. 276.

Fig. 277.

pressure being exerted in one direction when going ahead, and in the reverse direction when going astern. Fig. 276 shows an arrangement which has often been adopted, in which the rubbing surfaces of the block are completely lined with white metal, and which arrangement has generally given satisfaction. The cap is filleted into the bottom half of the bearing, and oval holes are fitted in the base-plate to allow of adjustment in the fore and aft direction when wear takes place. This adjustment is necessary, otherwise the propeller would gradually wear its way forward and cause the cranks, eccentrics, &c., to be out of line with the corresponding parts of the engines, besides bringing side stresses on the crank-arms and bearings.

Another form of thrust block has often been fitted of similar general design, but containing separate brass thrust rings fitted in the bearing to form the rubbing surfaces. These are made in halves, and arranged so that they may be renewed when necessary. Both these plans of thrust block have, however, been generally superseded by a type which permits the position of each of the thrust rings to be adjusted inde- pendently by means of nuts and screws. This block, Fig. 277, con- sists of a hollow trough A, which is kept supplied with lubricant, and ordinary plummer-block bearings B at each end. The shaft collars are formed as in the previous examples, but of larger diameter, and the parts against which the shaft collars bear consist of separate pieces shaped similar to horse-shoes, so that they can be removed and replaced without disturbing any other part. These 'horse-shoe' collars, C, fit between the collars on the thrust shaft, and are fixed in position or adjusted by nuts on two screwed bars, D, attached one on each side to the hollow trough foundation. The wedges F, sometimes fitted, also enable the block to be adjusted bodily. The horse-shoe collars are lined with white metal on each side, in which a groove is cut for the lubricating oil, and separate lubrication tubes are provided for the ahead and astern faces. Small bolts E are fitted to the collars, to prevent them rising from their proper positions.

Thrust blocks are carried on strong plate bearers generally fixed to not less than three frames of the ship, and wedges or screws are fitted to the foundation plates to enable the position of the thrust blocks to be adjusted bodily within certain limits if required. The holes in the base of the thrust block, for the holding-down bolts, are made elongated to admit of this. An ordinary plummer block should always be fitted close to the thrust bearing to carry the weight of the shaft, so that the thrust bearing will only have to sustain the thrust of the propeller and not take any of the weight of the shaft.

In single-screw ships the thrust of the propeller has sometimes been taken on a disc on the stern post fitted with lignum-vitæ segments. (See Chapter XXV.)

Rotary engines.—Having now described the usual arrangements for producing the rotary motion of a shaft, which motion is essential for marine propulsion, we will consider an example of the 'rotary engine' which is being used to a small extent for this purpose, viz. the marine steam turbine introduced and perfected by the Hon. C. A. Parsons, of Newcastle. 'Rotary engines' are those in which the steam causes a rotating motion by direct action on the shaft, without the intervention of any mechanism such as a crank and connecting rod.

Parsons' marine steam turbine.—This machine consists of a hollow cylinder which rotates on its axis, and is provided with a large number of inclined blades arranged in a ring, and well secured in grooves in the revolving cylinder or drum. There are a series of such rings of blades along the length of the cylinder, and between each ring of revolving blades there is a corresponding ring of similar blades fixed in the outer casing containing the revolving drum, but inclined at a different angle to that of the revolving blades, the moving and fixed blades being practically similar, but with angles reversed.

Fig. 277*a* shows the relative arrangement of fixed and revolving blades and the direction of motion of the revolving blades and steam.

The angles and curvature of blades are so arranged that the velocity of the revolving blades and steam causes the latter to enter the moving blades with a velocity parallel to their surfaces ; and similarly, on leaving the moving blades the combination of the velocity of these blades with the velocity of the steam along the inclined surface of the blade causes the final velocity of steam on exit from these blades to be parallel to the axis of the turbine.

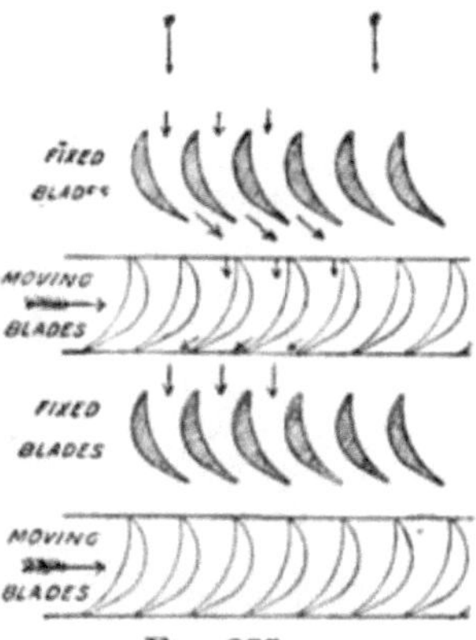

FIG. 277*a*.

The steam then proceeds through the next series of fixed blades, and so on till the condenser is reached. The impulse of the steam as it leaves the fixed blades and impinges on the revolving blades causes the turning effort on the shaft. The arrows in Fig. 277*a* indicate generally the direction of flow of the steam in its passage through the blades.

Fig. 277*c* shows a vertical section through the high-pressure turbine cylinder of H.M.S. ' Viper,' with the revolving drum shown in elevation. The boiler steam, after passing through a strainer, enters the steam orifice A, and thence to the hollow belt B, and then enters the turbine through orifices which are formed all around the cylinder. It now proceeds through the fixed and revolving blades along the narrow passage between the cylinder and revolving drum. At C an enlargement of diameter occurs, the steam therefore expands and becomes of lower pressure. It then passes through the second series of fixed and revolving blades along the larger space between cylinder and drum until the point D is reached, where a further enlargement of cylinder diameter takes place with consequent further expansion of steam, still further expansions taking place at E and F till the exhaust orifice G is reached.

In H.M.S. ' Viper ' this orifice G leads the exhaust steam to the low-pressure turbine fitted on a separate propeller shaft, there being two shafts on each side the ship. The construction of this turbine is similar to the one illustrated, further considerable enlargements of cylinder and expansion of steam taking place, till exhaust to the condenser occurs at a low pressure. A large relief valve, discharging on deck, is fitted on the branch H, in case any undue pressure occurs

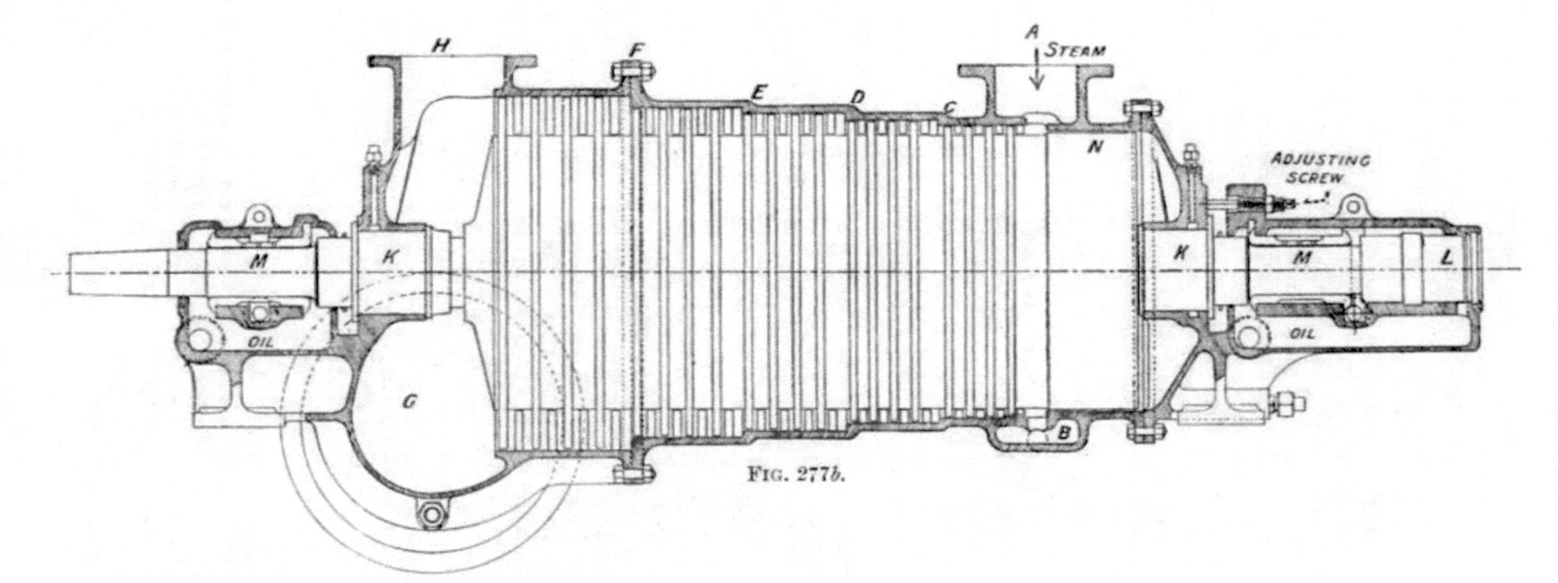

FIG. 277b.

which would be in excess of the safe pressure for the low-pressure turbine.

At K K special forms of glands are fitted, consisting of a series of narrow revolving rings, the small pipes shown being fitted to supply steam to these glands, so that in case of leakage no air will enter through the gland to the central space which is in connection with the exhaust. A similar gland is provided at the part N to prevent leakage of steam to this central space. The diameter of the enlarged part N, called the 'dummy piston,' is proportioned so that the steam pressure on it together with the thrust of the propeller is practically equal to the astern force due to the action of the steam on the revolving blades. Any differences between these forces is taken by a small external thrust-block, fitted in the usual manner, at L, with a cap provided with a small screw for adjusting purposes.

The bearings M must be very carefully lubricated, owing to the high speed of rotation of the shaft. They are therefore supplied with oil under pressure by a pump fitted for that purpose, the oil inlet and outlet orifices being indicated on the drawing, the oil passing through a cooler surrounded by water on its way to the bearings. The speed of rotation of the turbine with its shaft and propellers is considerable, viz. 1,000 to 1,400 per minute, so that very careful balancing of all the revolving parts is required. An oil ring is fitted at each end between the oil chamber and the turbine to prevent any oil creeping along the shaft to the turbine.

All the blades are fixed to the cylinder casing and revolving drum by being recessed in them as shown in Fig. 277c, and are secured at the correct distance apart by wedges inserted between them in the recesses. It will be seen, therefore, that the angles of the blades cannot be altered, so that the turbine only works in one direction, and in order to secure astern working a separate turbine has to be fitted on the shaft with blades arranged in a reverse direction. When going ahead, steam is shut off from this turbine, and when required to go astern steam is shut off from the ahead turbine and turned on to the astern one. This type of turbine

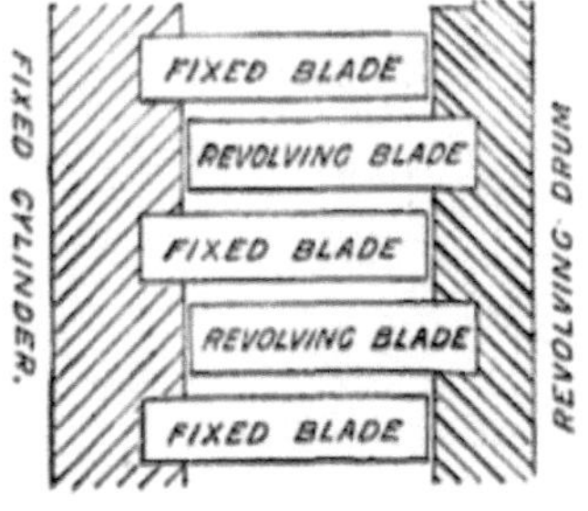

FIG. 277c.

has been already tried in a small vessel, the 'Turbinia,' with success and economical efficiency of the steam. With this form of engine it will be seen that very considerable expansion of the steam is possible ; about 100 expansions can easily be arranged for, while there is no alternate heating and cooling of the surfaces exposed to the action of the steam, so that a fair amount of economy when working at high pressure can be obtained. The amount of expansion given is, however, constant, and as reduction of speed can only be obtained by lowering the initial pressure of steam, much less benefit from expansion is then realised, so that at low speeds the consumption of steam per horse-power may be expected to be considerably in excess of the consumption at high powers. No ready means has yet been devised for ascertaining the horse-power being exerted by these turbines.

The principal difficulty in devising a satisfactory rotary steam-engine has been the excessive speed with which steam issues from an orifice under even moderate pressure, and Mr. Parsons' device of splitting up the total fall of pressure into many stages and using a succession of turbines is successful in reducing the necessary speeds required to more practicable limits.

Another form of turbine, viz. that by De Laval, is also used for land work, but not for marine. In this type there is a single set of blades working at a much higher speed than the Parsons combination, which speed is reduced to more practicable limits by helical gearing outside.

CHAPTER XXII.

PROPULSION.

Resistance of ships.—In considering the question of the propulsion of ships, it will be necessary in the first place to explain briefly the general nature of the resistance experienced by ships in their passage through the water, which resistance has to be overcome by the action of the propeller. The most important element is the frictional action of the water itself on the skin of the ship. Water is not a perfect fluid, and when it is disturbed its particles will exercise friction, both on each other and also on the surface of any body past which they move. If a well-formed ship with a clean bottom be towed through the water, the water will open out at the bow, and follow round the sides of the ship in well-defined currents, called '*stream lines*,' closing in again under the stern, so that the counter-pressure under the stern thus caused tends to balance the head resistance to the ship's motion.

If the run aft be not sufficiently fine to allow the water to close in under the stern properly, an eddying wake would be formed under it, which would increase the direct or head resistance to the motion of the vessel. The surface or wave-making action constitutes another source of resistance. From the bows of all ships in motion, waves are formed, to a greater or less extent, which in most cases pass away from the ship in divergent directions ; and the energy expended in creating these waves is wasted.

Elements of total resistance.—The three elements constituting the total resistance to the ship's motion are, therefore :—

1. Frictional resistance, due to the gliding of the particles of water over the rough skin of the ship.

2. Eddy-making resistance, due to a wake at the stern.

3. Surface disturbance or wave-making resistance.

The first of these is by far the most important. In well-formed ships the second is small and need only be considered in exceptional cases. The third element, due to surface disturbance, may in some cases be of considerable importance. This cause of resistance may be reduced to a minimum by making the lengths of entrance and run of the ship sufficiently great for her required maximum speed ; for a certain speed of a ship there are minimum lengths of entrance and run which must be given in order to reduce the loss from surface disturbance to reasonable limits. This condition is more affected by the length of run than by length of entrance ; and the entrance may be reduced to a certain extent without entailing so great a loss of efficiency as would result from a similar decrease in the length of the run.

For every ship there is a certain limit of speed, beyond which any addition can only be obtained at the expense of a very rapid increase in the resistance ; and this is attributed to the wave-making action. Up to the above limit the resistances due to the eddy and wave-making elements are comparatively small, and the total resistance is approximately proportional to the frictional resistance, and varies practically as the square of the speed. Beyond this limit the total resistance has been found to vary as the cube and still higher powers of the speed.

Frictional resistance. — Frictional resistance varies with the amount of the immersed surface of the ship, with the co-efficient of friction of the skin in water, and also depends upon the length of the surface, and the velocity with which the particles of water glide over it. The length has an important influence. For example, in some experiments made by the late Mr. Froude, it was found that a plane 8 feet long coated with varnish, moving at a speed of 600 feet per minute, experienced a resistance of 0·325 lb. per square foot, whereas the resistance opposed to a similar plane 50 feet long moving at the same speed was only 0·25 lb. per square foot, or one-fifth less. For greater lengths, up to 300 or 400 feet, the resistance per square foot was about the same as for the 50-foot length. The skin resistance of a ship may be regarded as practically the same as that of a plane of the same area as the immersed surface of the ship, with similar ratios of length to depth.

Summary of principal facts. — Sir William H. White, in his 'Manual of Naval Architecture,' gives the following summary of the principal facts relative to the total resistance offered to the motion of a ship when towed, or propelled by sails, through the water. The effect of the action of the propeller in increasing the resistance will be pointed out further on.

1. 'That *frictional resistance*, depending upon the immersed surface of a ship, its degree of roughness, its length, and (about) the square of the speed, is not sensibly affected by the forms and proportions of ships, unless there be some unwonted singularity of form or want of fairness. For *moderate* speeds, this element of resistance is by far the most important ; for *high* speeds it also occupies an important position—from 45 to 60 per cent. of the whole resistance, probably, in a very large number of classes when the bottoms are clean ; and a larger percentage when the bottoms become foul.'

2. 'That *eddy-making resistance* is usually small, except in special cases, and amounts to some 8 or 10 per cent. of the frictional resistance. A defective form of stern may cause largely increased eddy-making.'

3. 'That *wave-making resistance* is the element of the total resistance which is most influenced by the forms and proportions of ships. Its ratio to the frictional resistance, as well as its absolute magnitude, depend upon many circumstances, the most important being the forms and lengths of the entrance and run in relation to the intended full speed of the ship. For every ship there is a limit of speed, beyond which each small increase in speed is attended by a disproportionate increase in resistance ; and this limit is fixed by the lengths of the entrance and run—the "wave-making features of a ship."'

The sum of these three elements constitutes the total resistance offered by the water to the motion of a ship towed through it, when the depth of water is great in proportion to the speed. In a steamship there is also an augmentation of resistance due to the action of the propellers.

Effect of wind and waves.—The laws of resistance given above relate only to smooth water, and do not take any account of the action of the wind and waves, which action, with the resultant pitching and tossing, will evidently cause the resistance of a ship in a seaway to be very different from that in smooth water, and it is impossible to make a theoretical estimate of the difference. It is, however, clear from general observation and experience that length, size, and weight in ships tend to give them greater facilities for maintaining their speed in a seaway, and this is conclusively shown by the regularity with which large ocean steamers make their voyages under all conditions of wind and sea.

In order to make a complete investigation of the theory of propulsion, so far as it has yet been developed, it would be necessary to employ somewhat extensive mathematical reasoning which would be beyond the province of this treatise, so we shall confine ourselves to summarising, with only slight use of mathematical expressions, the leading principles and deductions that illustrate the action of a propeller in the water.

Principles of momentum and work.—The action of propellers is best analysed by the principle of momentum, by which the effect of a force is estimated by multiplying it by the *time during which it acts* instead of the *space through which it acts*, as in the principle of work.

If a body move from rest in a straight line under the action of a constant force P, then after t seconds

$$P\,t = \frac{W}{g}\,v,$$

where $W =$ the weight of the body,
$v =$ velocity in feet per second,
and $g =$ the accelerating force of gravity.

The product, $\dfrac{W}{g}\,v$, is called the momentum of the body; so that the force multiplied by the time through which it acts is equal to the momentum of the body; if the body had initially a given velocity, 'change of momentum' should be substituted for momentum.

If $t = 1$, then $P = \dfrac{W}{g}\,v$, that is, *the force acting is equal to the momentum or change of momentum generated per second.*

If in the time t the body has moved through a space x, we have also

$$P\,x = \frac{W\,v^2}{2\,g}.$$

Now, $\dfrac{W\,v^2}{2\,g}$ is half the 'vis-viva' of the body, so that the force multiplied by the *distance* through which it acts (or the work done) is equal to half the vis-viva generated; if the body had initially a given velocity the work done would be equal to one-half of the change in the vis-viva.

Therefore, in the simple case of a constant force acting on a body, in a given direction, if it be considered by the *time* during which it acts, its measure is the momentum or change of momentum produced; whilst if it be considered with respect to the distance through which it acts, it should be estimated by the change produced in the half vis-viva.

The general action of propellers can best be understood by considering, first, a few elementary examples.

Pressure of a jet on a fixed plane.—In the first place, by the application of the principle of momentum, the pressure produced on a fixed plane by the impact of a jet of water striking it perpendicularly, as shown in Fig. 278, is easily ascertained. Any particle is at first moving with a velocity v, perpendicular to the plane, and after a certain time it is deflected, and moves parallel to the surface of the plane, so that the momentum, perpendicular to the plane, becomes zero, being destroyed by the action of the plane. This is on the assumption that nothing in the nature of a rebound occurs, and that all the motion perpendicular to the plane is destroyed. This is true for all the particles in the jet, so that the effect of the plane is to destroy the whole momentum of the jet, which originally had a uniform velocity v perpendicular to the plane.

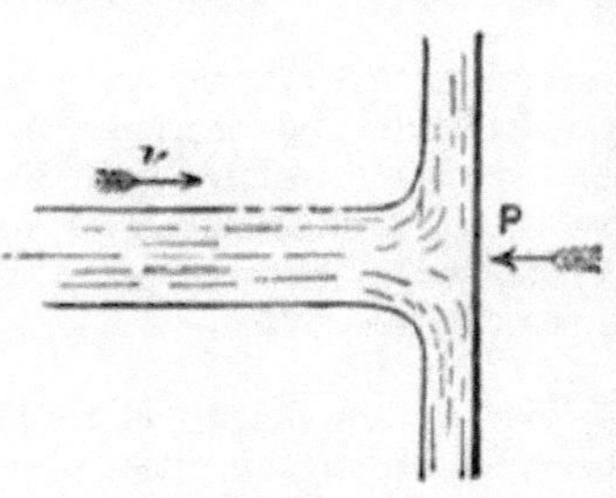

Fig. 278.

If A = area of the jet in square feet, v its velocity in feet per second, and W the weight of a cubic foot of water, $W A v$ = weight of water that strikes the plane per second.

The original momentum of the water delivered by the jet, in one second, perpendicular to the plane was

$$= \frac{W}{g} A v \times v = \frac{W}{g} A v^2.$$

This is entirely destroyed by the action of the plane, and consequently the pressure on the plane will be

$$P = \frac{W}{g} A v^2.$$

It is evident that the greater the quantity of water acted on per second, the greater will be the pressure produced; and this is equally true with respect to the action of propellers.

When a vessel is propelled by the action of any propeller worked by forces within the ship herself, the total momentum of the sea and ship is necessarily zero, and any forward momentum generated by the passage of the ship is exactly balanced by the backward momentum generated by the propeller. We will now proceed to consider actual propellers, commencing with a definition.

The 'race of a propeller' is the technical name given to the stream of water driven sternward by the propeller.

Jet-propeller.—This is the simplest form of propeller, but one that has been rarely used, for reasons that we shall see. In this case, water is drawn from the sea by a pump through orifices in the bottom, and projected sternwards through orifices either at the sides or stern. The water acted on was originally at rest. It is drawn into the ship, and consequently caused to move forward with a velocity V = the speed of the ship, and is lastly projected sternward with a velocity v, which we will suppose to be known.

The final velocity of the issuing water with respect to still water is therefore = $(v - V)$, and if A = the joint sectional area of the orifices, in square feet, the number of cubic feet of water acted on per second is = Av. The weight of the water leaving the ship per second is therefore WAv, and the total sternward momentum per second of the issuing jets is

$$= \frac{W}{g} Av\,(v - V).$$

From the principles previously stated, this must be equal to the reaction produced, or the *thrust of the propeller*.

If R be the thrust of the propeller,

$$R = \frac{W}{g} Av\,(v - V) \qquad . \qquad . \qquad . \qquad . \quad (1)$$

For sea-water $\dfrac{W}{g}$ is equal to 2 approximately.

It is evident that the thrust of a jet-propeller is theoretically independent of the position of the orifice, whether above or below the water level.

Theoretical efficiency of the jet-propeller.—The efficiency of the jet-propeller, if the loss from friction of the passages, shock, &c., be neglected, can now be ascertained. The work done in forcing out the jets of water is equal to one-half the vis-viva generated ; or,

$$= \frac{W}{2g} A\,v\,(v - V)^2.$$

The useful work done in propelling the ship = RV.

$\therefore$ Total work done per second $= RV + \dfrac{W}{2g} A\,v\,(v - V)^2$

$$= \frac{W}{2g} A\,v\,(v^2 - V^2)\ \text{from (1)}.$$

The efficiency of the propeller $= \dfrac{\text{useful work}}{\text{total work}}$.

$$= \frac{RV}{\dfrac{W}{2g} A\,v\,(v^2 - V^2)} = \frac{\dfrac{W}{g} A\,v\,(v - V)\,V}{\dfrac{W}{2g} A\,v\,(v^2 - V^2)} = \frac{2V}{v + V}$$

This is theoretically the maximum efficiency that any propeller can attain, as it is assumed that all the water is projected directly sternwards, and all the losses from friction of passages, shock, &c., are neglected, conditions which are far from being even nearly obtained in practice. It is assumed, for example, that the water enters the orifices at speed V, and that its velocity is *gradually* accelerated up to the speed v, so that all the energy in the supply-water to the pump is utilised. In practice much of this is lost, and in some designs practically all. The smaller is v for a given value of V, the greater is the efficiency.

From the formula (1) we see that the thrust mainly depends on the product A v, and that the smaller the value of v the greater must be the value of A for the same thrust. Since the efficiency becomes a maximum when $v = $ V, which is the smallest value v can have, it follows that theoretically the larger A is made the more efficient would be the performance. Generally, A is made as large as practical considerations will admit, so as to keep v, the speed of the race, as small as possible ; the sternward momentum of the race with respect to still water representing a loss, and the higher its velocity the greater will be the loss from shock, &c. With reference to screw-propellers, as we shall see in a later portion of this chapter, this principle requires modification.

Advantages and disadvantages of water-jet propulsion.—The advantages claimed for water-jet propulsion in warships consist in the freedom from damage in action by wreckage or grounding, greater control of motion of the ship from deck without altering the motion of the engines, and possession of large pumping power in case of a leak.

In practice they are at a great disadvantage, owing to the magnitude of the frictional resistances and the difficulty of operating on a sufficiently large body of water on this plan ; and instead of being more efficient than other propellers, as they should be theoretically, they are in practice much less efficient. Their defective action therefore, due to the resistance of passages, &c., combined with the practical objections to the fitting of large orifices in the ship's side, either above or below the water, places the jet out of the region of practical propellers, except under very special circumstances, such as in lifeboats, &c.

Results of trials.—The 'Waterwitch' is the only example of a ship with a jet-propeller in the Royal Navy, and her trials demonstrated the inefficiency of the system. With 760 I.H.P. the 'Waterwitch' attained a speed of 9·3 knots, displacement 1,160 tons. The 'Viper,' twin-screw gun-vessel, of somewhat similar dimensions but inferior in form, attained a speed of 9·6 knots with 696 I.H.P., displacement 1,180 tons. The quantities of water acted on by the two kinds of propellers were very different. In the 'Waterwitch' the quantity of water passing astern per second was about 150 cubic feet, while the twin screws of the 'Viper' acted on over 2,000 cubic feet per second, or about fourteen times as much.

In 1883 one of the second-class torpedo boats by Messrs. Thornycroft & Co. was fitted with a turbine, and great skill and care were exercised to insure the best results. Efficiency of astern working was subordinated to that of ahead working, and the water inlet was placed at the bottom, and made into a scoop to utilise as much as possible of the energy of the entering water. All sudden changes of angles and velocity of water were avoided. On the comparative trials between the hydraulic boat and the other boats of equal size fitted with screw-propellers, it was found that the speed of the hydraulic boat was no greater than could be attained in the screw boats with about half the power. The actual results were : Hydraulic boat, I.H.P. 167, speed 12·6 knots. Screw boat, I.H.P. 170, speed 17·3 knots. The efficiencies were analysed as follows : Screw boat : Engine, ·77 ; screw propeller, ·65 ; total efficiency, ·5. Hydraulic boat : Engine, ·77 ; jet-propeller, ·71 ; circulating pump, ·46 ; total efficiency, ·254. The screw boat was therefore nearly double as efficient as the hydraulic, the principal loss in the latter being in the pump.

Feathering paddle-wheels.—With feathering paddle-wheels the floats are supposed to act in a direct sternward direction, and to enter and leave the water normally, the area of the race of both paddles being equal to that of a pair of floats. In ordinary radial paddle-wheels there is much local agitation and disturbance of the water, due to their oblique action on entering and leaving, which complicates the question, and the area of the race is not so clearly defined.

Before being acted on by the floats the water is assumed to be at rest, and therefore, relatively to the ship, it would have a sternward velocity V, equal to the speed of the ship.

Let v be the final velocity of the race *relatively* to the ship, and A = the area of a pair of floats, one on each side of the ship, then the sternward momentum generated per second is equal to R, the propelling reaction, or $R = \dfrac{W}{g} A v (v - V)$, as in the jet-propeller.

The propelling reaction R acts on the paddle floats, and the velocity of the floats is assumed to be v, the same as that of the propeller race relatively to the ship ; therefore the engine has to overcome a resistance R through a space v in one second. Hence, as regards the efficiency of the paddles the energy exerted in propelling is $= R v$, and the useful work done is clearly $= R V$.

Therefore the total work wasted is equal to

$$R (v - V),$$

and the efficiency is

$$\frac{R V}{R v} \text{ or } \frac{V}{v},$$

which is theoretically not so great as in the jet-propeller, other things being equal.

The work wasted in producing the race is equal to the half vis-viva generated

$$= \frac{W}{2 g} A v (v - V)^2 = \tfrac{1}{2} R (v - V).$$

This, therefore, only amounts to one-half the total power wasted, the remainder being absorbed in producing the violent churning and agitation of the water which is always produced by paddle-wheels. In practice the loss from this cause would be even more than one-half of the total power wasted, for in the above investigation we have neglected the resistance to forcing the floats in and out of the water, which considerably increases the work of the engine.

The expression $\dfrac{V}{v}$ must therefore be regarded as the maximum possible efficiency with these propellers.

Radial paddle-wheels.—In paddle-wheels with radial floats only the float for the time at the bottom of the wheel is vertical, and giving direct sternward velocity to the water. All the others act obliquely and have a vertical as well as a horizontal reaction, the former, although absorbing a large proportion of the power of the engines, being wasted, so far as propulsive effect is concerned. The greater the immersion of the wheel, the greater will be the loss due to the vertical component of the pressure on the float. These wheels, therefore, should be so designed that at the maximum load draught of the ship, they should not be immersed more than one-quarter the diameter of the wheel; for beyond this limit the loss from the vertical reaction increases at a very rapid rate.

With these propellers it is impossible to determine, with accuracy, the area and speed of the race. Various assumptions may be made, but they are now of little practical value, as the use of the feathering paddle is almost universal for important vessels in which this means of propulsion is employed.

Objections to paddle-wheels.—The chief objection to the employment of paddle-wheels for ocean navigation arises from the practical difficulties attending the variation in immersion during long voyages, owing to the lightening of the ship by the consumption of coal, stores, &c. Even with feathering wheels, in which the floats are approximately vertical when in the water, the loss from forcing the floats in and out of the water, churning, &c., is much increased when the wheels are deeply immersed; and it is evident that if the wheels are to be sufficiently immersed at the end of a long voyage they must have been too deep in the water on starting. Even if water ballast be used to overcome this difficulty a larger expenditure of engine power would be necessary. For short voyages, in which the draught of water is comparatively unchanged, paddle-wheels may be advantageously employed, and they are almost essential for propulsion in many shallow rivers, where the depth of water is insufficient to admit the use of screws.

For ocean navigation, however, they have been superseded by the screw, for in addition to the loss of efficiency from alteration in draught, paddle-wheels are objectionable in consequence of the racing and straining of the machinery due to the rolling motion in a seaway, causing the paddles to often emerge from the water on one side and be correspondingly depressed on the other. For vessels of war the exposure of the paddles and engines to injury by shot and their interference with the deck arrangements render them doubly inadmissible. The paddle-wheel, as a propeller, is now only employed in the few special cases suitable to this form of propeller.

Screw-propeller.—The action of a screw-propeller is much more complex than that of the two types of propellers previously discussed, and is due mainly to the following causes :—

1. The action of the propeller on the water is oblique instead of direct.

2. The velocities of the several particles of water acted on by the screw are different from each other.

3. The screw acts on water that has previously been set in motion by the ship.

The difficulties attending an exact mathematical investigation of the action of screw-propellers are consequently so great that the problem is not yet solved. No formula yet in existence will give an accurate value for the thrust of an ordinary screw, even when working in undisturbed water, while for the case of propellers working behind actual ships the problem is still more difficult and complicated. The principles involved may, however, be easily understood. Oblique action, other things being equal, is always a cause of loss of efficiency in a propeller, and the fact that, in spite of this, the screw is a practically efficient propeller is explained by the circumstance that it operates upon a much greater quantity of water than could be acted on by a pair of paddle floats, or by any other propeller in a ship of the same size in the same time, and, as has been proved previously, the efficiency of any propeller depends to a large extent on the quantity of water acted on. The screw is the form of propeller best adapted to fulfil this condition.

It will now be desirable to define a few of the technical terms that will frequently be used.

Diameter.—The diameter of the screw is the diameter of the circle formed by the tips of the blades when revolving. The area of this circle is called the 'disc area' of the screw.

Pitch.—The pitch of the screw is the distance through which the screw would advance *in one revolution* provided it revolved in an unyielding medium such as a solid nut.

Speed of screw.—The speed of the screw is the distance it would advance *in a unit of time*, supposing the screw to be working in a solid nut. This is obviously equal to the pitch of the screw multiplied by the number of revolutions made per unit of time.

Slip.—In consequence of the screw-propeller working in a yielding medium, the speed of the ship is generally less than the speed of the screw. The difference between the speed of the screw and the speed of the ship is called the slip of the screw.

If v = speed of the screw.

V = „   „   ship.

$v - V$ = slip of the screw.

$$\frac{v - V}{v} = \text{slip of the screw expressed as a fraction of the speed of the screw} \quad . \quad . \quad . \quad (2)$$

$$\frac{v - V}{v} \times 100 = \text{percentage of slip.}$$

This, however, is only the *apparent* slip of the screw. It assumes the screw to be acting on water previously at rest, which can never be the case with the water operated on by the screw-propeller of a ship. The friction of the ship on the water during its passage causes a wake to follow her, so that the screw-propeller acts on water already set in motion. The velocity of this stream must therefore be considered, in order to obtain the *real slip*, which represents the true value of the backward velocity impressed on the water by the propeller. The speed at which the water follows the ship depends on her form, and is difficult to ascertain, so that the slip generally referred to is the apparent slip only and not the real slip.

If we assume the water to be a stream of velocity μ and of sufficient breadth, the original velocity of the water acted on, relatively to the screw, is $V - \mu$, while its final velocity is v, so that the *real slip* will be $\dfrac{v - (V - \mu)}{v}$

or $$\frac{v + \mu - V}{v} = \text{real slip} \quad . \quad . \quad . \quad (3).$$

Negative apparent slip.—From the nature of the medium in which the screw-propeller works, it is clear that in every case there must necessarily be *positive real slip*, as it is the change in the backward momentum of the water which causes the propelling reaction or thrust; but it is not difficult to imagine cases in which the water following the ship has such an initial velocity that the *apparent slip* might be *negative*—that is, the speed of the ship might be greater than that of the screw-propeller. From the formula (3) above, it will be seen that if μ be considerable, V may be greater than v quite consistently with a positive value for the real slip, in which case the apparent slip would be negative. This has sometimes occurred, and before the matter was sufficiently understood gave rise to a vast number of theories to account for its existence.

Possibly in some cases the apparent negative slip may be attributed to some extent to the difficulty of correctly estimating the true mean pitch of an ordinary screw. The method adopted practically is to divide each blade by a number of circular arcs at equal distances apart, as in Fig. 300, and to measure the pitch or pitches at each arc separately. It is generally found that the pitches at the various radii are somewhat different ; and frequently at each radius the pitch of the leading part differs from that of the following part of the blade. The arithmetical mean of all the pitches thus measured, for all the screw-blades, is called the 'mean pitch' of the screw ; but considering the different velocities with which the several sections pass through the water, and their different obliquities and areas, it is by no means certain that this method gives the true mean pitch of the propeller as regards its propulsive effect, and a comparatively small error in estimating the mean pitch might considerably affect the calculated apparent slip of the screw.

Propeller race.—The action of the screw-propeller is to drive sternward a cylindrical column of water, usually called the 'propeller race,' and the thrust of the screw is measured by the sternward momentum generated in this race in a unit of time. The area of this race is approximately equal to that of the screw disc, less that of the boss of the screw, the race being in fact approximately a revolving annular column. In consequence of the obliquity of the propelling surfaces, the race receives a rotatory as well as a sternward motion, and this centrifugal action causes a certain loss of thrust. The race of a screw-propeller may be conceived to be a series of concentric cylinders of water moving sternward, and rotating at different velocities. It is evident that the thrust must be diminished both by the centrifugal motion and by the frictional action of the particles of water.

Augmentation of resistance due to action of screw-propeller.— The most important feature in the action of a screw-propeller, as affecting its efficiency, is the effect it produces on the water under the stern of the ship. In the absence of the propeller the water displaced at the bow by the passage of a well formed ship, would close in under the stern and cause a forward pressure there. The action of the screw withdraws this water, and consequently diminishes the pressure of water under the stern, which is equivalent to increasing the resistance of the ship, as compared with the natural resistance, or the resistance experienced by the ship when towed at the same speed. The *resistance augmentation* varies exceedingly, depending on the shape of the stern of the ship and the size and position of the screws relatively to the vessel. The late Mr. Froude experimented, and considered about 40 per cent. to be the augmentation for a single-screw ship with a full run, and thick stern- and rudder-posts, a large percentage being accounted for by these posts alone. Later experiments have indicated for single-screw ships from 20 to 40 per cent., depending on the form, and the stern- and rudder-posts ; the lower value would be for a very fine ship. For twin-screw ships it also varies considerably, say from 5 to 25 per cent. The smaller value is, as before, for vessels of very fine form and usual position of screw. In the 'Iris,' and other twin-screw ships of similar form, the increase is 10 to 12 per cent. It may be very considerably reduced by placing the screw some distance behind the ship.

Mr. Froude proved by experiment that if a single screw were placed, from one-third to one-quarter of the extreme breadth of the ship, clear from the stern, the increase of resistance due to its action was only one-fifth of that ordinarily produced. Even omitting the practical objections to such a position, it must not be thought, however, that such a change would be entirely beneficial, for although the ship's resistance would be reduced, yet the propeller would be further removed from the following wake of water, so that it is less able to utilise the energy existing in this wake. The initial velocity of the following wake causes the thrust of the propeller to be greater than if the water were undisturbed.

General conclusions.—Notwithstanding these defects the screw-propeller has proved itself practically to be the most efficient propeller. It has entirely superseded the paddle-wheel for ocean navigation, as it is very slightly affected by the two causes which have such a serious prejudicial effect on the efficiency of paddle-wheels—viz. variation of immersion and rolling in a seaway—and is protected from shot by being below the surface of the water.

The considerations relative to the action of screw-propellers point to the conclusion that the greater the area the greater will be the efficiency. This is generally true, but it is subject to modification in practice. It is most important that the highest part of the screw-blades should be a sufficient depth below the surface of the water to prevent air to any considerable extent mixing with the propeller race, by air being drawn down or breaking the surface of the water, which would decrease the quantity of water acted on by the screw. For so long as the air does not obtain access to the blades, the full atmosphere pressure is available for causing the water to flow to the propeller, but when this is reduced by access of air the flow is diminished, and the efficiency lessened. As the lowest point of the screw-blade must, in ordinary ships, be above the keel, these considerations limit the maximum diameter that can be advantageously given to the screw.

With screw-propellers revolving rapidly it is evident that there must be a considerable waste of power in overcoming the edgewise and frictional resistance offered by the water to the motion of the screw. The power expended in this work is in many slow-moving engines estimated at about 4 per cent. of the total I.H.P. developed by the machinery, while with fast-running engines it will exceed this. The frictional resistance of the circumferential part of a large screw, moving at a high velocity, is much greater than that of the part nearer the boss, and this modifies in practice the proportions arrived at from theoretical considerations. The disc area in ordinary screw ships varies from one-half to one-quarter of the immersed midship section of the ship, one-third being a good average value.

The most important consideration relative to the efficiency of a screw-propeller is the facility offered for the free and unrestricted flow of a plentiful supply of water to be operated on, and this is attained by making the after run of the ship with as fine lines as possible, but was not fully understood when screw-propellers were first introduced.

Guide-blade propeller.—Mr. Rigg proposed a screw having fixed blades, called 'guide-blades,' placed immediately behind the revolving propeller, so arranged that the rotating water leaving the revolving part is discharged on to the fixed guide-blades, which are inclined at the reverse angle to the blades of the screw, so that the rotation of the water is gradually destroyed, and the water caused to be moving directly astern on leaving the guide-blades. A thrust is therefore exerted on the guide-blades which is added to the propulsive power.

Screw-turbine propeller.—Mr. Thornycroft in his 'screw-turbine' propeller, Fig. 279, has adopted these guide-blades, and added other features having for their object the gradual acceleration of the motion

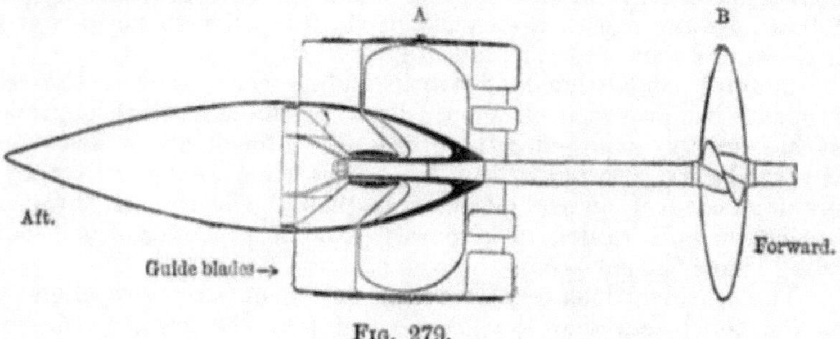

Fig. 279.

of the water by the screw. In the ordinary propeller the leading edge acts suddenly on the water it meets, and, as we have seen, such sudden action causes loss. In Thornycroft's screw-turbine the screw is made to revolve in a tunnel, A, and the boss of the screw is of increasing diameter from forward to aft, so that the area for the passage of water inside the tunnel is gradually reduced. The water enters the tunnel with the velocity of the vessel, and passing through the diminishing area gradually increases its velocity. The screw is of considerably in-creasing pitch to suit this gradual increase of velocity, and at the after end are placed the fixed guide-blades, with a long tail forming a prolongation of the boss to allow of the water gradually returning to the velocity corresponding to the larger area.

The thrust on the fixed guide-blades is found to be considerable, and the whole device forms a propeller, which by its principle is able to act on a smaller quantity of water than an ordinary one. It is thus suited to shallow draft vessels, and many steamers for operating on the Nile have been made on this principle. This propeller is, however, very inefficient when going astern, so that for astern working a separate small ordinary propeller, B, is fitted.

Messrs. Yarrow & Co., in similar boats for the Nile, obtain a light draught by allowing the propellers to rotate in a tunnel formed in the stern, so that the top of the screw may be considerably out of water. The action of the propellers fill the tunnel, so that the former are fully supplied with water.

Twin screws.—Twin screws have now been employed in the Royal Navy for many years and with very satisfactory results. The system has also been in many cases applied to passenger steamers of the mercantile marine, and is gaining favour in that service. The area of the propeller race has by this means been much increased, and trials of single- and twin-screw ships in the Royal Navy show that the propulsive efficiency of twin screws is rather greater than that of single screws.

The duplication of the machinery in twin-screw ships also prevents a total collapse in case of accident ; for if one set of engines broke down, the other set would be capable of propelling the ship at a fair rate of speed, so that she might speedily reach a port. By the use of twin screws the manœuvring power of the ship is greatly increased, for by working one screw ahead and the other astern the ship may be turned in her own length without necessitating any speed of ship, and this may be of great importance in an action. The ship could also be steered by the propellers alone, independently of the use of the rudder, if necessary in case of accident. The mechanical arrangements in a twin-screw ship with vertical engines enable the hull to be subdivided into longitudinal watertight compartments, by fore-and-aft bulkheads, separating the respective engine and boiler rooms, which adds greatly both to the strength and safety of the ship.

Low power working with twin screws.—It was at one time thought that with twin screws the most economical method of working at low powers was to stop one engine in order to get rid of its friction, and develop all the powers in the remaining engine, using helm as necessary to maintain a straight course. Numerous comparative trials have, however, been made in the Royal Navy, with the result that the most economical method of working was shown to be when using both screws, although the power developed in each engine may become very small.

Triple screws.—This system has not been fitted in the Royal Navy, but various war vessels in France, Germany, and the United States, several of which have been recently tried, have been provided with triple screws. On this plan three independent sets of engines are fitted in separate watertight compartments working three separate screws, one at the centre line, and one at either wing. The engines of the centre screw are placed abaft those of the wing screws, those for the two wing screws being arranged in a similar manner to those of a twin-screw vessel. By this means, with very large maximum powers, the engines become of more moderate size, and more easily stowed in war vessels ; but the principal reason for the adoption of this plan lies in the expectation that when steaming at low powers, the centre engine only can be used, so that the engine will be of moderate size for the power developed. It will therefore, as compared with the twin-screw system, be more economical in consumption of fuel *per I.H.P.* at low powers, while the constant friction of the engines at work will be much reduced.

On the other hand, however, the drag of the two idle screws adds considerably to the resistance of the vessel, so that it is quite possible the consumption of fuel for a given distance steamed by the vessel may be increased. Experience alone will decide whether this system is on the whole advantageous for such low power working.

CHAPTER XXIII.

CO-EFFICIENTS AND CURVES OF PERFORMANCE.

Co-efficients of performance.—For many years at the Admiralty the following co-efficients have been used to indicate the resistance and propulsive efficiency of ships approximately.

Let A = area of immersed midship section of the ship in square feet.

D = displacement of the ship in tons.

V = speed of ship in knots.

Then,

$$\text{1st co-efficient} = \frac{A\,V^3}{I.H.P.}$$

$$\text{2nd co-efficient} = \frac{D^{\frac{2}{3}}\,V^3}{I.H.P.}$$

These are based on the assumption that the resistance offered by the water to the motion of the ship varies as the square of the speed, and that, consequently, the power required to overcome this resistance would vary as the cube of the speed. This is only true for moderate speeds, but the co-efficients calculated from these formulæ have been very useful for comparing the relative performances of ships, especially when somewhat similar in form, and have been valuable, in the case of a new design, as data for approximating to the I.H.P. necessary to drive the ship at an assumed maximum rate of speed. On the whole, the second co-efficient, in which the efficiency is referred to the two-thirds power of the displacement, has been found to be the more trustworthy, giving a fairer measure of the resistance than the midship section co-efficient, especially in dealing with ships that are not similar in form.

It is, however, a well-known fact that at the higher rates of speed the resistance of ships often varies at a very much higher power of the speed than the square, and these co-efficients, though they have done good service, are not now sufficiently accurate, and fail to indicate many points of importance which are shown by more correct methods.

Curves of I.H.P.—In cases where an accurate analysis is required, trials at several different rates of speed, varying from the maximum to speeds as low as from three to four knots per hour, are made, and the I.H.P.s for the respective speeds shown in a graphical form by the construction of diagrams, in which the speeds are set out as abscissæ, and the corresponding horse-powers as ordinates. Having determined a sufficient number of points, a fair curve is drawn through them, and the I.H.P. corresponding to any intermediate speed can then be ascertained by simply drawing the vertical ordinate from the point representing the speed required.

The details of construction of these curves of I.H.P. are shown in Fig. 280. In this case the speeds at which the ship was tried are those marked A, B, C, and D, and the corresponding horse-powers are shown on the scale of I.H.P. by the points E, F, G, and H. By drawing the dotted horizontal and vertical lines as shown in the diagram, the points P, Q, R, and S are obtained. It is clear that when the horse-power is zero the speed will also disappear; so that if a fair curve be drawn through the points P, Q, R, and S, to touch the horizontal base line at the origin, where the speed is zero, it will represent the

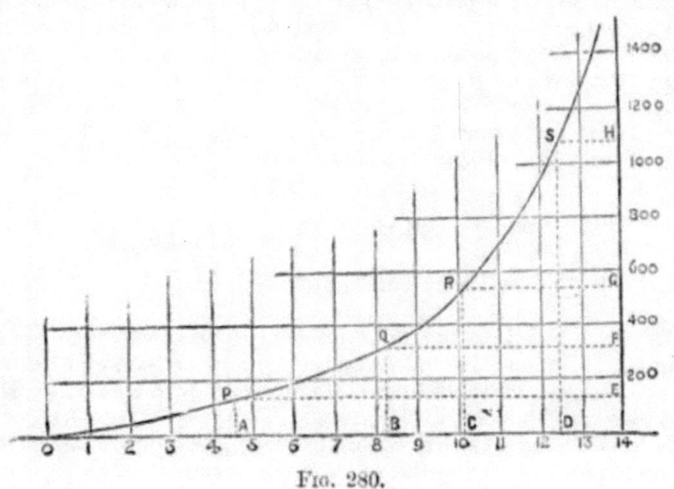

Fig. 280.

varying relations between the I.H.P. and the speed of the ship; or, in ordinary language, the curve of the I.H.P. of the ship. From these diagrams many important facts are learnt.

Curves of indicated thrust.—In 1876 the late Mr. Froude proposed the substitution of the '*indicated thrust*' of the propeller for the I.H.P. as ordinates of the diagram.

The I.H.P. of itself is not altogether reliable as a measure of the propulsive efficiency, as it combines in one item the performances of the ship, machinery, and propeller. It was deemed desirable to reduce the I.H.P. to a force factor by dividing it by the speed of the propeller, the result being what he termed 'indicated thrust.'

The indicated thrust may be estimated either by—

1. Multiplying the mean effective pressure on the pistons in pounds by twice the length of the stroke in feet, and dividing the product by the pitch of the propeller in feet; or

2. Multiplying the I.H.P. by 33,000 to bring it to foot-pounds, and dividing the product by the pitch of the propeller in feet multiplied by the number of revolutions per minute; which is the speed of the propeller in feet per minute.

The indicated thrust is therefore equal to—

$$\text{Piston pressures in lbs.} \times \frac{\text{twice the stroke in feet}}{\text{pitch in feet}}$$

$$\text{or} = \frac{33,000 \text{ I.H.P.}}{\text{pitch in feet} \times \text{revolutions per minute}}.$$

Having calculated the indicated thrusts for the trial speeds of the ship, a curve is constructed, with the speeds as abscissæ, as in the I.H.P. curves, but with the indicated thrusts as ordinates instead of the I.H.P.s.

Fig. 281 is an example showing the construction of the indicated thrust curve. Vertical ordinates, equal to the indicated thrusts at

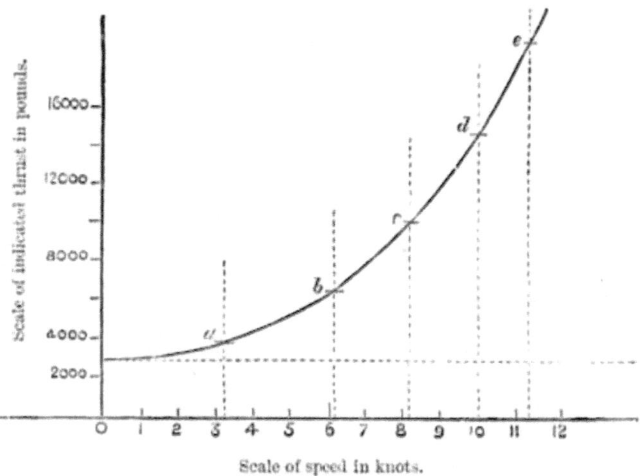

FIG. 281.

the respective speeds, are set up, and a series of points, a, b, c, d, and e, are thus obtained, through which a fair curve is drawn.

Components of total power exerted.—The power exerted in the cylinders of a marine engine when analysed can be resolved into several component parts, which show the amount usefully expended and the distribution of the losses.

The following are the components :—

1. Useful thrust, or ship's true resistance.

2. Augment of resistance, due to the action of the propeller in diminishing pressure under the stern of ship, less the gain due to the action of the following wake.

3. Equivalent of friction and resistance of the screw-blades in their motion through the water, and the necessary loss by slip.

4. Equivalent of friction due to the piston packings, glands, and dead weight of the working parts, &c., which constitutes the initial or slow-speed friction of the engines.

5. Equivalent of friction of the engines due to the working load.

6. Equivalent of the duty of any pumps worked off the main engines, such as air-pump generally, and feed- and bilge-pumps often.

As regards the second element, when a vessel of good form is towed through water the water follows the motion of the ship and closes in at the stern, so that the pressure on the stern is the same as that on the bow. By the action of the screw, however, the stern currents of water are withdrawn, so that the pressure on the stern is diminished, and therefore the resistance to motion is increased. This is a source of loss. Again, the friction of the hull of the vessel causes a body of water, known as the 'frictional wake,' to follow her at a certain speed compared with still water. Now as compared with the effect of a propeller acting on water previously at rest the action may be considered to be the same as if a body of water of volume and speed equal to the frictional wake at the propellers, were impinging on them, causing a force to be exerted on the screws, and thence on the ship. This represents a gain, and item 2 is the difference between the loss represented by increased resistance due to the action of the screw, and the gain due to the presence of the frictional wake.

Constant friction of engines.—It was observed by Froude, on drawing the thrust curves, that they do not descend to the thrust zero when the speed disappears, but tend to cross the vertical axis at some distance above it, representing a considerable amount of thrust at the zero of speed. This apparent thrust when the speed is reduced to zero, and when there can be no real thrust, represents the thrust equivalent of the initial or constant friction of the engines. If a horizontal line be drawn through this point of intersection, the height thus cut off from the thrust ordinates would represent the deduction to be made from them in respect of the constant friction, and the remainder of the ordinates between the new base line and the curve would represent approximately the variations of indicated thrust excluding the constant friction.

The point of intersection of the curve with the vertical axis may be found approximately geometrically as follows. The lowest point in

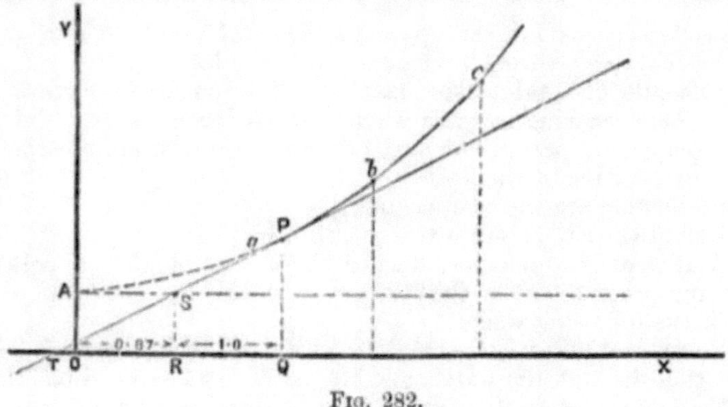

Fig. 282.

the curve found by trial should, if possible, correspond to a speed of three or four knots. For these speeds the resistance has been found to vary approximately as the 1·87 power of the speed.

In Fig. 282 let $a\,b\,c$ represent the lowest portion of the thrust curve corresponding to speeds of about from three to six knots, say. From any point P near the lower end of the curve, draw the tangent P T. Divide the abscissæ O Q at the point R in the ratio 0·87 to 1, so that O R is to R Q as 0·87 is to 1, and through R draw the ordinate R S cutting the tangent in S. If a horizontal line be drawn through S, cutting the vertical axis O Y in A, A will be the point through which the thrust curve will pass, and O A will represent the thrust equivalent of the initial or constant friction of the engines.

It is very essential for even approximately determining the initial friction geometrically, that the ship should be tried at a low speed, say three to four knots, for the lower the speed at which the observations are taken the more correctly should the equivalent of the constant friction be determined.

Unfortunately in practice this method cannot be relied on to give accurate results at present. Large numbers of such curves have been obtained, and a considerable variation is presented in the estimates of initial friction as so ascertained.

Froude's analysis of total power.—From experiments made by Mr. Froude on single-screw ships he concluded that generally, in ships of ordinary form, only from 37 to 40 per cent. of the total power exerted by the engines is utilised in the useful thrust of the propeller, and he estimated the various items of the total distribution of the power for a slow-moving single-screw vessel such as were common at that time. His estimate, arranged in a somewhat different form for clearness, was as follows, at full power :—

	Percentages
Dead load or constant friction	13
Friction due to the working load	13
Work expended on air-pumps, feed-pumps, &c., worked by main engines	6·9
Loss due to slip	9·1
,, ,, friction of screw	3·8
,, ,, augmentation of resistance (or thrust deduction)	15·5
Effective horse-power	38·7
Total	100·0

The sum of the first three items represents the loss due to the mechanism, and amounts to 32·9 per cent., so that the efficiency of the mechanism of the engine was estimated to be only 67·1 per cent.

It is known, however, with later information, that the amount of loss stated for the third item, which was based on land practice at that time, was over estimated, as also probably were the first two items, so that the engine efficiency must have been higher than 67·1 per cent. and the losses at the screw correspondingly greater.

Distribution of power in modern vessels.—With a modern high-speed engine the distribution of total power is quite different from the estimate of Froude given above. In the first place, a continuous reduction of dead-load friction has been effected in recent years, due to improved design and workmanship and to the use of much higher pressures and piston speeds, which has resulted in much smaller engines and shafts for a given power.

The estimates, also, must necessarily vary with the arrangement of pumps at the engines. In some vessels not any pumps are worked off the main engines, so that Froude's third item would vanish altogether, assuming the indicated power to be that developed in the main cylinders only. In the Royal Navy only the air-pumps are worked from the main engines, and these are now made considerably smaller than at first, and the power required for working them is correspondingly small.

For a good modern example of naval twin-screw vessel with fast-running, high-pressure engines, the distribution of power may be taken to be as follows, approximately :—

	Per cent.
Dead-load friction	6
Working-load friction	7
Air-pump working	1
Loss at propeller by slip, blade friction, and augmentation of resistance, allowing for gain due to speed of wake	33
Balance, or effective horse-power	53
	100

The sum of the first three items represents the engine losses, and amounts to 14 per cent., corresponding to an engine efficiency of ·86. The amount of power delivered to the screw is therefore 86 per cent., also 33 per cent. is lost by the action of the screw before the remainder is transmitted to the thrust block. The efficiency of the screw is therefore

$$\frac{86 - 33}{86} = 61\cdot6 \text{ per cent.}$$

The dead-load friction has in many engines been ascertained by actual test. With the horizontal engines of H.M.S. 'Iris' it was shown to represent 8 per cent. of the full power. It is generally from 5 to 10 per cent., depending on the type of machinery, but in special small quick-running engines it is sometimes smaller even than the lower figure.

The relative importance of this dead-load friction increases as the power being developed is reduced, which partially accounts for the fact that it is not economical to reduce the speed of a vessel beyond a certain point.

Information to be obtained on service.—The application of these thrust curves may be made the source of much valuable information with reference to the efficiency of performance of machinery. War-ships on ordinary service steam at various speeds, often very low, so that a series of points at the lower end of the curve, which are difficult to get before the ships proceed on service, can be usually obtained. This is the most important part of the curve, so far as the determination of the initial or constant friction of the engines is concerned. Indicator diagrams are generally taken daily, so that in course of time a considerable number of diagrams are taken, showing the performance of the engines under a great variety of circumstances.

The base line might be divided to represent revolutions per minute, instead of speed of ship, which is generally more difficult to obtain accurately, and for each number of revolutions at which diagrams have been taken, ordinates showing the indicated thrust should be set up, and the fair curve drawn through the points thus obtained will approximately represent the thrust curve. In order to ascertain the initial or constant friction of the engines, we then proceed as described previously.

It is a usual custom for engineers to tabulate, for their own information, the average horse-power, coal, &c. required when the engines are working at various speeds. These tabulated results only represent a number of isolated facts, but when they are shown in the form of a curve the general law underlying the facts can be more readily ascertained and more valuable information obtained.

Curves of coal consumption. Economical speed.—The construction of curves for all such records is recommended, especially as regards the

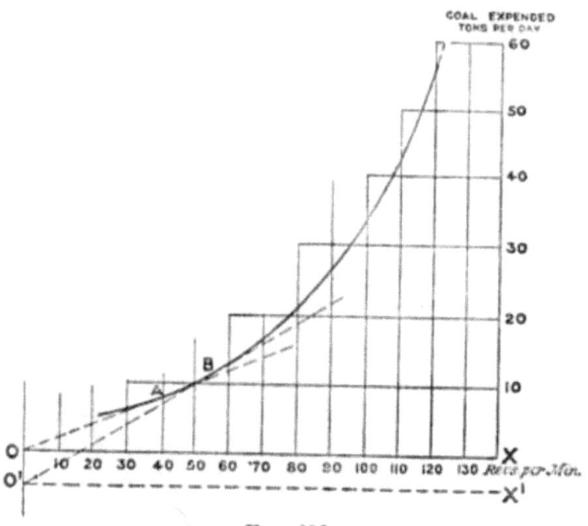

FIG. 283.

consumption of coal per day corresponding to various rates of speed of ship or revolutions of engines. A number of runs must be made at various speeds and the coal used carefully measured, the various points ascertained being set off on a diagram and a fair curve drawn through them. This curve, like the thrust curve, if produced to the axis does not intersect it at the zero point.

Such a curve will give by simple measurement the consumption of coal per day for any intermediate speed. One such curve is shown in Fig. 283. It is also easy to ascertain the most economical speed for the engine and the coal consumption at that speed. For if we draw a tangent from o to the curve meeting it at A, it is evident that the ratio of $\dfrac{\text{coal consumption}}{\text{speed}}$, i.e. the tangent of the angle A o x is least at the point A, and is greater for any other point on the curve, so that A will be the most economical speed of the engine. It will be seen, however, that the range of speed about this point at which the consumption is practically unaltered is considerable, and this being so it will generally be advantageous to select the higher limit of speed.

When the steaming distance of the ship for a given quantity of coal is under consideration, the amount of coal necessary to be expended for purposes other than the main engines must be taken account of. This is done by drawing a line o′ x′ at a distance below o x equal to the consumption per day for auxiliary purposes, such as electric lighting, culinary purposes, distilling drinking water, &c. The most economical speed of the ship is therefore obtained by drawing a tangent from o′ to the curve meeting it at B, which gives a greater speed than if the consumption for auxiliary purposes were not taken account of. The reason why the slowest speed is not the most economical will be understood from what has gone before ; it lies in the increased proportionate waste by constant friction as the power is diminished, and the proportionately increased loss by radiation from boilers, steam pipes, &c., and the greater proportionate consumption of coal for the constant auxiliary services of the ship.

Amount of consumption for auxiliary purposes.—The consumption of coal on board warships for auxiliary purposes—i.e. for purposes other than propelling the vessel—is very considerable. This service includes the consumption for culinary purposes, warming ship, distilling, electric lighting, working guns, &c., and often amounts during the whole of the commission of a warship to much more than that expended in propelling the vessel, owing to the intermittent nature of the steaming generally required. The following amounts are the consumptions of coal for auxiliary purposes in modern war vessels : Large 1st class battle ships, 10 to 15 tons ; 1st class cruisers, 8 to 15 tons ; 2nd class cruisers, 5 to 8 tons ; and 3rd class cruisers, 3½ to 6 tons. The actual amount depends on the number and extent of the auxiliary machinery fitted, and tends to increase in the newer ships owing to the larger quantity of fresh water used, extensive electric light installations, fitting of refrigerators, &c.

CHAPTER XXIV.

PADDLE-WHEELS.

Radial paddle-wheel. — The simplest form of paddle-wheel is generally known as the common or radial paddle-wheel. In this wheel the floats are bolted direct to the arms of the wheel, and consequently the pressure they produce on the water is always perpendicular to the radius, and the only float that produces a direct sternward reaction is the one at the bottom of the wheel, all the others having a vertical component tending to raise or depress the vessel, which is wasted so far as propulsion is concerned.

Width of floats.—The extreme width of the floats should not exceed one-half the width of the vessel, so that the combined width of the two paddle-wheels should not be greater than the width of the ship. In sea-going steamers the width of float generally does not exceed one-third the width of vessel. In still water the greater the width of float the more effective the wheel, as the required area of race can be obtained with less immersion, and the loss from oblique action is thereby reduced. This condition, however, is limited by the practical difficulties involved in supporting the overhanging end of the paddle-shaft. In rough weather extreme width would be objectionable from many causes.

Immersion of wheels.—The depth of immersion of paddle-wheels is practically limited by the draught of water of the vessel, as it is evidently undesirable to allow the lower edge of the propeller to be below the keel. The immersion of the wheels must also depend on their diameter, for if the floats act too obliquely on entering and leaving the water, a large proportion of the power would be wasted in producing vertical reactions. As an extreme case, we may point out that a radial paddle-wheel immersed to its centre would be of no value as a propeller.

In general the greatest immersion of a paddle-wheel should not exceed one-half the radius, or one-fourth the diameter of the wheel. When sea-going steamers were used for long voyages, the immersion at starting was about one-half the radius, and the mean draught for the voyage about one-third the radius of the wheel.

For effective working, the tops of the floats, when in their lowest position, should always be some distance below the surface of the water. In large sea-going paddle steamers the top of the lowest float was usually about 18 to 20 inches below the surface, at mean draught ; in smaller vessels from 12 to 15 inches. In river steamers the immersion is generally much less, say from 3 to 6 inches ; but these boats always work in smooth water, and their draught is practically constant. In sea-going steamers the immersion of the floats at their lightest draught should not be less than 6 inches.

Number and pitch of floats —In radial paddle-wheels the number of floats is generally made equal to the number of feet in the diameter of the wheel, which practically sets them at about 3 feet apart from each other. In some fast ships, to reduce vibration, they have been set closer than this, or from 2 to $2\frac{1}{2}$ feet apart. If the floats be set too closely together the water will not escape with sufficient freedom from between them, whilst if too far apart the vibratory action will be excessive. The number and pitch of floats should be so arranged that there will always be at least three floats immersed at the same time.

Reefing paddle-wheels.—The floats are secured to the radial arms of the paddle-wheels by hook-bolts, in such a manner that if the draught of the vessel be increased, the floats may be readily unshipped and secured in other positions nearer the centre of the wheels. This operation is usually called *reefing the paddle-wheels*, and is equivalent to reducing the effective diameter of the wheel and the immersion of the floats, and thereby diminishing the loss from oblique action. Reefing is desirable when by increased draught it is found that the wheels cannot be driven fast enough to utilise all the steam generated in the boilers. This operation, by decreasing the resistance, enables all the steam generated to be used, and the piston speed increased, with a consequent gain in the power and speed of the ship.

The only points of advantage of the radial over the feathering paddle-wheel are its lightness, simplicity, and cheapness of construction. There are no working parts in it, and defects can be readily made good at little cost. Its propelling efficiency, however, is much less than that of the wheel with feathering floats, and the improvements in design and workmanship have made the latter so practically trustworthy, for the comparatively few services for which paddle-wheels are now required, that the radial paddle-wheel may be regarded as altogether a propeller of the past.

Feathering paddle-wheel.—In order to obviate the disadvantages resulting from the oblique action of the floats of radial paddle-wheels, especially in cases where the draught of the vessel varied considerably, feathering paddle-wheels have been introduced. The general form and arrangement of these propellers are shown in Figs. 284 and 285. The wheel consists of a wrought-iron framework, secured to a strong cast-iron centre or boss, keyed on the end of the paddle-shaft. The floats, instead of being fixed to the arms of the wheel, are carried on joint-pins, and their motion is controlled by the action of an eccentric, through rods and levers, in such a manner as to keep the floats approximately normal to the effective surface during their passage through the water, so that the whole of the thrust will be in a sternward direction. Its efficiency is at least 10 per cent. greater than that of the radial paddle-wheel when both work under suitable conditions, and the economy and efficiency resulting from its use far more than compensate for its increased first cost and expense of maintenance.

It is however more complicated, and requires more care and attention, than the radial wheel. It is very important that the working parts should be sufficiently strong to withstand the shocks to which

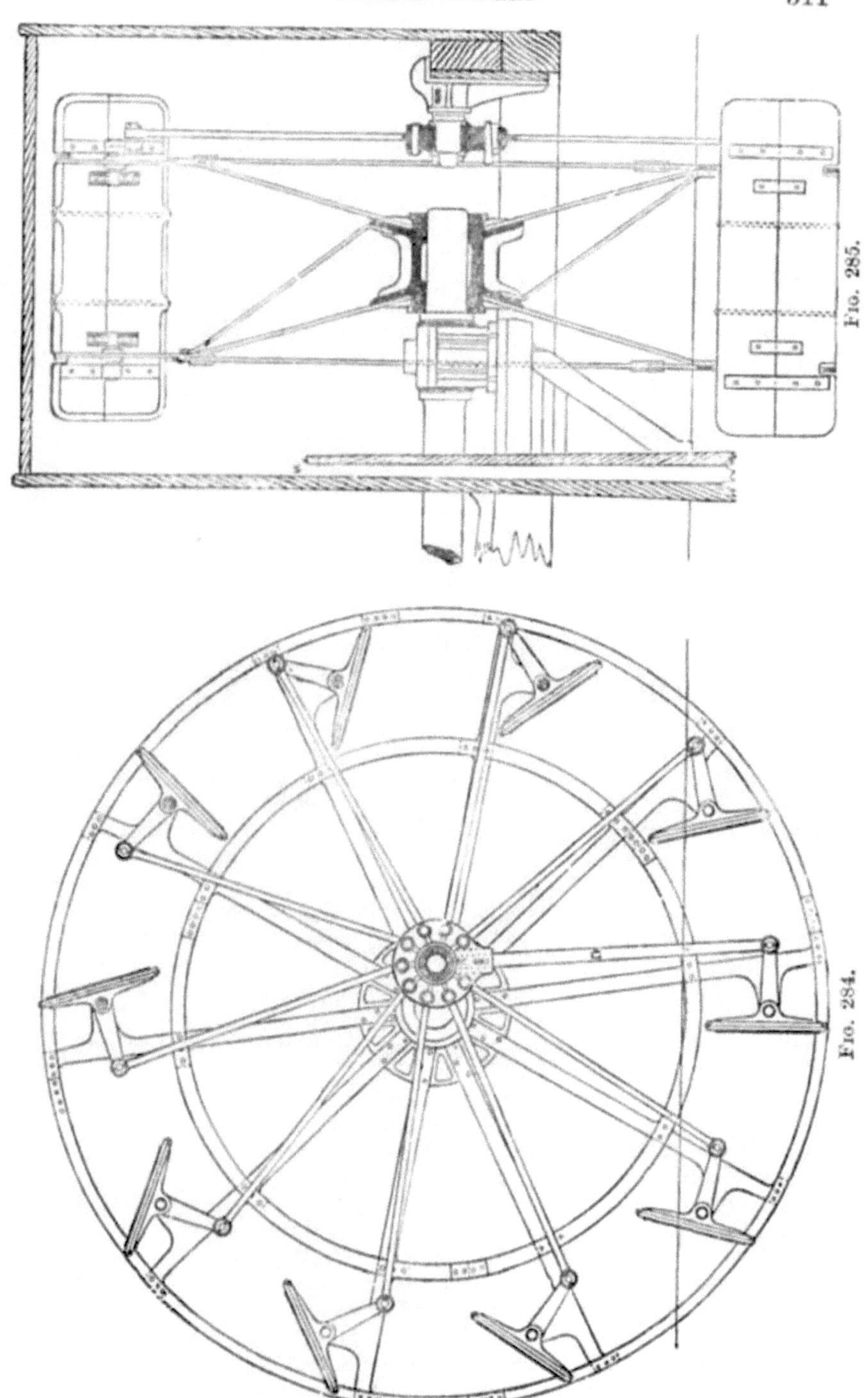

Fig. 285.

Fig. 284.

they are exposed, without undue straining, for damage to any part of
the feathering apparatus is liable to paralyse the action of the entire
wheel.   These wheels are consequently made much heavier than the
radial wheel, and are more difficult to properly support.

This complication and liability to serious injury might possibly have
tended to prevent their being extensively used for long sea voyages, in
preference to the simpler radial wheels, which, if damaged, could be so
much more easily repaired.   As, however, the paddle-wheel for ocean
navigation has been entirely superseded by the screw-propeller, this
point need not be further discussed, and there can be no doubt that for
short voyages, river navigation, and towing purposes, for which alone
paddle-wheels are now used, feathering floats possess very great
advantages, enabling the wheels to be made of less diameter and width,
and in consequence of their increased efficiency the indicated horse-
power of the engines may be proportionately reduced for a given speed.

Dimensions and pitch of floats.—The floats in feathering paddle-
wheels are generally placed about twice as far apart as the floats in the
radial wheel ; that is, the pitch of the floats is usually about six feet.
They are also made deeper, say about twice the depth of the common
float, for in this case the area of the race, or stream driven back on
either side of the ship, is equal to the width multiplied by the depth of
the float instead of the width of float multiplied by the depth of
immersion, as is assumed to be the case with the radial paddle-wheel.

Eccentricity of feathering apparatus.—The method of determining
the throw and position of the eccentric necessary to produce the proper
action of the floats in the water may be easily explained by means of a
skeleton diagram.   In Fig. 286 let A represent the centre of the paddle-
shaft, and K the centre of the eccentric pin or sheave that produces the
necessary movement of the paddle-floats, the correct position of which
is required to be found.   For simplicity, the floats are supposed to be
jointed at their centres.   In practice this is not exactly the case, the
joint being just behind the float, and as close to it as possible.   In an
actual design, this would render necessary a slight modification in the
details of the following method of determining the eccentricity, but the
deviation is small, and there will be no difficulty in making the required
correction when the principles involved are understood.   The circle
B C D E F G, drawn with A as centre, through the centres, or joints, of the
floats, may be taken to represent the paddle-wheel circle.   Let w w
represent the water-line, B and D being the points in which it is cut by
the paddle-wheel circle.

Consider three floats in the positions shown by B, C, and D, one just
entering the water, the second at its lowest point, and the third just
leaving the water.   In order that the motion of the floats through the
water should be correct, moving as nearly as possible edgewise,
relatively to the water in the paddle race, the directions of the faces of
these floats produced, should meet at the point F, at the top of the
paddle-wheel circle.   If, therefore, from F, the highest point of the
circle, straight lines, F B, F C, and F D are drawn, these will represent
the directions of the faces of the paddle floats at these respective points.

From the centres of these three floats, B, C, and D, draw the float-
levers, B*b*, C*c*, D*d*.   These are usually at right angles to the float, and their
lengths are about three-fifths of the depth of float.   These values are

arbitrary, and subject to convenience in any particular design ; but the angle seldom deviates much from a right angle, and the proportionate length of lever given above is generally suitable. Having thus determined the points, *b*, *c*, and *d*, to which the radius rods from the eccentric have to be jointed, it is only necessary to find by plane geometry the centre, K, of the circle passing through them. K will then be the centre, and A K the throw, of the eccentric necessary to produce the required motion of the floats.

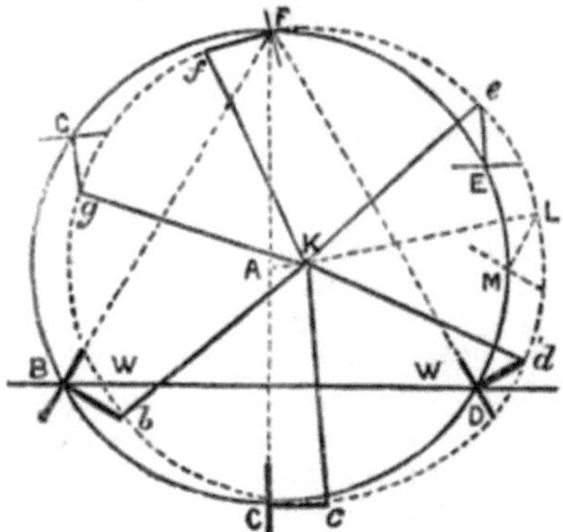

Fig. 286.

The velocity of the propeller race is clearly represented by the circumferential velocity of the circle B D F G, and the effect of the motion produced by the action of the eccentric, thus determined, will be to cause the floats, while *in the water*, to move as nearly as possible edgewise, relatively to the propeller race, and thus prevent loss from oblique motion. By drawing floats in other positions, it will be seen that their action when *out of the water* is far from being free from vertical reactions, but these, operating only on the air, may be neglected.

Paddle-shaft bearings.—The shaft carrying the paddle-wheel is called the paddle-shaft, and is sometimes supported by two bearings, one on the ship's side, and the other on a beam, called the *sponson* or *spring beam*, on the outside of the paddle-box. In this case, the feathering apparatus has to be worked by a large eccentric on the paddle-shaft, to which the radius rods are attached.

Overhung wheels.—The most general arrangement, however, is that shown in Figs. 284 and 285, in which the paddle-wheel is overhung and supported by a single bearing on the ship's side, the outer bearing being dispensed with. In this case the feathering motion is produced by attaching the radius rods to a sheave working on a pin carried by a bracket fixed to the outer side of the paddle-box, in the proper position, eccentric to the wheel, to produce the required movements of the floats.

Driving and radius rods.—In the feathering apparatus, one of the guide or radius rods, called the driving rod, is rigidly fixed to the eccentric, to make it rotate about the axis K. The remainder of the rods are simply jointed to the eccentric, as well as to the float-levers, with pins. In Fig. 284 the driving rod is marked D. All the joints in the feathering apparatus should be bushed either with gunmetal, white metal, or lignum-vitæ.

Details of paddle bearings.—The outer bearings of paddle-wheels, when they are so fitted, cannot be examined when the engines are at work. Guide-boards or troughs are therefore fitted on the side of the paddle-box, so that the water carried up by the wheel is caused to constantly run on these bearings to prevent their overheating. This splashing and churning action of the wheel on the water is also often utilised for the purpose of keeping a small tank, fitted inside the paddle-box, always full of water, to be used, if necessary, on the bearings of the paddle and intermediate shafts which are above the water-line. The water-service pipes for these journals are also, in general, connected with the delivery-pipe from one of the auxiliary pumping engines of the ship.

When the paddle-wheels are overhung, and carried by a single bearing on the ship's side, the journal should be made of larger diameter, and considerably longer than is necessary when an outside bearing is fitted, to resist the increased pressure and strains. There should also be thrust collars on the journal, to prevent end motion when the ship rolls. The bearings for paddle-shafts in the Royal Navy are generally made of gunmetal, though they are sometimes made of lignum-vitæ strips, as in the case of bearings for screw-shafts. When so fitted the shafts should be cased with gunmetal.

Stuffing-box on ship's side.—The hole in the ship's side through which the paddle-shaft passes is either fitted with an ordinary stuffing-box, or covered with a leather disc to prevent the passage into the ship of water carried round with the paddle-wheel.

Disconnecting apparatus.—In paddle-wheel tug-boats, gear is usually fitted to enable the wheels to be disconnected from each other, and each engine worked independently, to facilitate the manœuvring of the vessel. In many cases an ordinary disconnecting clutch is fitted on the intermediate shaft for this purpose.

Another plan consists in fitting a cast-iron disc on the intermediate shaft, in lieu of a crank-arm. This is driven by feathers on the shaft, over which it may be drawn back, clear from the crank-pin, when the engines are required to be worked independently. Engines of this class, of large power, should be fitted with auxiliary steam starting-engines and starting-valves to facilitate handling.

In the more recent paddle-wheel tug-boats in Her Majesty's service a pair of cylinders, forming a compound engine, has been attached to each crank. The shafts for each wheel may either be connected by a clutch coupling, or left quite independent of each other, for the engines will be entirely under control whether they are coupled or not.

CHAPTER XXV.

SCREW-PROPELLERS.

EACH blade of a screw-propeller may be regarded as a small portion of the thread of a screw of great pitch, and of considerable depth relatively to the pitch. The generation of the surface of a propeller blade of uniform pitch may be conceived from the following geometrical construction.

Let A A', Fig. 287, represent the axis of the screw. Suppose a line A B, perpendicular to A A', to move uniformly along A A', and at the same time to revolve uniformly around it. It is clear that the extremity B of the arm A B will travel on the surface of a cylinder, and will trace out a spiral curve B B' on that cylinder. The same will be true of every point in the line A B; the point C, for example, traces out the curve C C', therefore the surface swept out or developed by the line A B will be a spiral or screw surface.

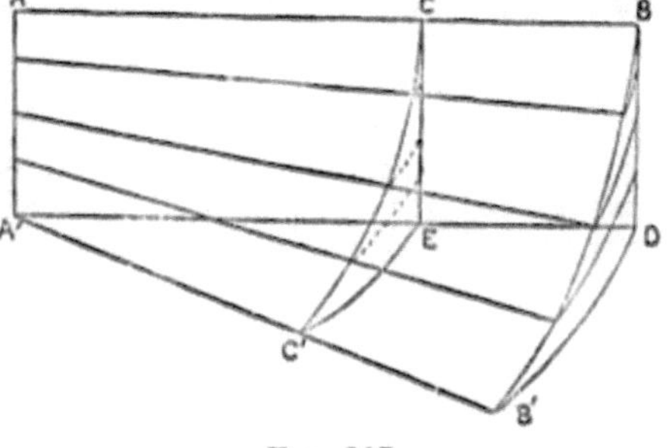

FIG. 287.

Pitch of the screw.—If the line A B made a complete revolution around A A', the distance of A' from A at the end of the revolution would be the *pitch of the screw.* It is the distance between two consecutive threads measured parallel to the axis.

Length of screw.—An actual screw-blade consists only of a portion of a complete convolution ; and the extreme dimension of the blade, measured parallel to the axis, is called the *length of the screw.* In Fig. 287 this is represented by the line A A'. The aggregate length of all the screw-blades is equal to the length of the screw multiplied by the number of blades.

Angle of the screw.—The angle B B' D, between the curve and the plane A' D B' perpendicular to the axis, is called the *angle of the screw,* at the radius A B. It is evident, if the pitch be constant throughout, that the smaller the radius the greater will be the angle of the screw, the angle C C' E, for example, being considerably greater than the angle B B' D. The relations between the pitch, circumference, and angle of the screw may be shown by means of a right-angled triangle, having the pitch as perpendicular and the circumference as base, the tangent of the angle of the screw being equal to the pitch divided by the circumference. In Fig. 288, let A B represent the pitch and B C the circumference of a screw, to any given scale. Then the angle

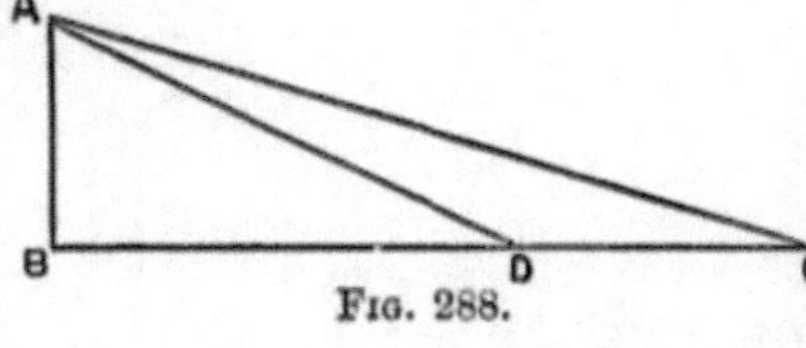

FIG. 288.

A C B will represent the angle of the screw at the end of the blade. The pitch being assumed the same throughout the blade, the angle at any other part of the blade may be found by determining the circumference B D at the given part, and joining A D; the angle A D B being the required angle.

Form of blade.—Screw-blades are made of a great variety of forms. The effect of form of blade has not yet been fully ascertained, but the shape suitable for one ship does not always prove equally efficient for a different ship. As a rule it would appear that form has little peculiar value as regards propulsive efficiency, though it may have some influence on the amount of vibration produced ; the main points to be considered are, the pitch and surface of the blades in relation to diameter.

The work absorbed in friction and the disturbing effect on the stream-line motions must necessarily have some effect in determining the most suitable shape of the blade, but this has not yet been reduced to exact calculation.

In consequence of the increased angle of the screw-blade as it approaches the axis, the inner part of the blade, if the boss be small, has very little propulsive efficiency, and only absorbs power in churning the water. This was very noticeable in the earlier forms of screw-propellers, in which the boss was only about twice the diameter of the shaft, so that the inner portions of the blades were nearly in a fore-and-aft direction. In these screws also, the length of the screw, or, in other words, the length of the projection of the blades on a fore-and-aft plane, was constant throughout the blades, so that the side view of the screw was rectangular. The ends of the blades were, therefore, very broad, and absorbed much power in surface friction, owing to their great velocity.

An endless variety of different patents have been originated on the question of the form and arrangement of screw-propeller blades, many of them peculiar and complicated, but they have all failed on trial to give the results anticipated.

Hirsch screw.—A variety of screw much favoured at one time was the Hirsch screw, a four-bladed example of which is shown in Fig. 289. In this propeller the blades are curved forward, the axis of the blade being approximately a spiral curve, instead of a straight line as usual, the pitch also increases towards the circumference, and there are other minor peculiarities. The method of obtaining the curve of the centre line of the blade is shown by the dotted construction.

It was supposed that this curved form of blade tended to resist the centrifugal motion of the particles of water acted on by the propeller, and that vibration was diminished by the action of the blade being gradual.

Griffiths' screw.—Mr. Robert Griffiths was probably the most successful of the early designers as regards propeller proportions. He substituted for the central inefficient portion of the screw a large spherical boss, one-third the diameter of the propeller, which would revolve without agitating the water. This principle is now adopted for most screw-propellers, though the bosses are not usually so large as in the earlier Griffiths' screws. The general diameter of the boss in screw-propellers as now fitted is about one-fifth to one-quarter the diameter of the propeller. In the Griffiths' screw also, the outer ends of the blades, which revolve at the highest velocity, were considerably narrowed, to reduce loss from friction. The widest part of the blade was about four-tenths of the radius from the centre, the blade being somewhat pear-shaped. The tips of the blades were bent forward to the extent of about one-twenty-fourth of the diameter of the propeller.

The proportions of Griffiths' two-bladed propeller are :—

Width of blade at tip	0·07	pitch
Greatest width	0·167	,,
Width at root	0·11	,,
Aggregate length of two blades	0·24	,,

The two-bladed propeller shown in Fig. 290 is an example of a somewhat modified form of Griffiths' screw fitted to a vessel with a lifting screw.

Propeller arrangements for old masted ships. — Before describing the modern arrangement of propellers and shafting, some space will be devoted to that of the early single-screw vessels, which were supplied also with sail power. Such vessels were intended at times to proceed under sail alone, and disconnecting couplings were fitted to enable the propeller to revolve freely without moving the engines. This was usually effected by fitting one of the couplings with bolts, that could be readily withdrawn by means of screws. A friction strap was fitted, to hold the propeller during the time the bolts were being withdrawn or replaced, and a thrust-bearing abaft the disconnecting coupling prevented the shaft being drawn back by the propeller when revolving while disconnected.

The resistance offered when under sail by the propeller was still great, and to obviate this one of the following plans was adopted :—

1. To lift the screw entirely out of the water.

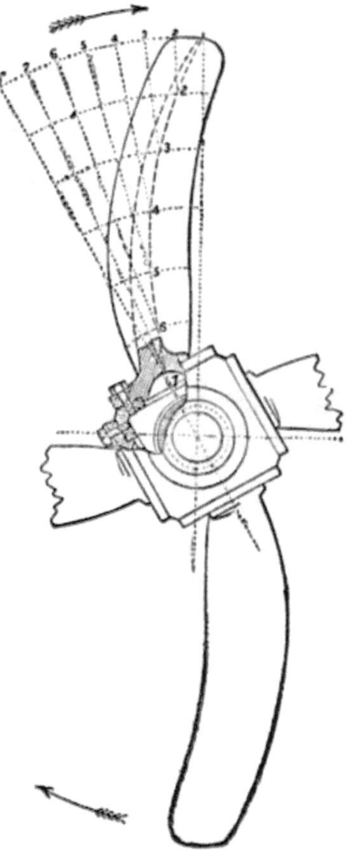

FIG. 289.

2. To arrange the *blades* of the screw so that they could be 'feathered,' that is, turned round on the boss, so as to be approximately in the fore-and-aft direction.

3. The fitting of 'Mangin' screws with narrow blades behind each

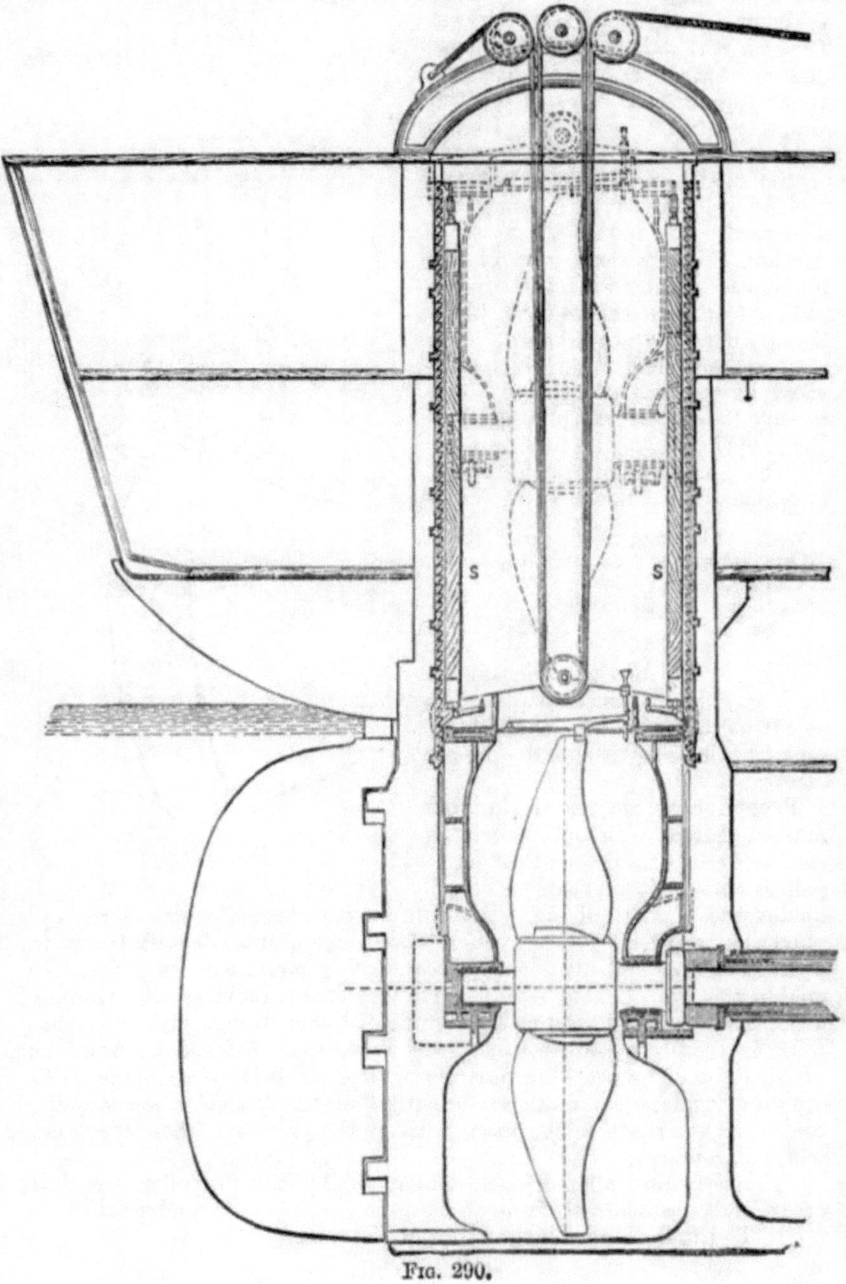

Fig. 290.

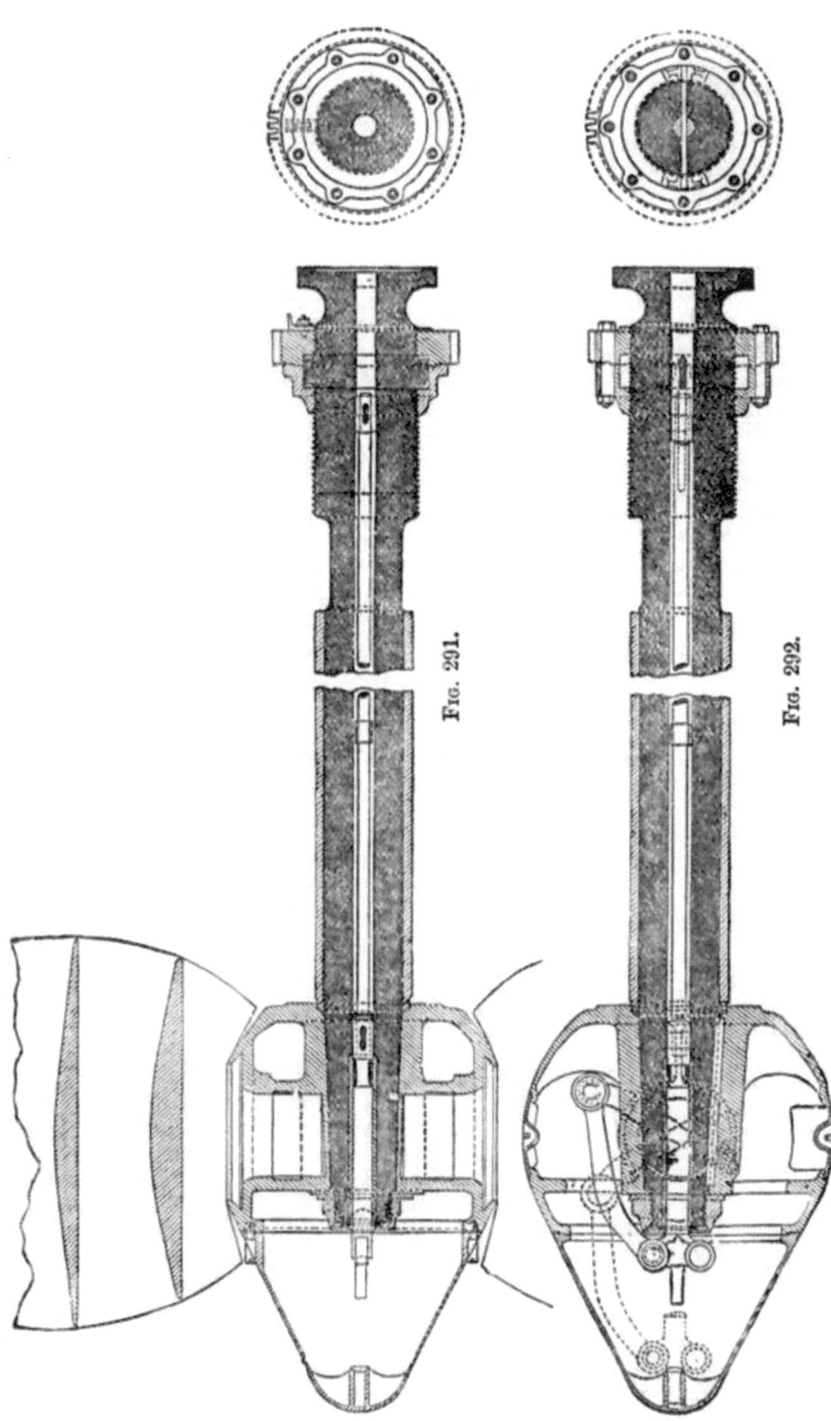
FIG. 291.
FIG. 292.

other, to reduce their transverse width and enable them to be more completely masked by the stern post.

Lifting screws.—The earlier single-screw ships in the Royal Navy were fitted on the first plan. A screw propeller of this description, with the necessary fittings, is shown in Fig. 290. On the end of the screw-shaft a gunmetal coupling called the *cheese-coupling* is keyed, having a rectangular slot running across it. The boss of the screw is cast with journals on its forward and after sides. The foremost journal has a T-head which fits into the slot in the cheese-coupling, by which the rotation of the shafting is transmitted to the propeller when in place. These journals are carried by bearings, fitted with strips of lignum-vitæ, in the ends of a frame called the 'banjo-frame.'

When lowered into the working position, these bearings drop into brackets or 'chairs' bolted to the stern- and rudder-posts. The banjo-frame works in guides on the stern- and rudder-posts, having ratchet teeth with safety catches to hold the propeller, in case of accident to the lifting gear while the screw is being raised. It is secured in the working position by struts, called 'Samson posts,' s, which butt against brackets at the top of the screw-well.

There were many serious objections to the application of lifting screws, also many practical difficulties attending their management and efficient maintenance, so that attention was soon turned to the design of arrangements enabling sails alone to be used without undue increase of resistance from the propeller when fixed vertically. The second and third of the above plans were therefore introduced.

Feathering screw.—In this the blades can be turned in an almost fore-and-aft direction, so that they produce but little retarding effect on the vessel. Mr. R. R. Bevis is the designer of probably the best of such arrangements, shown in Figs. 291 and 292. A short shaft or spindle, at the root of each blade, passes inside the hollow boss, and has an arm attached to it. The stern-shaft is hollow, and rods are carried through the shaft, from the ends of the arms to a collar near the forward end of the shaft, which collar can be moved forward or backward by a nut working over a thread cut on the outside of the shaft. The dotted lines in Fig. 292 show the arms when the blades are set at the working angle, and the full lines their positions when the blades are feathered and placed

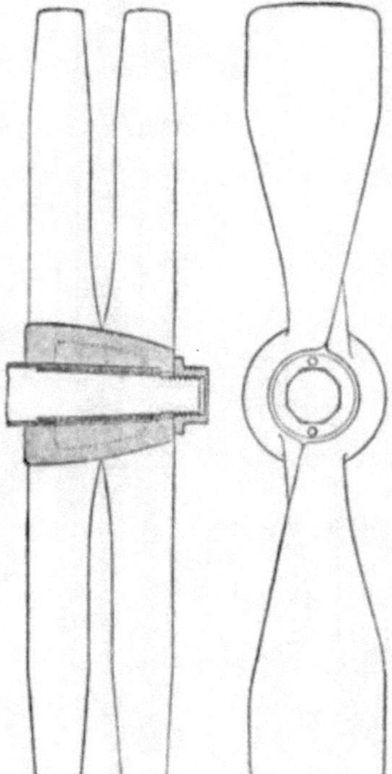

Fig. 293.

in a fore-and-aft direction. These propellers have been fitted to a large number of steam yachts and to several of the older ships in the Royal Navy.

Mangin screw-propeller.—The Mangin screw-propeller is shown in Fig. 293. It may be regarded as a two-bladed propeller in which each blade is cut in halves, with one half set immediately behind the other on the shaft, so that the width it occupies is only one-half that of an ordinary two-bladed screw, and its retarding effect on the ship would be correspondingly reduced. When the aggregate area of the four blades is equal to that of the two blades of an ordinary screw, there is little difference in the efficiency.

Modern screw-propellers.—These arrangements for providing for the application of sail power in steam vessels are now practically obsolete. Twin screws are now universal in the large vessels of the Royal Navy, and as sail power is thus not required to provide for possible breakdown of the machinery, the masts and sails, which are inconvenient and interfere with the fighting efficiency of a warship, are not now fitted. The following paragraphs describe the usual screw-propellers now fitted to various classes of vessel.

Number and pitch of blades.—The usual number of blades in screw-propellers are two, three, and four. Three- and four-bladed propellers appear equally efficient and suitable for large vessels. The blades are, except in small screws, cast separately from the boss, and are secured to it by bolts, generally forged of naval brass, manganese bronze, &c. Three- and four-bladed screws are now the most general. Two-bladed screws used to be fitted in cases where it was intended to lift the propeller out of the water when the ship was under sail.

The four-bladed screw-propeller with a single-screw ship has the effect of reducing *vibration* compared with a two-bladed screw, being more continuous in its action. There appears to be no advantage from any point of view in increasing the number of blades beyond four.

The pitch of the blades is generally uniform, but sometimes the pitch of the leading half of the blade, or the part that first acts on the water, is made less than that of the following half, to make the action gradual and decrease shock.

Material of propellers.—In the mercantile marine, screw-propellers are often made of cast-iron, for cheapness, the blades being cast on the boss so that the whole propeller forms a single casting. In the Royal Navy, and often in the mercantile marine, the screws are generally made of gunmetal, manganese bronze, phosphor bronze, &c. A cast-iron boss with manganese bronze blades is a common fitting in the mercantile marine, while in vessels such as torpedo-boat destroyers, a steel boss with blades made of some special alloy of bronze is common.

Screw-propellers can be made much thinner and lighter of gunmetal than of cast-iron, and still lighter if made of manganese bronze or some similar alloy. By this means the edgewise resistance is reduced, and by making the blades separate from the boss the whole screw is not destroyed in the event of damage to a single blade. Spare propeller-blades are always carried.

In some ships cast-steel is used for screw-propellers to thin the blades, but their backs have been found to suffer considerably from corrosion. This has been remedied in some cases by fitting a brass sleeve on the blade at this part.

Alteration of pitch.—The holes in the blade flanges of large propellers are made elongated, to allow the pitch of the screw to be adjusted slightly if necessary, by turning the blade round on the boss and fixing it in a different position. The extent of the variation of pitch allowed is from 2 to 3 feet. Filling pieces of brass or lignum-vitæ are supplied, for the spaces on either side of the bolts.

A slight alteration of the pitch is often found by the steam trials of vessels to be necessary to secure the best results. It is also desirable in some cases, especially in old vessels, when the working pressure of steam in the boilers is reduced as they become worn, for the *weight* of steam that can be produced by the boilers is practically constant for moderate alterations of pressure, and consequently, at the reduced pressures, the *volume* of the steam generated will be greater than at the original pressure. If it be desired to utilise all the steam at the lower pressures, it is generally necessary to drive the engines faster, and to do this the pitch of the screw requires to be reduced. With the much greater life of modern boilers, and having in view the margin of power generally existing when new, this operation is now much less common.

Shape of blades.—The acting surface or '*front*' of the blade, that is, its after face, preserves the exact geometrical form ; the form of the forward face or '*back*' of the blade is modified by the thickness neces-sary for strength, and is not a true screw-surface. The transverse sections of the blades approximate in shape to semi-ellipses, shallow at the ends and becoming fuller towards the root. The sections at various radii of a modern screw-propeller, and the angle of the screw at that section, are shown in Fig. 297.

As regards the form of blade, although the numbers of ideas on this point are innumerable, yet gain does not appear to be effected in practice by departing much from the elliptical form with the extremities of the transverse axis at the centre and tip respectively, as shown in Fig. 297. This is now the general form of the expanded surfaces of the blades of H.M. ships, and it has given more satisfaction on the whole than other shapes. The surfaces of the blades should be made as smooth as possible, to reduce friction.

Propeller diameter and pitch.—Many rules have been proposed for determining the most suitable diameter, area, &c., of screw-pro-pellers, but they fail to be of much service unless the conditions are very similar, so that most propellers are now designed from experience obtained in previous similar vessels, and the results of trials made with differently proportioned screws. In the Royal Navy experiments with model screws are made in the large tank at Haslar, and most of the screws for large naval vessels are now proportioned from trial data obtained from this source.

These experiments are made on screws of elliptical form with the extremities of the axes at the centre and circumference of the screw respectively, the breadth of the ellipse being one-fifth the diameter. It appears that there is a wide range of 'pitch ratio,' i.e. the ratio of pitch to diameter, which can be adopted without material change of efficiency, provided in all cases that the amount of blade area allowed is properly proportioned to the pitch ratio adopted. As the diameter is reduced, so the pitch should increase for the standard elliptical blade, and the blade area will also be reduced.

The power and revolutions of the engines being first determined,

and the speed estimated, the results of the experiments may be indicated
in the form of a curve, a sample of which, for a large battleship, is shown
in Fig. 294. This curve gives the corresponding pitches and diameters
for either three-bladed or four-bladed propellers of the standard shape, the
pitch being practically the same for either three- or four-bladed screws.
Any diameter inside the limits shown can be adopted, provided the
corresponding pitch given by a vertical ordinate is also used. For
example, the dotted vertical line A B C shows that for a pitch of

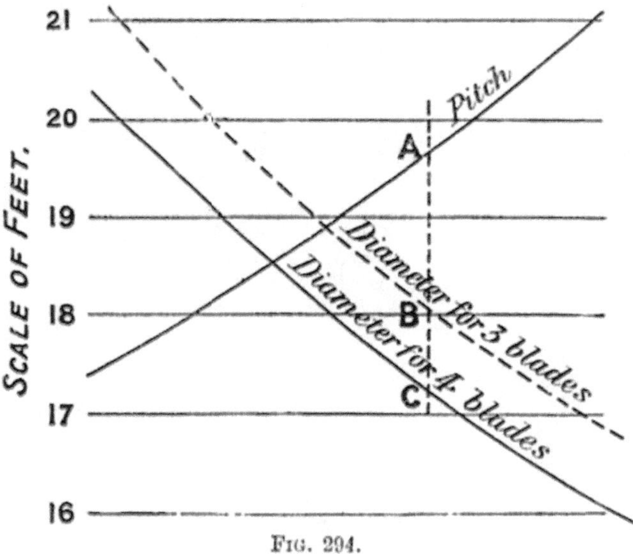

FIG. 294.

19·6 ft. the corresponding diameter for a four-bladed screw is 17 ft.
3 in., and for a three-bladed screw about 18 ft. It will be seen that
the variation of pitch and diameter permissible is considerable.
Generally a point near the middle of the curves is selected. Knowing
the shape of the standard blade and the size of the boss, the blade area
can then be calculated.

With torpedo boats and destroyers the system of actually trying
various propellers has been found essential, and it is very remarkable
how appreciable an effect even apparently small changes in propellers
have on the speeds of the boats.

Expanded surface of blades.—This is the surface obtained by
assuming the actual width of the blade at various distances from the
centre to be laid off on a plane surface ; this area may be imagined to
be obtained by flattening or untwisting the propeller-blade, and is
shown at A in Fig. 297. The area provided is as follows in the recent
vessels for Her Majesty's Navy :—For four-bladed propellers of battleships, ·012 to ·014 square foot per I.H.P. ; for three-bladed propellers
of quick-running cruisers, ·007 to ·009 square foot per I.H.P., while for
the quicker running torpedo-boat destroyers it varies between ·005
to ·007 square foot per I.H.P.

In the mercantile marine the areas are larger. They vary considerably, depending on the speed. For ocean single-screw passenger steamers, however, ·02 sq. ft. per I.H.P. is a common value, while ocean cargo steamers have considerably more area, ·06 sq. ft. per I.H.P. being not uncommon.

Strength of propeller-blades.—The propeller-blade should be strong enough to withstand its share of the twisting moment on the shaft, but it should be weaker than the shaft with reference to the straining action of a blow from a hard substance on the tip of the blade. The moment of resistance of the blade in going from the boss to the tip should also diminish faster than the moment of such a blow, so that if fracture resulted it should take place as near to the tip of the blade as possible, so that the broken blade may be still useful for propulsion.

In Fig. 295 let A represent the axis of the shaft, the circle G D H the boss of the propeller, and A B a radius drawn from centre of shaft to tip of blade. Let A C, perpendicular to A B, represent the calculated thickness of blade near the axis, and join C B. Then the triangle B A C will represent the section through the centre of a blade that fulfils the condition of gradually diminishing in strength from the centre to the tip, since the strength of any section varies as the square of the depth. In practice the end of the blade cannot be reduced to a point as shown ; so from B, a distance B E must be set off equal to the minimum practicable thickness, and a line E F drawn parallel to the face A B. The point F will then be the point at which it will give way if fractured by a blow on the tip.

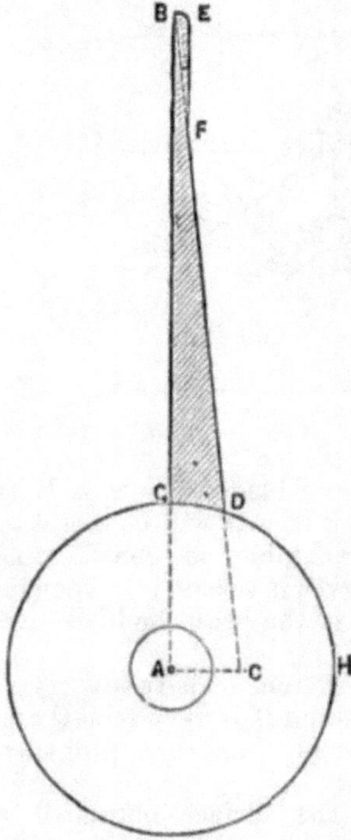

Fig. 295.

Details of modern propellers.—Figs. 296 to 298 show the usual form of four-bladed screw-propeller now fitted in the Navy. The blades are bolted to a boss, about a quarter the diameter of the propeller, secured on the end of the screw-shaft. The hole through the boss, and the shaft, is tapered, and the screw is driven by the action of a longitudinal key or feather let into the shaft, and fitting into a suitable key-way cut in the boss. The end of the shaft is screwed, and the propeller boss is kept in its place by means of a cap-nut, secured by a keep-plate, which prevents corrosive action of the water on the end of the shaft.

The nut and end of the propeller have a conical tail-piece secured over them, to reduce the loss by eddying motion and to prevent fouling of ropes, &c. The gunmetal liner on the shaft is recessed into the boss, and a small stuffing-box fitted to prevent the access of water to the shaft at its junction with the propeller. The holes in the flanges of the blades are elongated, as previously described, to enable the pitch of the screw to be adjusted, and brass or lignum-vitæ stops are fitted between the bolts and the edges of the holes to prevent the blade shifting.

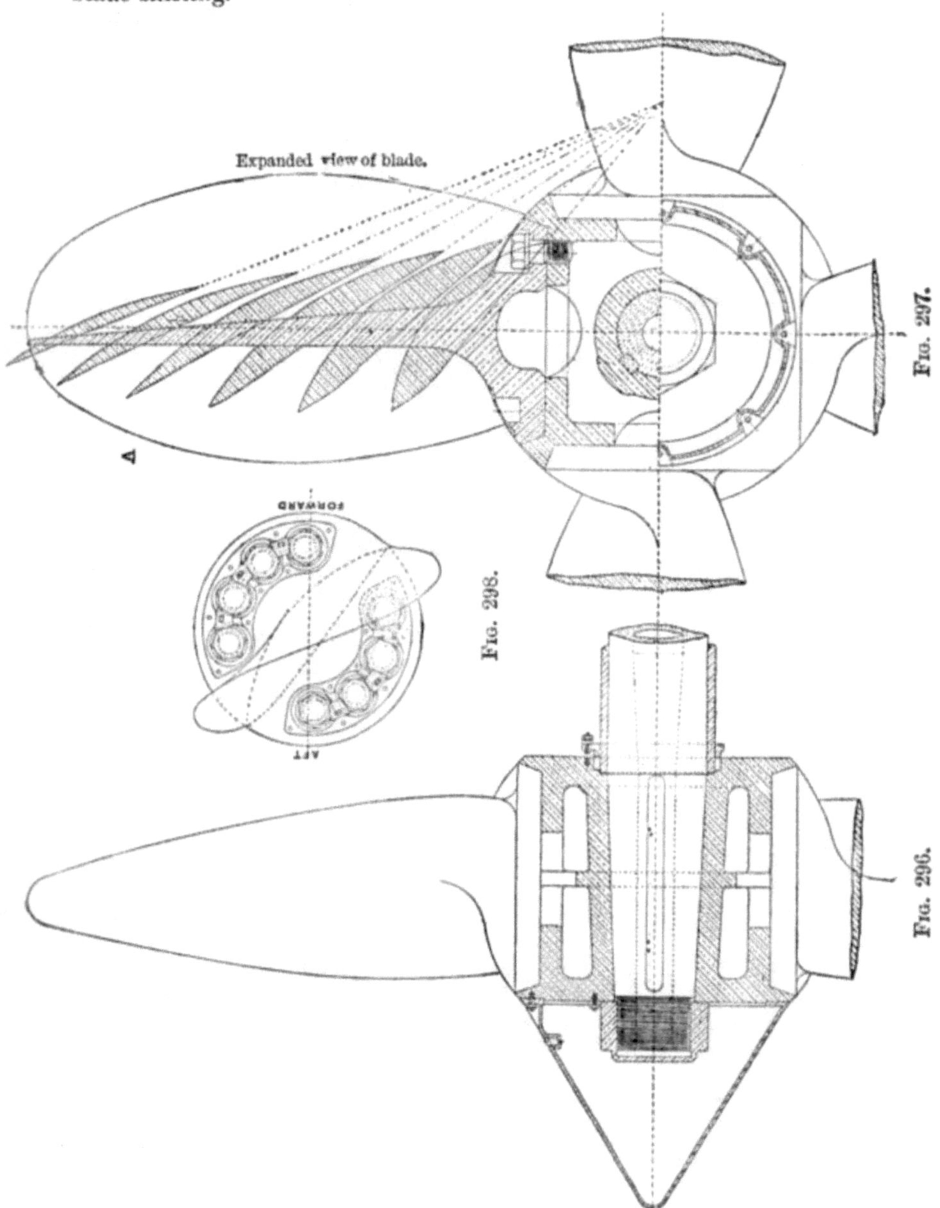

The flanges of the blades are recessed into the boss, and the heads of the bolts securing the blades are recessed into the flange, these latter recesses being covered with plates. Keep-plates are fitted between the bolt-heads to prevent any slacking back. By this means the spherical form of the boss is preserved, and resistance in the water reduced.

The whole of the propeller, except the bolts, is usually of gunmetal,

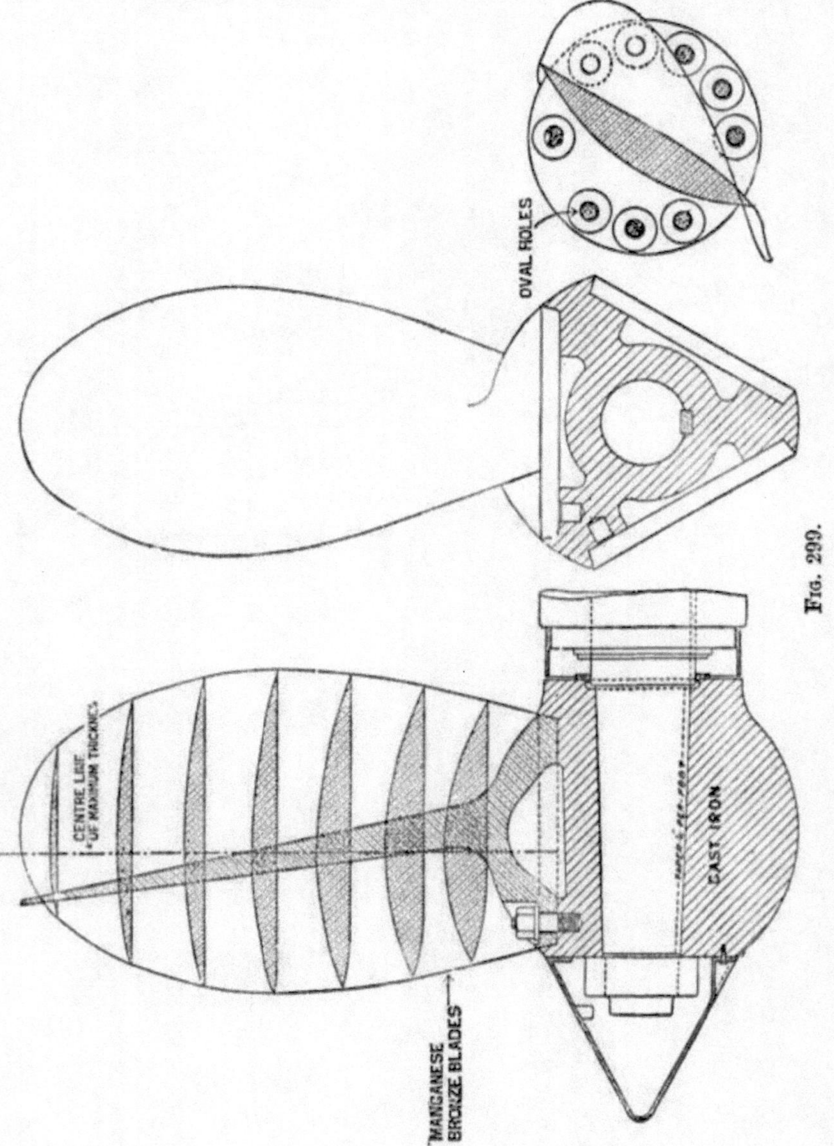

the bolts being made of some forged metal, such as naval brass. The blades are often of manganese bronze. The three-bladed screws are of similar construction.

Fig. 299 shows a three-bladed propeller as fitted in the mercantile marine. Its construction is somewhat similar to the preceding. The boss is, in this case, of cast-iron, the blades are of manganese bronze, and provision is made for slightly altering the pitch by elongating the bolt-holes.

Fig. 300 shows a propeller of entirely different construction, and represents that of a torpedo-boat destroyer, making about 400 revolutions per minute. These screws are generally three-bladed, and have a certain amount of slope astern as we proceed from boss to tip. The blades in the example shown are keyed to the boss, but they are often cast in one with it.

Stern-tube.—Where the shafting passes through the hull of the ship and enters the water, special means are provided to insure the watertightness of the hull, and to obtain sufficient support for the shafting. This consists of the '*stern-tube*,' which, in ships of the Royal Navy, is generally made of gunmetal, while in merchant steamers it is frequently made of cast-iron. In wood and composite ships the stern-tube is fitted in a wrought-iron or steel casing built into the stern of the ship, and bored out to receive it. This additional casing is also fitted in the Royal Navy to most steel ships with twin screws. Figs. 301 to 303 show the stern-tube.

The outer casing or tube is called the shipbuilder's stern-tube, and consists of a tube of steel plate built into the framework of the vessel. At the ends, where the engineer's stern-tube bears on it, steel stiffening bushes are fitted. These are bored out to fit the bearings on the engineer's tube. The bushes are attached each to two frames of the vessel, specially stiffened to carry and distribute the weight of the shafting. With twin screws, where the shafting leaves the ship at the side, the frames and plating are bossed out to surround the stern-tube for some distance aft. The stern-tube is generally placed in its bearing from inside the ship, a flange being provided on the forward end for the attachment to the ship.

The bearings, or rubbing parts, of the stern-tube are fitted with strips of lignum-vitæ, between which the water can pass freely to lubricate the shaft. Originally brass bearings were used, but it was found that they wore away very rapidly, as with metal on metal under water, the pressure that can be safely carried is much less than with lignum-vitæ. The lignum-vitæ at the after end of the tube is now often carried in a separate bush made in halves, which can be withdrawn for examination at any time without removing the shaft.

To prevent water passing into the ship, a stuffing-box is fitted where the shaft leaves the stern-tube at the inner end, with a gland known as the 'stern gland' which, when the engines are at work, is slackened to allow a little water to run through and keep the rubbing parts cool. A cock and passage are fitted as shown, to enable water to be drawn off when required, to ascertain the temperature of the rubbing surfaces. Gear is fitted to the stern gland to insure all the nuts being screwed up and slacked back equally. The six nuts and pinions being marked A in the figure, while the keeps for securing the circular rack are marked B, and are three in number. Fig. 304 shows the stern-tube of a single-screw mercantile vessel, which will be readily understood from the preceding description.

Stern shafting.—The length of propeller shafting, which passes

THREE STEEL STUDS
G.M. NUTS
TAPER 1 INCH TO THE FOOT
STEEL RING
STEEL PIN AT FORD END
SEE SECTION FOR CONTINUATION OF TAIL PIECE
ANGLE AT POINT
ANGLE AT ROOT

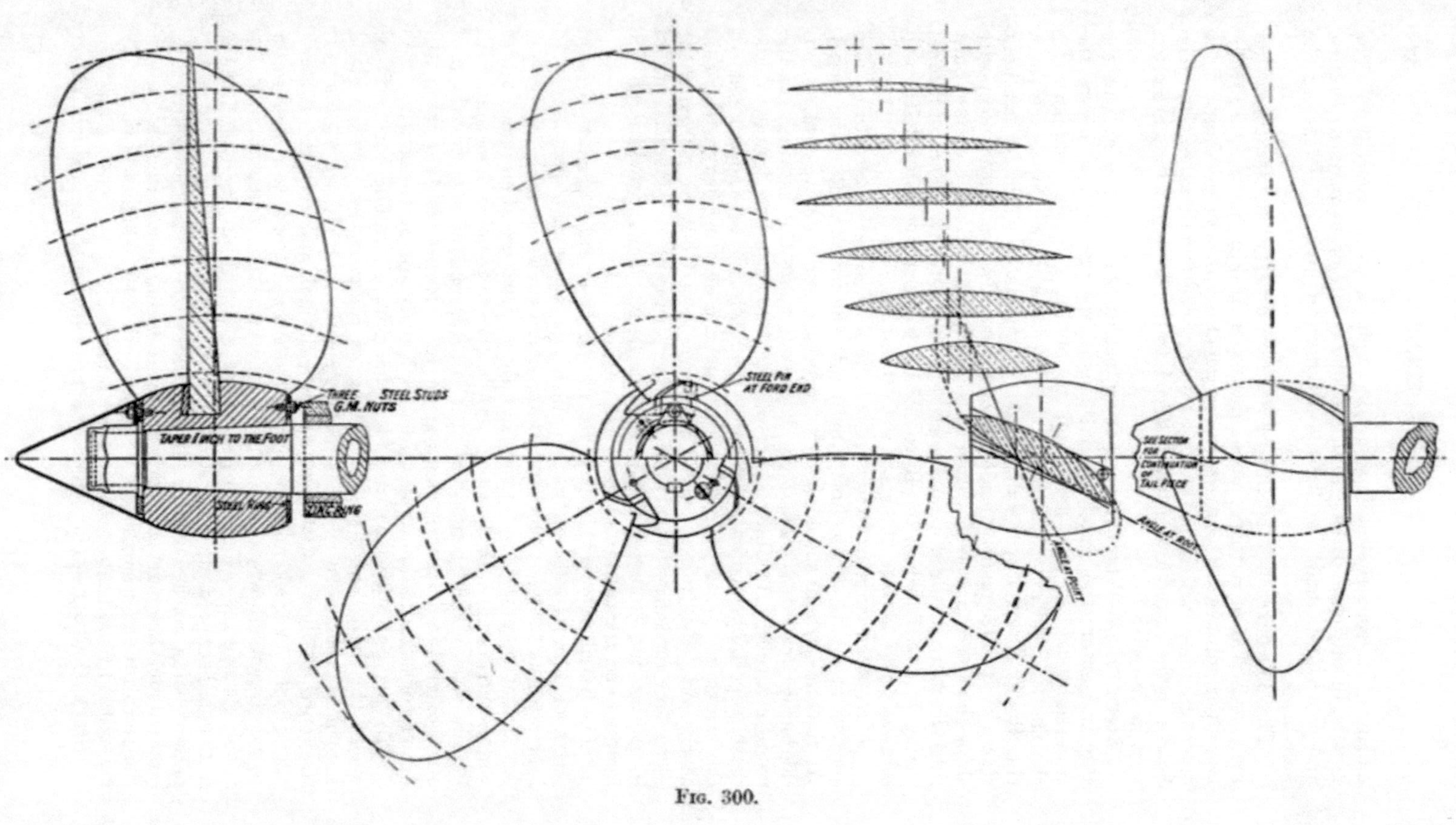

Fig. 300.

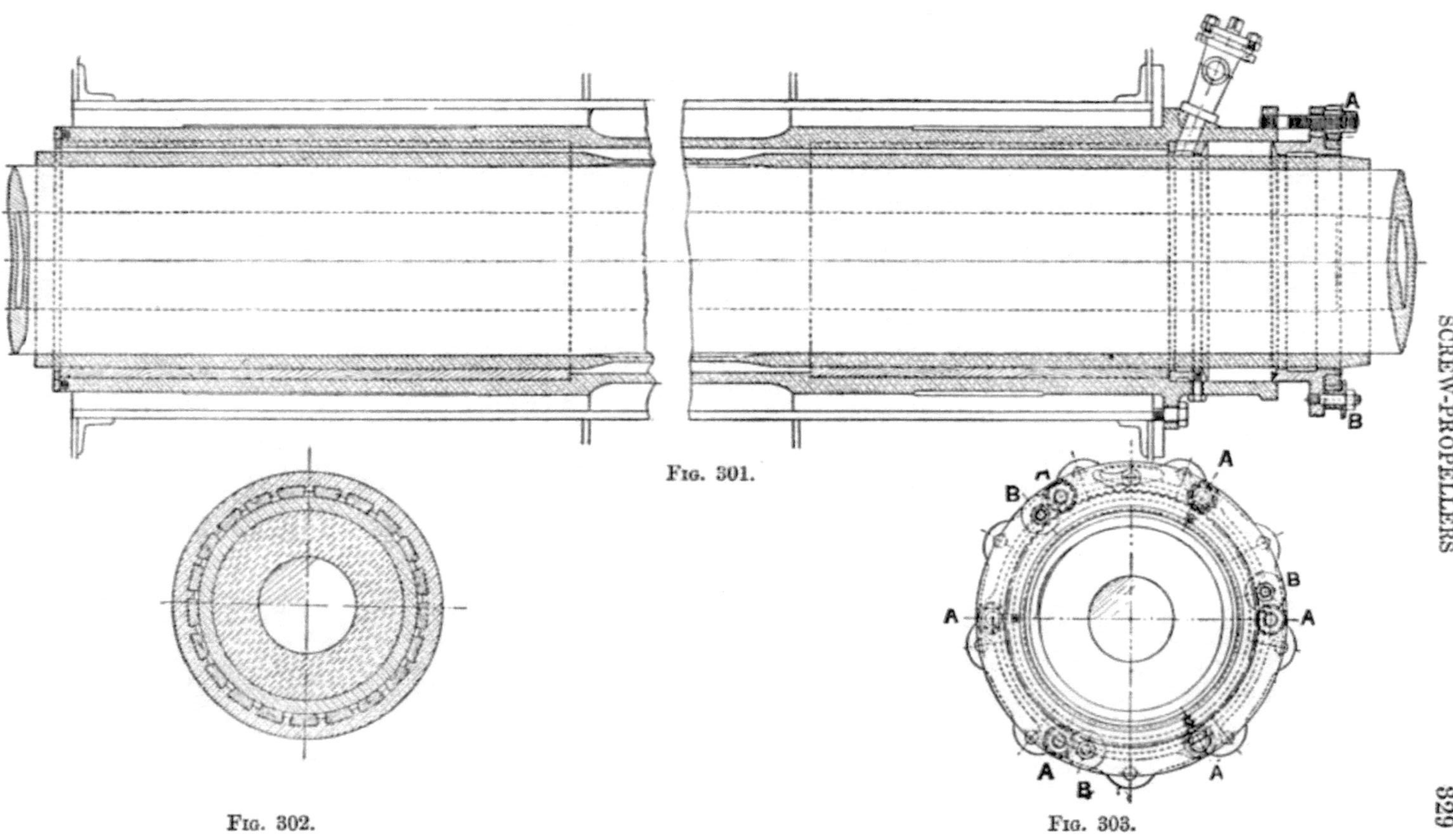

Fig. 301.

Fig. 302.

Fig. 303.

through the stern-tube, is covered with a gunmetal sleeve or casing. This is generally cast separate, and after being turned and bored is forced on by hydraulic power, after being slightly warmed. Sometimes this casing is cast around the shaft, which in this case is usually grooved, to prevent the sleeve turning, the shaft itself being made hot before the metal is cast around it, but the greatest care is necessary to prevent the shaft bending and to insure a sound casting. The former method is the better.

The casing inside the stern-tube is in one piece unless it is too long to be so cast, in which case it is fitted in two lengths tightly filleted into each other, and usually brazed at the junctions, for if there should be any leakage, the shaft will decay at the joints from galvanic action. Two methods of forming this joint are shown in Figs. 305 and 306. Studs should be screwed through the casing into the shaft to prevent any change in its position by the working of the engines. The parts of the casing at the ends of the shaft which work in the lignum-vitæ bearings should be thick and fit solidly on the shaft. The intermediate portion, which simply protects the shaft from the action of the water, is generally made much lighter. In the mercantile marine, the intermediate portion of the sleeve is frequently dispensed with, the shaft being cased with gunmetal only at the bearings, and the centre part either left bare or lapped with wire and painted. This construction is shown in Fig. 304.

Arrangements for copper sheathed vessels.—If the vessel be sheathed with wood and coppered, the copper exercises a powerful galvanic action on all exposed steel surfaces under water, so that in twin-screw ships it is necessary to cover the whole of the shafting under water with gunmetal sheathing similar to that described for the shafting in the stern-tube. In this case the casing is always in lengths, tightly filleted into one another, and in addition well brazed at the junctions. The space between the shaft and the casing is usually filled with some protective material. Any couplings in the shafting under water will also require to be fitted with a gunmetal casing. Sketches of the gunmetal casing over the coupling under water are given in Figs. 307 and 308. Whether the ship be sheathed with copper or not, the part of the shafting which passes through the stern bracket in twin-screw ships is always cased with gunmetal, which works on lignum-vitæ placed in a bush fitted to carry it, in the stern bracket.

Thrust arrangements.—In the older single-screw ships, the propeller being situated at a very strong part of the hull, arrangements were made for part of the forward thrust to be taken directly on the stern-post ; a ring or disc, lined with lignum-vitæ, was fitted on the after-face of the stern-post for the forward end of the propeller boss to press against and drive the ship forward (see Fig. 290). The whole of the astern thrust was taken inboard by an ordinary thrust bearing on the shaft such as is described in Chapter XXI. In addition, when lifting screws were fitted, as there was no rigid connection between the propeller and shafting, an additional disc fitted with lignum-vitæ was required, at the after end of the propeller on the rudder-post, to take the backward thrust, the rudder-post being made strong enough for this purpose.

In twin-screw vessels the propellers cannot press directly on the

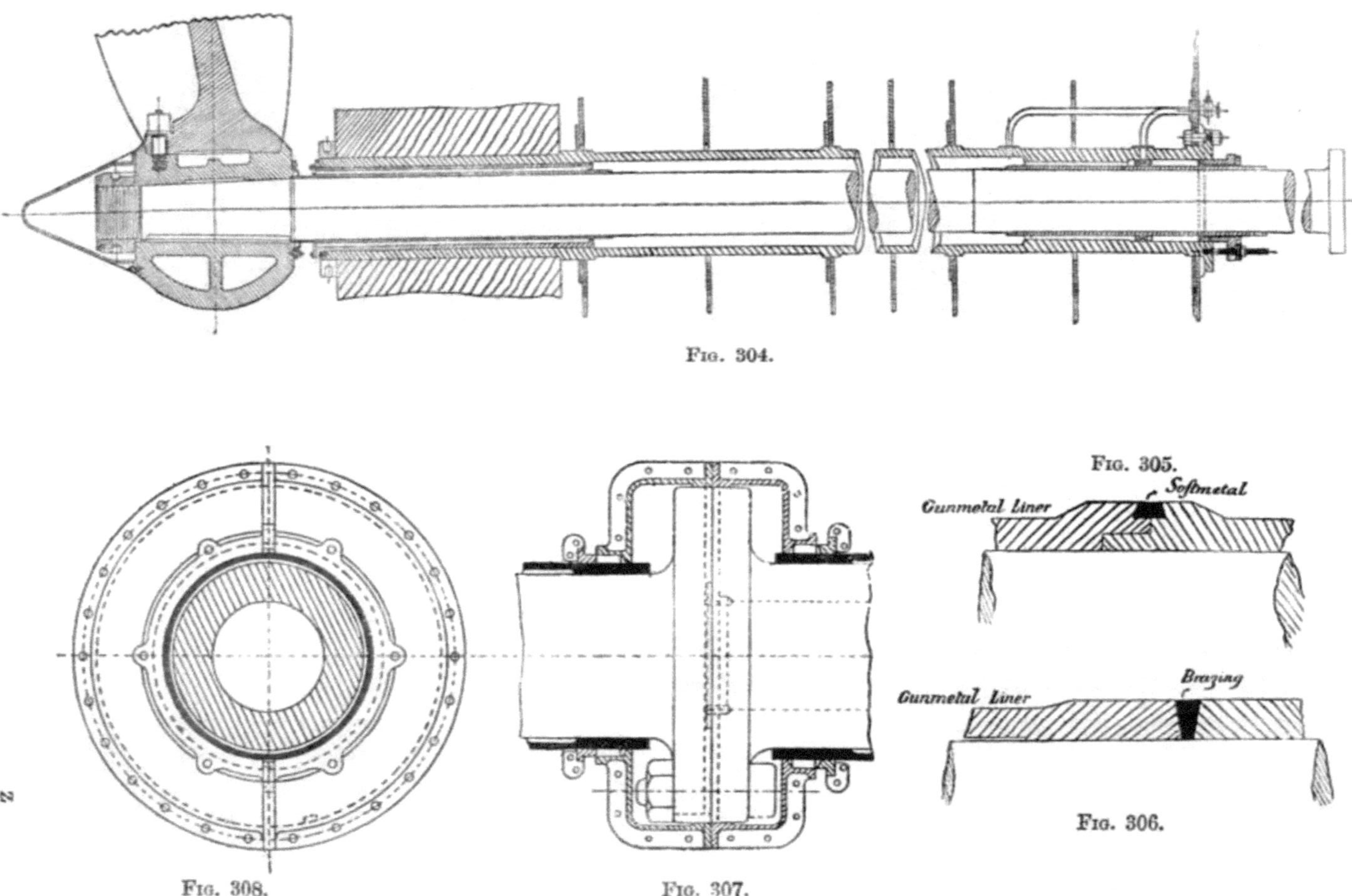

Fig. 304.

Fig. 305.

Fig. 306.

Fig. 307.

Fig. 308.

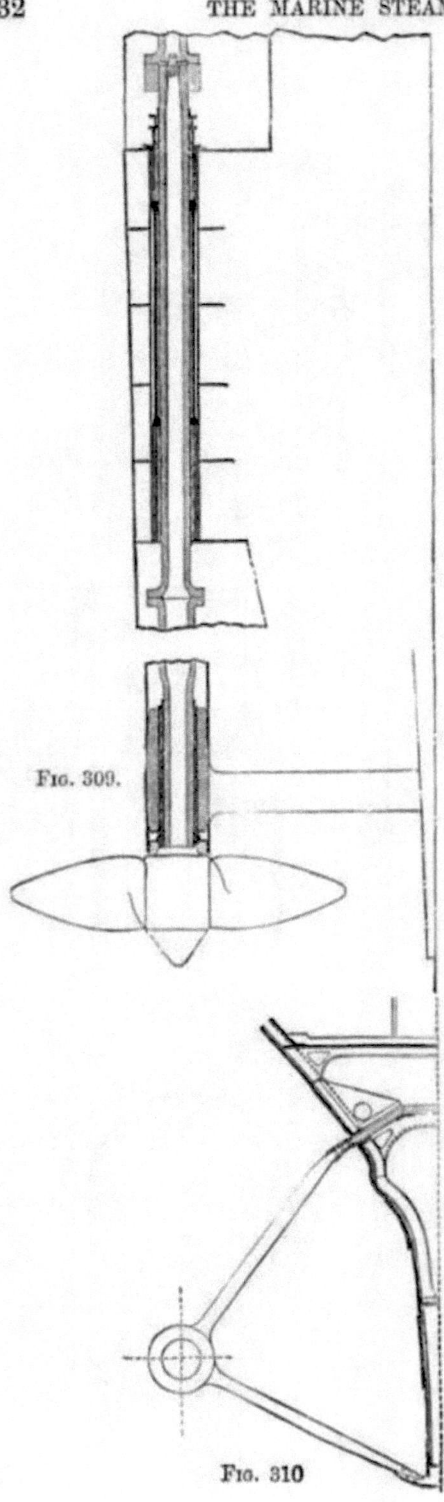

Fig. 309.

Fig. 310

stern, and the shaft brackets are incapable of taking the thrust, so that in such cases both ahead and astern thrusts must be wholly taken inboard, by means of a thrust-block on the shafting.

This system of taking the whole of the thrust both ahead and astern by means of a thrust-block fitted inside the vessel is a satisfactory method, the thrust-blocks being very efficient. They can be always under observation, and can be easily adjusted and kept in proper order. Besides being adopted for twin-screw ships, its convenience has led to its adoption in single-screw ships, so that the single-screw mercantile marine vessels are also generally without any outboard thrust arrangements, and depend on the inboard thrust-block to take the whole thrust. In Fig. 304, showing the stem tube and propeller of a modern single-screw mercantile vessel, there is no outer thrust bearing.

Shaft Brackets. — In twin-screw ships, the propellers on either side of the ship usually work outwards when driving the ship ahead; but in many recent war-vessels, as the result of experiments made in the Admiralty experimental tank at Haslar, they are made to turn inwards. These experiments, made on models, indicated a slight increase in efficiency, so that, as it is more convenient from the engineer's point of view for the screws to turn inwards, the starting platforms being then both in the front of the engines at the middle line, the plan has been adopted in many ships for the Royal Navy. Experience with engines so arranged has, however, caused some adverse criticism as regards the power of the screws to turn the ship when working one ahead and one astern, which appears to be reduced.

The after parts of the propeller shafting pass outside the ship and work in bearings close to the propellers, carried by brackets secured rigidly to the hull. In the older high-speed ships, in which the after run is very fine, the length of the shafting outside the ship is so great that intermediate bearings, between the stern-tube and the after-bracket, have been fitted, but the resistance of these additional bracket-bearings is great, and they have not often been fitted to modern vessels. In modern ships, hollow steel shafts, of enlarged diameter between the bearings to give increased stiffness, are fitted, to dispense with the intermediate bearings and their resistance.

Figs. 309 and 310 show the stern and propeller fittings of modern high-speed twin-screw warships. The bush carrying the lignum-vitæ in the after bracket is in these sketches withdrawn by removing the propeller and drawing the bush aft, but as this involves considerable work, these bushes in the more modern vessels are made in halves, and arranged so that it can be withdrawn forward so that the propeller need not be disturbed.

CHAPTER XXVI.

THE INDICATOR AND INDICATOR DIAGRAMS.

WE will now proceed to describe the apparatus which enables the engineer to ascertain many facts of the greatest importance as to the action of the steam inside the cylinder. This instrument is called the steam-engine indicator, or, shortly, the 'indicator.' Unfortunately, even when the indicator has told us all it can, regarding the interior economy of the steam-engine, there remains much respecting which our knowledge is very imperfect.

The steam-engine indicator is an instrument which shows the pressure of steam in the cylinder at each point of the stroke of the piston. This pressure varies considerably, and is shown for both the outward and inward strokes, which enables the effective pressure at any point of the stroke of the piston to be ascertained, and the mean effective pressure on the piston during the stroke to be calculated.

General features of indicators.—The general features of the instrument are as follows :—A pencil is attached by means of a system of levers to the piston of a small cylinder of known area, open to the atmosphere at the top, and connected by means of stopcocks and pipes to either end of the engine cylinder as required. When the stopcock is open, so as to place the bottom of the indicator cylinder in connection with one end of the engine cylinder, the indicator piston, carrying the pencil, is moved up and down by the varying pressures of the steam, the motion of the indicator piston being resisted by the action of a spiral spring of known elastic force. A sheet of paper is fixed on a barrel, which is caused to revolve backward and forward in a manner coincident with the motion of the engine piston, and on this moving paper the pencil traces a curve or diagram, from which, at any given part of the stroke of the engine, the corresponding pressures of steam in the engine cylinder may be measured. From the mean effective pressure ascertained from this diagram the I.H.P. of the engines is ascertained. This determination of the horse-power is the principal use of the indicator. By means of the indicator diagram, however, many other particulars relative to the action of the steam in the cylinders, and the adjustment and condition of the slide-valves and pistons, may be ascertained ; and many improvements that have been made in the performance and efficiency of steam-engines have been largely assisted by the application of this instrument.

The following important particulars may be seen by inspection of the diagrams :—

(1) Whether the admission of steam is early or late, the amount that the initial pressure in the cylinder is below the boiler or receiver

pressure, and whether the pressure is well maintained up to the point of cut-off or not.

(2) The part of the stroke of the piston at which the admission of steam to the cylinder is cut off, and whether the cut-off is sharp or gradual.

(3) At what point and pressure the steam is admitted to the condenser.

(4) The amount of back pressure or vacuum, whether the reduction is obtained quickly or not, and the amount of compression at the end of the stroke.

It must be borne in mind, however, that as the indicator shows only the pressure at each point of the stroke, the engineer has to account for peculiarities in the form of the diagram by reasoning, and errors are here often committed.

The indicator in a crude form was invented by James Watt. Since his time its construction has been simplified and perfected, McNaught being one of the earliest to effect improvements.

McNaught's indicator.—In the McNaught indicator, which did excellent service with engines fitted with low steam pressures and moving at slow speeds, the pencil is attached directly to the indicator piston, so that their extent of motion is the same. Consequently, they are unsuitable for quick-moving, high-pressure engines, as the necessarily long springs used in them have to be instantly compressed to a considerable extent on the admission of steam, and in quick-moving engines this causes violent oscillation of the pencil and a series of undulations resulting in a serrated diagram which is almost useless as an indication of the action of the steam in the cylinder.

Modern indicators.—To obtain satisfactory diagrams it has been found necessary to fit springs of high tension so as to permit of only a small motion of the piston. This reduces vibration, but to obtain a sufficient height of diagram it necessitates that the motion of the pencil be much greater than that of the indicator piston. The various types of modern indicators differ principally in the means of producing this multiplication, while still keeping the pencil moving in a straight line, and preserving a constant ratio (4 to 6) between the motions of piston and pencil. The difficulty with such motions is not so much to make the pencil move in a straight line, as to insure that it also moves, throughout its range, exactly the same number of times faster than the indicator piston.

The following features are common to all modern indicators, sketches of two of which are given in Figs. 312 and 313. At the lower end of a cylindrical case, A B, is the small steam cylinder in which a piston works practically steamtight, with as little friction as possible. To the lower end of this cylinder a straightway cock, c, is fitted, shown only in Fig. 312, with its end screwed to enable it to be attached to the nozzle of a right-angled three-way cock, called the *indicator cock*, which is connected by pipes to the two ends of the engine cylinder, so that the indicator may be placed in communication with either side of the piston as desired, enabling the two diagrams showing the pressures of the steam on both sides of the piston to be taken on one card. Sometimes the indicator is connected directly to each end of the cylinder, so as to get separate diagrams, which is often desirable in very quick-moving engines, especially in cases where a fair lead of pipes cannot be readily obtained to enable the two diagrams to be taken on the same sheet.

The upper end, B, of the cylinder is always open to the atmosphere; also, to enable a connection to be made between the under side of the indicator piston and the atmosphere, small holes are made in the shell and plug of the cock C, so that when this cock is shut as regards the supply of steam to the indicator, these small holes open up a connection between the bottom of the indicator and the atmosphere.

A spiral spring of known tension is attached to the piston and also

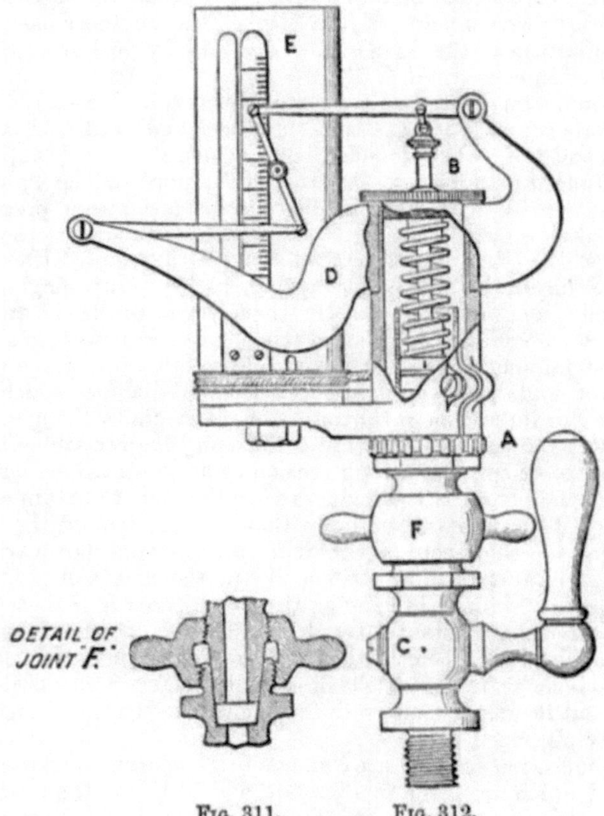

Fig. 311.   Fig. 312.

to the top of the casing, and this spring resists the motion of the piston, when acted on by the steam pressure underneath, or by the atmospheric pressure above when the pressure of steam below is less than that of the atmosphere.

The pencil is generally a small brass wire, the paper being specially prepared to enable the wire to mark it. E is a brass drum on which the diagram paper is wrapped and held by clips. This paper cylinder is caused to revolve around a vertical axis by means of a cord deriving its motion from any reciprocating part of the engine that has the same motion as the engine piston, the extent of motion being suitably reduced by means of levers, &c., to cause the paper cylinder to make about three-fourths of a revolution for each stroke of the engine. The tension is kept on the string, and the paper cylinder brought back to its original position as the engine piston returns, by the action of a spring inside the drum, E. It is very important that the point to which the cord is attached has an exactly corresponding motion to that of the engine piston, but on a smaller scale.

Richards' indicator.—This instrument was the first of the modern indicators with reduced travel of piston to come into use, and its application has for many years been very successful. A sketch of this instrument is given in Fig. 312.

The pencil, instead of being attached directly to the piston-rod, as in the early indicator, is worked by a lever of the third order, the extent of the motion of the piston being only one-fourth that of the pencil, which latter has an extreme travel of $3\frac{1}{8}$ inches. The parallelism of the pencil is maintained by an arrangement of light steel rods, carried by a movable brass bracket, D, fitted on the top of a cylinder. This bracket can be moved round the cylinder by hand, to bring the pencil on or off the metallic paper wound round the barrel.

Crosby's and other 'high-speed' indicators.—Another type of indicator has come into extensive use during the last few years for obtaining improved diagrams from engines of high pressure, working at high rates of speed, such engines as those of torpedo boats, and torpedo-boat destroyers, which often run at over 400 revolutions per minute, with steam pressures of 250 lbs. per square inch in the boilers. It will be readily understood that obtaining satisfactory diagrams from such engines is a work of some difficulty.

In the Richards instrument the rods of the parallel motion are made very light, but it will be seen that there are several rods in the neighbourhood of the pencil, which move up and down through the same distance as the pencil. At very high pressures and speeds, therefore, the momentum of these moving rods produces a slight disturbance in the diagram, and it is important to reduce the weight of the moving parts in the neighbourhood of the pencil as much as possible when the indicator is intended for use with exceptionally high pressures and speeds.

There are several types of indicator in which this is sought to be accomplished, two of which, Crosby's and Darke's, have been used in the Royal Navy for some years, and have given satisfaction. Crosby's high-speed indicator is shown in Fig. 313. In this indicator the motion of the indicator piston is reduced to only one-sixth that of the pencil. The parallel motion and pencil attachment are very light, and the moving parts are few in number, so that there is very little disturbance of the diagram due to the momentum of comparatively heavy moving parts. The spring of the pencil drum is in this indicator a short spiral, instead of a volute spring, as in most other indicators. The upper side of the indicator piston is open to the atmosphere by means of the hole shown. The remaining features of the apparatus will be readily understood from the diagram.

Method of taking indicator diagrams.—The indicator pipes from both ends of the cylinder must first be blown through to clear them from water. The indicator being fixed in position, the string is connected to the indicator lever, and its length adjusted by means of a running loop, to give the proper movement to the paper cylinder. A sheet of prepared paper is stretched smoothly on the paper cylinder, and the ends secured by the spring clips. The indicator cock, and the cock c, are then opened, and the indicator piston allowed to move up and down *till the apparatus is thoroughly warmed* before any part of the diagram is drawn. This will be after a few revolutions of the engine. The handle of the stop cock c should then be turned horizontally to the position in which the bottom of the indicator piston is in communication with the atmosphere.

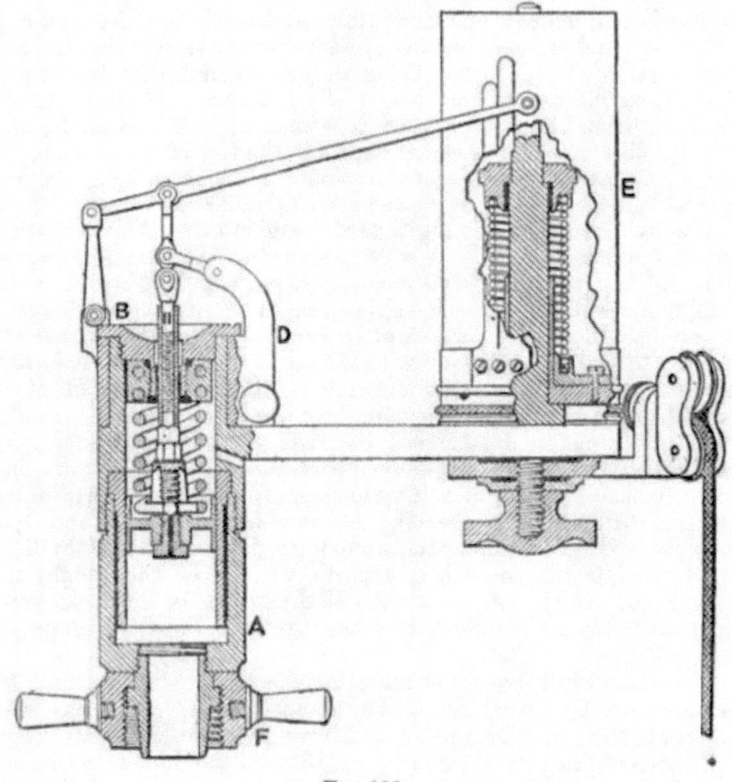

Fig. 313.

In this position the pencil, on being pressed against the revolving paper, will trace a straight line, which will represent the atmospheric pressure, and is called the atmospheric line of the diagram. This is marked c d in Fig. 314.

The cock c on the instrument is then opened for steam, and the indicator cock below it set to make connection with one end of the engine cylinder ; the indicator piston will move up and down according to the variation of pressure in the cylinder, and if the pencil be slightly pressed against the paper the combination of the motions of the paper and pencil causes the latter to trace out a curve such as A B D R C in Fig. 314. A stop is fitted to the revolving arm which prevents the pencil being pressed too heavily against the paper. The pencil traces the part A B Q D during one stroke of the piston, and on the return stroke traces the lower part D R C.

This diagram shows the pressures of the steam on one side of the piston only, during a complete revolution. To ascertain the pressures on the other side of the piston, the indicator cock must be so placed as to open up communication between the indicator piston and the opposite end of the cylinder, when a similar diagram, but reversed, will be obtained. The cocks are then closed, and the diagram removed from the drum.

On the diagrams, besides the time and date, there should be marked the scale of the diagram—i.e. the number of pounds pressure each vertical inch represents—the amount of steam and receiver pressures, and the vacuum shown by the gauges, also the number of revolutions per minute the engine was making at the time the diagram was taken, and the fraction of cut-off of the steam, as shown by the indexes of the links.

Absolute pressure at any point.—If a horizontal line be drawn at a distance below C D, equal, on the given scale, to the atmospheric pressure, say 14·7 pounds per square inch, this line O N will be the *zero line*, or line of no pressure, and all ordinates measured from this base line will represent *absolute pressures* of steam per square inch.

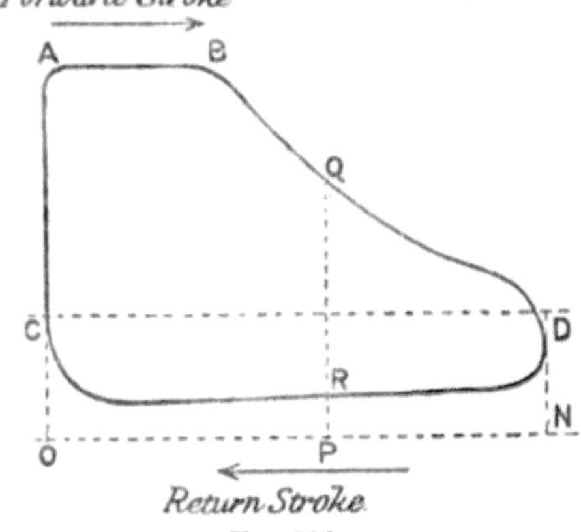

Fig. 314.

The total length O N of the diagram represents the length of stroke of the piston of the engine, and at the part of the stroke represented by the point P—i.e. when the piston has travelled the fraction $\dfrac{O\,P}{O\,N}$ of its stroke—the forward absolute pressure on the piston will be P Q. When the piston has completed its stroke, and returned to the position P on the return stroke, the absolute pressure on the same side of the piston is represented by P R. This pressure P R is now a back pressure—that is, it resists the motion of the piston.

Mean pressure.—It is clear that the mean of all the distances, such as P Q, will be the mean *forward* pressure during, say, the forward stroke, while the mean of all the distances such as P R will be the mean *back* pressure during the return stroke. The difference between these two pressures—that is, the mean of all the distances, such as Q R, or the mean height of the indicator diagram—is the *mean effective pressure* on this side of the piston during two strokes.

We also have a similar diagram from the other side of the piston, the average height of which gives us the mean effective pressure on the other side during two strokes. It follows, therefore, that the mean of the average heights of the two diagrams gives us the total mean effective pressure on the piston, to determine which is the principal use of the indicator diagram.

It should be carefully observed, however, that any particular distance, such as Q R, measured from the *same indicator diagram* does not give us the effective pressure on the piston at that point, for the effective pressure at any time is the difference between the forward pressure on one side of the piston and the back pressure *on the other side*. To exhibit, therefore, the forces acting on the piston at each point of the stroke, the forward pressure line of one diagram must be combined with the back pressure line of the other diagram.

Fig. 315 shows this combination. In this figure the diagrams from the two sides are distinguished by full and dotted lines, and the diagram showing the forces acting on the piston at any point of one stroke is shown by the shaded area. For instance, at any point P the resultant pressure on the piston is M N. It will be seen that reversal of the force occurs at the point S, where for an instant no force is acting on the piston, after which, at any point T the resultant pressure on the piston is negative, of amount U V, and tends to bring the piston to rest.

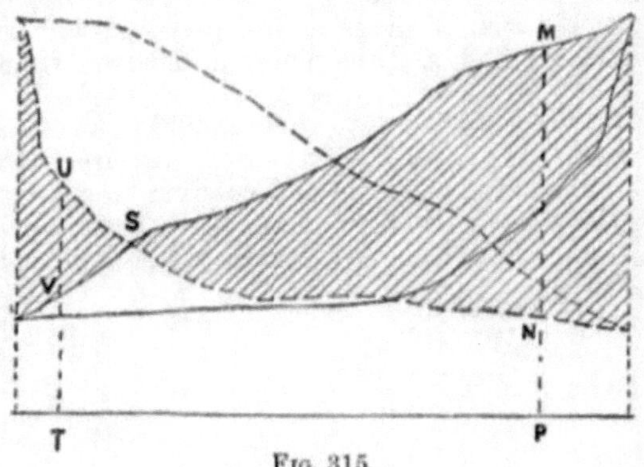

Fig. 315.

Unless these leading principles be well understood some erroneous ideas will be formed when inspecting an indicator diagram, as regards the distribution of force throughout the stroke.

We will now consider the manner in which the performance of the engine can be deduced from actual indicator diagrams.

Theoretical diagram. — In the first place we will take the theoretical diagram which was explained in Chapter XI., and point out the deviations of actual diagrams from this, resulting from various causes. This theoretical diagram is similar in form to the actual diagram, but much more simple in construction. It is repeated in Fig. 316, and is made up of the admission line, steam line, expansion line, exhaust line, and vacuum line, as indicated in the figure, with the atmospheric line, and the zero or base line, and in its construction it is assumed that (*a*) the full pressure of the boiler steam acts suddenly on

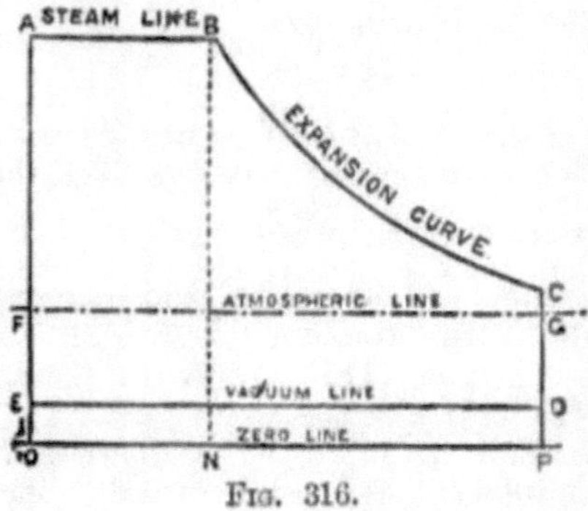

Fig. 316.

the piston at the beginning of the stroke, and remains constant up to the point of cut-off ; (*b*) that the expansion is continued to the end of the stroke ; (*c*) that the communication with the condenser is opened at the end of the stroke, the pressure falling suddenly to that in the condenser ; and (*d*) that the back pressure remains constant during the whole return stroke.

Form of expansion line.—The exact form of the expansion curve for various conditions of wetness of steam and reception of heat has been discussed in Chapter XII. For most practical purposes, however, the curve is sufficiently accurate when made a common hyperbola—i.e. with the absolute pressure varying inversely as the volume. The following is a useful construction for drawing the hyperbola :—

Let o A represent the absolute pressure of steam and A B the quantity of steam expanding, B being the point of cut-off, o x is the zero line or line of no pressure. Draw B N perpendicular to the zero line. Produce A B and take any point K in it ; join o K. From L, where

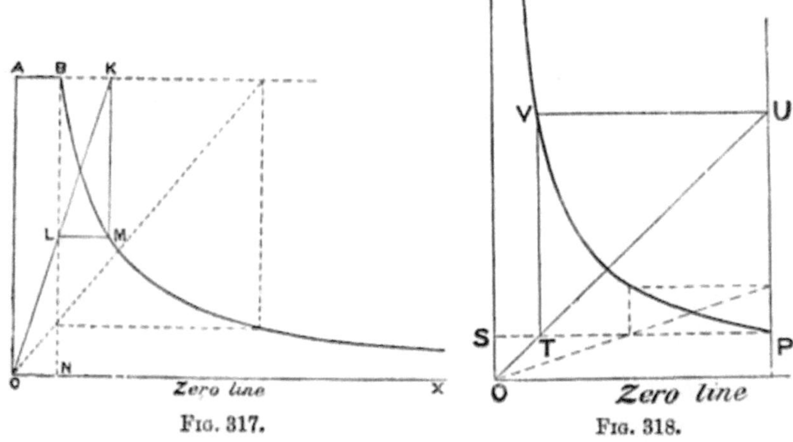

FIG. 317.

FIG. 318.

o K intersects B N, draw L M parallel to the zero line, and from K draw K M perpendicular to it ; the point of intersection, M, of these lines is a point on the hyperbola. A series of such points can easily be obtained, and a curve drawn through them is the hyperbola.

A compression curve is drawn in a similar manner, thus :—In Fig. 318, let P be the point at which compression commences ; draw P S parallel to and P U perpendicular to the zero line. Take any point T in P S, and join o T meeting P U in U. Draw U V parallel to and T V perpendicular to the zero line, and their intersection V is a point on the compression curve. A series of such points being found, the curve drawn through them will be a hyperbola, representing approximately the compression of the steam.

We will now point out the deviations from the theoretical diagram that exist in an indicator diagram taken from an actual engine whose various parts are properly fitted and adjusted.

Wire-drawing on steam side.—Wire-drawing is the technical name for the reduction of pressure which steam undergoes by its passage through contracted areas, and by which its efficiency is reduced. We will consider first the steam side.

If the initial pressure actually shown by the indicator be compared with the boiler pressure, a perceptible difference is always observed. This difference in the cases of high-speed engines with long steam pipes and moderate sized steam ports is often very considerable. A certain difference of pressure must always exist between boilers and cylinders, otherwise the steam would not flow from one to the other. The steam line of an actual diagram therefore necessarily always falls below the boiler pressure line. The admission pressure also generally falls a little as the piston advances and its speed increases, owing to the area of steam ports generally fitted being insufficient to admit steam fast enough to maintain the full pressure. Owing to the very large size which would be required for the slide-valves and cylinder ports of modern high-speed engines in order that no slope of the admission line should take place, a slight sloping of this line is generally allowed at full power in such engines, as this feature is of less importance than the reduction in size of passages and ports, and inertia of the moving slide-valve.

This difference of pressure and sloping of admission line as the stroke proceeds is, therefore, practically necessary to a certain extent, and when not excessive is not to be regarded as a defect. In large quick-moving engines this feature is always noticeable in their full-power diagrams. The difference between the boiler pressure and the mean initial pressure varies considerably with the speed and design

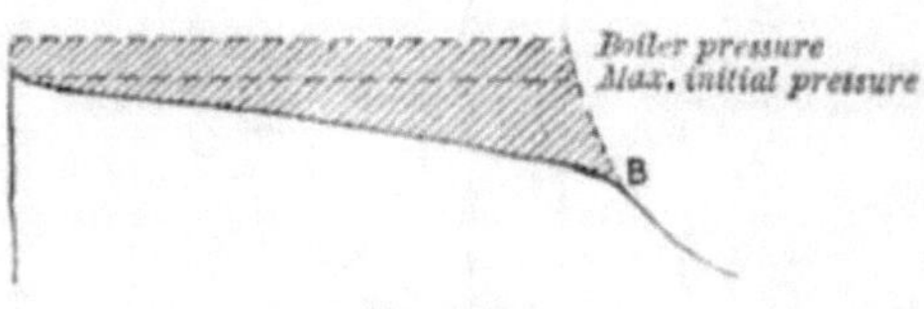

Fig. 319.

of the engine. Even in engines of high pressure and speed it ought not, in cases where reducing valves are not fitted, to exceed 10 per cent. of the absolute boiler pressure.

It can be shown by analysis that the fall of pressure due to this is proportional to the square of the speed of the piston, and also proportional to the density of steam—i.e. practically to its pressure.

The apparent loss due to this wire-drawing is the shaded area of the diagram in Fig. 319 ; but the actual loss is not so great as this, as the wire-drawing has the effect of drying the steam, so that the heat equivalent of some of this apparently lost work re-appears in the steam. With ordinary slide-valves the cut-off also is not absolutely sudden, as is assumed in the theoretical diagram, but gradual ; so that, instead of having a point at B, the actual diagram would be somewhat rounded, as shown.

Wire-drawing during exhaust.—Again, on the exhaust side, in a simple engine or low-pressure cylinder, as the steam must flow from cylinder to condenser, there must be a difference between the actual back pressure and the pressure in the condenser. This difference is more or less dependent on the freedom of the exit passages and pipes for the steam from the cylinder to the condenser. The difference between the vacuum line of the diagram and that in the condenser is generally from 2 to $2\frac{3}{4}$ lbs., or 4 to $5\frac{1}{2}$ inches of mercury at the maximum power of naval engines, while at the power for continuous steaming it is about $1\frac{1}{4}$ to $1\frac{1}{2}$ lbs., or 2 to 3 inches of mercury.

To obtain a sufficiently free exhaust the communication with the condenser is opened before the end of the stroke, say at nine-tenths to eleven-twelfths of the stroke, this being necessary to insure the vacuum being nearly complete when the piston commences its return stroke, owing to the exhaust not opening suddenly, but gradually. This early release and gradual opening causes the 'toe' of the diagram to be rounded off, as in Fig. 320 at C D.

Compression or cushioning.—The theoretical diagram assumes that the back pressure remains constant during the whole return stroke. In practice the connection with the exhaust pipe is closed at some point E before the end of the stroke, and the steam then remaining in the cylinder is compressed behind the piston until just before the end of the stroke, its pressure rising to F, when fresh steam enters and a new stroke commences (see Fig. 321).

The imprisoned steam forms a 'cushion,' which tends to bring the piston gradually to rest at the end of the stroke, and greatly reduces the sudden force that would otherwise come on the engine, owing to

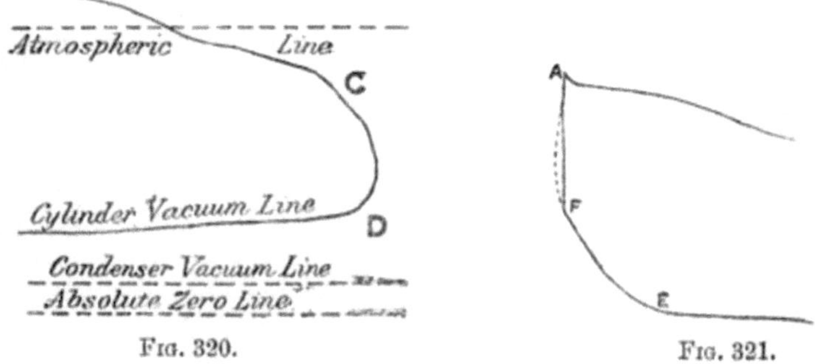

FIG. 320. FIG. 321.

the admission of steam of full boiler pressure at the end of the stroke. This action is called 'compression' or 'cushioning,' and has the effect of greatly reducing shocks to the mechanism.

Compression, as we shall see later on, also greatly reduces the loss from clearance. The corner E F of the diagram is called the compression, or cushioning corner.

Pre-admission.—To increase the opening to steam at the beginning of the stroke, which would otherwise be deficient and not permit the steam pressure being maintained sufficiently, the admission of steam occurs at F, just before the completion of the return stroke; the steam pressure then at once rises to the admission pressure, and the compression curve E F gives place to the admission line F A.

Clearance.—In the construction of the theoretical diagram of Fig. 316, it has been assumed that the piston travels the whole of the volume of the cylinder, and that the expansion curve B C represents the expansion of a quantity of steam whose volume is A B, the volume swept out by the piston. Actually, however, not only is there a small space between the piston and the cylinder cover at the end of the stroke, but the passages between the cut-off valve and the cylinder are also of considerable volume. The sum of these spaces—i.e. the volume of the ports and passages between the piston at the end of its stroke and the slide-valve face—is called the *clearance volume*.

These are spaces through which the piston does not move, but which are filled with steam on admission. The quantity of steam expanding in the cylinder is, therefore, not only that in the volume swept out by the piston, but that in the clearance spaces as well. In actual engines this clearance volume varies considerably ; but usual values for large marine engines are as follows, in fractions of the stroke volume, which is a convenient way of representing it.

Let c = fraction of stroke whose volume is equivalent to the clearance, then

$$c = \frac{\text{volume of clearance space}}{\text{area of piston} \times \text{length of stroke}}.$$

In large marine engines in the Royal Navy, the values of c are usually as follows :—For flat slide valves 12 to 19 per cent., for piston valves 21 to 25 per cent. In the mercantile marine with large engines the clearances vary usually as follows :—For flat slide valves 10 to 15 per cent., for piston slide valves 12 to 20 per cent. In special cases these values are often considerably exceeded ; for example, in one torpedo-boat destroyer the clearance in the H.P. cylinder, with a piston valve, is 34 per cent.

Effect on indicator diagram.—The effect of clearance on the indicator diagram is most conveniently represented by measuring off, away from the diagram (Fig. 322), a distance $o\,o'$, equal to the length of the stroke the clearance amounts to ; thus $o\,o' = c$. O P. The quantity of steam expanding is now A′ B, instead of A B, and the hyperbolic curve of expansion must be constructed, as indicated by full lines, by lines radiating from the centre o'. The effect is that the expansion curve lies above that which would be obtained by neglecting the clearance, which in the figure is represented by the dotted lines and curve.

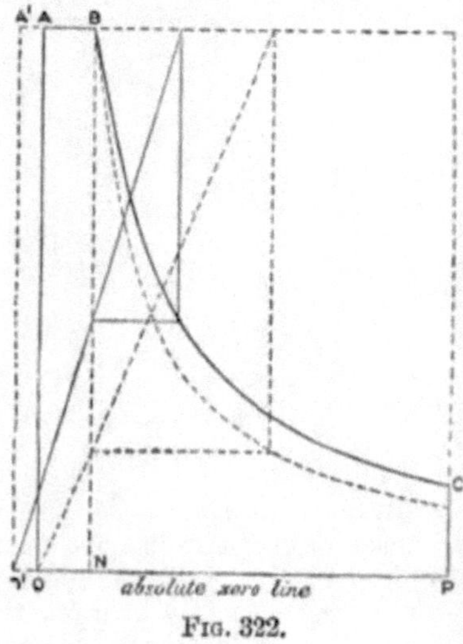

Fig. 322.

In some old Woolf engines the clearance volume was as great as two-fifths the stroke volume, and the alteration of expansion curve resulting from this was very great. In all marine engines, however, the influence of clearance is considerable, so that it is absolutely essential that the clearance should be known and allowed for, as above, before comparisons of any value can be drawn between the actual expansion curve and the theoretical.

The apparent ratio of expansion before clearance is allowed for, is

$$\frac{O\,P}{O\,N} = r' \text{ say } \therefore O\,N = \frac{O\,P}{r'}$$

The real ratio of expansion allowing for clearance

$$= \frac{O\,O' + O\,P}{O\,O' + O\,N} = \frac{c\,.\,O\,P + O\,P}{c\,.\,O\,P + \dfrac{O\,P}{r'}} = \frac{c + 1}{c + \dfrac{1}{r'}}$$

For example, suppose the apparent ratio of expansion of steam in the cylinder, as shown by the cut-off gear, to be 8 times, and the total clearance spaces to be one-eighth of the total capacity of the cylinder, which is not an excessive value :—

Then the actual rate of expansion $r = \dfrac{\frac{1}{8} + 1}{\frac{1}{8} + \frac{1}{8}} = 4\frac{1}{2}$,

so that the actual rate of expansion of steam will only be $4\frac{1}{2}$ times, instead of 8 times, as indicated by the position of the piston at the point of cut-off.

The effect of clearance is to diminish the efficiency of the expansion and cause waste of steam ; for at the beginning of each stroke all the clearance spaces must be filled with steam, which rushes in from the slide casing and does no work during its admission. In cases of high expansion in a single cylinder, unless special care be taken to reduce the clearance as much as possible, the loss from this cause may become very considerable.

Effect of cushioning on efficiency.—The waste of steam resulting from clearance is reduced by the compression at the end of the return stroke, and if the compression be so great as to raise the pressure in the clearance spaces, just before the point of admission, to the initial pressure of the steam, loss from clearance is practically prevented, as no steam is required to pass from the slide casing into the clearance space. It is evident, however, that the mean pressure of the steam during the stroke is reduced by the considerable amount of cushioning required, and if this amount of cushioning were allowed at full power the size of the cylinders would have to be increased on this account, so that this is not generally done. At lower speeds and powers, with the slide gear linked in, this amount of compression can often be usefully effected. In cases in which engines are worked at very high rates of expansion in a single cylinder, it is always advantageous to use a high degree of compression, not only to reduce loss from clearance, but to prevent shock to the machinery on the change of the stroke by the sudden admission of steam of high pressure to the cylinder.

Faults indicated by diagrams.—The form of diagram obtained from an actual engine in good order and properly adjusted does not differ much from the theoretical diagram, the principal deviations being in the rounding of the corners.

It must be clearly understood that the only fact absolutely given by the indicator diagram is the actual pressure of the steam on the piston during the stroke. In order to draw reliable conclusions from the diagrams, a correct knowledge of the action of the steam in the engine is necessary, and careful study is required to enable the information contained in the diagram to be properly understood.

In dealing with the indicator diagrams of a triple or other compound engine, it should be remembered that the steam line of any cylinder succeeding the high pressure is itself an expansion curve, so that it must not be expected to be parallel with the atmospheric line ; again, the back pressure line of the high pressure and succeeding engines, except the low pressure, also represents the expansion, or compression, of steam in the receiver, often in a complicated manner, so that deviations from the horizontal must often be looked for here.

A few of the more important causes affecting the forms of diagrams are as follows. The diagram taken is generally that of a simple engine, but the corresponding deductions for other diagrams can easily be made.

Steam and exhaust openings too small.—This is the most serious defect that can be shown by a diagram, as it is one that is generally due, not merely to incorrect adjustment of the parts, but to faulty construction, and can only be remedied by enlarging the cylinder ports and passages, which in most cases would involve the substitution of new cylinders.

Fig. 323 is an illustration of the effect on the diagram in this case. On the steam side the insufficiency of steam opening is shown by loss of initial pressure and wire-drawing, while on the exhaust side, in consequence of the restricted area of the exhaust passages, the steam will not be able to escape freely, so that the back pressure will be increased and the vacuum not fully attained until the piston has traversed some portion of its return stroke, the vacuum line sloping downward from D to E instead of being horizontal. It is evident that wire-drawing during the exhaust is more injurious than during admission, as it affects nearly the whole length of the diagram during the return stroke, increasing the average back pressure, and thereby reducing the power of the engine.

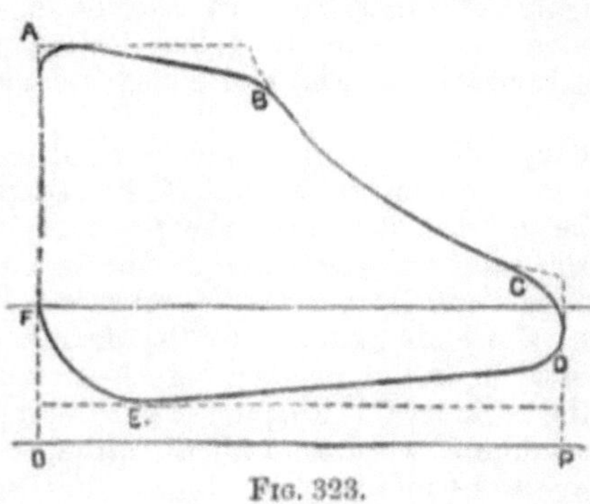

Fig. 323.

Area of cylinder ports and passages.—In the design of engines, the cylinder ports and passages should be made sufficiently large to prevent to as great an extent as possible the fall of pressure during admission. The proper proportion that the area of the ports and passages should bear to that of the cylinder depends upon the steam pressure and piston speed. The following rule is used for calculating the port area :—

$$\frac{\text{area of port}}{\text{area of piston}} = \frac{\text{speed of piston in feet per minute}}{5{,}000 \text{ for H.P. ; } 6{,}500 \text{ for I.P. ; or } 8{,}000 \text{ for L.P.}}$$

Where possible, however, these figures should be reduced by about 10 per cent. to increase the areas. The area of steam pipe and also the maximum opening for steam is about 70 per cent. of the port area, and the area of exhaust pipe 20 per cent. greater than the port area. It is most important to arrange for the free and unrestricted exhaust of the steam from the cylinder at the end of the stroke, for any defect in this action causes a much more serious reduction of power of the engines than would arise from deficiency in the area of opening for admission. It is usual to make the exhaust ports and passages at least 50 per cent. greater than the maximum steam openings for this reason.

Suppose the slide-valve incorrectly set on the rod, the eccentric being set at the proper angle of advance.—In this case one end of the valve will have insufficient lap on the steam side and too much on the exhaust, and at the other end of the valve the errors will be of an opposite character. The valve will therefore at one end admit steam too early, continue the admission too long, and cut-off too late, while at the opposite end the operations will be reversed. On the exhaust side, the valve, at the end with early and lengthened admission, will commence to exhaust late and the period of the exhaust will be shortened ; at the other end the exhaust will begin early and continue for an increased portion of the stroke. The diagram will therefore be of the character shown in Fig. 324, the faults in the diagrams from *opposite* sides of the piston being of *opposite* natures.

Suppose the slide-valve correctly set, that is, with the proper lead at each end, but the eccentric secured in a wrong position on the shaft.—If the angle of advance be too small all the actions of the

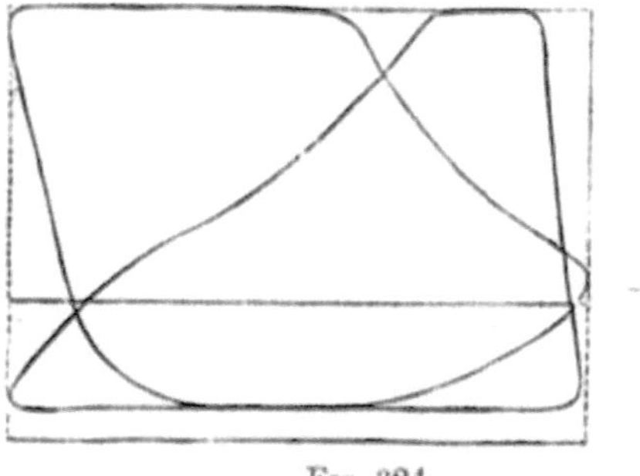

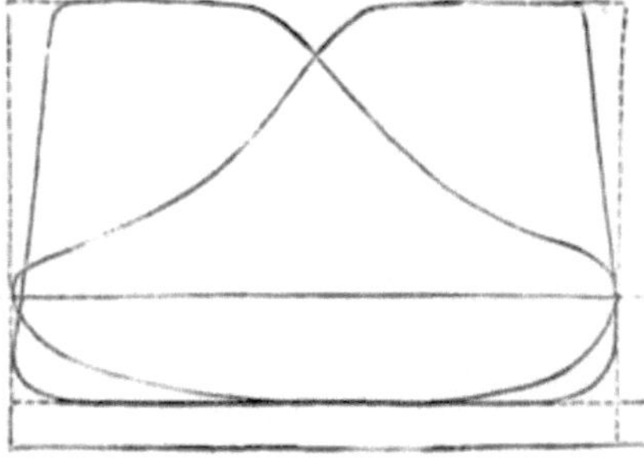

Fig. 324.   Fig. 325.

slide-valve for *both* sides of the piston will be too late, the diagram being as shown in Fig. 325, the admission lines sloping inwards and both compression corners being small or non-existent. The late release has the effect that the back pressure does not fall to the condenser pressure till some fraction of the stroke has been performed. This defect is a more serious one than that next described, in which the operations are too early.

If the angle of advance be too great, all the operations on *both* sides of the piston will be too early. The early release causes a considerable fall of pressure before the end of the stroke, and the compression becomes excessive. This form of diagram is approximated to when the steam is worked expansively by the use of the link motion. The effect of 'shortening the link,' as it is technically called, is to shorten the stroke and increase the equivalent angle of advance of the eccentric, by which the actions of admission, cut-off, release, and compression are all made earlier. When not excessive these features of the diagram should not be regarded as defects. Fig. 326 shows an actual diagram from a triple-expansion engine, taken when 'linked in' considerably, from which the effect on the diagram can be seen.

In both these examples the faults in the figures, from the *opposite* sides of the piston, are *similar* in character, and not opposite as in the case of the valve being wrongly placed on the rod. These defects may be remedied by moving the eccentric on the shaft, and setting it with the proper angle of advance, to give the slide-valve the required lead, &c.

Leaky slide-valves and leaky pistons.—If the valves are leaky steam will continue to enter the cylinder after the admission is nominally cut off. In consequence of this the expansion line will rise above the proper or normal curve, the pressure being increased by the leakage during expansion. This would involve a loss of efficiency, and should be guarded against, especially in slow-moving engines, in which the percentage of loss would be the greater. On the other hand, if the piston leak, steam will pass from the steam to the exhaust side of the piston during the stroke, which would cause the pressure during expansion to be lower than it would otherwise have been, the pressure being reduced by the leakage. This is a serious defect, because the steam which passes the piston goes direct to the exhaust, without doing useful work in that cylinder.

In a stage-expansion engine any steam leaking past the piston of a high-pressure or intermediate cylinder does useful work in the succeeding cylinders, so that the loss would not be so great.

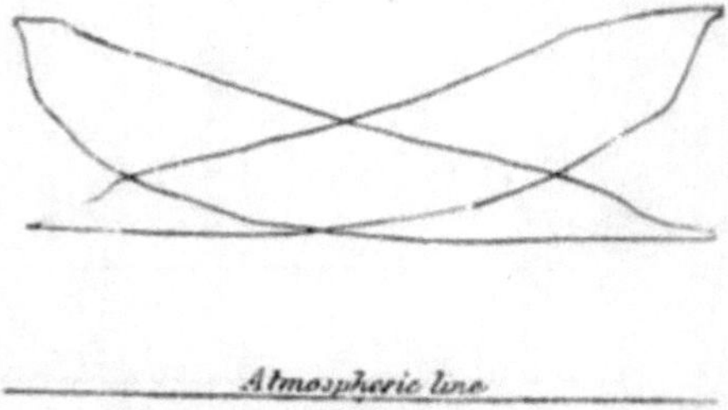

The condition of the valves and pistons of an engine as regards leakage is a matter of importance as regards its economy, and insufficient attention is often paid to this question. It is not usually to be detected by a simple inspection of indicator diagrams, as, unless the leakage be excessive, its influence on the form of the diagram is not great.

[Fig. 326.

The proper method to pursue in order to determine whether the pistons and valves are in good condition is to test them by steam pressure, when the engine is at rest, by fixing the piston in some position in which the slide-valve is closed, and applying steam to one side of the piston by means of the starting valves or other means ; the leakage of the piston may be observed by the use of an open cock at the other end of the cylinder, such as the indicator cock. By admitting steam to the slide jacket with the valve in the closed position, and opening cocks at each end of the cylinder, the leakage of the slide-valve can be observed. By such means it can be readily ascertained if the pistons and slide-valves are approximately in an efficient condition.

Useful information can be obtained from the indicator diagram by selecting a point about two-thirds along the expansion curve, and ascertaining by construction, by the method described previously, the point on the corresponding hyperbola which has the same pressure as that at a point just after cut-off. The clearance and zero lines must first be drawn (the amount of clearance in the cylinders of the engines should be known by the engineer of every steam vessel). Vertical and horizontal lines are then drawn through the point P selected, Fig. 327, the former meeting the pressure line at the point near cut-off in Q. Join O Q and complete the rectangle P R; then R is on the hyperbola corresponding to the point P. The relation between the point R and the point S on the actual diagram gives us some information of the kind sought, if it be compared with the similar relation shown on a diagram taken when the engine was new, or known to be in an efficient condition, and when the conditions as regards steam jacketing, pressure, &c., are the same. The correct relation between R and S will depend on the type of engine and whether steam jacketed or not. If R lies beyond the proper position on the outside, leaky slide-valves should be suspected,

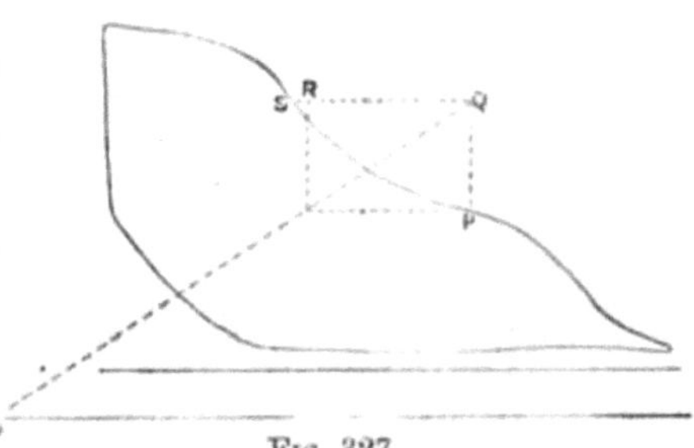

FIG. 327.

while if R lies on the other side of the proper position, i.e. towards the vertical axis, a leaky piston is the probable cause, and it should be tested.

In engines with efficient steam jackets and the parts in good condition, the points R and S should not differ by any considerable amount, R generally lying a little outside the diagram. In new engines, if a very considerable difference between these points occurs, investigation will be desirable.

All the defects hitherto discussed influencing the form of the diagram are due to alterations affecting the power and efficiency of the engine. We will now mention a few external causes which affect the form of the diagram only, and which must be carefully avoided if correct inferences as to the action of the steam are to be drawn.

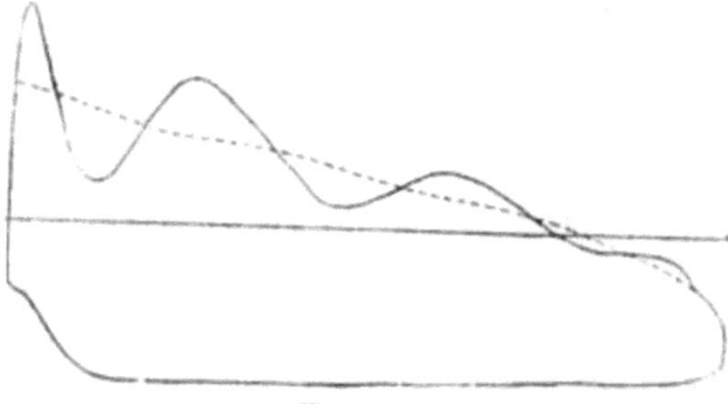

FIG. 328.

Undulation or vibration of the pencil.—This, if it occur, is due to the weakness of the springs, especially when of considerable length. It should be avoided by selecting stronger springs, and indicators having pencil motions suitable to the speed of the engine, as explained previously. If undulations do occur, it will be more correct to calculate the horse-power from a dotted line drawn midway between the crests and hollows, as shown in Fig. 328, than from the actual diagram itself.

Friction of the indicator.—When this occurs it opposes the motion of the indicator piston, and therefore tends to make the indicated forward pressure less and the indicated back pressure greater than is correct, and so to make the indicated work appear less than is really exerted. In practice, if the instruments are kept in order this will not exist, because the indicator pistons are always made with a slight degree of leakage, so as to make them as nearly as possible frictionless. Sometimes, however, dirty matter is carried into the indicator cylinders with the steam, which would increase the friction, and it is necessary that the instruments should be frequently examined and cleaned to insure correct results being obtained. In cases of high expansion, if the indicator piston be too tight, the defect is sometimes shown by a series of steps on the diagram, the piston, instead of following the steam freely, descending in jumps in consequence of the friction.

This can be tested for one position of indicator piston by drawing the atmospheric line when the pencil has been gradually released, (1) after the indicator piston has been depressed by the finger, (2) after it has been raised by the finger. The two lines should coincide if the condition is satisfactory.

Position of the indicator.—If the position of the indicator is such that a rapid current of steam passes across the nozzle, the steam pressure shown on the diagram will be thereby reduced. Sudden bends, great length and smallness of diameter in the indicator pipes, also tend to reduce the indicated pressure given by the diagrams.

Length of string.—The length of the string should be carefully adjusted before taking the diagram, for if it be either too long or too short the paper cylinder will come to rest before the piston reaches the end of its stroke. The pencil will consequently trace a vertical line when it should be inclined, which will cause the corners to be square and incorrect, and the effect will be the same as if a vertical line were drawn, cutting off a portion of the proper diagram.

Calculation of horse-power from indicator diagrams.—By means of the indicator diagram we are enabled to measure the mean effective pressure on the piston, and consequently, as the area of the piston, length of stroke, and number of revolutions per minute are known, the I.H.P. of the engine can be readily calculated.

If P = mean effective pressure on the piston in lbs. per square inch,
and A = net area of piston in square inches :

then $P \times A$ = total pressure on the piston in lbs.
and if L = length of stroke in feet,
N = No. of revolutions of the engine per minute,
then $2 L \times N$ = speed of piston in feet per minute.

Therefore $P \times A \times 2 L \times N$ = the number of foot-pounds of work done per minute.

Consequently, since one I.H.P. is equal to 33,000 foot-pounds done per minute, the I.H.P. developed in the cylinder in question will be

$$\text{I.H.P.} = 2\frac{\text{PLAN}}{33{,}000}.$$

In this formula A is the mean *net* area of piston. The area of piston-rod must be subtracted from that of the piston, as the pressure does not act on the former area. Similarly with a tail rod, should the engine be so fitted. In strict accuracy, supposing p_t and a_t the mean effective pressure and net area of the front part of the piston, and p_b and a_b the similar quantities for the back part of the piston, the horse-power will be :—

$$\text{I.H.P.} = \frac{\text{NL} \, (p_t \, a_t + p_b \, a_b)}{33,000}.$$

a_t is generally not the same as a_b on account of the area of the piston-rod. They are generally so nearly equal, however, that the error made by substituting $\frac{1}{2} (a_t + a_b)$ for each of them is inappreciable. This is what is done to arrive at the simple and usual formula :—

$$\text{I.H.P.} = \frac{2 \, \text{PLAN}}{33,000}.$$

In this expression, P and N are the only variables for the same cylinder. It is therefore usual in practice to combine the constant quantities to further facilitate calculation. The *cylinder constant* for any engine is clearly

$$= 2 \, \frac{\text{L A}}{33,000} = \text{C say}$$

A being the mean net area of piston.

This constant, multiplied by the mean pressure calculated from the diagram and by the revolutions of the engine per minute, will give the I.H.P. of the cylinder,

$$\text{or, I.H.P.} = \text{C} \times \text{P} \times \text{N}.$$

If there be more than one cylinder, the powers developed in the several cylinders must be added together to obtain the total I.H.P., care being taken to remember that the scales used in the cylinders of a stage-expansion engine vary with the pressure.

Calculation of mean effective pressure from the indicator diagram.—The following is the method commonly adopted for ascertaining the mean effective pressure from a pair of indicator diagrams.

The total length of the diagram is divided into ten equal parts, and vertical ordinates are drawn at the middle points of the spaces thus formed. The first and last ordinates will then each be $\frac{1}{20}$th of the length of the diagram from the end, and the common distance between the several ordinates will be equal to $\frac{1}{10}$th of the length of the diagram. This method of division is shown on the diagrams of Fig. 334.

Diagrams are taken from *each* side of the piston, and the lengths of the several ordinates, intercepted between the forward and back pressure lines of one diagram, are measured on the required scale, added together, and divided by 10. The same process is carried out on the other diagram, and the mean of the two means thus obtained gives the *mean effective pressure* for the complete double stroke of the engine, which is used in calculating the I.H.P.

To facilitate calculation, the lengths of the ordinates are usually measured successively on a strip of paper, the second ordinate commencing at the end of the first, and so on. The total length thus obtained is measured on a scale made ten times as great as the scale of the diagram, so that the mean pressure may be read off at once.

The other method used for ascertaining the mean effective pressure is by the use of the 'planimeter.'

Calculation of steam used as shown by the indicator diagram.—
From the indicator diagram the quantity of steam, and consequently
of water, used per I.H.P. per hour, as accounted for by the indicator
diagram, may be ascertained. The values calculated from the
diagrams are not, however, representative of the actual amount
of water passing through the engine, but are always less than the
actual quantities of steam used, and often very considerably so,
because they do not include the waste of steam due to liquefaction in
the cylinders, radiation, and other causes. Relatively, however, as
showing the differences in the performance of similar engines, or of
the same engine working under different circumstances, this application
of the diagram is of value, and some information may be gained from
such calculations, provided their real meaning and limitations be
clearly understood.

From what has been said before it is clear that the working steam
in the cylinder consists of two parts, viz. (*a*) the portion that passes
through the engine at each stroke, being received from the slide
casing at the beginning of the stroke and exhausted from the cylinder
during the return stroke, and (*b*) the cushion steam, viz. that part of

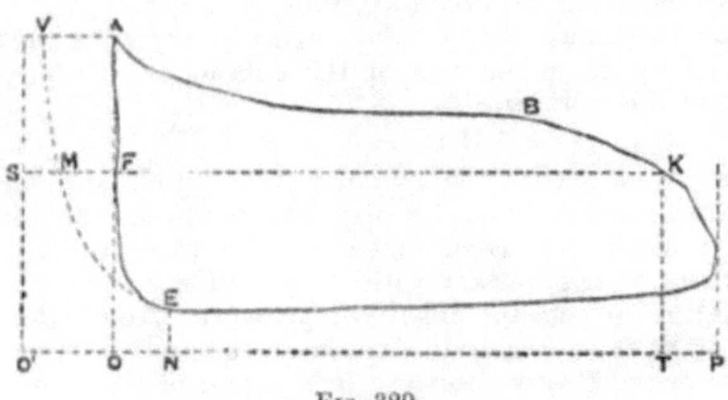

Fig. 329.

the steam which is present in the clearance spaces and cylinder when
compression takes place, and which is retained in the cylinder and
compressed till the end of the stroke. This volume of steam, therefore,
does not leave the cylinder at all, but is alternately compressed and
expanded at each stroke.

The consumption of steam does not include this cushion steam. We
have, therefore, to ascertain the quantity of steam that *leaves the cylinder*
during each stroke. To do this we must select a point, say K, Fig. 329,
on the expansion curve in such position that it is undoubtedly
before release has taken place ; then clearly at the point K in the expansion the total volume of steam present is S K.

Let E be a point on the back pressure line, just after the exhaust
has closed and compression begun, then the quantity of steam of
volume O′N and pressure N E is retained in the cylinder and does not
leave it. This quantity must therefore be deducted from the total
quantity just before release, viz. the volume S K of pressure T K, to
obtain the quantity leaving the cylinder and used per stroke. To
reduce these quantities to the same pressure we draw a saturation
curve through the point E meeting the horizontal line through K in M.

Then s M will be the volume of the cushion steam when its pressure is K T, which steam does not leave the cylinder, therefore the difference— i.e. the volume represented by M K—on the same scale that O P represents the stroke volume, is the amount of steam that leaves the cylinder at each stroke, so that this quantity, at pressure K T is the consumption of steam per stroke as accounted for by the indicator diagram. This quantity may be termed the *working steam*, while the remainder, viz. s M, is termed the *cushion steam*.

Theoretical diagram of a stage-expansion engine.— It was explained in Chapter XVIII. that the total expansion of steam successively in the cylinders of a compound or multiple-expansion engine is theoretically the same as if it had been carried out entirely in the low-pressure cylinder only. We will take first the simplest possible case, in which there is no clearance and no wire-drawing, and that there are receivers between the cylinders so large that the pressure in them remains constant, there-fore the back pressure in the smaller cylinder, and admission pressure in the larger cylinder of any pair, remain constant and equal to the receiver pressure. Let us further assume that the expansion in each cylinder reduces the pressure to the back pressure in the cylinder, and therefore to the admission pressure in the succeeding one.

It is clear that in any multiple-expansion engine, when it has been running sufficiently long to have as-sumed a steady condition, *the quantity of steam entering and leaving any cylinder is the same throughout.* In actual engines, of course, part of this steam exists in the form of water. Let A B D C be the high-pressure dia-gram of this engine (see Fig. 330),

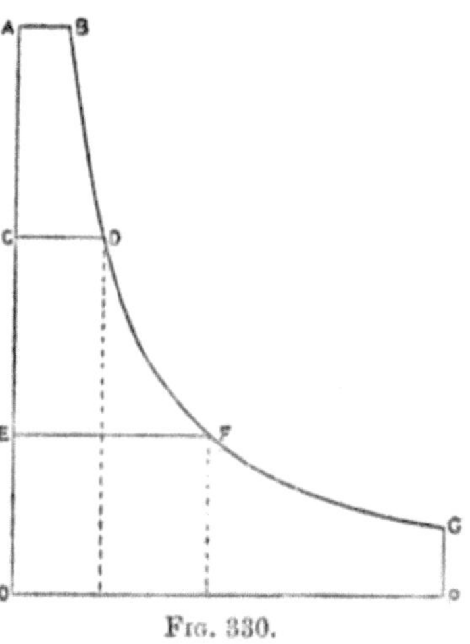

Fig. 330.

then the volume C D of steam at the receiver pressure O C leaves the high-pressure cylinder and enters the receiver; also, as the same quantity of steam enters the intermediate cylinder up to the point of cut-off, there-fore C D is the admission line of the intermediate-pressure diagram, and its expansion curve, as the quantity of steam expanding is the same, will be D F, a continuation of the hyperbola B D. The intermediate-pressure diagram is therefore C D F E, where E F is the volume of the inter-mediate cylinder. Similarly, E F to P O is the low-pressure diagram where O P is the final volume of steam—i.e. the volume of the low-pressure cylinder. The expansion curve, therefore, is exactly the same as if the volume of steam A B of pressure O A had been expanded in a single cylinder of volume O P.

This assumption of a large receiver and constant receiver pressure is one extreme case ; the assumption of no reservoir at all is another ex-treme case, which is dealt with at the beginning of Chapter XXXIII.

With the proportions of cylinders necessary from practical con-siderations, the powers developed in the various cylinders would be very unequal, that in the low pressure greatly preponderating, while the necessary cut-offs would be inconvenient.

To obtain greater equality in the powers developed in each stage it is necessary to lower both receiver pressures, which is done by making the cut-off in the low-pressure and intermediate-pressure cylinders later than before. A greater volume of steam is therefore drawn from the receivers per stroke, so that as the total weight of steam passing into the other cylinders must still be equal to that discharged from the high-pressure cylinder, the pressure gradually falls in the receiver till the pressure is such that the volume being taken by the receiving cylinders equals the quantity discharged from the high-pressure cylinder.

Let us suppose the cut-off in the intermediate cylinder, Fig. 331, altered so that the volume of steam admitted is increased from c d to c′ d′ ; then c′ d′ being the volume of steam admitted, as its weight remains unaltered its pressure must be o c′, and c′ d′ will be the steam line of the intermediate-pressure diagram. The pressure at release in the high-

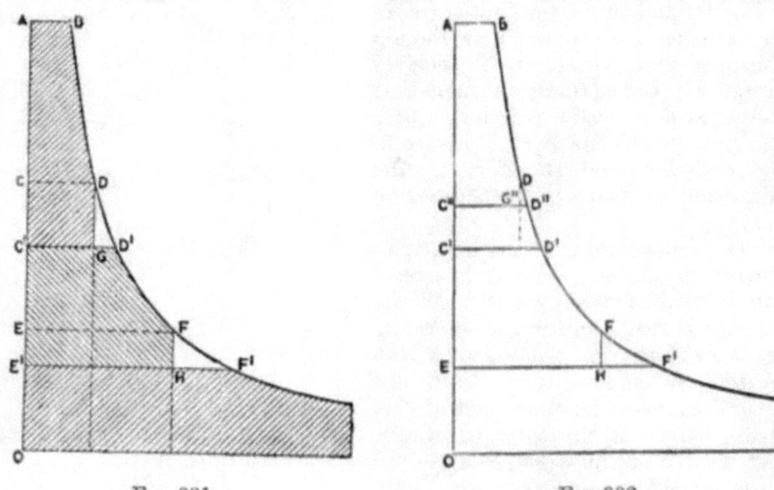

FIG. 331.FIG. 332.

pressure diagram, viz. o c, remains unaltered, and is now greater than o c′, the pressure in the receiver, so that on release from the high-pressure cylinder a sudden drop of pressure occurs represented by d g. The triangular area d g d′ therefore disappears, and is mostly lost. A similar action takes place between the intermediate pressure and the low pressure, and the sketch shows the effect of making the cut-off in low-pressure cylinder later—viz. from e f to e′ f′.

Effect of altering the cut-off in the intermediate or low-pressure cylinder.—The preceding reasoning enables us to understand the effect of altering the cut-off in the various cylinders of a triple-expansion engine on the distribution of the power. Suppose we consider the intermediate-pressure diagram c′ d′ f h e, Fig. 332. Now if we cut off earlier in this cylinder, as the *weight of steam passing through it remains the same*, its initial pressure must be increased. If the cut-off is made earlier, so that the volume admitted is reduced from c′ d′ to c″ d″, the pressure of steam in the receiver will be altered from o c′ to o c″ : this will have the effect of increasing the power developed in the intermediate-pressure cylinder and reducing that developed in the high-pressure cylinder, the total power remaining practically constant. The intermediate diagram will be increased to c″ d″ f ii e, and the high pressure reduced to a b d g″ c″. Similarly, making the cut-off later in the intermediate-pressure or low-pressure cylinder of a triple expansion engine has the effect of reducing the work done in that cylinder and increasing the work done in the preceding cylinder, the total work remaining practically unaltered.

Making the cut-off later in the high-pressure cylinder has, of course, the effect of increasing the total power of the engines. In this case the work done in *each* of the cylinders is increased, as the quantity of steam passing through the engines is increased. Similarly, if the cut-off is made earlier the power is reduced throughout.

In a naval engine, owing to the proportions that have to be adopted, although the cut-offs at full power are comparatively late in all cylinders, the high-pressure cylinder still does less and the low-pressure more than its proportion of the work. At reduced powers the cut-offs are made earlier in all cylinders, so that the proportion of power gradually increases in the high-pressure cylinder, and is gradually reduced in the low-pressure, till at very low powers the high-pressure does more than its proportion, and the low-pressure cylinder less.

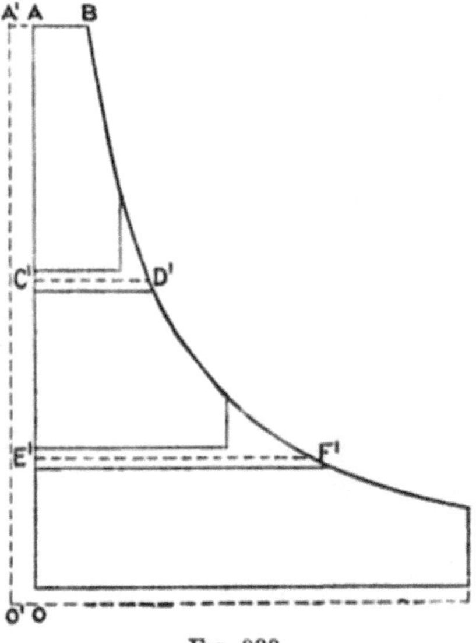

Fig. 333.

The independent linking-up gear fitted to most vessels enables the slide-valves of the low-pressure and intermediate cylinders to be linked up more than the high-pressure when so working, so that if required the receiver pressures can be raised, and the proportion of power developed in their cylinders be brought to nearer an equality with that being developed in the high-pressure cylinder.

These diagrams enable us to clearly see the effect of all such alterations of relative cut-off in the various cylinders on the distribution of the power.

Theoretical diagram taking account of clearance and wire-drawing between cylinders.—Clearance greatly affects the preceding calculations, and is a very complicated factor. We will consider here the case of an engine in which the clearance volume is the same in all cylinders, with no compression. The construction is then the same, except that the hyperbolic expansion curve is drawn with axis o′, instead of o, o o′ being the clearance volume, as shown in Fig. 333.

The effect of wire-drawing between the cylinders is to raise the back pressure line of the high-pressure diagram, and to depress that of the intermediate-pressure diagram a little above or below the receiver pressure o c', and similarly for the lines between the intermediate-pressure and low-pressure cylinders.

Approximate theoretical indicator diagrams from an engine.— Proceeding as above, rounding off the corners, and allowing a little excess back pressure beyond c' d' and initial pressure in the inter-mediate-pressure cylinder below c' d' of amounts depending on the type of engine, and obtained from experience, we are enabled to roughly approximate to the indicator diagrams to be expected from a given engine.

Having dealt with the theoretical diagram we proceed to consider the case of indicator diagrams from actual engines, and the process of combining them to obtain as much information as possible.

Process of combining diagrams of actual stage-expansion engines.—The scales of pressures and volumes of the indicator diagrams obtained from any compound engine differ for the various cylinders, so that it is customary for various purposes to combine all the diagrams, so as to exhibit on the same scale and on one diagram the changes of pressure and volume undergone by the steam during its passage through all the cylinders. Such a diagram may also roughly exhibit the effect produced with that which would be theoretically obtained by the steam expanding in a single cylinder.

The diagram may be combined in various ways, depending on the purpose for which it is required. In every method the effect of clearance is absolutely necessary to be taken account of to obtain even an approximate idea of the action taking place. In stage-expansion engines certain large sources of loss appertaining to simple engines, losses not shown by the diagrams, are avoided, while other losses are introduced, consisting of the losses between the cylinders due to sudden expansion, friction, and wire-drawing, which it is most important to reduce to the smallest possible extent. The process of combination of diagrams gives graphically an approximate idea of these losses, and enables us to study their further reduction.

Usual method.—The usual method of combination is as follows. The diagrams when combined must be of such relative length as to represent the stroke volumes of their respective cylinders, while the scale of pressures must be identical.

A scale of volumes and pressures having been decided upon, each of the diagrams to be combined is divided into a certain number of equal lengths, and ordinates are erected at the middle of each of these divisions. The low-pressure stroke volume is set off on the zero line to the agreed scale, and the atmospheric line drawn above it on the proper scale of pressures. A distance o o' is then set off equal to the clearance volume of the low-pressure cylinder, as shown in Fig. 334. The distance o p is then divided into the same number of equal parts as the original diagram, and ordinates erected at the centre of each as before. The several ordinates of the original low-pressure diagram are then carefully measured, and transferred on the new scale to the corresponding ordinate on the combined diagram, and curves drawn through the ends of the ordinates to represent as closely as possible the original diagram.

The intermediate diagram is then served in a similar manner, the end of its diagram being placed at M, such that L M is equal to the clearance volume of the intermediate cylinder on the agreed scale of volumes, and M N, representing the stroke volume of the intermediate cylinder, is then divided as before, and the intermediate diagram constructed. Similarly for the high-pressure diagram. The various distances A C, L M, and O'O represent the clearance volumes of the respective cylinders. We have now a combined diagram such that at any point, say V, the pressure of steam and volume occupied are represented by V T and V S. A hyperbola or saturation curve is generally drawn through the estimated point of cut-off to complete the figure.

Such a diagram gives, when comparing on the same basis engines of different design, an approximate idea of the amount of wire-drawing, and losses between the cylinders. For design work also the proportion between the area of the actual indicator diagrams and that of the hyperbolic enclosure gives us a fraction known as the *design factor*, which becomes useful in estimating the size of cylinders required for similar engines.

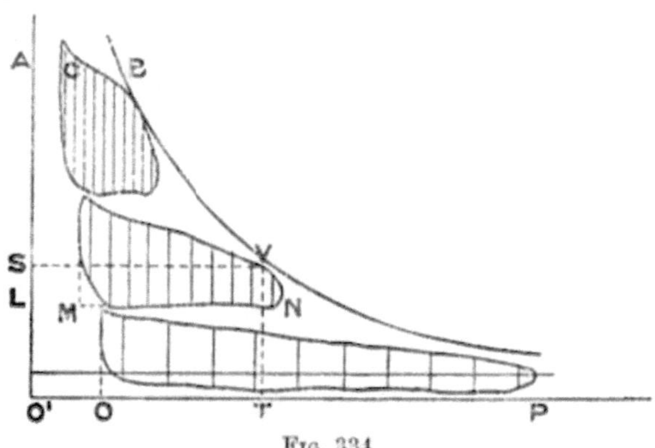

Fig. 334.

A set of indicator diagrams taken from the engines of H.M.S. 'Powerful' are given in Fig. 335, while the combination of these diagrams is shown in Fig. 336. It will be seen that their expansion curve, if drawn to touch the three diagrams, falls considerably below the hyperbola. The spaces between the three diagrams represent approximately the losses due to the resistance of the passages between the cylinders, while the spaces between the release lines and the dotted expansion curve represent approximately the losses from sudden expansion on admission to the receivers.

Referring to Fig. 336 it must be observed that, owing to the varying amounts of clearance volumes, the quantity of steam expanding in the three cylinders is different, so that one continuous curve, either hyperbolic or saturation, cannot really represent the expansion curves of the three diagrams, but, provided its limitations are understood, useful information may still be obtained from such a diagram. To study the form of the expansion curves more accurately, a hyperbola should be drawn for each diagram through its point of cut-off.

It is often found that the diagrams when combined in this way overlap one another, and there is nothing wrong in this being so, for any given point in the steam line of the intermediate diagram, for instance, does not correspond with the point on the high-pressure back-pressure line on the same ordinate. The point of correspondence must be obtained by calculation, knowing the relative position of the pistons from the arrangement and sequence of the cranks.

Combination to exhibit the real losses of pressure by wire-drawing between cylinders.—A useful diagram may be obtained by setting out the back pressures of one diagram, when in connection with the receiver, and on the same ordinates the forward pressure of the succeeding diagram *at the same instant.* A convenient plan is to do this in such a manner that the abscissæ represent the number of degrees one of the cranks has travelled through, while the ordinates represent the pressures in the cylinders when they are in connection with the

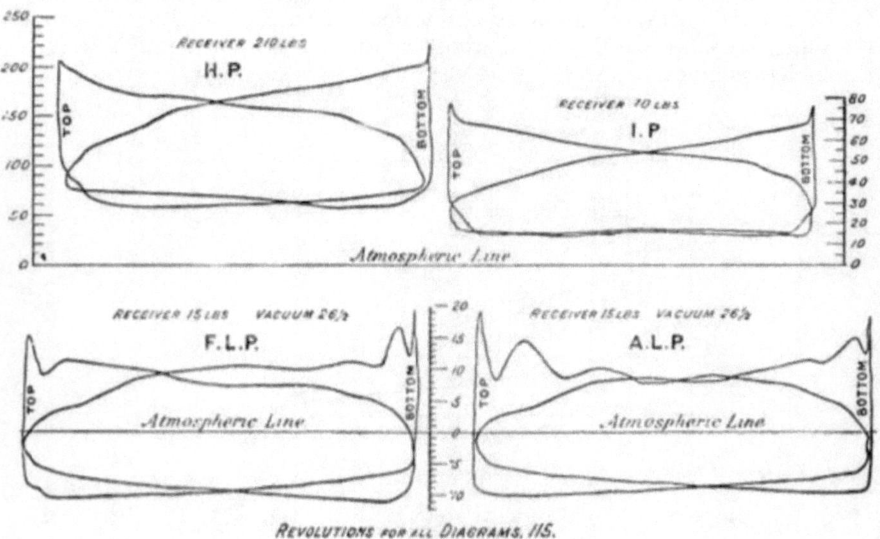

Fig. 335.

receivers. The parts of the diagrams to be so treated would be those between release and compression in the high, and between admission and cut-off in the intermediate, and similarly for the back pressure of the intermediate and the steam line of the low. Sometimes the entire diagrams are thus transformed, but little useful information can be extracted except from the parts mentioned. When these parts are thus transformed, the overlapping previously referred to will be found to have disappeared, and the loss of pressure by wire-drawing at any point is seen.

Fig. 338 shows this combination for the diagrams of H.M.S. 'Powerful' previously dealt with. The full lines in each case represent the pressures in each cylinder when in connection with the receiver, the dotted lines representing the pressures when the cylinder is not in connection with the receiver. The actual loss by wire-drawing can be seen at any point. It will be useful for students to draw such a diagram for themselves from a given set of indicator cards.

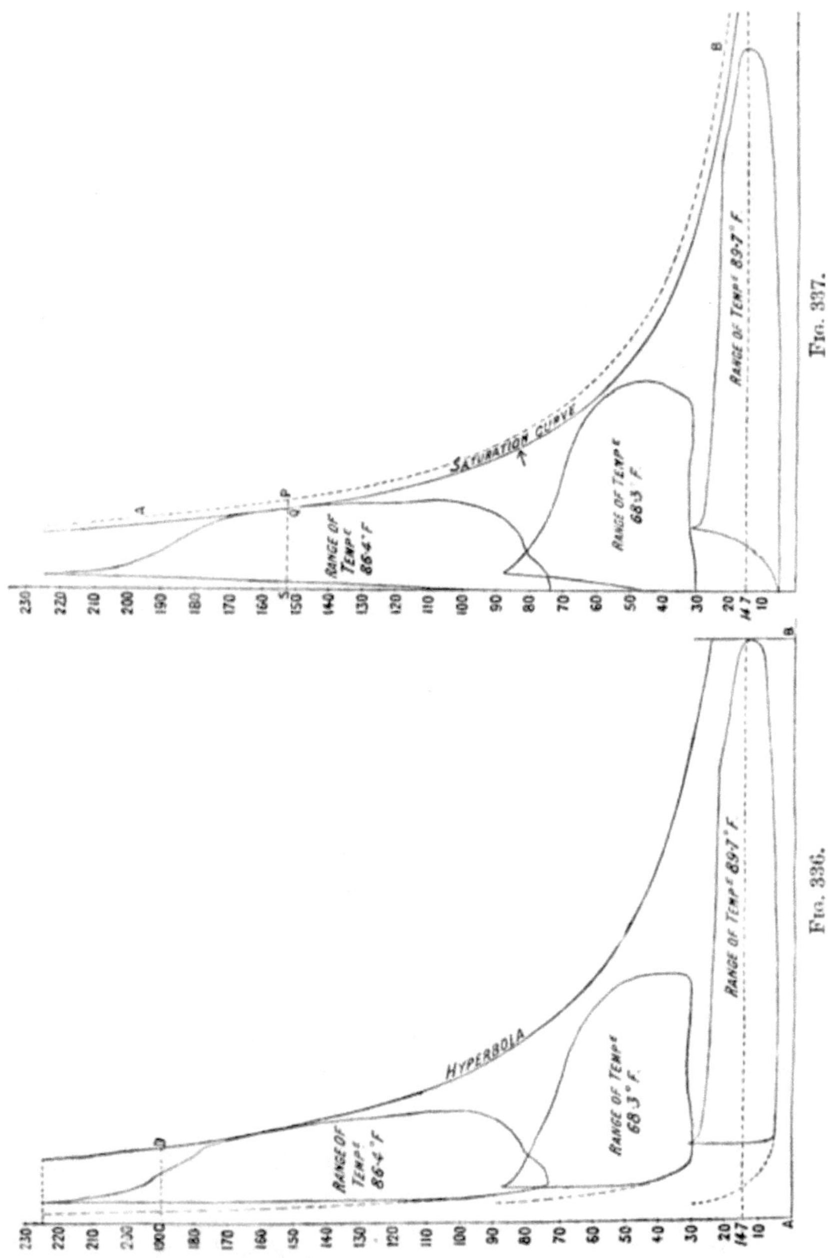

Combination to exhibit the distribution of water in the cylinders.— The preceding combined diagram indicates the volume and pressure of the total amount of steam in the various cylinders, which, as previously explained, is of varying quantity, owing to the different amounts of the cushion steam. An important plan of combining the diagrams is to convert them in such a way that this varying cushion steam is eliminated, so that the diagrams will represent the volume and pressure of the 'working steam'—i.e. the weight of steam discharged from each cylinder per stroke—which amount is constant for all the cylinders. The saturation curve will then be the same for all the diagrams. To do this it is necessary to subtract from the volume of steam at each pressure on the diagram a quantity equal to the volume the cushion steam would occupy at that pressure. The method already described must be pursued to obtain this, the saturation curve E M, of Fig. 329, being continued to the initial pressure. The diagrams are then redrawn by setting off from the line of zero volume, abscissæ equal to the horizontal distances of the indicator diagram from

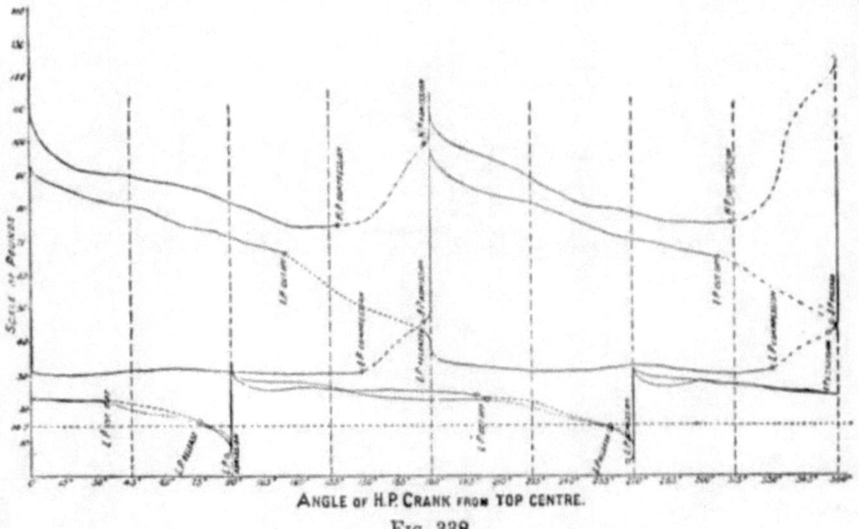

Fig. 338.

this saturation curve. Taking the diagram, Fig. 329, for example, this would be converted to Fig. 339, such that if o M' of this figure is equal to o s on the original diagram, M' F' = M F, and M' K' = M K.

The indicator diagrams in Fig. 336 have been thus transformed in Fig. 337. The area of the respective diagrams has not been altered by this transformation, but they now represent the changes of volume and pressure in all the cylinders of the constant quantity of *working steam*. To obtain the full advantage from the study of such a diagram, the quantity of feed-water used in the cylinders per stroke must be known. If this be known, a saturation curve for that quantity of steam is drawn, as A D in Fig. 337. If any horizontal line, such as s P, be now drawn, when the steam is shut off from the receivers, s Q will represent the volume of steam present in the cylinder and Q P the volume of steam condensed in the form of water.

Generally, however, the quantity of water used is not known, but

useful information may still be obtained from the diagram by drawing
a saturation curve which just touches the diagram.   This will then be
a *curve of uniform wetness*, equal to the smallest wetness shown by the
diagrams, and the relative liquefaction as the steam passes through the
various cylinders will be indicated by the relation of the diagram to
this curve.

This curve is drawn for the combined diagrams of H.M.S.
'Powerful' in Fig. 337, from which it will be seen that the wetness of the

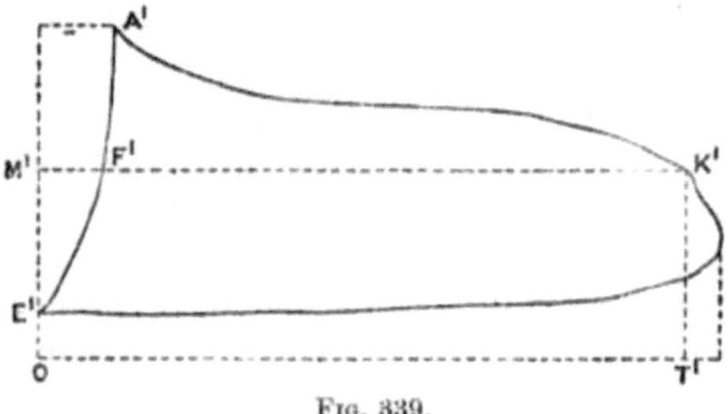

FIG. 339.

steam is greater in the I.P. and L.P. cylinders than in the H.P., but
the difference is not great.   The pressures maintained in the cylinder
jackets influence this.   On this occasion the jacket pressures were
lower than the initial pressures in the various cylinders, and had higher
pressures been maintained, the converted diagrams would probably all
have touched the saturation curve, indicating a constant amount of
moisture present in each cylinder.

CHAPTER XXVII.

PUMPING, WATERTIGHT, AND FIRE ARRANGEMENTS.

THE facilities for pumping out water from steamships, in case of a hole being made in the skin below the water-line, are much superior to anything that is possible in sailing vessels, in which the whole of the work has to be performed principally by manual labour. A statement of the fittings usually adopted in steamships, and of the precautions necessary in order to insure or increase their efficiency, will therefore be useful. The hand-pumping arrangements are practically the same in all ships, whether steam or sailing, and we shall consider only the special arrangements which are, or may be, fitted to all ships possessing steam power.

The pumping arrangements should be of such a nature that they may be used whilst the main propelling engines of the ship are at work, so that the ship may be able either to proceed to the nearest port in case of accident, whilst the pumps keep the water from rising too high, or, in extreme cases, that the ship may be kept afloat long enough to be run into shallow water or conveniently beached. In calculating the pumping power of the ship under the adverse circumstances supposed, it must not be assumed in cases where the pumping power depends on the speed of the main engines, that these could be worked at full power, for it is probable that under these conditions the engines could not be expected to work at more than about half power.

Circulating pump.—The pumps for circulating water through the engine main condensers may be considered as the main reliance in case of considerable leakage. These pumps are fitted with bilge as well as sea suctions, to be used in case of need, the circulating water being drawn from the bilge instead of the sea. Additional pipes to discharge the water directly overboard without passing through the condensers are sometimes fitted.

If the pumps be reciprocating and worked by the main engines, their efficiency and power would be reduced in the same ratio as the revolutions of the engines, which could only be worked at reduced power under the circumstances. If the circulating pumps be worked by separate engines, as is always now the case in the Royal Navy, the above limitation would not exist.

Circulating pumps, when worked by separate engines, are usually centrifugal, and it is known that for the small lift required to pump out a ship, the quantity of water that can be thrown by a comparatively small centrifugal pump is considerable.

In the Royal Navy the efficiency of the circulating pumps for bilge purposes is always tested prior to the receipt of the machinery. In the latest battleships four centrifugal pumps, each about 3 ft. 6 in.

diameter, are fitted for the main engine condensers, and each of these is capable of discharging at least 1,200 tons of water per hour from the bilges when worked at a speed not exceeding 300 revolutions per minute.

Precautions to insure circulating pumps drawing water.— Precautions have to be taken to insure the efficient working of centrifugal pumps for the purpose of lifting water. For ordinary work in ships, their only office is to circulate the water, both the inlet and outlet orifices being below the surface. They cannot in all cases be relied on to lift the water from any considerable depth, and they should be placed as low down in the ship as possible, which is the most simple way of insuring that they will draw readily, in the excitement consequent on the ship making water rapidly. It is also necessary that they should be fully charged with water at starting, and kept fully supplied when at work, for any air getting into the suction pipes interferes with the action of the pumps, and any considerable quantity would stop them from pumping. Self-acting non-return valves should therefore be placed at the bottoms of the suction pipes, as low down as possible in the bilge, so that the whole length of the suction pipes will be filled with water before starting the pumps to draw from the bilge. The suction pipe should also be of sufficient area to keep the pump fully supplied with water, without requiring too high a velocity in the pipe. In some cases inefficient action of these pumps for bilge purposes has been due to the smallness of the supply pipe, the water not being able to enter the pump sufficiently fast to keep it fully charged.

Situation of pump and engine.—Large engine power required.— Though the pump itself should be close to the bilge, the engine for working it ought, if possible, to be at a high level, so as to be out of reach of the water in case of its rising rapidly, as the full discharge of a centrifugal pump under these circumstances requires a high speed of revolution.

This arrangement has been carried out in several of the older naval ships, the pump being placed in a horizontal position in the bilge, where it acts most efficiently, and worked by a vertical shaft carried to a considerable height and attached to the crank shaft of a horizontal engine. No engine can work long with water surrounding it, turning the cylinders into condensers, and stopping the engines. This arrangement, while very suitable for pumping efficiency, is generally inconvenient as regards the other engine-room fittings, and has not been carried out in any recent ship, or for some years.

Another point that should be kept in view in designing these pumps is the provision of large engine power; for in the case of a serious leak, when the water rises and gathers on the fires, or prevents the firemen from working in the stokeholds, the pressure of steam will drop, and may become even less than the atmospheric pressure. It is for this reason that the engines are made considerably larger than required for merely circulating water under ordinary circumstances.

The valves for changing the suction of the centrifugal pumps from the sea to the bilge, are arranged to be worked from the starting platform, and to enable this to be done quickly in case of need, the valves in the sea and bilge suction pipes are often coupled together so that they may be worked by a single lever.

Several instances have been recorded in which ships seriously injured have been kept afloat long enough to run to harbour, or to enable the passengers and crew to be saved, by the application of the circulating pumps.

Main engine bilge pumps.—Formerly the majority of all steamships, including warships, were fitted with bilge pumps worked direct by the main engines, and this is still the common practice in the mercantile marine.

These pumps are not fitted so much to provide for extraordinary leaks as to clear the bilges of the water that drains into them from pipes, bearings, &c., and other ordinary leakages from various causes. They are, however, usually much larger than is required for these purposes alone, even when the ordinary leakages are comparatively large, so that where so fitted their action should be taken into account in calculating the pumping power of a ship. The plungers of these pumps are always working with the main engines, so that they are not made as large as might otherwise be the case ; for it would be difficult to keep the plungers and barrels sufficiently lubricated to prevent over-heating, and a considerable addition would be made to the constant friction of the engines, which is already large. Larger pumps would also necessitate larger discharge pipes, valves, &c., which would be inconvenient and often impossible. In modern warships separate bilge pumping engines are fitted instead of pumps worked by the main engines.

A small pump is, however, still fitted in the most recent warships, which is arranged to be worked by hand, and either from the air pump levers or by an eccentric sheave or pin on the engine-shaft to assist in dealing with the water service and other drainage water. Its size is so small, however, as to be inappreciable as regards a leak in the vessel.

Fire and bilge engines.—The fire pumps and those for ordinary bilge pumping work are often pumps of different pattern. This has sometimes been the case in the Royal Navy, but for many years past in this service they have been of the same construction, and can be used at will for either of these purposes.

At least two such pumps are fitted in all except the smallest ships, and they are sometimes distinguished by the names of ' main ' and 'auxiliary' fire and bilge pumps. In large battleships and cruisers there are four of these pumps, two in each engine room, each of the four being capable of pumping 80 to 120 tons of water from the bilges per hour, while smaller cruisers are supplied with two such pumps, each capable of discharging 60 tons in the case of second class cruisers, and 40 tons in third-class cruisers, per hour. The pumps are large enough to remove these quantities with revolutions not exceeding 60 per minute and a steam pressure of two-thirds the maximum boiler pressure, and they form a means of pumping water out of the ship auxiliary to the main circulating pumps. They are used to clear the bilge of water and oil which finds its way there from bearings, drain pipes, &c. A sketch of one type of these pumping engines, with two cylinders and double-acting pumps, is shown in Fig. 340.

Double cylinders are desirable for these engines to facilitate starting ; and the slide-valves are made with very little lap, to insure

the engines starting readily in any position of the cranks, economy in
the use of the steam being in these cases a minor consideration.

Separate steam pumps are fitted for latrine purposes in modern
large warships. These 'latrine pumps' discharge sea-water into the
fire main direct for use in connection with the sanitary system.

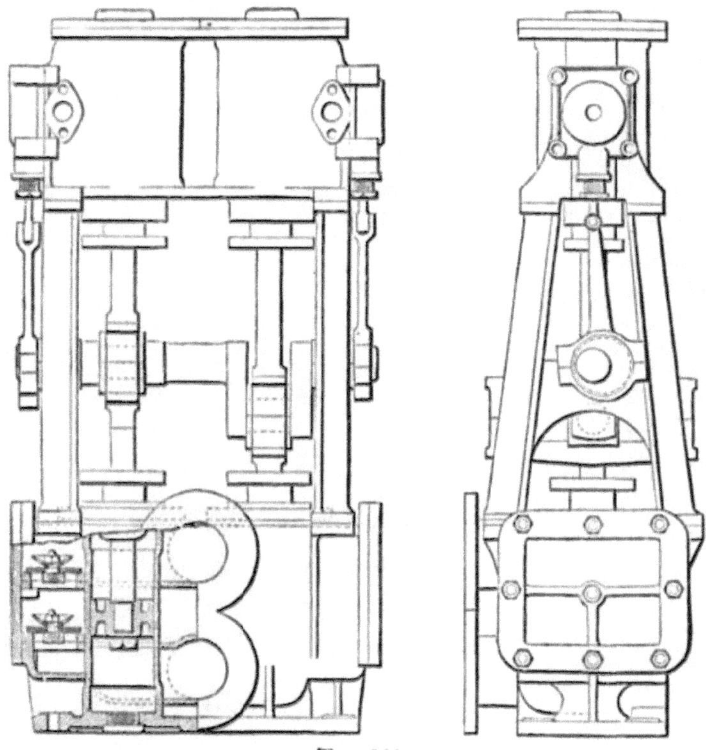

Fig. 340.

Friedmann's bilge ejector.—This apparatus is a modification of
the Giffard's injector, sometimes used for feeding boilers, the number
of nozzles being increased so as to give the steam several suction
orifices instead of one. The steam is conducted to a tuyere about one-
half the diameter of the steam pipe, and then passes successively through
a series of intermediate tuyeres, through which the water is drawn from
the hold, and expelled from the ship through the discharge pipe.

This apparatus occupies little space and its capacity is considerable,
but it consumes a large quantity of steam and would not be economical
for general use. Several of the old armour-clad ships are fitted with
Friedmann's ejectors to deal with the coal spaces, the water from which
may contain quantities of coal-dust, but they are not fitted in modern
vessels.

Usual bilge ejectors.—Small bilge ejectors, with a single orifice,
are fitted to steam launches, pinnaces, &c., and have been found
by experience to clear the boats of water efficiently. The steam

pipe is $\frac{1}{2}$-inch to $\frac{5}{8}$-inch diameter, with a $\frac{1}{4}$-inch orifice, and the discharge-pipe is $\frac{3}{4}$-inch to $\frac{7}{8}$-inch diameter. Such ejectors have been found by experiment to be sufficiently powerful to force water out of the bilges faster than it would flow in when a plug, about one inch diameter, in the bottom of the boat was removed.

Bilge ejectors of more powerful type are also fitted in all torpedo boats and torpedo-boat destroyers. These vessels are divided into several watertight compartments, and a steam bilge ejector is fitted in each of the large compartments, each being sufficiently powerful to discharge 30 tons of water per hour from the bilges.

Pulsometer.—This is a peculiar pumping arrangement acting by the direct pressure of the steam on the water which used to be fitted in many steamships of the mercantile marine, especially for ballast pumps, and appears to have given satisfaction. The whole of the steam used, however, is lost, so that with high-pressure steam their use has become inadmissible.

Flow of sea-water through a hole.—Although the steam pumping appliances supplied to ships most perfectly equipped in this respect are very valuable, most ships would be in great danger in case of serious damage below the water line if they had only the pumping arrangements to rely on. The quantity of water that would flow into a ship through a hole may be calculated approximately as follows :—

Let H = depth of hole below the water line in feet,
      A = area of hole in square inches,
and g = accelerating force of gravity.

Then, if V = velocity of flow into the ship in feet per second,
$$V = \sqrt{2\,g\,H} = 8 \sqrt{H} \text{ approximately.}$$

The number of cubic feet of water that would flow into the ship per second is therefore equal to

$$\frac{A \times 8 \sqrt{H}}{144} = \frac{A \times \sqrt{H}}{18}.$$

For example, supposing a hole in a vessel 12 inches in diameter, 16 feet below the surface of the water. The area of this hole is equal to 113 square inches, so that the rate at which the water would begin to flow into the ship would be $= \dfrac{113 \times \sqrt{16}}{18} = 25$ cubic feet per second, or 90,000 cubic feet per hour. This divided by 35 will give the number of tons per hour ; so that a hole 12 inches in diameter, 16 feet below the water, would be capable of admitting into the ship $\dfrac{90,000}{35} = 2,570$ tons of water per hour. Therefore a comparatively small hole in the bottom of a ship would be sufficient to absorb all the available pumping power that could be provided.

Watertight compartments.—The pumping arrangements can, even when most complete and efficient, only be regarded as an auxiliary in cases where the ship sustains considerable damage below the water line, such as from collision, &c. ; and the only complete safeguard is the division of the hull into as many watertight compartments as is possible, consistent with the requirements of the ship, so that the effects of any injury may be localised. The pumping arrangements could, in cases where the damage is not serious, or the leak not considerable. be utilised to keep the defective compartment sufficiently free from water to enable the damage to be wholly or partially repaired.

As shown above, however, in cases where the injury is so serious as to admit large bodies of water, the pumping appliances would not be powerful enough to keep the compartment free, unless collision mats or other leak stoppers can be applied. In this case the pumps are, however, very valuable for dealing with water in adjacent compartments due to local straining of bulkheads, double bottoms, &c.

The watertight compartments are formed by constructing iron or steel watertight bulkheads across the ship at certain sections. In large war vessels there is a further subdivision by a longitudinal bulkhead at the middle line of the vessel, and also in the coal bunker and wing spaces, and by horizontal iron or steel watertight decks. In many warships the middle-line bulkhead extends throughout the engine and boiler rooms, but in the most modern they are confined to the engine room only. This middle-line bulkhead is also fitted in some passenger steamers, with twin screws.

When the vertical bulkheads do not terminate at a watertight deck, their upper edges should be carried to a sufficient height above the load water line to prevent the water in an injured compartment flowing over the tops of the bulkheads into the adjoining compartments, even when the ship is at the greater immersion due to the injured compartments being full of water. The height to which the bulkheads are carried above the load water line should be proportioned to the volumes of the respective compartments, in order to insure safety without unduly increasing weight.

Watertight doors.—The communication between the various compartments is maintained by means of sliding watertight doors, sketches of which are given in Figs. 341 and 342. When the door is worked in a vertical direction it is raised and lowered by means of a screw, as shown in Fig. 341. When the watertight door slides horizontally, it is worked by means of racks and pinions, the racks being fixed on the back of the door itself, as shown in Fig. 342. The gear for working these doors should be on the main or upper deck, above the water line, and in positions readily accessible in case of emergency. Means should also be provided for working the doors from below when required. Wedges are fitted on the doors and at the ends of the guides, so that when the door is shut it may be pressed tightly against the inner face of the guide to prevent the passage of water.

To promote uniformity and prevent mistake, the gear for working watertight doors should be fitted in such a manner that the door may be closed by a right-hand motion. Every precaution should be taken to keep the guide grooves clear and the gear in good working order, so that there may be no difficulty in closing the doors in case of necessity, when any mistake may be not only inconvenient but fatal. When the doors are open, the bottom grooves, which are the most liable to become choked, are covered with plates or sills, fitted to open out automatically by the closing of the doors. The doors in watertight bulkheads should be as few as possible in number, and placed at as high

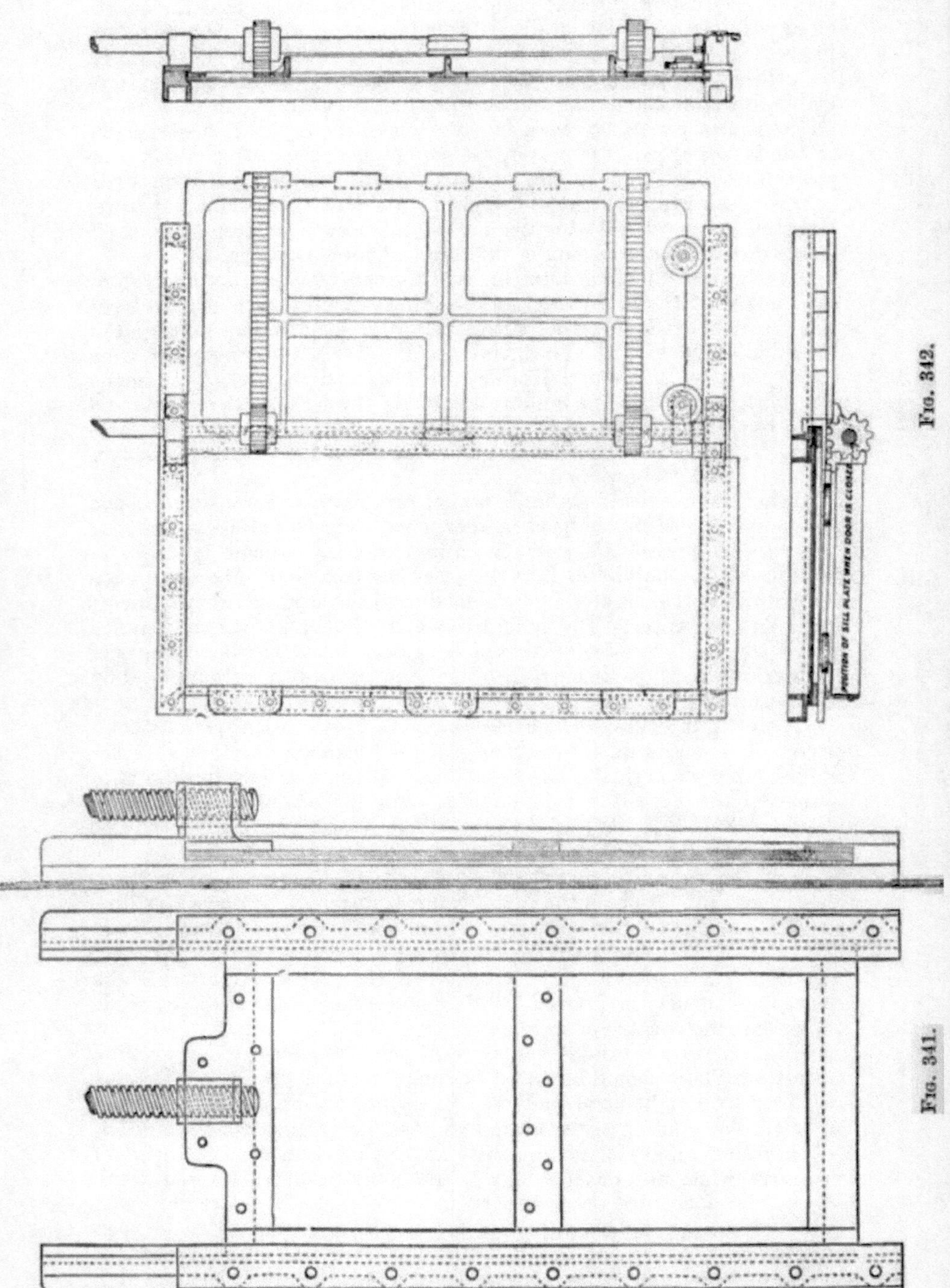

FIG. 342.

FIG. 341.

a level as circumstances will allow, in order to increase the efficiency of the watertight arrangements.

Special provision is made for quickly closing from the hold, the doors in the large spaces forming the engine and boiler rooms, and these doors should be kept well up from the inner bottom. Vertical doors are capable of more rapid and certain closing than horizontal doors, and are fitted for all important doors in the hold space. The quick closing is now effected by fitting a quadruple-threaded screw of coarse pitch for the door, while for ordinary vertical closing doors the screw is a double-threaded one.

Sluice-valves.—Small sluice-valves are usually fitted in the lower parts of the watertight bulkheads to allow the water to be drained from one compartment to another if required. These valves should be arranged to shut with a right-hand motion, and the rods, &c., for working them should be carried to the same height, and to the same positions, as the gear for working the watertight doors. Cocks are sometimes provided in certain parts instead of sluice-valves.

Double bottom.—The safety of most ships in the Royal Navy is very much increased by the construction of a 'double bottom.' This consists of an inner watertight skin, at some distance from the outer skin, extending for about two-thirds to three-fourths of the total length of the ship. The distance between the inner and outer skins at the bottom of the ship is generally about three or four feet, depending on the size of the ship; and above the turn of the bilge, the inner skin is continued by vertical bulkheads carried up above the water line, and forming what are called the 'wing passages.' The double bottom and wing passages are divided into many small compartments by longitudinal and transverse bulkheads.

In H.M.S. 'Majestic,' for example, there are 46 compartments in the hold space, 48 in the double bottom, and 36 in the coal bunkers and wings, making a total of 130 watertight compartments in the ship. To enable the surfaces of the double bottoms, wing passages, &c., to be examined, cleaned, and painted, two manholes are made in the inner skin for each of the several compartments. The manhole doors are screwed down over the holes, generally with red-lead putty between the faces, so as to make watertight joints. The duplicate manhole facilitates ventilation.

Considerable damage may be done to the outer skin of a ship fitted with a double bottom without endangering her safety, for unless the inner skin be broken no water can enter the hold. The compartments in the double bottom are also so small that the filling of several of them would have but comparatively little effect on the immersion or the trim of the ship.

Water ballast.—In some cases the double-bottom compartments have been utilised for the carrying of water ballast, and in this way they have proved useful as the ship became lighter from any cause. Some are also appropriated as reserve tanks for the stowage of fresh water for the use of the boilers.

Suction and discharge arrangements of fire and bilge pumps.— These pumps are fitted with separate suction pipes leading to the following parts :—Forward and after ends of engine room, with a continuation to the screw tunnel from the latter; main engine saveall ;

each boiler compartment ; the main suction pipe, described below ; salvage system of the vessel ; and to the sea ; the valve boxes and pipes being so arranged that each pump can draw from any of these parts. The pumps deliver water either overboard direct, to the engine room, or to the fire main, a large air vessel being fitted in connection with the latter. Fig. 342a shows a general arrangement of the valve-boxes and suction and delivery pipes of a large ship.

A A are pumps ; B B are directing valve-boxes to which the bilge suctions are led. These valves are of the non-return type, excepting

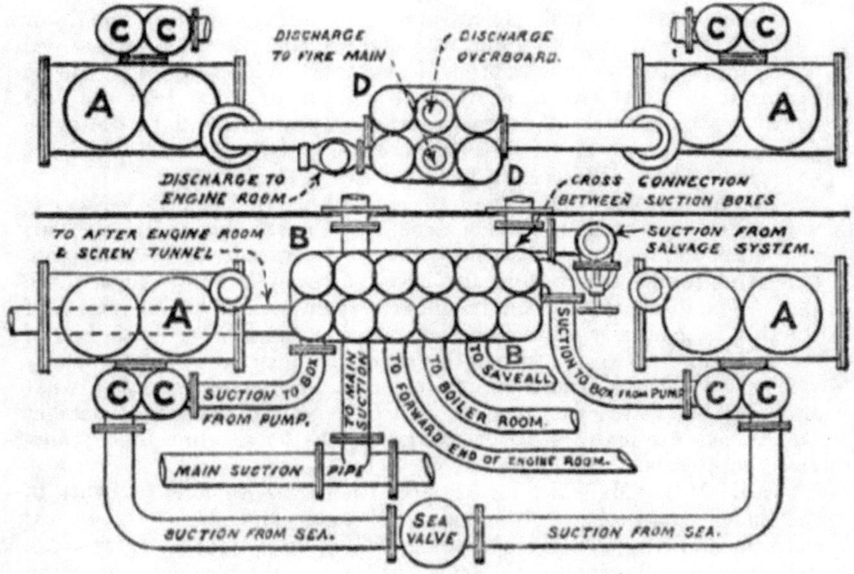

FIG. 342a.

in the case of the two valves on the right, which form a connection with the corresponding box in the other engine room ; C C are shut-off valves from sea, and bilge directing valve-box, respectively, so that one pump in each engine room can be worked on the sea whilst the other is on the bilge. D D are directing valve-boxes for discharge either to fire main, overboard, or to engine room.

The connection to the main suction permits the steam pumps being used on all the ship's double bottoms, as explained later. Should the main engine saveall suction of these pumps or the saveall pumps themselves become choked, the sluice-valve M (Fig. 342b) affords a direct connection with the engine room bilge suction.

The valves in B B being non-return prevent the possibility of sea-water passing into the vessel when the sea suction is open. In addition to these, in the cases of long lengths of suction pipes, it is generally the practice to fit additional non-return valves on the ends of the pipes to facilitate the pumps drawing.

Main suction pipe.—The steam bilge pumping engines are, as described above, connected through a branch on the directing valve-boxes with a pipe termed the *main suction*, A A A, Fig. 342b, which is in large ships 6 inches in diameter in wake of the double bottom, and tapers slightly from this part to the ends of the vessel. This pipe has branches, each with a separate stop valve, leading into each double bottom and watertight flat compartment, and also to pockets in the bilges above the double bottoms in the machinery spaces, for the purpose of pumping them out. Sluice-valves are fitted on the watertight flats beyond the double bottom proper for draining water above the flats to the suction pipes. The ship's large hand pumps are also connected to this suction pipe, and are arranged so that either pump can draw from any compartment.

The main suction pipe can also be utilised for filling the double bottom compartments when required, by connecting the valve-box with the sea suction, but to guard against the accidental introduction of salt water into the tanks appropriated for storage of reserve feed-water, portable connections are used between these tanks and the valve-boxes.

Main drain pipe and general drainage arrangements.—To further facilitate the pumping out of the hold of a ship divided into several compartments, large galvanised steel drain pipes are fitted. Fig. 342*b* shows the arrangement of drain pipes, main suction pipe, and general drainage arrangements for the machinery compartments and adjacent spaces in a modern battleship. In this case the main drain pipes D D D are 15 inches diameter throughout the length of the machinery spaces, and are continued beyond these spaces, as far as the double bottom and watertight flats extend, but are gradually reduced in diameter, and the extreme ends are carried up so as to drain water from the forward and after parts of the protective deck.

The drains, E E E, from the wing spaces and bunkers adjacent to the machinery spaces lead directly into the bilges of these compartments, and the main drain receives the water by means of sluice-valves F F F. Outside the machinery spaces, where not convenient to flood the bilges, the drains lead direct to the main drain pipes.

Sluice-valves are fitted to the main drain pipes at each watertight bulkhead, and where the main drain is fitted in duplicate, or where it has branch connections leading into another watertight compartment, non-return valves, G G G, are fitted to provide against the drainage from one compartment flowing into another, in case the sluice-valves are unintentionally open. The main drain pipes terminate in large sluice-valves at the forward and after bulkheads of the engine rooms ; these valves regulate the flow of water to the engine room compartments, the two engine room compartments being connected by a large sluice-valve at the middle line bulkhead. The main drain pipe is intended to deal with considerable quantities of water, which flow into the engine-room bilges, and if so large in amount that the ordinary steam bilge pumps are unable to deal with it, it can be pumped out by the circulating pump through its bilge suction, waterways being provided in the engine bearers for free access to these suctions.

For convenience the main drain pipe was, in the older ships, carried through the double bottom, but it was not in connection with it, and was fitted only for the drainage of compartments in the hold of the ship. In modern ships the drain pipes are not run through the double bottom, various accidents to the outer skin of the vessel and consequent fracture of the drain pipe having shown the danger of such a lead.

ENGINE ROOM
ENGINE ROOM SAVEALL
ENGINE ROOM
ENGINE ROOM SAVEALL
FOR'D BOILER ROOM.
D MAIN DRAIN
MAIN SUCTION
To Main Circulating Pump Bilge Suction Valve
Main Circulating Pump Bilge Suction Valve
Stop Valve
Suction from Double Bottoms
To Ships Hand Pump
Water Tight Division in Double Bottom
Sluice Valve Horizontal
Connection to Steam Pump
Mud Box
Drain from Bilges
To Flood Valve Box from Sea Valve

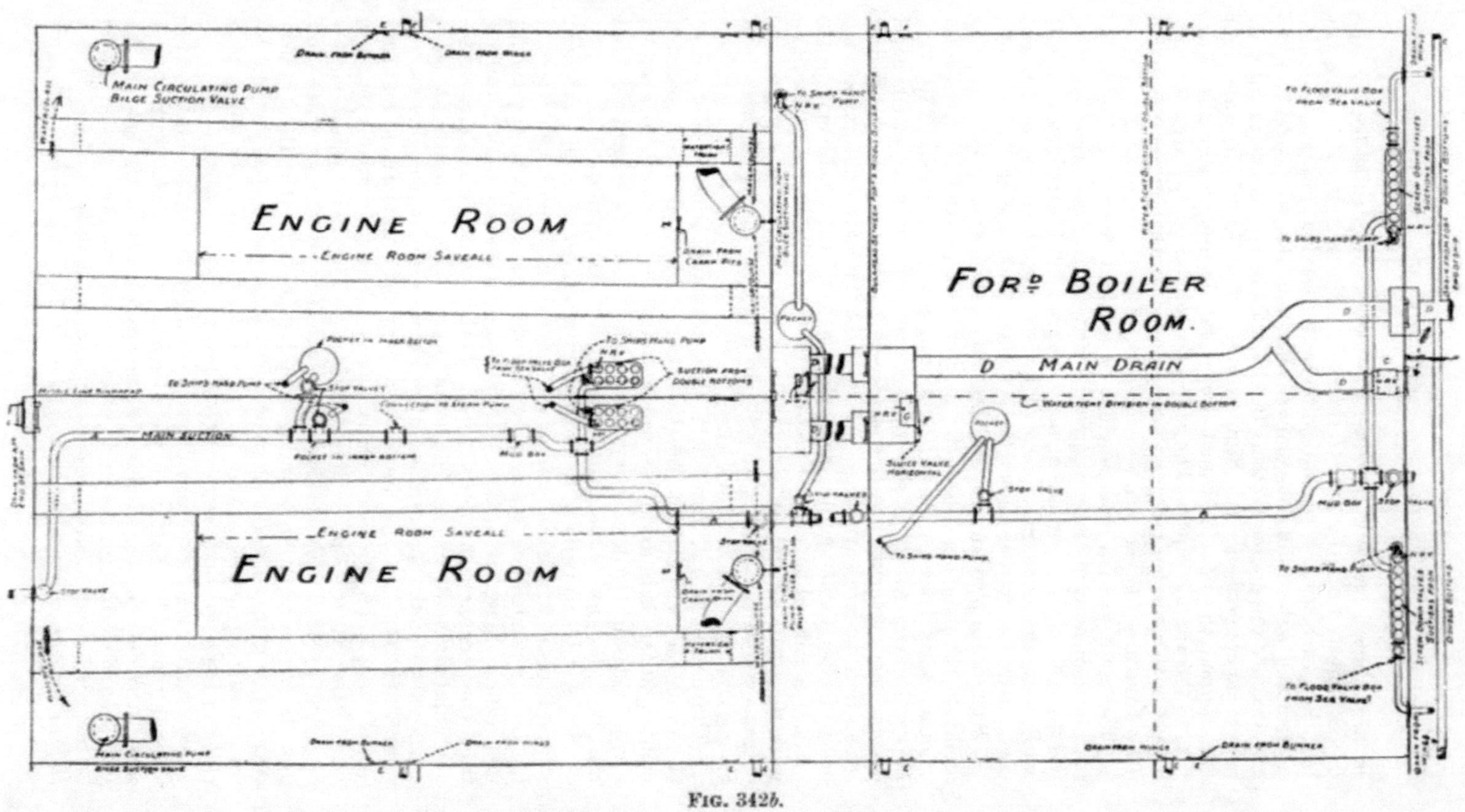

FIG. 342b.

They are now always placed above the inner bottom.   Arrangements are made for flushing the main drain pipes near the ends direct from the sea, and chains are sometimes fitted for clearing them when choked.

Drainage of small amount can be dealt with as follows :—

(1) In double bottoms and under watertight flats beyond the double bottoms :—By ship's hand pumps direct or by the main suction.

(2) Machinery spaces over double bottoms :—By the ship's hand pumps direct ; through the main suction pipe by the ship's hand pumps or steam bilge pumps ; or by the ordinary steam pump bilge suction.   Other spaces over double bottoms and over the watertight flats at ends of double bottoms :—By draining into the main drain, or to the compartments under the watertight flats by means of sluice-valves.

(3) From bunker compartments at sides of engine and boiler rooms :—By sluice-valves to engine and boiler rooms, the water being then dealt with as at (2).

(4) From wing compartments adjacent to the machinery spaces :— By running to bilges of machinery compartment by pipes with sluice-valves at the bulkhead.   From wing compartments beyond the machinery spaces and at the ends above the protective deck :—By running direct to the main drain and thus to the engine room bilges.

Drain cisterns.—In the older warships the main drain pipes are connected to large drain cisterns, and the small pump suctions are led to these, arrangements being made so that the cisterns overflow into the engine room bilges when the circulating pumps are required.

Flooding cocks.—To the most dangerous parts of the ship, such as the magazines, shell- and spirit-rooms, &c., flooding pipes are led, connected with the sea by Kingston or other valves and sea-cocks in the ordinary manner, so that in case of fire the compartment may be flooded with water from the sea.   Special precautions have to be taken to prevent these cocks being tampered with ; and, as a rule, there is between the ordinary sea-cock and the compartment an additional cock or valve, which is locked, and can only be opened by the officer entrusted with the key.

Arrangements are also made in warships so that when they are in dry dock these parts may then be flooded from the shore water pipes, by means of branches on the flooding system, fitted for this purpose.

Fire-main.—All the fire and bilge and latrine steam pumps, except any worked off the main engines, also the ship's hand pumps, are fitted with sea suctions, and are arranged to deliver the water into a pipe called the fire-main, which is carried fore-and-aft in the ship, with branches leading to different parts as required.   At various points in the fire-main, delivery valves with suitable screwed nozzles are fitted, to which hoses may be connected to direct water on any required spot. Non-return valves should be fitted at the junctions of delivery pipes from pumping engines with the fire-main, and the pumps should have sufficient power to produce the necessary pressure in the main.

For dealing with small fires, small bib-valves are fitted to enable water to be quickly drawn off in buckets, to avoid the delay which might be caused by rigging a hose.

Besides the branches on the fire-main for the sanitary arrangements, others are fitted for washing-out boilers and guns, for running through hawse-pipes when working cables, and for capstan water service.

CHAPTER XXVIII.

AUXILIARY MACHINERY AND FITTINGS.

In modern steamships, especially in those of the Royal Navy, the auxiliary machinery and fittings are of great importance. In H.M.S. 'Powerful,' for example, there are ninety-nine different auxiliary steam-engines for various purposes in addition to the main engines of the ship. In the battleships of the 'Majestic' class there are 72 auxiliary steam-engines and 32 hydraulic turning engines, lifts, bollards, &c. Those vessels are really huge floating war machines, where all the principal operations for working, steering, and fighting are performed by steam or hydraulic power with little manual labour, so that the vessel's efficiency will depend largely on the condition of the machinery department.

The enumeration of the various kinds of work on board ships that are now done by steam power would be sufficient to show the importance of this part of the duty of the engineer. In addition to the main propelling engines, steam power is used for ventilating the ship and supplying air to the boilers ; weighing the anchor ; steering ; pumping ; working turrets, and loading, training, and working the guns ; compressing air for charging and launching torpedoes ; putting torpedo and other boats into and lifting them out of the water ; distilling fresh water ; producing electricity for lighting the vessel and for search lights ; for refrigerating purposes ; for actuating the machines supplied in the workshop ; lifting coal into the vessel, &c.

The development of electrical science has now rendered possible the transmission in a very efficient and economical manner of the power generated in the dynamo to electric motors for various purposes in different parts of the ship, and this is taken advantage of to work ventilating fans, &c., in confined spaces, where the heat of steam pipes would be objectionable. It also reduces the complication, as the necessary wire leads can be run along in places where steam and exhaust pipes would be most difficult. Such motors will probably be much more extensively used on board ship in the future than they are at present.

Steering engine.—Figs. 343 and 344 show an arrangement of steam steering engine which has been largely fitted and found efficient. The shaft A, leading to the tiller, is driven by the engine through a system of toothed gearing, which reduces the speed of revolution to a sufficient extent to obtain the necessary turning moment to work the rudder readily, when the ship is moving at full speed.

The speciality in this engine is the fitting by which it is stopped when the helm is moved to the required angle, the rudder being held

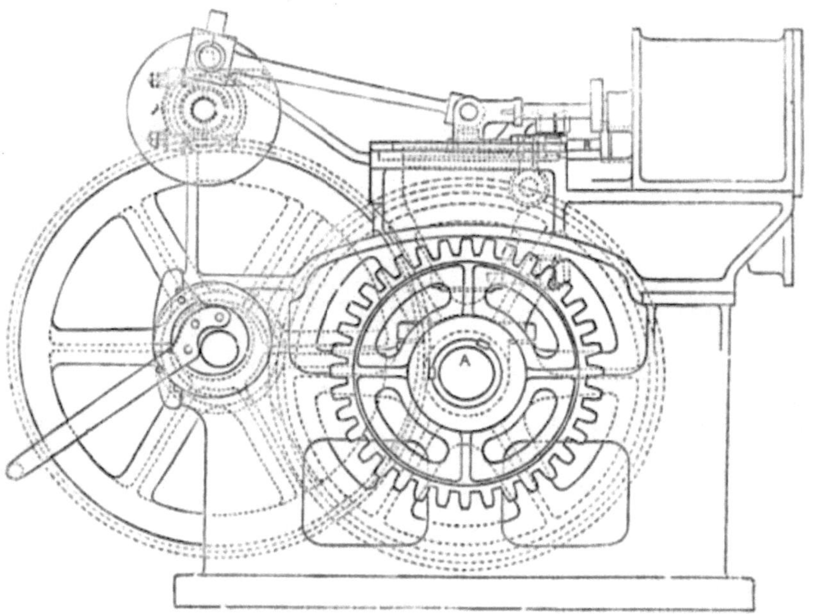

Fig. 343.

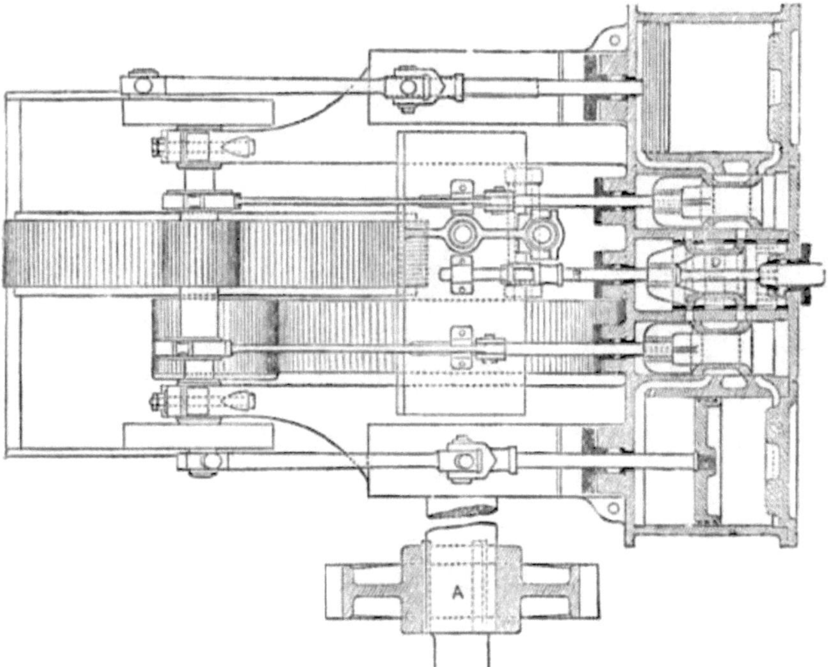

Fig. 344.

in this position until the engine is again moved by the working of the steering wheel. A sketch of this arrangement to an enlarged scale is shown in Fig. 345. The starting and reversing valve D, Fig. 344, is a differential valve, similar to that described in Chapter XVII., and it is actuated by means of shafting and gearing, led from the engine to the steering wheels placed at various parts of the ship. The rod of this reversing valve is marked R on the diagrams, and is actuated by the rising and falling of the screw S, operating on the bell-crank lever working on the fulcrum B, Fig. 345. The screw S is caused to revolve by the action of the spur-wheel C, which is worked by the several steering wheels in the ship. On the shaft A a bevel wheel E is fixed, which, as the shaft revolves, works the nut F, and thus causes the screw S to rise or fall according to the direction of rotation. This gear is so arranged that when the engine is started in any direction by the working of the steering wheel, the action of the wheels E and F tends to move the starting valve back to its central position, and thus to stop the engine.

There are, therefore, two forces acting on the valve : the one from the steering wheel, worked by hand, which moves the valve as may be required to start the engine in the direction necessary to put the rudder to starboard or port as desired ; and the other from the engine

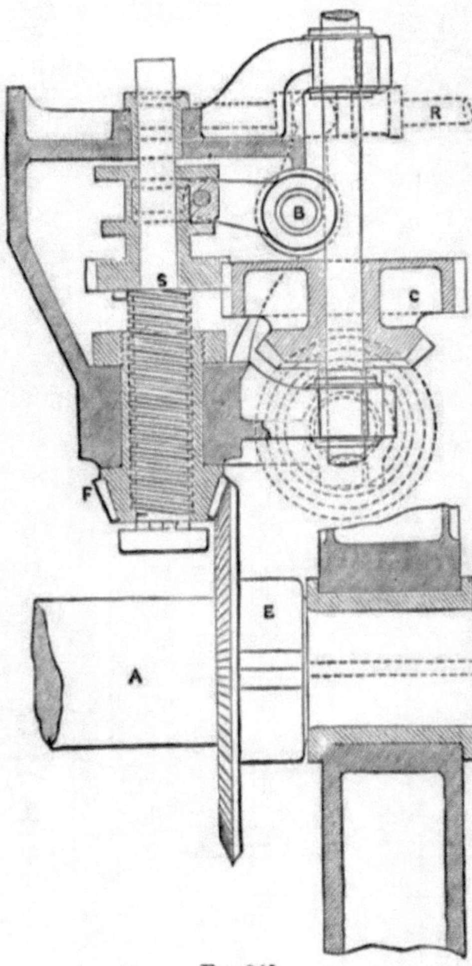

Fig. 345.

itself, which always tends to replace the valve in its central position and stop the engine. Consequently, the engine only keeps in motion while the steering wheel is being worked, and as soon as the steersman ceases turning the wheel the steering engine stops, and the rudder remains fixed in the position to which it has been put until it is again moved by the steersman.

Instead of transmitting the motion of the steering wheel to the engine by means of shafting and bevel wheels, *Brown's ' Telemotor '* is fitted in several recent warships of the Royal Navy, in which the motion is transmitted by water pressure in small pipes, a certain motion of the piston of a water cylinder, called the ' transmitter,' at the steering position on deck, producing a similar motion in the piston of a water cylinder, called the ' receiver ' cylinder, near the steering engine, by means of which the reversing valve is moved by a simple form of lever, so arranged that the resulting motion of the engine works the engine controlling valve back to its middle or ' stop ' position. Means are provided for preventing inaccuracy due to changes of volume of the fluid through differences of temperature or losses from joints, and for reducing inaccuracy from leakage past the pistons.

Steam steering wheels. — The wheels which work the reversing valve of the engine, called steam steering wheels, one of which is shown in Fig. 346, are fitted on pedestals which contain stops to prevent the wheels being turned too far in either direction, which would cause the rudder to be placed at too great an angle, and strain and endanger the steering gear. The number of turns of the steering wheel from hard a port to hard a starboard is arranged to be eight, and more revolutions than this are prevented by projections on the sliding nut A, which, when the maximum number of turns have been made, engage with corresponding stops pinned on the shaft, so that the wheel cannot be moved further. The wheel also works an index finger on the top of pedestal, which shows the steersman the position of the rudder.

Gear between engine and rudder. —The steering engine sometimes works, through its shaft, a barrel on which wire ropes are wound, which lead to the end of the tiller as in the ordinary hand steering gear.

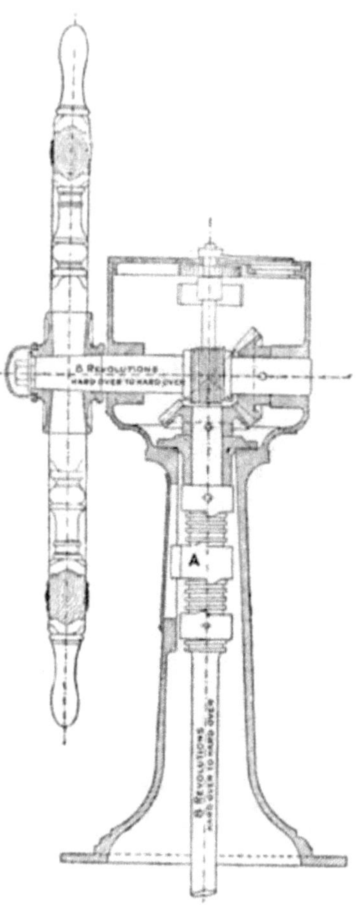

Fig. 346.

This, however, is not so suitable for steam power, as there is risk of the ropes being strained if the engine be moved quickly ; and the holes in the bulkheads of the ship through which the ropes pass cannot be made watertight.

In all gear worked by steam power, the arrangements should be as rigid and mechanical as possible, and shafting and gearing be adopted if practicable, in preference to ropes or chains. The holes in the bulkheads of the ship through which the shafting is carried can then

be made watertight by suitable stuffing-boxes. More generally, therefore, and in all warships except those of the smallest class, shafting is
carried from the steering engine to the after part of the ship, where it
actuates the rudder by means of suitable gearing.

Details of rudder gears.—One arrangement which has been found
efficient is 'Rapson's slide,' largely used in battleships, and shown in
Figs. 347 and 348.   With this arrangement there is a sliding frame,
travelling on guides or rails running transversely across the stern of the
ship, and the slide is pulled on one side or other of the middle line by a
pitch chain, A, having tightening screws, and actuated by the steering
engine through a 'sprocket' or chain-working wheel, B, below the slide.
The sprocket is rotated by the steering engine or hand steering gear,
whichever is connected.

The end of the tiller, C, is parallel and of rectangular section and a
swivelling block carried by the sliding frame fits over it.   As the steering engine moves the sprocket wheel, the sliding frame moves along the
guides and carries with it the end of the tiller, which slides in the
swivelling block, the latter rotating slightly in the horizontal plane to
suit the angle of the tiller.

The arrangement shown is that of a modern battleship with two
steering engines and hand steering gear ; the wheels and clutches shown
explain how either steering engine or the hand gear can be used to
operate the rudder.   By turning the small wheel shown in connection
with the clutch levers the three slots are turned round, and these are so
arranged that only one clutch is in gear at the same time.   The wheels
are loose on the shaft, while the clutches work on feathers, and the one
in gear drives the steering shaft.

Another arrangement, which is designed to increase the turning
moment on the rudder as its resistance increases, is Harfield's compensating steering gear, shown in Figs. 349 and 350.   In this gear the
engine drives a horizontal bevel wheel, A, loose on the vertical spindle,
but which, by means of a clutch keyed to the vertical spindle, rotates
an eccentric pinion, B, on a vertical shaft.   This eccentric pinion gears
with a rack, C, so shaped as to always engage with the eccentric pinion,
while moving about a fixed centre.   The force is transferred to the
rudder by means of double rods which simply transmit the force from
the fixed axis to the rudder-head, but do not alter it, so that when
examining the action of the gear the fixed centre may be considered to
be the rudder-head.

Assuming the engine to exert a constant turning moment on the
vertical shaft, it will be seen that when the rudder is central the
longer radius of the eccentric pinion acts on the rack, and the motion
is comparatively rapid and the force exerted small.   As the rudder
increases its angle, and therefore its resistance to motion, the smaller
radius of the eccentric pinion comes into operation, and the force
exerted is correspondingly increased.   A worm leading from the hand
steering position, gearing with a worm-wheel D, also loose on the vertical spindle, are provided to enable hand power to be also used, the
clutch being the means of transference from steam to hand power.   To
prevent risk of accident when this transference takes place it is necessary that the rudder pins should be shipped, so as to secure the rudder.
These are shown in Figs. 349 and 350.

Hydraulic steering gear.—In many ships hydraulic power has

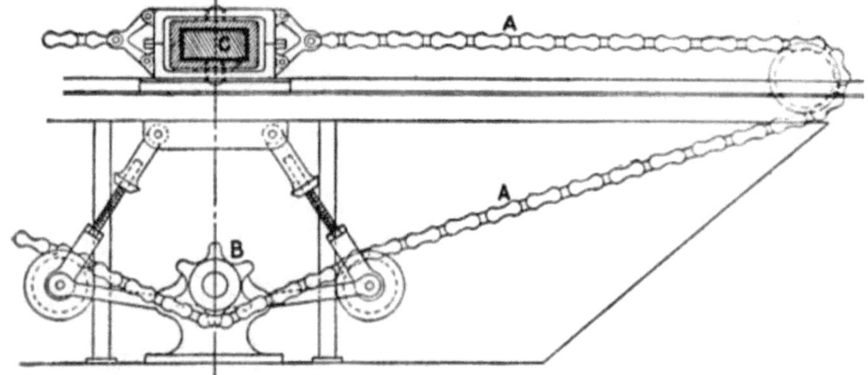

FIG. 347.

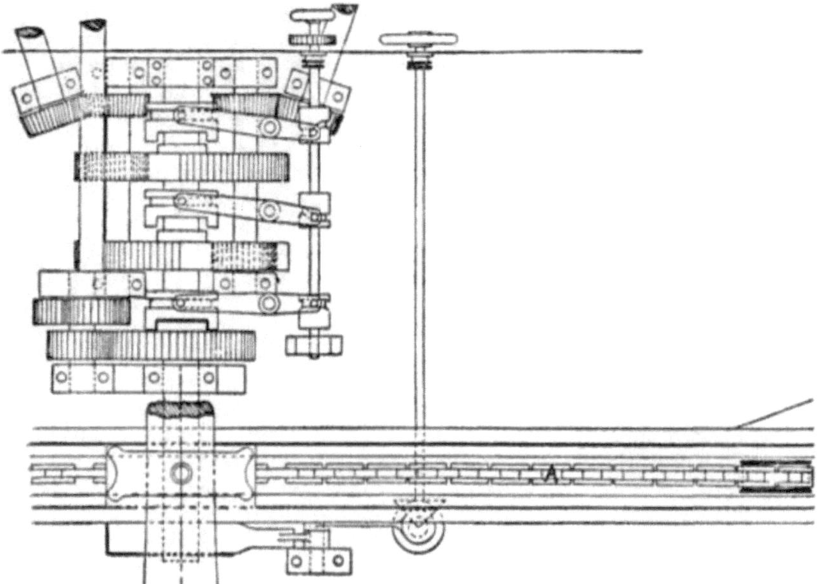

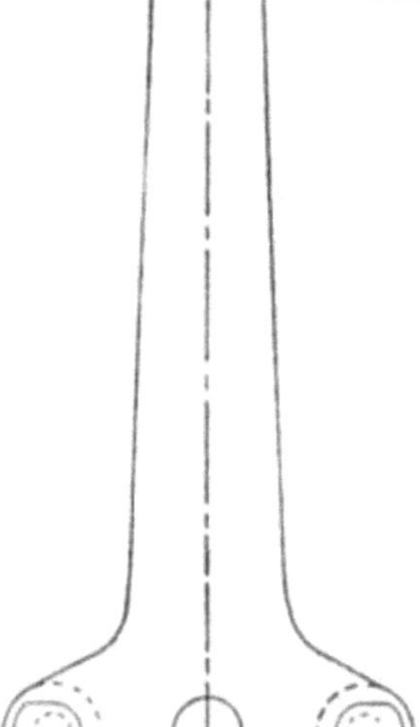

FIG. 348.

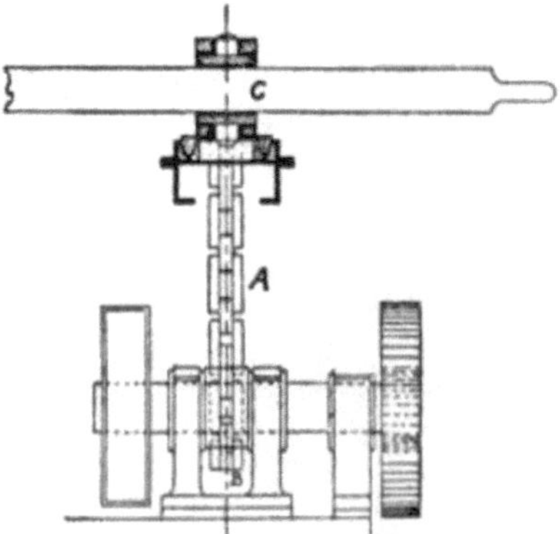

FIG. 347a.

C C

been used, instead of steam power, for working the rudder, and various plans have been adopted for utilising water pressure for this purpose. In several ships that have been fitted with this kind of steering gear, the hydraulic pressure has been utilised for other auxiliary purposes, such as for working cranes, winches, reversing gear for main engines, &c.

The advantages of steam or hydraulic power for steering in the case of large ships need no discussion. It places the control of the ship practically in the hands of one man, who is enabled to place the rudder hard over to starboard or port, when the ship is steaming at full speed, with little exertion, perfect safety, and in very much less time than would be required with hand gear, even when worked with a large number of men. It is, however, essential that the steering apparatus should be simple in construction and arrangement, and safe and reliable in operation, so that much skill, care, and attention are required to be devoted to the design of the whole of the details of the gear to reduce complexity and promote efficiency to as great an extent as possible.

Capstan engine and gear.—The capstans of steamships of any considerable size are worked by steam, the power being usually applied through the medium of a worm-wheel, keyed on the lower end of the spindle, which is driven by a worm worked generally by an engine fitted for this purpose only. A large warship would be fitted at the forward end with duplex cable holders for working $2\frac{3}{8}$-inch cable, one on each side of the ship, with a combined warping capstan and cable holder at the middle line. Each of these spindles is carried through the decks to the capstan engine flat, where the worm-wheels are fitted on their spindles, a suitable bushed step being provided in the bed-plate for taking the weight of the spindle and cable holder or capstan.

The worms driving these worm-wheels are generally worked from the crank shaft of the capstan engine by steel mitre gearing with helical teeth, arranged with suitable clutches so that the cables may be both hauled in or both veered, or one hauled in and the other veered, simultaneously, without reversing the engine. In the case of the centre forward capstan, in order to meet the case of working by hand by means of capstan bars, the worm-wheel is loose on the spindle and driven by a disc keyed to the shaft and placed immediately above the worm-wheel. The clutch-gear provided at the capstan engine enables the direction of the cable holders to be reversed.

The capstan engines are fitted with reversing valves, which may be actuated from the cable working deck, so that any desired motion can be obtained. When the capstan is being worked by steam power the safety pawls fitted for hand working should be kept securely lifted to prevent accident, the gearing of the engine itself being sufficient to hold the capstan in any position.

Cable holders.—These are generally of cast-steel and arranged to run loose on their shafts, as shown in Fig. 351. They are fitted with friction plates of wrought-steel and brass, shown in the lower part of the figure, and cast-steel driving-discs keyed firmly to the spindles. The friction plates are actuated by a cast-steel compressing nut, so that by turning this nut in the proper direction it gives compression to the friction plates, and so enables the driving disc to work the cable holder.

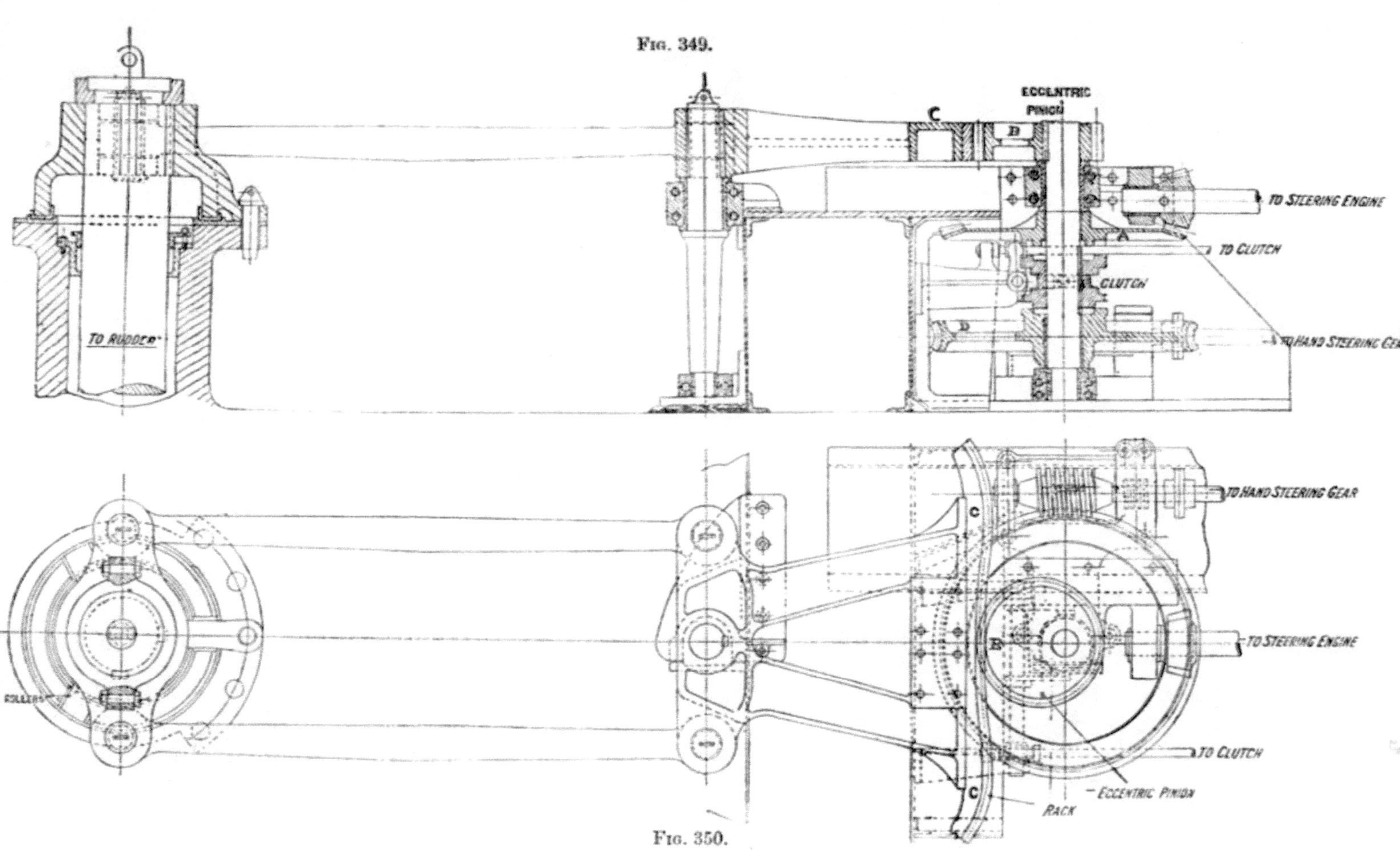

Fig. 349.
ECCENTRIC PINION
C
B
A
TO STEERING ENGINE
TO CLUTCH
CLUTCH
D
TO RUDDER
TO HAND STEERING GEAR
TO HAND STEERING GEAR
C
B
TO STEERING ENGINE
TO CLUTCH
ECCENTRIC PINION
RACK
C
ROLLERS
Fig. 350.

The centre line capstan cable holder, Fig. 352, is securely keyed to the spindle, and is provided also with a smaller cable holder above it, for 1¼-inch chain to perform the operation of catting the anchor. Means are also fitted to enable this centre capstan to be worked by hand, either from the upper deck or some intermediate one.

An *after capstan* and engine is also fitted in the largest vessels in a similar manner to the forward capstan, and suitable for working a smaller size of cable, say 1⅝-inches. Portable whelps for working steel-wire hawsers are also fitted, one of these being indicated in position at the left of Fig. 352.

Limitation of force exerted by capstan engine.—The cylinders of all auxiliary engines should be made large enough to enable the engines to be efficiently worked with reduced pressures of steam. In the case of the capstan engine, it is therefore necessary to prevent the possibility

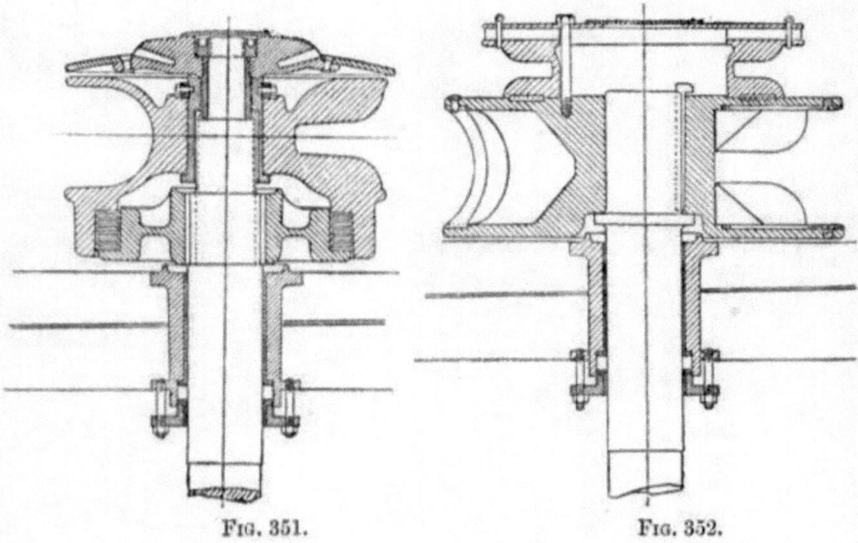

Fig. 351.   Fig. 352.

of excessive strains being brought on the chain cables when higher steam pressure is being used. The maximum pressure to be allowed in the steam chest of the engine is such that a pull of more than two-thirds of the proof-strain of the cable cannot be exerted by it. To effect this, reducing valves are sometimes fitted, but more generally in the Royal Navy a pressure gauge with prominent mark showing the maximum pressure, is fitted on the engine side of the stop-valve, so that the attendant can regulate the opening of the windlass stop-valve accordingly.

The use and advantages of hydraulic machinery.—Hydraulic power is largely used in battleships for working the heavy guns. For this purpose it has many advantages. The principal reasons for its adoption are :—

1. It is noiseless and steady in working.
2. It is easily controlled over a large range of speed.

3. It is always ready for use, no preliminary preparation such as warming, being required.

4. As the parts of the machinery are cool, its use is not objectionable in magazines and confined spaces, and if any part is injured it can immediately be handled for repair.

5. There is no fear of explosion if a pipe or machine be struck by a shot.

6. On account of the high working pressure used, the machine can be kept small and light.

7. It is specially adapted for absorbing the energy of recoil of the guns.

Hydraulic pumping engine.—A constant supply of water at a pressure of 800 to 1,100 lbs. per square inch is maintained by large steam pumping engines, two of which are fitted in each battleship. A small auxiliary engine is fitted in addition for use when the machinery is being cleaned and repaired. A sectional elevation of one of the main pumping engines, showing the principal parts, is given in Fig. 353. This engine, which is of the horizontal tandem compound type, has two sets of steam cylinders and pumps secured to one bed-plate, and coupled to a crank-shaft with cranks at right angles to each other.

The H.P. cylinder is placed between the L.P. cylinder and the shaft. The L.P. piston has two piston-rods, which pass through chambers cast on the sides of the H.P. cylinder, and are secured to a crosshead to which the H.P. piston-rod and the pump ram are also secured. The slide-valves are arranged horizontally on the tops of the cylinders, and are both driven by one eccentric through a rocking shaft and levers. As the piston-rods and pump ram are connected to the same crosshead, most of the force of the steam is transmitted directly to the water in the pump. These pumping engines are not fitted with flywheels, and the resistance of the pumps being constant it is necessary to maintain the full steam pressure practically throughout the stroke. The point of cut-off is at ·95 of the stroke.

The pump piston has a sectional area equal to twice that of the ram, and is kept watertight in one direction by two L leathers.

The action of the pump is as follows.—During the out-stroke of the ram, water flows into the pump through the suction valve A, and fills the barrel. At the same time the water in the annular space B in front of the piston is driven out through the delivery valve C. While the ram is moving into the barrel during the return or in-stroke, the water in the cylinder is forced out through the intermediate valve D, half passing into the annular space around the ram, and the other half being forced through the delivery valve. The pump therefore delivers water during both strokes, but only draws water through the suction valve during one stroke. The delivery of water from the two pumps is very regular, and the arrangement has the advantage of keeping a constant pressure on the packing of the ram, which reduces leakage and prevents the entrance of air during the in-stroke   This is very important, as the presence of air in hydraulic machinery causes irregularity of working and may seriously increase the stresses on the parts.

As the water is used for working a considerable number of machines which are used intermittently, the demand on the pumps may be very irregular, and the speed of the engines must frequently and rapidly

Speed Govern.
Exhaust steam stop valve
Steam stop valve
Relief valve
Hyd's Govern.
L.P. Cylinder
H.P. Cylinder
X
C
D
B
A

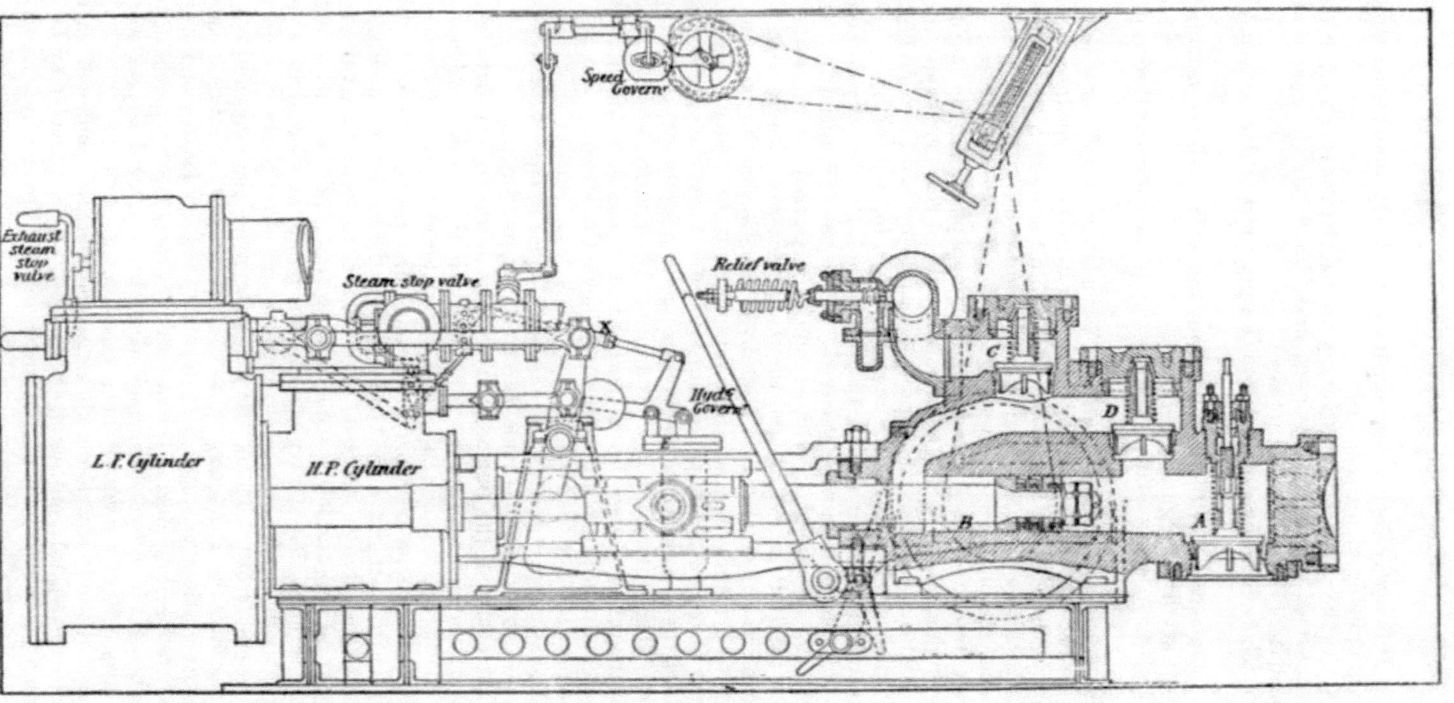

Fig. 353.

change. If friction and the inertia of the moving parts were negligible, it would be necessary only to provide constant steam pressures on the cylinders high enough to balance the required pressure in the pumps, and the engine would automatically vary its speed so as to maintain a nearly uniform water pressure. Small pumps made on this principle are fairly satisfactory, and are used in H.M.S. 'Rupert.'

Hydraulic governor.—For large pumps, however, the variations of water pressure would be too great, and some means of regulating the steam pressure is required. The necessary variations of speed are too sudden and frequent to admit of hand control, and an automatic pressure governor is generally used. A section through one of these governors is shown in Fig. 354. A small hydraulic cylinder B is connected to the delivery pipe of the pumps. A plunger A which works in it is pressed down by springs, which are so proportioned that the plunger cannot rise until the water pressure reaches 950 lbs. per square inch and will have risen through its full travel when the pressure reaches 1,150 lbs. Leakage between the ram and cylinder is prevented by the cup leather C, shown unshaded in the figure. The upper end of the plunger is connected to a throttle valve in the steam pipe, and when the plunger is at the top of its stroke this valve

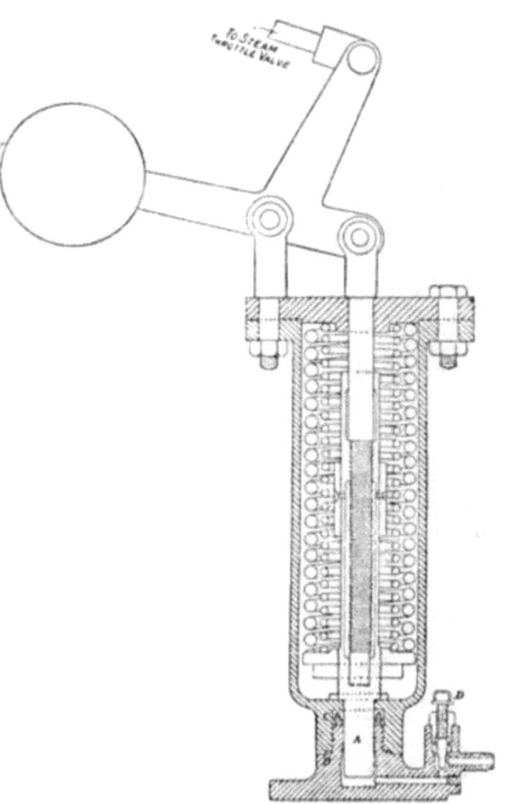

Fig. 354.

is nearly closed, only allowing sufficient steam to pass to keep the engines moving slowly at 4 to 6 revolutions per minute, the water delivered from the pumps being returned to the suction tank through the relief valve shown in Fig. 353, loaded to about 1,100 lbs.

When one or more hydraulic machines are started, the pressure in the delivery pipe falls, and the springs force the plunger down and open the throttle valve until the speed of the engine increases sufficiently to bring the pressure back to the normal. To prevent a too sudden variation in speed a small valve D is fitted between the governor cylinder and the delivery pipe. This is regulated to only allow a slow motion of the plunger. To prevent the dangerous racing which would result if a pipe burst or the suction tank became empty, and which would cause the plunger of the hydraulic governor to fall to the bottom of its cylinder and so admit full steam pressure to the engines, a centrifugal speed governor is fitted (see Fig. 353). The water used in the various machines is returned to the suction tanks. To reduce the friction of slide-valves, &c., and to prevent corrosion of internal steel parts, soft soap and mineral oil are mixed with the water.

Hydraulic gun-turning engines.—Hydraulic turning engines are used for rotating the gun turntables of turrets and barbettes. The turntables are carried on a number of flanged coned rollers, which move between accurately turned roller paths, one of which is secured to the ship and the other to the underside of the turntable. The rollers are kept at the correct distances apart by two circular rings of steel plate, which carry the axis pins of the rollers. The rollers and upper roller path are made of forged steel, and the lower path of cast-steel. Bronze racks are secured to the peripheries of the turntables. Pinions on vertical shafts gear with the racks, and the turning engines are connected to the shafts at the lower ends through suitable gearing.

The engines are of the three-cylinder oscillating type, and water is admitted and exhausted from each cylinder by a slide-valve which is moved by a crank pin on the cylinder trunnion. The valve-box also contains a reversing slide-block which by its movement starts, stops, reverses, and regulates the speed of the engine. As these blocks are large and the pressure high the friction between the working faces is great and they could not well be moved by hand. A small hydraulic reversing cylinder is therefore provided for this purpose. The piston-rod is connected to a weigh-shaft, which moves the three reversing slides simultaneously when water is admitted to one end or the other of the reversing cylinder by a small slide-valve, which is moved by handwheels fitted in the turntable close to the gun sights. The gearing is so arranged that the position of the reversing slide always corresponds to a definite position of the handwheel.

A brake is fitted on the engine shaft which comes into action automatically when the water pressure at the engine falls below a certain amount. This insures that the turntable shall always be under control. Duplicate engines and gearing are provided for each turntable. These hydraulic engines work very smoothly at any speed. They are quite free from any risk of dangerous racing, even if all load is removed, as the hydraulic resistances in the engine itself increase very rapidly as the speed rises.

In some ships the engines have been fitted in the turntables, the racks being secured to the structure which supports the lower roller path. In recent vessels care has been taken to arrange the parts of the turntable, and the guns and machinery fitted in it, so that the centre of gravity of the whole is situated on the axis of revolution.

In addition to working the turning engines, the hydraulic power is also used for working a number of hydraulic machines for loading and working the guns, raising ammunition, &c. All important machines, pipes, &c., are duplicated, and in the later ships each operation can be performed by hand if necessary, though at a much slower speed. In some ships electrical motors are fitted to perform a few of the operations of working the guns in case of break down of the hydraulic machinery.

Steam turret-turning engines.—The earliest turret ships were provided with steam turret-turning engines, the engine being controlled by a balanced differential valve similar to that described in Chapter XVII., which can be worked from the turret as well as at the engine. Steam-engines have also been fitted in H.M.S. 'Barfleur' and 'Centurion' for this purpose.

Air compressing machinery.—Machinery for compressing air for the purpose of charging and sometimes launching Whitehead torpedoes is now fitted in nearly all warships. The types of engines and pumps used for this purpose vary in design and arrangement, but in all of them the compression is done in two or more cylinders with successively decreasing diameters. The drawings, Figs. 355 and 356, of a two-stage compressor will serve to illustrate the principle. Fig. 356 is a vertical cross section through Fig. 355, on a larger scale, to indicate the detail more clearly. The pump has a cylinder A fitted in a casing B, through which latter, water is circulated to carry off the heat caused by the compression of the air. In this cylinder a combined piston and cylinder C, attached to the piston-rod of the engine, works. Air is drawn into the large cylinder on the down stroke through the annular valve D.

A little water and oil is admitted into the large cylinder during the suction stroke and, passing in as spray with the air, assists in carrying off the heat of compression. During the up stroke the air is compressed and forced through a number of holes past the valve E (shown unsectioned in the figure) into the moving cylinder. Only one of these small holes is shown. On the next down stroke more air enters the large cylinder through the inlet valve, and the air in the small cylinder is forced out through the delivery valve F. The air next passes through a coil of copper wire, G, in the water casing, where it is cooled. The cooling water is circulated through the casing and also through the condenser H, in which the injection water is produced by condensation in a small steam coil, by the action of the moving cylinder which, in combination with suitable valves, one of which is shown at K, acts as a pump. Each cylinder of the compressor and also the casing is provided with a safety-valve.

The compressors are arranged in sets of one, two, or three, on one bed-plate. Each can compress 10 cubic feet of air to a pressure of 1,700 lbs. per square inch in 70 minutes. When working at their maximum capacity, the machines run at about 350 revolutions per minute. Special machines for torpedo boats and destroyers run at 500 revolutions per minute.

Separator column.—After leaving the cooling coils the air passes through a separator column L, where the injection water is removed. The separator column is formed of a steel tube with caps screwed on the ends. The top cap carries an inlet and outlet valve, and the lower one has a drain valve. A short length of pipe M is screwed to the inlet orifice, and extends down the inside of the tube for a portion of its length. The water and air on entry are therefore directed downwards, the water falling to the bottom and the air rising and passing out through the outlet valve to the reservoir. The drain valve requires to be opened frequently to blow out the accumulation of water. In a

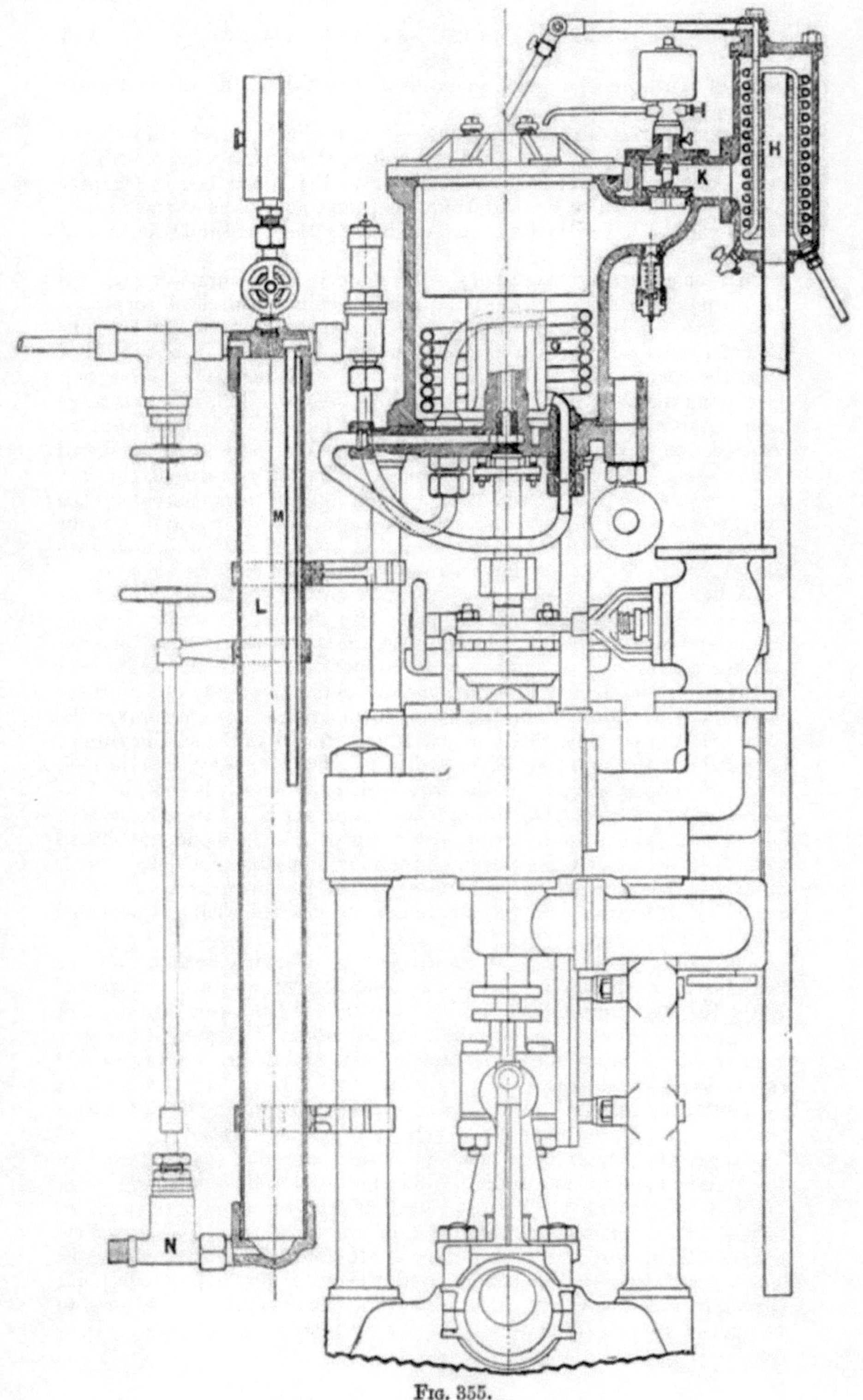

Fig. 355.

recent form the action is automatic, the valve being opened by the weight of the water which collects in a cup supported by a spring, and to which a balanced piston valve is connected.

Air reservoirs and pipes.—The air is stored in reservoirs of steel tubes arranged in groups of fifty. The tubes are fitted with gunmetal caps at the ends, and are connected together by screwed unions and connecting pipes. The tubes are about 3 inches in diameter, $\frac{3}{16}$-inch thick, and 6 feet long, and a reservoir of fifty tubes has a capacity of about $11\frac{1}{4}$ cubic feet. The whole of the air fittings are tested by a water pressure of 2,550 lbs. per square inch, the maximum working air pressure being 1,700 lbs. per square inch. The air is distributed to the torpedo tubes through copper pipes of $\frac{3}{4}$-inch internal diameter, the main leads being fitted in duplicate.

In all torpedo gear and fittings the greatest reliability and accuracy are necessary, as such very high pressures and sudden impulses have to be dealt with. Every precaution must be taken to prevent leakage, and too great an amount of care cannot be exercised in the fitting of every detail of the gear.

Boat-hoisting engines.—In most large ships, engines arranged to drive suitable winch barrels are now fitted for the purpose of placing the torpedo and other boats into the water, or of lifting them, and landing them in position on board in fixed crutches. Two engines and winch barrels are necessary, one for lifting the boats out of the water, and the other for 'topping' the derrick and bringing the boats inboard. These should be quite independent of each other. The derrick is hinged on a swivel or ball joint supported by a bracket secured to the mast or signalling pole.

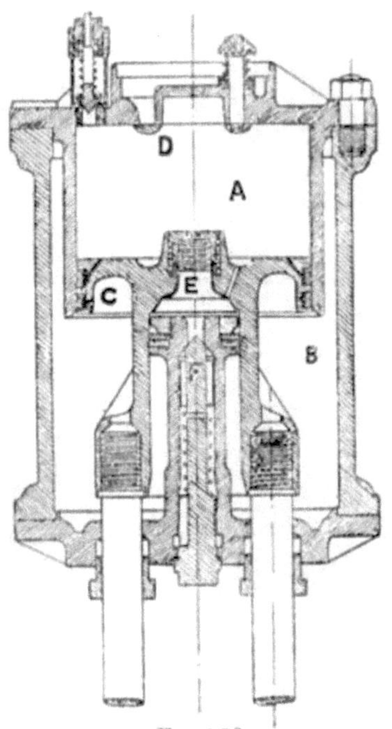

Fig. 356.

Ventilating engines.—In most vessels blowing engines are required for the purpose of providing a supply of fresh air for the crew spaces, as well as for the ventilation of the engine and boiler rooms. The engines are arranged to drive rotary fans, which draw air from ventilating shafts, and distribute it through the ship by ventilating trunks with openings in the several compartments. The outlets from these ventilating pipes are generally fitted with light gridiron valves, so that only such as may be required may be opened at any time. In modern warships, with closed stokeholds, blowing-fans and engines are also fitted for accelerating the draught in the boilers.

Ash-hoisting engines.—Small engines to drive winch barrels are fitted in most steamships for the purpose of lifting the filled ash buckets, &c., from the stokeholds, to enable the ashes to be thrown overboard. Some of these engines are fitted with reversing gears, so that the

buckets are both raised and lowered by steam, or friction gear may be
fitted to allow the barrel to be disconnected from the engines so that
the bucket may descend by its own weight, the rate of descent being
regulated by a brake. Overhead rails are fitted on the upper deck,
from the top of the ash-tube to the shoots at the ship's sides, to facilitate
the discharge of the ashes, &c. A voice-pipe or gong is fitted for
signalling between stokehold and deck.

See's ash ejector.—Various arrangements have been devised to
obviate the necessity of raising the ashes to the deck and thence discharging them. A steam ash ejector has been fitted in several vessels, but its
low efficiency and the necessity of preserving fresh water renders such apparatus now inadmissible. Another and much more economical arrangement is
See's ash ejector shown in Fig. 357. In this apparatus, which is fitted in
many large passenger steamers in which the raising of ashes on deck is
objectionable, the ashes are placed in a trough leading to a pipe, a jet of water
at a pressure of about 200 lbs. per square inch from one of the pumps is
then admitted, and scours the ashes along the pipe into the sea. A small
valve is fitted to permit the entry of air into the pipe during the discharge.
The apparatus is simple and efficient.

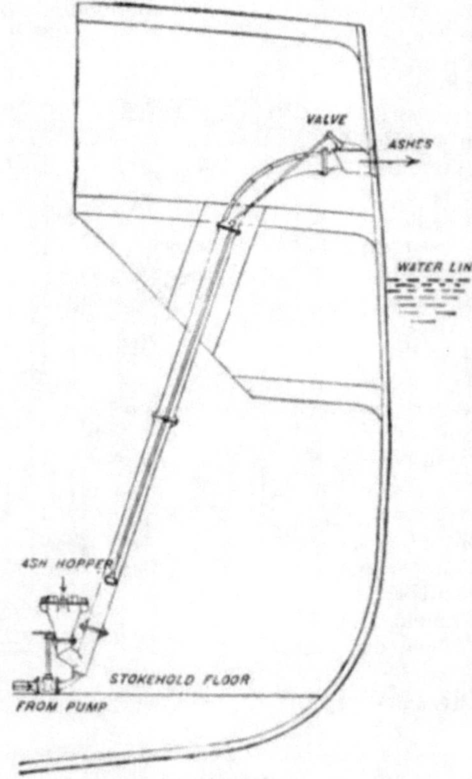

Fig. 357.

Feed-pumps.—For delivering the feed-water from the feed-tanks to the
boilers, pumps of a variety of designs have been employed. For many
years in the Royal Navy feed-pumping engines of similar type to the
bilge-pumping engine of Fig. 340 were employed, except that the pump
valves were made of metal instead of indiarubber, as in the bilge- and
fire-pumps. These pumps have a constant stroke regulated by a crank
shaft, and the valves are worked by eccentrics. They gave satisfaction
for many years with steam of moderate pressures, even when they
worked at high rates of speed. With the high steam pressures now
used this design has not been so satisfactory, and it has recently given
place to others, larger and slower in speed, and generally with slide-
valves worked by a tappet action from the piston-rod either of its own

engine, or of its fellow engine if of the 'duplex' variety. Fig. 340 will serve as an illustration of the crank-shaft variety of feed-pump, the valves, however, being altered to the metallic type. We will illustrate two varieties of well-known feed-pumps of the other type, viz. Weir's and Belleville's.

Weir's feed-pump (Figs. 358 to 361) is a vertical pump, double acting, with a set of inlet and discharge valves for each end of the pump arranged at the upper part of the barrel. The valves are a series of small ones milled out of solid metal and give a large area with a small lift. In each valve-seat, for engines of say 1,500 to 1,600 I.H.P., there would be about seven of these valves in the suction part, and four in the discharge part. There is generally a single cylinder and single pump, with a separate liner fitted for the pump piston to work over, the pump piston packing being in the latest variety made of vulcanite. Sometimes solid pump pistons are fitted.

The steam valve arrangement is rather complicated and not generally understood, but in view of the very considerable number of these pumps in use in the Royal Navy and mercantile marine, and the importance of maintaining them in proper condition, we will explain the action in detail. It consists of a main valve for distributing steam to the cylinders, and an auxiliary valve for distributing steam to work the main valve. The main valve moves horizontally from side to side, being driven by steam admitted and exhausted from each end alternately; the auxiliary valve is actuated by a lever with fixed fulcrum worked by the rod of the pump. This auxiliary valve moves on a flat face on the back of the main valve as shown in Figs. 360 and 361, and in a direction at right angles to the latter.

Both the main and auxiliary valves are simply slide-valves, but the former is half round, the round side working on the correspondingly shaped cylinder port face, while the back of the valve is flat. Both ends of the main valve are lengthened so as to project beyond the port face (see Fig. 361), and are turned cylindrical with flat ends. Caps are fitted on each of these ends, forming cylinders which are closed at the mouths by the flat ends of the main valve, which act as pistons, the length of stroke the piston can make being the full travel of the valve.

The auxiliary valve face has three ports (see Fig. 360), the centre one being the exhaust, and the two side ports being steam passages led through the piston ends of the main valve. The right-hand cylinder port passage is led through the left-hand end of the piston, the other passage being similarly led to the other end of the valve. These ports admit steam to the two small caps or cylinders at each end of the valve alternately, by which it is thrown from side to side.

Besides these ports, two other ports are formed on the auxiliary valve face leading to, and corresponding to, two ports on the half-round main valve face for admitting steam to the top and bottom of the cylinders. These ports on the auxiliary valve face are arranged to cut off steam before the end of the stroke and so reduce the speed, but the expansion chambers at each end of the main valve are fitted with bye-passes to admit steam for the full stroke when desired. This may be necessary, for instance, when starting the pumps, as then the cylinders may be full of water. These bye-passes are formed by notches cut in the edges of the caps, and may be opened or shut by turning the caps

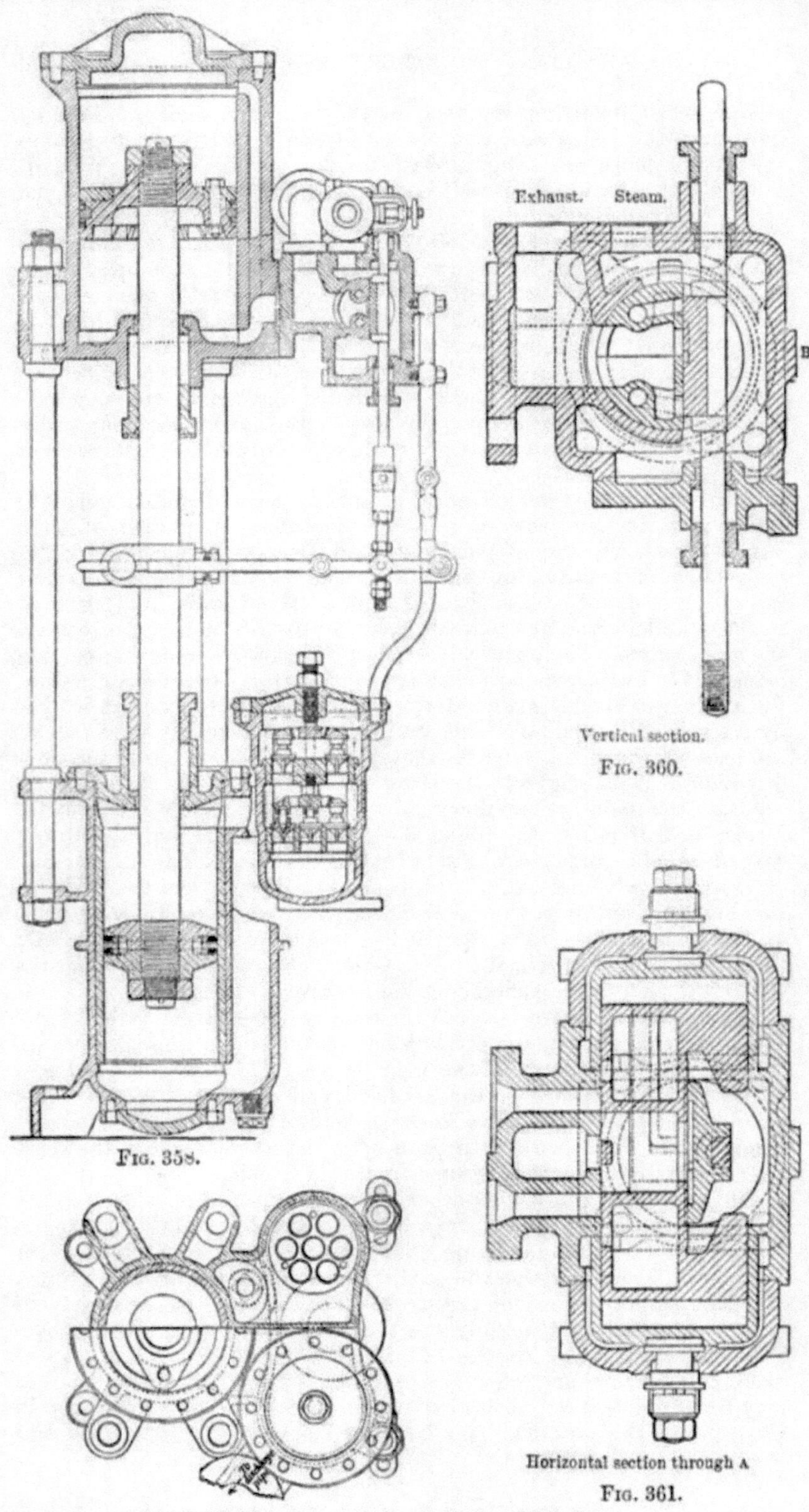

Vertical section.

FIG. 360.

FIG. 358.

Horizontal section through A

FIG. 361.

by means of the spindles at each side of the valve chest, and thus give a definite cut-off. There are separate bye-passes for up and down strokes, and the silent working of the pumps depends on the proper regulation of these bye-passes.

The auxiliary valve and face act just like an ordinary single-ported slide-valve, except that, besides the vertical movement of the auxiliary valve, the *valve face* moves across the auxiliary valve when the exhaust port is open to one of the chambers at the end of the main valve ; the other chamber being in this position open to the steam, the valve is thrown over until the exhaust is cut off, which acts as a cushion. In this position the main and expansion ports are full open for the return of the piston, which moves at a rapid rate until the expansion is closed ; then at three-quarters stroke the auxiliary valve closes the expansion ports, and the speed is reduced towards the end of the stroke, when the auxiliary valve opens the exhaust and throws the main slide for the return stroke.

Examinations necessary.—The steam valve must be overhauled as often as the main slide-valve of the propelling engine, as it works under far more severe conditions as to pressure, being between the boiler pressure and the condenser. It is not, as might appear from its shape, a piston-valve, but is an ordinary slide-valve, and as such must be kept tight by facing up in the usual way. It is most important that the curved ribs between the steam and exhaust ports should have a good bearing, and if they show signs of losing this, they must be filed and scraped in the usual way. There is practically no wear on the valve itself, so long as it is bearing properly on the bars ; and it is only when it loses the bearing that it wears at all. If the high-pressure steam is allowed to leak past the bars, it speedily cuts them away, and hence the importance of the faces being regularly looked to and kept in proper order. A little attention from time to time will insure this. As the auxiliary valve holds the main valve up to its face, after bringing up the bearing it may be necessary to put a liner between the valve spindle and back of valve to hold it up if it is slack. After lining up, the valve should be moved backward and forward by hand to see that it is not too tight. The face on the auxiliary valve must also be kept in good working order. The remaining parts require no special remark.

The Belleville feed-pump.—Figs. 362 and 363 show one form of this, viz. the horizontal variety. Most recent examples are, however, vertical. The pump is double acting, the steam cylinder having an ordinary flat slide-valve without lap, worked by the curved lever shown, which is moved at each end of the stroke by a projection on the pump-rod. A passage is provided at each end, so that steam is admitted uniformly all round the cylinder barrel, and not at the top only, which avoids bending forces on the rod. The steam pressure remains constant, therefore, till near the end of the stroke, when the projection strikes the valve lever and commences to close the steam valve, so that the steam pressure falls, and the motion would cease but for special fittings provided. Before the piston can commence the return stroke it is necessary that the valve should not only be closed but pushed sufficiently far over to reopen for steam on the other side.

To enable the steam already in the cylinder to complete the stroke and throw the valve over to the opposite side, an orifice is provided at each end of the pump-barrel, closed by the levers shown and communicating with the suction chamber, so that when the pump piston nears the end of its stroke it strikes one of these levers and opens the orifice to the suction chamber, so that the pressure in the pump falls, and the steam in the cylinder, although cut off, is enabled by its expansive force to complete the stroke and reverse the steam valve, when the motion continues in the opposite direction.

The suction and discharge valves are a series of small ones, generally eight in number at each end, four for suction and four for discharge. Small holes, about $\frac{1}{16}$-inch diameter, are made through the

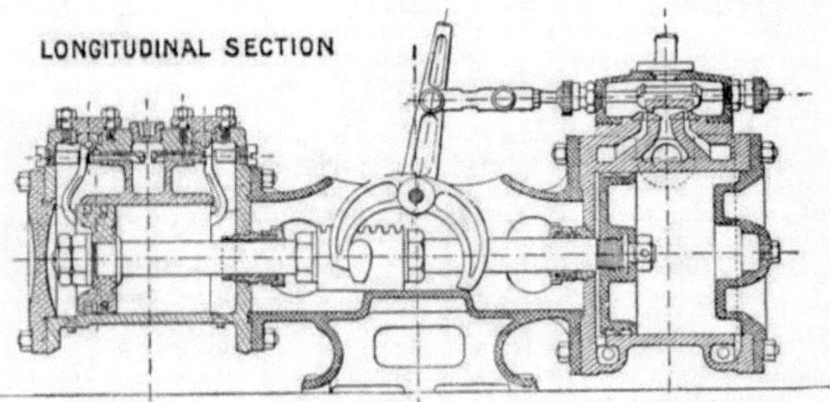

Fig. 362.

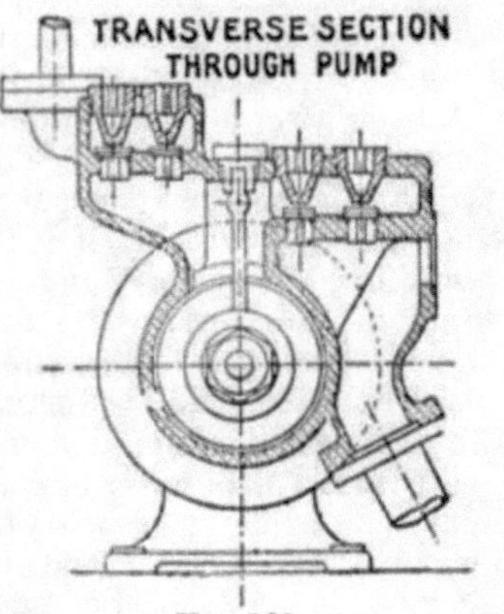

Fig. 363.

levers into the orifice leading to the suction chamber, so that a small quantity of water is always escaping from the pump-barrel, which causes the pump to keep slowly in motion even when the valves on the boilers are closed. This small hole is fitted at the lever centre shown in the transverse section.

Feed-water heaters.—The advantage of supplying the boilers with feed-water approximating in temperature to that of the boiler has long been recognised, although the exact manner in which the practice should be conducive to economy has always been uncertain. Its beneficial effects as regards boiler preservation and reduction of racking stresses due to variations of pressure are well established. Even when the heating steam is taken from the boiler direct, so that theoretically there is neither a gain nor loss of heat by the process, large numbers of vessels in which such feed heaters are fitted report an appreciable gain in economy, and that when using the feed heaters, steam is more easily maintained than when they are not in use. When the heating steam is taken from the last receiver of the engine, or the exhaust steam of any engine, a gain in economy can be shown to exist theoretically. Feed-water heaters are now largely fitted in the mercantile marine, and results justify their adoption. They are also being fitted in vessels of the Royal and U.S. Navies.

Weir's feed heater and regulator, Fig. 364, takes steam from the final receiver of the engine after it has done most of its work. It enters the heating chamber through a circular perforated ring, and there mixes with the cold feed-water, which is admitted through the spring loaded valve on the cover. The heated water falls to the bottom of the heater, whence it is removed by the feed-pump. A galvanised iron float is fitted to the bottom of the heater, which communicates by means of levers with the steam valve leading to the feed-pump, by which means the level is kept constant in the heater and the pumps are prevented from drawing air. The heat causes any air in the feed-water to be liberated, whence it can be drawn off by the cock on the top of the heater to the condenser or atmosphere.

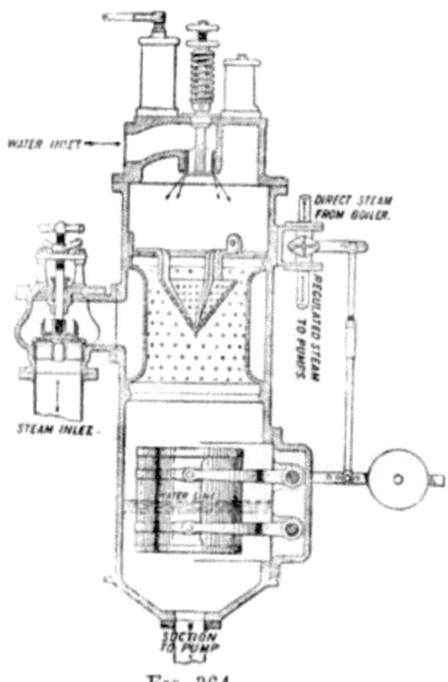

Fig. 364.

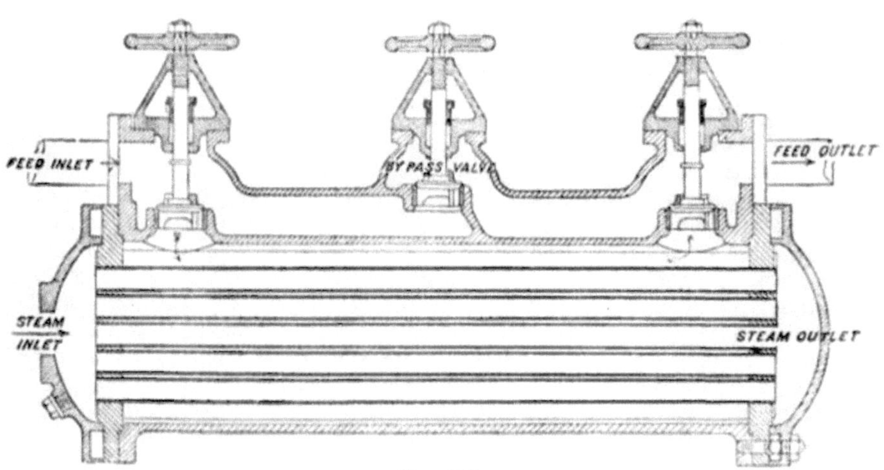

Fig. 365.

Kirkaldy's feed heater.—In this apparatus, shown in Fig. 365, the steam does not mix with the feed-water, but the latter is conducted

D D

through tubes, on the other side of which is the heating steam which is drawn from the boilers, or sometimes the exhaust steam from various auxiliary engines. It is therefore a surface-heater of similar construction to a surface-condenser, the tubes being rolled into tube plates in the ordinary manner. Bye-pass valves are fitted, so that when necessary the feed-water can be passed direct without passing through the heater.

There are also many other makers who have specialities for feed-water heating.

Auxiliary condenser.—In the earlier ships the exhaust steam from the auxiliary engines was led into the main-engine condensers in order to prevent loss of fresh water, a connection to the waste steam pipes being also fitted. The number of auxiliary engines in modern ships is so great that the unavoidable leakage into their cylinders seriously affected the vacuum in the main-engine condensers, and when the main engines were not at work the auxiliary engines had to exhaust into the atmosphere, causing considerable waste of fresh water, unless other complications were introduced. To remedy this, separate auxiliary surface condensers are now fitted to receive the exhaust steam from all the auxiliary engines of the ship. These auxiliary condensers are fitted with independent circulating pumps, and with air-pumps that deliver into the hot-wells or feed-tanks, so that the condensed steam may be returned to the boilers by the feed-pumps.

They are of identical construction with those of the main condensers described in Chapter XX. Figs. 366 and 367 show details of the circulating pump, air-pump, and engine for an auxiliary condenser as commonly fitted in the Navy, metallic bucket, foot, and head valves being fitted. One engine serves for both pumps, the air-pump being worked below the crank shaft by means of double rods from the engine crosshead. Fig. 368 shows the arrangement of the auxiliary condenser and the pumps and pipes in connection.

The number and size of the auxiliary engines being considerable in a modern warship, the necessary auxiliary condensing power is also large. In the latest battleships there are two auxiliary condensers, one in each engine room, the combined cooling surface being 2,200 square feet.

Grease filters.—In Chapter X. the absolute necessity has been explained of preventing the entry of grease or oil in the boilers of vessels working with high-pressure steam. The best way to effect this desirable object is to limit as far as possible the use of oil for the internal parts of the engines. Many engines are capable of working efficiently without the direct admission of oil into the cylinders and slide-valves, the amount which finds its way inside owing to the necessary use of oil on the piston-rods and slide-rods being sufficient for internal lubrication. The machinery of torpedo boats and destroyers is found to work well under these circumstances indeed, all oil cups are now omitted on such engines. The same method of treatment is now extended in many cases to larger engines with satisfactory results. Grease filters are, however, a necessity in any case, as even the quantity of oil that enters through the piston-rods gradually becomes considerable.

The types of grease filters are very numerous, but space will only

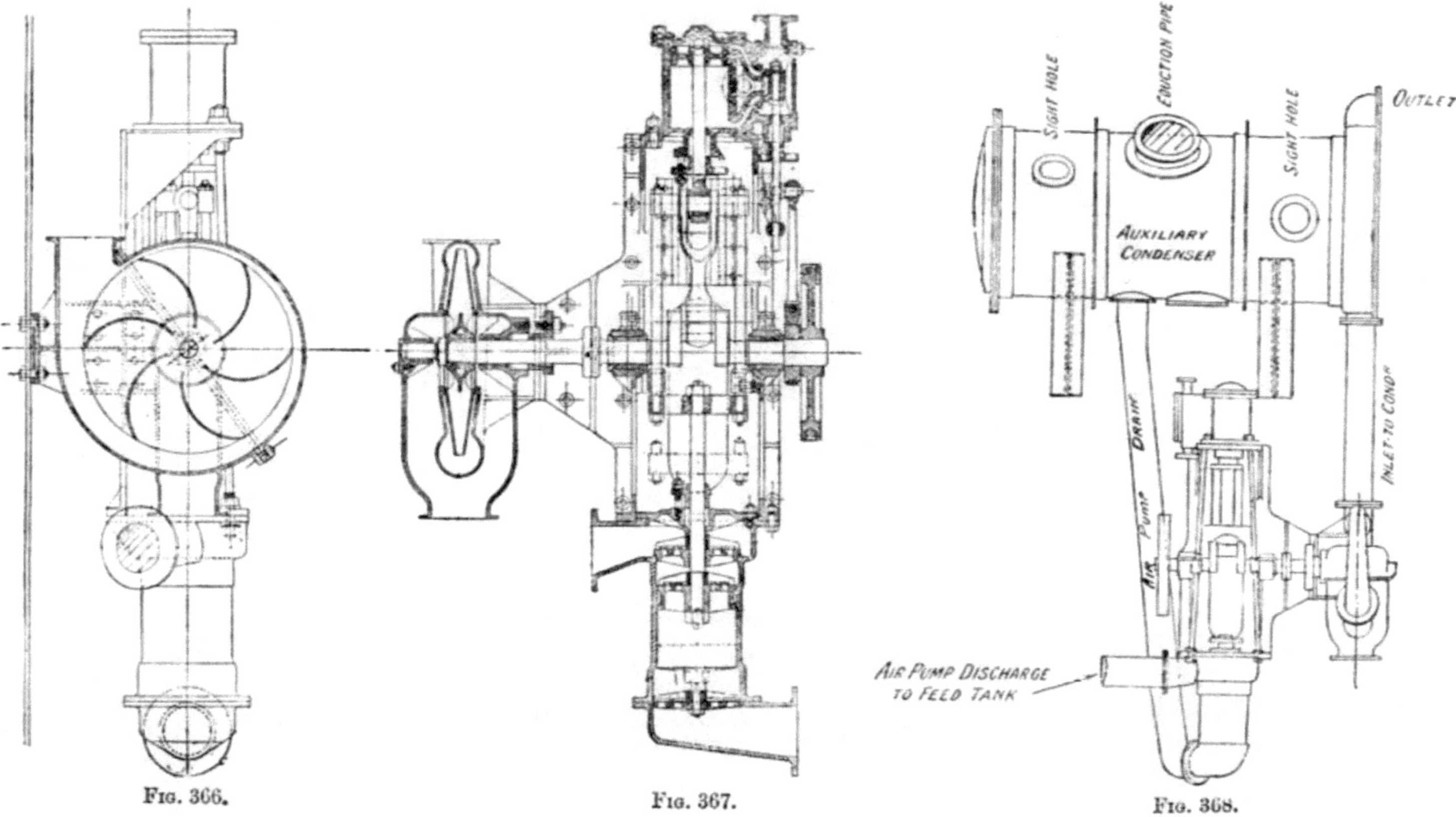

Fig. 366.

Fig. 367.

Fig. 368.

admit of one such being described. We select for illustration Harris's grease filter, fitted in the 'Campania,' H.M.S. 'Terrible,' and large numbers of other vessels. It consists of a considerable number of annular gratings threaded consecutively on a central spindle as shown in Fig. 369. On each of these gratings is fitted one or two sheets of filtering medium, consisting of towelling or flannel supported by wire gauze. These layers of filtering medium are shown at A A, in the sectional half of the diagram on the left. The gratings are so constructed that a large central space, B, is formed for the reception of feed-water, whence it enters to the spaces between the flannels through holes as shown, and after passing the flannels it makes its exit through similar holes in the circumference, shown in elevation on the right of the diagram, and proceeds to the outlet orifice. The course of the water is shown by

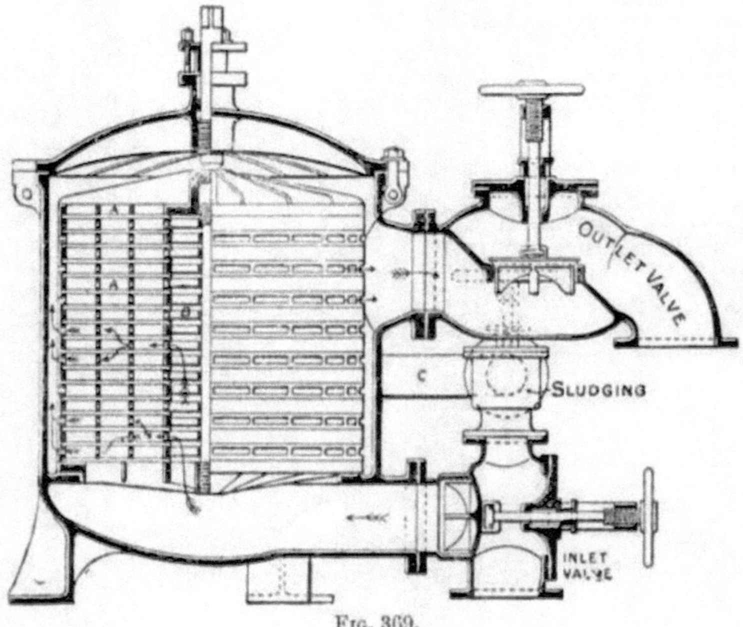

Fig. 369.

the arrows. This arrangement provides a large filtering area in a comparatively small space. When the cloths become dirty an arrangement of pipes, C, leading the inlet water to the reverse side of the cloths, and a steam cleaning jet, are provided, so that the grease can be washed off by a reverse current of water, a pipe and valve being supplied for carrying off the grease.

Governors.—The object of the governor is to maintain uniformity of motion of the engines when the resistance experienced is varied from any cause. In a marine engine considerable diminution of resistance may ensue in rough and stormy weather from the pitching motion of the ship when the propellers rise partly out of the water and increase the speed of the engines, causing what is technically called 'racing of the engines.'

The governor for a land engine usually consists of a pair of heavy balls rotated by the engine, which fly outward under the action of centrifugal force and close the throttle valve. This is not suitable for marine purposes, as the action of gravitation on the balls would be affected by the motion of the ship, so that the forces acting would become irregular, and other devices have therefore to be adopted.

The early marine governors were fitted to act directly on the throttle valve and required to be made large and heavy, as the motion produced on the valve was due entirely to the work accumulated in the flywheel. They therefore absorbed a considerable amount of power in working, and their action was not sufficiently rapid for modern engines. To decrease the weight and increase the sensibility of governors for marine engines, the more recent instruments of this class have been designed to cause the revolving or governing part of the apparatus to actuate a small valve only, for the purpose of admitting steam to a small governor cylinder, in which a piston connected to the throttle valve works. As the governing apparatus has only to work a small balanced valve, it may be made very light, so that the rapidity of action of the gear is by such means much increased.

Others still lighter and simpler are those in which, like the former, the governing apparatus is set in motion by the engine itself when the speed is increased, and in addition the force to close the valve comes also *from the main engine.* This is effected by arranging by various devices that the inertia of a moving weight causes an engagement with and closing of the throttle valve, by direct connection with some reciprocating part of the marine engine.

In each of the governors previously mentioned it will be noticed that an increased speed of the engine is required before the governor gear can operate, and they cannot anticipate and prevent such increase. This defect caused them originally to be of doubtful value, as it was combined with sluggishness in action, the throttle valve being generally closed only after the racing was over. The more modern instruments are, however, much more efficient, and are fitted in most large mercantile vessels making regular passages at high speeds.

Another entirely different class of governor is that which acts by variations of pressure at the stern of the vessel near the propeller, and not from engine speed variations. Racing being caused by diminished immersion of the propeller, it is accompanied by a diminution of pressure of water at that part which can be utilised to actuate the throttle valve. Such governors may therefore anticipate and prevent any increase of speed, and are more perfect in principle. Unlike those of the preceding class, however, they would have no effect in case of serious increase of speed due to such an accident as a broken shaft or propeller.

One of each of these types of modern governor will be described, commencing with the latter type.

Dunlop's governor.—This governor, shown in Fig. 370, consists of a sea-cock at the stern of the ship, opening into an air vessel or air chamber, A, so constructed that, by opening the sea-cock, water flows into the air vessel, and compresses the air contained therein to a pressure equivalent to the head of water outside the ship.

From the top of the air chamber a pipe B is led to the underside of an airtight elastic diaphragm, forming part of an apparatus in the engine room. On the upper side of the diaphragm is a spiral spring, with means of adjusting its compression to balance the air pressure below the diaphragm. From the centre of the diaphragm a connection is made to the slide-valve of a small steam cylinder D, so constructed that its steam piston moves in exact accordance with the movements of the diaphragm. This steam piston is connected by suitable gear to the throttle valve of the engine whose speed is to be controlled.

The sea-cock being open, any variation of head of water outside

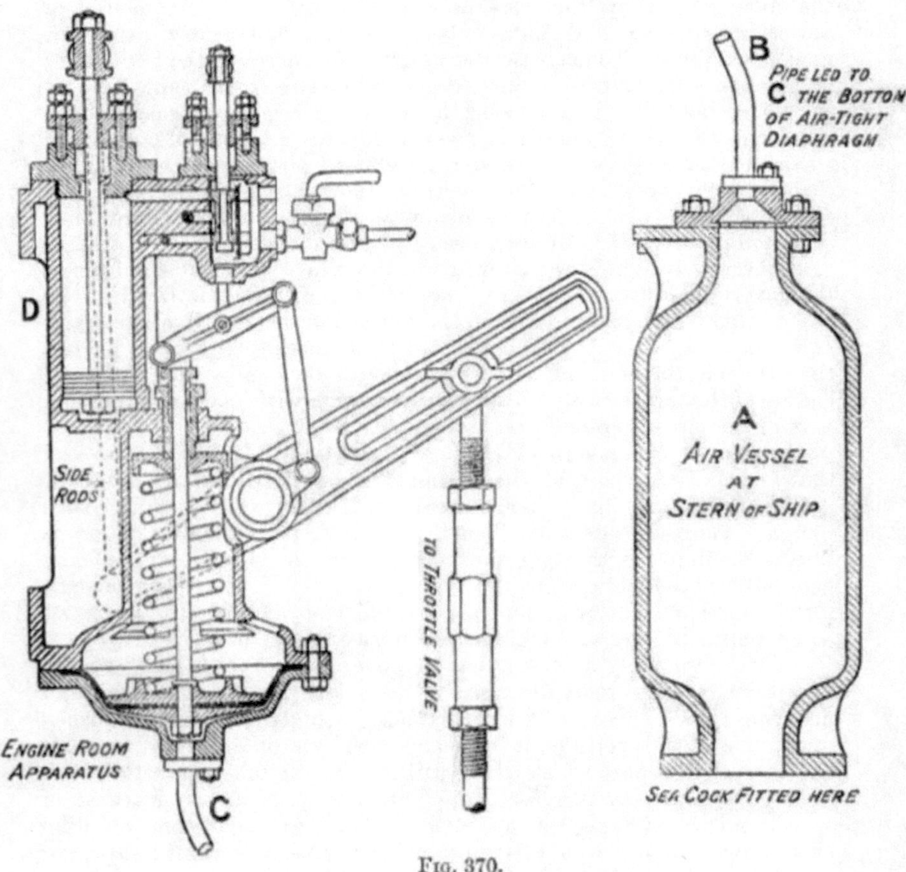

FIG. 370.

the ship is accompanied by an in-flow or out-flow of water through it, and consequently a variation in the pressure of the air contained in the air vessel, and also under the diaphragm of the engine-room apparatus, causing the diaphragm to move through such part of its travel as is requisite to enable the compression of spring and air pressure to balance one another again. Every movement of the diaphragm is followed by a corresponding movement of the governor steam piston, and consequently of the throttle valve of the engines under control, the time taken between the variation in the head of water at the stern of the ship and the moving of the throttle valve being practically nothing.

The governor therefore anticipates any increase in the speed of the engines due to the propeller rising out of the water, and does not depend upon a variation in the speed of the engines to be controlled, before it acts. By adjusting the balance between the spring and the air pressure under the diaphragm, the diaphragm begins to fall and the throttle valve to close when the tips of the propeller blades rise to any desired distance from the surface of the water. The air vessel should be fitted as far aft in the screw tunnel as possible, the hole through the side of the vessel being placed about one-fourth the diameter of the propeller below the level of the centre of the shaft. The reports of the action of this governor in the mercantile marine are very satisfactory. It is fitted in the 'Campania,' 'Paris,' and many other vessels.

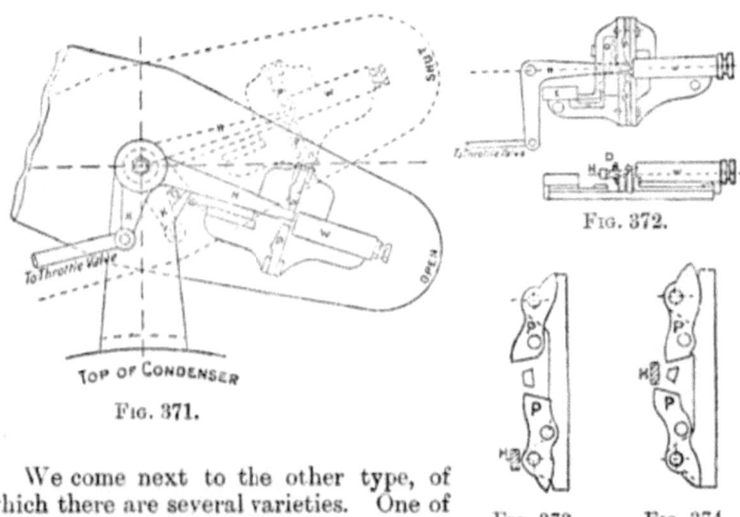

Fig. 371.

Fig. 372.

Fig. 373.

Fig. 374.

We come next to the other type, of which there are several varieties. One of them—viz. *Brown's emergency governor gear*—has already been described in dealing with reversing arrangements (see Chapter XVII.). Another example is the following, viz. :—

Aspinall's governor.—This governor consists of a hinged weight, w, operating two pawls, P, P, carried on a frame which is bolted to a pump lever, or other reciprocating part, as shown in Figs. 371 and 372. One of these pawls always projects, while the other lies close against the frame as shown on a larger scale in Figs. 373 and 374. The throttle-valve lever is so arranged that it is moved by these pawls when they project from the frame.

Under normal circumstances the lever H is in its lowest position and the throttle valve wide open, while the upper pawl projects and the lower one lies back as shown in Fig. 373, which represents the governor at the top of the stroke. The governor then travels freely past the throttle handle H without moving it. When the revolutions of the engines are increased by about five per cent. above the normal speed, the weight, w, is left behind on the downward stroke, and therefore moves upwards relatively to the frame and is kept in that position by a detent arranged for this purpose. This movement of the weight reverses the position of the pawls, causing the bottom one to project and the upper one to be brought back. The bottom pawl then engages with lever H, lifting it throughout the whole upward stroke to the position shown by dotted lines in Fig. 371, and thus shutting off steam by closing throttle valve, the pawls being as shown in Fig. 374, which again represents the governor at the top of the stroke.

On the return stroke the detent is lifted by passing the lever H, liberating the weight w, which if the racing has stopped, falls, and the position of the two pawls is again altered, the top pawl now engaging with the lever H, depressing it, and thus reopening the throttle valve. If the racing has not stopped, the pawls remain as in Fig. 374, and the throttle valve remains closed. An emergency gear is also provided at E, the details not being shown in the figure, which only comes into operation in case of very excessive racing, such as on losing a propeller, or breaking a shaft, in which case an additional arm situated at A, is left behind and locks the weight w in the 'shut off' position, thus preventing the reopening of throttle valve.

Distilling apparatus.—The fresh water used on board ship for drinking, washing, culinary purposes, and for making up the waste of the feed-water for the boilers, &c., is produced from sea-water by the process of distillation. In addition to its convenience, there is no doubt that this practice has added greatly to the health of the Navy, as the water thus obtained is perfectly pure, which is impossible to insure in shore water in many ports of the world.

The distilling condensers first fitted were for drinking water only, and were simple condensers for the steam produced in the boilers, and any impurities in the boiler water often found their way by priming, &c., into the distiller. For this reason a separate boiler was usually fitted for distilling and auxiliary purposes, which was not fed with the greasy surface-condenser water, but with clean sea-water. This boiler was of such construction as to facilitate, as far as possible, the removal of the scale formed by the evaporation of the sea-water. The losses of feed-water by leakage of glands, joints, &c., were made up by the admission of the required amount of sea-water, generally by a small cock on the condenser which placed the steam and water spaces in connection.

As pressures of steam increased, this practice became inconvenient, and the admission of sea-water and formation of scale in the boilers became objectionable, so that fresh feed-water to make up waste became imperative. Other arrangements were therefore made, and separate evaporators were fitted which produced vapour from sea-water by contact with tubes filled with steam, taken either from the boilers direct, or from the receivers of the engine. They are really small boilers, with heat obtained from steam passing through tubes, instead of, as in an ordinary boiler, by heat obtained directly from the combustion of coal. This vapour is conducted to the distilling condensers for production of fresh drinking water, and a portion to the main or auxiliary condenser for making up the deficiency of boiler feed-water. The scale is thus deposited in the evaporator, which is specially constructed to admit of its ready removal. This evaporator, with the usual distilling condenser in connection, is spoken of as a 'double distiller,' as the resulting drinking water is obtained by the agency of two distillations of water, first in the boiler and secondly in the evaporator. The condensed primary steam is returned to the boiler.

There are many varieties of evaporators and condensers in use for marine purposes, but they all act on the same principle.

Normandy's evaporator.—In this variety the evaporating tubes are all straight and rolled into tube plates at their ends, as shown in Fig. 375. The steam from the boilers enters these tubes through the pipe shown, and evaporates the surrounding sea-water and is itself condensed and returned to the boilers. The steam generated outside the tubes is conveyed by one of the two valves shown, either to the auxiliary condenser for feed make-up purposes, or to the distilling condensers for production of drinking water. The resulting scale is deposited in the evaporator, from whence it is cleaned out at intervals. To facilitate cleaning, the nest of tubes is hinged about a vertical axis near the door, so that by unbolting the top and bottom connections to the steam and drain pipes, the nest of tubes can be revolved and brought outside the barrel and conveniently cleaned. An automatic valve is fitted at the steam outlet which prevents undue production of vapour and possible consequent priming. The sea-water for the evaporator is supplied by one of the pumps shown on the right. It takes its supply from a feed box containing a float, which maintains a constant level in the feed box.

Normandy's condenser.—The steam from the evaporator enters the condenser through the pipe A, and passes through the two series of tubes shown, the upper set being the condensing and the lower the cooling tubes. The casing is kept filled with cold sea-water, which enters at the orifice B, at the bottom, and flows out through the upper orifice C, which is kept some distance from the top of the chamber, so that the hottest sea-water is not discharged overboard. The sea-water feed for the evaporator in connection with the condenser is taken from this hot sea-water so as to promote economy of evaporation. An air pipe D with cock is fitted to allow the air evolved from the condensing water in the casing by heat to pass into the outlet pipe leading to the sea. Pipes with small hooded orifices open to the atmosphere are fitted to allow sufficient air to enter to properly aerate the water, and this is drawn away with the fresh water.

The condensed water rises from the lower chamber through the pipe F, and overflows down the pipe G to the pump suction, so that the cooling tubes of the condenser are in this case always full of water and the fresh water drawn off is cold. A cock is fitted at the bottom of pipe F, which can be set so that the condensed water leaves direct and does not rise up the pipe F and overflow. In this case the level of the water in the cooling tubes will be much lower, so that more of the surface is devoted to condensing and less to cooling, so that a larger quantity of fresh water is made but delivered at a higher temperature. The distilled water is pumped by means of a small steam donkey-pump into test tanks, and from these tanks it flows by gravity to the water tanks in the hold of the ship. The quality of the water in the test tank is occasionally tested.

In a large number of merchant steamers and ships of the Royal

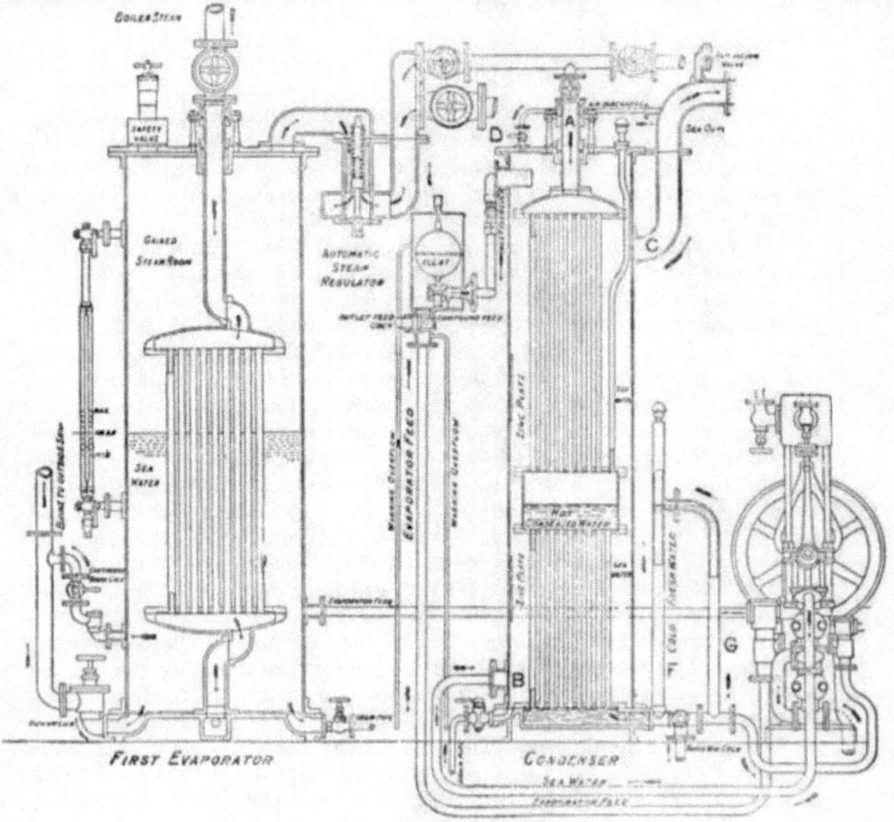

Fig. 375.

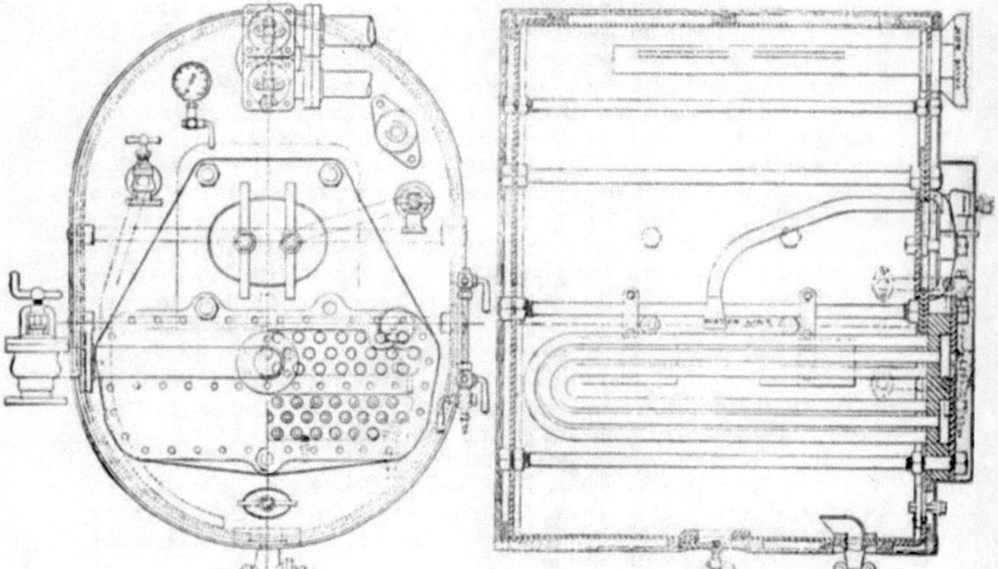

Fig. 376.

Navy, other kinds of fresh water-making machinery have been fitted.
Weir's, Kirkaldy's, and Caird & Rayner's evaporators are the most
generally employed, and have proved efficient.

Weir's evaporator, Fig. 376, consists of a cylindrical shell in which
the heating surface is composed of a series of U-shaped tubes expanded
into a tube plate. This series of tubes forms a nest, which can be removed from the shell when necessary to scale the tubes. The two ends
of the tubes communicate with two separate chambers ; the ends in the

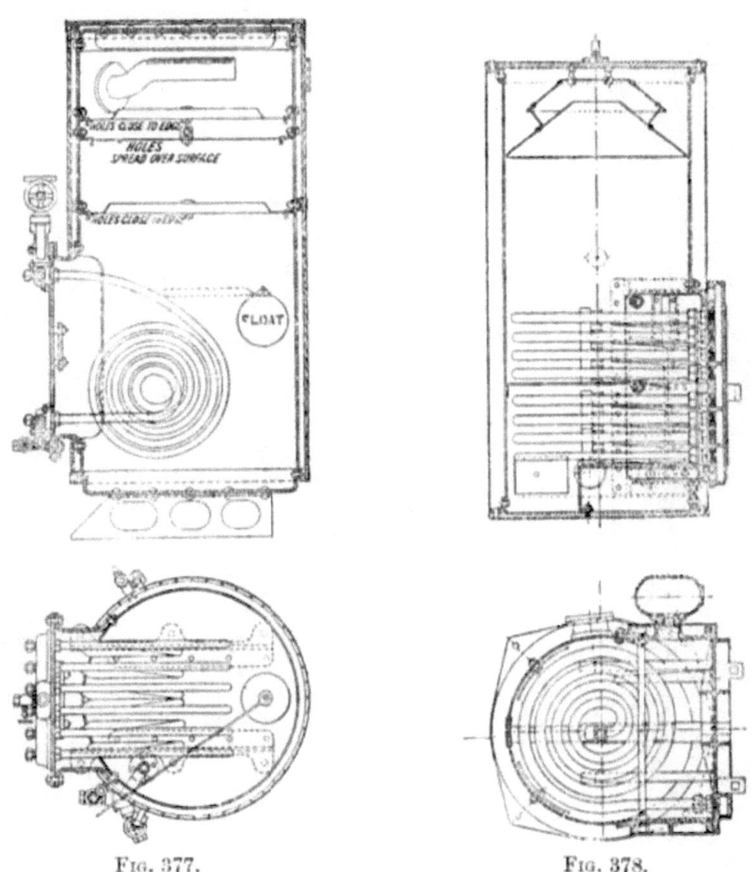

FIG. 377.   FIG. 378.

admission chamber are open, but the outlet ends of all except one
of the lowest are contracted by brass plugs, each having a small hole
as an opening to the outlet chamber. This tube is left open at the one
end, but the other end is connected directly with the drain valve, and
any steam which may pass through the small holes in the contracted
ends is condensed and returned through the evaporator before it
escapes. Besides the inlet and outlet steam valves and feed-valve, a
gauge glass to show the water level in the evaporator, safety valve,
pressure gauge, blow-off cock, and brine valve are fitted. The sea-

water is supplied by means of a small pump.   The action is the same as in Normandy's evaporator.

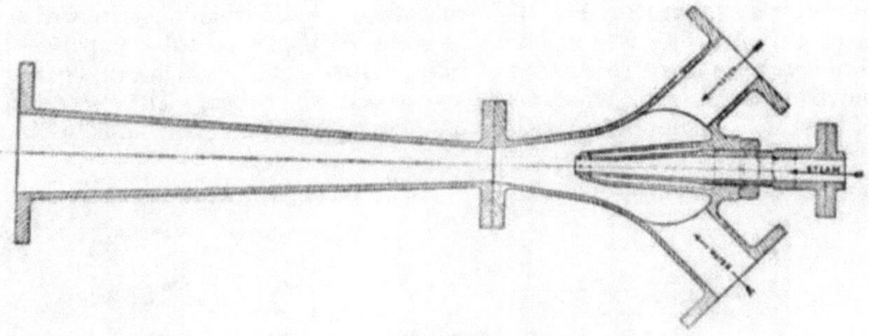

FIG. 379.

Kirkaldy's evaporator is also largely fitted in the mercantile marine and Navy.   It consists of a cylindrical shell with evaporating tubes in the lower part, but curved in a different manner to Weir's, as indicated in Fig. 377. An automatic feed-valve is fitted to maintain a fixed water level.

Caird & Rayner's evaporator is also similar, the tubes being curved horizontally in the manner shown in Fig. 378. The apparatus by Kirkaldy and Caird & Rayner are extensively fitted in torpedo-boat destroyers and torpedo boats, for which they are very suitable on account of their lightness.

Steam injectors for filling fresh water tanks.—As explained in Chapter XX, the fresh water produced by the evaporators is stored for boiler purposes in the reserve fresh-water tanks.   These tanks are filled with fresh water from the shore if convenient opportunities present themselves, generally by means of water boats alongside the vessel.   The fresh water is generally drawn from the water boats and discharged into the engine feed tanks by means of a steam injector, a sketch of which is shown in Fig. 379.   The centre orifice is supplied with steam, and water is allowed to flow in from either side of the ship and be discharged by the steam jet into the tanks.   From the engine feed tanks the water overflows into the reserve fresh-water tanks, where it remains until required for the boilers.

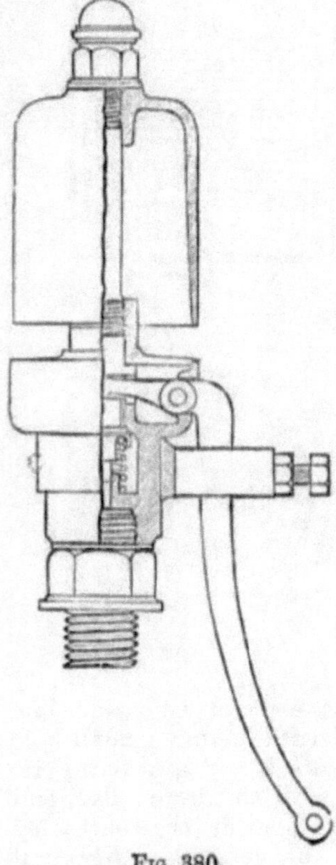

FIG. 380.

Steam fog-whistle.—All steamships are fitted with steam whistles or sirens for signalling purposes, and for indicating the position of the ship in case of fog, &c. A sketch of a steam whistle for use with moderate steam pressures is shown in Fig. 380. The sound is produced by the vibrations caused by steam issuing from the narrow annular orifice against the thin edge of the bell of the whistle. The bell is screwed on to enable its distance from the steam orifice to be adjusted to suit the pressure of steam used. The steam pressure acts on the top of the valve and tends to keep it closed, as also does a spiral spring. The valve is opened by a lever, and string or wire, led to some convenient place for working it.

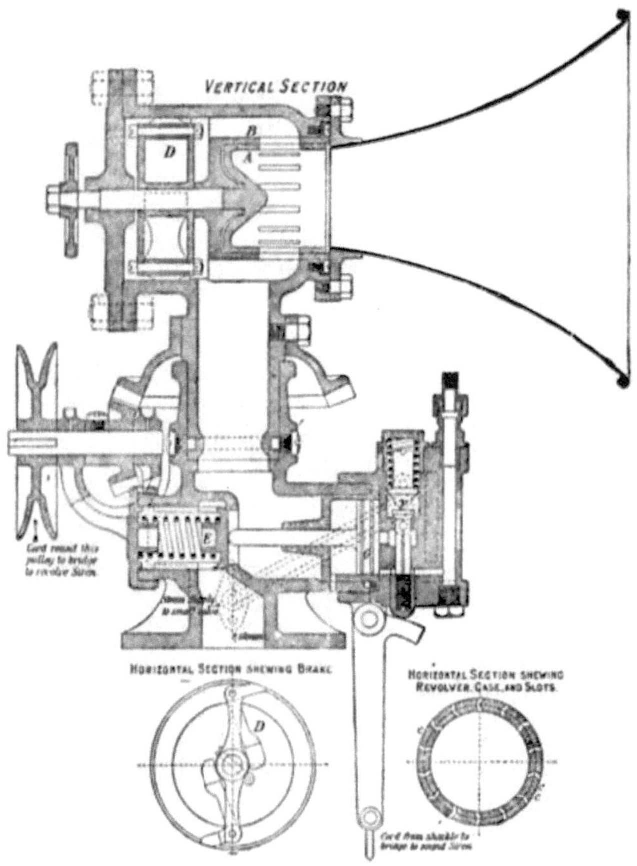

Fig. 381.

The siren is another and much more powerful instrument for signalling purposes at sea. In Holmes & Ingrey's siren, adopted in the Royal Navy and illustrated in Fig. 381, the steam passes through a number of narrow slits on the surfaces of two cylinders with horizontal axes, the inner one of which, A, revolves within the other, B, which is fixed, and the steam then issues to the atmosphere through a trumpet-mouthed orifice to increase the volume of sound. To assist in starting the siren, should the main slits not be opposite one another, a small number of auxiliary slits, c, are made in the outer cylinder, so that should the main slits be closed, one of these auxiliary slits must be open. A brake D, shown in detail, is fitted to the revolving cylinder to prevent its speed being excessive. The centrifugal force causes the two arms to press against the surrounding barrel, and the friction thus produced limits the speed. The bell mouth can be turned so as to point in any desired direction by the bevel gearing and pulley, worked from the navigating position.

With high steam pressures, as the valve lifts against the pressure the force required to be exerted becomes too great for proper manipulation, and the main valve, E, which admits steam to the siren, is moved by a small piston G, which is actuated by a much smaller valve F. When the siren is desired to be sounded this small valve is worked from the bridge, and high-pressure steam is thus admitted to the piston, which is forced forward and opens the steam valve of the siren. These auxiliary valves are also fitted to steam whistles when the pressure is very great.

In the Royal Navy the most recent practice is to fit two steam sirens for signalling purposes, so arranged as not to be both masked by the funnel or other fittings when signalling in any direction, the steam whistle having been reported as practically of no service.

Telegraphs—The necessary orders from the deck to the engine rooms and to the principal auxiliary engines of the ship are usually transmitted, by means of shafting and gearing, to index pointers which work over dials suitably engraved. The apparatus consists of two parts : a transmitter on the bridge and a receiver in the engine room. Loud gongs are fitted in the receiver, the hammers being worked by a sprocket wheel on the index spindle, to call attention to the moving of the telegraph. The gongs are of different tones to help to distinguish between orders for ahead and astern. Reply gongs are fitted to indicate to the officer on deck that the order has been received. The tell-tale informs him when it has been executed.

In the latest type of apparatus (Chadburn's) adopted in the Navy the orders are transmitted by a wheel on the side of the standard, one revolution of the wheel being made for each order. In the receiving portion a self-centering arrangement is supplied, which insures the pointer moving to the centre of each division and prevents misunderstanding of the order transmitted.

Electric telegraphs.—In some ships electric telegraphs have been fitted for transmitting orders, but the mechanical details of this system have not been sufficiently perfect to cause its general adoption. It would, however, be in many cases an advantage if electricity could be utilised for this purpose, especially in ships in which communication has to be made between stations at considerable distances from each other ; and it is probable that the difficulties that have hitherto been experienced in the arrangements of details of the gear will shortly be successfully overcome, and that electric telegraphy will become thoroughly reliable for transmitting all the necessary orders on board ships. It cannot be said to be so at present.

Voice-pipes and Telephones.—To facilitate communication, voice-pipes with mouthpieces at their ends, are fitted from the deck to the main and auxiliary engine rooms, and between such other parts of the ship as may be considered necessary.

For the long important leads of voice-pipes they are made 2 inches in diameter, clothed with a non-conducting composition and suspended with some insulating material, in order to exclude as far as possible external noises. The ends at noisy stations are provided with two flexible ends with large indiarubber fittings, so that each ear can be covered, and the end pressed so as to fit the shape of the head, in order to assist in exclusion of noise. Electric call-bells and indicators are fitted to attract attention. The smaller and less important voice-pipes are made $1\frac{1}{4}$ inch in diameter and fitted with whistles at their ends for attracting attention. With long lengths of voice-pipe led to the engine-room or other noisy places, communication by voice-pipe when going at full speed is generally difficult, and in recent war vessels telephones are fitted for such communication with excellent results.

Tell-tale apparatus.—Standards and dials, with revolving pointers driven by the main engines through shafting and gearing, are fitted in convenient places visible from the working positions, to enable the officers on deck to satisfy themselves as to the speed and direction of the engines when going in and out of harbour, picking up buoys, or executing manœuvres. By inspecting these dials they are able to see when and how correctly an order is carried out.

Refrigerating engines.—A new class of auxiliary steam-engine has recently come into use on board ships, consisting of the refrigerating machines which are fitted in large numbers of passenger vessels and vessels carrying cargoes of meat in the mercantile marine, and in all recent battleships, and most recent cruisers and gunboats of the Royal Navy, for maintaining a low temperature in a small separate provision room, called the refrigerating chamber. A few smaller machines for making ice only, have also been fitted on smaller ships. There are various systems on which such machines are made for reducing a room to a low temperature.

Cold-air system.—This is one of the simplest, and is shown in Fig. 382. The machine consists of a tandem compound engine with cylinders A and B having piston slide-valves on the same spindle worked by a single eccentric. This engine supplies the motive power of the apparatus. On two other cranks, side by side, are placed the two cylinders, C and D. C is called the compressing cylinder and D the expanding cylinder. D is provided, by means of a slide-valve and expansion valve working on its back, with means of sharply cutting off the inlet of air when it enters the expanding cylinder. The compressing and expanding cylinders are double acting. A cooling chamber constructed like a surface-condenser, with a pump for circulating the cooling sea-water through it, completes the apparatus.

The action is simple, and as follows. The power exerted by the engine A B moves the pistons of C and D up and down. Air is drawn into the cylinder C through the inlet valves E E from the surrounding atmosphere or from the cold room, it is compressed on the return stroke into the air cooler, and the work done on it appears as heat in the air. This heated air, passing through the tubes of the air cooler, is cooled by the circulating water, and is then led to the valve chamber of the expanding cylinder D. The compressing cylinder is supplied with

DELIVERY F E SUCTION
A
D C B
AIR DELIVERY
WATER
DELIVERY F E SUCTION
EXHAUST
WATER INLET
PUMP LEVER
AIR COOLER,
OR
CONDENSER
CONDENSER
PUMP
WATER OUTLET
COLD AIR OUTLET

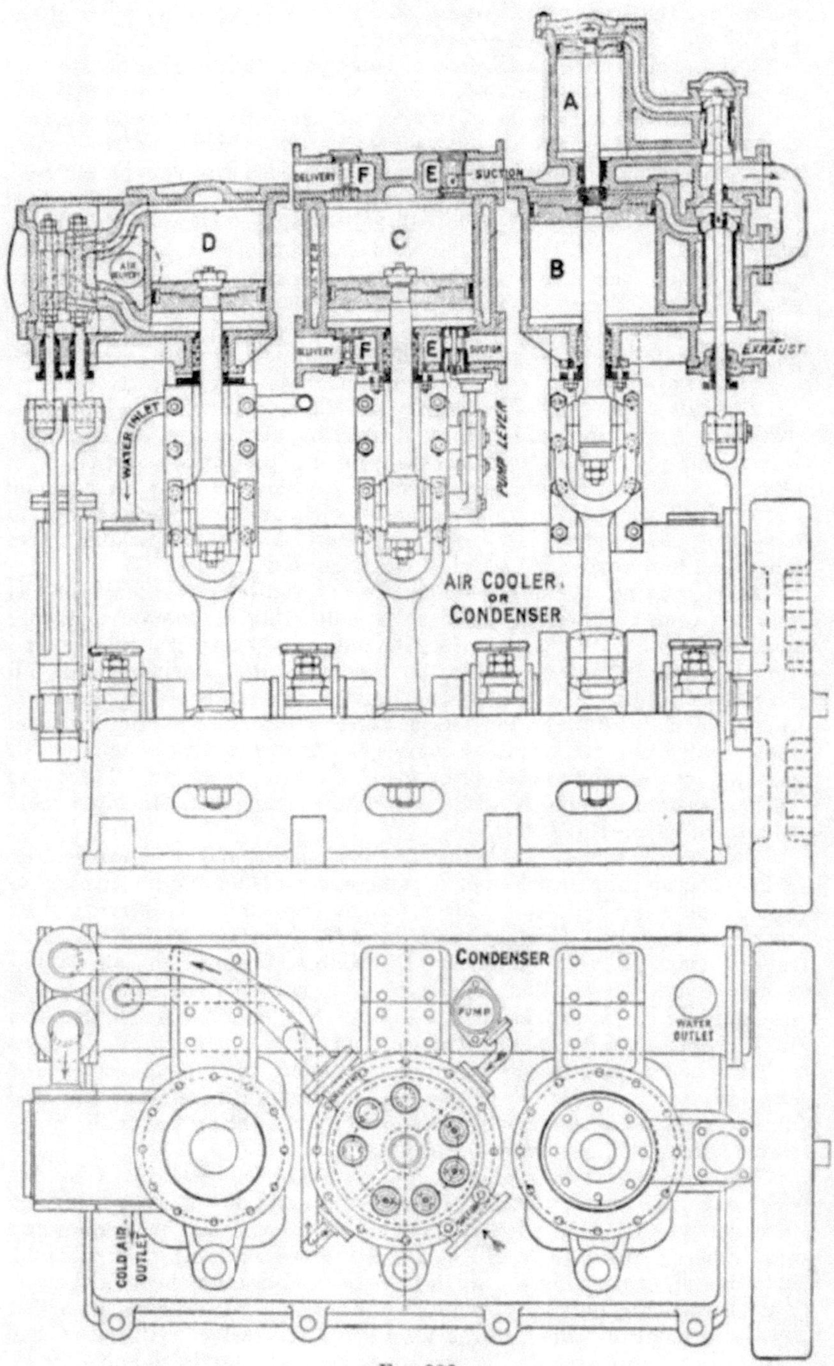

Fig. 382.

a water jacket through which the circulating pump delivers the cooling water on its way from the air cooler to the sea. The tubes of the cooler may be made tight by screwed glands and packing, or may be simply rolled in the tube plates, the latter plan being sufficient. In the cylinder D the cut-off valves are so arranged that the proper quantity of air is admitted before supply is cut off, and during the remainder of the stroke the air expands, and therefore does work on the piston, and heat is expended in the process in exactly the converse manner to the generation of heat in the compressing cylinder. As, however, the air has been deprived of its surplus heat in the air cooler, the heat equivalent of the work it does is absorbed from itself and a considerable lowering of its temperature results.

Snow box. Refrigerating chamber.—This cold air is then exhausted through the exhaust orifice of the slide-valve in the usual manner, and conducted first to the 'snow box' (a small accessible chamber in which the snow formed from the moisture is deposited), and thence to the cold chamber, in which the supply of meat or provisions is kept, and where it displaces air of higher temperature. The refrigerating chamber is insulated by lagging its bulkheads, ceilings and floor with silicate cotton or other non-conductor, a teak lining being fitted over this to form the inside surface. The chamber is generally divided into two parts, one being the cold meat storage room and the other the vegetable room, as different temperatures are required to properly preserve the different classes of provisions.

Carbonic acid system.—Another well-known plan, which is both successful and efficient, is the carbonic anhydride system of Messrs. J. & E. Hall, in which carbonic anhydride is passed round and round in the circuit. This system is fitted in many ships in the mercantile marine, and in some war vessels, and is illustrated in Fig. 383.

The machine consists of three parts : a compressor, condenser, and evaporator. The compressor draws in heated and expanded gas from the evaporator and compresses it. The compressed gas then passes to a condenser, consisting of coils, in which the warm compressed gas is cooled and liquefied by reduction of temperature caused by the action of the cooling sea-water. From the condenser the cool liquid carbonic anhydride is conveyed into the evaporator, consisting of coils, where it vapourises and expands, absorbing heat in the process, and cooling the surrounding brine which is in contact with the coils. This cold brine is circulated by a small pump to the refrigerating chamber, where it is conducted though a long series of rows of cooling pipes, termed 'grids,' which are placed at the roof of the chamber. The cold brine grids in this position set up a circulation of air, the cold air descending and being replaced by less cold air, which is cooled in its turn. Any moisture in the air is condensed on the grids, and appears as frost on the pipes. The large quantity of cold brine present in the pipes forms a considerable reserve of cooling medium, enabling the chamber to be maintained cold for a considerable period after the machine is stopped, so that the latter need not be run more than a few hours per day. All openings in the cold room should evidently be only through the ceiling.

Action of the system.—Under atmospheric pressure the liquid CO_2 would evaporate at 120° F. below zero, but its temperature of evaporation rises with the pressure in a similar manner as water. At a pressure of 500 lbs. per square inch it boils at a temperature of 30° F., so that cold water may be used to supply the heat for boiling it. The pressure in the evaporator is therefore regulated to the required temperature of the cooling water, so that a considerable pressure is necessary in the evaporator. The compressor draws the gas from the evaporator, and compresses it to the liquefying pressure, the heat due to the compression being absorbed by the cooling water in the condenser coils, and the gas in these coils becomes liquid before its exit. The liquid is then boiled in the evaporator coils, cooling the surrounding brine by the heat absorbed during the evaporation. The compressor gland is made tight by cupped leathers with glycerine forced between them at

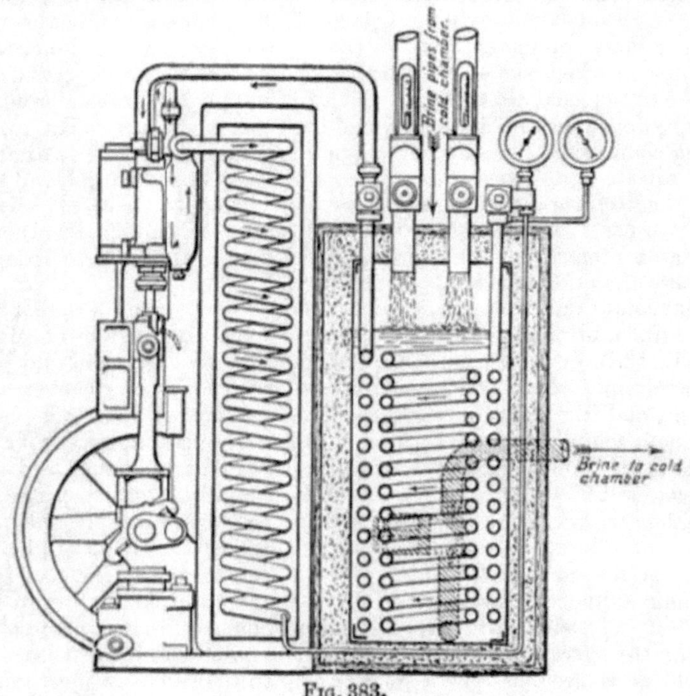

Fig. 383.

a pressure superior to that in the compressor, so that no escape of gas can take place. The small quantity of glycerine which enters the compressor is drained off occasionally from a separator through which the gas passes on its way to the condenser.

These machines are more efficient in economy of cold production than the dry air machines, although less simple. Carbonic anhydride is supplied in steel cylinders to replenish the supply, but as war vessels may often be on such service that replenishment may be difficult, more of the cold air machines are being fitted at present in the Navy than the carbonic acid machines.

Electrical machinery.—The dynamos used on board ships for internal illumination, and for working search lights and motors are of the direct driven type, and are shown generally in Figs. 384 and 385.

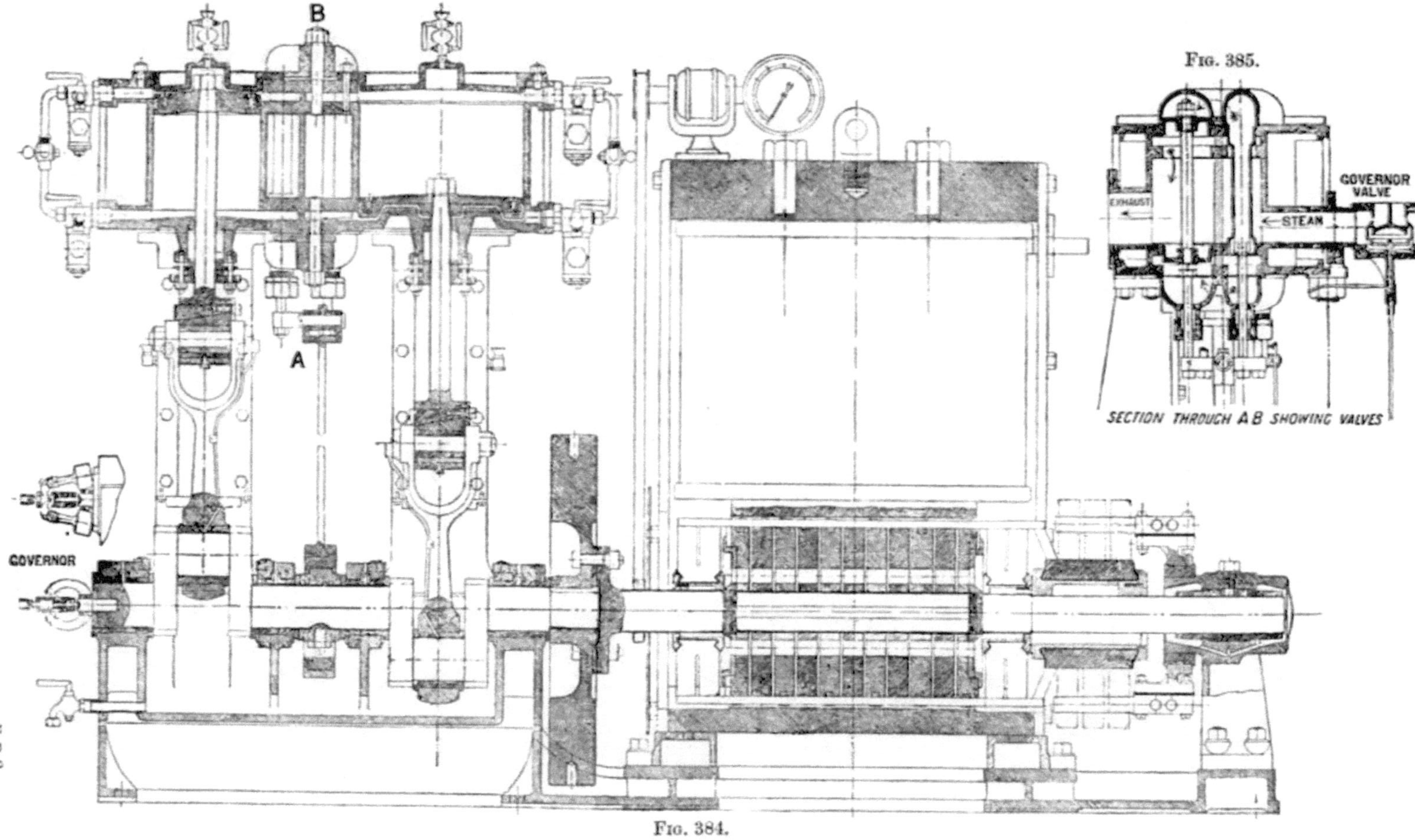

B
A
GOVERNOR
Fig. 385.
GOVERNOR VALVE
EXHAUST
STEAM
SECTION THROUGH A B SHOWING VALVES
Fig. 384.

Each set of machines usually consists of a compound-wound dynamo with its armature shaft coupled to the crank shaft of a vertical double acting open-type steam-engine. The engines have two cylinders side by side, and the two cranks are 180 degrees apart. Most of the engines are compound, but some simple engines are in use in ships where the steam pressure is low. The pistons and other reciprocating parts attached to each crank are carefully balanced, and a heavy fly-wheel is fitted on the engine shaft, at the dynamo end, which conduces to steady running. A governor is fitted to the other end of the crank shaft and operates on a balanced throttle valve. In the sketch, Fig. 385, the two valves are worked by the same eccentric, the H.P. top port being open to steam by the amount of the lead, the exhaust from the H.P. proceeding as shown by the dotted arrow through the lower chamber to the bottom port of the L.P., while the upper port of the L.P. is open to the exhaust.

Type of dynamos.—The dynamos are usually of the inverted two-pole type, and are carried on an extension of the engine bed. They have drum armatures and the field magnets are compound-wound to give a constant pressure of 80 volts for any current from zero to the maximum, while the speed of the engine is maintained constant. The usual speed is 320 revolutions per minute. The machines used in the Royal Navy are proportioned for maximum currents of 100, 200, 400 or 600 ampères, and generally three sets of engines and dynamos are fitted in each ship.

All the machines are connected to a switch-board placed in a central position. From the switch-board the current is distributed to the various circuits for lighting, motors, &c. This board is so arranged that a circuit can be quickly changed from one machine to another, but no circuit can receive current from two machines at the same time. The most recently fitted dynamos are of the iron-clad type, the field magnet coils and the armature being almost entirely surrounded by iron. The object of this arrangement is to reduce to a minimum the leakage of magnetic lines of force which may affect compasses or chronometers in the neighbourhood of the machines. An illustration of a machine of this type, with its engine, &c., is given in Fig. 384.

Construction of armatures.—The armature core of the dynamo is built up of thin discs of soft iron slipped over metal sleeves which are keyed on the shaft. The discs are insulated from each other by thin sheets of asbestos paper in order to prevent loss of energy and heating due to eddy currents, and are kept in place by clamping plates and end nuts.

The conductors on the armature which carry the current are made up of copper wires twisted together and pressed to a rectangular sec-tion. They are insulated by a covering of varnished tape. Usually two lengths of bars are used. They are placed round the periphery of the armature longitudinally, long and short bars alternating, their ends overhanging the core ; all the ends at one end of the armature pro-jecting the same distance. Projections are fitted into the core at intervals which drive the conductor bars. These projections are insu-lated by mica slips. The bars are kept in place by bands of steel or bronze binding wire tightly wound on and soldered. Mica strips are placed under the bands to prevent injury to the insulation of the bars.

Each bar is connected at each end by bent copper strips to bars almost diametrically opposite to it, so that the whole of the bars and end connections form one closed circuit. The projecting end of each long bar is also connected to the nearest commutator segment, the number of segments being equal to the number of long bars. Two or more pairs of brushes bear on the commutator to collect the current, so that any brush may be lifted off without interrupting the circuit.

Field magnet windings.—The field magnet winding consists of shunt and series coils, wound on a frame which fits over the upper pole piece. The shunt coils are of small wire and are of high resistance. The ends of the wire are connected to the machine terminals. The greater part of the magnetisation is due to these coils, so that at full speed, and when no current is being taken from the machine, the electric pressure is normal, i.e. 80 volts.

The series coils are formed of thick copper bars and convey the whole current generated. They provide additional magnetisation proportional to the current flowing in them, and so compensate for the additional pressure required to force this current through the machine. By the combination of the two sets of coils the pressure is thus independent of the current, so long as the speed is constant.

In the largest machines there are two distinct armature windings laid on side by side, the bars of the two windings alternating as also do their respective commutator segments. The two windings are connected in parallel by the brushes which all have a bearing rather wider than the angular width of two commutator segments.

Commutator.—To obtain satisfactory working the commutator must be kept true, and should be frequently examined to see if flats are being formed on it. These are due to unequal wear of the segments, generally from sparking, and they rapidly increase if neglected. If slight, they may be removed by filing while the machine is running slowly with the brushes off. If considerable, the commutator must be turned up. This is generally done in place, using a lathe slide rest clamped to the bed plate; the engines being run as slowly as possible. After turning the commutator should be polished.

Brushes.—The brushes must be carefully filed to fit the commutator curve, and to bear evenly from side to side. The most satisfactory way is to make a pair of hard wood or metal clamps, to hold the brush while being filed, having their ends of the correct shape. The brushes must be carefully set in the holders with all the tips of each set in a line, and the tips of the two sets bearing simultaneously on diametrically opposite commutator segments. Generally two segments are marked at their ends with crosses to assist in this adjustment. The electrical parts of the machine rarely require attention but should be occasionally tested to see that the insulation of the circuits is good.

Adjustment of bearings.—The engines should be very carefully adjusted to obtain quiet running. The centre line of the shafts should be maintained at its original height, which is usually slightly above the axis of the bore of the pole pieces. If so adjusted part of the weight of the armature is borne by a vertical force due to the uneven distribution of the magnetic flux of the field magnets, and this relieves the bearings. A gauge, by which the distance of the tops of the shaft journals below the planed parts of the bed can be readily measured when the caps and upper brasses are removed, is useful for this purpose.

To insure steady running a heavy fly-wheel and good governor are necessary, and the latter should be kept in good condition and adjustment. When the load on the machine is gradually taken off the increase of speed at no load should not exceed 5 per cent., and when suddenly removed the temporary increase should not exceed 10 per cent.

The governor.—The governor should be frequently examined to insure its parts working freely without backlash, as friction causes the objectionable defect known as 'hunting.' This is a defect to which sensitive and not very stable governors are often subject.

If the governor gear is stiff and a reduction of load on the engine occurs, the governor does not act until the engine has increased its speed sufficiently for the increased centrifugal force to overcome the spring and the frictional resistances. When this speed is reached the valve will commence to close, but as the centrifugal force and the resistance of the spring are nearly equal for all positions of the valve, and because the friction of the parts in motion is less than their friction in repose, the valve will continue to close until the energy of motion of the gear has been absorbed by the frictional resistances and the work done in overcoming the unbalanced part of the spring's force. The resulting valve opening will be too small for the normal speed and the engine will be slowed too much. The opposite action will now commence, resulting in a periodic rise and fall of speed and a very unpleasant variation of light from the lamps to which the machine is supplying current. This hunting may be stopped by closing the stop-valve until the control of the engine is taken from the governor, and the speed of the engine is slightly below that for which the governor is set. When the load is steady the valve may be gradually reopened.

It is well always to keep a nearly constant pressure of steam up to the governor valve. In some cases a reducing valve is used, but, in the absence of this, careful regulation of the stop-valve will much assist the governor which will not closely control the speed under varying load if the steam pressure is also varying.

This regulation of the steam is much easier if a pressure gauge is fitted between the stop and governor valves.

Adjustment of governor.—A good way to adjust an engine governor is as follows. Overhaul the gear to see that the whole of the parts are well fitted and free, and that there are no flats worn on the ends of the short arms of the governor balls. Next try the governor valve. It should be free but sufficiently steamtight when closed to reduce the engine speed below the normal with full steam pressure and no load.

After reconnecting the parts, the engine should be started without load, and the speed increased by gradually opening the stop-valve until the governor balls fly out to their widest position. By means of a trammel and marks on a part of the engine frame and on one of the bell cranks of the governor gear, it may be seen when the governor balls reach this position. The corresponding speed should not be more than 5 per cent. in excess of the normal speed, full steam pressure being used. If necessary the tension of the governor spring should be altered to adjust this speed. The rod connecting the governor valve to the gear should now be shortened by the adjusting nut provided, until the stop-valve can be fully opened without any further increase of speed. This adjustment insures that the permanent increase of speed when the load is gradually removed shall not exceed the limit allowed. The increase due to sudden removal of the load will depend on the relation which the moment of inertia of the fly-wheel and other moving parts of the engine bears to the time taken by the governor to close the valve.

When the load is put on, the speed will be reduced and the governor will open the valve until the steam opening is sufficient. The amount of the variation of speed for full load and no load will depend on the sensitiveness of the governor and on the steam pressure, a greater steam opening, and therefore a greater movement of the balls, being required when steam is low than when it is high. By small adjustments of the tension of the regulating spring the normal speed may be obtained for average load, and if the steam pressure is kept fairly constant the variation of speed due to change of load will be quite small.

Over-compounding.—It should be noted that to maintain a constant electrical pressure at the machine terminals, a perfectly compounded dynamo requires to be driven at constant speed. It is usual to slightly over-compound direct driven machines, so that the small loss of electrical pressure due to the fall in speed necessary to change the position of the governor when the load is increased, is compensated for by the increase of pressure produced by the increase of current flowing in the series coils of the machine. This action also tends to reduce the effect of the resistance of the leads between the dynamo and the lamps.

Effect of increase of temperature.—During the first few hours of running, the electric pressure at the dynamo terminals will fall gradually, due to the increase of resistance of the machine circuits as the temperature increases. After a time the temperature will become constant and no further variation of pressure will occur. It will generally be found that to maintain the full pressure the speed requires to be a few revolutions above the normal, the amount of increase depending on the temperature of the surroundings.

CHAPTER XXIX.

RAISING STEAM AND GETTING UNDER WAY.

In this chapter the procedure of raising steam in the boilers and getting the engines under way will be described. It will be assumed that the engines have not been worked for some time, the boilers being empty.

Filling the boilers.—When preparing to raise steam, the boilers are filled with water to some distance above the ordinary working level, say to about three-fourths the height of the gauge glass, to allow for the losses that occur during the warming of the engines. In modern vessels clean fresh water should always be used unless absolutely unobtainable. Salt water can be used in ships with jet condensers, and is also permissible in some of the older vessels in which the steam pressure is less than 90 lbs. per square inch, and in which salt water make-up for boiler feed is a necessity. When clean fresh water is not available, every care should be taken to avoid the necessity of filling the boilers from shallow depths, or for using impure water of any kind, and if in harbour the boilers should be filled at high water, but in no case should the water be taken from refitting basins.

Boilers may be filled with fresh water, (*a*) by means of a hose from the jetty, or water-boat alongside, through one of the upper manholes, (*b*) by connecting the hose to the boiler-emptying valve, or (*c*) by the auxiliary feed engine from the reserve fresh-water tanks.

When ships are without steam power, either (*a*) or (*b*) is adopted, and when steam power is available in the ship (*c*) is the most usual plan, the supply to the auxiliary feed-pumps being maintained in the reserve fresh-water tanks by the ship's injectors. In the first case (*a*) is the more expeditious method, as it allows a full ingress for the water, at the same time providing full egress for the air, and it is the method generally adopted.

In plans (*b*) and (*c*) provision must be made for the escape of air by opening the safety valves, air, water-gauge drain, test, and hydrometer cocks, the latter three being closed as the water reaches their respective levels, the others when the water has reached the required level.

Boilers may be filled with salt water by means of the surface blowout apparatus if the water level of the boilers is below the sea level, as is usually the case ; or if this be not sufficient, it may be supplemented by means of a hose through one of the upper manholes, or connected to the boiler-emptying valve, the supply being procured by the ship's hand-pumps through the fire main ; or when steam is available, by the auxiliary feed engine from the sea direct.

Raising steam.—Prior to lighting fires the following points should be attended to :—

Boiler room procedure.—Fill the boilers as described above, then having removed or opened the funnel covers, the funnel guys should be slackened, to allow for the expansion of the funnel ; the cowls on the downtake tubes should be worked and trimmed to the wind; and any dampers in the uptakes should be opened wide. Any forced draught fittings, including the air-pressure gauges, should be examined, and there should be no combustible material in proximity to the boilers. A reserve of fresh water should, if practicable, have previously been provided in the reserve tanks. The main and auxiliary stop-valves on the boilers should be opened sufficiently wide to allow a free passage of steam to the engines, the necessary amount being determined by experience, also any valves in the steam pipes leading to the auxiliary engines to be used should be opened wide, except the valves at the engines themselves. The safety valves should be closed, so that the heated air and vapour will pass from the boilers to the main and auxiliary steam pipes, gradually raising their temperature.

Engine room procedure.—The following valves in the main steam pipe should be opened, viz. bulkhead stop-valves ; intermediate screw-down valves ; regulating and manœuvring valves ; connecting valve in pipe between engine rooms : valves to cylinder jackets, main circulating engine, starting engine, starting valves, and steering engine, if steam for the latter is to be taken from main steam pipe.

The silent blow-off valve should be closed. The jacket drain valves should be opened to the condensers, and the cylinder and slide-casing drains to the bilge.

The exhaust valves on the auxiliary condensers and the inlet and discharge valves of the main and auxiliary circulating pumps should be opened, the air-cocks being kept open till each condenser is full of sea-water. As soon as any fresh water accumulates in the condenser, test its freshness, to ascertain whether the tubes and packings are free from leakage.

All crank-pits and working parts generally should be examined for obstructions, and the main engines turned through a complete revolution by the hand-turning gear, after which the turning gear should be disconnected and secured. It is also advisable to run the links from full gear ahead to full gear astern by hand before connecting the steam starting engine.

All feed-tank fittings should be examined, and the suction valves for the main and auxiliary feed engines opened. The indicator and revolution counter gear should be connected and adjusted. Any relief cocks for backs of slides and balance pistons should be opened.

Generally.—It should have been ascertained that all joints are made and glands packed ; all securities for working parts and holding-down bolts are in position ; all lubricators are connected and clear, the oil lubricators being filled and the necessary worsteds ready ; all pressure and vacuum gauges connected, with their shut-off cocks and cocks at gauges open ; all drain-cocks on the various steam and exhaust valve boxes and pipes are open and connected to the drain tank direct, the direction cocks on the steam traps being so arranged. All auxiliary engines necessary for getting under way and steaming should be turned through one revolution by hand ; all steam and exhaust connections, except those on the engines themselves, should be open ; and all oil lamps, including those for pressure and water gauges on the boilers, should be properly trimmed for use before the dynamo engine can be started.

Laying fires.—The method of proceeding will depend on whether steam is urgently required or otherwise, but for definiteness we will describe a normal case of raising steam in a three-furnace tank boiler in which, to insure a gradual increase in the temperature of the various parts, and to diminish, as far as practicable, the stresses due to their expansion, the time allowed is rarely less than eight hours. The three furnaces would often be lighted together, and no fixed rule can be given as to the absolutely best procedure in this respect, but the practice of first lighting one furnace only, and after an interval dealing with the others, is perhaps the best plan, and this will be described.

A measured quantity of coal is placed on the floor-plates in front of each of the boilers which are to be used ; the bars of each furnace should then be '*primed*'—i.e. covered throughout with a layer of average-sized pieces of coal. One furnace, usually the lowest, is next '*wooded*'—i.e. pieces of firewood, so arranged as to facilitate the access of air to all parts, are placed at the furnace mouth, over a bed of oily waste, shavings, &c. The wood is next '*topped*'—i.e. the space between the wood and the furnace-crown is practically filled with pieces of hand-picked coal.

Lighting fires.—To light the fires the oily waste, &c., is kindled, at the same time the furnace door is left wide open, and the ash-pit doors closed, so that a good draught is insured through the fire, and the flame is carried over the coal laid on the furnace bars and tends to ignite it. Both the furnace and ash-pit doors of the other furnaces are kept closed to prevent the access of cold air. Lighting the fire in one furnace tends to set up circulation in the water, and promotes uniformity of temperature throughout the mass.

As the fire burns it is continually topped with hand-picked coal, and after about two hours there will be a fairly substantial fire at the mouth of the furnace. After this has been done, it is usual to light one or both of the wing fires from the fire in the central furnace. These fires are made at the front of the bars and constantly topped with hand-picked coal, the furnace and the ash-pit doors of these furnaces being arranged similarly to those of the middle furnace. If only one wing furnace is lighted at first, the other would be similarly treated about one hour afterwards.

Spreading fires.—After about four hours the centre fire is *spread*— i.e. the fire which till now has been on the front of the furnace is spread over the partially ignited coal on the remainder of the bars—after which this furnace door is closed and ash-pit door opened, so as to admit the air underneath the furnace bars and so promote the combustion of coal throughout. The other fires are similarly treated at about the fifth or sixth hours, at the discretion of the person in charge.

About this time the water should be boiling and pressure begin to show in the gauges. The rate of combustion can now be regulated by the amount of opening given to the draught-plates, and depends on the time at which steam is required to start the engines.

If steam be required for an emergency all the fires would be lighted simultaneously and spread earlier than described, but rapid raising of steam in water-tank boilers is to be deprecated, except in cases of absolute necessity.

When steam shows in the boilers. Boiler room procedure.—Soon after steam pressure begins to show on the pressure gauges, the safety valves should be lifted from their seats for a short period, and this should be repeated when the steam pressure is near its maximum. Each water-gauge cock on boilers and separators should be worked and test cocks tried, to see they are clear, and the water gauges tested frequently whilst the pressure is rising. The pressure gauges should be watched to see that each shows practically the same pressure, which should be the case if all the main stop-valves and the pressure gauge cocks are open and the gauges in good order.

The openings allowed for the main and auxiliary stop-valves depend on the amount of steam required and on experience, but they are sometimes opened fully, if there is no tendency in the boilers to prime. Frequently also, in the case of long stokeholds, it is found beneficial to open those nearer the engines less than those more distant, so as to equalise the supply of steam from each boiler, and to enable this to be properly effected the initial opening of the valves should not be great.

In the engine room.—The regulating valves should be closed and the manœuvring valves regulated so that the cylinders may be warmed up gradually. The main and auxiliary circulating pumps should be started as soon as possible, to prevent the condensers becoming heated from the drainage and exhaust steam ; also the auxiliary air-pump, to keep both the auxiliary and main condensers free from condensed water. This latter duty is in some cases performed by some other engine.

As soon as the pressure is sufficient the drain-tank engine should be started, and the direction cocks on the steam traps of the steam and exhaust pipes should be set to allow the drainage to pass through the traps. Special care should be taken with the drainage of the main and auxiliary steam and exhaust pipes, and the separators, where so fitted, should also be kept well drained. Accumulated water in pipes is a common cause of accident. It may break down the engine by entering the cylinders, or, by being set in motion by the steam, cause fracture of a valve box or pipe, should its motion be suddenly arrested or changed. This water hammering action must be carefully guarded against.

The main and auxiliary feed-pumps should be tested by pumping from the feed-tanks, and the latter also from the reserve fresh-water tanks, and delivering into the boilers. They should be again tested against the full steam pressure before the main engines are reported ready.

Any other necessary engines in the stokehold should be worked for trial, and it may be necessary to keep the stokehold fans slowly revolving for ventilation, but they should not, except in cases of necessity, be used for rapidly urging the fires and quickly raising steam.

Warming the engines.—The cylinders should be warmed as

follows :—(*a*) by use of the steam jackets where so fitted ; (*b*) by allowing the links to pass frequently from full gear ahead to full gear astern, at the same time permitting a very small amount of steam to pass through the manœuvring valves, and thus through the cylinders to the condenser ; (*c*) by occasionally opening the auxiliary starting valves. The cylinder and slide casing drains should be used to keep the engines clear of water, but unnecessary waste of steam should be avoided.

As regards (*a*), the jacket steam and collector drain valves should be regulated to keep the proper pressure in the jackets, whilst at the same time insuring their efficient drainage ; e.g. the valves should be so set that the collector is kept about one-third full of water by the gauge glass. (*b*) This is easily done in the case in which an 'all-round' starting gear and engine is fitted, as the starting engine can be set slowly rotating continuously in the same direction, care being taken that the quantity of steam admitted at any time by the manœuvring or auxiliary starting valves is not sufficient to move the engines. If the engine be fitted with independent linking up gear on the various cylinders the gear should be set in the full cut-off positions. (*c*) When the starting valves are fitted to admit steam to the receiver pipes they should be kept slightly open. When fitted direct to the cylinders, their direction will require reversal to top and bottom of cylinder alternately.

The electric-light machinery should be started on the circuits in the various machinery spaces as soon as there is sufficient steam. The glands on the stern tubes should be slackened to permit of a slight leakage through them, the fire and bilge engines being used on the bilges as necessary, and the crank-pit save-all pump started if separate.

The main water-service valves should be opened, and just before starting, water should be allowed to circulate through the backs of the ahead crosshead guides.

The telegraphs and voice pipes should be tried as to working and correctness, and the steam connections to the siren and whistle should be opened, the pipes drained, and the whistle and siren tried and left with their steam connections open. Funnel guys should now be adjusted.

As soon as there is sufficient steam pressure the steering engine should be put in gear. Having first ascertained that the locking gear is out and the rudder otherwise free, it should be first worked at the engine itself by putting the rudder to both extreme positions, leaving it at the middle position. The controlling gear for the deck steering position should then be connected, and the engine run hard over each way from the bridge. Both rudder and steering wheel should be placed in the amidship position before connecting up.

The engineer in charge, having satisfied himself that the above particulars have been attended to, and that steam is raised to about the required pressure, with the fires properly burnt through, the correct water level in the boilers, and the feeding arrangements satisfactory, and also that the cylinders are thoroughly warmed and drained, should, about ten minutes before the main engines are required, see that all worsteds and other main engine lubricating arrangements are set in working position, and obtain permission from the deck to try the main engines, to insure that they are under proper control, both in the ahead and astern directions.

Starting and stopping.—Although from deck considerations it is often of importance to move the engines as little as possible before unmooring, it is nevertheless most desirable that the engines should make at least one complete revolution in each direction under steam before they are reported ready for getting under way, and, if there are no special reasons to the contrary, they should be allowed to make a few complete revolutions in each direction in order to ascertain that they are under control and can be readily handled before weighing anchor or slipping moorings. This trial should not be sufficient to produce any way on the ship.

Having received permission and seen that everyone is clear of the engines, drain the main cylinders and slide-casings and the cylinders of the starting engine, and work this engine for putting the links into full gear ahead. Open the manœuvring valve, but not too wide, when, provided the high-pressure crank is not on the dead centre, if the high-pressure slide-valve is in such a position as to admit steam to that cylinder, and the cylinders are properly warmed and drained, the engines should start. If the high-pressure slide-valve is closed, or practically so, the auxiliary starting valves must be used, when no difficulty should be experienced in starting. The manœuvring valve should now be closed, the links be put into the full astern position, the manœuvring valve opened as before, and the engines allowed to revolve in that direction for a few revolutions, when the manœuvring valve should be closed and the links centred, so as to stop the engines.

After stopping it should be noted to what degree the main condenser retains the vacuum shown on the gauge, which will give an indication of its freedom or otherwise from air leaks. The revolution tell-tale should now be in gear. The engines should now be reported ready for getting under way, and the cylinders and slide-casings then kept drained as necessary, the proper pressures being maintained in the cylinder jackets and their drains suitably adjusted. The engines will then be in readiness to be started immediately in response to orders received by the engine-room telegraphs.

Precautions : **(1) opening the manœuvring valve.**—This should not be opened sufficiently wide to start the engines rapidly, as this might cause damage to the cylinders and pistons if the former should happen to be not properly drained, or cause sudden reduction of the pressure in the boilers, and possibly sudden ebullition and consequent passage of water directly from the boilers to the cylinders. The amount of opening required should, however, be quickly given. If the main regulating valve be used for starting, a very small amount of lift will be sufficient, and additional care is necessary to prevent too rapid starting.

(2) Shutting the steam supply-valve whilst reversing the links.—With flat slide-valves, and especially if the engine is at rest, this should always be done, as the initial friction of such slide-valves is considerable, and even if the starting gear is strong and sufficiently powerful it relieves it of considerable stress. With many of the older starting gears, and with unlubricated flat slide-valves there is sometimes risk of straining the gear. If the engine is moving, the stress on the gear is much less. Independently of this, however, most engines have a certain position from where they start less readily than from others, and if steam is on and the starting gear be slow in action, the gradual admission of steam after the links pass the central position often causes the engines to move into this unfavourable position, while if the steam is not admitted till the links are in full gear it permits of more direct control over the movements of the engine, as a greater volume of steam is admitted to the cylinder through the slide-valve.

This applies especially to the older compound engines, with flat high-pressure slide-valves, and with little margin of power in the reversing engines. With modern triple-expansion engines, after once under way, and when time of reversal becomes a consideration, this practice is not an absolute necessity, as the starting engines and reversing gear are sufficiently powerful to move the link gear over quickly enough without closing the steam supply valve. When cylindrical slide-valves are fitted, little additional work is brought on the starting engine and the closing of the steam supply valve is unnecessary.

(3) **Use of the auxiliary starting or pass-valves.**—These valves should be worked with judgment, or possibly their use may defeat the object in view, and prevent the engine from starting.

(*a*) With pass-valves. In triple-expansion engines with valves fitted so as to admit steam to the intermediate and low-pressure *receivers*, care must be taken in the slide-valve setting of the engines that the whole of the main slide-valves cannot be closed to the admission of steam at any position of the cranks. In handling the engines by means of these pass-valves, only that valve should be used which will be effective in producing a turning moment in the required direction of the shaft. For example, suppose that when the high- and low-pressure slide-valves are closed to steam, but the intermediate slide-valve is open, that the pass-valves leading to both receivers are opened. The effect will be to put steam on the proper side of the intermediate piston from the intermediate receiver, whilst owing to steam having been admitted to the low-pressure receiver, it finds its way through the intermediate exhaust to the other side of the intermediate piston, thus tending to neutralise the effect of the other pass-valve, at the same time the other two cylinders are of no use for starting purposes, the result being that the engine may not start. If steam is admitted only to the low-pressure receiver, besides producing no effect in starting, it is also objectionable for the reason that the exhaust pressure tends to force a flat intermediate slide-valve off its face.

The correct auxiliary valve to open in the above case is obviously that to the intermediate receiver only, when the turning force available for moving the engine is due to the pressure on the intermediate piston less any adverse force due to the same pressure acting through the exhaust on the high-pressure piston. With the above fittings the turning force available can generally only be due to the receiver pressure acting on the difference of areas of two adjacent cylinders, and as the steam has also to fill the whole of the receiver, and generally portions of two cylinders—viz. the steam side of one and the exhaust part of the preceding—they are sometimes slow in their action. For this reason starting valves are by some preferred to be fitted to supply steam directly and independently to each end of each of the intermediate and low-pressure cylinders.

(*b*) When such starting valves are fitted, the force available will be due to the starting pressure acting at least on the area of one of these cylinders, and frequently may be due to that pressure acting on the sum of the areas of the low and intermediate-pressure cylinders. Owing to the smaller space to be filled with steam, their action is, when correctly used, more rapid than the preceding variety. With these fittings, however, more care is required to admit the steam to those ends of the cylinders which will cause the motion of the pistons to rotate the cranks in the direction corresponding to the position of the links, or similar complications to those previously described will occur, besides which, in the case of flat slide-valves, there is a liability to force these valves off their faces; more consideration as to the side of the piston to which it is necessary to admit steam is required than with pass-valves, so that the latter are the more simple in use.

The auxiliary starting valves should therefore be used as little as possible, and then with care as to direction. When an engine becomes locked by the injudicious use of the starting valves, the cylinders should be freed from the steam as quickly as possible, and this is most readily accomplished by closing the starting valves and main regulating or manœuvring valves, and putting the links into full gear in the opposite direction, at the same time opening the cylinder and slide-casing drains, thus permitting the steam in the engines to pass through the exhaust passages to the condenser and to the bilge as necessary. The engine should then be moved in this direction, after which the link-gear should be quickly reversed, when, if mistakes are not repeated, the engines will readily start.

Most of the earlier compound engines were fitted with flat slide-valves on the high-pressure cylinder, and these are with inexperienced operators very liable to be forced from their faces when starting the engines by starting valves. This defect is shown by a sudden rise of pressure in the low-pressure receiver, which generally causes the relief valve to lift and steam to escape to the engine room.

Should this happen the regulating or manœuvring valve and starting valves should be closed, the link-gear be worked to and from its mid position in both directions, in order to relieve the low-pressure receiver from pressure, and the cylinder and receiver drains be opened to relieve the pressure in the cylinders, after which the link-gear should be middled and the regulating valve be suddenly opened, and the reversing engine worked so as to move the link-gear a short distance to and from the mid positions in both directions, when the slide-valve will usually assume its normal position.

(4) **Warming cylinders.**—If this is not attended to, difficulty will be experienced in starting owing to the considerable condensation of the entering steam, and the consequent accumulation of water will be conducive to damage to the cylinders and pistons, unless great attention be paid to the drainage arrangements. Abnormal stresses are also brought on the cylinder casings by expansion through the sudden admission of steam to comparatively cold surfaces.

(5) **Draining cylinders.**—Previously to trying the main engines, the cylinders and slide casings should be blown through by the use of

the starting valves, &c. This permits any excess of oil present to pass direct to the bilge. When under way these directing cocks should be turned to discharge to the condensers.

In vessels fitted with horizontal engines in which the main condenser is higher than the lowest part of the low-pressure cylinders, difficulty has frequently been experienced in preventing accumulation of water in the low-pressure cylinders, especially when the vessel is under way, as the difference of vacuum in the condenser and low-pressure cylinders is not sufficient to overcome the resistance of the drain pipes and to lift the water from the cylinder to the condenser. To meet this difficulty small evaporators have been fitted below the lowest parts of the cylinder, and the cylinder drain pipes led to them, a live steam coil being used to evaporate the drain water. The usual drainage arrangements to bilge are also provided.

(6) **Accumulation of fresh water in condensers before starting.**— It is of importance to prevent this accumulation, especially when the main air-pumps are of long stroke and consequently have a large bucket velocity. This is now usually effected by a suction from either the auxiliary air- or hot-well pump, which pump must be kept working. If this be not attended to, the main air-pump may become glutted with water on starting, and great stresses be suddenly brought on all parts of the air-pump. It also usually entails a loss of fresh water through the air-pump relief arrangements. The water accumulates from steam and water passing through the engines during the warming process, and from the use of the silent blow-off. Accumulation may also be due to leaky condenser tubes or joints of tube plates, and this should always be ascertained whilst the engines are being prepared for starting by drawing off some and testing it. If leaking to any extent, it is advisable, if time be available, in order to prevent the access of salt water to the boilers, that the defect be made good before getting under way ; if not, the first opportunity should be taken to effect the repair.

(7) **Condenser pumps.**—The main circulating pumps should be kept running sufficiently fast to insure the condensers being cool, and any drain cocks or other fittings which may admit air to the main condensers should be adjusted to prevent this. The auxiliary circulating pump and air-pump should also receive attention, so that the auxiliary condenser remains cool and free from water, which insures efficient drainage from those cylinders and slide casings led to the auxiliary exhaust pipe and from the cylinder jackets. It also relieves back-pressure from the auxiliary engines generally.

(8) **Safety valves blowing off or steam pressure rising too high.**— This should be prevented to avoid the loss of fresh water, and inconvenience from noise and water on deck. If the steam pressure tends to rise faster than required, the fires should be checked as follows. The stokehold fans should be run at a speed only sufficient for ventilating purposes, while the draught plates on the boilers should be closed, and the fires should not be disturbed more than actually necessary. If the pressure still continue to rise beyond that required, the silent blow-off valve should be slightly opened so as to pass the steam direct to the main condenser. This should always be done with caution, and care taken that (a) the valve is opened gradually, so as not to shake the condenser tubes more than necessary, otherwise leaky tubes may result,

(*b*) the pump for emptying the condenser of fresh water is at work, (*c*) the silent blow-off is shut before the main engines are started. The steam pressure should be checked in this manner when easing or stopping the engines.

Starting of engines deferred.—In cases where some considerable time elapses between the first trying of the engines and the order to start being received on the engine-room telegraph, in addition to the preceding, the starting engine should be worked occasionally from full gear ahead to full gear astern, so as to prevent accumulation of pressure in the receivers and keep the working parts free.

Procedure when main engines are under way.—When the engines are under way the suction from the auxiliary air-pump or hot-well pump to the main condenser should be shut, and the speed of the main circulating pumps be regulated to the requirement of the main condenser. The engine-room tell-tales should be taken out of gear, except in the case of warships steaming with a fleet, in which case they may still be required. Special attention should be paid to the bearings and all working rods to see that they are keeping cool, also to the engine-room gauges, to see that the vacuum is maintained in the condensers and that the jacket and receiver pressures are correct. The engines should be worked slowly for a time, and then the regulating valve slowly opened, so that the speed is gradually increased and no sudden demands are made on the boilers, which would result in a lowering of steam pressure and possibly passage of water with the steam into the cylinders. This also allows the fires to gradually burn through and attain a sufficient incandescent body for maintaining the required speed without undue forcing, and brings the maximum stresses uniformly and gradually on the various parts of the engines and boilers. Especial attention should be paid to the lubrication of the thrust-block at this period, as during the process of starting and till the ship is fairly under way the thrust on it is in excess of the normal amount.

Adjustment of link gear.—When fairly under way the link motions should be adjusted to the cut-off which will give the required number of revolutions of the engines, with the regulating valve practically wide open, to obtain in the high-pressure slide-chest a high steam pressure, in order to promote economy of fuel, unless the cut-off required would be too early for smooth and regular working, in which case the link motion should be set for the earliest practical cut-off and the steam pressure adjusted accordingly. This point occurs generally at or before 2-10 stroke, or at such rate as develops either (*a*) an excessive compression loop at the top corner of the indicator diagram, (*b*) too considerable a falling away of the high-pressure admission pressure due to wire-drawing, or (*c*) a jerky motion of the valve gear. The nature of the limit will depend on the design of the valve gear, and especially the amount of compression in the high-pressure cylinder at full power. With many valve gears, however, the jerky motion referred to, imposes the limit of efficient working. When this point is reached there is no alternative except to obtain further reductions of power by lowering the initial steam pressure.

Independent linking-up gear.—This should now be adjusted, depending on the speed required, so as to regulate the proportion of power developed in the several cylinders. Experiments should be made, as far as possible, when making passages, with the view of determining the best distribution from the point of view of economy, the cut-off in the high-pressure cylinder being always as early as practicable. The best distribution for various rates having been thus determined, the engines can, when fairly under way, be at once properly set, if continuous working at that speed is expected.

Jacket pressures. Scrooping or grunting.—The cylinder jacket pressures should be regulated, and it should be borne in mind that the higher the pressures in the jackets the less will be the loss from 'exhaust waste' due to liquefaction and the consequent wasteful transfer of heat direct to the exhaust. The most efficient plan, considering only the action of steam, would be to carry steam of the full boiler pressure in each of the cylinder jackets, including the low-pressure, but even if this were done it would be insufficient to entirely prevent loss from this cause. Owing, however, to mechanical considerations connected with the wear of the internal parts, as the amount of internal lubrication in high-pressure marine engines is always reduced to a minimum, it is not possible to carry out the principle to this extent, especially in the low-pressure cylinder. The jacket pressures should generally not fall below the initial pressure in the cylinder—i.e. the preceding receiver or steam-pipe pressure—in which case the amount of moisture present in the cylinders will be considerable. In some cases where wear is feared the high-pressure steam jacket supply is taken from the high-pressure slide casing. The pressure which can be safely carried can only be determined by experience, and this will vary with the amount of lubrication entering the cylinder through the piston- and slide-rods, the material of the rubbing surfaces, and their adjustment.

If any 'scrooping' occurs, which can be made to disappear by lowering the jacket pressure, the limit will have been reached, but it should not be too hastily assumed that noises of this kind are caused by the jackets. Scrooping often occurs when the speed of the engines is reduced by throttling the steam, which wire-draws and dries it. The boiler pressure should therefore be adjusted to the requirements of the engines, provided it is not reduced below that required for readily starting from any position.

Feed-water temperature.—Where the circulating pumps are fitted in duplicate, as usual in the Navy, only one should be worked, and the speed of this should be reduced until the temperature of the feed-water is as desired. With feed-water heaters there is no limit to the lowness of this temperature except that of efficiency. Without them the effect on the boiler has to be considered, and under these circumstances it is not advisable to reduce this temperature below 100° F., so as not to unduly magnify the racking strains on the boiler due to differences of temperature. With feed-water heaters the temperature may be rather lower with advantage. When working at low power it will often be found that it is impossible to run the circulating pump so slowly as would be required from these considerations without risk of its stopping altogether. If this be so, in order to avoid this danger, and at the same time where feed-water heaters are not fitted, to prevent the feed-water being too cold, the circulating water valve should be gradually closed until the feed-water is of the correct temperature, with the pump running at a speed which will avoid danger of stopping.

Supply of feed-water.—The water level in the feed-tanks should be constantly observed. If automatic float gear is not fitted, the speed of the feed-pumps should be regulated so that the suction is always covered with water to avoid air entering the pumps and the boilers. If additional feed-water is required beyond that which the evaporators are producing, it should be obtained from the reserve fresh-water tanks by opening the suction from this part to the main condenser or air-pump.

If when the engines are working steadily any considerable discharge takes place from the overflow-pipe on the feed-tank, the engine-room watchkeeper should at once warn the stokehold staff, and ascertain the cause, which may be due to the feed-pumps stopping or failing to deliver sufficient water to the boilers, or to the boiler feed-valves not being sufficiently open. Prompt action under these circumstances has prevented many accidents.

CHAPTER XXX.

MANAGEMENT OF ENGINES UNDER WAY—ENGINE AND BOILER DEFECTS.

IN this chapter, and the succeeding, particulars are given relative to the care and management of the machinery and boilers, which are to some extent based upon the instructions contained in the ' Steam Manual ' now in use in the Royal Navy. A few of the most usual defects in engines and boilers are also dealt with, and suggestions given as to their suitable treatment.

Before taking charge of a watch the engineer should satisfy himself by personal inspection that all bearings are working well and are in a proper state of lubrication, that the water in the boilers is at the proper working height, that the water in the bilge is not excessive, and that as far as can be seen there are no recent defects of importance in machinery or boilers. He should read the recent entries in the engine-room register, and make himself acquainted with any special orders. Pending these inspections the engineer about to be relieved remains in charge. He should also receive information from the off-going engineer, showing that no increase of density in the boilers has taken place, or, if the water has become salt, that it does not exceed the density allowed, and also as to what special cocks and valves are open in the department. The information as to these points should be verified by the oncoming engineer as soon as possible after taking charge.

When in charge of the watch he should leave the engine-room platform as little as possible, so as to execute expeditiously any order received from the deck or stop the engines in case of accident. As his duties require his occasional absence from the engine-room platform, he should instruct one of the subordinate watchkeepers in the manipulation of the engines, and this watchkeeper should be always on the starting platform during his occasional absence.

In addition to any special orders received, the watch has to carry out the usual routine orders, and note their execution in the engine-room register. The principal are—

Hourly.—Quantity of coal used ; steam pressure in the boilers and at engines ; vacuum in main condensers ; air pressure in stokeholds, if any ; total number of revolutions ; depth of water in the bilges.

At least each watch.—Density of the feed-water and of the water in each of the boilers in use ; temperatures of feed-water, engine and boiler rooms, coal-bunkers, on deck, and sea-water ; quantity of fresh water made for drinking purposes and used for make-up feed (measured if possible, otherwise estimated); amount of ashes produced; and description of any work done in the department.

Other notations in register.—The other necessary notations of work done to be entered in the register beyond that occurring each watch are as follows :—

Daily.—The alkalinity of the boilers in use; temperature of bunkers when fires are not alight. Take indicator diagrams and insert horse-power, &c., which should be done more frequently should any material variation occur in the working condition of the engines. Moving of any auxiliary engines not in use; working the siren and whistle; examination of controlling shafting of the steering engine, and statement of condition.

Four times per week.—Removing bunker lids for ventilation purposes where bunkers are not automatically ventilated, and replacing them after three hours. Even where automatic ventilation is fitted it is desirable as a precautionary measure to frequently remove the lids.

Weekly.—Lifting safety valves of, and testing density and alkalinity of water, in boilers not in use; working the various cocks and valves, especially those of sea connections; condition of all telegraph gear; working all watertight doors, sluice, drain, and ventilating valves.

Use of oil.—Each watch is allowed certain fixed quantities of the various oils, which have been ascertained by experience to be sufficient for the good working of the machinery. Every endeavour should be made to keep within the quantities allowed. The principal used are olive oil, for external bearings; or, in cases *where the load is not heavy*, a mixture of olive and mineral oils is used for this purpose. Mineral oil is used for internal lubrication and for piston, slide, or freshwater pump-rods, and on any other fittings where it can get mixed with the feed-water. Colza or rapeseed oil is used for lamps.

Cleanliness.—This is essential for health and the efficiency of the machinery department. In a well-ordered engine room, each watch, in addition to the general duties, is responsible for a definite portion of the cleaning work. During long steaming periods, especially in tropical climates, the bilges require constant attention; and those parts which are not easily accessible under way should, whenever practicable, be frequently washed through, and be freely supplied with disinfectants.

Density of water in the boilers.—It is the usual practice, when under steam, to test the water in the boilers by the hydrometer every watch; and when not under steam, once each week. As a rule, if sea-water necessarily has access to the boilers, no brining or emptying is necessary until the density reaches 25 degrees, or $2\frac{1}{2}$ times the density of sea-water, but it should not be allowed to exceed 40 degrees. The selection of the most suitable density in any particular case must depend on the experience gained principally as to the condition of the boilers on the examinations after steaming. With surface condensation, if only salt-water make-up feed is available, the rise of density should not exceed one degree daily, a daily increase of two degrees being considered excessive.

In the more recent vessels, in which fresh water, either from the reserve tanks or from the evaporators, should always be available to make up losses, practically no rise of density should take place, and a rise of two degrees in three days is considered excessive. When an excessive rise of density does occur, steps should be taken to ascertain the cause and to remedy the defect. It is now very rarely that the density in such vessels rises to the above given limits, and it is generally only necessary under way to get rid of the grease or other impurities from the surface by opening the brine cocks occasionally. The deposition of scale in the boiler does not depend so much on the density at which the water is kept as on the quantity of sea-water that enters. The higher density has, in the case of boilers fed from surface condensers with salt-water make-up, been found beneficial as regards cleanliness as well as economy.

Change of water.—On service, in order to exclude air, in the absence of which oxidation is small, it is desirable to keep the water in the boilers without change as long as practicable, whether the fires are alight or not, the boilers being only emptied when necessary for examination, cleaning, or repair. This will require to be done much oftener with boilers fed with sea-water than with those fed from surface condensers, as in the former case scale is continually being deposited on the heating surfaces while the boilers are at work. Experience as to the condition of the boilers on the examinations can be the only guide as to the greatest amount of steaming to which it is safe to expose them without cleaning. This depends principally on the amounts of solid and greasy matter admitted with the feed-water.

When filled with fresh water, with the condenser tubes tight, and sea-water make-up, it has been found that on an average, boilers should be cleaned after twenty-five days' continuous steaming at moderate speeds. Intermittent steaming under the above circumstances tends to cause the scale to accumulate on the furnace crowns, in which case cleaning has been found necessary after fires have been alight sixteen days. The higher the density at which they are worked, the longer they can be kept going without cleaning.

When distilled water is used for make-up feed, and a moderate amount of oil is used for internal lubrication, no difficulty is found in steaming for thirty days continuously at moderate speeds without removing the greasy deposits from the boilers, but it depends entirely on the amount of oil used. In many cases, using little oil and with efficient grease filters, much longer periods than this can be run without opening up.

Chemical tests.—It is necessary that the water in the boiler should be prevented from becoming acid by decomposition of lubricants or other causes. If it be kept in a neutral or alkaline state it will possess little corrosive properties. In order to ascertain the chemical condition of the water, a small quantity should be drawn off every day when the boilers are at work, and once a week when not at work, and tested with litmus paper. If the water is acid, it may be neutralised by putting a little soda in the condenser or hot-well, from whence it will be pumped into the boilers with the feed-water. The use of lime also has the effect of keeping the water in the boilers alkaline, and lime dissolved in a special tank and then admitted to the feed-water is used in preference to other such substances with Belleville boilers.

Uniformity of temperature and pressure.—Sudden changes of temperature and pressure during the working of the boilers should be prevented ; the smoke-box doors should only be opened when absolutely necessary, as in tank boilers the cold air affects the tube ends, which, being thinner than the tube plates, are liable to shrink and leak; but this is of little importance with water-tube boilers.

The boilers should not be emptied by blowing out except in cases of urgency, as this produces strains, and consequently leaks, especially in tank boilers. When steam is no longer required, the boilers should be closed up, the fires allowed to burn out, and the water cool gradually, so that the boilers may contract uniformly, and prevent undue strains on any part. When all is cool, the ashes and clinkers, &c., may be drawn out of the furnaces, and any fuel not entirely consumed should be saved. The water is, when cool, run out from the boilers —if necessary for examination, cleaning, or repair—into the reserve fresh-water tanks if it be clean and fresh, or if otherwise to the bilge. With tank boilers, the practice of drawing fires shortly after the engines are stopped is objectionable, as the cold air entering the furnaces is liable to cause leakage at the fire-box ends of the tubes, and in the joints of the combustion chambers and backs of the furnaces.

Stoking and economy of fuel.— Care is required in the working of boilers to promote economy of coal. The fires should be stoked carefully and regularly, the steam pressure and water level kept constant, and no waste allowed by steam blowing off from the safety valves, which should always be kept tight to prevent leakage. The cinders and small coal that fall into the ashpits should be reburnt, and the fires not unnecessarily forced or disturbed. The wing firebars should be placed close to the sides of the furnaces, to prevent the fire being too fierce close to the plates. If there are stay-nuts or other projections in the line of fire-bars, the wing-bars should be cast with recesses to fit over them, so that they may be quite close to the plates. In corrugated furnaces the wing-bars should be cast to fit the corrugations.

To diminish the quantity of cold air admitted at one time, also to reduce the bad effects of this air striking the tube plates, no two furnace doors of the same boiler should be open at the same time, and the firing should be done quickly, the furnace doors only being kept open a short time. When using Welsh coal in ordinary tank boilers under natural draught, five to six inches is a good thickness of fire, which should be increased when working under forced draught. With Belleville boilers a rather thinner fire than this gives the best results. The fires in all boilers should be maintained in the same condition to equalise steam production, and kept as free from clinker and slag as possible to insure access of air through the bars.

The amount of clinker can be judged by the brightness or otherwise of the bars when viewed from below. In addition to the partial removal of clinker during every watch, each fire is consecutively thoroughly cleaned ; for which purpose it is burned low, and all clinker and slag, with most of the fire, is removed from the furnace bars. During the cleaning the uptake damper of this furnace, if fitted, should be closed, and fan draught reduced to prevent much access of cold air. To reduce fluctuation of steam pressure only one fire is cleaned at the same time, and only one fire in the same boiler during the same watch, if practicable. When working under natural draught with When coal, it is generally arranged that each furnace is cleaned once during each twenty-four hours, or oftener with higher rates of combustion or with inferior coal.

It is important to keep the tubes and smoke-boxes free from soot and ashes. Soot doors are now generally fitted, so that this can be done as regards the smoke-boxes without opening the smoke-box doors. For the tubes, brushes are supplied for use when steam is not raised ; but under way the cleaning is done by means of the steam-jet. Under natural draught this is usually carried out on each boiler once in forty-eight hours, and, owing to the discharge of small ashes, &c., on deck, is done at night during the first and middle watches. During the operations of cleaning fires or tubes, the tendency of the steam pressure is to fall, and despatch is therefore essential.

Losses of feed-water.—All losses should be reduced to a minimum, and a supply of fresh water to make up the losses should be provided. Losses occur through leakages from boilers, engine glands, and drains of various kinds, air-pump and other fresh-water pump-rods, defective pipe joints, lifting of safety and relief valves of boilers and engines, air-pump relief when engines are suddenly started, feed-tanks over-flowing to bilge, using the siren and whistle, sweeping tubes by steam, scumming boilers, leaky cocks and valves, &c.

The above losses amount on an average to from $\frac{1}{4}$ ton of water for each ton of coal burnt when steaming at high powers, to $\frac{1}{2}$ ton of water per ton of coal at low powers, the increase being due to the losses by auxiliary machinery being comparatively large and practically constant at all powers. Losses of feed-water are replenished either from fresh water carried in the reserve tanks, or by using the evaporators in connection with one of the engine condensers.

Use of oil for internal lubrication.— In modern high-pressure marine boilers the principal danger to be guarded against is the mineral oil deposit on the furnaces and combustion chambers. The oil used for the lubrication of the cylinders and slide-valves is carried over into the boilers, and sometimes forms a black carbonaceous scale, which is an almost perfect non-conductor of heat, even when not more than $\frac{1}{16}$-inch thick. In order to prevent as far as practicable access of oil, all internal lubrication of the main and auxiliary machinery should be reduced to a minimum, and oil on piston-, slide-, air-, and feed-pump rods should not exceed that necessary for good working. It is generally found unnecessary to admit lubricant directly to the internal parts of the engines, as that which enters the cylinders by means of the piston- and slide-rods is found to give sufficient lubrication for the internal parts. All grease extractors and filters should be kept in working order, and frequently cleaned.

Feed-water increasing in quantity.—If without the use of the evaporators for make-up or of additional feed, the water in the boilers shows little or no loss, or should be gaining instead of losing, the reason should be ascertained. Test the feed-water, and if there are no indica-tions of salt, the gained water is fresh, so that the *make-up* feed-valves on the suction to reserve fresh-water tanks should be examined to see that they are not open or leaking, or that the auxiliary feed-pump suction to the reserve fresh-water tanks is properly closed.

Should the feed-water be salt to any degree, ascertain the cause, and remedy it at the first opportunity. Saltness is occasioned principally by defective condenser tubes or tube glands, stay-nuts, tube-plate joints, &c., leakage through the sea connections of the auxiliary feed-pumps, or priming of the evaporator, and there are other minor causes.

Fan engine stopping.—Should this occur when under air pressure, the damper in the fan trunk should be closed to prevent loss of air pressure and the speed of the remaining fans correspondingly increased. The cause, which is generally defective lubrication, should be remedied and the fan re-started as soon as possible.

Flaming at the funnel.—If this occur see that the cowls on deck are trimmed to the wind and the fans are running sufficiently fast ; the fires should be levelled and reduced in thickness, and where the furnace doors are so arranged, as much air as practicable should be admitted over the top of the fire. It is generally due to unconsumed gas—i.e. carbonic oxide—bursting into flame on meeting the oxygen of the air at the top of the funnel. Reducing the thickness of the fire admits more oxygen for combustion. It may even be necessary, in torpedo operations at night, when the boilers are not being pressed and conceal-ment is desirable, to slightly open the furnace doors to prevent flaming.

Furnace bars melting.—Any such bars should be replaced by re-moving the fire from the part affected, and checking the air supply to that furnace by closing the damper and draught-plates, also easing the fans. The bars are generally slid into their places by means of fire-irons, or by tying the bar to a slice, and dropping it in place. The cause will often be found to be the absence of water from the ash-pans or fires being unduly thick.

Priming.—The passage of water with the steam from the boilers to the engines, technically called *priming*, is most objectionable, and when it is severe, unless proper precautions be taken, may lead to dangerous consequences, such as the cracking of cylinders or covers by the blows due to the thumping of the pistons at each end of its stroke.

Priming arises either from unduly forcing a boiler, more especially if the design be defective, or from bad management.

Points in design affecting priming.—As regards design, this should provide for the proper circulation of water, absence of local ebullition, and the free escape of the steam generated ; otherwise there will be danger of priming when the boiler is being forced. These points are favoured by :—

(*a*) *Ample water spaces* round the sides and backs of the combus-tion chambers and between the tubes. In large boilers, the clear space between the tubes should never be less than one inch, and this might be increased with advantage in a horizontal direction if space and weight are available ; also, the lower rows should be kept well clear of the tops of the furnaces.

(*b*) *Volume of the steam space being sufficiently large.*—If the space allowed provides too small a reserve for steam, fluctuations of pressure are caused, and irregular ebullition, which may cause water to pass over with the steam. The volume per maximum horse-power with cylin-drical boilers should not be less than from ·5 cub. ft. at 60 lbs., to ·2 to ·25 cub. ft. at 155 lbs. pressure, and more should be allowed if possible. The limit to which the volume may be reduced depends on the type of boiler, for in torpedo-boat destroyers this value has been reduced to ·05 and ·06 cub. ft., with pressures varying from 180 lbs. to 200 lbs. per sq. in., without any detrimental effects due to priming, but in these cases the directions of the steam and water currents have been especially provided for.

(c) *Sufficient area of the water surface.*—The larger this area the less is the quantity of steam per unit of surface which passes from it, and consequently the more gradual is the escape of the steam.

(d) *Suitably arranged internal steam pipes.*—These should, where practicable, be arranged so as to collect the steam uniformly from all parts of the boiler, and be placed as far as practicable from the water level. They are often arranged as two complete pipes running the entire length of the boiler, and are provided either with small holes or slots on their upper surfaces. The total area of these orifices should not be less than twice the area of the pipe leading from the boiler.

Bad management as causing priming—

(a) *Starting the engine or increasing speed too suddenly.*—This is a most injudicious practice, as it rapidly lessens the pressure of the steam in the boiler, and consequently the corresponding temperature. The temperature of the water will therefore be in excess, and violent ebullition and possibly priming follows.

(b) *Too much water in the boiler.*—This produces small steam space and water surface, with their consequent bad effects.

(c) *Uneven firing*, or uneven forcing of different boilers. Uneven firing causes different rates of combustion with various furnaces, interfering with the normal circulation and producing irregular local ebullition. Boilers nearest the engines, or having a freer supply of air to the furnaces, frequently do more work than others in a set, unless the supply from them is regulated, which is usually done by partially closing the stop-valves from those boilers.

(d) *Impurities in the water*, such as the presence of too much soda, from not having sufficiently washed out the boilers after having used soda for cleaning them, or from the use of soda in cleaning the condenser tubes, causes priming. In many types of boilers it is certain to result in priming, even at moderate speeds. Boilers of the locomotive type are especially sensitive to this action, certain qualities of fresh water from the shore even setting up a strong tendency to frothing and priming. Mud or excess oil will also cause priming. They do this in various ways, sometimes presenting a resistance at the water level to the passage of the steam generated, causing local, intermittent, and violent actions.

To stop priming.—If it be general in all boilers, reduce the speed of the engines and decrease the rate of combustion by easing the fans or shipping the draught plates, care being taken to keep sufficient water in the boilers, the auxiliary feed system being used if necessary.

If only one or two boilers in a set are priming, the cause will be local and be generally due to improper management. In this case the stop-valves on these boilers should be partially closed and the rate of combustion checked. If due to management, either (a), (b), or (c), as soon as the water is quiescent and at its working level, the stop-valve should be gradually opened and the boilers gradually worked up to the required power.

If all the boilers prime, due to (d) impurities in the water, the practice of allowing the feed-tanks to overflow to the bilge, and using clean fresh water from the reserve feed-tanks and distilling plant till the water in the boilers is mostly renewed, together with the use of the surface blow-off to remove impurities, is beneficial. Formerly, when sea-water was generally used, the same result was obtained by keeping the surface blow-out open and using sufficient salt-water feed. If the cause is the presence of soda, the only cure is to have the boilers emptied and washed out.

If, after all precautions have been taken, and with good working conditions, it is found that on the engine reaching a certain speed the boilers still prime, it may be concluded that they are being forced beyond their immediate capabilities, and the generation of steam will have to be reduced for safe working.

Indications of priming.—1st. By the water in the gauge glasses of the boilers being considerably agitated and not showing a constant level, broken water often passing continuously through the glass. If due to dirt in the boilers, the water in the gauge-glass becomes discoloured.

2nd. The separator, if fitted, gets filled with water, and its drain should be kept open to prevent as much water as possible from passing to the engines. If a separator be not fitted, the drains on the valve-boxes in the line of steam pipe should be kept open for this reason.

3rd. Water comes over into the slide casings and cylinders, and causes a knocking at the ends of the stroke. If the priming become excessive this causes the cylinder relief valves to lift, and may be dangerous if too great to be relieved quickly. The drain cocks on the cylinders and slides should be kept open and the speed of the engines reduced.

4th. Even slight priming causes the speed of the main and other engines to be reduced, which reduces also the speed of the air-pump, while, as the quantity of steam and water passing into the condenser is increased, the vacuum in the condenser becomes reduced, often considerably. As the water carried over with the steam evaporates during exhaust, the back pressure in the cylinder is increased. The air-pumps also may be overcharged and the feed-tanks quickly filled.

Broken gauge-glass.—The cocks on boiler should be immediately shut, and the glass replaced without delay. The new glass should be free from flaws or scratches, with ends ground square or fire-finished, and of the correct length. If too long it would restrict the passage of steam to the glass, if too short the packing may work over the edges of the glass. In the later Admiralty pattern gauges the correct length of the glass is stamped on the framing. Before replacing it the whole of the old packing should be removed, and the screws of the adjusting glands made easily workable.

The packing is then placed on the glass, and while screwing up the bottom gland, the glass should be kept in contact with the metal of the lower cock. Care should be taken not to screw up the upper gland hard before the lower one, as this may lift the glass and perhaps allow the lower packing to choke the orifice. The glands should at first be only screwed up hand-tight, after which the *steam* and *drain* cocks should be opened a small amount to heat the glass gradually, when after a short interval the *water* cock should be gradually opened, and then the drain cock closed, the steam and water cocks being then fully opened gradually, and the glands adjusted as required. These precautions are necessary to prevent fracture of the glass.

The glass should now be tested by closing the steam cock and opening the drain, when water should rush out freely. Next close the water cock and open the steam cock, when steam should freely rush out. Next close the drain and open the water cock, and *note carefully how the water rises in the glass.* It should rise smartly to the water level of the other glass.

Draining water gauges.—When, in the ordinary course, gauge-glasses are blown through or drained, by opening the drain cock, if the water rises slowly, but eventually stops at the same level as in the other glass of the boiler, this will indicate a partial choking of the lower passage. The choking of the upper or steam passage is an occurrence which very seldom happens. It would be indicated, however, by a rapid rise of the water level to a higher position than shown on the other gauge, due to condensation of the vapour in the upper part of the glass when cut off from the boiler.

To endeavour to clear glasses with such indications, blow through the steam and water cocks separately, shutting one before blowing through the other ; but if this be not successful, then the passages will require to be cleared by removing the screwed plug, and passing a small rod through the passages, removing the glass if necessary, steam being lowered in the boiler.

When the water gauges are not fitted directly on the boilers, but either on short stand-pipes or steady pipes, there will be a connecting passage between the upper and lower arms, in addition to that through the water gauge, and this has an important influence when dealing with defects in gauges, which must be carefully borne in mind. Suppose, for example, that the orifice in the stand-pipe leading to the steam space is choked (refer to Fig. 93) ; if, when testing such a gauge, the water cock be shut and the steam cock blown through, water would be blown out, ascending the stand-pipe from the lower orifice, and unless the presence of the stand-pipe is remembered, this might lead to the erroneous conclusion that the passages were clear. Under these circumstances the glass would be practically full of water, so that it would be wrongly concluded that there was too much water in the boiler.

For this reason it is usually insisted that the short stand-pipes fitted in the Navy (see Fig. 93) shall not be less than two inches in the bore, so that there will practically be little or no risk of their choking. With the long stand-pipes fitted in the mercantile marine (Fig. 94), cocks are fitted at each end of the stand-pipe. When these cocks are fitted the orifices of the stand-pipe can also be tested, for by shutting the top one and blowing through the bottom, and *vice-versa,* it can be ascertained if they are both clear. The complete testing of such a gauge-glass and fittings, therefore, involves four distinct operations— viz. the independent testing of top and bottom orifices of the gauge-glass, and the same for those of the stand-pipe.

To ascertain whether a glass is full of water.—When filled with water well above the top cock, the water runs through the glass without a break when using the drain only, and if the water be clean no movement will be seen through the glass, and it is sometimes difficult to tell whether it be full or empty. In this case shut the top and bottom cocks and open the drain, when, if the glass be full, the water will be seen gradually falling in the glass. Next shut the drain and open the bottom cock, keeping the top cock closed, when the water will be seen rising in the glass.

Water out of the gauge-glass.—The action required will depend on the cause and the time since the water was last seen in the gauge-glass; it will require judgment to determine whether it is advisable to put on all the feed available or to draw fires. If the stokehold watch-keeper is reliable, and is sure that the loss was due to an irregularity in feeding, and that the water-level could not possibly be much below the bottom of the glass, also that the feeding arrangements are in good order, then all available feed should be concentrated on that boiler, including the auxiliary feed service, till the water appears in the glass, when the ordinary feed arrangements should be again used.

Although not visible in the glass, further information can be obtained as to the lowness of the water by closing the top cock, when, if the lower orifice in the stand-pipe or boiler is covered with water, it will immediately rise in the glass, owing to condensation of steam in the upper part. This practice should, however, only be resorted to under such circumstances, and will then be some guide to the person dealing with the defect as to the nature of the further steps required, having in view the position of this lower orifice in relation to the highest parts of the heating surfaces.

If, however, the boiler has lost its water through failure of the feed-valves on the boiler, or the feed-pumps to act efficiently, excessive leakage, or excessive priming, the following steps would usually be taken.

(a) The draught plates should be shipped, to prevent as far as possible any leakage passing into the stokehold.

(b) The fires should be drawn, or extinguished by the drenching apparatus, if fitted.

(c) All steam stop-valves on the boiler should be closed.

(d) When the fires are practically out, the safety valves might be slightly lifted to reduce the pressure, if in excess.

(e) If there be leakage into the combustion chamber or furnace, the fans should be kept running to insure the vapour passing to the funnel rather than into the stokehold.

If the feed-pump be working and not increasing the water in the boilers, the water supply arrangements should be examined to see that only the proper valves are open, and that there is water in the tank from which it is drawing. Leaky or split boiler tubes sometimes account for the persistent failure of the feed-pumps to maintain the water level. If the pump is working very rapidly the cause will generally be shortness or absence of the supply of water. To ascertain that the feed-valve on the boiler is working correctly the beat of the valve should be felt at each stroke, and the temperature of the feed-pipe near the boiler ascertained to be practically that of the feed-water.

This valve may not have been working efficiently and have allowed the passage of hot water back to the feed-pump. If jammed open, tapping with a hammer often frees it.

The passage of hot water from the boiler to the feed-pipe will affect the efficient working of the pump, as the delivery valves are seldom quite tight, which causes the pump casings to get hot, and consequently increases the elastic force of the vapour on the suction side of the plunger, and prevents the foot-valves from properly lifting, and decreases, or even entirely stops, the supply to the pump. In this case a bucket of cold water thrown over the pump barrels often causes the pump to start working. If the check-valve cannot be got to work correctly, the pump should be shut off and the auxiliary pump only used for supplying the boiler, and the valves examined and refitted as soon as practicable.

A feed-pump may also become inoperative through (a) the feed-water being too hot, when the action previously described occurs in the pump barrels. Beyond 130° Fahr. they cannot generally be relied on. (b) Accumulation of air in the passages between the suction and delivery valves, for which special outlet valves or cocks should be provided at the highest parts ; or air may be admitted owing to the glands of the pump plungers not being tight enough.

Most accidents and breaks-down of pumps occur during the operation of starting them in a hurry, when they are probably imperfectly drained, &c. ; and, considering the fact that the auxiliary feed-pump, when required at all, is generally wanted quickly, it is a good plan to keep both pumps slowly at work, when in case of any derangement of one the other can be increased in speed at once and without danger of accident.

Condensers.—The ends of the condenser tubes should be kept tight, new packings being fitted as required, to prevent mixture of sea-water with the feed. This is a point of importance, and the feed-water should be tested regularly to ascertain whether or not it is fresh. If the condenser tubes are leaking considerably, care should be taken to prevent water passing to the cylinders when the engines are standing, and the ends of the defective tubes should be repacked on the first convenient opportunity. The tubes should be frequently examined and tested to ascertain if any are perforated, and they should be kept as clean as possible to preserve their efficiency.

Defective vacuum.—The effect of priming in reducing the condenser vacuum has already been referred to. The most usual causes of defective vacuum are as follow :—

1. Insufficient supply of cooling water through the condenser tubes, causing only a partial condensation of the vapour.

This may occur through (a) condenser sea-valves becoming partially closed, or the passages or ends of the tubes becoming choked. In small ships of shallow draught, *weed-traps* are frequently fitted between the inlet valve and the circulating pump, and should be occasionally cleared. Choking of the grating of the inlet valve most frequently occurs with the auxiliary condenser. In later designs arrangements have been fitted for permitting one of the reciprocating pumps to discharge through this orifice with a view of clearing it ; but if not, a diver is sent down. When the ends of the tubes are choked, the obstructions may be removed through the hand-holes on the covers after emptying the condenser.

(b) If the vacuum suddenly diminishes, the circulating pump may have decreased speed or possibly stopped, in which case the cause should be immediately sought and removed. If due to any cause not immediately removable, such as hot bearings or other defect in the mechanism, it will be necessary to stop the circulating engine to cool or adjust it. Meanwhile, the other pump should be started, or the valve connecting the supply from the other engine room should be opened. If this cannot be done rapidly, the main engines must be eased down or stopped.

2. Dirty condenser tubes.—When foul from grease on the steam side or muddy deposits on the water side, their heat-conducting power is considerably reduced. It may sometimes be advisable to clean the tubes by filling the steam side of the condenser with a hot solution of soda, and allowing it to remain for some time, care being taken that as little as possible of the solution is afterwards introduced into the boilers with the feed. In a condenser in which steam passes through the tubes, the grease may be cleaned by means of a hot solution of caustic potash or soda, passed through the tubes by means of a brush with a long wire handle. When the tubes are very dirty—especially in recent practice, where the area of cooling surface is much less than formerly—it may be necessary to remove the tubes from the condenser and thoroughly clean them.

3. Defective action of the air-pump due to (*a*) defective valves. If the pump is a horizontal double-acting one, either the head- or foot-valves defective will reduce the vacuum. In a vertical single-acting pump, as long as the bucket and head-valves or bucket and foot-valves are intact, the pump will work satisfactorily and the vacuum will be practically unimpaired, especially if the bucket and foot-valves are correct ; but should the bucket valves be displaced, the effect in spoiling the vacuum soon becomes apparent, even when the head- and foot-valves are both intact.

Indiarubber valves become defective through contact with mineral oil or hot water, which renders them plastic and causes them to swell, when they may overlap or their working surface become indented into the grating. When this occurs, if they are not too defective, the remedy is to trim the valves, and, if necessary, reverse them. India-rubber valves will last longer if they are occasionally soaked in a solution of soda. Metal valves last much longer than indiarubber, and vessels frequently serve a three years' commission without disturbing or replacing any of the original metallic air-pump valves. When they do become defective, it is through distortion or breakage.

(*b*) Air-pump plunger too tightly packed. This causes the barrel to work warm, and consequently raises the temperature and pressure of the vapour, hence reducing the vacuum. Pending a convenient time for the refitting of the packing, the pump should be worked with as much water as can be afforded, so as to cool the barrel, the extra supply being obtained from the reserve tanks, that not required for the boilers being again returned to the tanks.

(*c*) Leak in the air-pump rod glands. This practically only applies to horizontal air-pumps, for with vertical bucket pumps this gland is not exposed to a vacuum. It is, however, a most effective cause of reduction of vacuum in a horizontal double-acting pump, where the gland is in direct communication with the space between head- and foot-valves.

(*d*) Leaky plunger. This impairs the exhaustion of the pump, and hence a higher pressure in the condenser is required to lift the foot-valves. In a vertical single-acting pump the effect produced is the same as when the bucket valves are slightly deranged.

(*e*) If the pump be badly designed, either as regards size or more generally in regard to excessive clearance volumes at the ends of the stroke, a poor vacuum will result.

4. Air leaks direct into the condenser, which may occur through glands of main piston-rods, and slide-rods, and air-pump rods when worked directly off the piston, not being properly adjusted, and especially the low-pressure cylinder relief valves, drain cocks, or other fittings and joints, being either off their seatings due to dirt, &c., open to the atmosphere, or having slack glands. The expansion joints on receiver and eduction pipes not being properly packed or adjusted are frequent sources of loss of vacuum. One of the various fittings on the condenser itself may be left open or not properly adjusted, especially those out of sight, such as the drain cock on the air-pump suction pipe, and the connection to reserve fresh-water tanks, especially when these are empty. Leaks from glands and drains of any auxiliary engines and pipe connections in communication with the main condenser are common sources of loss of vacuum, especially if the engines are not at work—*e.g.* those from starting engines, feed engines, and additional main circulating pumps, where so fitted.

5. A defective gauge occasionally leads to erroneous conclusions as regards the vacuum. This defect can generally be detected by comparison of the indications of the compound and vacuum gauges on each condenser. The cock on the pipe leading to the gauge will sometimes be partially closed, or the gauge connections to the pipe leaky. A check on the gauges can be obtained from an indicator diagram, and comparing the back pressure line with the vacuum on gauge.

Hot piston-rods.—A rise of temperature in piston- and slide-rods above that of the normal working conditions is generally accompanied by a smell of burning oil ; and if the rod cannot be felt, heating can always be confirmed by syringing a few drops of fresh water on the rod, when, if *hot*, the water will hiss and run off in a spheroidal condition, and, if very hot, oil applied in a similar manner will cause a dense smoke. If not very much above its normal temperature—that is, *a warm rod*—the gland which contains the soft packing should be slackened, and the rod be well supplied with mineral oil and a little fresh water from a syringe, the speed of the engines being reduced slightly if considered necessary. The use of tallow is very effective as far as cooling the rod is concerned, but should not be used, as it gets introduced into the feed-water and thence to the boiler.

When the rod is much heated—that is, *a hot rod*—the gland should be slacked as before, and the load removed from the rod to prevent it bending, for which purpose, and also to give it a greater chance of cooling, the engines should be considerably reduced in speed, or stopped if considered necessary. The rod should first be cooled by oil only, applied with caution. Never put the water service on a *hot* rod, as it is seldom heated uniformly throughout the circumference, and sudden cooling of one part more than the other is liable to cause distortion and bending, more especially with hollow rods. Piston-rods always require especial attention, for, with metallic packing, hot rods may cause a serious breakdown and delay owing to the melting of the soft metals used in the packing, permitting them to run, and often cut the rods. The principal causes of hot piston-rods are as follow :—

1. Glands not properly packed.—Where asbestos or Tuck's packing only is used, care is required to insure that the packing is not ragged, too much worn, or too hard, that the proper size and number of turns are used, that the joints of each turn are broken so as not to be in line, and that the gland is screwed up squarely.

With metallic packing as described in Chapter XIX., if properly fitted, no abnormal stress can be brought on the rod, as the springs are so adjusted that when the box is jointed no more pressure is brought on the rod than practice has proved can be done with immunity from heating. In this case the gland with the soft packing is only of secondary importance, but care should still be taken to see that it is packed squarely.

2. Neck-bush and gland too tight on the rod, causing unnecessary friction.

3. Piston-rod not working centrally in the stuffing-box gland and neck-bush. In vertical engines this may be due to

(a) Wear of the crosshead guide not being properly lined up ;

(b) Gudgeon-pin brasses wearing unequally in a vertical direction, more especially where the top end of the connecting rod has two bearings.

(c) Crank shaft wearing bodily forward due to thrust-block not being properly adjusted.

(d) If cylinders are bolted together, proper allowance may not have been made when adjusting the various bearings to permit of the rod being central when the cylinders are hot.

(e) There is also with horizontal engines the wear of the pistons downward, due to their weight.

4. Insufficient lubrication.—The piston-rods are continuously lubricated by pipes led to holes at the stuffing-box, as shown in Chapter XIX, but they are so important as regards good working of the engine that this should not be entirely depended on, but be assisted with an occasional application of mineral oil from a syringe.

Causes of hot bearings :—

1. Deficient surface. The pressure between the working surfaces thus becomes so great as to prevent a film of the lubricant passing between them.

2. Working surfaces not being in line, causing abnormal local pressures and abrasion.

3. Bad fitting, so that the pressure is not uniformly distributed over the working surfaces.

4. Stopping of lubrication, which is the most usual cause.

5. Presence of gritty substances in the bearings.

6. Lubrication improperly applied. As a general rule the oil should be led to the bearing at a point of low pressure. If led to near the point of greatest pressure suitable oil ways should be cut to allow the oil to enter the bearing.

When feeling a bearing to ascertain its temperature, care should be taken to feel the actual bearing itself as close as possible to the rubbing surfaces.

Cooling hot bearings.—The following are general principles :—

(*a*) Where the heating is known to have been gradual, and the bearing is *warm* only. In this case supplement the oil supply with the water service. If the temperature still increases the bearing should be slightly slackened, or otherwise adjusted, according to the description of bearing. With main bearings, thrust and plummer blocks, stern glands, and many others, this can be done without stopping, but for gudgeon pins, crank-heads, &c., the engines must be stopped. When stopped, the bearing should be thoroughly cooled before starting again, and in the cases of crank-head and gudgeon pins care must be taken not to slacken sufficiently to cause any considerable hammering, which would tend to do damage in other ways.

In the case of hot bearings it is often advantageous to add a little powdered blacklead or sulphur to the oil, to assist in carrying off the heat generated by the friction. The blacklead or sulphur should be sifted through bunting, to cause it to be quite free from lumps and grit. If, after the preceding, the bearing still heats, the engine must be stopped and the bearing properly examined, lubricators cleared, and bearing refitted as necessary before attempting to again run at a high speed.

(*b*) When a bearing is *suddenly* found to be *hot*. The engine should be slowed down, and, if necessary, stopped, and the bearing be practically cooled with oil before the application of any water, as the immediate use of water may fracture the bearing through causing sudden local contractions. Caution is always necessary in the application of cold water.

Special precautions are required with all bearings when the engines are working with increased speed in the astern direction, as the normal conditions as to pressure are reversed. This specially applies to the thrust and crosshead guide bearings, where entirely different surfaces are brought into contact, and particularly to the latter, where the area of the astern working surface is generally considerably less than on the ahead side.

The bearings which require most careful watching are those in which one of the rubbing surfaces will soon become plastic when over-heated, such as ordinary white metal, which melts at about 400° Fahr. The bearings so fitted are: crank-heads, main bearings, and plummer blocks almost invariably ; and gudgeons or top-end bearings, eccentric straps, crosshead guides, and thrust bearings generally. The use of white metal is also being extended, with advantageous results. When fitted it is the practice at high speeds to assist the oil lubrication with a little water, which forms a lather. This lather is not only an efficient lubricant, but as it will neither form nor remain on a hot bearing it is a good visible guide to the working condition.

Use of water service.—Water should, however, be used as little as possible, as if not applied with care it corrodes and destroys the bearing surfaces. If in any case water is used on the bearings during the working of the engines, the supply should be discontinued some time before stopping, and oil only used instead, so that the journals may become coated with oil and preserved as far as possible from rusting after the engines are stopped ; also, the caps and brasses should be removed at the earliest opportunity for examination, and if used on the connecting-rod ends or main bearings the bolts should be drawn, cleaned, and coated with a preservative—either tallow or mineral oil and blacklead—before being replaced.

Stern tube bearing.—The condition of this bearing should be ascertained by feeling the bottom part of the gland, and testing the temperature of the water which runs through the cock fitted at the bulkhead. If warm, the circulation of water should be increased by slacking back the gland and opening the water service cock on the bulkhead as necessary.

CHAPTER XXXI.

ENGINES DONE WITH—EXAMINATIONS, ADJUSTMENTS, AND GENERAL INFORMATION.

Engines done with.—When the ship arrives in harbour and the engines are finally done with, the regulating and stop-valves should be closed, the worsteds taken out from the lubricators, cylinder and jacket drains opened, the engines *wiped down while warm* to clean off the grease, &c., adhering to them, and the bilges should be pumped out by one of the auxiliary engines before the steam pressure in the boilers is too low. All sea connections should be closed, and the condenser casings and pipes drained to prevent corrosion. If the engines are not likely to be used for some time, the covers and doors of the foot and delivery valve chambers should be taken off and all the water drained out of the condensers, hot wells, and feed-tanks, which should then be kept dry. The covers and doors need not be rejointed until it is necessary to again prepare for steaming.

If the ship has been for a considerable period under steam, advantage should be taken of the interval to make a thorough examination and adjustment of the working parts and to remedy all defects. The man-hole doors on cylinder covers, or with small cylinders the covers themselves, should be removed, and the junk-rings of the pistons taken off for examination of the springs, &c. The pistons and the insides of the cylinders should be cleaned and oiled, and the junk-rings replaced. The manhole door should not be rejointed, so that the internal parts may be kept clean and free from rust until again required for steaming. The slide casing doors should be removed, slide-valves examined, and taken out if necessary, the surfaces cleaned and oiled, defects, if any, made good, packing rings adjusted or refitted, and covers rejointed. The packings of all the glands that have not been renewed for some time, or which show signs of leakage, especially those on the cylinders and condensers, should be examined, and renewed or refitted where necessary. The condenser doors should be taken off for examination of the packings at the ends of the tubes.

All the bearing surfaces, working parts, and fastenings should be examined and adjusted. The bolts of the bearings should be drawn back and thoroughly cleaned and coated with preservative as previously described. The coupling bolts of the screw shafting should be examined, and some of them drawn back to insure that they are in good order.

The boilers and mountings, as practicable, should be examined, and defects made good, and all auxiliary machinery should be examined, adjusted, and repaired if required.

During the time the ship remains in harbour after the examinations have been completed and defects made good, all main and auxiliary engines and gear should be kept clean and oiled, and partly turned round every day by the hand turning gear. The slide-valves of each of the engines should be worked daily by the starting gear, and levers and other working parts moved occasionally to prevent them from sticking. The sea and bilge cocks or valves of the pumps should be opened and closed daily, except those leading to the condenser, and the watertight doors, sluice-valves, Kingston, flooding, and other sea-cocks and valves, and the cocks or valves of the fire-main, should be worked regularly every week to insure their being kept in proper working order.

Examinations after being at rest a considerable time.—The 'Steam Manual' governing procedure in the Royal Navy requires that when a vessel has been lying in reserve the undermentioned parts of the machinery, with the gear attached to them, should be examined and, if movable, worked, to ascertain that they are in good order before steam is allowed to be raised, the result of the examinations being certified in writing by the officers who make them :—(1) Main and auxiliary stop-valves ; (2) safety-valves ; (3) brine-valves, pipes, and Kingston valves ; (4) steam and water gauge cocks and pipes ; (5) feed-cocks, valves, and pipes, drain-cocks and pipes to all boxes, and all other mountings ; (6) separators, steam pipes, expansion and other joints ; (7) stop, regulating, reducing, and slide-valves ; (8) auxiliary starting valves, hand and steam starting gear, and all relief cocks and escape valves ; (9) sea suction and discharge valves, and other valves and cocks in connection with the surface condensers, main-engine pumps, and auxiliary engines ; (10) the shaft couplings, nuts, cotters, keys and pins connecting the working parts, and all other important fastenings of the machinery should be sounded and overhauled ; (11) pistons, and especially fastenings of junk-rings ; and (12) piston-rod nuts and guards, and any attachments to the pistons.

Adjustment of main bearings, crank-pins, and gudgeons.—This is a most important matter, and one that should always be given personal attention to by the engineer in charge of the machinery. It is very necessary that the connecting rod and crank-shaft bearings should be kept properly adjusted, and that the engines should not be allowed to work with the journals slack. This would in the latter case leave the shaft improperly supported, while in the former case the hammering of the pistons on the crank-pins at each stroke causes a serious increase of bending strains on the crank-shaft which, from the nature of the case, it is difficult to reduce to exact calculation. Many broken shafts have been ascribed to this cause.

The main bearing and connecting-rod brasses should be screwed up tightly on to the stops or liners and not left loose. The corners of large nuts—i.e. for main bearings, crank-pins, crosshead or gudgeon bearings, &c.—should be numbered, and one or two well-defined lines marked on the caps, so that the positions of the various corners can be measured in relation to these lines and recorded. Knowing the pitch of the thread of bolts, the distance the corner of each nut requires to be moved through for an adjustment of $\frac{1}{200}$ of an inch or any other distance can be easily calculated. A record should be kept for all large bearings, which will obviate repeated markings by centre-punch, chisel, &c., which is confusing and leads to error.

It is impossible to lay down a hard and fast rule for the amount of slackness from 'hard home' at which large revolving or oscillating bearing surfaces should be worked. This must always be a matter of experience, as all adjustments when cold are subject to alteration when under working conditions, due to various causes.

To adjust the amount of slackness in large bearings the use of lead wire is very common, a small piece of such wire $\frac{1}{16}$ inch diameter being inserted along the axis between the cap and the shaft or pin, and the nuts screwed up evenly till the thickness of the wire corresponds to the desired amount of play measured on a wire gauge. The position of the nuts should now be carefully observed, and after removing the wire the distance pieces and thin packing strips should be so fitted that when the nuts are screwed up tightly against the packing pieces the corners of the nuts are in the observed position. All white metal lined bearings should be worked with as little play as possible. When the engines are new a greater play is necessary than subsequently, when the bearings, after having worked some time, can be gradually adjusted for a smaller amount of play.

After adjusting crank-head and gudgeon bearings, they should be tested by moving them along the pins by means of a crowbar in several positions, to see that they are free, which of course they should be. Gudgeon brasses should be tested with the connecting-rod at its greatest angle with the line of centres, as these tend to wear oval, and the hardest parts must be quite free.

When time is important and there is a heavy knock which requires removal from a bearing, an old rule, expressed by 'halving the knock,' may be followed. This consists in removal of liners, tightening nuts hard home, noting the distance they have moved through, and then adjusting them slacked back to half this distance.

With horizontal engines great care is necessary before adjusting the bearings to insure that the shaft or pin is bearing hard against the bottom brass, otherwise there may be much more play than intended and shown by the lead wire. For this purpose it is necessary to turn the engines by the turning gear in such direction that the pins or shaft will be pressed against the back brass prior to the adjustment being carried out. With vertical engines the weight of the various parts tends to effect this object, but the engines should also be turned in this case.

Adjustment of other working parts.—Especial care is necessary with the link motion, as most of the wear takes place in the ahead position, so that only a portion of the wear can be taken up, and unless the links are trued up for all positions of the block there must always be a slackness in the ahead position.

Adjustment of eccentrics may best be effected by testing their freedom with the ends disconnected from the rods or links.

The crosshead slippers are generally adjusted by moving the crosshead as near as possible to the cylinder, displacing the piston-rod packing, and lining up till the rod is equidistant from the hole in the cylinder for the packing. In the fore-and-aft direction, however, the rod will, when cold, often be found not to be quite equidistant, owing to the expansion of the cylinders when hot. For this reason the adjustment should also be tested when hot by turning the engine in such a direction that the slipper which is being adjusted is pressed home on the guide, and noting if the piston-rod is true for each point of the stroke. For this purpose it will be obvious on consideration that if the ahead slipper is being adjusted the turning gear must be worked so as to move the engine in the astern direction, and *vice-versâ*. Marks should be made on the crosshead when the engines are new and corresponding marks on the guide, with gauges fitted between them, which can be applied at any time, and which will also indicate the amount of lining up required.

The outsides of the crank and propeller shaft journals should always be marked when new, as a guide to indicate when the shafting is working forward from the wear of the thrust collars. From these marks the proper adjustment of the thrust-block is made in the fore-and-aft direction.

All bearings that have been adjusted should be carefully watched for a time after being under way.

Relief rings for flat slide-valves.—It is necessary that these rings should be properly adjusted, to insure steamtightness without too great a pressure on the working faces. If they be slack, the equilibrium of the valve is destroyed, which increases the stress on the eccentrics and gear, and a loss of efficiency will ensue from the passage of steam to the condenser or receiver from the back of the valve, without performing work in the cylinder. If too tight, the friction is increased, and unnecessary strains are brought on the eccentrics and slide-gear.

Pistons.—Great waste of steam will ensue if the pistons leak and allow steam to pass from the steam to the exhaust side, and thus, in the case of the low-pressure cylinder, to the condenser, without the performance of any work. The metallic packing ring should, therefore, always be kept pressed against the working surface of the cylinder. Advantage should frequently be taken of opportunities for taking off the junk-ring for inspection of the piston springs. In the case of horizontal engines, the pistons have a tendency to wear down and allow the steam to pass over them to the condenser. They and the guide surfaces should be kept lined up to the central position, and the metallic packing rings should be turned some distance round as they become worn. When horizontal pistons are fitted with back supporting rods or trunks, the guides should be lined up and adjusted as required, to prevent, as far as possible, the weight of the piston from resting on the bottom of the cylinder.

The condition of the pistons and valves should be tested for tightness, as the indicator diagram is of little or no service as regards this important defect, for leakage of steam, except under exceptional circumstances, has so little effect on an indicator diagram that its detection by this means can seldom be effected.

The pistons and valves can, however, be tested when the engine is at rest by thoroughly warming it and then fixing the piston in some position and admitting steam to one side by the starting or pass-valve, and noticing the amount of steam passing to the other side by means of the indicator cock, or lifting the escape valve or drain cock. The tightness of the valves can also be tested in this manner. Steam should be kept in the steam jackets while this is being done. Periodical testing in this manner and comparison with the original condition will often locate many defects.

Boiler tests.—To promote safety in the working of the boilers, and to serve as a guide for the reduction of the load on the safety valves when it may become necessary, it is desirable that the boilers should be tested by water pressure at regular intervals. To carry out this test, the boilers are first filled, care being taken that they are practically free from air, and the pressure is then produced by pumping additional water into them, by means of one of the steam pumps if fires are alight in other boilers, and, if not, by a hand pump or by one of the pumps specially supplied with fittings for this purpose. During the application of the water pressure, the boiler should be carefully examined and gauges used to detect any change of form in the furnaces and combustion chambers. The thickness of the plates should also be periodically ascertained by drilling small holes through them. The test-holes are afterwards tapped and filled with screw rivets.

The Admiralty rule is that, provided during the examination no indication of weakness is observed, the water pressure test should be double the working steam pressure in all boats' boilers, and in large water-tank boilers where the steam pressure is 90 lbs. per square inch and under ; if above 90 lbs. and not over 155 lbs. steam pressure, 90 lbs. above the working pressure ; and with water-tube boilers to $1\frac{1}{2}$ times the working pressure. If any sign of probable permanent deformation be detected, the test should be stopped, and the working pressure is, if originally not more than 90 lbs. on the square inch, then limited to two-fifths of the pressure arrived at before such indications were seen ; and if the working pressure be originally above 90 lbs. and not above 155 lbs. per square inch, the reduced working pressure is not to be more than 90 lbs. less than, or in the case of water-tube boilers two-thirds of, the test pressure arrived at before such indications were seen.

This reduced pressure is used until the defect, if local, can be made good and the proper test pressure applied If the drill test should show unusual thinness in any part, the water pressure should be very carefully applied, to prevent injury being caused from over-pressure. In all cases it should be carefully noted whether there is permanent set. The Admiralty practice as regards amount of test pressure is followed generally by other foreign navies. The Board of Trade and Lloyd's, however, require a test of double the working pressure.

Ventilation of coal bunkers. Precautions to prevent accidents.— Considerable care is necessary to prevent accident from explosion of gas in coal bunkers. The coal-shoots should always be kept quite clear of coal to permit the gas to escape through the grated covers on the deck. Ventilating pipes are usually carried from the upper parts of the bunkers to the funnel casings, to allow the impure air and gases as they form, to pass away freely to the atmosphere. Inlet pipes are also fitted to admit fresh air, and these are led to the upper parts of the bunkers, as far as possible from the outlet orifices, so that the ventilation may be from the surface, and not through the body of the coal. The ventilating pipes from the several bunkers should be independent of each other, and always kept quite clear and open for ventilation, except when under forced draught, if closed stokeholds are fitted.   In special cases, where coal bunkers are not provided with permanent ventilating arrangements, comprising a separate inlet and outlet, care must be taken that the bunker lids are taken off frequently to keep the bunkers well ventilated.   This should be done at least four times a week for not less than three hours at any one time.

The ventilation of bunkers, especially those without permanent ventilating fittings, should be tested by using safety lamps before sending men to work in them, and whenever the coal bunker lids are removed, lights should not be brought near the openings until the accumulated gas has been allowed to escape.   Special precautions should be taken in this respect for a few days after coaling.   Small tubes with screwed deck-plates are fitted in the bunkers at regular intervals, about ten feet apart, to enable the temperature to be ascertained.   This should be done frequently, and if the temperature is rising means should be adopted for increasing the ventilation and getting rid of the gas.

Wet coal to be avoided.—Moisture sometimes causes a rapid generation of heat and gas, especially when the coal contains a considerable quantity of pyrites.   Wet coal should not be shipped, and the coal should be kept as dry as possible after it is in the bunkers.   Ships should not be coaled on rainy days if it can be avoided, and bunker lids should be replaced as soon as possible after coaling to prevent water passing into the bunkers when the decks are being washed.

CHAPTER XXXII.

MATERIALS USED IN CONSTRUCTION.

THE most extensively used material in the construction of engines and boilers is iron, using the term in its inclusive sense to comprise cast-iron, wrought-iron, and steel; which, though differing so greatly in qualities, are but different forms of the same material.

Iron is very rarely found in the metallic state, but is generally combined with oxygen and carbonic acid, and mixed to a greater or less extent with clay and earthy matters. In this condition it is called *iron ore*, of which there are many varieties.

British iron is made from the ores known as red hæmatite, clay iron-stone, and black-band, but principally from the two latter.

Cast-iron.—Cast-iron is obtained from the iron ore by the process known as 'smelting.' The substances employed in smelting are: (1) the ore itself; (2) the fuel, which produces heat by its combustion and supplies carbon; (3) the air, which supplies oxygen for the combustion of the fuel, and for combination with the carbon in the ore; and (4) a flux, generally lime, which promotes fusion of the ore and combines with the earthy portion, forming a slag.

The iron, after it is reduced from the ore, is drawn off from the blast-furnaces, run into a series of shallow gutters or grooves, and broken into short pieces, about 2 or 3 feet long. It contains in its composition a proportion of carbon, from 3 to 5 per cent., and is known as *pig-iron* or *cast-iron*. Only a part of this carbon is actually in chemical combination with the iron—say, from 1 to about $2\frac{1}{2}$ per cent.—the remainder being diffused throughout the mass in the form of graphite or plumbago.

From its low first cost, its strength, and the facility with which it can be cast into any form, *cast iron* is extensively used in all engineering work. In the marine steam-engine, the cylinders and covers, slide casings and valves, framing, plummer blocks, and many other parts, especially those of intricate form, are generally made of cast-iron, and often the pistons and condensers. In land and mercantile marine engines the stop- and safety-valve boxes are also usually made of cast-iron, and in land engines the steam-pipes also.

The properties of different brands of cast-iron vary very widely according to the quality of the ore from which they are produced, and to the proportion of carbon actually combined with the iron. The iron that contains the greater quantity of carbon in combination is called *white cast-iron*, from the appearance of the fracture. It is very hard and brittle, and unsuitable by itself for foundry purposes. It is known in the market as No. 8 pig.

At the other end of the scale is *grey cast-iron* (No. 1 pig), in which the greater proportion of the carbon is diffused throughout the mass in small particles of blacklead or graphite, which give to the fracture a greyish colour. This is much softer and tougher than the white iron, and is generally used in making castings, being mixed with some of the whiter varieties, or with good scrap cast-iron, to give it sufficient strength and hardness for various purposes. Cast-iron with properties intermediate between those of white and grey iron is often called *mottled cast-iron*, and its nearness in composition to white or grey pig is indicated by numbers intermediate between 1 and 8.

Cast-iron is improved in strength and closeness of texture by re-melting in the foundry cupola, the quantity of uncombined carbon being thereby reduced. The grey pig-iron as received from the blast-furnaces is not altogether suitable, alone, for engine castings, especially in cases where hard and smooth working surfaces are required. In such cases it is desirable to mix with it a proportion of good scrap cast-iron, from old engine castings, to increase both the strength and uniformity of the casting. The proportion of scrap varies from 30 to 70 per cent. according to the degree of hardness required.

Unequal contraction in cooling.—The great objection to the use of cast-iron, especially for parts that have to sustain severe and inter-mittent stresses, is the uncertainty that exists as to its actual strength in any particular instance, in consequence of the unequal and unknown stresses brought on the material during the process of cooling in the mould. The initial stress is sometimes so great that the casting is found fractured on being taken out of the mould, before it has been subjected to the action of any external force, and it must in any case weaken the casting. The amount of contraction varies with the size and thickness of the casting and with the quality of iron used. In thin castings the contraction is about $\frac{1}{16}$-inch per foot, whilst in thick castings it is as much as $\frac{1}{8}$-inch per foot.

To prevent unequal contraction as far as possible, sudden variations in the thickness of the several parts should be guarded against, and sharp corners should be avoided. Suitable arrangements should also be made to cause the rate of cooling of the different parts of the casting to be as nearly uniform as possible. Unless proper precautions are taken this unequal contraction will often cause distortion of form in castings of irregular shape, and it is therefore an advantage to make the castings as symmetrical in form and uniform in thickness as is consistent with the purposes for which they are required.

Cast-iron is also liable to have its strength reduced by the existence of *blow-holes* or gas-bubbles underneath the surface, which cannot generally be discovered by any ordinary inspection or test, if they should be at any depth below the surface. If near the skin of the iron, they may be discovered by tapping the casting with a hammer.

In consequence of these defects, cast-iron is an unreliable material for structures of irregular form that have to sustain intermittent heavy loads, and a large margin of strength should be allowed when it is employed. It, however, has the advantages of cheapness and stiffness, and at present it is the only material that can be used for many parts of the machinery. If it can be avoided it should not be used in parts that have to withstand unequal and irregular temperatures ; as it is an unreliable material for parts that are exposed to unequal temperatures or subject to blows.

Several serious accidents have occurred from the bursting of cast-iron stop-valve boxes when steam has been admitted to them without previously taking the precaution of draining out the cold water that had accumulated in the valve-boxes and steam-pipes. For this reason gunmetal is generally used in the Navy for stop- and safety-valve boxes of marine boilers, but they are sometimes of cast-steel. In the mercantile marine they are commonly of cast-iron.

The strength of cast-iron under the action of a crushing load is much greater than when exposed to tension, its resistance to crushing being from 80,000 to 110,000 lbs. per square inch, whilst its average tenacity is only from 16,000 to 18,000 lbs. per square inch. It is, therefore, more suitable for parts that are exposed to compression than for those that have to sustain stretching or tension.

For the cast-iron used by the Admiralty the minimum tensile strength is 9 tons per sq. inch, and the minimum transverse breaking load for a bar 1 inch square loaded at the middle between supports 1 foot apart at least 2,000 lbs.

The soundness or compactness of a casting is promoted by casting it under pressure. Consequently cylinders, pipes, &c., should be cast in a vertical position, with a *head* or additional column of metal above, whose weight serves to compress the mass of metal in the mould below. The dross and gas-bubbles ascend into the head, which is cut off when the casting is cool.

Malleable cast-iron.—By imbedding an iron casting in oxide of iron, or powdered red hæmatite, which consists almost entirely of peroxide of iron, and keeping it at a high temperature for a sufficient time, which will vary with the size of the casting, a portion of the carbon contained in the iron will unite with the oxygen in the oxide, and the casting will be converted, to a greater or lesser extent, into a material resembling mild steel or wrought-iron. This material is much cheaper than wrought-iron or steel ; but the process is only applicable to comparatively small articles of fairly uniform thickness.

Malleable cast-iron is not generally used for important parts of machinery, but the junction-boxes for the Belleville boiler tubes are made of malleable cast-iron, and the material gives satisfaction in this situation, although exposed to high pressures and temperatures.

Wrought-iron.—Wrought-iron, in its pure state, is simply metallic iron, without admixture or combination with any other element, and produced from cast-iron by the processes of refining and puddling, or by the use of a Bessemer converter.

Wrought-iron was at one time universally employed for the construction of the boilers, shafting, piston and connecting-rods, and nearly all the moving parts of the engines, especially those that are subject to severe and varying strains. It is tough and strong, and has a fibrous structure, which renders its resistance to tension much greater than its resistance to compression. It is malleable and ductile, and though it can only be fused with difficulty and at a very high temperature, it possesses the property of *welding*, when raised to a white heat (say 1,500° to 1,600° Fahr.), which enables two pieces of iron to be firmly united or welded together by hammering.

The fibrous structure which the best wrought-iron shows is produced by the processes of manufacture, but vibration tends to reduce it to the crystalline condition, and this probably accounts for numerous fractures of parts subject to vibration and intermittent strains, the fractures in most cases showing crystalline or granular surfaces. General experience shows that if wrought-iron shafts, such as railway axles, marine-engine shafting, &c., which are exposed to intermittent stresses, be designed with the ordinary factor of safety used for machinery, they are liable to fracture after running for a certain period, and in such cases the appearance at the fractured part is crystalline. These parts are, therefore, generally made larger than at first sight appears necessary, so as to give increased stiffness and reduce the intensity of the torsional stresses on the particles.

The tensile strength of good iron forgings made from scrap-iron is about 22 tons per square inch with the grain and 19 tons across the grain.

Case-hardening.—The outer skin in many wrought-iron pieces of machinery is made hard, to resist friction, by the process of case-hardening, which consists in imbedding the article in some carbonaceous substance, and raising it to a red heat, by which means the outer layers acquire sufficient carbon to convert them into hard steel. One of the most convenient is finely powdered yellow prussiate of potash, with which the iron is sprinkled, heated to redness without access of air, and afterwards cooled in water. The depth of the hardening will depend on the time occupied in the process. In marine engines, the pins of the link motion and many other similar parts and small nuts are usually made of iron, case-hardened, or of steel. The gudgeon pins of wrought-iron or mild steel are also generally so treated when they work on a gunmetal surface.

Steel.—The term *steel* is applied to all compounds of iron and carbon in which the proportion of combined carbon does not exceed 1·5 per cent. The properties of the materials thus included under a common name vary, however, very greatly, according to the amount of carbon they contain. When the percentage of carbon is below 0·5, the material is called *mild steel*, and possesses few of the qualities popularly attached to steel, and in point of fact very closely resembles the best wrought-iron. The hardness and tenacity of steel, and its capability of fusion, increase as the percentage of carbon becomes greater.

Steel is produced in general either by the addition of carbon to wrought-iron, or by the abstraction of carbon from cast-iron. The former method, although more complex and expensive, is preferred for making the higher classes of steel required for tools, &c., as wrought-iron can be obtained in a greater state of purity than cast-iron. The second method is employed for making large quantities of steel rapidly and cheaply, such as that required for ordinary plates, bars, rails, &c.

Steel is distinguished from wrought-iron by its capability of being cast into a malleable ingot, so that uniformity of structure may be insured; and, above a certain percentage of carbon, also by its possessing the property of *tempering*, which enables it to be hardened by sudden cooling, a property valuable in the manufacture of cutting tools; or softened by gradual cooling from a high temperature. The mild steel used for engine forgings and boiler plates, which only contains from 0·15 to 0·30 per cent. of carbon, is destitute of hardening qualities.

Bessemer steel.—In the Bessemer process for making steel, molten pig-iron is poured into a vessel called a *converter*, through which a stream of air is blown by a strong blast. The oxygen of the air first removes the silicon and manganese, and then unites with the carbon and carries it away. After all the carbon has been removed, the proper proportion of carbon required to make the steel is introduced by the addition of a quantity of special molten pig-iron (*Spiegel-Eisen*). The steel thus made is poured into ingots, and afterwards hammered, rolled, and worked as required. The process has to be a rapid one, however, and it is difficult to judge as to the correct time to stop the action of the blast. Irregularities are often found in the finished product.

Acid and basic Bessemer processes.—There are two Bessemer processes, depending on whether the converter has an acid lining of 'ganister' or whether it is a basic lining of 'dolomite.' The resulting steel is termed either 'acid' or 'basic' Bessemer steel. The difference consists principally in the action on any phosphorus contained in the molten pig-iron. With the basic lining the phosphorus is eliminated by the presence of lime in the converter.

With the acid lining, however, the lime cannot be added, as they combine with each other, so that the phosphorus remains. The pig-iron used with this process, therefore, must not contain more than the amount of phosphorus allowable in the steel; while with the basic process large quantities of phosphorus are permissible in the pig-iron.

Siemens-Martin steel.—In the *open hearth* process of making steel the great heat produced by a Siemens regenerative furnace dissolves in a bath of molten pig-iron the ores of iron, either in a raw state or in a more or less reduced condition. The oxygen in the ore unites with the carbon of the molten pig-iron to form carbonic oxide, which passes off as gas. Usually, steel or wrought-iron scrap is added in addition to the iron ores. The principal advantage of this system of producing mild steel is that it is not dependent on a limited time for its results, as is the case in the Bessemer process. The heat of the furnace is such that the fluid bath of metal, after having been reduced to the lowest form of decarbonisation, may be maintained in that condition for any reasonable length of time, during which samples may be taken and tested, and such additions made to it as may be necessary to adjust it to the required quality, and uniformity in all the ingots produced may thus be insured. To further improve the quality of the material, a small quantity of *Spiegel-Eisen* and ferro-manganese is generally added. There are both acid and basic processes for Siemens-Martin steel, the differences being similar to those described above for Bessemer steel.

Properties of mild steel.—Mild steel can be worked well at a red heat, and can be bent cold into most ordinary forms. It, however, possesses the peculiar property of becoming brittle at a temperature between about 400° and 600° Fahr., which is technically known as a *blue heat*, from the colour of the fracture at that temperature. Care should therefore be taken to prevent any work being done on the material after it has fallen to this dangerous limit of temperature.

All plates or bars that have had much work done on them while hot should be subsequently annealed. The annealing, if possible, should be performed simultaneously over the whole of the plate or bar in question, and care should be taken to prevent the access of air to the furnace, or the impinging of the flame on the material during the process. After the material has been raised gradually to a red heat, it should be taken out of the furnace and allowed to cool slowly. Annealing is not necessary in cases where the whole of the plate has been heated and bent or flanged at one heat.

Steel made by the Siemens-Martin process is now extensively used for engine forgings and for boiler plates and tubes, instead of wrought-iron. To insure soundness the ingots from which the plate or forging is made should be cast with a large head. During the solidification the lower part of the ingot has to feed itself from the head, forming a funnel-shaped cavity usually known as 'the pipe,' which is essential for the ingot to be sound. The head must be long enough to allow the whole of this pipe to be cut away and the forging to be made from the sound metal below it.

The tensile strength of steel used in boiler work is between 27 and 30 tons per square inch, with an elongation in 8 inches of length of not less than 20 per cent. before fracture. For steel forgings the Admiralty permit the strength to be between 30 and 35 tons, with an elongation of 27 per cent. For crank and propeller shafting the limits are between 28 and 32 tons, with 30 per cent. elongation.

Whitworth's fluid compressed steel. — Sir Joseph Whitworth's system of producing sound steel ingots, free from blow-holes and suitable for the best engine forgings, consists in subjecting the metal while setting in the ingot mould to great hydraulic pressure, and by this method steel of very great uniformity and strength is produced. This has been extensively used for shafting, cylinder liners, and many other purposes. In the Whitworth system the whole of the forging is performed by suitable and powerful hydraulic presses, no hammering whatever being employed, but the ingot gradually squeezed to the required form. There can be little doubt that this system is superior to the use of steam hammers, and it is now the common practice of other leading steelmakers.

Steel castings. — In modern engines the frames, bedplates, pistons, and many other parts have been made of mild cast-steel, and this has enabled reductions of weight to be effected.

The greatest difficulty to be overcome in making mild steel castings is to prevent 'draw' in the metal from the contraction while cooling in the mould. The steel requires a temperature of about 4,000° Fahr. to melt it, as compared with 2,000° Fahr. for cast-iron, and the contraction of the steel casting is as much as $\frac{5}{16}$-inch per foot. Steel castings cannot be 'fed' as in the case of iron ones, and consequently the head must be of sufficient size and suitably arranged to allow of this feeding action taking place, and the milder the steel the greater this will be. This forms the 'pipe' in the head, which is generally an index of a sound casting, for if the casting in contracting does not feed from the head, it must feed from itself and become unsound. All steel castings after being taken from the mould should, without first being allowed to cool, be reheated and annealed to insure molecular equilibrium and freedom from internal strains.

For ordinary steel castings the Admiralty require the strength to be between 28 and 35 tons per square inch, with elongation in 2 inches of not less than 15 per cent.

Nickel steel.—The tensile strength and elasticity of steel is very considerably increased by adding to it a certain percentage (about 5) of nickel. This combined material has not been used extensively as yet in this country.

After iron and steel, the materials most generally used in the construction of the machinery are copper, tin, zinc, lead, and their alloys.

Copper.—This metal is red in colour and very soft, malleable, and ductile when cold. It cannot be welded, and does not make good castings. It can, however, be readily worked cold, and it is consequently used principally for making steam and other pipes which require to be bent cold. At high pressures and temperatures large copper steam pipes have been found liable to split, and many accidents have occurred recently owing to this. In such pipes in the Navy steel is now always used, or the copper steam pipes are sometimes lapped round with copper wire secured at the ends.

For most purposes it is too soft and weak to be used by itself, but it is the principal element used in forming the various alloys included under the terms 'gunmetal' and 'brass,' which are so extensively used in various parts of the machinery.

Although the term 'brass' is often applied indiscriminately to all alloys of copper with tin or zinc, its use, strictly speaking, should be confined to alloys of copper and zinc only, those made with copper and tin being known as gunmetal or bronze. A little zinc is usually added to the gunmetal alloys to facilitate casting.

Gunmetal or bronze.—This alloy is considerably harder than copper, and offers much greater resistance to crushing, which makes it suitable for many parts of machinery. It is easily fusible, and forms good, sound, and strong castings. It is therefore extensively used in the marine steam-engine for making cocks and valves of all descriptions, condenser and other pumps and fittings. Gunmetal is much used for bearing surfaces in machinery, as it is sufficiently hard and durable to prevent excessive wear, but less so than iron or steel, so that the bearing will wear instead of the journal. The alloys of copper and tin increase in hardness and brittleness as the percentage of tin is increased. The ordinary gunmetal used in machinery is much tougher than cast-iron, and is, therefore, more suitable for parts that are subject to shocks. In consequence of its resistance to corrosion, it is very suitable for pumps, valve-boxes, propellers, and other parts exposed to the action of water, and is largely used for all such fittings in preference to cast-iron, though its first cost is much greater.

The proportions of copper, tin, and zinc in the gunmetal ordinarily used vary to some extent with the nature of the article produced. In the Navy the proportions generally are copper 88, tin 10, zinc 2. For engine bearings the proportion of tin may be somewhat increased, the following being an analysis of metal suitable for this purpose :

copper 85, tin 10, and zinc 5. The tensile strength of good gunmetal, such as that used for bolts, &c., may be taken at about 10 to 14 tons per square inch. The Admiralty specify their gunmetal to be of at least 14 tons per square inch.

Brass.—Ordinary brass which is used for cheap castings, where strength is not important, is an alloy composed of about two parts of copper to one of zinc, and is yellower in colour and much softer than gunmetal. It is not suitable for parts exposed to compression, and is not used for making important engine castings.

Brass tubes.—If the proportions of copper and zinc in the alloy be suitably arranged, the brass produced will be malleable, and may be rolled into sheets or drawn into tubes or wire. The condenser-tubes and internal steam and feed-pipes in the boilers are generally made of this material. The proportion of copper in the condenser tubes is generally 70 per cent., with the addition of 1 per cent. of tin to prevent corrosion, the remainder being zinc.

Muntz-metal.—This is composed of about 60 parts of copper to 40 parts of zinc, with frequently 1 per cent. of lead to assist malleability. This material can be rolled hot into bars, plates, and sheets, and has been largely used for making rods, bolts, &c., as it possesses considerable tenacity. It has, however, been found that if Muntz-metal bolts are in contact with copper or gunmetal in sea-water, galvanic action ensues, which speedily decomposes the Muntz metal, the zinc in the compound being destroyed. It is equal in tenacity to that of good wrought-iron.

Naval brass.—This action appears to be very largely reduced or practically prevented by the addition of a little tin to the metal. An alloy composed of 62 parts of copper, 37 parts of zinc, and 1 part of tin, which for distinction is known by the name of *naval brass,* is now used instead of Muntz-metal for all such fittings. The addition of the tin does not prevent the naval brass being forged with quite as much facility as Muntz-metal.

There are various descriptions of special bronzes used which have a strength considerably above that of ordinary gunmetal.

Manganese bronze consists of gunmetal with the addition of a small proportion of ferro-manganese. Its strength when rolled is about 28 to 30 tons per square inch. This is a favourite metal for propeller blades.

Phosphor bronze, consisting of copper and tin with a little phosphorus added, is also considerably used.

Aluminium copper and bronze.—Aluminium when added to copper sheets and brass improves their qualities in a marked degree, especially as regards reduction of corrosion. Various alloys, termed aluminium copper and bronze, are now under trial in the Navy, and they seem destined to be most useful to engineers in the future.

Zinc.—Besides its uses in various alloys (brass, Muntz-metal, &c.), connected with the machinery, slabs of zinc are used for the protection of boilers. Rolled zinc is preferable to cast zinc for this purpose. Zinc is also used for coating iron that is exposed to the action of water or moisture, thus preventing its corrosion and decay. The zincing is performed by immersing the iron article, after it has been thoroughly cleaned by fire or acids, in a molten bath of zinc, by which means it becomes coated with a layer of zinc, which increases in thickness according to the length of time that the article is kept in the bath. This is termed zincing or galvanising by the 'hot' process.

The steel boiler tubes now being used in most water-tube boilers are also coated externally with a thin coating of zinc which is generally electrically deposited. This coating of zinc is sometimes obtained by the 'hot' or dipping process, and the internal surface has also some-times been so treated. In the British Navy only the outside surface is coated, and this is effected in the following manner :—The tubes are first cleaned bright by being pickled in weak hydrochloric acid till all scale formed during manufacture is removed, after which, and immediately before zincing, the tubes are immersed for not more than half an hour in a weak sulphuric acid bath, the ends of the tubes being plugged during the latter process. On removal from the sulphuric acid the tubes are well brushed and thoroughly washed and immersed in the electro depositing bath till the required amount of zinc is deposited, this being about $1\frac{1}{4}$ ozs. per square foot. This is known as the 'cold' process.

Lead.—Lead is not used alone in any part of the marine engine, except occasionally in the form of weights for balancing certain moving parts, but it is used in combination with other soft metals for making the white-metal alloys for bearing surfaces.

CHAPTER XXXIII.

THEORETICAL INDICATOR DIAGRAMS OF STAGE EXPANSION ENGINES.

To determine the relative proportions of the cylinders of stage expansion engines, and the points of cut-off in each to produce the most uniform strains on the shafting, and enable the work due to the expansion to be most fully realised, theoretical indicator diagrams showing the action of the steam in the several cylinders are very useful. For simplicity, we will neglect the effects of the release before the end of the stroke, the compression, the resistance of the passages between the cylinders, &c., simplicity being of more importance than extreme accuracy, especially as allowance can easily be made for the compression, early release, &c., after the diagrams have been drawn, if the principles involved are clearly understood.

Let V represent the volume of the large cylinder ;

v the volume of the small cylinder ;

U the volume of the intermediate reservoir ;

R = total rate of expansion ;

Rate of expansion = r in high-pressure cylinder, and ρ in low-pressure ;

λ = ratio of cylinders ; so that $R = r\lambda$;

ϕ = ratio of reservoir to h.p. cylinder ; so that $U = \phi v$;

p_1 = initial absolute pressure in the high-pressure cylinder.

Since a volume $\dfrac{v}{r}$ of steam entering the high-pressure cylinder at pressure p_1, occupies finally a volume V at pressure $\dfrac{p_1}{R}$, we shall have $\dfrac{v}{r} = \dfrac{V}{R}$.

Compound engines with cranks at 0 deg. or 180 deg. apart, but without an intermediate reservoir.—In Fig. 386, O B represents the initial absolute pressure of the steam on its admission to the high-pressure cylinder, and B C is the line of pressure during admission. At C the steam is cut off and expands in the small cylinder to D, the end of the stroke, when the communication is opened to the large cylinder, and the steam exerts a forward pressure on the large piston and a back pressure on the small piston. This part of the action

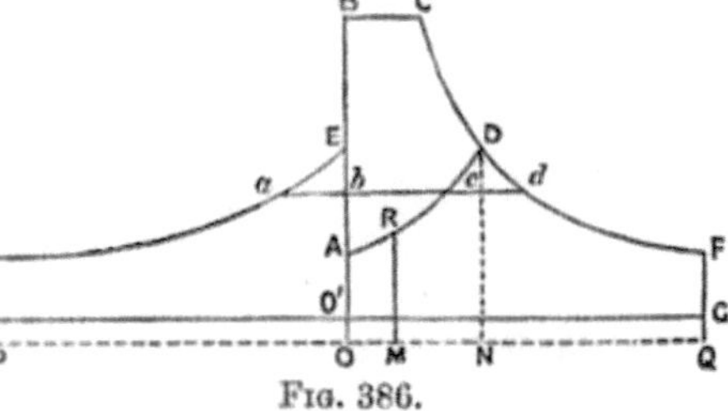

FIG. 386.

of the steam is represented by the two curves, D A and E F, the ordinates of D A representing the back pressures on the small piston and the corresponding ordinates of E F the forward pressures on the large piston. O P is = V, the volume of the large cylinder, and O N = v, the volume of the small cylinder. At the end of the stroke of the large piston the communication is opened to the condenser, and the pressure falls to P G, the constant condenser pressure. These diagrams may be combined as follows :—Draw any straight line, $a\,b\,c\,d$, parallel to P O Q, and intersecting the two diagrams, and lay off on it $c\,d = a\,b$, then $b\,d = b\,c + c\,d$ represents the total volume occupied by the steam when its absolute pressure is $O\,b$, and 'd' is a point on the indicator diagram which would be formed if the steam had been expanded in the large cylinder only. By drawing a sufficient number of horizontal lines and laying off the proper distances on them, any number of points can be found, and the diagram can be reasoned about as if the whole of the action had taken place in one cylinder only. The pressure at any point in the forward stroke of the large piston, and back stroke of the small piston, is easily obtained. At any point M in the return stroke of the small piston, the total volume occupied by the steam is $(v - x) + x\,\dfrac{V}{v}$, where $x = NM$.

Therefore the pressure $M\,R$

$$= p_1\frac{v}{r} \div \left\{ v - x + x\frac{V}{v} \right\} = p_1\frac{v}{r} \div \left\{ v + x\left(\frac{R}{r} - 1\right) \right\} = \frac{p_1\,v}{vr + x(R - r)}$$

Compound engines with cranks at 0 deg. or 180 deg. apart, but with an intermediate reservoir.—This is a case that seldom occurs in practice unless the reservoir be used for the purpose of reheating the steam on its passage from the high- to the low-pressure cylinders. It is, however, interesting to examine the effect of the reservoir on the diagram, because in any case the passages between the cylinders form a sort of reservoir—in some cases not an inconsiderable one.

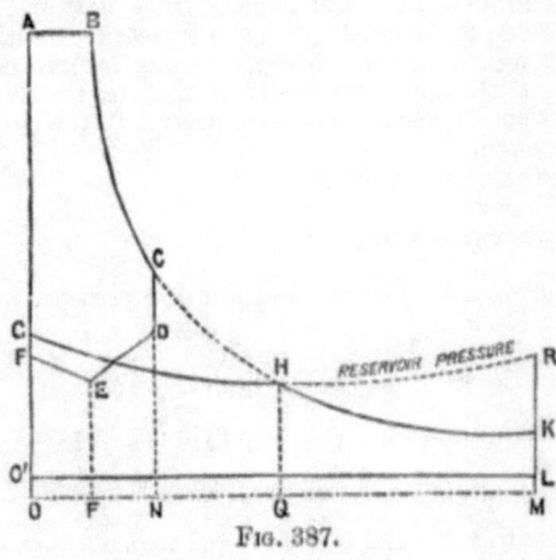

Fig. 387.

Let p_r = pressure in the reservoir immediately before the high-pressure cylinder exhausts into it. O A, Fig. 387 = p_1 = initial absolute pressure of the steam in the high-pressure cylinder. At B the steam is cut off and expands to C, the end of the stroke of the high-pressure cylinder. At this point the communication is opened to the reservoir, and a volume, v, of steam at pressure $\dfrac{p_1}{r}$ is admitted to the reservoir; consequently the pressure N D will be $= \dfrac{p_r U + \dfrac{p_1 v}{r}}{v + U}$. This is, of course, equal to the initial pressure O G in the low-pressure cylinder. The steam now acts on the low-pressure piston until $\dfrac{1}{\rho}$-th of the stroke of the low-pressure piston has been performed, when the admission to the large cylinder is cut off. At this point the steam occupies the volume $\left(1 - \dfrac{1}{\rho}\right) v + U + \dfrac{V}{\rho}$, and its pressure is therefore

$$= \frac{p_r U + \dfrac{p_1 v}{r}}{\left(1 - \dfrac{1}{\rho}\right) v + U + \dfrac{V}{\rho}} = \frac{p_r \phi + \dfrac{p_1}{r}}{\left(1 - \dfrac{1}{\rho}\right) + \phi + \dfrac{\lambda}{\rho}}.$$

This part of the action of the steam is represented by the curve G H in the low-pressure diagram, and D E in the high-pressure diagram. After the steam is cut off, it expands in the cylinder to the final pressure $\dfrac{p_1}{R}$, while in the reservoir it is compressed to the pressure p_r, represented by $MR = OF$. It only remains to determine p_r in order that the diagrams may be completely drawn. We can easily find p_r from the fact that a volume $\dfrac{V}{o}$ of steam

at pressure $\dfrac{p_r \phi + \dfrac{p_1}{r}}{\left(1 - \dfrac{1}{\rho}\right) + \phi + \dfrac{\lambda}{\rho}}$ occupies finally a volume V at pressure $\dfrac{p_1}{R}$.

Therefore
$$\frac{p_r \phi + \dfrac{p_1}{r}}{\left(1 - \dfrac{1}{\rho}\right) + \phi + \dfrac{\lambda}{\rho}} \cdot \frac{V}{\rho} = \frac{p_1}{R} V$$

$$\text{or,}\ p_r \phi + \frac{p_1}{r} = \frac{\rho p_1}{R} \left\{ \left(1 - \frac{1}{\rho}\right) + \phi + \frac{\lambda}{\rho} \right\}$$

$$\text{but } R = \lambda r$$

$\therefore$ by substitution and reduction we get $p_r = \dfrac{p_1}{R} \left\{ \left(\dfrac{\rho - 1}{\phi}\right) + \rho \right\}$

The diagram can now be completely drawn. If the reservoir pressure p_r be not so great as the pressure of release in the high-pressure cylinder, $\dfrac{p_1}{r}$, there will be a fall of pressure on the admission to the reservoir, and the work due to expansion will be partly lost. If these pressures be equal we have :—

$$\frac{p_1}{r} = \frac{p_1}{R} \left\{ \frac{(\rho - 1)}{\phi} + \rho \right\}$$

$$\text{or } \frac{R}{r} = \lambda = \frac{\rho - 1}{\phi} + \rho\ ;\ \text{therefore } \rho = \frac{\phi \lambda + 1}{\phi + 1}.$$

From this equation in any given case ρ can be determined, so that there shall be no loss on admission to the reservoir. When $\phi = o$, $\rho = 1$; this is the case previously discussed. Taking $\phi = 1$, that is, taking the volume of the reservoir equal to that of the high-pressure cylinder, we have $\rho = \dfrac{\lambda + 1}{2}$.

In this case, if λ be greater than 3, ρ will be greater than 2, consequently arrangements should be fitted to cause the cut-off in the low-pressure cylinder to be before half-stroke if the work due to the expansion is to be fully realised.

The following table gives a few values of rates of expansion necessary in the low-pressure cylinders of compound engines of this type when there is no fall of pressure on the admission to the reservoir.

$\lambda =$		1	2	3	4	5	6
	$\phi = 1$	1	$\dfrac{3}{2}$	2	$\dfrac{5}{2}$	3	$\dfrac{7}{2}$
ρ for	$\phi = 2$	1	$\dfrac{5}{3}$	$\dfrac{7}{3}$	3	$\dfrac{11}{3}$	$\dfrac{13}{3}$
	$\phi = 3$	1	$\dfrac{7}{4}$	$\dfrac{10}{4}$	$\dfrac{13}{4}$	4	$\dfrac{19}{4}$

We now pass on to consider the type of compound engine most generally used, viz. engines with two cylinders, side by side, acting on cranks at right angles to each other, and having an intermediate reservoir. The cases in which the cut-off in the low-pressure cylinder is after half-stroke, and before half-stroke respectively, must be discussed separately.

Two cylinder compound engines with cranks at right angles to each other, having an intermediate reservoir, the cut-off in the low-pressure cylinder being after half-stroke.—It will be necessary in the first place to find an expression for the distance of the high-pressure piston from the end of its stroke, when the steam is cut off in the low-pressure cylinder.

Let O A (Fig. 388) be the position of the crank of the low-pressure cylinder

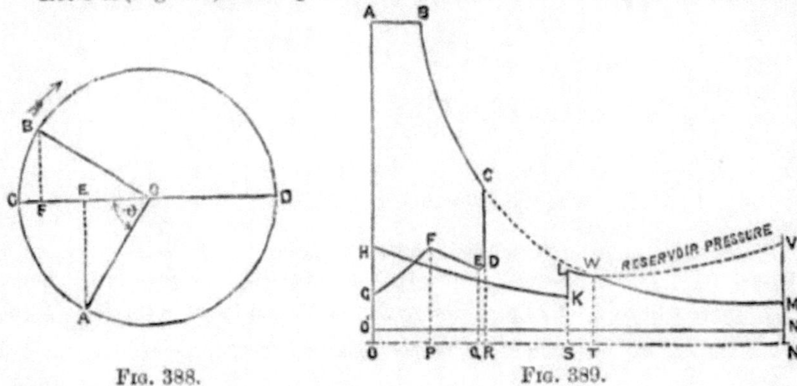

Fig. 388.   Fig. 389.

when the steam is cut off; O B the corresponding position of the crank of the high-pressure cylinder.

Then $\dfrac{D E}{D C} = \dfrac{1}{\rho}$ and $\dfrac{C F}{D C}$ = fraction of stroke performed by the high-pressure piston, when steam is cut off in the low-pressure cylinder $= \dfrac{1 - \sin\theta}{2}$

$$\frac{D E}{D C} = \frac{1}{\rho} = \frac{1 + \cos\theta}{2}$$

from which, $\cos\theta = \dfrac{2 - \rho}{\rho}$ and $\sin\theta = \sqrt{1 - \cos^2\theta} = \dfrac{2}{\rho}\sqrt{\rho - 1}$

$$\text{Therefore, } \frac{C F}{D C} = \frac{\rho - 2\sqrt{\rho - 1}}{2\rho}$$

In the following investigation we will denote this by m; consequently the fraction of the small cylinder that is occupied by the steam that acts on the low-pressure piston at the point of cut-off is $= (1 - m)$.

The following table gives some values of $(1 - m)$ for different values of ρ:—

$\rho =$	·5	·55	·6	·65	·7	·75	·8
$1 - m =$	1	·998	·990	·977	·958	·933	·9

In Fig. 389, O A represents the initial pressure of steam in the high-pressure cylinder. At B the steam is cut off and expands to C, the end of the stroke of the high-pressure piston, when the communication is opened to the reservoir and the pressure falls to R D. After this the steam expands in the reservoir and low-pressure cylinder until it is cut off in the latter. This part of the action of the steam is represented by the curve D E, Q E being the pressure at the point of cut-off. From this point the steam is compressed behind the high-pressure piston until it has completed half its return stroke, when its pressure is represented by P F. At this point the admission to the low-pressure cylinder commences, and the steam expands in the low-pressure cylinder until the end of the return stroke of the high-pressure cylinder, when its pressure is O G.

The low-pressure diagram is easily deduced from this. The initial pressure O H is, of course, equal to the back pressure P F at the middle of the return stroke of the high-pressure piston. The steam expands in the low-pressure cylinder until half-stroke, when its pressure, S K, is obviously equal to O G. At this point the high-pressure cylinder, containing steam at the pressure R C, opens to the reservoir, and the pressure rises to S L, S L being equal to R D. From L the steam expands in the reservoir and low-pressure cylinder to W, the point of cut-off, T W being equal to Q E. From W the steam in the cylinder expands to the final pressure N M, while that in the reservoir is compressed to V, N V being equal to the initial pressure in the low-pressure cylinder. At M the communication to the condenser is opened, and the pressure falls to N N',—the constant condenser pressure.

We will now give the algebraical expressions for the pressures at the different points, in order that the diagrams may be drawn in any given case. Since the total rate of expansion is R, the final pressure, N M, in the low-pressure cylinder is $= \dfrac{p_1}{R}$. The final pressure, R C, in the high-pressure cylinder is $= \dfrac{p_1}{r} = \dfrac{p_1 \lambda}{R}$.

The steam in the low-pressure cylinder is expanded ρ times : consequently at the point of cut-off, the pressure, T W, is $= \dfrac{p_1 \rho}{R}$. This is also the pressure, Q E, in the reservoir at the point of cut-off, and we have, therefore, steam at the pressure $\dfrac{p_1 \rho}{R}$ occupying a volume U $+ v (1 - m)$. This steam is compressed behind the high-pressure piston until the beginning of the next stroke of the low-pressure piston, when its volume has been reduced to U $+ \dfrac{v}{2}$, and its pressure has been increased to

$$\frac{p_1 \rho}{R} \cdot \frac{U + v (1 - m)}{U + \tfrac{1}{2} v} = \frac{p_1 \rho}{R} \cdot \frac{\phi + (1 - m)}{\phi + \tfrac{1}{2}}$$

which is the initial pressure O H ($= $ P F $= $ N V) in the low-pressure cylinder. This steam is driven before the high-pressure piston, and drives the low-pressure piston before it till half-stroke, when its volume is U $+ \tfrac{1}{2}$V, and the pressure S K is, therefore,

$$= \frac{p_1 \rho}{R} \cdot \frac{U + v (1 - m)}{U + \tfrac{1}{2} V} = \frac{p_1 \rho}{R} \cdot \frac{\phi + (1 - m)}{\phi + \tfrac{1}{2} \lambda}$$

But at this point the high-pressure cylinder, containing a volume v of steam at pressure $\dfrac{p_1 V}{R v}$, opens to the reservoir, and the pressure becomes

$$= \frac{\dfrac{p_1 \rho}{R} \left\{ U + v (1 - m) \right\} + v \dfrac{p_1 V}{R v}}{v + U + \tfrac{1}{2} V} = \frac{p_1}{R} \cdot \frac{\rho U + \rho v (1 - m) + V}{v + U + \tfrac{1}{2} V}$$

$$= \frac{p_1}{R} \cdot \frac{\rho \left\{ \phi + (1 - m) \right\} + \lambda}{1 + \phi + \tfrac{1}{2} \lambda} = \text{S L} = \text{R D}.$$

Thus all the points have been obtained, and the diagrams can be drawn.

Fig. 389 has been drawn for cylinders having a ratio of 4 to 1; the steam being cut off at half-stroke in the small cylinder, and at ·55 of the stroke in the large cylinder. The initial pressure O A = 70 lbs., and the condenser pressure N N′ = 3 lbs. per sq. inch. The volume of the reservoir has been taken equal to the volume of the small cylinder.

It will be seen that there is a considerable drop of pressure on the admission to the reservoir, with a corresponding increase in the reservoir pressure, which produces a sudden jump in the low-pressure diagram. In an actual case this jump would be lessened by the effect of the release before the end of the stroke, and of throttling in the passages between the cylinders, and it would appear more in the form of a curve convex to O N.

It will also be seen that a large portion of the work due to expansion is lost, and consequently that the engine is not economical so far as the *theoretical* action of the steam is concerned. This sudden fall of pressure without the performance of work would possibly have the effect of heating the steam somewhat, but there would still be a loss when there is a fall of pressure, as only a percentage of this heat can be converted into mechanical work. If the work due to expansion be fully realised, this drop will become zero and we shall have—

$$R\,C = R\,D.$$

$$\text{or } \frac{p_1\,V}{R\,v} = \frac{p_1}{R} \cdot \frac{\rho\left\{U + v\,(1-m)\right\} + V}{v + U + \tfrac{1}{2}V}$$

$$\text{or } \frac{V}{v} = \lambda = \frac{\rho\left\{U + v\,(1-m)\right\} + V}{v + U + \tfrac{1}{2}V}$$

$$\frac{\rho}{\lambda} = \frac{v + U + \tfrac{1}{2}V}{U + v\,(1-m) + \dfrac{V}{\rho}}$$

But $V = \lambda\,v$, and $U = \phi\,v$. Then, by substitution, we get

$$\frac{\rho}{\lambda} = \frac{1 + \phi + \tfrac{1}{2}\lambda}{(1-m) + \phi + \dfrac{\lambda}{\rho}}$$

$$\rho\left\{(1-m) + \phi\right\} + \lambda = \lambda + \lambda\,(\phi + \tfrac{1}{2}\lambda) \cdot$$

Solving for λ we get, $\lambda = -\phi \pm \sqrt{\left\{2\rho\,(1-m+\phi) + \phi\right\}}$

Of course the positive sign of the radical must be taken, as λ cannot be negative. From this equation, if ρ and ϕ be given, we can find the value of λ, that would prevent fall of pressure on the admission to the reservoir.

The following table gives a few values of λ, for different points of cut-off, that satisfy the foregoing conditions :—

$\dfrac{1}{\rho} =$	·5	·55	·6	·65	·7	·75	·8
$\rho =$	2	1·82	1·67	1·54	1·43	1·33	1·25
λ for $\phi = 1$	2	1·88	1·76	1·66	1·57	1·48	1·4
λ for $\phi = 2$	2	1·86	1·74	1·63	1·53	1·44	1·36
λ for $\phi = 3$	2	1·85	1·73	1·61	1·51	1·42	1·33

Two cylinder compound engines with cranks at right angles to each other, having an intermediate reservoir, the cut-off in the low-pressure cylinder being before half-stroke.—The action of the steam in this case is very similar to that in the last case, with the exception that when the high-pressure cylinder opens to the reservoir the communication with the low-pressure cylinder is closed, so that the increase of pressure takes place only in the reservoir, and tends to increase the initial pressure in the low-pressure cylinder. This is shown in Fig. 390, M being the point corresponding to the release from the high-pressure cylinder, and the steam is compressed to V, N V being the initial pressure in the low-pressure cylinder.

There will be a slightly different value for the quantity $1 - m$. In Fig. 391

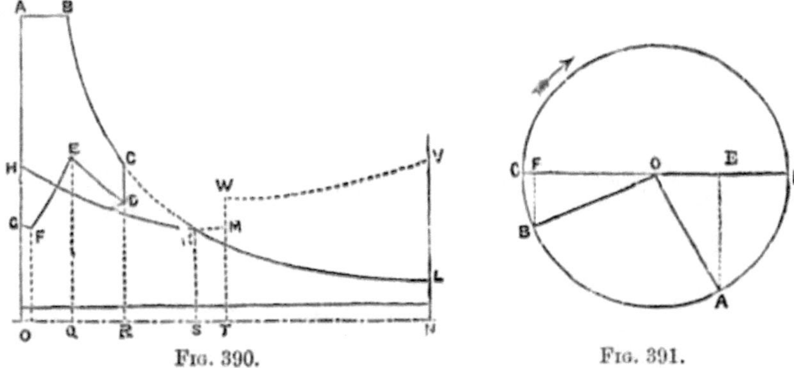

FIG. 390.

FIG. 391.

let O A be the position of the low-pressure crank at time of cut-off; and O B the position of the high-pressure crank.

$$\frac{D\,F}{D\,C} = m = \frac{1 + \sin\theta}{2}\,;\quad \frac{D\,E}{D\,C} = \frac{1 - \cos\theta}{2} = \frac{1}{\rho}$$

$$\therefore\ \cos\theta = \frac{\rho - 2}{\rho}\,;$$

$$\text{and } \sin\theta = \sqrt{1 - \cos^2\theta} = \frac{2}{\rho}\sqrt{\rho - 1}.$$

$$\therefore\ m = \frac{\rho + 2\sqrt{\rho - 1}}{2\rho} \text{ and } 1 - m = \frac{\rho - 2\sqrt{\rho - 1}}{2\rho}.$$

The following table gives the values of $1 - m$ for a few values of $\dfrac{1}{\rho}$.

$\dfrac{1}{\rho} =$	·2	·25	·3	·35	·4	·45
$1 - m =$	·01	0·067	0·043	0·023	0·008	0·003

The final pressure in each of the cylinders is the same as before, viz. in the low-pressure cylinder, $N\,L = \dfrac{p_1}{R}$, and in the high-pressure cylinder,

$R\,C = \dfrac{p_1}{R}\cdot\dfrac{V}{v} = \dfrac{p_1\lambda}{R}$. The pressure at cut-off, $S\,K = \dfrac{p_1\rho}{R}$.

At this instant the volume occupied by the steam is $U + v\,(1 - m)$.

At half-stroke the volume is reduced to U, and the pressure, T M, is therefore $= \dfrac{p_1\rho}{R}\cdot\dfrac{U + v\,(1 - m)}{U} = \dfrac{p_1\rho}{R}\cdot\dfrac{\phi + (1 - m)}{\phi}.$

At this instant the high-pressure cylinder containing a volume, v, of steam at the pressure $\dfrac{p_1}{R}\dfrac{V}{v}$ opens to the reservoir, and the pressure becomes

$$\frac{\dfrac{p_1 \rho}{R}\left\{ U + v(1-m) \right\} + v\dfrac{p_1}{R}\dfrac{V}{v}}{v + U}$$

$$= \frac{p_1}{R} \cdot \frac{\rho\, U + \rho v (1-m) + V}{v + U} = \frac{p_1}{R} \cdot \frac{\rho\left\{ \phi + (1-m) \right\} + \lambda}{1 + \phi} = T\,W = R\,D.$$

At the end of the stroke of the low-pressure piston this steam occupies the volume $U + \tfrac{1}{2} v$, and its pressure is therefore,

$$= \frac{p_1}{R} \cdot \frac{\rho\, U + \rho v (1-m) + V}{U + \tfrac{1}{2} v} = \frac{p_1}{R} \cdot \frac{\rho\left\{ \phi + (1-m) \right\} + \lambda}{\phi + \tfrac{1}{2}}$$

which is the initial pressure, $O\,H = N\,V$, in the low-pressure cylinder. F is the point in the return stroke of the high-pressure piston corresponding to the point of cut-off in the low-pressure cylinder. Consequently the pressure $P\,F = S\,K = \dfrac{p_1 \rho}{R}$. The pressure $O\,G$ is $= T\,M$. Thus all the points have been determined and the diagrams can be drawn in any given case.

Fig. 390 has been drawn for the same engine as Fig. 389, the total expansion was also the same, the only difference being that in this case the steam has been cut off at ·4 of the stroke in the low-pressure cylinder instead of ·55 as in the previous example.

There is in this case also a fall of pressure on the admission to the reservoir, with a corresponding increase in the pressure. The drop is, however, not so great nor so injurious, as it tends to increase the initial pressure of the steam in the low-pressure cylinder instead of the pressure at the middle of the stroke. All the work due to the expansion, however, is not realised, and there is still a considerable loss. If there were no drop we should have $R\,C = R\,D$,

$$\text{or } \frac{p_1}{R} \cdot \frac{V}{v} = \frac{p_1}{R} \cdot \frac{\rho\left\{ U + v(1-m) \right\} + V}{v + U}$$

Putting $V = \lambda v$, and $U = \phi v$, we get $\dfrac{\lambda}{\rho} = \dfrac{(1-m) + \phi + \dfrac{\lambda}{\rho}}{1 + \phi}$

$$\lambda (1 + \phi) = \rho\left\{ (1-m) + \phi \right\} + \lambda$$

$$\frac{\lambda}{\rho} = \frac{(1-m) + \phi}{\phi}.$$

From this we get the following table :—

$\dfrac{1}{\rho} =$	·2	·25	·3	·35	·4	·45
$\rho =$	5·0	4·0	3·33	2·86	2·50	2·222
λ for $\phi = 1$	5·5	4·27	3·48	2·92	2·52	2·228
$\phi = 2$	5·25	4·13	3·41	2·89	2·51	2·225
$\phi = 3$	5·17	4·09	3·38	2·88	2·507	2·224

The numerical values of the expressions for the pressures at the different points can be easily found in any given case, as the values of $(1 - m)$ are given in the tables.

On reference to the preceding table, it will be seen that with this type of engine, if the ratio of cylinders is more than two to one, the cut-off in the low-pressure cylinder should be arranged to take place before half-stroke, to prevent loss from sudden expansion, and consequently an expansion valve would be required on the low-pressure cylinder in order to enable the full benefit of the expansion of the steam to be realised.

Three cylinder compound engines with cranks at equal angles.—There are three cases :—

1. When both low-pressure cylinders are open to the reservoir at the time that the high-pressure cylinder exhausts into it ; that is, when the cut-off in each low-pressure cylinder is after 0·75 of the stroke.

2. When only one low-pressure cylinder is open to the reservoir when the high-pressure exhausts into it ; that is, when the cut-off in each low-pressure cylinder is between 0·25 and 0·75 of the stroke.

3. When neither of the low-pressure cylinders is open to the reservoir when the high-pressure cylinder exhausts into it ; that is, when the cut-off in each low-pressure cylinder is before 0·25 of the stroke.

(1) *Cut-off in the low-pressure cylinder after* 0·75 *of the stroke.*

By reference to Fig. 392, showing the positions of the several cranks, when the steam is exhausted from the high-pressure cylinder to the reservoir, it will be seen that if o p and o q represent the low-pressure cranks and o r the high-pressure crank, while one low-pressure cylinder gets steam at one-quarter stroke, the other does not get its supply until the piston has traversed three-fourths of its stroke, and is near the point at which cut-off takes place. The work done by the two low-pressure cylinders would in consequence be very unequal, so that this case would not occur in practice. In all three cylinder compound engines the cut-off in the low-pressure cylinders should be arranged to take place before 0·75 of the stroke.

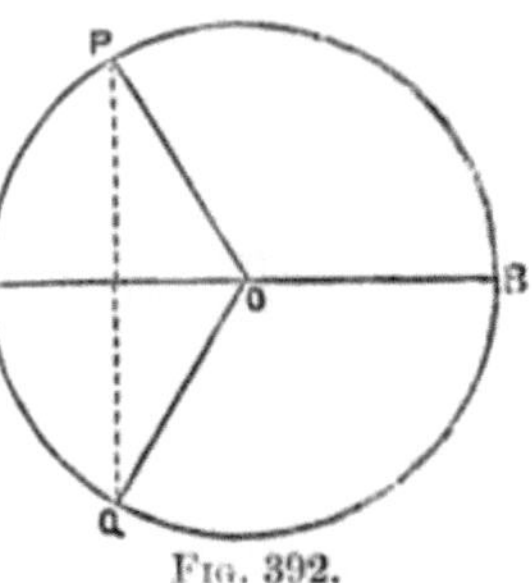

Fig. 392.

the low-pressure cylinders should be arranged to take place before 0·75 of the stroke.

(2) *Cut-off in the low-pressure cylinders between* 0·25 *and* 0·75 *of the stroke.*

This is the most general case that occurs in practice.

Let v = volume of the high-pressure cylinder.

V =   „   each low-   „

U =   „   the intermediate reservoir.

R = total ratio of expansion.

r = ratio of expansion in the high-pressure cylinder.

ρ =   „   „   each low-   „

λ = ratio of each low-pressure cylinder to the high-pressure cylinder.

ϕ = ratio of the intermediate reservoir to the high-pressure cylinder.

So that $V = \lambda v$; $U = \phi v$; and $R = 2 \lambda r$.

Also, for brevity, let the symbols α and β represent the low-pressure cylinders, and γ the high-pressure cylinder.

In the first place it will be necessary to investigate expressions for the distances of the high-pressure piston from the ends of the stroke when each of the low-pressure pistons are at the points of cut-off.

In Fig. 393 let O P, O Q represent the positions of the cranks of the low-pressure cylinders a and β respectively, and O R the position of the crank of the high-pressure cylinder γ at the point of cut off in a.

$$\text{Then} \quad \frac{AC}{AB} = \frac{1}{\rho} = \frac{1 - \cos \theta}{2}$$

$$\text{or} \quad \cos \theta = \frac{\rho - 2}{\rho}$$

$$\sin \theta = \sqrt{1 - \cos^2 \theta} = \frac{2}{\rho} \sqrt{\rho - 1}$$

At this point the distance of the high-pressure piston from the end of its stroke is represented by B D, so that the fraction of the high-pressure cylinder open to the reservoir is represented by

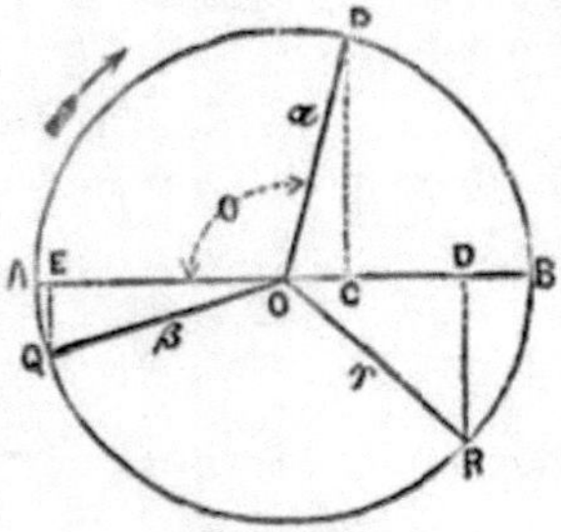

$$\frac{AD}{AB} = \frac{1 + \cos (\theta - 60^\circ)}{2}$$

$$= \frac{1 + \tfrac{1}{2} \cos \theta + \tfrac{1}{2} \sqrt{3} . \sin \theta}{2}$$

$$= \frac{3 \rho + 2 \sqrt{3 (\rho - 1)} - 2}{4 \rho} = l, \text{ say}$$

$$\frac{AE}{AB} = \frac{1 + \cos (\theta + 60^\circ)}{2}$$

Fig. 393.

$$= \frac{1 + \tfrac{1}{2} \cos \theta - \tfrac{1}{2} \sqrt{3} \sin \theta}{2} = \frac{3 \rho - 2 \sqrt{3 (\rho - 1)} - 2}{4 \rho}$$

Let this expression be denoted by m.

The following table gives values of l and m for different values of ρ :—

$\frac{1}{\rho} =$	0·25	0·30	0·35	0·40	0·45	0·50	0·55	0·60	0·65	0·70	0·75
$\rho =$	4·0	3·33	2·86	2·50	2·22	2·0	1·82	1·67	1·54	1·43	1·33
$l =$	1·0	·997	·988	·974	·955	·933	·906	·875	·838	·797	·748
$1 - l =$	0·0	·003	·012	·026	·045	·067	·094	·125	·162	·203	·252
$m =$	·250	·203	·162	·126	·094	·067	·044	·026	·010	·003	0·00

In investigating the nature of the diagram let us first assume that the cut-off and the final pressures in each of the low-pressure cylinders are the same.

In this case the final pressure in each of the low-pressure cylinders is $= \frac{p_1}{R}$; and the cut-off pressure in each low-pressure cylinder $= \frac{\rho p_1}{R}$.

Let the theoretical diagrams be represented by Figs. 394, 395, and 396 ; Fig. 396 being from the high-pressure cylinder γ and Figs. 394 and 395 from the low-pressure cylinders a and β respectively. Also let the pressures at the different points be denoted by the letter p, with the suffix corresponding to the number of the point on the diagrams.

First trace the action of the steam in the cylinder a.

The total volume occupied by the steam at the point of cut-off in a is

$$= U + \frac{V}{\rho} + lv$$

and the pressure at this point is $= \frac{\rho p_1}{R} = p_{12}$.

This is also $= p_{16}$ and $= p_{3}$.

At quarter-stroke of a, *just after* the high-pressure cylinder has exhausted into the reservoir, the volume occupied by the steam is

$$= U + v + \frac{V}{4}$$

and the pressure is therefore

$$= \frac{\rho\, p_1}{R} \cdot \frac{U + \dfrac{V}{\rho} + l\,v}{U + \dfrac{V}{4} + v}$$

$$= \frac{\rho\, p_1}{R} \cdot \frac{\phi + \dfrac{\lambda}{\rho} + l}{\phi + \dfrac{\lambda}{4} + 1} = p_4 = p_{11}.$$

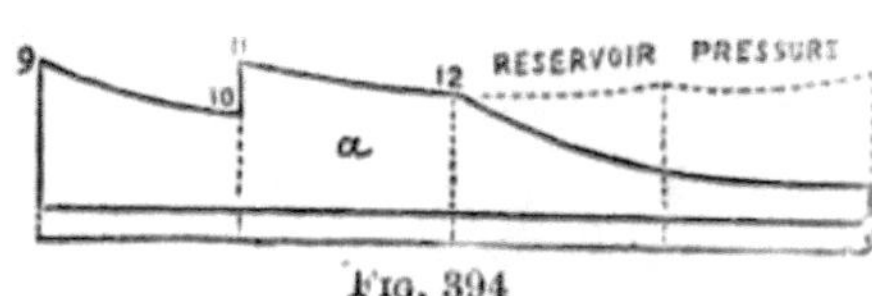

Fig. 394

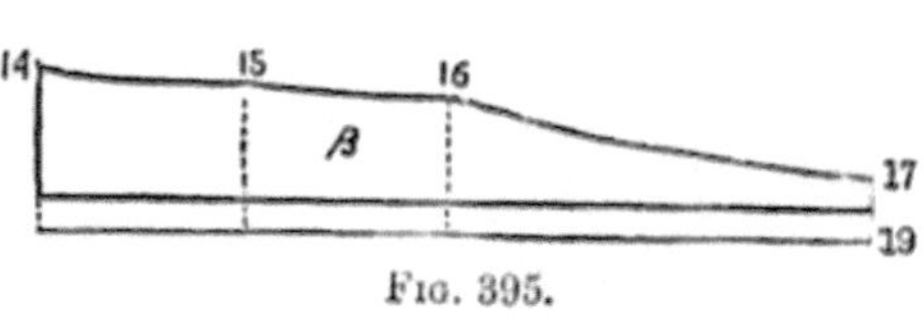

Fig. 395.

The volume occupied by the steam in the reservoir, &c., *immediately before* the high-pressure cylinder exhausts is $= U + \dfrac{V}{4}$; and its pressure is represented by p_{10}.

At this point a volume, v, of steam at a pressure $\dfrac{p_1}{r}$ is admitted to the reservoir from the high-pressure cylinder and the pressure rises to p_{11}, the steam then occupying the volume, $U + \dfrac{V}{4} + v$.

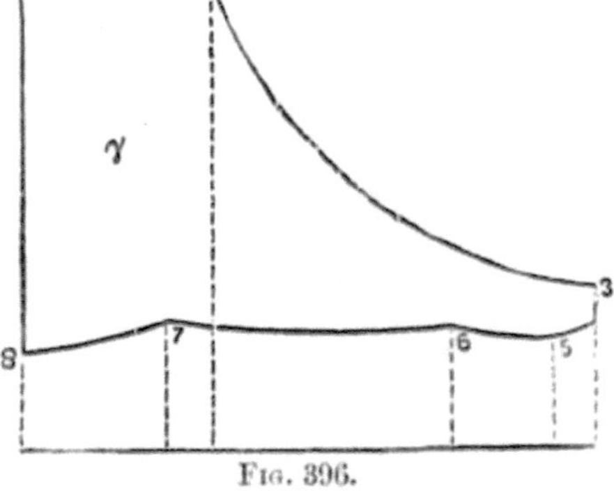

Fig. 396.

Therefore we have,

$$p_{10}\left(U + \frac{V}{4}\right) + \frac{p_1}{r}\,v = p_{11}\left(U + \frac{V}{4} + v\right) = \frac{\rho\, p_1}{R}\left(U + \frac{V}{\rho} + l\,v\right)$$

$$\text{or } p_{10} = \frac{\dfrac{\rho\, p_1}{R}\left(U + \dfrac{V}{\rho} + l\,v\right) - \dfrac{p_1}{r}\,v}{U + \dfrac{V}{4}}.$$

But $r = \dfrac{R}{2\lambda}$. Therefore $\dfrac{p_1}{r} = \dfrac{2\lambda\, p_1}{R}$

$$\text{and } p_{10} = \frac{p_1}{R} \cdot \frac{\rho\left(U + l\,v\right) + V - 2\lambda v}{U + \dfrac{V}{4}} = \frac{p_1}{R} \cdot \frac{\rho\left(\phi + l\right) - \lambda}{\phi + \dfrac{\lambda}{4}} = p_5 \text{, also.}$$

After the steam is cut off in a, the steam remaining in the reservoir is compressed behind the high-pressure piston, until the commencement of the stroke of β.

The volume of steam in the reservoir at cut-off of a is $= U + l\,v$.

At the commencement of the stroke of β this has been altered to $U + \dfrac{3}{4}v$;

and the pressure is therefore $= \dfrac{\rho\,p_1}{R} \cdot \dfrac{U + l\,v}{U + \dfrac{3}{4}\,v}$

$$= \frac{\rho\,p_1}{R} \cdot \frac{\phi + l}{\phi + \cdot75} = \text{initial in } \beta = p_{14} = \text{also } p_6.$$

This steam acts on the piston of β and is acted on by the high-pressure piston till quarter-stroke of β, when a is ready to commence its return stroke. The volume occupied by the steam at this point is $= U + \dfrac{1}{4}\left(V + v\right)$, and the

pressure is, therefore, $= \dfrac{\rho\,p_1}{R} \cdot \dfrac{U + l\,v}{U + \frac{1}{4}(V + v)}$

$= \dfrac{\rho\,p_1}{R} \cdot \dfrac{\phi + l}{\phi + \frac{1}{4}(\lambda + 1)} = \text{initial pressure in } a, = p_9 = p_{15} = p_7.$

Until the point of cut-off in β, this steam acts on the two low-pressure pistons, and is acted on by the high-pressure piston. At the point of cut-off in β, the volume occupied by the steam is

$$= U + \frac{V}{\rho} + (1 - l)\,V + m\,v$$

and the pressure is, therefore,

$$= \frac{\rho\,p_1}{R} \cdot \frac{U + l\,v}{U + \dfrac{V}{\rho} + \left(1 - l\right)V + m\,v} = \frac{\rho\,p_1}{R} \cdot \frac{\phi + l}{\phi + \lambda\left(\dfrac{1}{\rho} + 1 - l\right) + m}$$

$= p_{16}$, the pressure at the point of cut-off in β.

By the assumption previously made, viz. that the pressures at the points of cut-off in the cylinders a and β are to be the same, this must be equal to $\dfrac{\rho\,p_1}{R}$.

$$\text{Therefore, } \frac{\phi + l}{\phi + \lambda\left(\dfrac{1}{\rho} + 1 - l\right) + m} \text{ must be} = 1$$

$$\text{or } \phi + \lambda\left(\frac{1}{\rho} + 1 - l\right) + m = \phi + l \ \therefore \ \lambda = \frac{l - m}{\dfrac{1}{\rho} + 1 - l}.$$

From this we see that only when a certain relation exists between the ratios of cylinders and the point of cut-off in the low-pressure cylinders, can the final pressures and rates of expansion be the same in each of the low-pressure cylinders.

From the foregoing equation the necessary ratios of cylinders for certain points of cut-off, in order to make the final pressures in the low-pressure cylinders the same, can be readily found, and a few values are given below :—

$\dfrac{1}{\rho} =$	0·25	0·30	0·35	0·40	0·45	0·50	0·55	0·60	0·65	0·70	0·75
$l =$	4·0	3·33	2·86	2·50	2·22	2·0	1·82	1·67	1·54	1·43	1·33
$\lambda =$	3·0	2·62	2·28	1·99	1·75	1·52	1·34	1·17	1·02	0·88	0·75

From this table it appears that in the majority of cases in general practice, the expansion and cut-off will not be exactly the same in the two low-pressure cylinders. In general, if the steam is cut off at the same part of the stroke in each of the two low-pressure cylinders, the final pressures will be different; or if the final pressures be the same the points of cut-off will be different.

First assume the final pressures the same in each of the low-pressure cylinders, but the cut-offs different.

Let ρ represent the ratio of expansion in a.

    ,, ρ_1 ,,   ,, β.

The same method of reasoning must be applied as in the previous case, and it will be found that the only pressure that is altered is p_{16}.

This becomes

$$p_{16} = \frac{\rho\, p_1}{R} \cdot \frac{\phi + l}{\phi + \lambda \left(\dfrac{1}{\rho_1} + 1 - l_1 \right) + m_1}$$

where l_1 and m_1 are the values of l and m corresponding to the ratio of expansion ρ_1.

The final pressure in β, p_{17}, is, therefore,

$$= \frac{\rho}{\rho_1} \cdot \frac{p_1}{R} \cdot \frac{\phi + l}{\phi + \lambda \left(\dfrac{1}{\rho_1} + 1 - l_1 \right) + m_1}$$

But by supposition this is equal to the final pressure in a,

$$\text{or } \frac{p_1}{R} = \frac{\rho}{\rho_1} \cdot \frac{p_1}{R} \cdot \frac{\phi + l}{\phi + \lambda \left(\dfrac{1}{\rho_1} + 1 - l_1 \right) + m_1}$$

$$\text{or } \frac{\rho}{\rho_1} = \frac{\phi + \lambda \left(\dfrac{1}{\rho_1} + 1 - l_1 \right) + m_1}{\phi + l}$$

$$\rho\,(\phi + l) = \rho_1 \left\{ \phi + \lambda\,(1 - l_1) + m_1 \right\} + \lambda$$

$$\text{or } \rho_1 = \frac{\rho\,(\phi + l) - \lambda}{\lambda\,(1 - l_1) + \phi + m_1}.$$

As ρ and ρ_1 are not very different, it will be sufficiently accurate for practical purposes to take l_1 and m_1, the same as l and m. In this case the value of ρ_1 for any given value of ρ can be obtained.

Secondly.—Assume that the cut-off is the same in each of the low-pressure cylinders, so that, generally, the final pressures would be different.

Let p_a represent the final pressure in a.

    ,, p_β ,,   ,, β.

We shall be sufficiently accurate if we assume that $\dfrac{p_1}{R}$, which is the pressure due to the total expansion, is a mean between p_a and p_β.

$$\text{or, } \tfrac{1}{2}\left(p_a + p_\beta \right) = \frac{p_1}{R}$$

The expressions for the pressures at each of the points will be exactly similar to those previously given, with the exception that p_a must be substituted for $\dfrac{p_1}{R}$.

The expression for the pressure at the point of cut-off in β is

$$p_{16} = \rho\, p_a \cdot \frac{\phi + l}{\phi + \lambda \left(\dfrac{1}{\rho} + 1 - l \right) + m} = \rho\, p_\beta \text{ by hypothesis.}$$

$$\text{Therefore } \frac{p_a}{p_\beta} = \frac{\phi + \lambda \left(\dfrac{1}{\rho} + 1 - l \right) + m}{\phi + l}$$

From this equation the ratios of the final pressures in the two low-pressure cylinders to each other can be found ; and then from the equation,

$$\tfrac{1}{2}\left(p_a + p_3\right) = \frac{p_1}{R}$$

the actual final pressures may be obtained.

(3) *Cut-off in low-pressure cylinders before quarter-stroke.*

In this case the receiver is never in communication with more than one low-pressure cylinder at the same time.

This case would seldom occur in practice except possibly when the engines were being worked at reduced power. In engines in which the combined volume of the low-pressure cylinders is more than four times that of the high-pressure cylinder, loss from sudden expansion on admission to the receiver can only be avoided by cutting off the admission to the low-pressure cylinders before quarter-stroke, but practical considerations do not admit of this being done, so that the case is of little practical interest, and is not dealt with further. It will be a useful exercise, however, for the student to go through the investigation and ascertain the form of the diagrams.

Triple-expansion engines with cranks at 120°, and cut-off in cylinders between 0·25 and 0·75 of stroke.

(*a*) First *with LP crank leading* :—

Let v_1, v_2, and v_3 be the volumes of HP, MP, and LP cylinders.

w_1 and w_2 = volumes of 1st and 2nd reservoirs

r_1, r_2, and r_3 = ratios of expansion in HP, MP, and LP cyls.

$$\lambda_1 = \frac{\text{MP cyl.}}{\text{HP cyl.}} \quad \text{and} \quad \lambda_2 = \frac{\text{LP cyl.}}{\text{HP cyl.}}$$

R = total ratio of expansion.

Then $R = \dfrac{v_3}{v_1} r_1 = \lambda_2 r_1$; $v_2 = \lambda_1 v_1$; and $v_3 = \lambda_2 v_1$.

Let $w_1 = \phi_1 v_1$ and $w_2 = \phi_2 v_2$

Let O P (Fig. 397) be the position of MP crank at cut-off in the MP cylinder,

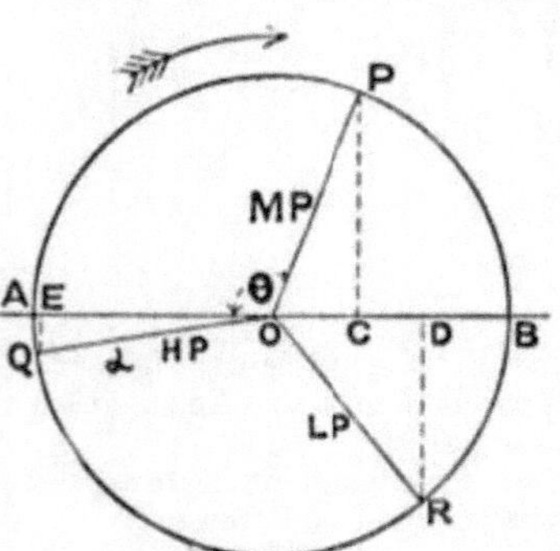

Fig. 397.

then

$$\frac{AC}{AB} = \frac{1}{r_2} = \frac{1 - \cos\theta}{2}$$

therefore $\cos\theta = \dfrac{r_2 - 2}{r_2}$

and $\sin\theta = \sqrt{1 - \cos^2\theta} = \dfrac{2}{r_2}\sqrt{r_2 - 1}$

The distance of the HP piston from the end of the stroke is $= AE$, so the total volume of steam is $w_1 + \dfrac{AE}{AB}$ (HP cyl.) $+ \dfrac{AC}{AB}$ (MP cyl.)

$$\frac{AE}{AB} = \frac{1 + \cos(\theta + 60°)}{2} = \frac{-\tfrac{1}{2}\sqrt{3}\sin\theta + \tfrac{1}{2}\cos\theta + 1}{2} = \frac{3r_2 - 2\sqrt{3(r_2 - 1)} - 2}{4r_2} = m$$

say.

Table for values of m will be found on p. 468. We can now determine the various cut-off and terminal pressures in the three cylinders.

Thus, if p_1 be initial pressure in HP cyl.

Cut-off pressure in HP cyl. $= p_1$

Terminal „ „ HP „ $= \dfrac{p_1}{r_1}$

$$\text{Cut-off pressure in MP cyl.} = \frac{r_2 p_1}{\lambda_1 r_1}$$

$$\text{Terminal } \quad \text{,, } \quad \text{MP } \text{,, } = \frac{p_1 v_1}{r_1 v_2} = \frac{p_1}{\lambda_1 r_1}$$

$$\text{Cut-off } \quad \text{,, } \quad \text{LP } \text{,, } = \frac{r_3 p_1}{\lambda_2 r_1}$$

$$\text{Terminal } \quad \text{,, } \quad \text{LP } \text{,, } = \frac{p_1}{\lambda_2 r_1}$$

Let the theoretical diagram be as shown in fig. 398.

First trace the action of the steam in the MP cylinder and exhaust from the HP cylinder.

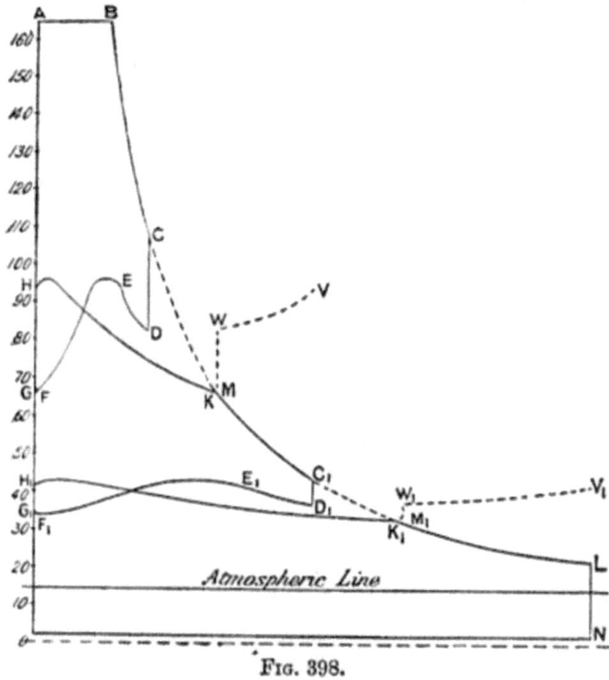

Fig. 398.

The total volume occupied by the steam at the point of cut-off in the MP cylinder is $w_1 + \dfrac{v_2}{r_2} + mv_1$, and the pressure is $\dfrac{r_2 p_1}{r_1 \lambda_1}$.

This is $p_K = p_F$.

At 0·75 stroke of the MP cylinder, just after the HP cylinder has exhausted into the reservoir, the volume occupied by the same steam is $w_1 + v_1$ and for the pressure p_D we have $p_D (w_1 + v_1) = p_K (m v_1 + w_1) + p_C \times v_1$

$$p_D = \frac{\dfrac{r_2 p_1}{r_1 \lambda_1} \left(m v_1 + w_1 + \dfrac{\lambda_1}{r_2} v_1 \right)}{w_1 + v_1} = p_W$$

This steam is now compressed by HP piston until at E the MP opens to steam. The pressure at E, p_E is given by

$$p_E (\cdot 75 \, v_1 + w_1) = p_D (v_1 + w_1)$$

$$p_E = p_D \frac{v_1 + w_1}{\cdot 75 \, v_1 + w_1}$$

As the MP piston moves slowly while the HP piston moves quickly the compression still goes on until $\lambda_1 \times$ (velocity of MP piston) = velocity of HP piston (i.e. until the volume of steam contained in the receiver and between the two pistons begins to increase).

Then expansion takes place, as the MP piston sweeps out a greater volume than the HP, until at F the steam is cut off in MP cylinder. We then have just before cut-off in MP cylinder, volume $_F = \left(\dfrac{v_2}{r_2} + w_1 + m\,v_1\right)$ and $p_F = $ cut-off pressure in MP.

For the remainder of the HP stroke the steam is compressed by the HP piston until just before admission, when we have

$$p_G\,w_1 = p_F\,(m\,v_1 + w_1) \therefore p_G = p_F\,\frac{(m\,v_1 + w_1)}{w_1}$$

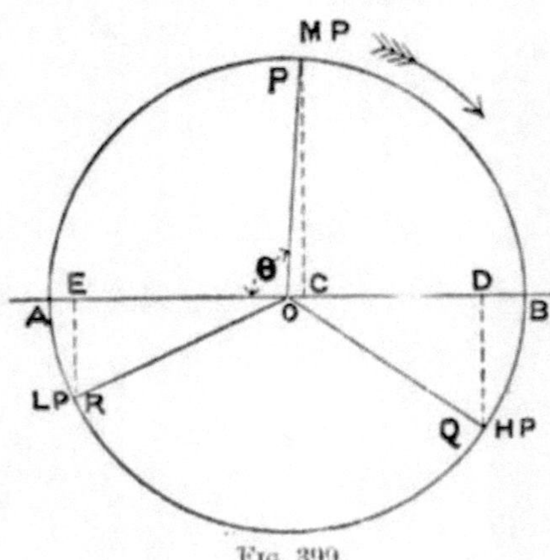

FIG. 399.

We have now all the points on the exhaust line of HP diagram and on the steam and reservoir pressure line of MP diagram.

The LP steam line and MP exhaust is obtained in exactly the same way.

Fig. 398 shows the diagrams obtained by these means with cut-off in each cylinder at 0·65 of stroke, the cylinder ratios being as $1 : 2\frac{1}{2} : 5$, the volumes of the receivers each being equal to $1\frac{1}{2}$ time the volume of the preceding cylinder and the initial pressure 165 lbs. absolute.

(b) Next consider the same engine but *with HP crank leading*.

Suppose in Fig. 399 the MP to be on the point of cut-off, then

$$\frac{A\,C}{A\,B} = \frac{1}{r_2} = \frac{1 - \cos\theta}{2} \therefore \cos\theta = \frac{r_2 - 2}{r_2}$$

$$\text{and } \frac{A\,D}{A\,B} = \frac{1 + \cos\theta}{2}\,60° = \frac{1 + \frac{1}{2}\cos\theta + \frac{1}{2}\sqrt{3}\,.\,\sin\theta}{2}$$

$$= \frac{3\,r_2 + 2\sqrt{3}\,(r_2 - 1) - 2}{4\,r_2} = l\ \text{say}.$$

Then the cut-off and terminal pressures for the different points can be obtained as before with the LP crank leading, the final volumes in each case being the same.

First consider the exhaust line of the HP diagram and the MP steam-line (Fig. 400).

At cut-off in MP diagram the volume is $\dfrac{v_2}{r_2} + l\,v_1 + w_1$, and pressure at cut-off $= p_M = \dfrac{r_2\,p_1}{\lambda_1\,r_1} = p_E$, E being where the HP piston has travelled $A\,B - A\,D$ on the return stroke, or $(1 - l)$ stroke.

This steam is now compressed by the HP piston until the MP again opens to steam.

We then have at F (just before the MP opens to steam)

$$p_F\,(·25\,v_1 + w_1) = p_E\,(w_1 + l\,v_1)$$

$$\therefore p_F = \frac{w_1 + l\,v_1}{·25\,v_1 + w_1}\,p_E.$$

The pressure will still rise due to compression by the HP cylinder until the increase of volume due to steam admitted to MP cylinder becomes equal to the decrease due to the motion of the HP piston or until

$$\frac{v_2}{v_1} \times \text{velocity of MP piston} = \text{velocity of HP piston, or}$$

$$\lambda_1 \times \text{velocity of MP piston} = \text{velocity of HP piston.}$$

At end of HP stroke just before exhaust the volume of steam is

$$\cdot 25 \, v_2 + w_1 \text{ and its pressure} = p_G$$

$$\therefore p_G \,(\cdot 25 \, v_2 + w_1) = p_E \,(w_1 + l \, v_1) \text{ and } p_G = \frac{w_1 + l \, v_1}{\cdot 25 \, v_2 + w_1} \, p_E.$$

To find the pressure directly after exhaust by the HP cylinder we have

$$p_C \, v_1 + p_G \,(\cdot 25 \, v_2 + w_1) = p_D \,(v_1 + \cdot 25 \, v_2 + w_1)$$

or

$$p_D = \frac{p_C \, v_1 + p_G \,(\cdot 25 \, v_2 + w_1)}{v_1 + \cdot 25 \, v_2 + w_1}.$$

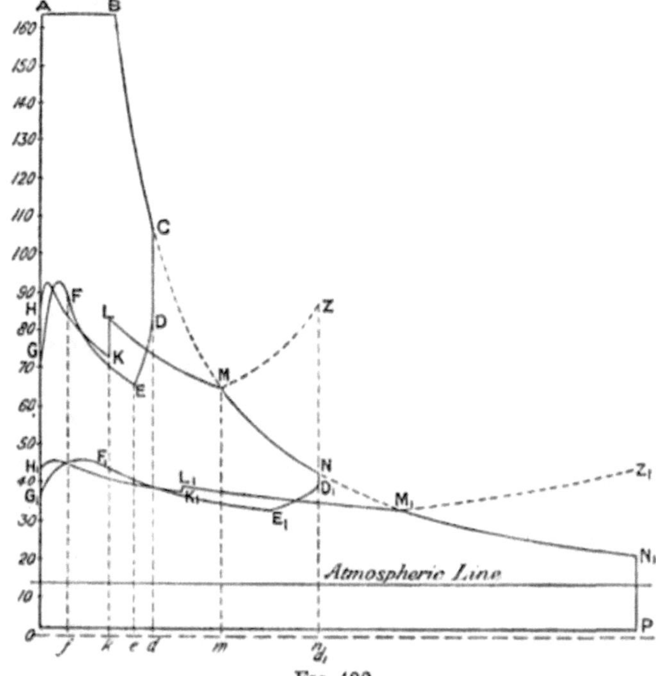

Fig. 400.

The initial pressure in MP cylinder p_H is $= p_F$.

All the pressures have now been found for exhaust line of HP, and this gives the pressures on the steam line of MP diagram and reservoir pressure.

After cut-off in MP cylinder the steam is compressed and not in contact with MP piston until $p_Z = p_H$.

The positions of the points E, L, K, &c., must now be determined. Thus, considering points D and E, $d\,e$ is the distance moved through by the HP piston while the MP moves from angle of 60° with line of centres to the point of cut-off, or if θ_c is the angle of cut-off $\left(\dfrac{1 - \cos (\theta_c - 60)}{2}\right)$ = fraction of stroke moved through by HP piston

$$= \frac{BD}{AB} \times \text{stroke} = (1 - l) \text{ stroke}$$

Again, ef is the distance moved through by the HP piston while the MP moves from cut-off to release
$= (\cdot 75 - 1 + l)$ stroke $= (l - \cdot 25)$ stroke. Also from F to G $= \cdot 25$ stroke.

Considering the steam line of MP diagram, the MP piston moves through 60° while pressure alters from p_H to p_K, therefore $ok = \cdot 25$ stroke.

Hence for the part from L to M, $km = \left(\dfrac{1}{r_2} - \cdot 25\right)$ stroke

and for the expansion line M N, $mn = \left(1 - \dfrac{1}{r_2}\right)$ stroke.

The exhaust line of the MP and steam line of the LP are obtained in exactly the same way, the only difference being alterations in r_1, r_2, w_1, &c., to the corresponding value r_2, r_3, w_2, &c.

Fig. 400 shows the diagram calculated for the same engine and proportions of cut-off, &c., as in the previous case.

Four cylinder triple-expansion engine with two LP cranks at right angles (i.e. engine with four cranks at right angles) and cut-off after half-stroke in each cylinder.—This, as regards cut-off, is the general case in practice.

Let P_1 = initial pressure in HP cylinder.

v_1, v_2, and v_3 the volumes of HP, MP, and one LP cylinder.

w_1 and w_2 the volumes of the two reservoirs.

r_1, r_2, and r_3, ratios of expansion in the three cylinders.

$$\lambda_1 = \frac{\text{MP cylinder}}{\text{HP cylinder}} = \frac{v_2}{v_1}.$$

$$\lambda_2 = \frac{\text{one LP cylinder}}{\text{MP cylinder}} = \frac{v_3}{v_2}.$$

ϕ_1 and ϕ_2 = ratios of reservoirs to HP cylinder and MP cylinder.

or $w_1 = \phi_1 v_1$, and $w_2 = \phi_2 v_2$.

R = total ratio of expansion.

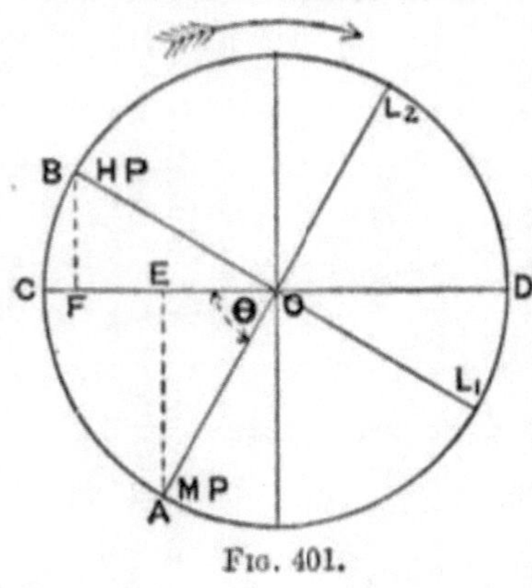

Fig. 401.

In the first place it will be well to notice that only two consecutive cylinders are considered at the same time (in the case of LP steam lines we consider the MP and both LP). Thus first consider the exhaust line of the HP diagram and steam line of the MP diagram.

To find an expression for the distance of the HP piston from the end of the stroke when steam is cut-off in the MP cylinder, let O A be the position of the crank of the MP cylinder at cut-off; O B the corresponding position of HP crank (Fig. 401). Then $\dfrac{DE}{DC} = \dfrac{1}{r_2}$ and $\dfrac{CF}{DC}$ = fraction of stroke

performed by the HP piston when steam is cut off in MP piston $= \dfrac{1 - \sin\theta}{2}$;

$$\frac{DE}{DC} = \frac{1}{r_2} = \frac{1 + \cos\theta}{2} \quad \therefore \cos\theta = \frac{2 - r_2}{r_2}$$

and $\sin\theta = \sqrt{1 - \cos^2\theta} = \dfrac{2}{r_2}\sqrt{r_2 - 1}$

$$\therefore \frac{CF}{DC} = \frac{r_2 - 2\sqrt{r_2 - 1}}{2r_2} = m \text{ say.}$$

Hence the amount of the HP cylinder which is filled with steam at the same pressure as the reservoir and MP cylinder at the point of cut-off, is equal to $(1 - m)$.

Table of values of $1 - m$ will be found on p. 462.

In Fig. 402 O A represents the initial pressure of steam in the HP cylinder. At B steam is cut off and expands to C at end of stroke of HP piston and then communication is opened to the reservoir and the pressure falls to the point D where pressure $= p_D$. After this the steam expands in the reservoir and MP cylinder until it is cut off in the latter. This part of the action of the steam is represented by the curve D E ; p_E being the pressure when this cut-

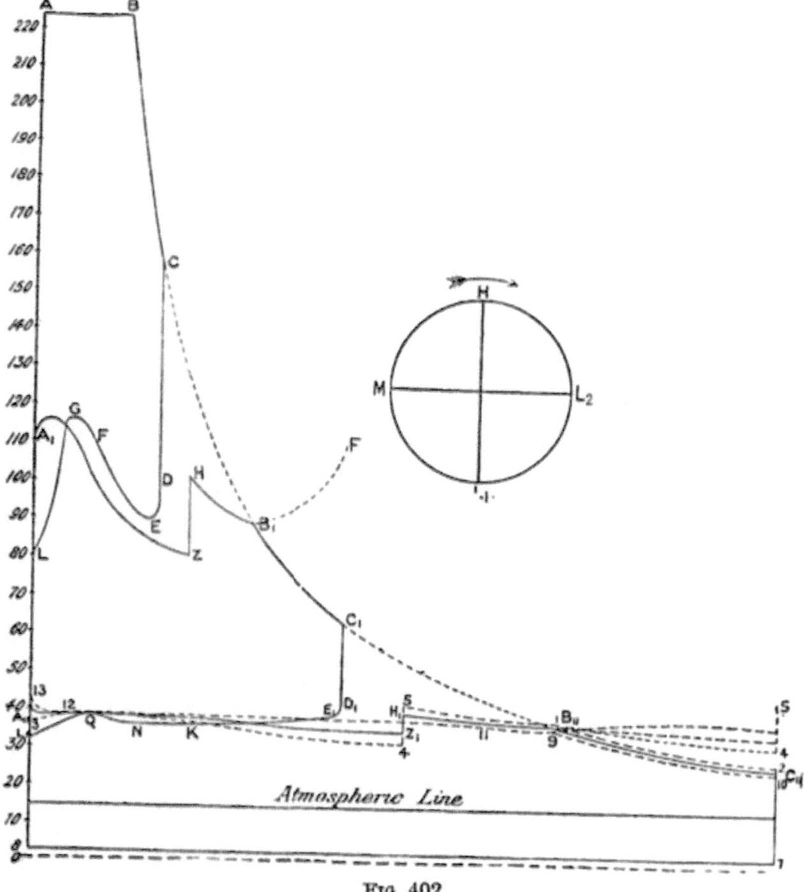

FIG. 402.

off takes place. From this point the steam is compressed behind the HP piston until it has completed its half-stroke at F and pressure $= p_F$ when the MP opens to steam. The MP piston, however, though larger than the HP piston, moves much slower than the HP, and hence the total volume of the steam between the two pistons decreases in volume and, therefore, increases in pressure until the volume becomes a minimum. This is evidently when the rate of increase of volume due to motion of MP piston is equal to the decrease of volume due to motion of HP piston. After this the steam expands and pressure falls to the point L when the pressure is p_L.

The steam line of the MP diagram is deduced from this back-pressure line of HP cylinder. The initial pressure $= p_{A1}$ is, of course, equal to the pressure at the middle of the back-pressure line of the HP cylinder, i.e. $= p_F$. The pressure now follows the back-pressure line of the HP, rising to a maximum $= p_G$ and then falling to a pressure equal to p_L at half-stroke. The HP now exhausts into the reservoir and the pressure rises to H, where $p_H = p_D$, and then again falls to B_1, due to expansion, the point of cut-off in the MP cylinder, p_{B1} being equal to p_E. From B_1 the steam expands to C_1 in the MP cylinder, while the reservoir pressure rises to F due to compression by the HP piston, p_F of course being the initial pressure of the MP cylinder $= P_{A1}$.

Now consider the MP exhaust line and the steam lines of the two low-pressure cylinders. For convenience in obtaining the mean diagram, the two low-pressure diagrams are drawn to twice the volume scale of the MP and the HP diagrams, but to the same pressure scale.

When the MP cylinder opens to exhaust the pressure falls to D_1, where the pressure is $= p_{D1}$. After this the steam expands to E_1, where one LP cuts off, as till then both the LP cylinders are open to steam. The two LP cylinders may be called L_1P and L_2P for shortness. Then after E_1 the reservoir pressure still falls, as L_2P is open to steam, to K when L_1P cylinder opens to steam, and the pressure falls more rapidly to N when the pressure is the same as at cut-off in the L_2P cylinder. The steam in the reservoir is now compressed by the MP piston, and expanded behind the L_1P piston, and hence as the MP piston is moving quicker than the L_1P, the pressure rises to a maximum at Q, and then falls to L_1 owing to expansion in L_1P cylinder. The steam line of the two LP diagrams are obtained from this MP exhaust line.

Thus the initial pressure of L_2P diagram at 13 is equal to p_{D1}, and falls to cut-off point 9 in the same way that the pressure falls from D_1 to K. The steam in L_2P cylinder then expands to 10, and opens to exhaust the pressure falling to the constant back-pressure line 7.8.

The initial pressure of the L_1P diagram is at $3 = p_3$, and is equal to the pressure at half-stroke in the exhaust of the MP diagram, and steam line of L_2P diagram. Almost directly after L_1P opens to steam L_1P cylinder cuts off and then the pressure rises in the same way as from N to Q, and then falls to 4 at half-stroke. The MP now opens to exhaust into the reservoir, and the pressure rises to $5 = p_{D1}$ and then again falls to 1, where steam is cut off, and expands in the cylinder, and then exhausts to the condenser.

The reservoir pressures are also shown. We can now obtain algebraical expressions for the pressures at the different points in order that diagrams may be drawn in any given case.

Since the ratio of expansion in HP cylinder is $= r_1$, the final pressure in HP cylinder $= p_C = \dfrac{P_1}{r_1}$, and final pressure in MP cylinder is $= \dfrac{P_1}{r_1 \lambda_1}$, therefore the cut-off pressure in the MP cylinder is $= \dfrac{P_1 r_2}{r_1 \lambda_1}$. This is also equal to the pressure in the reservoir at E, and we have therefore steam at the pressure $\dfrac{P_1 r_2}{\lambda_1 r_1}$ occupying a volume $w_1 + v_1 (1 - m)$. This steam is compressed behind the HP piston until the beginning of the next stroke of the MP piston, when its volume has been reduced to $w_1 + \dfrac{v_1}{2}$, and its pressure increased to

$$p_F = \frac{\dfrac{P_1 r_2}{\lambda_1 r_1}\left(w_1 + v_1(1-m)\right)}{w_1 + \dfrac{v_1}{2}} = \frac{P_1 r_2}{\lambda_1 r_1}\left(\frac{\phi_1 + 1 - m}{\phi_1 + \frac{1}{2}}\right)$$

which is the initial pressure of MP diagram $= p_{A1}$. The steam is now **driven** by HP piston and drives the MP piston, but as the HP moves much faster than the MP the pressure is increased until the volume begins to decrease. This it will do when the $\dfrac{\text{vel. of MP piston}}{\text{vel. of HP piston}} = \dfrac{\text{HP piston area}}{\text{MP piston area}}$, or if $a =$ angle that the MP crank makes with the line of centres ; when $\lambda_1 \times v_o \sin a = v_o \cos a$, or when $\cot a = \lambda_1$.

The volume now occupied by the steam is $\frac{1}{2} v_2$ vers $a + \frac{1}{2} v_1$ vers $(90 - a) + w_1$

and its pressure is given by

$$p_\text{G} = \frac{\dfrac{\mathrm{P}_1 r_2}{\lambda_1 r_1}(\phi_1 v_1 + \overline{1 - m}\, v_1)}{\frac{1}{2} v_2 \text{ vers } a + \frac{1}{2} v_1 \text{ vers } (90 - a) + w_1}$$

After this the steam expands until its volume is $w_1 + \dfrac{v_2}{2}$

$\therefore$ pressure at L $=$ pressure at Z $= p_\text{L}$.

$$= \frac{p_\text{F}\left(w_1 + \dfrac{v_1}{2}\right)}{w_1 + \dfrac{v_2}{2}} = \frac{\mathrm{P}_1 r_2}{\lambda_1 r_1}\cdot\frac{(\phi_1 + 1 - m)}{\left(\phi_1 + \dfrac{\lambda_1}{2}\right)}$$

At this point the HP cylinder opens to exhaust, and we have an HP cylinder full of steam at pressure $= p_\text{C}$ admitted to the reservoir, and the final pressure p_D is given by

$$p_\text{D} = \frac{\dfrac{\mathrm{P}_1 r_2}{\lambda_1 r_1}\Big\{ w_1 + v_1(1 - m) \Big\} + v_1 \dfrac{\mathrm{P}_1}{r_1}}{v_1 + w_1 + \dfrac{v_2}{2}}$$

$$= \frac{\dfrac{\mathrm{P}_1 r_2}{\lambda_1 r_1}\Big\{ \phi_1 + 1 - m \Big\} + \dfrac{\mathrm{P}_1}{r_1}}{\left(1 + \dfrac{\lambda_1}{2} + \phi_1\right)} = \frac{\mathrm{P}_1}{\lambda_1 r_1}\cdot\frac{r_2(\phi_1 + 1 - m) + \lambda_1}{1 + \dfrac{\lambda_1}{2} + \phi_1}$$

Thus all points for the first reservoir are determined.

The calculations for the other diagrams are similar to the above, remembering that now there are two steam lines of the two LP engines and one back-pressure line of MP diagram to be considered in conjunction.

We now want an expression for $\dfrac{\mathrm{N\,D}}{\mathrm{C\,D}} = \dfrac{\mathrm{C\,K}}{\mathrm{C\,D}}$ when $\mathrm{L}_1\mathrm{P}$ is at point of cut-off (Fig. 403), and this is evidently the same expression as found before for the MP cut-off $= l$ say.

$$\therefore l = \frac{r_3 - 2\sqrt{r_3 - 1}}{2 r_3} \text{ and } \frac{\mathrm{D\,K}}{\mathrm{D\,C}} = 1 - l.$$

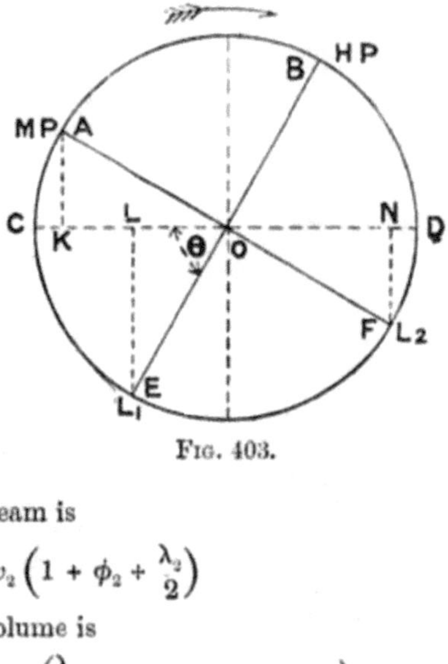

Let p_{D_1} be the pressure at D_1 in the second reservoir directly after exhaust from the MP cylinder, the volume of steam is

$$= v_2 + w_2 + \frac{v_3}{2} = v_2\left(1 + \phi_2 + \frac{\lambda_2}{2}\right)$$

This expands till cut-off in $\mathrm{L}_1\mathrm{P}$ when volume is

$$= \frac{v_3}{r_3} + l\, v_3 + (1 - l)\, v_2 + w_2 = v_2\left(\frac{\lambda_2}{r_3} + l\lambda_2 + (1 - l) + \phi_2\right)$$

Fig. 403.

And when L_1P is just opening to steam the volume of steam is

$$= \left(\frac{v_2}{2} + \frac{v_3}{2} + w_2\right) = v_2\left(\tfrac{1}{2} + \frac{\lambda_2}{2} + \phi_2\right)$$

Hence the pressure at cut-off in L_1P

$$= p_{D_1} \times \frac{1 + \phi_2 + \dfrac{\lambda_2}{2}}{\dfrac{\lambda_2}{r_3} + l\lambda_2 + 1 - l + \phi_2} = P \text{ say.}$$

The volume $\dfrac{v_3}{r_3}$ is now cut off from the reservoir in the cylinder L_1P, and we get the initial pressure in L_1P

$$= \frac{p_{D_1} \times \left(1 + \phi_2 + \dfrac{\lambda_2}{2}\right)v_2 - P \times \dfrac{v_3}{r_3}}{v_2\left(\tfrac{1}{2} + \dfrac{\lambda_2}{2} + \phi_2\right)} = P_3 \text{ say.}$$

At cut-off in L_2P we have this same steam in a volume

$$= lv_3 + \frac{v_3}{r_3} + w_2 + \left(1 - \frac{1}{r_3}\right)v_2.$$

Hence cut-off pressure in L_2P is given by

$$P_3 \times \frac{v_2\left(\tfrac{1}{2} + \dfrac{\lambda_2}{2} + \phi_2\right)}{lv_3 + \dfrac{v_3}{r_3} + w_2 + \left(1 - \dfrac{1}{r_3}\right)v_2} = P_2 \text{ say,}$$

and $\dfrac{P}{r_3}$ = terminal pressure of L_1, also $\dfrac{P_2}{r_3}$ = terminal pressure of L_2.

We can now obtain the cut-off pressures in L_1P and L_2P in terms of the one unknown quantity, p_{D_1}.

The weight of steam entering and leaving the engine is the same in one revolution. And this weight of steam is proportional to $p\,v$.

Let $K\,p\,v$ = the weight per revolution,

$$\therefore K\left(P\frac{v_3}{r_3} + P_2\frac{v_3}{r_3}\right) = \text{weight passed to condenser,}$$

and $K P_1\dfrac{v_1}{r_1}$ = weight entering engine. $\quad \therefore P\dfrac{v_3}{r_3} + P_2\dfrac{v_3}{r_3} = P_1\dfrac{v_1}{r_1}$,

which gives an equation for $P + P_2$, and knowing P and P_2 in terms of p_{D_1} we can find p_{D_1}, and thence P, P_2, and P_3. We have thus all the principal pressures. Thus p_{D_1} being known, the pressure falls to E_1 = cut-off pressure of L_1P, and then still falls to K, where pressure = initial pressure of $L_1 = P_3$, and then falls still quicker to N, when L_2P cuts off. As the MP piston now moves faster than the L_1P piston, we get a rise of pressure to Q, which is obtained as before by equating the rate of diminution of volume due to the MP piston to the rate of increase of volume due to the L_1P piston. The pressure then falls to L_1, when the MP again exhausts and the pressure at which point is equal to P_4.

It is easy then to fill in the steam curves for the two LP diagrams. Thus : 3, 4, 5, 1, 2, is the steam-line for the L_1P cylinder, and 13, 12, 11, 9, 10, is the steam line for the L_2P cylinder, found in exactly the same way as described for the steam line of the MP diagram. The mean LP diagram is the mean of these two, viz. A_{11}, Z_1, H_1, B_{11}, C_{11}. The back-pressure line is 7.8.

Four cylinder triple-expansion engine with two LP cranks opposite one another.—The next case to be considered is that of the same engine as in the previous case, with the cranks differently arranged, that is, having the intermediate crank opposite the high pressure and the two low pressures opposite each other, and at right angles to the other cranks, which is the usual arrangement. The two low-pressure cylinders therefore take steam and exhaust together. The diagram lines between the high pressure and the intermediate are evidently the same as the second case considered in this chapter, viz. a compound engine with cranks at 180° and with an inter-mediate receiver, and will be as shown at F E D C and G H K in Fig. 387. The diagram for the exhaust line of intermediate pressure and steam line of low pressure is the same as another of our previously investigated cases, viz. that of a compound engine with cranks at right angles, and will therefore be similar to G F E D C and H K L W M of Fig. 389, if, as is usually the case, the cut-off in the low pressure is after half-stroke. The diagram for this case can therefore be easily drawn from previous investigations.

In all these investigations the effect of clearance, always considerable, has been neglected for shortness and simplicity, but it is easily taken account of when the principles worked out above are understood, and it will be a useful exercise for the student to draw the last two diagrams, making the necessary allowances for cylinder clearance and compression.

APPENDIX

<hr>

(A.) *APPLICATION OF THE INDICATOR DIAGRAM TO DETER-
MINE THE STRESSES ON CRANK-SHAFTS. CURVES OF
TWISTING MOMENTS.*

For the sake of simplicity, suppose the obliquity of the connecting-rod and the weights of the reciprocating parts to be neglected.

Let Fig. 404 represent the crank-circle, O being the centre of the shaft, and suppose the forward pressure to be constant throughout the stroke, and equal to P. Then, it is clear that when the crank is in any position, O C, making an angle θ with the line of dead points, the twisting moment exerted will be $= P \times L \sin \theta$; where L represents the length of the crank. If, therefore, the crank-circle be divided into any number of equal parts, each subtending an angle a, the successive twisting moments will be, $P L \sin a$, $P L \sin 2a$, $PL \sin 3a$, &c.

The base line of the diagram of twisting moments is taken to represent the circumference of the crank-circle, and is divided into a number of equal parts representing equal angles of the crank with the line of dead points.

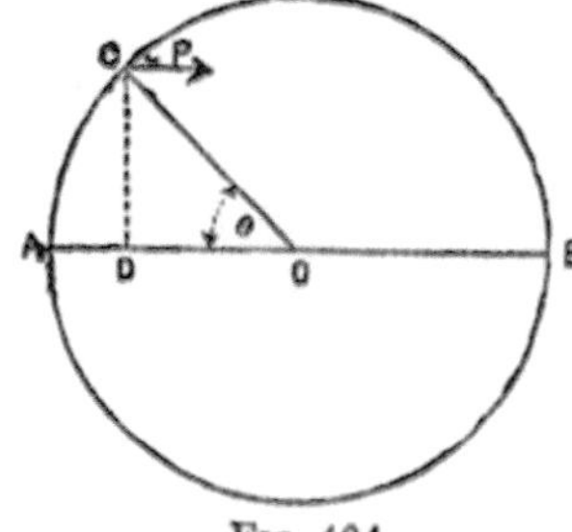

Fig. 404.

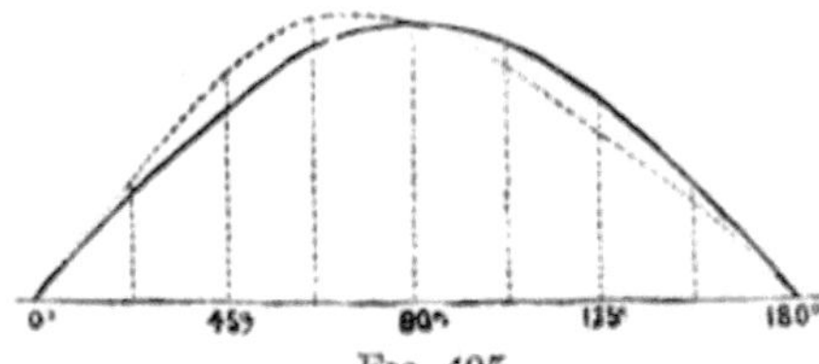

Fig. 405.

Ordinates are set up at these divisions equal to the twisting moment $(P \times L \sin \theta)$, for the corresponding angle, and a fair curve is drawn through the ends of the ordinates thus obtained.

In the case under consideration, the curve will be symmetrical, the obliquity of the connecting-rod having been neglected, so that the piston is supposed to have exact harmonic motion. This *curve of sines* is shown by the *full lines* in Fig. 405.

When the obliquity of the connecting-rod is taken into account the difference of speed of piston at the opposite ends of the stroke will be found to destroy the symmetry of the curve of twisting moments. By reference to Fig. 406, it will be seen that, if ϕ be the angle of the connecting-rod when the crank makes an angle θ with the line of dead points, the twisting moment, instead of being $= P \times L \sin \theta$ simply, is

$$= Q \times O\,C \sin O\,C\,D = Q \times L \sin (\theta + \phi)$$

where $Q =$ thrust on the connecting-rod $= \dfrac{P}{\cos \phi}$

$\therefore$ the twisting moment is $P \times L \dfrac{\sin (\theta + \phi)}{\cos \phi} = P.L (\sin \theta + \cos \theta \tan \phi)$

The second term in the bracket is always small, and when θ is greater than 90°, will be negative: so that it is clear that the curve will be fuller in the first quarter and less in the second quarter revolution, as shown by the dotted lines in Fig. 405.

If the crank-circle be divided into sixteen equal parts, each subtending an angle of $22\frac{1}{2}$°, the successive multipliers of P.L will be

	1	2	3	4	5	6	7	8	9
Connecting-rod, infinite	0	0·383	0·707	0·924	1·0	0·924	0·707	0·383	0
Connecting-rod = four cranks	0	0·428	0·834	1·015	1·0	0·833	0·580	0·338	0

In practice it is generally convenient to take P in tons, and L in inches, so that the resulting twisting moments are obtained in inch-tons.

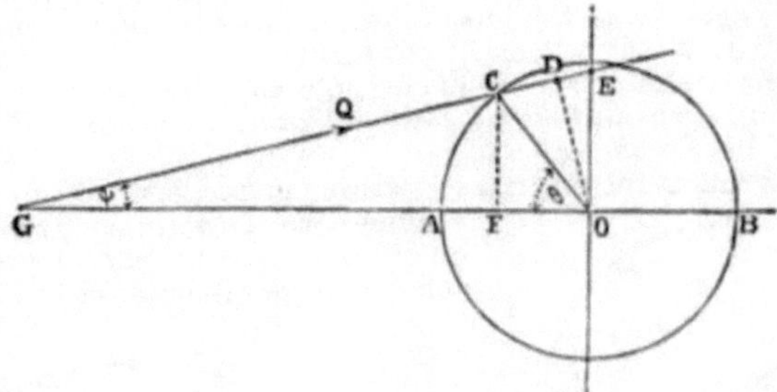

Fig. 406.

We now proceed to explain how actual indicator diagrams taken from the cylinders of an engine may be utilised to show the variations of the twisting moments on the crank-shaft throughout the stroke. The pressure on the piston will in this case vary at each point of the stroke, instead of being constant as before assumed, and the curve of twisting moments will be much less regular, and will fall very rapidly from the point at which expansion begins.

The base line of the diagram of twisting moments is divided into equal parts as before to represent the successive angles of the crank. Ordinates are drawn across the indicator diagram at the points corresponding to the respective positions of the piston for the several angles of the crank, which will give the pressure of steam per square inch on the piston for the given angle of the crank. This pressure multiplied by the area of the piston, by the length of the crank, and by the quantity represented by $\dfrac{\sin(\theta+\phi)}{\cos\phi}$ will give the corresponding twisting moment on the crank-shaft, or if

p = pressure measured on the diagram, in pounds.
A = area of piston, in square inches.
L = length of crank, in inches,

the twisting moment in inch-tons, exerted when the crank makes an angle θ with the line of dead points, is $= \dfrac{p\,A\,L}{2240} \cdot \dfrac{\sin(\theta+\phi)}{\cos\phi}$.

The values of the last term for successive angles of $22\frac{1}{2}$°, when the length of the connecting-rod is twice that of the stroke, which is its usual value in marine engines, are given above.

The ordinates of the curve of twisting moments, when the obliquity of the connecting-rod is taken into account, may be obtained geometrically as follows (Fig. 406) :—

The twisting moment is $= Q \times O\,D = \dfrac{P}{\cos\phi} \times O\,E \cos D\,O\,E$

but by similar triangles, $D\,O\,E = D\,G\,O = \phi$

$\therefore$ twisting moment $= \dfrac{P}{\cos\phi} \times O\,E \cos\phi = P \times O\,E.$

Consequently, for any angle of the crank, the ordinate of the curve of twisting moments will be proportional to the part O E of the vertical radius intercepted by a line drawn in the direction of the connecting-rod at the instant. For the corresponding angle of crank, if the connecting-rod were infinite, the twisting moment would be proportional to the vertical dotted line C F.

To obtain the combined twisting moments for the several cylinders of an engine, the curves representing the twisting moments for the respective cylinders are first drawn, the curve for the second cylinder commencing at the point corresponding to the angle its crank makes with the crank of the

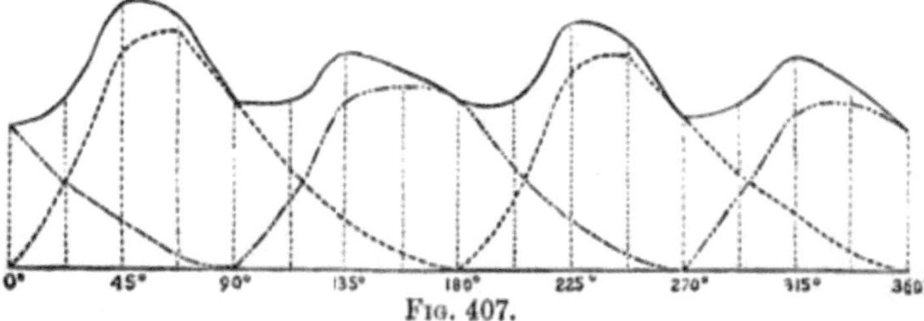

Fig. 407.

first cylinder, and so on. The ordinates of the curve showing the total twisting moment represent the sum of the ordinates of the twisting moments exerted by the several cylinders at the given angles.

An example of this is given in Fig. 407, which shows the twisting moments on the crank-shaft of a two cylinder compound engine with connecting rod four cranks long.

(B.) EFFECT OF THE INERTIA OF THE RECIPROCATING
PARTS OF THE ENGINES.

In the foregoing examples the pressure of the steam on the piston at any time, as shown by the indicator diagram, has been assumed to represent the pressure on the crank-pin for the corresponding part of the stroke. This, however, will be considerably modified by the inertia of the reciprocating parts of the engines. The angular velocity of the crank-pin is supposed to be uniform, the crank moving through equal angles in equal times, and the length of the connecting-rod infinite. The pistons, rods, &c., however, are at rest at the beginning of each stroke, their velocity gradually increases up to mid-stroke, when it reaches a maximum, after which the velocity decreases and becomes zero again at the end of the stroke.

The acceleration during the first half of the stroke can only be produced by the exercise of a pressure, which pressure must evidently be deducted from the steam pressure on the piston in order to obtain the actual pressure on the crank-pin. During the second half of the stroke, when the motion of the piston, &c., is being retarded by the action of the crank-pin, the work accumulated during the acceleration is given out in pressure, which has to be added to the steam pressure on the piston in order to get the total pressure on the crank-pin. The pressure producing the retardation is practically equal to that producing the acceleration, the only difference being due to the alteration in the velocity of the piston at opposite ends of the stroke resulting from the obliquity of the connecting-rod.

The effect of the inertia of the reciprocating parts, therefore, is to alter the distribution of the pressures on the crank-pin during the stroke; so that whilst, if friction be neglected, the total force that acts on the crank-pin during the stroke is equal to that acting on the piston, yet in the first half of the stroke the pressures on the crank-pin are less, and in the second half greater, than those on the piston. It is therefore clear that the variation of strains on the crank-shaft will be considerably affected from this cause, and it is important that the weights of the reciprocating parts should always be taken into account in constructing the curves of twisting moments.

From the laws of motion we know that if a body of weight W move from rest under the action of a constant acceleration force R, at the end of t seconds

$$R\, t = \frac{W}{g}\, v$$

where v = velocity in feet per second, and g = 32·2, the accelerating force of gravity.

If s be the space through which the body has moved in the time t,

$$v = \frac{2\, s}{t} \therefore R\, t = \frac{W}{g}\, \frac{2\, s}{t};\ \text{or } R = \frac{W}{g} \cdot \frac{2\, s}{t^2}$$

In the case of an engine the acceleration for the first few degrees of the crank is practically uniform, but it soon begins to diminish, and at mid-stroke, when the velocity has reached a maximum, and is for the instant uniform, the acceleration becomes zero. As a matter of fact the acceleration is absolutely greatest at the beginning of the stroke, and diminishes gradually up to half-stroke; though for the first two or three degrees the rate of diminution is so slow that for our present purpose it may be regarded as practically constant for the time under consideration. The difference between velocity and acceleration must be borne in mind. The acceleration is a maximum when the velocity is least, and becomes zero when the velocity reaches its maximum, and is for the instant uniform. This may be clearly seen when we remember that it is only *change of velocity* that requires the exertion of a force, so that, neglecting friction, when a body is moving uniformly no force is required to keep it in motion.

The inertia of a body may be defined as the property it has of, when at rest, remaining at rest, or when in motion continuing to move with uniform velocity unless acted on by some external force.

In the case of the reciprocating parts of the machinery of a steam-engine, if we apply the formula

$$R = \frac{W}{g} \cdot \frac{2\, s}{t^2}$$

we find that for the first degree of revolution, during which the acceleration is practically uniform,

if L = length of crank in feet, and n = number of revolutions *per second*, s = L × ·0001523; ·0001523 being the versine of an angle of one degree.

Also, $t = \dfrac{1}{360\, n}$; therefore, the force R necessary to produce the given celeration in the moving parts

$$= \frac{W}{g} \cdot \frac{2\, s}{t^2} = \frac{W}{g} \cdot \frac{2\,L \times ·0001523}{\dfrac{1}{(360\, n)^2}} = 1·227\ \text{W.L.}\, n^2$$

If N = number of revolutions *per minute*, R = ·00034 W.L.N².

If this be divided by the area of the piston in square inches, we shall get the equivalent pressure on the piston to produce the acceleration; which pressure must be deducted from that given by the indicator diagram at the beginning, and added to that given by the diagram at the end of the stroke, in order to obtain the actual pressures exerted on the crank-pin.

If p represents this pressure, and A = area of the piston,

$$p = \frac{R}{A} = 1\cdot227\,\frac{W\,L\,n^2}{A}\ \text{or} = \cdot00034\,\frac{W\,L\,N^2}{A}$$

In order, therefore, to obtain the pressures on the crank-pin at the respective portions of the stroke, a diagram showing the pressures required to accelerate or retard the reciprocating parts must be combined with the indicator diagram. The amount of acceleration will gradually diminish from the commencement of the stroke and become zero at mid-stroke, when retardation commences, and then gradually increases until at the end of the stroke it becomes equal to the acceleration at the beginning of the stroke. The diagram showing the accelerating and retarding forces will therefore be similar to Fig. 408.

Let A B represent the length of this diagram. A D = B E = p = pressure due to acceleration at the beginning, and retardation at the end, of the stroke.

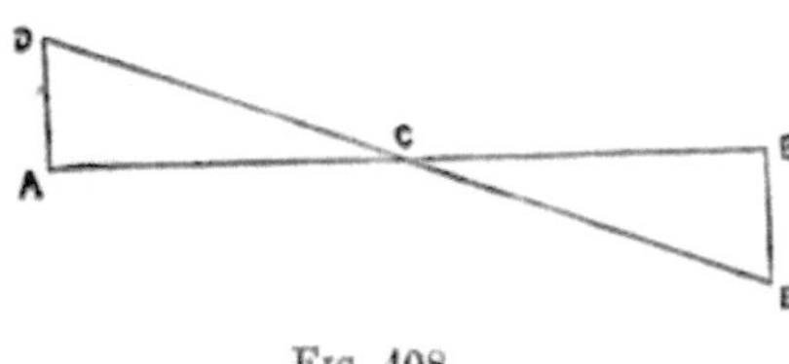

Fig. 408.

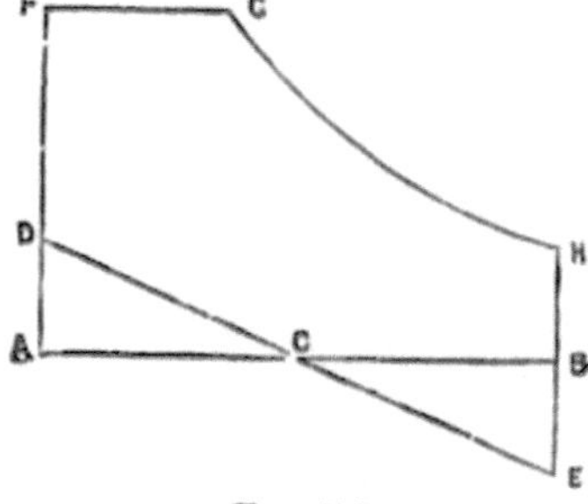

Fig. 409.

The straight line joining D and E will show the variation in the accelerating forces produced by the inertia of the reciprocating parts throughout the stroke. At C, the centre of the stroke, the acceleration is zero.

The combination of the two diagrams may perhaps be best illustrated by its application to a theoretical diagram. Let A F G H B, Fig. 409, be the indicator diagram; the initial effective pressure on the *piston* being A F and the final B H. A D = B E = pressure due to the acceleration of the reciprocating parts, calculated as before explained. Join D E. Then the effective pressure on the *crank-pin* at the beginning of the stroke is D F, and at the end H E. The varying pressures on the crank-pin during the stroke are given by the diagram D F G H E D, and are evidently much more uniform than those given by the indicator diagram A F G H B, which shows the steam pressures on the piston only. At the middle of the stroke the pressures on the piston and on the crank-pin are equal to each other.

In the case of an ordinary indicator diagram, the form of which is much less regular than that of the theoretical diagram, in order to obtain the pressure on the crank-pin, the acceleration diagram should be drawn as directed, and then the several ordinates of the indicator diagram decreased or increased by the values of the accelerating or retarding forces at the respective parts of the stroke, to form the diagram that gives the pressures on the crank-pin.

Fig. 410 is the diagram of twisting moments on the crank-shaft of the engine whose curve is shown in Fig. 407, when allowance is made for the inertia of the reciprocating parts.

In vertical engines the pressures on the crank-pin are also affected by the dead weight of the moving parts. This is equivalent to the addition during

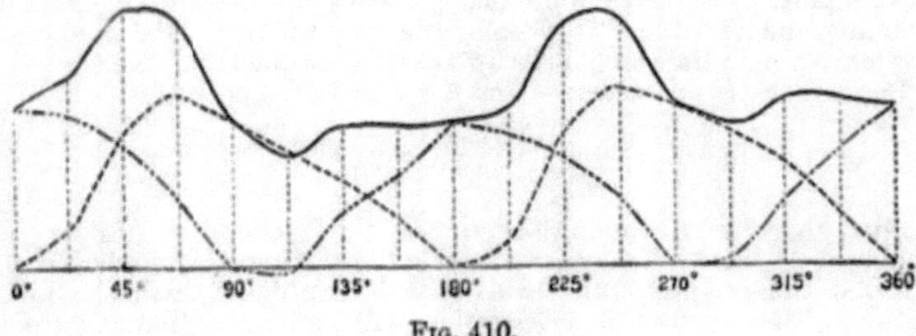

Fig. 410.

the down-stroke, and subtraction during the up-stroke of a pressure equal to the total weight of the parts divided by the area of the piston.

If p_1 = this pressure, $p_1 = \dfrac{W}{A}$ and the pressures to be subtracted from or added to the pressures on the indicator diagram will be those given by the acceleration diagram, plus or minus $\dfrac{W}{A}$, according as the stroke is down or up.

In the previous investigation of the forces produced due to the inertia of the moving parts the two following assumptions were made—
(1) that the connecting-rod was of infinite length,
and (2) that the velocity of the crank-pin was uniform.
Of these (2) is practically true, as engines have usually more than two cranks, and the turning moment does not vary much.
As regards (1), however, the small length of the connecting-rod alters the accelerating and retarding forces due to the inertia, the straight line D C E in Fig. 411 now becoming a curve as shown D_1 L E_1. The force is increased at

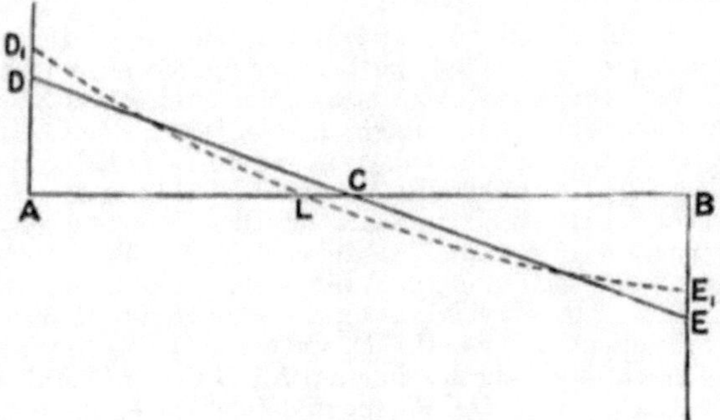

Fig. 411.

the beginning of the stroke and decreased at the end ; the point of no force L being moved, for the maximum piston velocity is not when the piston is at the middle of its stroke, but when at a distance C L from it, which is approximately when the connecting-rod and crank are at right angles.
To find the values of the forces due to inertia, we must find the acceleration of the parts, and then the forces being proportional to the accelerations we can find the forces. First, to find the velocities of the piston and crank. The piston motion is not now harmonic, although, as before, we suppose the crank to turn uniformly.

Let ϕ and θ be as in Fig. 412.

Then if I G is perpendicular to G O B and C I is O C produced, I is the instantaneous centre of the connecting-rod G C, and therefore

$$\frac{\text{velocity of G along G B}}{\text{velocity of C along crank circle}} = \frac{IG}{IC} = \frac{OE}{OC}$$

as the triangles O C E and C I G are similar.

Also $\dfrac{OE}{OC} = \dfrac{\sin OCE}{\sin OEC} = \dfrac{\sin (\phi + \theta)}{\cos \phi} = \tan \phi \cos \theta + \sin \theta$

and as ϕ is small $\tan \phi = \sin \phi$ approximately

$$\therefore \frac{OE}{OC} = \sin \phi \cos \theta + \sin \theta \text{ approximately.}$$

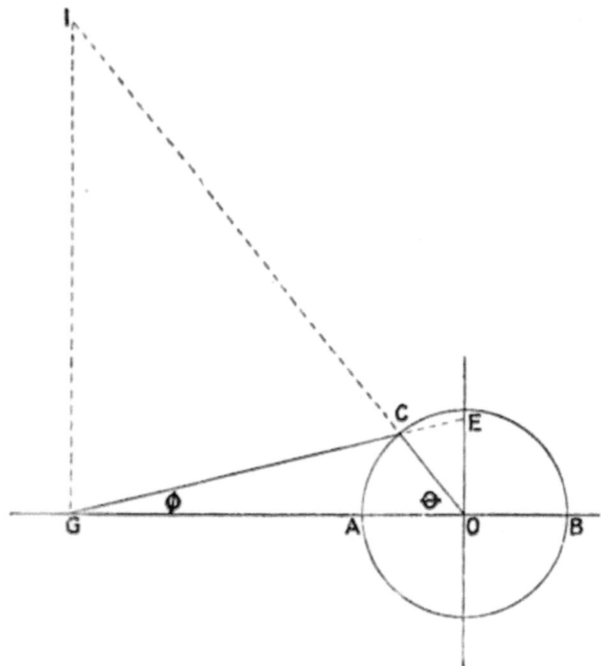

Fig. 412.

Let the connecting-rod $= n\,r$ where $r =$ radius of crank, and V_o and V be the linear velocities of crank-pin and piston respectively.

Then $\dfrac{GC}{OC} = \dfrac{\sin \theta}{\sin \phi} = \dfrac{n\,r}{r} = n$, or $\sin \phi = \dfrac{\sin \theta}{n}$.

Substituting these values we have

$$\frac{\text{Vel. of G along G A}}{\text{Vel. of C along crank circle}} = \frac{V}{V_o} = \sin \phi \cos \theta + \sin \theta,$$

$$\text{or } V = V_o \left(\frac{\sin \theta \cos \theta}{n} + \sin \theta \right) = V_o \left(\sin \theta + \frac{\sin 2\theta}{2n} \right)$$

The acceleration is given by differentiating with respect to t, the details of which we omit.

If W = weight of the reciprocating parts, the force due to the acceleration $= \dfrac{W}{g} \times$ acceleration, from which the accelerating or retarding force

$$= \frac{W}{g}\frac{V_o^2}{r}\left(\cos\theta + \frac{\cos 2\theta}{n}\right)$$

or, if p = the equivalent pressure per square inch of the piston,

$$p = \frac{W V_o^2}{g r A}\left(\cos\theta + \frac{\cos 2\theta}{n}\right)$$

$$= \cdot 00034\,\frac{W r N^2}{A}\left(1 + \frac{1}{n}\right)$$ at the beginning of the stroke when

$\theta = O^\circ$, n being the number of revolutions per minute, and A = area of piston in square inches.

Also $p = -\cdot 00034\,\dfrac{W}{A}\,r N^2\left(1 - \dfrac{1}{n}\right)$

when at the end of the stroke, and $\theta = 180^\circ$.

Also the point L can be obtained, for it is the point of no acceleration, and the piston has therefore a maximum velocity, which will occur approximately when the crank is at right angles to the connecting-rod, and therefore

$$C L = \sqrt{n^2 r^2 + r^2} - n r$$

Knowing the weights of the reciprocating parts of an engine, the curve of inertia can be constructed and applied to an indicator diagram, exactly as in Fig. 409, obtaining A D and B E from the expression just found and filling in the curve through L. The curve of turning moments is then obtained as before. In calculating the weights of the reciprocating parts the weight of the connecting-rod should be considered as concentrated at its two ends, the proportion of weight at each end being inversely as the distance of the end from the centre of gravity of the rod, so that less than one half of the weight is reciprocating.

Iron boilers.—The Surveyor is to fix the limits of weight to be placed on the safety-valves of passenger steamships. In performing this very responsible and onerous duty he must be very careful, as in the event of accident it will be necessary for him to satisfy the Board of Trade that he used due caution. On the one hand he must be careful as regards safety, and on the other hand he must not unduly reduce the pressure on a boiler.

Stays.—In the case of new boilers the Surveyors may allow a stress not exceeding 7,000 lbs. per square inch of net section on solid iron screwed stays supporting flat surfaces, but the stress should not exceed 5,000 lbs. when the stays have been welded or worked in the fire. The areas of diagonal stays are found in the following way:—Find the area of a direct stay needed to support the surface, multiply this area by the length of the diagonal stay, and divide the product by the length of a line drawn at right angles to the surface supported to the end of the diagonal stay; the quotient will be the area of the diagonal stay required. When gusset stays are used their area should be in excess of that found in the above way.

Girders.—When the tops of the combustion-boxes or other parts of a boiler are supported by solid rectangular girders the following formula should be used for finding the working pressure to be allowed on the girders, assuming that they are not subjected to a greater temperature than the ordinary heat of steam, and in the case of combustion chambers that the ends are fitted to the edges of the tube-plate, and the back-plate of the combustion-box:—

$$\frac{C \times d^2 \times T}{(W - P)\, D \times L} = \text{working pressure.}$$

W = width of combustion-box in inches.
P = pitch of supporting bolts in inches.
D = distance between the girders from centre to centre in inches.
L = length of girder in feet.
d = depth of girder in inches.
T = thickness of girder in inches.
N = number of supporting bolts.

$$C = \frac{N \times 1,000}{N + 1} \text{ when the number of bolts is odd.}$$

$$C = \frac{(N + 1)\, 1,000}{N + 2} \text{ when the number of bolts is even.}$$

The working pressure for the supporting bolts and for the plate between them should be determined by the rule for ordinary stays.

Flat surfaces.—The pressure on plates forming flat surfaces is found by the following formula:—

$$\frac{C \times (T + 1)^2}{S - 6} = \text{working pressure.}$$

T = thickness of the plate in sixteenths of an inch.
S = surface supported in square inches.
C = constant according to the following circumstances:—

C = 100 when the plates are not exposed to the impact of heat or flame, and the stays have nuts and washers, the latter being at least three times the diameter of the stay, and two-thirds the thickness of the plates.[1]

C = 90 when the plates are not exposed to the impact of heat or flame, and the stays are fitted with nuts only.

C = 67½ when the plates are not exposed to the impact of heat or flame, and the stays are screwed into the plates and riveted over.

C = 60 when the plates are exposed to the impact of heat or flame, and steam in contact with the plates, and the stays fitted with nuts and washers, the latter being at least three times the diameter of the stay, and two-thirds the thickness of the plates they cover.

C = 54 when the plates are exposed to the impact of heat or flame, and steam in contact with the plates, and the stays fitted with nuts only.

C = 80 when the plates are exposed to the impact of heat or flame, with water in contact with the plates, and the stays screwed into the plates and fitted with nuts.

C = 60 when the plates are exposed to the impact of heat or flame, with water in contact with the plates, and the stays screwed into the plates, and having the ends riveted over to form substantial heads.

C = 36 when the plates are exposed to the impact of heat or flame, and steam in contact with the plates, with the stays screwed into the plates, and having the ends riveted over to form substantial heads.

Where plates are stiffened by T or L irons, and a greater pressure is required than allowed above, the case should be submitted to the Board of Trade.

When a circular flat end is bolted or riveted to a cylindrical shell, S in the formula may be taken as the area of the square inscribed in the circle passing through the centres of the bolts or rivets securing the end, provided the angle ring or flange is of sufficient thickness.

When the riveted ends of screwed stays are much worn, or when the nuts are burned, the constants should be reduced, but the Surveyor must act according to the circumstances that present themselves at the time of survey, and it is expected that in cases where the riveted ends of screwed stays in the combustion-boxes and furnaces are found in this state it will be often necessary to reduce the constant 60 to about 36.

The flat ends of all boilers, as far as the steam space extends, should be fitted with shield or baffle plates, where exposed to the hot gases in the up-take; as all plates subject to the direct impact of heat or flame are liable to get injured unless covered with water.

Tube-plates.—The Surveyors should not in any case allow a greater compressive stress on the tube-plates than 8,000 lbs. which is that used in the following formula:—

$$\frac{(D - d)\ T \times 16,000}{W \times D} = \text{working pressure.}$$

D = least horizontal distance between centres of tubes in inches.

d = inside diameter of ordinary tubes in inches.

T = thickness of tube-plate in inches.

W = extreme width of combustion-box in inches from front of tube-plate to back of fire-box, or distance between combustion-box tube-plates when boiler is double-ended and the box common to the furnaces at both ends.

[1] If the diameter of riveted washers be at least two-thirds the pitch of the stays, and the thickness not less than the plates they cover, the constant may be increased to 150.

When doubling strips are fitted of the same thickness as the plates they cover, and not less in width than two-thirds of the pitch of the stays, the constant may be increased to 160.

When doubling-plates cover the whole of the flat surface the case should be submitted for the consideration of the Board.

Cylindrical boilers.—The Board of Trade consider that boilers well constructed, well designed, and made of good material should have an advantage in the matter of working pressure over boilers inferior in any of the above respects, as unless this is done the superior boiler is placed at a disadvantage, and good workmanship and material will be discouraged. They have therefore caused the following rules to be prepared :—

When cylindrical boilers are made of the best material with all the rivet holes drilled in place, and all the seams fitted with double butt straps each of at least five-eighths the thickness of the plates they cover, and all the seams at least double riveted with rivets having an allowance of not more than 75 per cent. over the single shear, and provided that the boilers have been open to inspection during the whole period of construction, then 5 may be used as the factor of safety. The tensile strength of the iron is to be taken as equal to 47,000 lbs. per square inch with the grain, and 40,000 lbs. across the grain. But when the above conditions are not complied with, the additions in the following scale should be made to the factor 5, according to the circumstances of each case :—[1]

A †	·15	To be added when all the holes are fair and good in the longitudinal seams, but drilled out of place after bending.
B †	·3	To be added when all the holes are fair and good in the longitudinal seams, but drilled out of place before bending.
C	·3	To be added when all the holes are fair and good in the longitudinal seams, but punched after bending.
D	·5	To be added when all the holes are fair and good in the longitudinal seams, but punched before bending.
E *	·75	To be added when all the holes are not fair and good in the longitudinal seams.
F	·1	To be added if the holes are all fair and good in the circumferential seams, but drilled out of place after bending.
G †	·15	To be added if the holes are fair and good in the circumferential seams, but drilled before bending.
H	·15	To be added if the holes are fair and good in the circumferential seams, but punched after bending.
I †	·2	To be added if the holes are fair and good in the circumferential seams, but punched before bending.
J *	·2	To be added if the holes are not fair and good in the circumferential seams.
K	·2	To be added if double butt straps are not fitted to the longitudinal seams, and the said seams are lap and double riveted.
L	·1	To be added if double butt straps are not fitted to the longitudinal seams, and the said seams are lap and treble riveted.
M	·3	To be added if only single butt straps are fitted to the longitudinal seams, and the said seams are double riveted.
N	·15	To be added if only single butt straps are fitted to the longitudinal seams, and the said seams are treble riveted.
O	1·0	To be added when any description of joint in the longitudinal seams is single riveted.
P	·1	To be added if the circumferential seams are fitted with single butt straps and are double riveted.
Q	·2	To be added if the circumferential seams are fitted with single butt straps and are single riveted.
R	·1	To be added if the circumferential seams are fitted with double butt straps and are single riveted.
S ‡	·1	To be added if the circumferential seams are lap and are double riveted.

[1] If the iron be tested, and the elongation measured in a length of 10 inches is not less than 14 per cent. with, and 8 per cent. across the grain, and the Surveyors are otherwise satisfied as to the quality of the plates and rivets, then 4·5 may be used instead of 5, and the minimum actual tensile strength of the plates used in calculating the working pressure.

T	·2	To be added if the circumferential seams are lap and are single riveted.
U	·25	To be added when the circumferential seams are lap and the strakes of plates are not entirely under or over.
V ‡	·3	To be added when the boiler is of such a length as to fire from both ends, or is of unusual length, such as flue boilers; and the circumferential seams are fitted as described opposite P, R, and S, but, of course, when the circumferential seams are as described opposite Q and T, V ·3 will become V ·4.
W *	·4	To be added if the seams are not properly crossed.
X *	·4	To be added when the iron is in any way doubtful, and the Surveyor is not satisfied that it is of the best quality.
Y ††	1·65	To be added if the boiler is not open to inspection during the whole period of its construction.

Where marked * the allowance may be increased still further if the workmanship or material is very doubtful or very unsatisfactory.

† When the holes are to be rimered or bored out in place the case should be submitted to the Board as to the reduction or omission of A, B, G, and I as heretofore.

‡ When the middle circumferential seams are double strapped or double riveted or lap and treble riveted and the calculated strength not less than 65 per cent. of the solid plate, S ·1 and V ·3 may be omitted. The end circumferential seams in such cases should be at least double riveted.

†† When surveying boilers that have not been open to inspection during construction, the case should be submitted to the Board as to the factors to be used.

The strength of ordinary joints is found by the following method :—

$$\frac{(\text{Pitch} - \text{Diameter of rivet}) \times 100}{\text{Pitch}} = \begin{cases} \text{percentage of strength of plate at} \\ \text{joint as compared with the solid} \\ \text{plate} \end{cases}$$

$$\frac{(\text{Area of rivet} \times \text{No. of rows of rivets}) \times 100}{\text{Pitch} \times \text{Thickness of plate}} = \begin{cases} \text{percentage of strength of} \\ \text{rivets as compared with} \\ \text{the solid plate.}[1] \end{cases}$$

Then take iron as equal to 47,000 lbs.[2] per square inch and use the smaller of the two percentages as the strength of the joint, and adopt the factor of safety as found from the preceding scale :—

$$\frac{(47,000[2] \times \text{least percentage of strength of joint}) \times \text{twice the thickness of the plate in inches.}}{\text{Inside diameter of the boiler in inches} \times \text{factor of safety}}$$

= pressure to be allowed per square inch on the safety valves.

Riveting, &c.—In the case of zigzag riveting the strength through the plate diagonally between the rivets is equal to that horizontally between the rivets, when diagonal pitch = $\frac{6}{10}$ horizontal pitch + $\frac{4}{10}$ diameter of rivet.

Plates that are drilled in place should be taken apart and the burr taken off, and the holes slightly countersunk from the outsides.

Butt straps.—Butt straps should be cut from plates and not from bars, and should be of as good a quality as the shell plates, and for the longitudinal seams should be cut across the fibre. When the straps are drilled in place they should be taken apart and the burr taken off and the holes slightly

[1] If the rivets are exposed to double shear, multiply the percentage as found by 1·75.

[2] See footnote on last page.

countersunk from the outside. When single butt straps are used they should be one-eighth thicker than the plates they cover.

The diameter of the rivets should in no case be less than the thickness of the plates of which the shell is made, but it will be found when the plates are thin, or when lap joints or single butt straps are adopted, that the diameter of the rivets should be in excess of the thickness of the plates.

Stays for dished ends.—Dished ends, unless of thickness required for a flat end, should be stayed; but when they are theoretically equal to the pressure needed, when considered as portions of spheres, the stays, when solid, may have a stress of 14,000 lbs. per square inch of net section, but the stress should not exceed 10,000 lbs. when the stays have been welded or worked in the fire, and such stays should be properly distributed. If they are not theoretically equal to the pressure needed they should be stayed as flat surfaces. Truly hemispherical ends subjected to internal pressure may be allowed double the pressure that is suitable for a cylinder of the same diameter and thickness. The ends should not be formed of less than four pieces.

All manholes and openings must be stiffened with compensating rings of at least the same effective sectional area as the plates cut out, and in no case should the rings be less in thickness than the plates to which they are attached. The openings in the shells of cylindrical boilers should have their shorter axes placed longitudinally. It is very desirable that the compensating rings round openings in flat surfaces be made of L or T iron. Cast-iron doors are not to be passed.

The neutral part of boiler shells under steam domes must be efficiently stiffened and stayed, as serious accidents have arisen from the want of such precautions.

Hydraulic test.—The boilers must be tested by hydraulic pressure to twice the working pressure in the presence and to the satisfaction of the Board's Surveyors.

Circular furnaces.—Circular furnaces with the longitudinal joints welded or made with a butt strap double riveted, or double butt straps single riveted :—

$$\frac{90{,}000 \times \text{the square of the thickness of the plate in inches}}{(\text{Length in feet} + 1) \times \text{Diameter in inches}}$$

= working pressure per square inch, provided it does not exceed that found by the following formula :—

$$\frac{9{,}000 \times \text{Thickness in inches}}{\text{Diameter in inches}} = \text{working pressure per square inch.}$$

The second formula limits the crushing stress on the material to 4,500 lbs. per square inch. The length is to be measured between the rings if the furnace is made with rings.

If the longitudinal joints instead of being butted are lap-jointed in the ordinary way, then 75,000 is to be used instead of 90,000, but where the lap is bevelled and so made as to give the flues the form of a *true* circle, then 80,000 may be used. When the material or the workmanship is not of the best quality, the constants given above should be reduced, that is to say— the 90,000 will become 80,000; the 80,000 will become 70,000; the 70,000 will become 60,000. When the material and the workmanship are not of the best quality, such constants will require to be further reduced, according to circumstances and the judgment of the Surveyor, as in the case of old boilers. Some of the conditions of best workmanship are, that the joints are either double riveted with single butt straps, or single riveted with double butt straps, and the holes drilled after the bending is done and when in place, and the plates afterwards taken apart, the burr on the holes taken off, and the holes slightly countersunk from the outside.[1]

Steel boilers.—The following should guide the Board's Surveyors when the general quality of the steel has been found suitable for marine boilers.

Tests.—The steelmakers or boilermakers should test one or more strips cut from *each* plate for tensile strength and elongation, and stamp both results on each plate or bar. When practicable the plates or bars should be so stamped that the marks can be easily seen when the boiler is constructed. The Surveyor is not obliged to witness the foregoing tests, although it is very desirable that he should when his other duties will allow him to do so, but he should see that all the plates and bars are properly marked. He should, however, select of each thickness at least one in four of these plates, either at the steel works or the boilermakers' works, and witness the testing of at least one strip or piece cut from each selected plate; but when the boiler plates exceed 15 feet in length, there should be a tensile test from each end, and when they exceed 20 feet in length and at the same time 6 feet in breadth, or exceed 2½ tons in weight, there should be a tensile test from each corner. In the latter cases the testing of each plate should be witnessed by the Surveyor. The mean of the results of the tests, if the latter fall within the Board's requirements as stated below, should be stamped on the plates. If a large number of failures take place in the 25 per cent. selected, the Surveyor should see more than 25 per cent. of the plates to be used in the boiler satisfactorily tested.

If, for the plates from which the Surveyor selects the above proportion, a greater stress is wished than is allowed for iron, tests for tensile strength and elongation should be made, also a few tempering and bending tests, and those

---

[1] The following examples will serve to show the application of the constants for the different cases that may arise:—

Furnaces with butt joints and drilled rivet holes
- 90,000 where the longitudinal seams are welded.
- 90,000 where the longitudinal seams are double riveted and fitted with single butt straps.
- 80,000 where the longitudinal seams are single riveted and fitted with single butt straps.
- 90,000 where the longitudinal seams are single riveted and fitted with double butt straps.

Furnaces with butt joints and punched rivet holes
- 85,000 where the longitudinal seams are double riveted and fitted with single butt straps.
- 75,000 where the longitudinal seams are single riveted and fitted with single butt straps.
- 85,000 where the longitudinal seams are single riveted and fitted with double butt straps.

Furnaces with lapped joints and drilled rivet holes
- 80,000 where the longitudinal seams are double riveted and bevelled.
- 75,000 where the longitudinal seams are double riveted and not bevelled.
- 70,000 where the longitudinal seams are single riveted and bevelled.
- 65,000 where the longitudinal seams are single rivetted and not bevelled.

Furnaces with lapped joints and punched rivet holes
- 75,000 where the longitudinal seams are double riveted and bevelled.
- 70,000 where the longitudinal seams are double riveted and not bevelled.
- 65,000 where the longitudinal seams are single riveted and bevelled.
- 60,000 where the longitudinal seams are single riveted and not bevelled.

In the case of upright fire-boxes of donkey or similar boilers, 10 per cent. should be deducted from the constants given above applicable to the respective classes of work.

for which no reduction of thickness is asked may be tested for resistance to bending and tempering only if preferred. In the latter case the tensile strength and elongation stamped on each plate should be reported by the Surveyor to the Board of Trade, along with the results of the bending and tempering tests. From the plates and bars, the tests of which have been stated to have been made by the steel maker, and not witnessed by the Surveyor, the Surveyor may, if he thinks it advisable, select any plates and bars after they are in the boiler yard and require specimens to be cut off and tested. If the results are not satisfactory the whole of the plates, except those which were tested and found satisfactory by the Surveyor, may be liable to be rejected.

The breadth of the test strips for tensile stress should be about 2 inches, and the elongation, taken in a length of 10 inches, should be about 25 per cent., and not less than 18 per cent. when tested in the normal condition, in which condition the Board prefers the tests to be made; but, if the plates are annealed, that is, heated to a red heat in a plate furnace, and immediately they are at that heat taken out and placed on the mill floor to cool, the elongation should not be less than 20 per cent. The test pieces must not be annealed after they are cut off from the plates.

When the plates are not taken out of the furnace immediately they are red hot, or if allowed to cool down in the furnace, or are covered with ashes or other non-conducting substance, it should be reported to the Board for their consideration and decision. The Surveyor should always report to the Board whether the plates have been annealed, or if in the normal condition when the test pieces were cut off. The test strips must be carefully prepared and measured, and they should be cut from the plate by a planing or shaping machine. The skin of the test pieces should not be removed by planing, shaping or otherwise, the edges only being planed or shaped, and in no case should the test pieces be prepared or reduced in size by hammering or otherwise working on an anvil.

The Surveyor should see that the plates for the manhole doors and for the rings round the openings for the doors, are tested in the usual manner.

The bending tests for plates *not* exposed to flame should be made with strips in the same condition as the plates, and occasionally also some temper tests should be made. Strips cut from furnaces, combustion-boxes, &c., should be heated to a cherry red, then plunged into water of about 80° and kept there until of the same temperature as the water, and then bent. The bending and tempering strips should be about 2 inches broad and 10 inches long, and they should be bent until they break, or until the sides are parallel at a distance from each other of not more than three times the thickness of plate.

When full allowance over iron is wished the tensile strength of the plates *not* exposed to flame should not be less than 27 tons, and should not exceed 32 tons, per square inch of section, and 27 tons should be the stress used in the calculations for cylindrical shells if the plates comply with all the conditions as stated herein, but for each ton the minimum tensile strength of the plate is above 27 tons, 1 ton may be added to the 27 provided the Surveyor witnesses the testing of all the plates. The tensile strength of furnace, flanging, and combustion-box plates may range from 26 tons to 30 tons per square inch.

Stays and rivet bars.—Stays and rivet bars should be tested for tensile strength and elongation, viz. one bar in 20 when the diameter of the bar does not exceed 1 inch; one bar in 12 when not over $1\frac{1}{2}$ inch; and one bar in 8 when the diameter exceeds $1\frac{1}{2}$ inch.

The tensile strength of stay bars should be from 27 to 32 tons per square inch, with an elongation of about 25 per cent. and not less than 20 per cent. in a length of 10 inches. Solid steel screwed stays which have not been welded or otherwise worked after heating may be allowed a working stress of 9,000 lbs. per square inch of net section, provided the tensile strength and elongation are as stated. Steel stays which have been welded or worked in the fire have been found to be unreliable, therefore they should *not* be passed. This does not apply to stay tubes welded longitudinally.

Rivet bars and rivets.—The tensile strength of rivet bars should be from 26 to 30 tons per square inch, with an elongation of not less than 25 per cent. in a length of 10 inches. The rivets before being tested should be carefully prepared, and the elongation should, when practicable, be taken in a length of 2½ times the diameter of the prepared part. The tensile strength of the rivets should be from 27 to 32 tons per square inch, and the contraction of area about 60 per cent.

Although the Surveyors may not in every case see the rivets tested, they should frequently select a few at the boilermaker's works, and mark them before they are prepared for testing.

If the original size of the bars for rivets or stays be reduced before testing it must be done in the lathe or by machine. Test pieces of any kind should not be prepared by heating or drawing down.

The rivet holes in the furnaces and shell seams should be *drilled*, but if it is wished to punch them and afterwards bore, or if wished to anneal the plates, the particulars of the punching and boring or annealing should be submitted to the Board of Trade for consideration before being done, but all punched holes should be made after bending.

In all cases where assent has been given for plates to be punched after bending and then annealed, the makers should stamp the plates with the words 'punched after bending and then annealed,' and in all cases where assent has been given for punching and afterwards boring plates the words 'punched and then bored' should be stamped on the plates.

Flat surfaces.—If the flanging plates and those exposed to flame comply with the foregoing conditions, the constants in the Board's rules for iron boilers may be increased as follows :—

The constants for flat surfaces when they are supported by stays screwed into the plate and riveted, 10 per cent. The constants for flat surfaces when they are supported by stays screwed into the plate and nutted, or when the stays are nutted in the steam space, 25 per cent. This is also applicable to the constants for flat surfaces stiffened by riveted washers or doubling strips, and supported by nutted stays. The constants for combustion-box girders 10 per cent. The constants for plain furnaces, 10 per cent.

Furnaces, corrugated.—When furnaces are machine made by Messrs. The Leeds Forge Co. of the Fox corrugated and Morrison suspension types, or by Messrs. John Brown & Co., Sheffield, of the Purves ribbed and grooved type, if they are practically true circles, and the plates not less than $\frac{7}{16}$ inch thick, the working pressure is found by the following formula :—

$$\frac{C \times T}{D} = \text{working pressure.}$$

C = 14,000 for Fox's corrugated and Brown's ribbed and grooved furnaces, and for Morrison's suspension furnace.
T = thickness in inches.
D = outside diameter in inches measured at the bottom of the corrugations when the furnace is of the corrugated or suspension type, or over the plain parts when it is of the ribbed and grooved description.

In Fox's corrugated furnaces the pitch of the corrugations and the length of the plain parts at the ends should not exceed 6 inches, and in Morrison's suspension furnaces the pitch should not exceed 8 inches, and the length at the ends 5 inches. In both descriptions of furnaces the depth from the top of the corrugations outside to bottom of corrugations inside should not be less than 2 inches, and the plates at the ends should not be unduly thinned in the flanging.

The plates of the ribbed and grooved furnaces should be formed by rolling, the ribs should not be less than $1\frac{5}{16}$ inches above the plain parts, and the depth of the grooves not more than $\frac{3}{4}$ inch, the length between the centres of the ribs not over 9 inches, and that of the plain parts at the ends not over 6 inches, and the ends rolled slightly thicker than the plain parts and not reduced at any part by flanging, &c., below the thickness of the body of the furnace. If the furnace is riveted in one or more lengths the case should be submitted for consideration.

Furnaces made up of flanged rings.—When horizontal furnaces of ordinary diameter are constructed of a series of rings welded longitudinally, and the end of each ring flanged, and the rings riveted together, and so forming the furnace, the working pressure is found by the following formula, provided the length in inches between the centres of the flanges of the rings is not greater than $(120\,T - 12)$, and the flanging is performed at one heat by a suitable flanging machine, and also the conditions which follow the formula are complied with :—

$$\frac{9,900 \times T}{3 \times D} \left(5 - \frac{l \times 12}{60 \times T} \right) = \text{working pressure.}$$

T = thickness of plate in inches.
l = length between centre of flanges in inches.
D = outside diameter of furnace in inches.

The radii of the flanges on the fire side should be about $1\frac{1}{2}$ inches. The depth of the flanges from the fire side should be three times the diameter of the rivet plus $1\frac{1}{2}$ inches, and the thickness of the flanges should be as near the thickness of the body of the plate as practicable. The distance from the edge of the rivet holes to the edge of the flange should not be less than the diameter of the rivet, and the diameter of the rivets at least $\frac{3}{8}$ inch greater than the thickness of the plate. The depth of the ring between the flanges should be not less than three times the diameter of the rivets, the fire edge of the ring should be about the termination of the curve of the flange, and the thickness not less than half the thickness of the furnace plate. It is very desirable these rings should be turned.

The holes in the flanges and rings should be drilled in place if practicable, but if not drilled in place they should be drilled sufficiently small and afterwards when in place rimered out until the holes are quite fair ; the holes should be slightly tapered and the heads of the rivets of moderate size.

After all welding, and after all flanging, and heating, each ring should be efficiently annealed in one operation.

Tube-plates.—A greater compressive stress should not be allowed on tube-plates than 10,000 lbs., which is that used in the following formula :—

$$\frac{(D - d)\,T \times 20,000}{W \times D} = \text{working pressure.}$$

D = least horizontal distance between centres of tubes in inches.
d = inside diameter of ordinary tubes in inches.
T = thickness of tube-plate in inches.
W = extreme width of combustion-box in inches from front of tube-plate to back of fire-box, or distance between combustion-box tube-plates when boiler is double-ended and the box common to the furnaces at both ends.

When full allowance is wished the rivet section, if iron, in the longitudinal seams of cylindrical shells should, when those seams are lapped, be at least $1\frac{3}{8}$ times the net plate section, and if steel rivets are used their section should be at least $\frac{23}{20}$ of the net section of the plate if the tensile stress of the rivets is not less than 27 tons and not more than 32 tons per square inch. In calculating the working pressure, the percentage strength of the rivets may be found in the usual way by the Board's rules ; but in the case of iron rivets the percentages found should be divided by $\frac{1\cdot3}{1}$, and in the case of steel rivets by $\frac{2\cdot3}{3}$, the results being the percentages required. If the percentage strength of the rivets by calculation is less than the calculated percentage strength of the plate, calculate the working pressure by both percentages. When using the percentage strength of the plate, 4·5 plus the additions suitable for the method of construction, as by the Board's rules for iron boilers, may be used as the nominal factor of safety, but when using the percentage strength of the rivets 4·5 may be used as the factor of safety. The less of the two pressures so found is the working pressure to be allowed for the cylindrical portion of the shell.

Local heating of the plates should be avoided, as many plates have failed from having been so treated. All plates that are punched, flanged, or locally heated, must be carefully annealed after being so treated. Steel plates which have been welded should not be passed if subject to a tensile stress, and those welded and subject to a compressive stress should be efficiently annealed. In other respects the boilers should comply with the rules for iron boilers.

Safety valves.—The provisions relating to safety valves are in substance as follows :—Every steamship of which a survey is required shall be provided with a safety valve upon each boiler, so constructed as to be out of the control of the engineer when the steam is up, and if such valve is in addition to the ordinary valve, it shall be so constructed as to have an area not less, and a pressure not greater, than the area of and pressure on the latter.

Cases have come under the notice of the Board of Trade in which steamships have been surveyed, and passed by the Surveyors, with pipes between the boilers and the safety-valve chests. Such arrangement is not in accordance with the Act, which distinctly provides that the safety valves shall be upon the boilers.

The area per square foot of fire-grate surface of the locked up safety valves, or (when there is more than one locked up safety valve on the boiler) the combined area of the locked up safety valves, should be not less than that given in the following table opposite the boiler pressure intended, but in no case should the valves be less than two inches in diameter. When, however, the valves are of the common description, and are made in accordance with the table, it will be necessary to fit them with springs having great elasticity, or to provide other means to keep the accumulation within moderate limits ; and as boilers with forced draught require valves considerably larger than those found by the table, the design of the valves proposed for such boilers, together with the estimated coal consumption per square foot of grate, should be submitted to the Board for consideration.

In ascertaining the fire-grate, the length of the grate should be measured from the inner edge of the dead plate to the front of the bridge, and the width from side to side of the furnace on the top of the bars at the middle of their length.

The safety valves should be fitted with lifting gear, so arranged that the two or more valves on any one boiler can at all times be eased together, without interfering with the valves on any other boiler. The lifting gear should in all cases be arranged so that it can be worked by hand either from the engine-room or stokehold.

Care should be taken that the safety valves have a lift equal to at least one-fourth their diameter ; that the openings for the passage of steam to and from the valves, including the waste-steam pipe, should each have an area not less than the area of the valves, and that each valve-box has a drain-pipe fitted at its lower part. In the case of lever valves, if the lever is not bushed with brass, the pins must be of brass; iron and iron working together must not be passed. Too much care cannot be devoted to seeing that there is proper lift, and free means of escape of waste steam, as it is obvious that unless the lift and means for escape of waste steam are ample, the effect is the same as reducing the area of the valve or putting on an extra load. The valve seats should be secured by studs and nuts.

SAFETY-VALVE AREAS.

Boiler Pressure	Area of Valve per square foot of Fire-grate	Boiler Pressure	Area of Valve per square foot of Fire-grat
lbs.	sq. in.	lbs.	sp. in
60	·500	105	·312
62	·487	110	·300
64	·474	115	·288
66	·462	120	·277
68	·451	125	·267
70	·441	130	·258
72	·431	135	·250
74	·421	140	·241
76	·412	145	·234
78	·403	150	·227
80	·394	155	·220
82	·386	160	·214
84	·378	165	·208
86	·371	170	·202
88	·364	175	·197
90	·357	180	·192
92	·350	185	·187
94	·344	190	·182
96	·337	195	·178
98	·331	200	·174
100	·326		

Size of shafting.—Main, tunnel, propeller, and paddle shafts must not be passed if found to be less in diameter than that found by the following rules, without previously submitting the whole case to the Board of Trade for their consideration. It will be found that first-class makers generally put in larger shafts than those found by the following formulæ.[1]

For compound condensing engines with two or more cylinders when the cranks are not overhung:—

$$S = \sqrt[3]{\dfrac{C \times P \times D^2}{f\left(2 + \dfrac{D^2}{d^2}\right)}}$$

$$P = \dfrac{f \times S^3}{C \times D^2}\left(2 + \dfrac{D^2}{d^2}\right)$$

where S = diameter of shaft in inches.

d^2 = square of diameter of high-pressure cylinder in inches, or sum of squares of diameters when there are two or more high-pressure cylinders.

D^2 = square of diameter of low-pressure cylinder in inches, or sum of squares of diameters when there are two or more low-pressure cylinders.

P = absolute pressure in lbs. per square inch, i.e. boiler pressure plus 15 lbs.

C = length of crank in inches.

f = constant from following table :—

NOTE.—Intermediate pressure cylinders do not appear in the formula.

[1] When shafts are proposed to be fitted whose diameters are less than 6 inches the case should be submitted for consideration.

For ordinary condensing engines, with one, two, or more cylinders, when the cranks are not overhung :—

$$S = \sqrt[3]{\frac{C \times P \times D^2}{3f}}$$

$$P = \frac{3 \times f \times S^3}{C \times D^2}$$

where S = diameter of shaft in inches.

D^2 = square of diameter of cylinder in inches, or sum of squares of diameters when there are two or more cylinders.

P, C, f, as before.

Constant	For two Cranks, Angle between Cranks	For Crank and Thrust Shafts	For Tunnel Shaft
f	90°	1047	1221
,,	100°	966	1128
,,	110°	904	1055
,,	120°	855	997
,,	130°	817	953
,,	140°	788	919
,,	150°	766	894
,,	160°	751	877
,,	170°	743	867
,,	180°	740	864
—	For three Cranks 120°	1110	1295

For paddle engines of the direct acting type multiply constant in this column suitable for angle of cranks by 1·4. (note against the "For Crank and Thrust Shafts" column)

For propeller shafts f should be 15 per cent. less than for crank shafts, but the portion of the propeller shaft forward of the stern gland, and all the thrust shaft with the exception of the part enclosed by the thrust bearing, may be of the same diameter as the intermediate tunnel shafting.

NOTE.—When there is only one crank the constants applicable are those in the table opposite 180°.

(D.) *LLOYD'S RULES FOR BOILERS AND MACHINERY.*
(Corrected to 1899.)

Use of steel in boilers.—When steel is used in the construction of boilers intended for vessels classed or proposed for classification in the Society's Register Book, the boilers shall be constructed in accordance with the requirements of the Rules, and the following conditions fulfilled.

The material of longitudinal stays and of plates for cylindrical shells is to have an ultimate tensile strength of not less than 27 and not more than 32 tons per square inch of section,[1] and that for screw stays and all other plates, between 26 and 30 tons per square inch. In all cases the ultimate elongation must not be less than 20 per cent. in a length of eight inches. Test pieces cut from the plates or bars are to be capable of being bent to a curve of which the inner radius is not greater than one and a half times the thickness of the plates or bars, both when in the normal condition and after having been heated uniformly to a low cherry red and quenched in water of 82° Fahrenheit.

[1] If the shell plates are to be flanged or welded, the ultimate tensile strength is not to exceed 30 tons per square inch.

Steel rivets are to be of soft and ductile quality, having a tensile strength between 26 and 30 tons per square inch, and are to be capable of withstanding the same tests as the plates are required to undergo.

A temper test is to be made from every plate intended to be used in the construction of boilers, and samples for tensile and cold bend tests are to be selected from each batch of plates, &c., submitted for approval, at least one of each test being taken from each cast or furnace charge from which the material has been produced. When plates are $1\frac{1}{4}$ inch thick or above, a tensile and a cold bend test are to be made from each plate.

The Society's Surveyor will attend at the steel works when necessary, and select the samples for testing before the plates are sheared to size, and these samples when marked by him for testing should, as far as practicable, be followed by the Surveyor through the different stages of preparation until the tests are completed.

The Society's Surveyor will require to have every facility placed in his way for tracing all plates to their respective charges.

The samples are taken for testing in order that the general quality of the material may be ascertained, and if any sample should fail to fulfil the conditions laid down, the plate from which the sample is taken must be rejected; and further tests should be made before any material, made from the same cast or charge as the failing sample, can be approved.

All the holes in steel boilers should be drilled; but if they be punched, the plates are to be afterwards annealed.

All plates that are dished or flanged, or in any way heated in the fire for working, except those that are subjected to a compressive stress only, are to be annealed after the operations are completed. No steel stays are to be welded.

Unless otherwise specified, the Rules for the construction of iron boilers will apply equally to boilers made of steel.

Cylindrical shells of iron boilers.—The strength of circular shells to be calculated from the strength of the longitudinal joints by the following formula :—

$$\frac{C \times T \times B}{D} = \text{working pressure in lbs. per square inch,}$$

where C = coefficient as per following table.

T = thickness of plate in inches.

D = mean diameter of shell in inches.

B = percentage of strength of joint found as follows—the least percentage to be taken :—

For plate at joint, $B = \dfrac{p - d}{p} \times 100$,

For rivets at joint $B = \dfrac{n \times a}{p \times T} \times 100$ with iron rivets in iron plates with punched holes,

$B = \dfrac{n \times a}{p \times T} \times 90$ with iron rivets in iron plates with drilled holes,

(In case of rivets in double shear 1·75 a to be used instead of a.)

where p = pitch of rivets.

d = diameter of rivets.

a = sectional area of rivets.

n = number of rows of rivets.

Note.—In any case where the strength of the longitudinal joint is satisfactorily shown by experiment to be greater than that given by this formula, the actual strength may be taken in the calculation.

TABLE OF COEFFICIENTS.

Description of Longitudinal Joint	For Plates ½ inch thick and under	For Plates ¾ inch thick and above ½ inch	For Plates above ¾ inch thick
Lap joint, punched holes	155	165	170
Lap joint, drilled holes	170	180	190
Double butt strap joint, punched holes	170	180	190
Double butt strap joint, drilled holes	180	190	200

NOTE.—The inside butt strap to be at least three-quarters the strength of the longitudinal joint.

Cylindrical shells of steel boilers.—The strength of cylindrical shells of steel boilers to be calculated from the following formula :—

$$\frac{C \times (T - 2) \times B}{D} = \text{working pressure in lbs. per square inch.}$$

D = mean diameter of shell in inches.

T = thickness of plate in sixteenths of an inch.

C = 21 when the longitudinal seams are fitted with double butt straps of equal width.

C = 20·25 when they are fitted with double butt straps of unequal width, only covering on one side the reduced section of plate at the outer lines of rivets.

C = 19·5 when the longitudinal seams are lap joints.

If the minimum tensile strength of shell plates is 28 or 29 tons per square inch instead of 27 tons these values of C may be correspondingly increased.

B = least percentage of longitudinal joint found as follows :—

For plate at joint, $B = \frac{p - d}{p} \times 100$,

For rivets at joint, $B = \frac{n \times a}{p \times T} \times 85$ with steel rivets in steel plates,

$B = \frac{n \times a}{p \times T} \times 70$ with iron rivets in steel plates,

(In case of rivets being in double shear, 1·75 a is to be used instead of a.)

where p = pitch of rivets in inches.

d = diameter of rivet holes in inches.

a = sectional area of rivets in square inches.

n = number of rivets used per pitch in the longitudinal joint.

NOTE.—The inside butt strap to be at least three-quarters the strength of the longitudinal joint.

NOTE.—For the shell plates of superheaters or steam-chests enclosed in the uptakes or exposed to the direct action of the flame, the coefficients should be two-thirds of those given in the above tables.

Proper deductions are to be made for openings in shell.

All manholes in circular shells to be stiffened with compensating rings.

The shell plates under domes in boilers so fitted, to be stayed from the top of the dome or otherwise stiffened.

Stays.—The strength of stays supporting flat surfaces is to be calculated from the smallest part of the stay or fastening, and the strain upon them is not to exceed the following limits, namely :—

Iron stays.—For stays not exceeding 1½ inches smallest diameter, and for all stays which are welded, 6,000 lbs. per square inch ; for unwelded stays above 1½ inches diameter, 7,500 lbs. per square inch.

Steel stays.—For screw stays not exceeding 1½ inches smallest diameter,

8,000 lbs.; and for screw stays above $1\frac{1}{2}$ inches diameter, 9,000 lbs. per square inch. For other stays not exceeding $1\frac{1}{2}$ inches smallest diameter, 9,000 lbs. per square inch; and for stays exceeding $1\frac{1}{2}$ inches smallest diameter, 10,000 lbs. per square inch. No steel stays are to be welded.

Stay-tubes.—The stress is not to exceed 7,500 lbs. per square inch.

Flat plates.—The strength of flat plates supported by stays to be taken from the following formula :—

$$\frac{C \times T^2}{P^2} = \text{working pressure in lbs. per square inch, where } T = \text{thickness of}$$

plate in sixteenths of an inch.

P^2 = square of pitch in inches, or if the pitch in the rows is not equal to the pitch between the rows, the mean of the squares of the two pitches.

C = 90 for iron or steel plates $\frac{7}{16}$ thick and under fitted with screw stays with riveted heads.

C = 100 for iron or steel plates above $\frac{7}{16}$ fitted with screw stays with riveted heads.

C = 110 for iron or steel plates $\frac{7}{16}$ thick and under fitted with screw stays and nuts.

C = 120 for iron plates above $\frac{7}{16}$ thick and for steel plates above $\frac{7}{16}$ and under $\frac{9}{16}$ thick fitted with screw stays and nuts.

C = 135 for steel plates $\frac{9}{16}$ thick and above fitted with screw stays and nuts.

C = 140 for iron plates fitted with stays with double nuts.

C = 150 for iron plates fitted with stays with double nuts and washers outside the plates, of at least $\frac{1}{3}$ of the pitch in diameter, and half the thickness of the plates.

C = 160 for iron plates fitted with stays with double nuts, and washers riveted to the outside of the plates of at least half thickness of plates and a diameter of $\frac{2}{3}$ of the pitch.

C = 175 for iron plates fitted with stays with double nuts and washers riveted to the outside of the plates when the washers are at least $\frac{2}{3}$ the pitch in diameter and of the same thickness as the plates.

For iron plates fitted with stays with double nuts and doubling strips riveted to the outside of the plates of the same thickness as the plates, and of a width equal to $\frac{2}{3}$ the distance between the rows of stays, C may be taken as 175, if P is taken to be the distance between the rows, and 190 when P is taken to be the pitch between the stays in the rows.

For steel plates other than those for combustion chambers the values of C may be increased as follows :—

$$
\begin{array}{ccc}
C = 140 & \text{increased to} & 175. \\
150 & ,, & 185. \\
160 & ,, & 200. \\
175 & ,, & 220. \\
190 & ,, & 240.
\end{array}
$$

If flat plates are strengthened with doubling plates securely riveted to them, having a thickness of not less than $\frac{2}{3}$ that of the plates, the strength to be taken from

$$\frac{C \times \left(T + \frac{t}{2}\right)^2}{P^2} = \text{working pressure in lbs. per square inch,}$$

where t = thickness of doubling plates in sixteenths and C, T, and P^2 are as above.

Note.—In the case of front plates of boilers in the steam space these numbers should be reduced by 20 per cent., unless the plates are guarded from the direct action of the heat.

L L

For steel tube-plates in the nest of tubes the strength to be taken from

$$\frac{140\,T^2}{P^2} = \text{working pressure in lbs. per square inch,}$$

where T = the thickness of plate in sixteenths of an inch.
     P = mean pitch of stay-tubes from centre to centre.

For the wide water spaces between the nests of tubes the strength to be taken from

$$\frac{C \times T^2}{P^2} = \text{working pressure in lbs. per square inch,}$$

where P = the horizontal distance from centre to centre of the bounding rows of tubes, and
     C = 120 where the stay-tubes are pitched with two plain tubes between them, and are not fitted with nuts outside the plates.
     C = 130 if they are fitted with nuts outside the plates.
     C = 140 if each alternate tube is a stay-tube not fitted with nuts.
     C = 150 if they are fitted with nuts outside the plates.
     C = 160 if every tube in these rows is a stay-tube and not fitted with nuts.
     C = 170 if every tube in these rows is a stay-tube, and each alternate stay-tube is fitted with nuts outside the plates.

The thickness of tube-plates of combustion chambers in cases where the pressure on the top of the chamber is borne by these plates is not to be less than that given by the following rule :—

$$T = \frac{P \times W \times D}{1600 \times (D - d)}$$

where P = working pressure in lbs. per square inch.
     W = width of combustion chamber over plates in inches.
     D = horizontal pitch of tubes in inches.
     d = inside diameter of plain tubes in inches.
     T = thickness of tube-plate in sixteenths of an inch.

Girders.—The strength of girders supporting the tops of combustion chambers and other flat surfaces is to be taken from the following formula :—

$$\frac{C \times d^2 \times T}{(L - P) \times D \times L} = \text{working pressure in lbs. per square inch,}$$

where L = width between tube-plates, or tube-plate and back plate of chamber.
     P = pitch of stays in girders.
     D = distance from centre to centre of girders.
     d = depth of girder at centre.
     T = thickness of girder at centre. All these dimensions to be taken in inches.

WROUGHT-IRON.

C =
  6,000, if there is one stay to each girder.
  9,000, if there are two or three stays to each girder.
  10,000, if there are four or five stays to each girder.
  10,500, if there are six or seven stays to each girder.
  10,800, if there are eight stays or above to each girder.

WROUGHT-STEEL.

C =
  6,600, if there is one stay to each girder.
  9,900, if there are two or three stays to each girder.
  11,000, if there are four or five stays to each girder.
  11,550, if there are six or seven stays to each girder.
  11,880, if there are eight stays or above to each girder.

Circular furnaces.—The strength of plain furnaces to resist collapsing to be calculated as follows :—

Where the length of the plain cylindrical part of the furnace exceeds 120 times the thickness of the plate the working pressure is to be calculated by the following formula :—

$$\frac{1{,}075{,}200 \times T^2}{L \times D} = \text{working pressure in lbs. per square inch,}$$

Where the length of the plain cylindrical part of the furnace is less than 120 times the thickness of the plate, the working pressure is to be calculated from the following formula :—

$$\frac{50 \times (300\ T - L)}{D} = \text{working pressure in lbs. per square inch,}$$

where T = thickness of plates in inches.

    D = outside diameter of furnace in inches.

    L = length of plain cylindrical part in inches, measured from the centre of the rivets connecting the furnaces to the flanges of the end and tube-plates, or from the commencement of the curvature of the flanges of the furnace where it is flanged or fitted with Adamson rings.

The strength of corrugated furnaces made of steel, on Fox's or Morrison's plan, to be calculated from

$$\frac{1{,}259 \times (T - 2)}{D} = \text{working pressure in lbs. per square inch.}$$

The strength of ribbed furnaces (with ribs 9 inches apart) to be calculated from

$$\frac{1{,}160 \times (T - 2)}{D} = \text{working pressure in lbs. per square inch.}$$

The strength of spirally corrugated furnaces to be calculated from

$$\frac{912 \times (T - 2)}{D} = \text{working pressure in lbs. per square inch,}$$

where T = thickness of plate in sixteenths of an inch.

    D = outside diameter of corrugated furnaces, or the outside diameter of the plain part of ribbed furnaces in inches.

The strength of Holmes' patent furnaces, in which the corrugations are not more than 16 inches apart from centre to centre, and not less than 2 inches high, to be calculated from the following formula :—

$$\frac{945 \times (T - 2)}{D} = \text{working pressure in lbs. per square inch,}$$

where T = thickness of plain portions of furnace in sixteenths of an inch.

    D = outside diameter of plain parts of the furnace in inches.

Safety valves.—Two safety valves to be fitted to each boiler and loaded to the working pressure in the presence of the Surveyor. In the case of boilers of greater working pressure than 60 lbs. per square inch, the safety valves may be loaded to 5 lbs. above the working pressure. If common valves are used, their combined areas to be at least half a square inch to each square foot of grate surface. If improved valves are used, they are to be tested under steam in the presence of the Surveyor; the accumulation in no case to exceed 10 per cent. of the working pressure. Each valve to be arranged so that no extra load can be added when steam is up, and to be fitted with easing gear which must lift the valve itself. All safety-valve spindles to extend through the covers and to be fitted with sockets and cross handles, allowing them to be lifted and turned round in their seats, and their efficiency tested at any time.

LLOYD'S RULES FOR DETERMINING SIZES OF SHAFTS.

The diameters of crank and straight shafts are not to be less than those given by the following formulæ :—

For compound engines with two cranks at right angles :—

Diameter of crank shaft in inches = $(\cdot04\,A + \cdot006\,D + \cdot02\,S) \times \sqrt[3]{P}$.

For triple-expansion engines with three cranks at equal angles :—

Diameter of crank shaft in inches = $(\cdot038\,A + \cdot009\,B + \cdot002\,D + \cdot0165\,S) \times \sqrt[3]{P}$.

For quadruple-expansion engines with two cranks at right angles :—

Diameter of crank shaft in inches = $\cdot034\,A + \cdot011\,B + \cdot004\,C + \cdot0014\,D + \cdot016\,S) \times \sqrt[3]{P}$.

For quadruple-expansion engines with three cranks :—

Diameter of crank shaft in inches = $(\cdot028\,A + \cdot014\,B + \cdot006\,C + \cdot0017\,D + \cdot015\,S) \times \sqrt[3]{P}$.

For quadruple-expansion engines with four cranks :—

Diameter of crank shaft in inches = $(\cdot033\,A + \cdot01\,B + \cdot004\,C + \cdot0013\,D + \cdot0155\,S) \times \sqrt[3]{P}$.

where A = diameter of high-pressure cylinder in inches.

B = diameter of first intermediate cylinder in inches.

C = diameter of second intermediate cylinder in inches.

D = diameter of low-pressure cylinder in inches.

S = stroke of piston in inches.

P = boiler pressure above atmosphere in lbs. per square inch.

The thrust shaft under collars to be of the same diameter as is required for the crank shaft, and the screw shaft at least $\frac{7}{10}$ the crank shaft diameter.

Intermediate shafting should be at least $\frac{15}{16}$ of the diameter required for the crank shaft.

NOTE.—The rules are intended to apply to two-cylinder compound engines, in which the ratio of areas of low- and high-pressure cylinders does not exceed 4·5 to 1; to triple-expansion engines in which it does not exceed 9 to 1; to quadruple-expansion engines in which it does not exceed 12 to 1; and in all cases, as regards the stroke, in which the length of stroke is not less than one-half the diameter or greater than the diameter of the low-pressure cylinder. Engines of extreme proportions beyond those limits being specially submitted to be dealt with on their merits.

INDEX